D0219081

Technical Communication

Technical Communication

Strategies for College and the Workplace

DAN JONES

University of Central Florida

KAREN LANE

Karen Lane Technical Consulting

New York   San Francisco   Boston
London   Toronto   Sydney   Tokyo   Singapore   Madrid
Mexico City   Munich   Paris   Cape Town   Hong Kong   Montreal

SENIOR VICE PRESIDENT AND PUBLISHER	Joseph Opiela
VICE PRESIDENT AND PUBLISHER	Eben W. Ludlow
DEVELOPMENT MANAGER	Janet Lanphier
DEVELOPMENT EDITOR	Linda Stern
MARKETING MANAGER	Christopher Bennem
SUPPLEMENTS EDITOR	Donna Campion
MEDIA SUPPLEMENTS EDITOR	Nancy Garcia
PRODUCTION MANAGER	Donna DeBenedictis
PROJECT COORDINATION, TEXT DESIGN, AND ELECTRONIC PAGE MAKEUP	Elm Street Publishing Services, Inc.
SENIOR COVER DESIGN MANAGER	Nancy Danahy
COVER DESIGNER	Keithley and Associates, Inc.
COVER PHOTO	© NASA
ART STUDIO	Burmar Technical Services
PHOTO RESEARCHER	Photosearch, Inc.
MANUFACTURING BUYER	Roy Pickering
PRINTER AND BINDER	Quebecor World/Taunton
COVER PRINTER	Coral Graphic Services, Inc.

For permission to use copyrighted material, grateful acknowledgment is made to the copyright holders on pp. 763–764, which are hereby made part of this copyright page.

Copyright © 2002 by Pearson Education, Inc.

All rights reserved. No part of this publication may be reproduced, stored in a retrieval system, or transmitted, in any form or by any means, electronic, mechanical, photocopying, recording, or otherwise, without the prior written permission of the publisher. Printed in the United States.

Please visit our website at http://www.ablongman.com/jones

ISBN 0-205-32521-1

2 3 4 5 6 7 8 9 10—QWT—04 03 02

Guidelines for Effective Communication

DEVELOPING CONTENT

Developing Ideas
Brainstorming Alone   87
Brainstorming in a Group   87
Effective Mind Mapping   88
Effective Freewriting   90

Researching Material
Planning Your Research   125
Getting Ready for the Interview   114
Planning the Interview   116
Practicing the Interview   116
Conducting a Telephone Interview   117
Creating a Questionnaire   120

Finding and Using Sources
Locating Information   126
Types of Sources   127
Finding Material in Other Libraries   127
Working with Your Information   131

Evaluating Sources
Assessing Print Sources   139
Planning an Online Search   148
Successful Online Searching   151
Evaluating Search Engines   161
Evaluating Internet Sources   164

WRITING AND EDITING

Organizing Material
Outlining   177
Using a Tree Diagram   179

Controlling Writing Style
Achieving an Informal Prose Style   606
Achieving Clarity with Technical Terms   214
Using Humor   224
Avoiding Gender Bias   226
Achieving Conciseness   343
Creating Style Guides   92

Styling Citations
Avoiding Plagiarism   182

Editing Drafts
Effective Developmental Editing   332
Effective Substantive Editing   333
Effective Copyediting   333
Revising Your Work   340

DESIGNING AND PRODUCING

Choosing an Effective Design
Design Principles   247
Document Triage   289

Using Type and Color
Using Color Effectively   269
Choosing Typefaces   256

Using Illustrations
Creating Informal Tables   302
Creating Formal Tables   303
Creating Bar Graphs   307
Creating Line Graphs   308
Creating Pie Graphs   309
Creating Pictographs   310

Creating Flowcharts   311
Creating Organizational Charts   313
Creating Schedule Charts   314
Creating Drawings   315
Creating Diagrams   316
Creating Maps   316
Using and Handling Photographs   318
Using Transparencies   451
Making Your Transparencies and Slides
    More Legible   456

Proofreading and Checking for Errors
Effective Proofreading   338

Brief Contents

Detailed Contents   *ix*
Tips Lists   *xxi*
Preface   *xxiii*

CHAPTER 1   Understanding Technical Communication   1

PART ONE   Getting Ready   31

CHAPTER 2   Audience and Persuasion   33
CHAPTER 3   Collaboration   53
CHAPTER 4   Planning   79
CHAPTER 5   Gathering Information   110
CHAPTER 6   Organizing and Managing Information   171

PART TWO   Writing, Designing, Illustrating, and Editing   195

CHAPTER 7   Achieving an Effective Style   197
CHAPTER 8   Designing Pages and Screens   234
CHAPTER 9   Illustrations   294
CHAPTER 10   Editing, Revising, and Evaluating   328

PART THREE   Job Search and Professional Development   365

CHAPTER 11   The Job Search   367
CHAPTER 12   Professional Growth   413
CHAPTER 13   Developing Presentation Skills   433

PART FOUR   Documents   463

CHAPTER 14   Correspondence   465
CHAPTER 15   Procedures, Processes, and Specifications   510
CHAPTER 16   Proposals   545
CHAPTER 17   Informal Reports   583
CHAPTER 18   Formal Reports   622
CHAPTER 19   Instructions   682

Appendixes   721

APPENDIX A   Mechanics of Good Prose   722
APPENDIX B   Grammar Issues   737
APPENDIX C   Documentation Styles   745
APPENDIX D   Other Documents   756

Index   *765*

Detailed Contents

Tips Lists xxi
Preface xxiii

CHAPTER 1
Understanding Technical Communication 1

In This Chapter 2
Technical Communication as
    an Essential Skill 2
    Technical Communication and You 2
    Defining Technical Communication 4
Technical Communication in College 5
    Typical Communication Challenges 5
    Communication Skills and Success in College 7
    Changes in Your College Environment 7
Technical Communication in the Workplace 8
    Typical Communication Challenges 8
    Communication Skills and Success
      in the Workplace 9
    Changes in Your Workplace Environment 10
Technical Communication and
    Social Action 11
    Social Contexts of Technical Communication 11
    Social Contexts for Communication Failures 12
    The *Challenger* Disaster as
      a Communication Failure 14
    The Costs of Ineffective Technical
      Communication 15
    The Benefits of Effective Technical
      Communication 15
    Apple Computer and Effective Technical
      Documentation 16
Technical Communication and
    Corporate Politics 17
    Understanding the Corporate Culture 17
    Communicating in the Corporate Culture 18
Technical Communication, Ethics, and
    Professionalism 19
    Ethics 19

Professionalism 19
    Ethics and Professionalism in College 20
    Ethics and Professionalism in the Workplace 20
Technical Communication and
    Collaboration 22
    Collaboration: The Pros and Cons 22
    Collaboration in the Electronic Age 22
Technical Communication, the Global Corporate
    World, and Diversity 23
    The Changing Workplace 23
    Technical Communication and Diversity 25
Technical Communication and Technology 26
From the Workplace 24
Checking What You've Learned 27
Exercises 28
    Review 28
    The Internet 28
    Ethics/Professionalism 29
    Collaboration 29
    International Communication 29
Resources 29

PART ONE
Getting Ready 31

CHAPTER 2
Audience and Persuasion 33

In This Chapter 34
Audience and Technical Communication 35
Approaches to Audience 35
    Categorical Approaches 35
    Heuristic Approaches 38
Secondary and Multiple Audiences 39
Audience and Levels of Technicality 41
    Highly Technical Prose 41
    Moderately Technical Prose 41
    Slightly Technical Prose 42

Nontechnical Prose   42

Technical Communication and Persuasion   43

Technical Documents as Persuasive
Documents   43

Technical Documents and Objectivity   44

Strategies for Persuading Audiences   44

Persuading by Appealing to Your Audience   45

Tips: Persuading an International Audience   46

Persuading by Establishing Your Ethos or
Credibility   46

Persuading by Strengthening Your Evidence and
Your Reasoning   47

From the Workplace   48

Checking What You've Learned   51

Exercises   51

Review   51

The Internet   52

Ethics/Professionalism   52

Collaboration   52

International Communication   52

Resources   52

CHAPTER 3
Collaboration   53

In This Chapter   54

Types of Collaboration   54

Divided-Labor Collaborations   55

Cross-Functional or Integrated Collaborations   56

Advantages of Collaboration   57

Disadvantages of Collaboration   60

Collaborating Effectively Face-to-Face   61

Tips: Face-to-Face Collaboration   61

Collaborating Effectively Online   63

Tips: Online Collaboration   63

Collaborating in Peer Reviews   64

Tips: Successful Collaboration in Peer Reviews   64

Tips: Benefiting from Reviews of Your Work   67

Improving Collaborative Skills   67

Enhancing Listening Skills   67

Tips: Improving Your Listening Skills   68

Handling Conflict   68

Tips: Ways to Handle Conflict   69

Negotiating   69

Tips: Negotiating Skills   70

Participating in Meetings   71

Tips: Attending Meetings Productively   71

Tips: Writing and Using an Agenda   71

Tips: Planning and Running a Meeting   72

Acting Ethically   73

Tips: Resolving Ethical Issues   73

From the Workplace   74

Checking What You've Learned   75

Exercises   77

Review   77

The Internet   77

Ethics/Professionalism   77

Collaboration   77

International Communication   77

Resources   78

CHAPTER 4
Planning   79

In This Chapter   80

Determining the Focus   80

Determining the Informational Needs of Your
Audience   81

Narrowing the Subject   81

Stating the Purpose   82

Limiting the Scope   84

Discovering Initial Ideas   85

Brainstorming   86

Tips: Brainstorming Alone   87

Tips: Brainstorming in a Group   87

Mind Mapping   88

Tips: Effective Mind Mapping   88

Freewriting   89

Tips: Effective Freewriting   90

Setting and Following Standards   91

Tips: Creating Style Guides   92

Determining the Style   94

Determining the Mechanics   95
Determining the Design   95
Managing Your Document   96
Estimating Time and Scheduling   97
Tips: Evaluating the Complexity of a Project   98
Tips: Breaking a Project into Smaller Units   98
Tips: Establishing a Schedule   98
Planning the Production   100
Creating the Document Plan   101
Using Planning Tools   101
From the Workplace   106
Checking What You've Learned   106
Exercises   107
Review   107
The Internet   108
Ethics/Professionalism   108
Collaboration   108
International Communication   108
Resources   108

CHAPTER 5
Gathering Information   110

In This Chapter   111
Research   111
Personal Knowledge   113
Interviewing   113
Researching for the Interview   114
Preparing for the Interview   114
Tips: Getting Ready for the Interview   115
Tips: Planning the Interview   116
Tips: Practicing the Interview   116
Conducting the Interview   116
Following Up on the Interview   117
Telephone and Mail Interviews   117
Tips: Conducting a Telephone Interview   117
Questionnaires and Surveys   118
Tips: Creating a Questionnaire   120
Focus Groups   121
Experimentation   122
Written or Recorded Information   124

Using the Library—Print Sources   125
Tips: Planning Your Research   125
Tips: Locating Information   126
Tips: Types of Sources   127
Tips: Finding Material in Other Libraries   127
Tips: Working with Your Information   131
Evaluating Print Sources   137
Tips: Assessing Print Sources   139
Using the Library—Electronic Sources   142
Tips: Planning an Online Search   148
Tips: Successful Online Searching   151
The Internet and the Web   151
Search Engines   156
Tips: Evaluating Search Engines   161
Search Indexes or Catalogs   162
Weaknesses of the Internet for Research   162
Evaluating Online Sources   163
Tips: Evaluating Internet Sources   164
From the Workplace   166
Checking What You've Learned   166
Exercises   169
Review   169
The Internet   169
Ethics/Professionalism   169
Collaboration   169
International Communication   169
Resources   170

CHAPTER 6
Organizing and Managing Information   171

In This Chapter   172
Organizing Information   172
Note Cards, Notebooks, and Computers   172
Databases   173
Outlines   175
Tips: Outlining   177
Trees   178
Tips: Using a Tree Diagram   179
Flowcharts   179
Storyboards   180

Evaluating Information   181

Reporting Information Ethically   182

Plagiarism   182

Tips: Avoiding Plagiarism   182

Paraphrasing Versus Direct Quotations   183

Copyright   185

From the Workplace   188

Checking What You've Learned   191

Exercises   192

Review   192

The Internet   192

Ethics/Professionalism   192

Collaboration   193

International Communication   193

Resources   193

**PART TWO
Writing, Designing, Illustrating,
and Editing   195**

**CHAPTER 7
Achieving an Effective Style   197**

In This Chapter   198

Style and Discourse Communities   198

Style and Genre   199

Kinds of Styles   201

Plain Style   201

Complex Style   202

Improving Your Writing Style at the Word
Level   203

Levels of Diction   203

Denotation and Connotation   206

Usage   207

Long Words   207

Abbreviations, Acronyms, Initialisms   208

Action Verbs   210

Active Voice   210

Passive Voice   211

Noun Strings   211

Nominalizations   212

Jargon   212

Tips: Achieving Clarity with Technical Terms   214

Ambiguous Modifiers   214

Trite Phrases or Clichés   214

Improving Your Writing Style at the Sentence
Level   215

Sentences and Technical Terms   215

Emphasis   215

Variety   216

Improving Your Writing Style at the Paragraph
Level   216

Writing on One Topic   217

Developing the Paragraph Topic   217

Achieving an Effective Flow   219

Providing Adequate Details   220

Handling New Information   220

Avoiding Ambiguous Reference   221

Improving Your Writing Style in Larger
Segments   221

Developing an Appropriate Tone   222

Tips: Using Humor   224

Avoiding Bias   225

Tips: Avoiding Gender Bias   226

Understanding Cultural Contexts   227

From the Workplace   226

Checking What You've Learned   228

Exercises   228

Review   228

The Internet   231

Ethics/Professionalism   232

Collaboration   232

International Communication   232

Resources   232

**CHAPTER 8
Designing Pages and Screens   234**

In This Chapter   235

Conventions and Expectations   235

Principles of Design   240

Simplicity   240

Symmetry   242

Consistency   244
Readability   245
Usability   245

Tips: Design Principles   247
Ways to Organize Space   247
White Space   247
Grids   249
Rules and Border Graphics   250
Headers and Footers   250
Text Lists   250
Typography   253
Typefaces and Fonts   253

Tips: Choosing Typefaces   257
Size   257
Weight and Color   258
Spacing: Letter, Word, Line, Paragraph   260
Alignment and Justification   263
Using Color   265

Tips: Using Color Effectively   269
Additional Design Principles for Screen
   and Web   270
Elements in Common with Paper-Based
   Pages   271
Elements Unique to Screen and Web   272
Designing Your Writing for Screen and Web   272
Improving Your Web-Page Prose Style   275

Tips: Writing for the Web   279
Designing the Interface   279
Interactivity   282

Tips: Organizing Online Space   283
On-Screen Color   285
Screen Resolution   287
Fonts   287
Browser Capability   288
Plug-Ins   288
Download Speeds   288
First Aid for Your Document Design   289

Tips: Document Triage   289
From the Workplace   290
Checking What You've Learned   290
Exercises   292
Review   292

The Internet   293
Ethics/Professionalism   293
Collaboration   293
International Communication   293
Resources   293

CHAPTER 9
Illustrations   294

In This Chapter   295
Appropriateness   295
Illustrating for Print   296
Illustrating for the Screen   299
Ethical Use of Illustrations   302
Tables   302
Informal Tables   302

Tips: Creating Informal Tables   302
Formal Tables   303

Tips: Creating Formal Tables   304
Graphs   305
Bar Graphs   305

Tips: Creating Bar Graphs   307
Line Graphs   307

Tips: Creating Line Graphs   308
Pie Graphs   309

Tips: Creating Pie Graphs   309
Pictographs   310

Tips: Creating Pictographs   310
Charts   311
Flowcharts   311

Tips: Creating Flowcharts   311
Organizational Charts   312

Tips: Creating Organizational Charts   313
Schedule or Gantt Charts   313

Tips: Creating Schedule Charts   314
Drawings, Diagrams, and Maps   314
Drawings   314

Tips: Creating Drawings   315
Diagrams   315

Tips: Creating Diagrams   316
Maps   316

Tips: Creating Maps   316
Photos   317
Tips: Using and Handling Photographs   318
Clip Art   319
Computer Illustrations   321
   Vector Programs   321
   Raster Programs   323
   Graphics Utilities   324
From the Workplace   322
Checking What You've Learned   325
Exercises   326
   Review   326
   The Internet   326
   Ethics/Professionalism   326
   Collaboration   326
   International Communication   327
Resources   327

CHAPTER 10
Editing, Revising, and Evaluating   328

In This Chapter   329
Editing   329
   Developmental Editing   330
Tips: Effective Developmental Editing   332
   Substantive Editing   332
Tips: Effective Substantive Editing   333
   Copyediting   333
Tips: Effective Copyediting   333
   Proofreading   336
Tips: Effective Proofreading   338
Revising   339
Tips: Revising Your Work   340
   Accuracy and Precision   340
   Appropriateness   341
   Conciseness   342
Tips: Achieving Conciseness   343
   Telegraphic Writing   346
   Concreteness   346
   Consistency   347
   Clarity   347
   Sincerity   348
   Negative Constructions   348
   Sentence Parallelism   349
Evaluating Drafts   350
   Review Cycles   350
   Style Review   354
   Peer Review   354
   Reviewing Large Projects   357
   Usability Testing   358
From the Workplace   356
Checking What You've Learned   360
Exercises   361
   Review   361
   The Internet   362
   Ethics/Professionalism   362
   Collaboration   362
   International Communication   362
Resources   363

PART THREE
Job Search and Professional Development   365

CHAPTER 11
The Job Search   367

In This Chapter   368
Where to Search   368
   School Career Counselors   368
   Job Fairs   370
   Trade Journals and Magazines   370
   Newspapers   371
   Employment Agencies   371
   Networking   373
   Professional Meetings   373
   Job Databases   374
   The Internet   375
Job Correspondence   375
   Application Letter   376
   Thank-You Letter   379
   Reference Letter   381
   Update Letter   381

Accept/Decline Letter   383
Resignation Letter   385
Résumés   388
General Requirements for Résumés   388
Designing Your Résumé   392
Tips: Résumé Design   392
Printed Résumés—Chronological
Organization   393
Printed Résumés—Functional Organization   394
Electronic Résumés   395
Tips: Word Choices for Scannable Résumés   399
Tips: Designing a Scannable Résumé   400
Portfolios   400
Tips: Creating Your Portfolio   401
Interviewing   402
The Informational Job Interview   402
Tips: Informational Interviews   403
The Job Interview   404
Tips: Interview Preparation   405
Conducting the Job Interview   409
Tips: Interviewing Job Candidates   409
From the Workplace   406
Checking What You've Learned   410
Exercises   410
Review   410
The Internet   411
Ethics/Professionalism   411
Collaboration   411
International Communication   411
Resources   411

CHAPTER 12
Professional Growth   413

In This Chapter   414
Career Development   414
Professional Organizations   415
Professional Journals   416
Finding Journals   416
Publishing Journal Articles   417

Online Forums   420
Conferences   421
Continuing Education   422
Seminars and Training on the Job   423
Degree and Certificate Programs   423
Individual Courses   424
Correspondence Courses and Other Distance
Learning   424
Professional Development through Establishing
Contacts   424
Networking   425
Chapter Meetings   425
Collaborating   426
Mentoring   426
Tips: Being Mentored   427
Tips: Mentoring   430
From the Workplace   428
Checking What You've Learned   430
Exercises   431
Review   431
The Internet   432
Ethics/Professionalism   432
Collaboration   432
International Technical
Communication   432
Resources   432

CHAPTER 13
Developing Presentation Skills   433

In This Chapter   434
Giving Oral Presentations   434
Kinds of Presentations   435
Impromptu, Outlined, or Scripted
Presentations   435
Informative or Persuasive Presentations   435
Preparation   436
Planning   436
Knowing the Audience   436
Researching   437
Organizing   437
Using Appropriate Language   437

Beginning the Presentation   437
Developing the Middle   438
Ending the Presentation   439
Practicing   439
Dressing Appropriately   439
Setting the Stage   440
Delivery   440
Relaxing   441
Controlling Nervousness   442
Establishing Eye Contact   442
Projecting   442
Using an Appropriate Pace   443
Using Gestures   443
Avoiding Distractions   443
Using Auditory Clues or Signposts   444
Expecting the Unexpected   444
Using Presentation Tools
    Appropriately   444
Watching the Time   445
Using Handouts   445
Letting the Audience Know You're
    Wrapping Up   445
Thanking the Audience   445
Presentation Tools   446
Models   446
Chalkboards and Dry-Erase Boards   446
Posters   448
Flip Charts   449
Transparencies   450
Tips: Using Transparencies   451
35-mm Slides   453
Computers and Presentation Software   455
**Tips: Making Your Transparencies and Slides
    More Legible   456**
Videos   456
From the Workplace   458
Checking What You've Learned   460
Exercises   461
Review   461
The Internet   461
Ethics/Professionalism   461
Collaboration   461
International Communication   461
Resources   462

**PART FOUR
Documents   463**

**CHAPTER 14
Correspondence   465**

In This Chapter   466
Letters   466
Parts of a Letter   467
Letter Formats   476
Tips: Formatting Letters   482
Patterns: Direct and Indirect   483
Types of Letters   485
Memos   493
Formats   494
Tips: Writing Memos   496
Tips: Styling Memos   497
E-mail   498
Advantages of E-mail   498
Disadvantages of E-mail   498
Sending E-mail and Attachments   501
Netiquette   503
Emoticons and Abbreviations   506
From the Workplace   504
Checking What You've Learned   507
Exercises   508
Review   508
The Internet   508
Ethics/Professionalism   509
Collaboration   509
International Communication   509
Resources   509

**CHAPTER 15
Procedures, Processes, and
Specifications   510**

In This Chapter   511
Definitions   511
Informal Definitions   511
Formal Definitions   512
Extended Definitions   513

Technical Descriptions   513

Processes   517

Policies and Procedures   519
  Company Policies   522

Tips: Company Policies—Planning   523

Tips: Company Policies—Reviewing   523

**Tips: Company Policies—Formatting and
  Producing   523**
  Other Procedures   524

Specifications   526
  Precision and Accuracy   527

Tips: Writing Effective Specifications   528
  Writing Specifications   528
  Presenting Specifications   529

From the Workplace   534

Checking What You've Learned   534

Exercises   537
  Review   537
  The Internet   538
  Ethics/Professionalism   538
  Collaboration   538
  International Communication   538

Resources   538

Exhibit 15.1: Procedures and Policies—National
  Institutes of Health Guidelines for Research
  Using Human Pluripotent Stem Cells   539

CHAPTER 16
Proposals   545

In This Chapter   546

The Proposal-Writing Process   546
  Planning   546
  Researching   547
  Writing   547
  Editing and Revising   547
  Producing the Proposal   547

Kinds of Proposals   548

The Request for Proposal (RFP)   549

Elements of a Proposal   551
  Abstract   552
  Introduction   557

Background on the Problem or Need   557
Description of What Is Proposed   558
Methods Section or Specific Plan
  Statement   559

Tips: Methods Section   559
  Schedule for Carrying Out the Plan   560
  Qualifications of Plan Participants   560
  Budget   560
  Conclusion   561
  Appendix   562

Tips: Proposal Writing   564

The Successful Proposal   565
  Following the Evaluation Criteria   565
  Pitfalls to Avoid   573

From the Workplace   572

Checking What You've Learned   574

Exercises   577
  Review   577
  The Internet   577
  Ethics/Professionalism   577
  Collaboration   577
  International Communication   577

Resources   577

Exhibit 16.1: Request for Proposal—STC Special
  Opportunities Grant Guidelines   578

CHAPTER 17
Informal Reports   583

In This Chapter   584

Types of Reports   584

Informal and Formal Reports   586

Common Types of Informal Reports   586
  Progress Reports   586
  Periodic Activity Reports   587
  Trip Reports   588
  Lab Reports   591
  Meeting Minutes   594

Tips: Writing Minutes   594
  Forms   596

Choosing the Most Appropriate Format   598

**Tips: When to Use Memo, Letter, or E-mail Format
  for Reports   598**

Strategies for Preparing Informal Reports   599
   Focusing   599
   Gathering Information   599
   Interpreting the Information   600
   Organizing   600
   Designing and Illustrating   601
   Writing and Revising the First Draft   601
   Using an Appropriate Prose Style   603

Tips: Achieving an Informal Prose Style   606
From the Workplace   604
Checking What You've Learned   606
Exercises   607
   Review   607
   The Internet   607
   Ethics/Professionalism   607
   Collaboration   607
   International Communication   608
Resources   609
Exhibit 17.1: Memo Report   610

CHAPTER 18
Formal Reports   622

In This Chapter   623
Informational and Analytical Reports   623
   Background Reports   624
   Feasibility Reports   625
   Recommendation Reports   626
   Empirical Research Reports   628
   Scientific Papers   633
Strategies for Preparing a Formal Report   636
   Focusing the Report   636
   Gathering Information   638
   Interpreting the Information   638
   Organizing the Report   639
   Designing and Illustrating the Report   640
   Writing and Revising Various Drafts   640
Common Elements in Formal Reports   641
   Letter of Transmittal   641
   Cover   642
   Title Page   642
   Abstract   642

Tips: Writing an Abstract   644
   Executive Summary   644

Tips: Writing an Executive Summary   645
   Table of Contents   646
   List of Illustrations   646
   Introduction   646
   Methods   647
   Results or Discussion   647
   Conclusion   648
   Recommendations   648
   Glossary and List of Symbols   648
   Appendixes   652
   References   654
   Index   654

Tips: Creating an Index   654
From the Workplace   652
Checking What You've Learned   655
Exercises   657
   Review   657
   The Internet   657
   Ethics/Professionalism   657
   Collaboration   658
   International Communication   658
Resources   658
Exhibit 18.1: Background Report—Computer
   Virus Vulnerabilities for Networked/
   Computer-Based Business Systems   659

CHAPTER 19
Instructions   682

In This Chapter   683
Instructions as Technical Prose   683
Elements of Instructions   684
   The Introduction   685
   Theory   685
   List of Materials, Tools, and Equipment   686
   Steps Involved   686
   Troubleshooting   687
   Warnings   687
   Other Elements   688
Strategies for Preparing Instructions   689
   Focusing   689
   Gathering and Interpreting Information   689
   Organizing   692
   Designing and Illustrating   695

Tips: Designing and Illustrating Instructions   695
   Writing and Revising   696
   Using an Appropriate Prose Style   697
Tips: Prose Style in Instructions   697
   Producing the Instructions   698
Testing Your Instructions   698
From the Workplace   698
Checking What You've Learned   699
Exercises   701
   Review   701
   The Internet   702
   Ethics/Professionalism   702
   Collaboration   702
   International Communication   702
Resources   702
Exhibit 19.1: Sample Instructions—How to Use
   Softwood in Woodworking   703
Exhibit 19.2: How to Install a Ceiling Fan in Your
   Home   716

APPENDIXES   721

APPENDIX A
Mechanics of Good Prose   722

Spelling   723
Capitalization   723
Punctuation   724
   Period   724
   Question mark   725
   Exclamation Point   725
   Comma   725
   Semicolon   726
   Colon   726
   Dash   727
   Hyphen   728
   Slash   728
   Apostrophe   728
   Quotation Marks and Ellipses   729
   Parentheses and Brackets   731
Marks of Emphasis—Bold, Underline, and
   Italic   731
Bullets   732

Abbreviations, Acronyms, and Initialisms   732
Numbers   733
   Measurements   734
   Fractions and Decimals   735
   Percentages   736
   Addresses   736
   Time   736
   Dates   736

APPENDIX B
Grammar Issues   737

Parts of Speech   738
   Noun   738
   Pronoun   738
   Verb   738
   Adjective   738
   Adverb   738
   Preposition   739
   Conjunction   739
   Interjection   739
Commonly Confused Words   739
Problematic Grammar Issues   741
   Fragments   741
   Run-on Sentences   741
   Comma Splices   741
   Dangling or Misplaced Modifiers   742
   Faulty Parallelism   742
   Subject–Verb Agreement   742
   Pronoun–Antecedent Agreement   742
   Pronoun Case   743
   Tense, Mood, Voice   743

APPENDIX C
Documentation Styles   745

Humanities   746
   MLA Style   746
   Chicago or Turabian Style   746
Social Sciences   746
Physical Sciences   746
Life Sciences   747
Electronic Sources   747

Within-the-Text Examples: MLA, Turabian, APA   748
  Page References in Paraphrased Material   748
  Author and Page References in Paraphrased and Quoted Material   748
Works Cited Examples: MLA, Turabian, APA, IEEE, CBE, Vancouver   749
  Books: One Author   749
  Books: Two Authors   749
  Books: Many Authors   750
  Corporate Author   751
  Reprint   751
  Chapter in a Book   752
  Article in a Journal   753
  Article in a Journal: Two Authors   753

Article in a Journal: Three or More Authors   754
Article in a Magazine or Newspaper   755

**APPENDIX D
Other Documents   756**

Literature Reviews   757
Writing Literature Reviews   758
Annotated Bibliographies   759
Writing Annotated Bibliographies   760
Resources   761

Credits   763
Index   765

Tips Lists

Chapter 2 Audience and Persuasion
Persuading an International Audience   46

Chapter 3 Collaboration
Face-to-Face Collaboration   61
Online Collaboration   63
Successful Collaboration in Peer Reviews   64
Benefiting from Reviews of Your Work   67
Improving Your Listening Skills   68
Ways to Handle Conflict   69
Negotiating Skills   70
Attending Meetings Productively   71
Writing and Using an Agenda   71
Planning and Running a Meeting   72
Resolving Ethical Issues   73

Chapter 4 Planning
Brainstorming Alone   87
Brainstorming in a Group   87
Effective Mind Mapping   88
Effective Freewriting   90
Creating Style Guides   92
Evaluating the Complexity of a Project   98
Breaking a Project into Smaller Units   98
Establishing a Schedule   98

Chapter 5 Gathering Information
Getting Ready for the Interview   115
Planning the Interview   116
Practicing the Interview   116
Conducting a Telephone Interview   117
Creating a Questionnaire   120
Planning Your Research   125
Locating Information   126
Types of Sources   127
Finding Material in Other Libraries   127

Working with Your Information   131
Assessing Print Sources   139
Planning an Online Search   148
Successful Online Searching   151
Evaluating Search Engines   161
Evaluating Internet Sources   164

Chapter 6 Organizing and Managing Information
Outlining   177
Using a Tree Diagram   179
Avoiding Plagiarism   182

Chapter 7 Achieving an Effective Style
Achieving Clarity with Technical Terms   214
Using Humor   224
Avoiding Gender Bias   226

Chapter 8 Designing Pages and Screens
Design Principles   247
Choosing Typefaces   257
Using Color Effectively   269
Writing for the Web   279
Organizing Online Space   283
Document Triage   289

Chapter 9 Illustrations
Creating Informal Tables   302
Creating Formal Tables   304
Creating Bar Graphs   307
Creating Line Graphs   308
Creating Pie Graphs   309
Creating Pictographs   310
Creating Flowcharts   311
Creating Organizational Charts   313
Creating Schedule Charts   314
Creating Drawings   315

Creating Diagrams 316

Creating Maps 316

Using and Handling Photographs 318

Chapter 10 Editing, Revising, and Evaluating

Effective Developmental Editing 332

Effective Substantive Editing 333

Effective Copyediting 333

Effective Proofreading 338

Revising Your Work 340

Achieving Conciseness 343

Chapter 11 The Job Search

Résumé Design 392

Word Choices for Scannable Résumés 399

Designing a Scannable Résumé 400

Creating Your Portfolio 401

Informational Interviews 403

Interview Preparation 405

Interviewing Job Candidates 409

Chapter 12 Professional Growth

Being Mentored 427

Mentoring 430

Chapter 13 Developing Presentation Skills

Using Transparencies 451

Making Your Transparencies and Slides More Legible 456

Chapter 14 Correspondence

Formatting Letters 482

Writing Memos 496

Styling Memos 497

Chapter 15 Procedures, Processes, and Specifications

Company Policies—Planning 523

Company Policies—Reviewing 523

Company Policies—Formatting and Producing 523

Writing Effective Specifications 528

Chapter 16 Proposals

Methods Section 559

Proposal Writing 564

Chapter 17 Informal Reports

Writing Minutes 594

When to Use Memo, Letter, or E-mail Format for Reports 598

Achieving an Informal Prose Style 606

Chapter 18 Formal Reports

Writing an Abstract 644

Writing an Executive Summary 645

Creating an Index 654

Chapter 19 Instructions

Designing and Illustrating Instructions 695

Prose Style in Instructions 697

Preface

Technical Communication: Strategies for College and the Workplace is the result of an unprecedented collaboration between a college professor and a practicing technical communicator. We hope our unique co-authorship reflects the best of college teaching and the best practices in industry as we help prepare students for success in college and in the workplace. Our text places special emphasis not only on professional skills but also on professional values. It instructs students in the basic and advanced techniques of the craft of communicating, but more than that, it clarifies the qualities that differentiate a practitioner from a professional: ethical values, commitment to quality, and productive interaction with peers, colleagues, employers, clients, and the public.

FOCUS ON PROFESSIONALISM

Technical Communication focuses on professionalism through individual chapters on the job search and professional growth; "From the Workplace" profiles; job-related emphasis on collaboration, teamwork, and peer review; "Choosing the Ethical Path" sidebars; extensive coverage of electronic communication and electronic research; and discussion of numerous communication tools. Throughout, students are shown how the strategies they are learning now will be directly applicable in the workplace.

Profiles of Professionals in Technical Fields

From the workplace Students will read about real people, people with diverse educational backgrounds, who are working in a variety of technical fields. A series of profiles throughout the textbook—"From the Workplace"—introduces systems analysts, programmers, engineers, managers, technical communicators, designers, and other technical professionals in their own words. First-person descriptions and discussions provide details on how their education and opportunities led these professionals to their present positions and how their communication skills have contributed to success in their careers. The emphasis in these profiles is not only on the current positions of those profiled but also on their sometimes unexpected career paths, and how their many qualities—skills, talents, aptitudes, and attitudes—and their opportunities made them successful. The profiles will give students a good idea of the value of what they are learning and motivate them to take seriously the advice and instruction they are receiving.

Observations and Advice from Professionals

In addition to the in-depth profiles, numerous quotations—observations and advice—from many technical professionals, reflecting on their experiences and the importance of effective communication, appear as sidebars in many chapters. As their individual titles suggest, these sidebars give students an insider's view of how the textbook topics directly relate to workplace issues. Some of them carry forward the instructional material of the chapters. Others review career-forming experiences. Still others are in the form of advice to new graduates as they enter the workplace. Finally, some provide anecdotal material that may be interesting to students for a variety of reasons: exhibiting humor, irony, or insight into how things really "work" in the working world.

Peer-Review Strategies

Technical Communication provides solid coverage of peer review accompanied by peer-review guidelines for many assignments. Peer review is not only a fact of life in the workplace; it also helps encourage good work and study habits for students whose usual inclinations may be to merge the writing, revising, and reviewing stages of document preparation when faced with a looming deadline. The text gives special attention to the importance of peer review for every draft that students write in an introductory course. When they are required to think critically about documents prepared by others, students sharpen their own writing and reviewing skills. Students learn the advantages of regularly reviewing the work of their peers and of having their own work reviewed.

Collaboration

Collaboration may be the one area scientific and technical majors as well as other future professionals are least prepared for as they enter the workforce. We emphasize teamwork and the collaborative process for exercises and projects, in addition to dedicating Chapter 3 to the subject and providing at least one end-of-chapter collaborative exercise in each chapter. Students will learn how to work productively on a team by learning how to work collaboratively on many of their school assignments. Moreover, the text's ancillaries—the *Instructor's Manual* and the Companion Website—are designed to be particularly useful in helping instructors evaluate collaborative work effectively.

Ethics and Professionalism

We emphasize ethics and professionalism. Ethical situations are flagged as they arise in a variety of contexts in "Choosing the Ethical Path" features within many of the chapters. In addition, an exercise on ethics and professionalism appears at the end of every chapter.

International Communication

This textbook offers strategies for communicating technical information to other cultures. In addition, at least one exercise concerning international technical communication is provided at the end of every chapter.

Electronic Communication

Technical communication is increasingly electronic. Therefore, a text that does not appropriately cover electronic media is one that will prove of limited value to the student entering the marketplace. Our text provides detailed treatment of electronic communication, including e-mail, netiquette, mailing lists, search engines, Web sites, multimedia, and other forums for electronic communication, with particular emphasis on using electronic media to convey technical information. The discussions are specific enough to be useful, but principle-based enough to remain timely for many years.

The Internet

Technical Communication includes extensive coverage on doing research using the Internet and on evaluating Internet resources. This area, which is important for every college student and technical professional, is changing so rapidly that students need coverage that is both current and timeless. We offer the latest information about online research, while emphasizing sound research practices that can be applied as technology and resources evolve.

In addition to an emphasis on obtaining information from the Internet in Chapter 5 and an exercise involving the Internet at the end of every chapter, we show students how to prepare information for publication online, including for the World Wide Web. Students increasingly are creating Web sites, not just for their own use but as consultants for companies in a variety of industries. When they leave school, the knowledge and experience they will have acquired from Chapter 8, "Designing Pages and Screens," will give them a good start with a skill much valued in the job market.

Interpersonal Skills

No matter how technically able they may be, students need to know how to interact with their peers, colleagues, clients, employers, and the public. Students require a variety of interpersonal skills: interviewing skills, presentation skills, and professional development skills. These topics are treated extensively in Chapters 3, 5, 11, 12, and 13, and in sections of several other chapters.

Correspondence and the Job Search

Most textbooks discuss correspondence as a whole only generally. Chapters 11 and 14 provide a more inclusive discussion of many kinds of correspondence. Both chapters give special attention to the job search and job correspondence, business correspondence of various types, and guidelines about how to determine the type of correspondence appropriate for most situations that students and technical professionals are likely to encounter. Chapter 12 is devoted entirely to professional development, to give students the chance to see beyond school to the issues professionals face as they negotiate the employment moves that are the usual accompaniment to most careers.

Computer Tools

A knowledge of computer tools is crucial in today's work environment. Many technical communication textbooks give little or no attention to the numerous tools college students and technical professionals may use to create their work. We give detailed attention to many tools—Web editors, templates, planners, productivity and research organizers, and more—to help readers create professional-looking documents. Here again, the discussion is specific enough to be useful, but not so tied to today as to be soon outdated.

OTHER FEATURES

Tips Lists and Checklists

 This text, emphasizing rhetorical context over a methods approach, offers many tip lists and checklists throughout. Students and professionals should be applying a process to the technical documents they create, a process that includes planning, researching, writing, designing, illustrating, editing, revising, and producing. However, this text also recognizes that each document students and professionals write has its own requirements and its own rhetorical situation. Stated simply, technical documents are written for specific purposes for particular audiences and involve contexts ranging from a need to know to a need to be persuaded. The goal is to provide readers with enough practical tips and checklists, along with other reference information, to help them create the most effective technical document for a particular context. Each chapter concludes with "Checking What You've Learned," which summarizes many of the major rhetorical principles and strategies covered in the chapter.

Style, Tone, and Bias

Some introductory textbooks mention style and tone, but few go beyond offering just the basics. Since control of style underlies all successful communication, we offer—in Chapter 7, an in-depth chapter on style—a more detailed treatment of the intricacies of style, tone, and bias in technical communication than is usually found in an introductory textbook. In addition, Chapter 10, "Editing, Revising, and Evaluating," discusses many strategies students can use to edit and revise their documents for style issues.

Resources

The reader will find resources for further reading at the end of each chapter. Topics introduced in the textbook can open the door to more in-depth treatments without having to create an encyclopedic (and hence less focused) textbook. By presenting a carefully selected mixture of classic and current resources, we direct students to reliable outside material they will find helpful both in school and eventually on the job.

Exercises

At the end of every chapter, a variety of exercises helps students remember and practice many of the key points of the chapter. Each chapter provides review exercises and specialized exercises concerning the Internet, ethics and professionalism, collaboration, and international communication.

ORGANIZATION

This textbook is organized into four major sections:

Part One, "Getting Ready"

Part Two, "Writing, Designing, Illustrating, and Editing"

Part Three, "Job Search and Professional Development"

Part Four, "Documents"

Communicating technical information is a multistep process. Our text uses a common-sense and practical approach to guide students through the various stages of preparation they need in order to achieve their objectives in their writing courses and on the job.

After an introductory chapter, "Understanding Technical Communication," Part One provides detailed chapters on the prewriting stages that are so important but that are often overlooked in students' other courses: identifying the relationship between audience and persuasion, collaborating, planning, and gathering and managing information.

Once the preliminary planning and research have been accomplished, students learn, in Part Two, how to control the elements of style, the appearance of their documents, the visual display of information, and the usability of their work.

Employment skills and professional growth have been areas often under-represented in textbooks, but in Part Three of our text, students are introduced to the practical intersection of school skills and work skills: the job market. We present a detailed discussion of job correspondence, résumés, portfolios, interviews, professional organizations and meetings, presentations, online forums, conferences, and opportunities for continuing education.

Part Four instructs students on how to select, plan, create, and produce a variety of specific kinds of technical documents. All of the strategies discussed earlier in the textbook can be applied to the many kinds of technical documents covered in this section: correspondence (letters, memos, e-mail), procedures and processes, proposals, informal reports, formal reports, and instructions.

Four appendixes provide discussion of mechanics (spelling, capitalization, punctuation, abbreviations, numbers), grammar, citation styles, and specialized documents (literature reviews and annotated bibliographies).

ANCILLARIES

Ancillaries include a comprehensive and full-featured *Instructor's Manual*, a resource-rich Web site, the CourseCompass course management system, and a large array of other teaching and learning aids for faculty and students.

Instructor's Manual

Each chapter in the *Instructor's Manual* provides the following major features:

- *Chapter objectives*—The objectives for each chapter are concisely described in a bulleted list.
- *Chapter summary and teaching notes*—The content of each chapter is summarized in a few key paragraphs, and major points deserving emphasis are highlighted.
- *Classroom activities and assignments*—Detailed suggestions are provided concerning class preparation, in-class activities, and computer-related activities.
- *An activity concerning the workplace profile*—Each profile covered in "From the Workplace" has a corresponding activity to challenge students to relate the technical professional's experiences to the other material in the text.
- *Additional assignments*—Many additional assignments are provided to supplement the exercises in the chapters.
- *Quizzes*—A brief quiz is provided for each chapter.
- *Photocopy and transparency masters*—Each chapter concludes with several convenient masters for class use.

Companion Website

The Companion Website for this text is designed to be a valuable Web resource for both instructors and students. The Instructor Resource section offers a rich array of materials to supplement in-class presentations and out-of-class assignments, including the following:

- *PowerPoint slides*—A set of slides outlines the main ideas of each chapter.
- *InterActivities*—These activities engage students quickly in the chapter topics.
- *Term project ideas*—These suggested projects require students to combine skills learned in several chapters.
- *Faculty FAQs*—The authors answer frequently asked questions from both new and seasoned technical communication instructors.

The Student Resource section provides tools for mastering both the theory and practice of technical communication:

- *Chapter overview*—The overview gives a preview of the chapter's main concepts.
- *Self-paced review quiz*—A quiz is provided for each chapter.
- *Examples and references to related documents on the Web*—Study questions for analysis accompany these resources.
- *Chapter review checklist*—The checklist covers topics students should know after reading the chapter.
- *The CyberLibrary*—This extensive list of Web references is valuable to technical communication students and professionals alike.

CourseCompass Course Management Cartridges

CourseCompass combines the strength of Longman content with state-of-the-art eLearning tools. CourseCompass is a nationally hosted, interactive online course management system powered by BlackBoard, leaders in the development of Internet-based learning tools. This easy-to-use and customizable program enables professors to tailor content and functionality to meet individual course needs. Longman's CourseCompass courses for English include a range of pre-loaded content, such as testing and assessment question pools, chapter-level objectives, chapter summaries, illustrations, Web activities, and an array of supplementary ebooks —all designed to help students master core course objectives.

Take Note!

Take Note! is a complete information-management tool for students working on research papers or other projects that require the use of outside sources. This cross-platform CD-ROM integrates note taking, outlining, and bibliography management into one easy-to-use package. ISBN 0-321-08232-X

The Longman English Pages Web Site

This updated site offers original content and provides you and your students with traditional and online resources for reading, writing, and research not only in technical communication but also in literature and composition. Features for instructors include teaching perspectives, sample projects, and online casebooks. Features for students include interactive tutorials and more than 25 student papers with layered annotations. Visit this Web site at **www.ablongman.com/englishpages**.

Literacy Library Series

This series offers informed, detailed guidelines for writing in academic, public, and workplace communities. Each booklet provides strategies for understanding the issues, audiences, and rhetorical conventions of each of these communities, as well as giving concrete advice and models for writing in these different communities.

Public Literacy ISBN 0-321-06498-4
Workplace Literacy ISBN 0-321-06499-2
Academic Literacy ISBN 0-321-06501-8

Researching Online, Fifth Edition

Researching Online by David Munger gives students detailed, step-by-step instructions for performing electronic searches; for researching with e-mail, listservs, newsgroups, IRC, and MUDs and MOOs; and for evaluating electronic sources. This resource also includes excellent coverage on writing for the Web. ISBN 0-321-09277-5

Composition on the Net, 2001

This excellent student supplement by H. Eric Branscomb and Doug Gotthoffer provides a thorough introduction to using the Web as a resource for college writing. It provides a comprehensive array of useful sites to help composition students begin their search and includes activities that encourage practical, hands-on use of the Web. This supplement also has a thorough section on evaluating sources on the Web. ISBN 0-205-33073-8

Visual Communication, Second Edition

This newly revised text by Susan Hilligoss of Clemson University introduces document-design principles and features practical discussions of space, type, organization, pattern, graphic elements, and visuals for a range of document types—including newsletters, brochures, and Web sites. ISBN 0-321-09981-8

Learning Together: An Introduction to Collaborative Learning

This brief guide to the fundamentals of collaborative learning by Tori Haring-Smith of Brown University teaches students how to work effectively in groups, how to revise with peer response, and how to co-author a paper or report. ISBN 0-673-46848-8

A Guide for Peer Response, Second Edition

This supplement, by Tori Haring-Smith of Brown University and Helon H. Raines of Armstrong Atlantic State University, offers students forms for peer critiques, including general guidelines and specific forms for different stages in the writing process and for various types of papers. ISBN 0-321-01948-2

ACKNOWLEDGMENTS

We are, first of all, indebted to the many authors whose works we list in the Resources section of every chapter. Their work provided us with a broad understanding of the major areas of technical communication. We also appreciate the work of the many authors we cite for various figures, tables, and textboxes throughout the book.

We are indebted to thousands of students in numerous introductory technical communication courses over the past 21 years who have given us a good perspective on what they need in an introductory textbook. We especially appreciate the many students who gave us permission to use samples of their work: Nancy Williams, Kay Collins, Russell Jarvis, Don Gentry, Robert Stultz, Lisa Trimarchi, Laura Martinez, and Ginger Puryear.

We called on the expertise of numerous professionals in a variety of fields, who generously shared their specialized knowledge. In particular, we acknowledge the help of Carole S. Hinshaw, head of the Reference Department, University of Central Florida Library, for her conscientious reading of the chapters on library research and her many excellent suggestions. Any errors in these areas that crept into this book are entirely our own fault or the result of the inevitable change in information through the passage of time. We also thank Corinne T. Russo of the University of Central Florida Career Resource Center, whose helpfulness and broad knowledge of the job-search field helped immensely in preparing Chapters 11 and 12. For help with the section in Chapter 5 on surveys and questionnaires, we thank Don Zimmerman of Colorado State University.

We owe a special thanks to Karla Kitalong, of the University of Central Florida, who reviewed the manuscript for the purpose of suggesting additional artwork. Her comments and suggestions were particularly helpful. Other technical communication faculty at the University of Central Florida—Madelyn Flammia, J. D. Applen, Paul Dombrowski, and Mary Ellen Gomrad—provided helpful suggestions along the way. David Gillette, of California Polytechnic State University, provided many excellent suggestions concerning the Web site for the textbook. For suggestions and continued support, we thank our friend and colleague, Gail Lippincott of the University of North Texas. Carol Shehadeh, of the Florida Institute of Technology in Melbourne, was primarily responsible for the Web site and provided many outstanding elements that will be useful to both students and faculty. We are indebted as well to Nancy Sadusky-Krantz for her remarkable work on the *Instructor's Manual*. Because of her efforts we are confident we have one of the best instructor's manuals a textbook could possibly have.

We much appreciate the contributions of the many professionals who generously agreed to be interviewed for the "From the Workplace" profiles and sidebar comments. Their insights and experiences unquestionably helped make this textbook a more useful, real-to-life book. We are also grateful to those professionals whose work we were, unfortunately, not able to include, not because of any lack of quality in the comments they provided us but only because of lack of space.

We also want to thank the reviewers of the textbook proposal or the manuscript: Ann M. Blakeslee, Eastern Michigan University; Nancy W. Coppola, New Jersey Institute of Technology; James Dubinsky, Virginia Technical Institute; Kevin LaGrandeur, New York Institute of Technology; Kenneth Rainey, Southern Polytechnic University; Carol M. W. Shehadeh; Katherine Staples, Austin Community College; Thomas L. Warren, Oklahoma State University; William J. Willamson, University of Northern Iowa; and Beverly Zimmerman, Brigham Young University.

We must thank Ginger Yarrow of Elm Street Publishing Services, Inc. Ginger worked closely and very professionally with us to ensure the entire production process went smoothly. Her assistant, Heather Johnson, provided timely support on numerous occasions. Marcy Lunetta, permissions editor, obtained a number of permissions for the textbook, and we are grateful for her efforts.

We are also grateful to many people at Longman Publishers: Ellen Darion, senior developmental editor, who worked with us on the first draft of the manuscript; Janet Lanphier, development manager; Donna DeBenedictis, production manager; Shaie Dively, photo researcher; Christopher Bennem, marketing manager; Nancy Garcia, media supplements editor; and William Russo, editorial assistant. We especially appreciate the guidance of Linda Stern, development editor for Longman Publishers. Under her direction, the myriad details of this project came together smoothly and professionally. So many of the strengths of this book's design and contents can be directly traced to her efforts. She pulled together the contributions of authors, artists, editorial staff, and production staff to help make the finished work much better than it otherwise would have been.

We undoubtedly owe our greatest thanks to Eben Ludlow, vice president of Longman Publishers, who invited us to work on this book, who ensured we had the resources we needed to publish it along with the supplements, and who provided invaluable support throughout the writing and publication process. All authors should be so fortunate as to work with someone as committed as he is to quality publishing.

Finally, each of us wants to thank some other special people:

I want to thank my co-author, Karen Lane, who worked tirelessly from the planning to the production of this textbook. Much of its quality is due to her thoroughly professional efforts. Of course, I also want to thank my wife, Carol, and my son, Sam, for their understanding and for providing me the time to complete this project.

Dan Jones
Department of English
University of Central Florida
djones@ucf.edu

My first thanks go to my co-author, Dan Jones. It would be impossible to overstate the importance of collaboration in a large project such as this, and Dan is the ideal partner in a collaboration. He is diligent and insightful and—unusual in my experience—totally without ego concerning his work. Writing this book has been a huge undertaking for both of us, and the fact that it went as smoothly and successfully as it did is a tribute to Dan's knowledge, professional high standards, and generosity of spirit.

I also owe a great deal to my family and friends, who put up with my absences, both mental and physical, necessitated by my being engaged in a project of this magnitude over the course of so many months. Not only were they understanding when I was not able to fulfill many of the responsibilities of friendship and home, but they were actively supportive and always encouraged me when I needed it. I particularly want to thank my parents for their extraordinary love and encouragement; my daughters, Deborah and Amanda, for their love and support and the joy their presence in my life has always brought; and my dear husband, Mickey, who patiently and lovingly anchored me when I most needed it.

Karen Lane
Karen Lane Technical Consulting
klane@klane.com

1

Understanding Technical Communication

Technical Communication as
an Essential Skill   2

Technical Communication in College   5

Technical Communication in the
Workplace   8

Technical Communication and
Social Action   11

Technical Communication and
Corporate Politics   17

Technical Communication, Ethics, and
Professionalism   19

Technical Communication and
Collaboration   22

Technical Communication, the Global
Corporate World, and Diversity   23

Technical Communication and
Technology   26

From the Workplace   24

IN THIS CHAPTER

Information—on history, theory, background, a fact, or a statistic—is useful and valuable, since it can lead to a broader understanding of a subject, an issue, a problem, or a trend. But information by itself isn't enough. When you use various strategies to apply what you know, you develop skills. Students in the technical disciplines and practicing technical professionals need diverse communication skills more than ever. As this introductory chapter illustrates, your communication skills are an integral part of your studies, and they will largely determine your success both in college and in the workplace. In an age of cross-functional teams (people from many departments working together as a team), a global economy, cultural diversity, and rapidly changing technology, your communication skills can be your biggest asset.

You will learn about:

- technical communication as an essential skill for college and the workplace. Your ability to communicate effectively will be a big factor in determining your career path.
- technical communication as a social action. You create documents for people to do, understand, or accept something, and you must consider that your audience may derive different meanings from those you intended in your communications.
- technical communication and corporate politics. Your ability to communicate effectively will help you handle adversity in the workplace.
- technical communication, ethics, and professionalism. Your documents are influenced by your values and by your behavior.
- technical communication and collaboration. You will work with others on many kinds of projects and will collaborate in many different ways.
- technical communication, globalism, and diversity. Your career and the companies you will work for are tied to a much larger economy than your local economy, and the people you meet both in college and in the workplace will constantly challenge you to handle cultural diversity.
- technical communication and technology. You will learn how keeping pace with the rapid changes in technology at home, in college, and in the workplace is yet another essential communication skill.

TECHNICAL COMMUNICATION AS AN ESSENTIAL SKILL

Technical Communication and You

As a college student, you will have many opportunities to communicate with your peers and your professors in writing, in oral presentations, and in other contexts. And if you are participating in an internship or working part- or full-time while taking college classes, you already know that you continue to face many communication challenges in the workplace. Once you complete your college studies and begin your career in earnest, you will continually be called on to communicate with all kinds of audiences in all kinds of situations using a variety of media. You don't have to be a technical-writing major to learn about technical communication. If you are a student majoring in a technical discipline or if you are a technical professional, you will find that technical communication is part of what you do in school or on the job. In effect, your communication skills are an integral part of who you are.

> Students majoring in a technical discipline write proposals, reports, and instructions.
>
> Technical professionals prepare many kinds of technical correspondence; write proposals, reports, manuals, and instructions; and give technical presentations.

It's common knowledge that communication skills are some of the most important factors in determining a person's success in the workplace. If you look at the characteristics and qualities of the most successful people at any company in any profession, you will find that by far the majority of these people are excellent communicators. They know how to plan, research, design, write, edit, evaluate, and produce effective technical documents. And they are confident and able presenters. In general, they have strong interpersonal skills. They know how to get what they want by using persuasion and by negotiating. Of course, luck, personality, friends in the right places, timing, and many other elements contribute to the potential for success on the job. However, excellent communication skills are among the most reliable predictors of success for you and your career.

What does success mean? It means accomplishing your goals. For you, that could be financial security, peer recognition, promotions, respect of others, or job satisfaction. Success is the accomplishment of what you set out to do. And success is not mostly a matter of luck or timing. Work on your skills—technical, interpersonal, and communication—and you will position yourself to succeed. Your communication skills are the concern of the course for which you are reading this textbook. You have been learning communication skills all your life, but the ones you will need to be successful in your career are not only extensions of what you already know but are also more specialized for the technical professions.

In a certain sense, communication skills overlap greatly with your technical and interpersonal skills. They are the unifying elements in bringing together what you know with those who need to know it. That means communicating not only your technical knowledge but also your understanding of the qualities and dynamics of a situation.

Defining Technical Communication

Communication is a very broad issue, encompassing all kinds of visual, auditory, emotional, and technical content. In this text, we are interested in technical communication. What does that mean?

Technical communication, like many other kinds of communication, is concerned with making a purpose clear to an audience. However, technical communication is more specialized than other kinds of communication (for example, essay writing) in many ways. Technical communication, unlike more general communication, concentrates more on meeting the information needs of the audience, on handling a specialized vocabulary, on creating a helpful design, and on providing illustrations wherever appropriate, for example. And while the same could be true in part of some other kinds of communication, technical communication emphasizes these features more consistently. (See Figure 1.1.)

Technical communication, with its typical emphasis on subjects concerning science and technology, is more specialized than other writing. Most often its subjects are the concerns of a particular discipline or profession; its aim is to provide information a specific audience can use. The primary aim of technical communication isn't to delight or entertain, but to provide information that needs to be understood, accepted, or used. It often has a specialized vocabulary, and effectively handling this specialized vocabulary presents one of the biggest challenges to those who write technical prose.

Technical communication is also different from other kinds of communication in the kinds of documents it typically generates—technical correspondence (letters, memos, e-mail), reports (a discussion of something that was done), proposals (an offer to do something), and instructions (a discussion of how to do something). You will learn more about these various types of documents (also called genres) later in this book.

> " " The primary aim of technical communication isn't to delight or entertain, but to provide information that needs to be understood, accepted, or used.

FIGURE 1.1

Components of Technical Communication

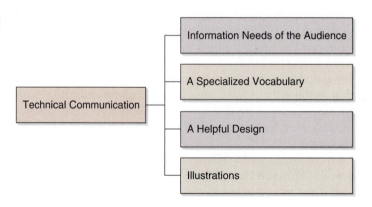

Learning how to create effective technical documents isn't easy. For example, you will determine specifically what you need to say about your subject for a well-defined reader using appropriate prose, and you will design that content in a particular genre (or kind of document). You may have to deliver the content in oral, rather than visual, form. And learning how to create and deliver an effective technical presentation requires a similar approach. For a presentation, the appropriate prose is not only the words you will say and the manner in which you say them, but the words you use in any visuals. In addition, appropriate design for the visuals is also a major concern.

Once you learn what you need to know to communicate technical information clearly, you will have an essential skill for a college student and, later, for a technical professional.

TECHNICAL COMMUNICATION IN COLLEGE
Typical Communication Challenges

If you are a college sophomore, junior, or senior, you have already spent a great deal of time completing many writing assignments and oral presentations. In high school you may have written research papers for your English, history, humanities, or science classes. And you may have taken many exams that required in-depth responses to essay questions. You probably also had to give oral presentations on everything from book reports to laboratory experiments.

In your college classes you no doubt continue to write research papers, give oral presentations, and take essay exams. As a student, you probably spend many hours taking notes, which you may even flesh out to help you during subsequent review. And, if you are taking one or more courses in the sciences, you are probably taking an accompanying lab for some of these courses. In the labs you probably take notes on your experiments and may also be required to turn in laboratory reports on what you have done.

Additionally, you may have created a home page or campus organization page on the Web (see Figure 1.2), and you probably are sending an increasing amount of e-mail. It's also likely that you have already been involved with at least one team project requiring you to work with your classmates. And, typically, you have been called upon to give oral presentations on many kinds of topics and issues in college, just as you did in high school.

In many respects, you spend much of your time in college learning how to solve problems. Of course, many of your courses require you to memorize terminology, dates, names, theories, and so on. However, many of your courses also teach you how to look at problems from many perspectives and how to consider many possible approaches for addressing these problems. Your writing assignments and oral presentations are essential in helping to shape your critical thinking and reasoning, while giving you a solid foundation in the knowledge you need in your discipline. And if the assignment requires research, you are also sharpening your research skills.

FIGURE 1.2

College Web Site
Main Page

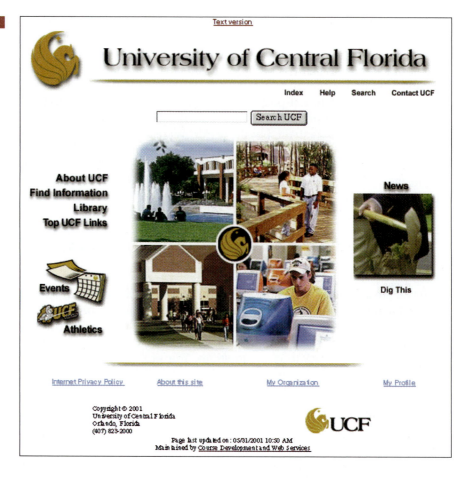

Communication is one essential tool you will always use for problem solving. You ask questions when you are not sure what the problem is or how you should approach it, you communicate constantly with your peers if you and they have been assigned to work on a project as a team, and you more than likely jot down notes to keep track of your thoughts as you consider various solutions. Written and oral communication are in every way an integral part of all of the problem solving you do in all of your college classes, regardless of your major. Simply stated, the primary purpose of much of the communication you do in college is to prove your understanding of the information you are learning and to improve your analytical or thinking skills.

As shown in Figure 1.3, you will have several different audiences as a college student. Your primary audience is typically a college professor or, in the case of some classes, a graduate teaching assistant. Sometimes your audience is a classmate if your teacher relies on peer review for drafts of your work. Often your audience is a group of your peers, particularly if you are working on a team assignment. It's not uncommon for your audience to know as much as or more than you about your subject.

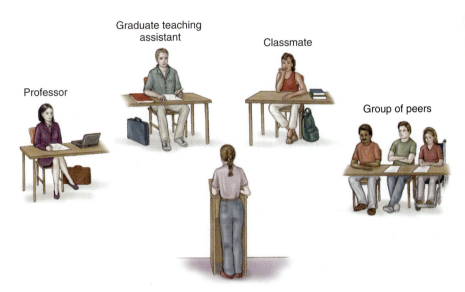

FIGURE 1.3

A College Student's Audiences

Communication Skills and Success in College

Your success in college is directly tied to your communication skills. Students who write well typically receive higher grades on papers, students who have strong interpersonal skills work with their peers and their professors much more effectively, and students who are able presenters deliver stronger oral presentations. Many students tend to focus exclusively on learning their disciplines—all of the necessary concepts, theories, terminology, and so on. Sometimes it's easy to lose sight of the fact that communication skills are an integral part of learning what you need to know about your discipline. Once you have begun your career, you will be constantly called on to communicate with people from all backgrounds. The more effectively you can communicate technical information to a wide variety of audiences, the more successful you will be and the more valuable you will be to your employer.

Changes in Your College Environment

College campuses and the way you learn in college are changing rapidly, and if you are to succeed in your college studies, you must learn how to adjust to these changes. Your college classes only faintly resemble the college classes your parents took a few decades ago. Today computer technology (computers, CD-ROMs, DVDs), the Internet (e-mail, chat rooms, the Web, distance learning via the Web), and multimedia classrooms with state-of-the-art video and audio are widely used in the college learning experience. Most college students today will make extensive use of these technologies during their undergraduate years, and many of their courses will require extensive use of these technologies as well. And, inevitably, these technologies are also changing the ways professors cover the content of their courses.

How is this change important to you? Your communication skills are both challenged by and shaped by the technologies and changes in teaching methods. The rapid pace of these changes compels you to learn how to communicate effectively in many new and different ways from college students just a generation before you. And the more skilled you are as a communicator, the better you will be able to adapt to all of these changes.

TECHNICAL COMMUNICATION IN THE WORKPLACE

Typical Communication Challenges

When you begin your career as a technical professional, you will find that the kinds of writing you do, your purposes for writing, and the audiences you write for are often quite different from those in college writing. And the situations requiring oral presentations are also quite different from those in your college classes.

Just as you spend much of your time in college learning how to solve problems, you spend a great deal of your time in the workplace learning how to solve problems, too. One major difference in your favor will be that you will have had at least some classroom experience behind you to help you determine how to approach the problems you encounter in the workplace. But the pressure to solve quickly and appropriately the problems you encounter is another difference, one that is not so helpful. The company or organization you work for exists to make a profit, and the problems you have been hired to address affect that profit. You will continually have to draw on a wide array of communication skills in addition to your knowledge and intuition to help you address the problems you have been assigned or that you discover.

The kinds of workplace writing you do will include

- correspondence (letters, memos, e-mail)
- notes
- manuals (instructions)
- proposals
- reports
- policies and procedures
- job descriptions
- performance evaluations
- promotional materials (posters, brochures, fliers)

Your purposes for writing may be simply

- to inform
- to describe
- to relate how something happened
- to persuade

ADVANCING YOUR CAREER

Regardless of your job title or position, following these general principles will help you make the most of your time at work and prepare you for those (perhaps unexpected) changes of employment:

- Never be afraid to ask questions or ask for clarification on a topic. The more you understand, the more you can contribute.
- Look for ways in which you can help your co-workers, your boss, and your employer. Willingness to use your talents—whether or not they fit into your job description—is always noticed.

—Paul Lockwood, team leader, Chicago, Illinois

- to explain why something was done or how to do something
- to solve a problem

Your audiences will include supervisors at all levels of management, peers or co-workers, subordinates, customers, vendors, various other technical professionals, investors, and the general public. Your readers may know as much as or far more than you do, or they may know far less than you about your subject.

Oral presentations in the workplace will include impromptu presentations during staff meetings, outlined presentations to clients and department supervisors, and scripted presentations at conferences or other professional meetings.

Other necessary skills are more subtle. You will have to develop your thinking skills, personal qualities, and interpersonal skills. You will have to learn

- how to determine what is and is not important information in a given context
- how to read between the lines in various contexts
- how to recall information from discussions accurately
- how to absorb and apply new information
- how to balance conflicting work demands
- how to organize yourself and others to accomplish tasks
- how to listen to the ideas and suggestions of others
- how to respond constructively to the ideas and suggestions of others

You may, for example, be assigned to improve the performance, reliability, efficiency, or some other quality of an engineering design, a computer program, a testing procedure, or a marketing method. Even trying to solve a seemingly minor problem may require weeks, even months, of work. Your employer will expect you to approach the problem creatively and effectively, expecting you to come up with solutions or answers or ways of further limiting the question. You will often brainstorm with team members and work collaboratively to come up with solutions. You will be expected to provide updates on your progress—orally in staff meetings and in writing via e-mail, memos, or perhaps an informal or formal report. Throughout the entire process you will be called on to use a wide array of communication skills in addition to many analytical skills.

Communication Skills and Success in the Workplace

Once you have begun your career in earnest, you will notice a lot of things during those first few weeks or months on the job. You will notice that some of your subordinates, peers, and supervisors have exceptional communication skills. (See Figure 1.4.) You will also notice that many subordinates, peers, and supervisors have weak communication skills. As the months and years pass, you will see that many of those whose strong technical knowledge is coupled

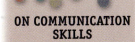

ON COMMUNICATION SKILLS

At best, the communication skills of new-hire graduates coming into the company are mixed. Colleges clearly do not make acquiring communications skills a requirement of computer degrees to the same level as acquiring software skills. It's not unusual to find evidence of poor communications skills in the first product produced by new-hire candidates—their own résumés.

—Rob Williams, software development manager, Lake Mary, Florida

FIGURE 1.4

The Value of Technical Communication Skills

Professionals with strong technical knowledge and exceptional communication skills are effective and successful in their fields.

with exceptional communication skills will be rewarded with employee awards, bonuses, pay raises, promotions, or other new job opportunities within the company. Many will leave to pursue even better opportunities elsewhere.

Employers know that people who are knowledgeable about their discipline and who also can communicate their knowledge in many different, effective ways make valuable employees. These typically are the employees most responsible for helping a company create quality products and provide quality services for clients. These are the employees who are, in effect, the backbone of a good company. In a very real sense, your success, the success of your career, and the success of the company that employs you are tied together by and dependent on knowledge skills, people skills, and, most of all, communication skills.

Throughout this book, you will read interviews with professionals in your own and other fields. The professionals featured have a variety of backgrounds and perform a variety of jobs. What they have in common is a reliance on their strong communication skills to make their work more effective and their careers more successful.

Changes in Your Workplace Environment

The professionals you will read about also demonstrate the value of adapting to the rapidly changing nature of the workplace, an environment that varies constantly because of changes in corporate practices, products, management, employees, clients, and technologies. Professionals often find themselves making myriad adjustments, from taking on new tasks and learning new tools to changing positions within a company to changing careers entirely. In fact, it's more likely you will have to adjust to such changes and even make major changes in your career than it is that you will do essentially the same work for the typical 30 to 40 years of a career.

How is this rapid change in the workplace significant to you? The answer is simple. Learning the content of your discipline is only one small part of what you'll need to know to keep up with these changes. The available knowledge in your discipline will continue to grow rapidly every year, and keeping up with new knowledge in your field will be only part of the challenge. Rapid changes in technology, in the tools to help you get your job done, are another important factor. You'll be constantly challenged to keep current. However, what employers require most is employees who are adaptable, imaginative, creative, and articulate. These are the people who most readily thrive in a rapidly changing and dynamic workplace. In brief, your communication skills will be an essential part of your ability to adapt to and cope with change.

> " "
> What employers require most is employees who are adaptable, imaginative, creative, and articulate.

TECHNICAL COMMUNICATION AND SOCIAL ACTION

Social Contexts of Technical Communication

A common misconception is that technology and science are neutral activities and therefore those who communicate in the technical professions must be as neutral and objective as possible in their communications. Far from being neutral, technology and science occur within social, cultural, historical, political, and other contexts.

Technical communication occurs in social contexts and therefore technical communication is a social action. This view of technical communication means that you write correspondence and other technical documents so that other people can understand, accept, or do something. Your communications do not exist for their own sake. They are communications intended for others and quite often require others to respond. Your documents evoke feelings from others, challenge their thinking, inform them of something they may know only a little about, tell them how to do something they didn't know how to do previously, or perhaps persuade them to accept an idea they were at first unwilling to accept.

From the reader's standpoint, the fact that technical communication is a social action means that your technical documents are often interpreted differently by different people for different reasons. The meanings of your documents are determined not only by you but also by your readers. Readers read your documents with many kinds of backgrounds, expectations, values, assumptions, and opinions, and, in doing so, they help shape the meaning of what you have written. In addition to what your audience brings to the interpretation of your document, your technical documents come with an underlying assumption: you are asserting that your representation of the material your documents contain is the appropriate one, the right one, the "real" one. Other writers may have a different view of the material and may present it quite differently.

For example, your job-application letter is aimed at a prospective employer to help you obtain a job interview, your technical memo may be a status report to your supervisor on your project, your proposal may ask experts for continued funding for an experiment, or your instructions may tell a novice user how to install a new device to a computer. In each instance, your readers likely will have questions that must be answered, reading habits that range from careless to painstaking, pressures that are beyond your control, deadlines you are unaware of, and personalities that range from agreeable to difficult. Your technical documents must be written (or your technical presentations given) with these social, or people-oriented, contexts in mind. And they must be crafted to reach an audience that likely has mixed interests, backgrounds, needs, and abilities.

Social Contexts for Communication Failures

The social contexts of technical communication may also be understood by looking at the reasons why too much technical communication fails and at the consequences of these failures. Much technical communication fails because so many people focus on what they want to say rather than on what the reader needs to read or the listener needs to hear. In effect, much technical communication fails because writers and speakers fail to consider the social contexts of their communications or, in a phrase, their obligations to the reader or listener.

Technical documents fail for many of the same reasons that other kinds of writing fail:

- readers are ignored
- the purpose is not clear
- the organization is weak
- the subject is not focused
- the document is too long
- the style is not effective (many words are inappropriate, many sentences are too long or poorly constructed, many paragraphs are too long, many paragraphs are not detailed enough)
- the tone is inappropriate for the audience and purpose
- the document has basic errors in mechanics (grammar, abbreviations, punctuation, spelling, capitalization, numbers)
- the document has not been adequately edited or revised
- the design makes the document too difficult to navigate easily

One study of writing in organizations notes five categories of problems that readers have with corporate prose as shown in Figure 1.5 (Redish). All of

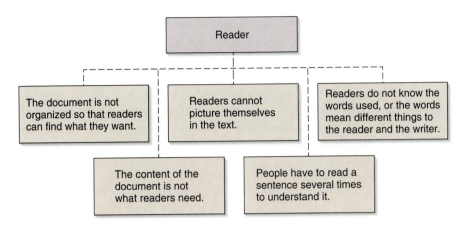

FIGURE 1.5

Problems Readers Have with Corporate Prose

SOURCE: Janice Redish. "Writing in Organizations," *Writing in the Business Professions*. Ed. Myra Kogen. Urbana: NCTE/ABC, 1989.

these problems are complex and have many causes. However, they all have one thing in common: writers failing to consider the reader. Writing technical prose is a social activity. Effective technical writing is audience based rather than subject based. Unfortunately, too much technical prose ignores the audience in a variety of ways:

- **Poorly organized documents:** People read for different purposes at different times. Sometimes people read to learn. Sometimes they read to do. Writers of technical prose must consider how people are using their documents so they can organize information in such a way that readers can find the necessary information easily. Good organization provides readers with a path they can easily follow. Without that path, they can't see connections and they can't follow the ideas the writer wants to convey.

- **Inappropriate content:** Writers too often focus on what they know rather than on what the reader needs to know. When writers write for themselves, they teach themselves what they already know. To reach readers who have not already mastered the material, writers have to be advocates for the audience and have users test the material to make sure the needed information is present and accessible.

- **Readers' not picturing themselves in the text:** A style can be so formal and abstract that it completely fails to clarify how or when to do a task. And when readers have to reread sentences to understand them, often it's because the writers put too many ideas in one sentence or created unnecessarily long and convoluted sentences.

- **Readers' not understanding the words writers use:** Writers of technical, bureaucratic, or business prose forget they are often writing to a complex audience (an audience whose members bring varied backgrounds to the task they are facing), they use inappropriate strategies for writing to multiple audiences, and they often assume their peers are familiar with professional jargon when they aren't (Redish 104–114).

> When writers write for themselves, they teach themselves what they already know.

The *Challenger* Disaster as a Communication Failure

There are many possible explanations for what caused the space shuttle *Challenger* accident on January 28, 1986, that killed seven people only 73 seconds after liftoff. (See Figure 1.6.) One key explanation is that a major communication gap occurred between management at one level and engineers at another. Various memos written at least five months before the accident warn about an O-ring erosion problem. Roger Boisjoly's July 31, 1985, memo, for example, warned that problems with the O-ring could result in "a catastrophe of the highest order—loss of human life." He concluded the memo by writing: "It is my honest and very real fear that if we do not take immediate action to dedicate a team to solve the problem with the field joint having the number one priority, then we stand in jeopardy of losing a flight along with all the launch pad facilities."

Roger Boisjoly's warning and warnings in numerous memos from other engineers and consultants were also ignored in subsequent months. Some warnings were ignored because of poor wording, others because of mounting pressures to launch, and yet others because no one could guarantee the launch would fail (ironically, engineers work to assure structural integrity; they don't offer guarantees that a structure will fail). The biggest point is that even the clearest and most direct memos on the issue were not interpreted in the same way by all of those who read them. Here was a tragic example of how technical documents are subject to the same social contexts as other kinds of writing.

FIGURE 1.6

U.S. Space Shuttle *Challenger*

The Costs of Ineffective Technical Communication

Ineffective technical communication also has its costs:

- Poorly written and poorly designed technical documents waste time. Readers must spend extra time trying to determine the purpose of the document if its purpose is not clear or if the language is obscure.
- Poorly written and designed documents decrease productivity. If employees are spending more time trying to understand both internal and external communications, they are spending less time doing the other things they need to do and were hired to do.
- Poorly written and designed documents may cause missed deadlines. Often because of poor organization or some other miscommunication, readers are not made aware that a response to a memo or e-mail message, for example, is required on a specific and perhaps urgent deadline.
- Poorly written and designed documents increase expenses. Printing jobs may have to be redone because of typos, design errors, or other problems.
- Poorly written and designed documents affect promotions and pay raises. If your communication skills are much weaker than those of a peer, the chances are good that your peer, not you, will receive upcoming promotions and pay raises.
- Poorly written technical documents affect prestige and morale. Your peers, subordinates, and superiors quickly will become aware of your communication skills and reward you or ignore you accordingly, actions which directly affect your prestige in the company and your morale as an employee.
- Poorly written and designed documents damage a company's reputation. Many companies spend a great deal of money paying staff to provide technical support, for example, in order to compensate for inadequate documentation of a product. If a company's product is difficult to use because of poor documentation (and poor technical support), clients or customers will find another company that does provide a quality product.
- Finally, poorly written and designed documents damage your reputation. If you cannot adequately make the purpose of communications clear, or if they are regularly filled with misspellings and other errors, people will doubt not only your communication skills but also your skills in other areas.

The Benefits of Effective Technical Communication

Unquestionably, effectively written and designed technical documents have numerous benefits:

- Effective technical documents save you and your readers time. Creating an effective document may often require more time initially, but as the

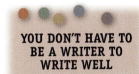

YOU DON'T HAVE TO BE A WRITER TO WRITE WELL

I am burdened with a masochistic enjoyment of writing. I am envious of those who write quickly and painlessly (and well). One of my idols is Norman Maclean who reportedly took ten years to write *A River Runs Through It.*

—Jack M. Watts, Jr., Ph.D., fire safety consultant, Middlebury, Vermont

author or one of the authors you will save time later by having to answer fewer questions about your document or having to provide fewer revisions. Your readers will save time because they will be able to find and understand the information they need more quickly.

■ Effective technical documents more often achieve their purpose. If you've done the necessary work of analyzing your audience, focusing your subject, and dealing with the many other contexts of your document, you will state your purpose where you need to state it, your audience will more readily recognize what results you are trying to achieve, and your audience will more likely understand, accept, or do what you want it to.

■ Effective technical documents often lead to better grades for college students and pay raises, promotions, and other kinds of recognition in the workplace. It should be obvious that quality work is rewarded whether it's in college or on the job.

■ Effective technical documents can save you money whether you are in college or in the workplace. The savings may be negligible in college compared to the savings in the workplace, but sometimes the savings in college can be substantial. For example, if you're working on a complex collaborative college document or project, and it's been created the way it should be, you can save money in printing by not having to reprint a botched job. Quality documents in the workplace can save companies thousands of dollars by avoiding unnecessary reprintings, generating fewer calls to technical support, wasting fewer hours for crisis management, and so on.

■ Effective technical documents may enhance your career in intangible as well as tangible ways. Intangible ways can't be quantified in terms of money or time. Intangibles such as pride, prestige, and high morale rise both in college and in the workplace as the result of a project that's been well done. You will find your reputation is enhanced; others will want to collaborate with you on other projects. You'll become known as someone who can be counted on to do a job the way it's supposed to be done.

Apple Computer and Effective Technical Documentation

During the 1980s, as the world's first popular computer, the Macintosh, was designed and built, technical writers worked alongside computer programmers to help make a difference in the design of the computer. Numerous questions from the writers caused the programmers to rethink their design. Even today, the programmers receive most of the recognition for designing the Macintosh, but without the technical writers and their contributions to the design, as well as their work on the documentation, the story of the Macintosh's success might have been quite different. Consider, for example, the work of Caroline Rose, technical editor of *Inside Macintosh*, the Macintosh's user man-

ON WRITING AND DESIGN

But whether I was writing, or whether other people were writing, I learned to listen very carefully to writers, because they're forced to look at every detail minutely, and if they say something is complicated, or they don't understand how to write about it, well, what could we have designed that makes it so difficult to write about? If it's not easy to write about, it's not easy to use. So I use writing as a guide for design. This puts writers in a very unusual position with respect to development— which people in development are somewhat surprised to learn about when it happens . . . but they're a great resource. So is customer service, if you can get feedback—if you keep records about what people ask and where they're having problems, it's extremely valuable. All those things go back into design.

—Jef Raskin, manager of publications at Apple Computer and manager of the Macintosh Project, 1979–1982

FIGURE 1.7

An Early Macintosh Computer

The Macintosh computer, whose user manual, *Inside Macintosh,* is a classic in the field of technical writing.

ual. It was largely because of her efforts that the manual for using the Macintosh was ready on time and was so easy to understand. *Inside Macintosh* is well known for its appealing illustrations and clear language, qualities that contributed to the enormous success of the Macintosh. (See Figure 1.7.)

TECHNICAL COMMUNICATION AND CORPORATE POLITICS

Corporations are discourse communities. A discourse community is a group of people who commonly associate with each other. You will learn more about discourse communities and how to communicate effectively to them in later chapters. (See Chapter 2, "Audience and Persuasion," and Chapter 7, "Achieving an Effective Style.")

Understanding the Corporate Culture

Every corporation has a distinct way of doing things. An organizational chart of the various departments and managers will provide one view of how a company compartmentalizes various tasks. For example, a typical mid-size company may have departments for human resources, quality control, marketing, and research and development. Each will have supervisors or directors

FIGURE 1.8

An Organizational Chart

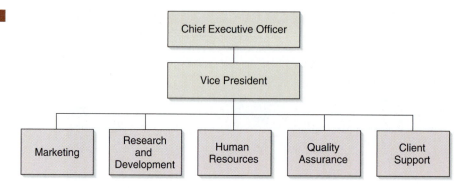

or managers, and higher up in the company will typically be various vice presidents and a chief executive officer. (See Figure 1.8 for an example of an organizational chart.) Such a hierarchy is only one way of understanding a particular discourse community, however. An organizational chart may not give you a real sense of who the most knowledgeable or most powerful people are within the company. To communicate more effectively within an environment, you will have to learn who the real decision makers are concerning the matter for which you are requesting action.

✳ Communicating in the Corporate Culture

THE POLITICS OF STYLE

Stylistic judgment is, last as well as first, always *political* judgment.

—Richard Lanham,
Revising Prose, 96

In addition to understanding the structure of a company, you also will have to learn the expected manner of communication within its environment. For example, you will have to determine when you should respond in writing to a communication. Sometimes doing so is optional, and sometimes it's best not to respond at all. And you will have to determine what the most effective or most preferred communication style is within the company. For instance, the company may prefer a more bureaucratic style over a plain style in communicating with clients. Or perhaps the humorous tone you establish in a letter will be seen as unprofessional when your aim is simply to make your letter more interesting to read. So before you select a style for a communication, consider your audience and the consequences your prose style will have, both for you and for the audience.

And don't forget that every corporate communication exists within certain contexts. For example, if you send a seemingly simple e-mail on restricting photocopying privileges for employees, instead of accomplishing your purpose of saving paper, you may paradoxically find the usage going up as disgruntled employees either ignore you or make a point of overusing the photocopier.

Finally, employees in every corporate culture experience pressures from within and without. There are constant pressures to succeed, to win against the competition (other employees, other teams, other departments, and other companies), to appease stockholders and supervisors, to meet deadlines, to gain recognition and rewards, to handle difficult personalities, to come in under budget, and so on. To communicate effectively in the corporate culture, you must learn how to play the politics or use the maneuvers or strategies best suited to your purposes.

TECHNICAL COMMUNICATION, ETHICS, AND PROFESSIONALISM

Ethics

Ethics, simply defined, is the examination of right and wrong conduct or behavior. Developing or adhering to your sense of ethics and learning how to deal with people whose notions of ethical behavior and its value differ from yours are essential communication skills. Working in today's highly technological society often challenges personal values and convictions, and you need to have a good sense of what your values are if you are to keep your integrity and character intact. Your ethics typically play a major role in shaping all of your communications, and you will find you often must make tough ethical decisions both in college and in the workplace.

> " " Your ethics typically play a major role in shaping all of your communications, and you will find you often must make tough ethical decisions both in college and in the workplace.

For example, in college you may be asked by a group member on a collaborative project to do far more than your share of the assigned work. Should you help the group member out? Should you politely refuse and suggest that the group member do his or her fair share of the work? Should you tell your professor about the student's failure to contribute equally? In the workplace, you may, for example, be asked as you prepare a presentation for a potential client to promise more than your company can deliver to increase the chances your company will win the contract. Should you refuse to do so? Should you be completely honest with the client regardless of what your supervisor tells you to do? Should you complain to someone higher in management at the company that employs you? These are just some of the many ethical situations you can find yourself facing.

Professionalism

Professionalism concerns more than your ethical behavior. It concerns how serious, responsible, and accountable you are about your studies in college or about your job duties in the workplace. Professionalism is a matter of attitude as well as of behavior. As an attitude, professionalism means taking your work seriously and taking pride in your work. As a behavior, professionalism means constantly trying to create the best work you can provide, whether it's a project, a document, or a presentation. Professionals are people who work to the best of their abilities at all of the courses in college and people who work to be the best employees they can be on their jobs. Of course, professionalism is, in a sense, a value or an ethic.

Ethics and Professionalism in College

Many college campuses have handbooks concerning the behavior of students, faculty, and staff on campus. These handbooks typically provide guidelines about everything from attendance to disruptive behavior. Handbooks are helpful because they establish minimal ethical standards and give all concerned at least some understanding of what is expected. They cannot ensure that everyone will follow the rules, but they create a climate that helps to foster ethical behavior. College students face ethical challenges just as anyone else does. As a college student you may see other students who are cheating on an exam, plagiarizing all or part of a research paper, stealing from their roommates, or lying to their friends. And you may also be faced with temptations by these and other situations. How you deal with such challenges reflects your ethical beliefs and how you incorporate those beliefs into your life.

Ethics and Professionalism in the Workplace

You may be wondering how ethics enters into the technical workplace. Aren't decisions on technical matters rather cut-and-dried? No, not at all. As a technical professional, you may be asked to misrepresent a product to some clients, you may know of others who falsely take credit for another's achievement, you may have colleagues who do not contribute their fair share to a team project, or you may see others steal supplies from the office. These and innumerable other possible ethical situations occur daily on college campuses and in offices throughout the world. How do you do what is right and avoid doing what is wrong? In a complex situation in which you face two equally tempting actions, how do you determine which action is best?

There are no easy answers to many of these questions. In addition to the codes of ethics mentioned previously, many ethical systems offer ways to resolve conflicts. You will have to choose the ethical system that makes the most sense to you, one you think you can adhere to no matter how difficult the choices you may face. Living an ethical life as a college student, as an employee, and as a person isn't easy. However, you can have an ethical life if you are determined to have one.

Many professions have a code of ethics that they expect their members to adhere to in their day-to-day activities. Providing a code of ethics creates a climate of expectations for professional standards and behavior. Some members may choose to ignore the code of ethics of their profession; you cannot make people who are inclined to act unethically behave ethically. However, a code of ethics can lend guidance, especially to newcomers to a profession. (See Figure 1.9.)

The code of ethics for a profession or organization typically appears in membership directories for the profession's major society or societies, in

Legality

We observe the laws and regulations governing our profession. We meet the terms of contracts we undertake. We ensure that all terms are consistent with laws and regulations locally and globally, as applicable, and with STC ethical principles.

Honesty

We seek to promote the public good in our activities. To the best of our ability, we provide truthful and accurate communications. We also dedicate ourselves to conciseness, clarity, coherence, and creativity, striving to meet the needs of those who use our products and services. We alert our clients and employers when we believe that material is ambiguous. Before using another person's work, we obtain permission. We attribute authorship of material and ideas only to those who make an original and substantive contribution. We do not perform work outside our job scope during hours compensated by clients or employers, except with their permission; nor do we use their facilities, equipment, or supplies without their approval. When we advertise our services, we do so truthfully.

Confidentiality

We respect the confidentiality of our clients, employers, and professional organizations. We disclose business-sensitive information only with their consent or when legally required to do so. We obtain releases from clients and employers before including any business-sensitive materials in our portfolios or commercial demonstrations or before using such materials for another client or employer.

Quality

We endeavor to produce excellence in our communication products. We negotiate realistic agreements with clients and employers on schedules, budgets, and deliverables during project planning. Then we strive to fulfill our obligations in a timely, responsible manner.

Fairness

We respect cultural variety and other aspects of diversity in our clients, employers, development teams, and audiences. We serve the business interests of our clients and employers as long as they are consistent with the public good. Whenever possible, we avoid conflicts of interest in fulfilling our professional responsibilities and activities. If we discern a conflict of interest, we disclose it to those concerned and obtain their approval before proceeding.

Professionalism

We evaluate communication products and services constructively and tactfully, and seek definitive assessments of our own professional performance. We advance technical communication through our integrity and excellence in performing each task we undertake. Additionally, we assist other persons in our profession through mentoring, networking, and instruction. We also pursue professional self-improvement, especially through courses and conferences.

FIGURE 1.9

STC Ethical Principles for Technical Communicators

As technical communicators, we observe these ethical principles in our professional activities.

Reprinted with permission from the Society for Technical Communication, Arlington, VA.

promotional literature (for example, brochures, and annual reports), and increasingly on Web sites. The Society for Technical Communication, for example, publishes its STC Ethical Principles for Technical Communicators in its annual fall membership directory.

TECHNICAL COMMUNICATION AND COLLABORATION

Collaboration: The Pros and Cons

Collaborating means working with others, and it is an essential job and social skill. Unfortunately, some people don't work effectively with other people. They don't want to share the workload because they don't like to delegate, they fear that the quality of the work will suffer if they allow others to share the workload, they don't like having to deal with the egos of others, or they don't like conflict. There are many other reasons, too.

Most of the time, collaboration is not a choice—it is a requirement. A professor may assign a group project, or an employer may form a team to work on a particular undertaking. Therefore, like it or not, teamwork plays a big role both in college and in the workplace. Students in a variety of disciplines may be required to work together on teams to produce a project. Employees in the workplace have to work in teams because of the complexity of the products they are creating or modifying. Although the drawbacks of collaboration are what you would expect when any group of individuals pull together as a team, the rewards can be more than commensurate with the aggravations. Since collaboration is a fact of working life, learn to appreciate its advantages and deal with its disadvantages.

Collaboration in the Electronic Age

Computers, the Internet, video conferencing technology, cellular phones, office phones, fax machines, and same-day or overnight express mail services are just some of many tools or services used to enhance collaboration both in college and in the workplace. More than ever, people can work together more easily on projects even though they may be thousands of miles apart. Of course, there still are and probably always will be some communication glitches, but today's technologies and those in development are making geographical distances between people less of a concern. However, the conveniences of these technologies or services don't replace the complex skills of knowing how to collaborate with others. If anything, the conveniences are making people with strong collaborative and other interpersonal skills even more valuable and in demand.

TECHNICAL COMMUNICATION, THE GLOBAL CORPORATE WORLD, AND DIVERSITY

The Changing Workplace

Today's workplace is international or global. Most major and mid-size corporations, and even many smaller companies, have clients outside of the United States. Employees who are comfortable dealing with an international clientele are in high demand. These employees will often know not only the language but also the cultural practices of the clients with whom they deal. Cultural practices are another area where the successful communicator will overcome barriers. And these cultural practices often directly affect the way people communicate with each other.

For example, Middle Easterners often use decorative language in their communications, including exaggeration, digression, and generalities. Americans prefer a much more direct or explicit style, one that gets to the main point quickly. In Japan and other Asian countries, people emphasize building trust before practicing business, a cultural value that influences their writing. A business letter, for instance, may inquire about the reader's family or health. The point of the letter may not appear until much later in the letter.

Some famous international marketing mistakes:

A General Motors auto ad with "Body by Fisher" became "Corpse by Fisher" in Flemish.

Pepsi Cola's "Come Alive With Pepsi" campaign, when it was translated for the Taiwanese market, became "Pepsi brings your ancestors back from the grave."

Coors translated its slogan "Turn It Loose" into Spanish, where it read as "Suffer From Diarrhea."

American Airlines advertised its new leather first-class seats in the Mexican market with the slogan "Fly in Leather," which meant "Fly Naked" in Spanish.

Electrolux, a Scandinavian vacuum manufacturer, used this slogan in an American marketing campaign: "Nothing sucks like an Electrolux."

Underlying cultural differences often impede understanding more than language problems. Any of us can learn more about cultural differences. We can learn, for example, what gestures, personal space, eye contact, and notions of time mean in other cultures. The American gestures for hitchhiking and our "Okay" sign are considered obscene in some other cultures. As for personal space, South Americans and Arabs are more comfortable at closer distances than we are. Japanese prefer more personal space than we do. Knowing how a culture distinguishes private space and intimate space can be very helpful in face-to-face communications. Eye contact varies from culture to culture as well. Our culture values direct eye contact while in many Asian cultures lack of eye contact shows respect. The notion of time can vary considerably among cultures, too. Our culture values promptness while arriving 45 minutes or more after a scheduled meeting would be the norm in many Latin American cultures.

Employees who know a second language and who are informed about cultural practices in other countries are an asset to any company. But anyone can learn to be culturally aware and sensitive to the needs and views of other groups.

From the workplace

Stacey L. Rush
Surface Water Systems Engineer
Kirkland, Washington

Stacey worked in accounting for many years before discovering what she now expects will be her life's work. Along the way, she went from being an apprehensive speaker to one who is comfortable and effective sharing information with the public, both in formal speaking engagements and out in the field.

It took a long time for me to find a career.

Before earning my civil engineering degree, I fell into the accounting field and remained there for 13 years. It was not what I truly *wanted* to do; it was just a job that paid the bills. I went back to college and discovered I actually enjoyed math and science courses, so I chose engineering as a major—first because it was interesting and second because I knew it would be marketable. In 1998, I earned a bachelor of science degree in civil engineering with an environmental emphasis.

While I was a senior in college, I attended a job fair sponsored by the University of Washington. When I saw the WSDOT (Washington State Department of Transportation) booth, my first thought was that designing highways would be the most boring job in the world. I went to the booth and spoke with the representatives anyway, and I found out they were looking for civil engineers with an environmental interest. I submitted a lengthy application, took a written and oral exam, and was subsequently hired into a wonderful position in their Water Quality Section. The focus of my job was to protect the lakes and streams near highway construction.

The newspaper led me to my current occupation. I noticed an advertisement in the paper for a stormwater engineer in the city where I live. While my responsibilities vary at the City of Kirkland, my main focus is the protection of surface water quality within or adjacent to the city. This protection is achieved through both public education and enforcement of the city code as it relates to stormwater. I truly enjoy the fact that I live and work in the same community. I can walk to work, and because I live here, I have an extra incentive to make sure the surface water is protected.

Communication on the Job

The ability to communicate thoughts in writing is important in every job. At my job, I create educational and enforcement documents, letters, memos, and e-mails on a daily basis. Documentation of my work is essential, especially in regard to city code enforcement. And although computers are an invaluable tool, they have still not replaced paper and pencils. I use pencils and a notebook at my desk and when I am out in the field.

Technical Communication and Diversity

More than ever, both college and the workplace have diverse populations. (See Figure 1.10.) You will see and work with people from all economic levels, family structures, religious backgrounds, lifestyles, military experiences, and geographic regions. People also will have different individual values, education, skill levels, ethnic backgrounds, gender, and physical and mental challenges. To communicate effectively in such diverse environments, pay attention to how other people perceive issues, so you can be sensitive to their concerns.

Learn to acknowledge, respect, and value differences on campus and in the workplace. Of course, becoming aware of differences is part of what your college education is all about. However, becoming more aware of diversity

At the City of Kirkland, most of my work involves other people. I work with maintenance crews, reviewers, inspectors, and other engineers. I also work with regulatory agencies, consultants, and the public. Not only do I work with other city staff; I also communicate with outside agencies and the public on a regular basis. Part of my job is to teach the public about water quality and environment-related issues. The ability to convey ideas effectively is extremely important, and you are often judged by your communication skills.

When I am in a parking lot inspecting storm drains, the general public often asks me what I am doing. When I speak to the public about code enforcement, most of the time they don't know that they are doing something wrong. These instances give me the opportunity for public education. Most of the people I meet are interested in preserving the good quality of our surface water; they just don't understand how their actions can adversely affect the water. Once I explain it, they are usually quick to comply.

Giving Presentations

After I graduated, I realized quickly just how important it would be for me to be able to speak effectively in front of groups. So now I volunteer for every opportunity to present material in front of co-workers and other people. The old saying is true: the more you practice the better you get. In one of my first presentations while still in college, my hand was shaking so much I was unable to use the laser pointer. It may be a while before I become an excellent speaker, but at least I don't dread the idea of speaking before a group anymore.

In the last few years, I have learned that *how* you present material is as important as the material being presented. I use pictures and bulleted lists in PowerPoint to prompt my thoughts, usually without any additional notes. I try to speak to the audience—as I would talk to another person—and not try to recite a memorized speech.

Speaking to different audiences has taught me a great deal. The first thing I learned is to use humor as much as possible. If you can engage your audience early they will be less likely to fall asleep on you. Second, know as much as you can regarding the background of your audience, and be able to adjust your speech accordingly. Third, try not to use too many acronyms or you will lose your audience. Finally, speak slowly and clearly, pausing to stress important items. I have a tendency to speak quickly, especially when I am nervous, so I make a conscious effort to slow down when speaking. Usually I can make a joke about my fast-talking during my speech and it seems to help relax everyone, including me.

I am fortunate that I have a career I enjoy and care about. It is important for me to feel that I am contributing something in my life, and by taking small steps toward protecting streams and lakes, I feel as if I am making a difference in my community. I know it sounds strange, but I actually love working with stormwater. There are so many options for a civil engineer; I plan to continue working or volunteering in the engineering field for the rest of my life.

FIGURE 1.10

Diversity in the U.S. College Population

The college student population is expected to change in the future: the percentage of white students will fall and that of minorities will rise.

SOURCE: Educational Testing Service.

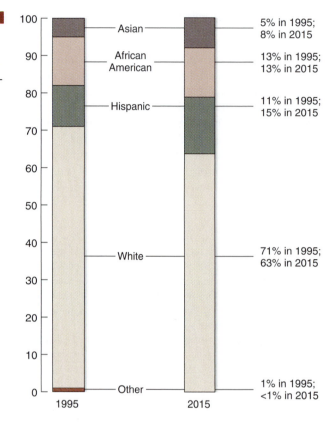

means much more than, for example, knowing the Equal Employment Opportunity Commission's hiring guidelines or embracing affirmative action. Becoming more aware of diversity means becoming more aware at a personal level, understanding that others very well may feel, think, believe, value, and act differently than you do. Becoming more aware of diversity means being sensitive to the many kinds of biases that can appear in your communications, whether they appear subtly, expressly, or without intent. It's important to find ways to recognize and avoid expressing biases.

TECHNICAL COMMUNICATION AND TECHNOLOGY

Everywhere you look—at home, on campus, and in the workplace—you will see how technology is increasingly changing how we live, study, and work. As shown in Figure 1.11, many homes now have offices complete with computers, printers, scanners, and fax machines. Many students have desktop computers, laptop computers, recorders, cellular phones, and electronic per-

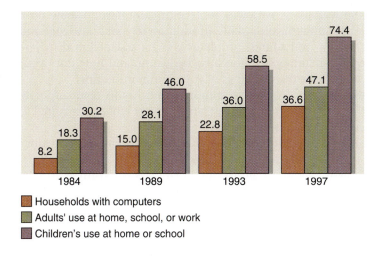

FIGURE 1.11

Percent Growth of Computer Use in the Home and Elsewhere

SOURCE: U.S. Census Bureau. Current Population Survey. October 1984, 1989, 1993, and 1997.

sonal digital assistants. And employees in the workplace have all of the above, as well as multimedia meeting rooms, video conferencing, and high-speed Internet connections. These and many more communication technologies have become integral to our lives, and the pace of change will only continue to accelerate. Keeping up with the rapid changes in technology at home, in college, and in the workplace is yet another essential communication skill.

Communication skills include more than knowing how to write effective letters, memos, proposals, and reports. Since all kinds of communication now occur electronically, knowing how to communicate comfortably and effectively in the electronic environment is essential to people in college and in the workplace. In addition, a great deal of communication in the workplace will be oral, not written. You may be called upon to give impromptu or outlined presentations at staff and department meetings and you will need to know how to use an assortment of presentation tools, ranging from overhead projectors to video. You may be called upon to represent your company at an off-site meeting. You may have to deal with clients over the phone, via videoconferencing, or in person. You will have many occasions to interview others for information, to negotiate, to network, to collaborate, and perhaps even to mentor or supervise. In all these activities, you will use many kinds of technologies to save time, money, and energy, and to represent both yourself and your company in the best way possible.

CHECKING WHAT YOU'VE LEARNED

- Why are your communication skills an integral part of who you are and a key factor in determining your personal and professional success?
- How do your writing assignments and oral presentations help shape your critical thinking and reasoning, besides providing you a solid foundation in the knowledge you need in your discipline?

- Once in the workplace, why will you continually have to draw on a wide array of communication skills, in addition to your knowledge and intuition, to help you address problems you are assigned or discover?
- Why is technical communication a social action, and how does your audience help shape the meanings of your communications?
- Every workplace is a discourse community and has its own corporate culture. Why will politics or maneuvering of many kinds be required to communicate successfully?
- Why is collaboration both in college and in the workplace a necessity? What are the many advantages and disadvantages of collaboration?
- The economy is essentially global. In which ways is sensitivity to how people in other cultures communicate necessary?
- Your own culture consists of people from many cultures and diverse ethnic backgrounds. How important it is to be aware of that diversity?
- The technology around you is rapidly changing. How do such rapid changes affect both those in college and in the workplace?

EXERCISES

REVIEW

1. Interview a professional (typically someone with five or more years of experience in a field). This person may be a friend, a relative, someone at the company where you are currently employed, or someone you contact for the first time. You may meet, talk over the phone, or e-mail this person. Ask how communication skills have been an essential part of his or her job. Bring your notes from the interview to class for discussion.

2. In a brief paragraph or two discuss what your expectations for this class were before the first class meeting. Now that you have listened to the introduction offered on the first day of class and have read this chapter, discuss how your expectations may have changed. If your expectations have not changed, discuss why. Bring your one or two paragraphs to class for discussion.

3. In a few brief paragraphs or a bulleted list, discuss some of the major concepts (for example, theories and ideas) you have studied so far in your discipline. Describe them so that people not in your discipline can understand what you have studied. Bring your paragraphs or list to class for discussion.

4. In a few brief paragraphs or a bulleted list, discuss some of the major tools or technology skills you have acquired so far. Also, discuss how you think these skills will be useful to you both in college and on the job. Bring your paragraphs or list to class for discussion.

5. In one or two paragraphs, discuss the kinds of writing projects (both individual and collaborative) you have been assigned in classes other than your English classes. Bring your paragraph(s) to class for discussion.

THE INTERNET

Using your favorite browser (for example, Netscape or Internet Explorer), find the Web site of a company you might like to work for. Discuss in several brief paragraphs how effectively the company projects a professional image on its Web site. Bring these paragraphs to class for discussion.

ETHICS/PROFESSIONALISM

Discuss in several detailed paragraphs an ethical choice you had to make concerning your job, college studies, or personal life. Discuss what factors made the decision difficult for you, and discuss how you resolved the situation. Bring the paragraphs to class for discussion.

 COLLABORATION

During class time, choose two other students in the class who may or may not have the same major as you do. Using no more than five minutes each, discuss with each other why you chose your major and where you expect to be in your career in five years. Identify the reasons you have in common for choosing your major, and identify any common points in your views of where you hope to be in five years. Take notes on what you tell the others and be prepared to share your comments with the rest of the class after this collaborative exercise is completed.

 INTERNATIONAL COMMUNICATION

Contact a friend, co-worker, or relative who regularly works with customers or employees from another country. Ask the person to describe some of the language, cultural, and other barriers that needed to be overcome in dealing with international clients. Provide this description in several detailed paragraphs, and bring these paragraphs to class for discussion.

RESOURCES

Bosley, Deborah S. *Global Contexts: Case Studies in International Technical Communication.* Needham Heights: Allyn and Bacon, 2001.

DuBrin, Andrew J. *Stand Out!* Paramus: Prentice Hall, 1993.

Lanham, Richard. *Revising Prose.* 3rd ed. New York: Macmillan, 1992.

Raskin, Jef. "Interview with Jef Raskin." *Making the Macintosh: Technology and Culture in Silicon Valley.* 13 April 2000. Online. Available at <http://library.stanford.edu/mac/primary/interviews/raskin/index.html>.

Redish, Janice. "Writing in Organizations." *Writing in the Business Professions.* Ed. Myra Kogen. Urbana: NCTE/ABC, 1989.

Rose, Caroline. "Caroline Rose on Technical Documentation." *Making the Macintosh: Technology and Culture in Silicon Valley.* 14 March 2000. Online. Available at <http://library.stanford.edu/mac/primary/interviews/rose/techdocs.html>.

PART ONE

Getting Ready

Chapter 2
Audience and Persuasion   33

Chapter 3
Collaboration   53

Chapter 4
Planning   79

Chapter 5
Gathering Information   110

Chapter 6
**Organizing and Managing
Information**   171

2

Audience and Persuasion

Audience and Technical Communication   35

Approaches to Audience   35

Secondary and Multiple Audiences   39

Audience and Levels of Technicality   41

Technical Communication and
    Persuasion   43

Strategies for Persuading Audiences   44

From the Workplace   48

IN THIS CHAPTER

Effective communication depends largely on understanding your audience. Understanding your audience means determining the information your audience needs in order to know, do, or accept something, determining your audience's preferences and biases, and understanding your audience's background, including its familiarity with your topic and receptiveness to your purpose. Being aware of the more subtly persuasive nature of technical communication is also important to effective communication.

You will learn about:

- the role of audience in determining your focus in your communications
- different approaches to audience: categorical and heuristic
- determining when your entire audience is a primary audience or whether secondary or multiple audiences should also be a concern
- the challenges of communicating to secondary and multiple audiences
- audience and levels of technicality: highly technical, moderately technical, slightly technical, and nontechnical
- the central role of persuasion in technical communication and strategies for persuading audiences

Perhaps the single most important principle of effective technical communication is that your audience largely determines or shapes everything you do.

Perhaps the single most important principle of effective technical communication is that your audience largely determines or shapes everything you do. If you want your communication to be effective, your audience should determine

- the planning and research that you must do
- the content you choose to discuss
- the purpose you establish
- the scope or depth of detail you provide
- the strategies you use for the opening, middle, and closing of your communication
- the organization of your topics
- the prose style of your sentences and paragraphs
- your design and illustration choices
- the overall tone or attitude of your communication
- the kind of document you write or presentation you give
- the editing, revising, and evaluating you do after you have completed your other work

THE USERS OF TECHNOLOGY

Developers, designers and documenters should meet with the users of the technology to understand their needs and the logistics of how they would actually use the technology.

—Rochelle Schwartz-Bloom, Ph.D., associate professor, Durham, North Carolina

Your audience must be your first and last consideration for these choices as well as many others.

Technical documents are also persuasive, and, of course, this quality is directly tied to audience. As a writer of technical prose, you are often doing more than informing or explaining. You often are trying to persuade your audience to agree with your point of view. In a grant proposal, for example, you try to convince a group of readers that a project is worthwhile and worthy of funding and that you and your team members are qualified to do the work. In a feasibility report, you try to convince readers that one course of action is preferable to another. In a letter of application, you try to convince readers that you are the best applicant for the job opening. These documents are obviously persuasive, but, in fact, all documents are persuasive in one way or another.

AUDIENCE AND TECHNICAL COMMUNICATION

Part of determining your focus is deciding what your audience needs to know, to do, or to accept. For that reason, you need to decide on the best means for getting your audience to understand or accept your purpose for writing. Many writers of technical prose are so preoccupied by what they know about a subject and what they want to write about it that they forget the most important reason for writing: to communicate with the audience.

Perhaps you've heard the statement about the secret to a successful business: location, location, location. One of the major secrets of successful writing is audience, audience, audience. This point may seem obvious and simple, but unfortunately most writers focus on their own view of the subject, purpose, and scope and not on their reader's view. You need to devote a lot of time to understanding your audience if your focus is to be properly defined.

APPROACHES TO AUDIENCE

Possible approaches to understanding your audience include using a categorical approach (for example, placing your audience into a well-defined niche determined by discourse community, background, or knowledge level) or using a heuristic approach (gathering information about your audience directly from the audience).

Categorical Approaches

A categorical approach to audience can be an effective way to gauge the expectations, assumptions, knowledge level, background, and other qualities of your audience if you don't know who your specific audience is.

Categorizing your audience by discourse community can provide helpful information. A discourse community, simply defined, is a group of people who share a common interest. A discourse community may be students in one class, students in one major, students on one campus, or all college students. A discourse community may be professionals in a discipline such as programming, engineering, science, law, medicine, or technical communication. Or a discourse community may be hobbyists with a particular pastime

A READER-CENTERED APPROACH

My career as a writer has taught me that reader-centered writing (a) tells readers what they need to know, not necessarily what you want to tell them, or at least puts the message in terms that are meaningful to the reader and answers the questions "So what?" "Who cares?" "What's in it for me?" (b) uses words, presentation, and graphics that are appropriate for the audience; (c) on Web sites, ensures that the navigation makes sense from the reader's point of view, which may not be the same as your company's structure (unless it's an intranet for company employees).

—Jean Weber, scientific and technical writer and editor, Queensland, Australia

such as quilting, sewing, gardening, ham radio, scuba diving, or chess. And, of course, there are many smaller discourse communities within larger discourse communities.

Members of a discourse community tend to share a common language or vocabulary, a common outlook, common values, and shared assumptions. They have certain expectations or standards for determining what constitutes knowledge in their community.

Some typical questions you need to consider about your audience include

- How similar are your readers? Are they all members of one discourse community? How much variation is there in their backgrounds and knowledge levels?
- Are there special preferences in this discourse community to which you need to give particular attention? Do you know what your readers expect when they read in their field?
- Are you sensitive to the values, expectations, and shared assumptions of this particular discourse community?
- Have you familiarized yourself with the documents people in this discourse community read?
- Are there particular political elements (tensions, relationships among people, histories, backgrounds) you need to pay particular attention to?

You may also categorize your audience by knowledge level. This approach takes the general view that most audiences can be divided into four categories: laypeople, executives, technicians, and experts. Two additional categories may also be useful: paraprofessionals and professionals. Of course, this approach basically groups audiences as a matter of convenience and is only partially helpful. It's important to keep in mind that the divisions in these categories are not so clear-cut; many audiences are combinations of the categories. All of us are laypeople concerning many subjects, and relatively few of us are experts. And some executives, for instance, read technical documents the same way technicians do and vice versa. Still, these categories can give you some helpful information concerning, for example, backgrounds and education levels, for at least an initial approach to your audience.

- **Laypeople:** Laypeople have little or no knowledge of the subject matter you are discussing and are unfamiliar with the basic terminology of the subject. Laypeople want to know enough to understand what they need to know, but typically don't want a very detailed discussion of the subject; they want to know enough to use or understand a new product.
- **Executives:** Executives are a specialized group of professionals who have decision-making authority in a company or organization. They have many years of experience in their field. Executives typically want to know the bottom line so that they can make informed decisions. They decide if and how a new product should be marketed. Executives

NOT READY FOR PRIME TIME

As a program manager, I often create written status reports on a program for an executive steering committee. Writing of the status of some reports that were part of the software product, but which were late in being completed, I wrote, "The reports are not ready for prime time yet."

Not thinking about my audience, I had used a phrase which was clear to me but not to my audience. I was comparing the reports to the *Saturday Night Live* Not-Ready-For-Prime-Time Players, a great group of actors who weren't totally polished but who were excellent at their craft. By that statement I meant to indicate that the reports were completed and functional but had a few cosmetic problems. I should have said so. The steering committee assumed the reports were in terrible shape.

—Bob Shapiro, senior program manager, Burlington, Massachusetts

have, typically, only a layperson's knowledge about a subject but sometimes are experts about a subject.

■ **Technicians:** Technicians are another specialized group of professionals. They may or may not have extensive knowledge about a technology. Technicians are the people who design and build everything from airplanes and yachts to computer operating systems. Often very practical in their outlook, they want to know how things work or why they won't work and want to see the schematics or other technical details of a problem.

■ **Experts:** Experts typically are defined as people who have advanced degrees in their field or 15 or more years of experience in their field, although many people who have advanced degrees or extensive work experience are not experts. Experts are well acquainted with the complex concepts and terminology of their field and typically have a keen interest in and a thorough knowledge of the underlying theory of a practice or product. They often work in academe or in the research and development areas of government and business. Experts commonly experience difficulty in communicating well with the layperson or nonspecialist.

■ **Paraprofessionals:** Paraprofessionals are people, such as college students or apprentices, who still are learning the essential discourse of their discipline or trade. They typically know much more about a subject than laypeople, but lack the experience of professionals, the decision-making authority of executives, the preoccupation with detail of technicians, and the extensive knowledge of experts. Paraprofessionals are still novices about many of the fine points of a discipline or trade; they are the inexperienced employees who will become much more seasoned after a few years on the job.

■ **Professionals:** Professionals are members of a discipline, trade, or profession who have been practicing in their field for at least a few years. They have college degrees or have completed extensive apprenticeships in a trade or craft and are thoroughly familiar with the standards and demands of their professions.

■ **Multiple or Combined Audiences:** Multiple or combined audiences are groups of people whose members may be a mixture of laypeople and executives, technicians, experts, paraprofessionals, or professionals. Such audiences are a common phenomenon in both academe and in industry, and effective communication with them requires a variety of skills and approaches.

> " "
> Paraprofessionals are still novices about many of the fine points of a discipline or trade; they are the inexperienced employees who will become much more seasoned after a few years on the job.

It's helpful to know which categories apply to your audience. If all the categories apply, you'll have more challenges in writing to the audience than if you were writing just to one audience. For example, typically a report will be read by experts and technicians as well as executives. Knowing this fact will help you to shape different parts of the report for the different audiences.

You may also discover that even your audience of one category has widely varied backgrounds. You may decide to ignore the least informed and appeal to the most informed. Or you may include supplemental information to help the less informed part of the audience, and you may refer this part of the audience to various beginners' books on your topic.

Knowing the categories for your audience is not enough. You also need to know if and why your readers are motivated to read your document, if they have certain apprehensions about the topic you are discussing, and if other psychological factors may be relevant. And you'll need to know how your audience will use your document and what it will want to read about as well as not want to read about. Where necessary, you may need to gather demographic information concerning age, gender, political preference, location, and so on.

Heuristic Approaches

When you gather information about your audience through direct questioning and observation, you are taking what is called a heuristic approach to analyzing your audience. Figure 2.1 summarizes the various avenues open to you when you use heuristic strategies. The strategies are explained here:

- **Gathering Quantifiable Information:** Gathering quantifiable information about your audience includes, for example, obtaining information about your audience's ages, spending habits, education, work experience, location, hobbies and interests, language(s), and physical limitations. Some common ways of obtaining this kind of information include surveys, questionnaires, and interviews. Any of these may be conducted in person, by telephone, mail, or e-mail, or via a form on a Web site, for instance. In some companies, technical support can be a valuable resource for providing some of this information by collecting some basic facts on those who call about a product.
- **Gathering Job Description Information:** Gathering information about the job descriptions of your audience includes looking at organization charts and job descriptions to see who may know more about

FIGURE 2.1

Heuristic Strategies

- Gathering quantifiable information about your audience
- Gathering information about the job descriptions of your audience
- Asking questions of and observing your audience at work
- Examining relevant documents pertaining to your audience and your document
- Working alongside your audience to gain hands-on experience (with a particular software program, for example)

your subject or to get a better idea of how your readers will respond to your document.

- **Asking Questions and Observing:** Gathering information by asking questions of and observing your audience at work includes, for instance, interviewing a few select members of your audience to verify information you are obtaining about your audience through other means.

- **Examining Relevant Documents:** Gathering information by examining any relevant documents pertaining to your particular audience and the document you are working on means reviewing various company documents to see what your audience is already familiar with or having difficulties with and seeing what kinds of design expectations you may be facing. Good documents to examine include notes from customer training, reports from the sales staff, maintenance reports discussing any problems, style guides, documents discussing reader expectations, and publications typically read by your audience.

   Of course, it's easier to examine sample relevant documents if you are employed by the company. However, many companies provide public access to at least some of their documents, and increasingly do so on the company's Web site. So a college student, for example, may gather information on some audiences within a company by accessing the company Web site and reviewing such documents as technical reports and troubleshooting notes used by employees who work in customer support, organization charts, product overviews, and annual reports.

- **Working Alongside the Audience:** Finally, gathering information by working alongside your audience to gain the same kind of hands-on experience it has often requires using the product or system that your audience is expected to use. Take notes on any difficulties or questions you have as a new user. Comment on any point that is unclear, any poorly chosen terms, and any weaknesses in organization, to mention only a few possibilities.

Through all these means you can gather valuable information that will help you obtain a much better understanding of your audience.

SECONDARY AND MULTIPLE AUDIENCES

Categorizing the audience and directly gathering information about the audience may only partly help you to overcome the difficulties of understanding for whom you are writing. Readers or listeners cannot be easily analyzed, categorized, or surveyed. Many will defy easy categorization, and surveys as well as other heuristic methods for analyzing audience may not always give you the understanding of your audience that you need. In addition to knowing about these common approaches for analyzing audience, you will also need to know more fully how to address other complex audience issues. You need to know when your entire audience is a primary audience or whether secondary or multiple audiences should also be a concern.

Primary audiences are the first or major intended readers or listeners for your document or presentation. As a college student, your primary audience for many assignments is your professor. For some projects and presentations your primary audience is your peers. In the workplace, your primary audience is the person or persons who will understand, assess, and act on your message. An effective strategy is to envision the audience sitting across from you, reading or listening to your every comment. Anticipate any questions or concerns the reader or listener may have and deal with them as you write or speak. Using a categorical approach to audience and collecting heuristic information are effective ways for understanding and handling this kind of audience.

Secondary audiences present more challenges. Secondary audiences are the other potential readers of your document or other audiences for your presentations. These are the people who also may receive a copy of your document. Often these are people you are aware of, but they just are not the most direct or most intended audience. And often secondary audiences consist of people you are unaware of. For example, secondary audiences for your presentations exist when people from your primary audience later share information about your presentation and your handouts with people who didn't attend.

You can anticipate and plan for secondary audiences in the documents you write and the presentations you give. In your documents, summaries and background discussions can be helpful for secondary audiences. For presentations, you can plan your handouts to be useful for both primary and secondary audiences by, for example, listing additional sources of information on your topic, providing a URL for a Web page about your presentation, or providing an e-mail address or other contact information.

> Perhaps the most common type of audience in the technical disciplines is a multiple or combined audience.

Perhaps the most common type of audience in the technical disciplines is a multiple or combined audience. Multiple or combined audiences typically consist of a combination of people from different discourse communities, different backgrounds and education levels (laypeople and executives, for example), and possibly primary as well as secondary readers or listeners. Writing one document or giving a presentation that will achieve its purpose with each of these audiences can be daunting. A layperson will expect you to use strategies to make the information more accessible—for example, definitions of terms and simpler language. An executive will want key information summarized. A technician will want greater depth of detail concerning the specifications for a project. And an expert will have many additional expectations.

Strategies for effectively communicating with multiple audiences include many of the strategies you would use for secondary audiences. In an informal report for multiple audiences, for example, you would use clear language, more examples, explanations, summaries, and background information for laypeople wherever appropriate; an executive summary or conclusions and recommendations for an executive audience; and schematics and detailed technical data, perhaps placed in appendixes, for technicians and experts.

AUDIENCE AND LEVELS OF TECHNICALITY

Often you will find that you cannot acquire an exact understanding of your audience. Instead, you will have only a general idea about who your audience is and its background. In such cases, you'll have to decide on the level of technicality you will use.

The level of technicality is determined by many factors including the complexity of the subject, general diction, technical terms, any definitions of technical terms, background information provided, explanations provided, details provided, the number of words per sentence, sentence structure, and sentence length.

Highly Technical Prose

In technical prose the highest level of technicality most often appears in writing by experts for other experts in a particular profession, field of study, or hobby. Few detailed explanations are given; technical terms are not defined. Only the essential facts, examples, or illustrations are provided. Knowledge of many facts, theories, and other essential information will be assumed. The following is an example of highly technical prose. (Note: FAMNN refers to Fuzzy ARTMAP neural network.)

> In this paper we introduced a variation of the testing phase of the FAMNN that we named FAMNN-m. We demonstrated that FAMNN-m exhibits a superior generalization performance compared to the generalization performance of FAMNN in the classification of noisy signals. These results are valid independently of the type of noise affecting the signals. Furthermore, the results are valid independently of the size of the ART architectures created. Also, we have shown that FAMNN-m does not require more classification time than FAMNN. The introduced modification of FAMMN was based on the fact that values of signal features which are distant from feature values that correspond to a pure noise signal, are affected more severely than values of signal features that are close. The proposed modification of FAMNN is especially suited for applications where it is required that the feature set captures only the shape characteristics of the signal and not its actual amplitude or average value. If the variance of the noise that contaminates the signals is estimated, then the FAMNN could adapt so that the classification results are further improved. In this paper, to illustrate our results, we have considered classification of textured images, which are a special case of 2-D signals.
>
> Dimitrios Charalampidis, Takis Kasparis, and Michael Georgiopoulos, "Classification of Noisy Signals Using Fuzzy ARTMAP Neural Networks." Unpublished article.

Moderately Technical Prose

Moderately technical prose is for people who are not experts but who have solid or strong technical backgrounds. Typically, you'll provide more explanation of a topic, some definitions of some terms, and some background information. An example of moderately technical prose follows.

> The term *hypertext* (coined by Ted Nelson in 1965) is commonly used to describe an electronic text composed of nodes (blocks of text) which are linked together in a nonlinear web. When viewing each node, certain words are highlighted to indicate that they "yield" to a separate node; these are anchors. By tracing from node to node, readers create their own paths in the textual network. The traditional dominance of a single author–fixed reading is overturned. Readers shape their own experience of the text not only at the subject level of interpretation, but at the object level of words on a page. The provision for shared authoring, links between previously distinct works, and innovative access methods all greatly alter the concept of the book.
>
> Laura Robin, "Hypertext Authoring Environment: A Critical Review." *Ejournal* 3.3 (November 1993). Online <http://carbon.cudenver.edu/~mryder/itcdatajournals.html>.

Slightly Technical Prose

Slightly technical prose is intended for people who have some technical knowledge or some technical background, but not as much as experts or those with strong technical backgrounds. Slightly technical prose typically has sentences with less complex sentence structure and typically uses shorter sentences and paragraphs. Technical terms are usually defined at least parenthetically or by a glossary. Examples, facts, details, background information, and explanations are also common. Two examples of slightly technical prose follow.

> There are several ways to include text in a PageMaker document, and we might as well start using the correct terminology; PageMaker calls documents publications, and so we will, too. Each publication can comprise one or more stories. A story is a continuous block of text that PageMaker recognizes as a single unit. For example, each article in a newsletter might be a separate story. A story can be as short as a single headline or as long as a chapter in a book.
>
> Rebecca Bridges Altman and Rick Altman, *Mastering PageMaker 5.0 for Windows.* (San Francisco: Sybex, 1993) 37.

> The third most common graphics format in your computer is BMP, short for "bitmap," the native format for Windows and OS/2. It's no good for transmitting graphics on the Internet, but it's the only format you can use for your Windows wallpaper.
>
> Judi N. Fernandez, *GIFs, JPEGs, & BMPs: Handling Internet Graphics.* (New York: MIS Press, 1997) 33.

Nontechnical Prose

Nontechnical prose is for people who have no technical background at all. Nontechnical prose avoids any technical terms or jargon, uses relatively short or simple sentences, and doesn't go into unnecessary detail or provide in-depth analysis. It chiefly aims to give a general overview. Only essential background is provided. Clear and simple explanations are provided throughout. An example of nontechnical prose follows.

> Design beginners tend to put text and graphics on the page wherever there
> happens to be space, often without regard to any other items on the page.
> What this creates is the slightly-messy-kitchen effect—you know, with a cup
> here, a plate there, a napkin on the floor, a pot in the sink, a spill on the floor.
> It doesn't take much to clean up the slightly messy kitchen, just as it doesn't
> take much to clean up a slightly messy design that has weak alignments.
>
> Robin Williams. *The Non-Designer's Design Book*. (Berkeley: Peachpit, 1994.) 27.

TECHNICAL COMMUNICATION AND PERSUASION

Technical Documents as Persuasive Documents

You may not think of your technical documents as persuasive documents. Perhaps you think you merely are making the subject as clear as possible to the intended audience. You see yourself as being fair, objective, unbiased, and knowledgeable about the subject, and you hope the audience will recognize your objectivity and understand or act accordingly on the information you provide. You don't think you're being persuasive; you believe you're being objective. So, you wonder, where does persuasion fit in?

The reality is that writers of technical prose write many kinds of overtly or directly persuasive documents, such as grant proposals, employment letters, and recommendation reports. But many people don't realize that any technical document is at least indirectly persuasive. Whether you are writing grant proposals, scientific journal articles, lab reports, or instructions, you have selected some information over other information for a purpose. In all cases, you are presenting a point of view, advocating a position, or presenting one way over many ways to understand, accept, or act on information.

The reasons for persuading an audience are many. You may want your audience to accept a course of action. You may want to persuade others to do what you want them to do. For example, working with others on a college assignment, you may want to persuade your group members to plan, research, and write a report on a topic you prefer instead of a topic they prefer. Or you may prefer to do certain tasks related to the collaborative project and will need to persuade the others that you are the best person for undertaking those tasks.

You may also want to persuade your audience to accept a claim. A claim is a point or assertion you want to prove. A typical claim you will encounter in the workplace is, "We should develop this product with these particular clients in mind instead of developing it for a broader base of clientele." Another example of a claim would be, "This feature of the program won't work because the program developers didn't devote enough time to debugging." You may want to persuade others to accept a claim that they may at first disagree with.

You may also want to persuade others to motivate them. In a collaborative effort, for example, the pace of the work for the entire team may fall behind schedule. You may want to motivate everyone on the team to get back on schedule and point out to them the many advantages of doing so.

Technical Documents and Objectivity

At this point, you may be wondering, "What about the value of objectivity? What role does it play in creating technical documents?"

Every discourse community has its own way of doing things. For example, the scientific community traditionally relies on objectivity, impartiality, the scientific method, and a supposedly nonexpressive writing style. In this view, writers of technical prose are seen as merely passing on information, much as a conveyor belt passes on packages from point A to point B. Writers are somehow seen as mere observers passing information on to readers. Some observers see objectivity as an important distinguishing characteristic of technical writing.

However, a different view suggests that writers—whether they are scientists, engineers, programmers, or professional technical communicators—are interpreters of information. And whether the writers are writing grant proposals, scientific journal articles, lab reports, or user manuals, they are representing a point of view, advocating a position, arguing for one way of understanding information or doing something rather than another way.

This view recognizes the creative and dynamic role that all writers of technical prose play when they write. Whether you are explaining how to use banking software or discussing Einstein's theory of relativity, you are advocating a point of view. Whether you are discussing an idea, product, organization, or service, you are an interpreter of technical information. Whether you are explaining a complex subject to peers or you are making a complicated and unfamiliar subject simpler and more familiar to a multiple or combined audience, you do so with much creativity, many strategies, and a constant manipulation of prose style.

STRATEGIES FOR PERSUADING AUDIENCES

Knowing how to be persuasive is one of the most important skills you can acquire. There is no one strategy that works best. Effective persuasion most often results from using a variety of strategies at the same time. Three major strategies are appealing to your audience, establishing your credibility, and strengthening your evidence and reasoning. Aristotle labeled these strategies pathos (emotional appeals to the audience), ethos (ethical appeals based on the character, reputation, or credibility of the writer or speaker), and logos (logical appeals to the audience's sense of reason).

Persuading by Appealing to Your Audience

Persuading others to accept a course of action, accept a claim, or be motivated is not easy. Others have reasons for doing things the way they do them, for thinking, believing, or acting one way instead of another. You need to consider carefully everything about your audience if you are going to achieve your persuasive goals.

1. **Consider the audience's attitudes:** From the outset, your audience may disagree with you, agree with you, or be neutral. You need to know what the audience's attitude is before you can best determine if you want to persuade it to abandon a position, continue believing something, or change its neutral position.

2. **Inform the audience of the advantages:** The strategy here is to let your readers or listeners know what's "in it" for them. You can be more persuasive in the workplace by connecting company goals and personal goals. Advantages may be personal, professional, or financial, to mention only a few possibilities. Financial advantages, of course, easily overlap with personal and professional. Personal advantages may include rewards (more free time, more recognition, reduced work load). Professional advantages for the company may include happier employees, higher morale, more efficiency, and reduced costs.

3. **Consider the audience's motivations and emotions:** People are motivated by many concepts and emotions—fear, anger, prejudice, patriotism, sympathy, power, prestige, safety, health, popularity, security. You may use many strategies to evoke these motivations and emotions. You may introduce humor to relieve some of the tension, you may heighten your audience's emotions about a topic, or you may appease the audience by conceding something. You may also negate the emotion concerning an issue by making an appeal based on objectivity, distance, or fairness, for example.

4. **Consider the ways the audience will react to you:** You can handle an audience in many ways and obtain different reactions with each strategy. You may be aggressive, respectful, or realistic, to mention a few possibilities. You can tell an audience to give you what you want, you can create sympathy by showing that you respect and share its values, or you can be realistic by pointing out various constraints for both you and the audience, such as company policies, time constraints, or legal constraints.

5. **Organize information to appeal to the audience:** The order in which you present your topic to an audience can be one of the most important factors in determining whether you will be persuasive. There are many ways to present information to audiences, for example, from points most important to your audience to points least important, from points most familiar to your audience to those least familiar, from the most challenging points to the least challenging (see

"Outlines" in Chapter 6). Also, if you know your audience will be receptive, then a direct pattern approach might be best. If you know your audience will be resistant, then an indirect pattern might be best (see "Patterns: Direct and Indirect" in Chapter 14).

6. **Consider other contexts for the audience:** The cultural background of your audience can be a big factor in many communication situations.

Persuading an International Audience

- Avoid jargon.
- Avoid overly long or complex sentences and big words.
- Avoid noun strings, nominalization (turning verbs into nouns), and verbalization (turning nouns into verbs).
- Avoid homographs (words spelled the same but having different meanings).
- Avoid idioms.
- Provide a glossary as an aid.
- Select graphics carefully to avoid culturally dependent images.
- Have a member of the target audience read the document.

Persuading by Establishing Your Ethos or Credibility

Don't underestimate the value of your ethos or credibility both for what you write and for your presentations. If your major aim is to persuade, your ethos or credibility can be your strongest asset. In many cases, your credibility can be more persuasive than the arguments or any other persuasive strategies you use. If your major aim is to inform, your credibility can lend more authority to your message.

You can establish your credibility in many ways:

1. **Know your subject:** Perhaps the most important way to establish your credibility is to know your subject extremely well and to show this knowledge throughout your document (or presentation). Your knowledge will show in your attention to detail and your technical accuracy. Readers and listeners respect people who obviously "know their stuff."

2. **Present your qualifications:** You may enhance your credibility by simply calling attention, whenever it's appropriate, to your qualifications or credentials. Discussing your qualifications is an expected part of a job application letter, a résumé, or a proposal, for example. However, you may call attention to your extensive experience in a variety of ways in correspondence and various technical documents other than proposals.

3. **Establish trust:** You may strengthen your credibility by showing your audience you are honest and sincere about the information you provide. In effect, you strengthen your credibility by establishing a relationship of trust with your audience. You establish trust by convincingly connecting your values and beliefs with the subject and the audience. Audiences will believe you can be trusted, that you share their goals and values, and that you are ethical.

4. **Respect the views of others:** You may strengthen your credibility by showing that you genuinely respect the audience's view of the issue. Writers or speakers undermine their credibility by being suspicious of the audience or by causing the audience to think it is being deceived in some way.

5. **Control your tone:** You may enhance your credibility by carefully controlling the tone of your document or presentation, by, for example, projecting an image of power or control when necessary, establishing a tone of deference or humility toward your audience, or showing you are aware of how delicate a matter or situation is. Establishing an objective tone will also help your credibility. If people think you are treating an issue (as well as opposing views) fairly, they tend to have more respect for what you write or say.

Persuading by Strengthening Your Evidence and Your Reasoning

Good evidence and sound reasoning (or logos) can also be essential in persuasion. Evidence is something that furnishes proof for your claim. Evidence may be direct, indirect, hearsay, or circumstantial. Typical kinds of evidence are examples, statistics, factual statements, and expert testimony. Consider the types of evidence that follow.

An Effective Example:

Technology isn't just for games and shopping. Inside the nation's classrooms, the Internet has become as common as chalk.

A Statistic:

As of last fall, 95 percent of schools had Internet access and 63 percent of public-school classrooms were wired.

A Factual Statement:

As schools add computers, the ratio of students per instructional computer with Internet access continues to drop.

Expert Testimony:

Dr. Terence Rainey, an expert on the impact of computers on education in public schools, argues that computers in the classroom will radically change the way students learn.

CHOOSING THE ETHICAL PATH

Some people commit errors of logic because they don't know what the common errors are, but, unfortunately, many deliberately use logic errors to mislead others into thinking something is true when it isn't.

From the workplace

Seth Maislin

Freelance Editor, Indexer, Information Architect, Instructor, Consultant
Arlington, Massachusetts

Seth is what might have been called, in earlier times, a Renaissance Man. He pursues many interests and works on developing his many talents. Seth is deeply interested in promoting professionalism in his various activities and he is always willing to help less experienced workers learn the ropes.

My undergraduate and postgraduate degrees are in optics, conferred at the University of Rochester, New York, the only university that offered an undergraduate optics program at that time. While at the university, I strove to achieve diversity of knowledge, something rarely available to engineers because of the academic requirements. Many of these subjects would prove helpful, particularly classes in creative writing, public speaking, linguistics, and foreign languages. I also had the opportunity to serve as a teaching assistant in mathematics and a writing tutor. Both experiences provided valuable early experiences in the art and challenges of instruction.

But in 1993 I left optics for good. I didn't leave it behind on purpose; rather I discovered book indexing, really by accident. Edmund Scientific Company publishes a catalog, and I happened to communicate with the layout artists at a time when they realized an index was behind schedule, so I got the job to create the index.

My education at the University of Rochester was valuable in that all education is valuable. My college education introduced me to the balance among working independently, being part of a team, and competing with peers. More directly, however, I was able to use my background in engineering and mathematics as a foot in the door with certain publishers. Although I was new to professional editing and indexing (and freelancing), I was very comfortable with the subject concepts. Good communicators in scientific and technical fields are apparently rare, so I had a definite advantage.

Freelancing and Consulting

My career began from a combination of networking through professional societies and simple cold-calling and résumé mailings. The first serious contract happened mostly by accident. During an introductory phone call, I was told they didn't use contractors; nevertheless, I spoke with an employee for half an hour, eager to learn about their business. Six months later they called me, looking for a contractor. I had no idea who they were! I had crossed them off my list 60 seconds into our initial conversation half a year before. But I had left an impression apparently, and that impression earned me several thousand dollars.

Sound reasoning also helps you to be more persuasive. In addition to, or as part of, the evidence you provide, audiences are also persuaded by the quality of your reasoning or logic. If you state a claim or main argument, how well do you support it with premises or supporting points? Is each premise a strong point in support of your claim? If you offer generalizations, do you support them effectively with specifics (deductive reasoning)? If you draw

Self-employment began with simple phone calls and mailings. But once it began, it snowballed. I marketed myself as special, presenting my engineering background as an asset. Eventually I became overworked, and realized I'd have to choose my clients and projects more carefully. This process took less than five years, and it continues today.

Discovering freelancing, particularly after the discomfort of a previous employment experience, seemed miraculous: I felt in greater control of my destiny. Further, editing and indexing projects were short, rarely lasting longer than two weeks. Since those early days I have been secure in the knowledge that I won't ever feel trapped in a job or a contract, because I can always do something different.

My recent job at Lycos came out of contracting as well. I was asked to work on-site at Lycos for a few weeks as a contractor. A recruiter, with whom I had spoken on many occasions about several topics, made the connection between my skills and interests and his client's needs. Once on site, I asked numerous questions, constantly displayed my work, and apparently made a great impression. They began to recruit me in earnest, and their offer was good enough that I chose to give up full-time freelancing, at least until they down-sized and I left their employ.

Today, I am consulting full time again. I believe I have already experienced all of the basic elements that will constitute my career future: consulting, teaching, and freelancing. Of course, I expect the media to change, the audience to evolve, the subject matter to diversify, and my own skill set to grow. In fact, I already insist upon it.

Meetings

People think this is crazy, but I love meetings. I attend lots of meetings and enjoy almost all of them. Perhaps it's because my work used to be exceedingly independent and because working at home can be isolating. The best meetings are those in which everyone has something to add, where people *don't* speak in turn, and where the leader of the meeting serves as a moderator and not a boss.

When I run meetings, my goal is to make sure conversation stays purposeful. I occasionally interrupt and clearly identify the issues, separating and defining them as best as possible. Then I let the meeting continue on its own. When every thread is either agreed upon or wanting for outside information, then the meeting is over.

Insider Advice

I attribute much of my success to my willingness to talk about myself and about the business. I have never been stingy with information, even financial information. People know they can speak to me to find answers, and that leads recursively to work and greater exposure, more opportunities to reach new audiences, and additional chances to grow as a person.

The best part of successful self-employment is that the concept of unemployment disappears. Job security is simply a myth, because there is always work, always a client, and always cash flow. Being able to rely on oneself instills much greater confidence than an employer can.

conclusions from the details or specifics (inductive reasoning), are your conclusions valid?

Of course, you must also be careful to avoid errors in logic. Don't be distracted from focusing on an issue through someone else's use of an *ad hominem* argument (attacking the person instead of refuting the belief). See Figure 2.2 for a list of some common tactics and faults.

FIGURE 2.2

Logical Fallacies

SOURCE: Adapted from "Stephen's Guide to Logical Fallacies." Available at <http://www.datanation.com/fallacies/index.htm>.

False Dilemma

Definition: A limited number of options (usually two) is given, while in reality there are more options.

Example: "America: Love it or leave it."

Slippery Slope

Definition: In order to show that a proposition P is unacceptable, a sequence of increasingly unacceptable events is shown to follow from P.

Example: "If I make an exception for you, then I have to make an exception for everyone."

Appeal to Force

Definition: The audience is told that unpleasant consequences will follow if it does not agree with the author.

Example: "You had better agree that the new company policy is the best bet if you expect to keep your job."

Attacking the Person (*argumentum ad hominem*)

Definition: The person presenting an argument is attacked instead of the argument itself.

Example: "You may argue that God doesn't exist, but you are just following a fad."

False Analogy

Definition: In an analogy, two objects (or events), A and B, are shown to be similar. Then it is argued that since A has property P, so also B must have property P. An analogy fails when the two objects, A and B, are different in a way that affects whether they both have property P.

Example: "Government is like business, so just as business must be sensitive primarily to the bottom line, so also must government." (But the objectives of government and business are completely different, so probably they will have to meet different criteria.)

Begging the Question

Definition: The truth of the conclusion is assumed by the premise. Often, the conclusion is simply restated in the premise in a slightly different form.

Example: "Since I'm not lying, it follows that I'm telling the truth."

CHECKING WHAT YOU'VE LEARNED

Audience Analysis

- Have you appropriately considered the discourse community of your audience?
- How does the discourse community affect the subject, purpose, scope, content, organization, style, design, and other elements of your document?
- Have you fully determined the background of your audience? Education level? Gender? Age? Attitudes toward the subject? Motives?
- Have you determined if there are any secondary audiences, and, if appropriate, have you provided useful information for the secondary audience?
- If you are addressing multiple audiences, have you used appropriate strategies for the multiple audiences?
- If the audience is too general or undefined, have you provided an appropriate level of technicality in your prose?

Persuasion

- Have you clearly determined what you want your audience to do, understand, or accept?
- Have you effectively used various strategies for considering audience? Attitudes? Motivations? Possible reactions?
- Have you considered the most effective way to organize your document for your particular purpose and audience?
- If your audience is multicultural, have you fully taken into account the many cultural factors you must consider?
- Have you effectively established your credibility with your audience?
- Have you used the most appropriate and effective evidence for your audience? Are the examples, factual statements, statistics, and expert testimony well chosen and convincing?
- Have you used sound reasoning for your purpose and audience? Are there any errors in logic?

EXERCISES

 REVIEW

1. Write a paragraph discussing some of the advantages of using a categorical approach to analyzing your audience.

2. Write a paragraph discussing some of the advantages of using a heuristic approach to analyzing your audience.

3. Create a list of documents you have written that had at least one primary audience and at least

one secondary audience. Also identify the audiences next to each document you list.

4. Write a paragraph discussing an occasion for which you had multiple audiences with different backgrounds and knowledge levels. Discuss whether or not you think you communicated effectively with all of the audiences. If not, discuss what you think you could have done to make your communication more effective.

5. Review the example of nontechnical prose concerning design beginners. Revise the paragraph to make it either moderately technical or slightly technical. Provide a list of the changes you made to create your revision.

 THE INTERNET

Find a Frequently Asked Questions list (FAQ) for a discussion list, a company, or an organization. Write several paragraphs discussing how effectively the list of questions and answers addresses the concerns of the intended audience or audiences.

 ETHICS/PROFESSIONALISM

1. After reviewing the strategies for persuading by appealing to your audience, make a list of ways you could use the strategies to be unethical. Also discuss what you think some of the consequences might be for such behavior.

2. After reviewing the strategies for persuading by establishing your ethos or credibility, make a list of the ways you might be able to use the strategies to your advantage during a meeting, a presentation, or an interview, for example.

 COLLABORATION

Working in small groups of two or three students, discuss the strategies of pathos, ethos, and logos as they are presented in this chapter. Try to reach a consensus on which of the three strategies your group thinks is the most important strategy for persuading an audience. Be prepared to discuss your conclusion with the class.

 INTERNATIONAL COMMUNICATION

Review the list of tips for persuading an international audience. Discuss why the tips will help an international audience to understand your communication more easily.

RESOURCES

Bosley, Deborah. *Global Contexts: Case Studies in International Technical Communication.* Boston: Allyn and Bacon, 2001.

Bushnell, Jack. "A Contrary View of the Technical Writing Classroom: Notes Toward Future Discussion." *Technical Communication Quarterly* 8.2 (Spring 1999). 175–188.

Hoft, Nancy L. *International Technical Communication: How to Export Information About High Technology.* New York: Wiley, 1995.

Laib, Nevin K. *Rhetoric and Style: Strategies for Advanced Writers.* Englewood Cliffs, NJ: Prentice Hall, 1993.

Lunsford, Andrea A., and John J. Ruszkiewicz. *Everything's An Argument.* 2nd ed. Boston: Bedford/St. Martin's, 2001.

3

Collaboration

Types of Collaboration   54

Advantages of Collaboration   57

Disadvantages of Collaboration   60

Collaborating Effectively Face-to-Face   61

Collaborating Effectively Online   63

Collaborating in Peer Reviews   64

Improving Collaborative Skills   67

Participating in Meetings   71

Acting Ethically   73

From the Workplace   74

IN THIS CHAPTER

Collaborating means working with others, and it is an essential college, job, and social skill. You will often work on teams in your classes, in the workplace, and in many different social settings. Your ability to collaborate effectively with others is an important factor in determining your college, career, and personal success.

You will learn about:

- the types of collaboration and how they work in a variety of settings
- the advantages and disadvantages of collaboration: how to make the most of collaboration and some typical pitfalls and how to deal with them
- collaborating effectively face-to-face: how to handle the most common kind of collaboration
- collaborating effectively online: how to handle an increasingly common kind of collaboration
- collaborating in peer reviews: how to critique the work of your peers
- improving collaborative skills: how to polish the skills you have and acquire others
- participating in meetings: how to get the most out of meetings
- acting ethically: how to abide by standards of behavior

WORKING AS A TEAM

At the beginning of any large project, a collaboration meeting should be planned. All parties involved should meet and get to know each other's skills and weaknesses. A project leader should be appointed at this time. All should agree on the writing style, audience, and other considerations. Next, a written project schedule with deadlines should be given to all team members so they will be aware of their respective roles in completing the project on time.

—Ann Vogt, technical author, Longwood, Florida

TYPES OF COLLABORATION

There are many kinds of collaboration. In college you may find yourself working with at least one other student to write a proposal and a report in an introductory technical writing class. Or you may be assigned to work on a team of two or more individuals to complete an assignment in a class in your discipline. Collaborative projects are becoming increasingly common in college classes because your professors recognize that much of the work you will do in the workplace will be collaborative.

In the workplace, you typically will be part of a much larger team. Regardless of the kind of job you have, you'll often find yourself working on projects with people from many different areas of the company. If you're a computer programmer, for example, you'll work not only with other programmers on a project, but with technical writers, managers, Web designers, quality assurance personnel, marketing people, and others.

There are many ways to describe the kind of collaborations in which you may participate, but essentially most collaborations will either be divided-labor or cross-functional collaborations.

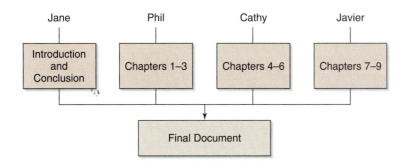

FIGURE 3.1

Horizontal Collaboration Model

Divided-Labor Collaborations

In a divided-labor approach, team members are given individual assignments or responsibilities. A divided-labor approach may be achieved in a horizontal model, a sequential model, or a stratification model.

In a horizontal model, team members divide a project into tasks so that each member is responsible for one part of the project. Students collaborating in this way would divide a writing project, for example, into three or four parts according to the number of people in the group. Each would be responsible for one particular section. Professional technical writers sometimes collaborate this way on large documentation projects in industry. The results of such an approach are mixed because group members will have their own styles, methods, attention to detail, and so on. Figure 3.1 shows the horizontal collaboration model.

Another common model is often referred to as the sequential model. In this model for a writing project, for example, one person typically would start a project by planning, designing, writing, editing, and revising. Another person then would take the work and review and evaluate it. A third person would further refine it and pass it on to a fourth. Overall, the results are more uniform than those of the horizontal model because everyone is looking at the same document and making contributions. Figure 3.2 shows the sequential collaboration model.

A third common model is the vertical division or stratification model. In this model, team members are responsible for the tasks they do best. In a

ASSISTING A DEVELOPER

It helps to be friendly and helpful. If you offer a developer assistance in checking the release notes for language errors, he'll also take your advice on language errors in the software, and hopefully in the long run, on design issues.

—Maaike Groenewege, technical writer, the Netherlands

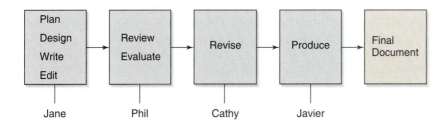

FIGURE 3.2

Sequential Collaboration Model

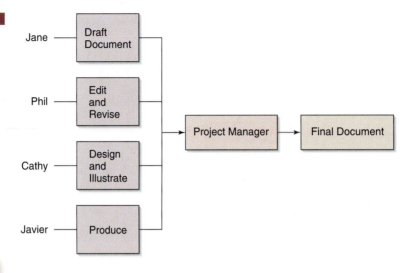

FIGURE 3.3

**Stratification
Collaboration Model**

THE VALUE OF CROSS-FUNCTIONAL TEAMS

If I could make one suggestion for improving the flow of information between developers, designers, and documenters it would be simply this: create cross-functional teams at product inception. Have those teams meet together on a regular basis (at least once a week). Involve the documentation specialist, designer, and developer from the first, and make certain that each team member feels on an equal footing with the other team members. It's amazing what happens when you put five to seven intelligent, skilled, dedicated people together on a team and teach them how to communicate with one another. Communication is the key!

—Marjorie Hermansen-Eldard, course developer, Orem, Utah

writing project, for instance, one member would draft the document, one would edit and revise, another would contribute the design and illustrations, a fourth would oversee production, and a fifth would serve as a project manager, coordinating the activities of everyone involved. Large documentation projects are often set up this way in industry, with technical writers and editors working under the supervision of a project or documentation manager.

The stratification model has the chief advantage of specialization. Each person is doing what he or she does best. In a large documentation project, for example, the entire document benefits from the special strengths of each team member. Another advantage of this method is that it follows the project team approach. Each person reports directly to the project manager, and team members feel that they are contributing equally instead of competing as in the sequential model. Figure 3.3 shows the stratification collaboration model.

Cross-Functional or Integrated Collaborations

In addition to collaborating by dividing tasks and responsibilities, you will often be required to collaborate with others throughout the entire process—from project inception to project completion—by sharing all or many of the same tasks and responsibilities. This model of collaboration is referred to as the cross-functional or integrated model. For example, as a programmer you may find yourself working on many of the same parts of the same project from beginning to end, not only with other programmers and other employees from your department, but with information designers, technical writers, managers, and other technical professionals from other areas of the company. Figure 3.4 shows the cross-functional collaboration model.

An important point to remember about collaborative approaches is that they are often much more effective than individual efforts. A well-planned and

FIGURE 3.4
Cross-Functional Collaboration Model

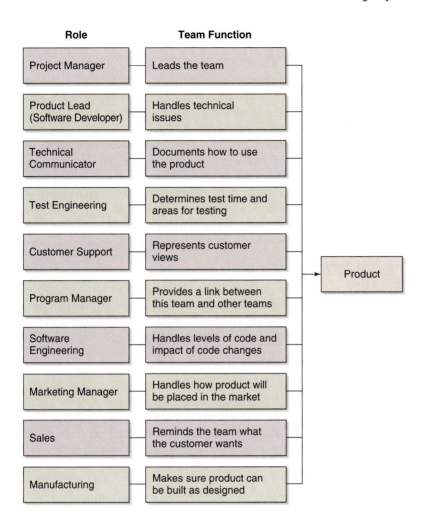

Role	Team Function
Project Manager	Leads the team
Product Lead (Software Developer)	Handles technical issues
Technical Communicator	Documents how to use the product
Test Engineering	Determines test time and areas for testing
Customer Support	Represents customer views
Program Manager	Provides a link between this team and other teams
Software Engineering	Handles levels of code and impact of code changes
Marketing Manager	Handles how product will be placed in the market
Sales	Reminds the team what the customer wants
Manufacturing	Makes sure product can be built as designed

Product

well-managed collaborative approach can be an enjoyable way to work on a number of projects.

ADVANTAGES OF COLLABORATION

The advantages of collaboration depend somewhat on the kind of collaboration—divided-labor collaboration or cross-functional. For example, if you're involved with a cross-functional model of collaboration, you may have a greater sense of having contributed equally to the project than if you had worked on only a small part of the project. Also, if you and your team members have all contributed equally, your project is more likely to have one voice and a sense of greater unity. In general, collaborations of all kinds have certain

TEAMWORK

Communication (within project teams) is highly personal and depends on the individuals involved. At the start of the project it is important for the project manager to articulate the expectations of all team members. Expectations should include the statement that team members should be prepared to supply the writers with information when asked and to review materials within the requested time frame. The manager sets the tone for the rest of the project team, and if he or she does not value documentation, the rest of the team will place less importance on it also. Once expectations have been set, it is up to the writers to understand the product, the technology, and the issues involved and then demonstrate that understanding in their own work. Competent people like to deal with other competent people and once that trust is established, information flows easily.

—Sharon Hopkins, documentation specialist, Burlington, Massachusetts

INTEGRATION OF SPECIALTIES

I recently had a rewarding experience working with a graphic designer. I had developed a new conceptual model for the user interface for an existing product. I met face-to-face with a designer and explained the motivation behind my idea. After an hour, we had sketches that the designer referred to for the next two weeks, when we met again to refine the product. Finally, the collaborative product was complete. This experience was so valuable to me personally because of the integration of specialties. The final product looked nothing like I imagined; instead it was considerably more attractive and functional, thanks to these consultations.

—Seth Maislin, freelance editor, indexer, information architect, integration manager, instructor, consultant, Arlington, Massachusetts

advantages compared to working alone on a project. The following are among the advantages.

Sharing the Workload

The most obvious advantage of collaboration is the sharing of the workload. Whether the group is two students working together on a report for a writing class or a team of ten individuals from various departments at a company, collaborating distributes the workload. The resulting work may be of much higher quality as the talents of the group members combine to improve the end result. In a true, equitable collaborative effort, team members contribute equal value and effort to the project. Although the division of labor is not always as equal as it should be, the effect of shared work—lightening the burden—should not be ignored. Additionally, many projects are too large for an individual to take on alone, so sharing the workload is essential.

Reducing the Project Time

As a corollary to sharing the workload, the time required to finish a job is often shortened. Unfortunately, this advantage can sometimes fail to materialize if the coordination of deliverables takes too much time. In general, however, a collaborative effort can take less time than an individual one.

Sharing Expertise

Teamwork can be superior to individual labor because team members will bring a range of skills to the table and can view critically and helpfully the work of the other participants. One thing that typically makes collaborative work enjoyable is how the collaboration becomes a learning experience for everyone involved. You learn from others as they learn from you.

Enhancing Creativity

Working with others on a collaborative effort can be much more fun than working on a project by yourself. If you're on a good team, you may find it exciting to work with others during the brainstorming and organizing phase of a project. In fact, you'll typically find that throughout the project, group work can often be exciting as you work toward a shared understanding with others—defining a problem, understanding its causes, proposing solutions, and recommending actions, for example. And you will find that you enjoy benefiting from their ideas and contributions as much as they enjoy benefiting from yours.

Of course, in many disciplines and professions, there are numerous examples of collaborations that led to amazing achievements: scientists James Watson and Francis Crick and the discovery of the helical structure of DNA, Orville Wright and Wilbur Wright and the first powered flight, and Steve Jobs and Steve Wozniak and the first Apple computer, to mention only a few. See Figure 3.5.

FIGURE 3.5

Famous Collaborative Teams

James Watson and Francis Crick were awarded the 1962 Nobel prize for physiology or medicine for their work on DNA; Steve Jobs, Steve Wozniak, and John Sculley founded Apple Computer in 1976; Orville and Wilbur Wright made the first successful flight in a motor-powered airplane, near Kitty Hawk, North Carolina, in 1903.

Sharing Responsibility

Another advantage is that you and your peers or co-workers are all responsible—often equally—for the project. Meeting the project deadline, achieving the expected quality, and fulfilling many other responsibilities can create stress for everyone involved. If the group is well managed and successful, all members have certain responsibilities and they have to fulfill those responsibilities. Doing so typically eases the pressure on everyone.

Sharing Recognition

If your project is particularly successful and if you have worked effectively with your group members, you will often enjoy the recognition that all of you receive for your efforts. And you will enjoy seeing some in the group being singled out for special recognition if they are deserving of special praise. Good teamwork can lead to much deserved recognition for members of the group.

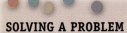

SOLVING A PROBLEM

We were working with a translation vendor who was not producing high quality work. We invited its representatives up to our offices for a meeting "to assess where we are and figure out the best way to move forward." The goal of the meeting was to get them aligned with our quality expectations and energize them to adapt their processes so that they could meet our expectations.

We could have had a drill-sergeant-type of meeting and read them the riot act (and wouldn't that have been more fun!). Instead, we had a meeting where we politely but firmly stated our expectations, gave examples of how they were not being met, reviewed their processes, and together agreed on changes in their process that would address their shortcomings. The vendor's logo and our logo appeared on the title slide for the presentation, and the title on the welcome slide was *Aligning the Partnership*. We achieved the desired results.

—Bob Shapiro, senior program manager, Burlington, Massachusetts

DISADVANTAGES OF COLLABORATION

As with the advantages, the disadvantages of collaboration also depend on the kind of collaboration. For example, a cross-functional collaboration is more difficult than a divided-labor collaboration. Just overcoming the scheduling problems presents one big challenge. The following are among the disadvantages.

Having Your Ideas Ignored

If you're not assertive during the group work, you may find that your ideas are ignored. In the dynamics of a group, often the more assertive individuals are able to persuade or even intimidate others into doing things their way. Your particularly good suggestion may be ignored because others prefer doing things their way even if their way isn't the most effective or appropriate way in this particular instance.

Having Ideas Miscommunicated

Depending on the type of collaboration used in a classroom or in a company, miscommunication can be a major problem. Individuals working alone and then reporting back to the group may not have a clear sense of their specific task responsibilities. They may produce work unrelated to the task at hand or work that in some other way misses the mark.

Doing More than Your Fair Share of the Work

You may find yourself working with others less motivated, disciplined, organized, or effective than you. If you are a particularly hard-working individual, you may find that you are contributing much more to the project than others on the team. You may have to deal with people who don't like to do their fair share, who want others to do most of the work, who don't take the time to do the necessary research and writing, who think they are too busy with other classes to work hard, who have always taken the easy way out, and so on.

Working with Difficult Personalities

You will encounter people with many kinds of personalities in collaborative work: those who are introverts and those who are extroverts, those who are aggressive and those who are passive. If, for example, you have several aggressive extroverts in your group, the progress of the group may be slowed by group conflict.

Working with People with Varied Skills

Just as personalities will differ in a collaborative effort, so will skills and abilities. You often will find yourself working with people as intelligent as, if not more intelligent than, you are and as skilled as, if not more skilled than, you are. However, you will also often find yourself working with others who are less intelligent and less skilled.

Sharing Responsibility

Sharing the responsibility was discussed earlier as an advantage; it may also be a disadvantage. If you're the project manager and you are supervising a weak team, you may end up taking all of the blame if the project fails. Or if the project fails, some team members may be unfairly blamed for the failure. Sometimes it can be difficult to identify who is chiefly responsible for the failure of a project.

Receiving Less Recognition for Your Contributions

You may receive less recognition in several ways. Group work often brings attention to the entire group but not necessarily to the individual contributions of team members. Also, you may not be given proper credit for your individual contributions, or others may take credit for what you contributed.

> **PROPRIETARY FEELINGS**
>
> People often feel very proprietary about the part they wrote, so if you come up with a suggestion to improve it they will often argue against it out of pride.
>
> —George Johnston,
> software development engineer,
> Redmond, Washington

COLLABORATING EFFECTIVELY FACE-TO-FACE

Face-to-face collaboration occurs frequently in college and in the workplace in all kinds of situations: class discussions; sessions in a campus computer lab; one-on-one meetings with peers, professors, supervisors, and project leaders; staff meetings; interviews; panel discussions; and group projects. Figure 3.6 shows a handy way to evaluate your group work.

Face-to-Face Collaboration

- Determine leadership duties early on. In college projects, the team or the professor will choose a group leader. In industry, the project leader often is the person responsible for seeing the project through to completion; in more complex projects, there may be several project leaders who report to different people.

- Determine the subject, purpose, scope, audience, and context for the document or project. See Chapter 2 and Chapter 4 for discussions of these topics. You must determine early in the project what you are doing, for whom, under what context and constraints.

- Organize the project effectively for the group. Organizing must be done earlier rather than later in the process. All group members need to know early on who will work on which tasks and what the entire project entails. It's helpful for every group member to have the big picture of the project in mind.

- Assign tasks to everyone in the group. Don't leave some group members with little or nothing to do or contribute.

(continued)

- Organize meetings effectively. The dynamics of the group won't work effectively if the group meetings aren't well planned.
- Determine a schedule for the project. Determining a schedule is another critical task that must be done early in the planning part of the project. (See Chapter 4.)

- Use brainstorming, mind mapping, and other techniques to encourage creative thinking. (See Chapter 4.)
- Be sensitive to cultural differences in the group. Many groups in college and in the workplace have members with diverse cultural backgrounds. Be aware of how

(continued)

FIGURE 3.6

Group Work Evaluation Form

Your Name _____

Your Group Project _____

Your Group Members _____   _____

_____   _____

Circle one term in each box.

Group Member	Contributed his or her fair share to all phases of the project	Participated actively in meetings	Was dependable, prompt, and courteous as a group member	Overall rating for this person's contributions to the group
Name: _____	Excellent Good Average Unsatisfactory Failing	Excellent Good Average Unsatisfactory Failing	Excellent Good Average Unsatisfactory Failing	Excellent Good Average Unsatisfactory Failing
Name: _____	Excellent Good Average Unsatisfactory Failing	Excellent Good Average Unsatisfactory Failing	Excellent Good Average Unsatisfactory Failing	Excellent Good Average Unsatisfactory Failing
Name: _____	Excellent Good Average Unsatisfactory Failing	Excellent Good Average Unsatisfactory Failing	Excellent Good Average Unsatisfactory Failing	Excellent Good Average Unsatisfactory Failing

people from different cultures react to the typical dynamics of a group.

- Be sensitive to gender differences in the group. Some groups allow one gender to dominate the group. It's important that all members of the group, regardless of gender, believe that they are equal partners in the group. Tasks should be distributed without regard to gender.
- Determine in advance how differences of opinion will be resolved fairly. You should decide early on if you will resolve differences, for example, by a vote of the members of the group, by drawing straws, by flipping a coin, or by appealing to someone outside the group.
- Determine how each group member's contribution will be reviewed and evaluated. In college, the professor typically reviews and evaluates each group member's contributions. Yet the professor also may ask each group member to review and evaluate the other members. A fair review and evaluation process should be in place in the workplace, too.

COLLABORATING EFFECTIVELY ONLINE

Now more than ever, college students and company employees are required to collaborate online. Online communication can be through direct e-mail, mailing lists, Web bulletin boards, or chat rooms. E-mail is a versatile tool that can be used to share ideas or send files back and forth for review and editing, possibly using a sophisticated online collaborative tool. Today's communicators must know how to work together effectively online.

Online Collaboration

- Keep in mind that you are communicating with other people.
- Agree on the method or methods for communicating online.
- Determine an appropriate level of style for your group communications.
- Be alert to peak times on the Internet if you want to communicate synchronously (everyone online and communicating at the same time).
- Establish an agenda in advance of your online meetings.
- Make sure someone saves all of the online work from each session.
- Use the tools you are most familiar with.
- Use asynchronous (not at the same time) methods for collaborating as well as synchronous methods.
- Use private communications when necessary.
- Be alert to new tools that can help you collaborate more effectively.

COLLABORATING IN PEER REVIEWS

Peer reviews are a common type of collaborative work used in college classes. Peer reviews may be face-to-face or completely online. In a peer review, you work with others—your peers—in a small group and follow specific criteria to critique their work while they critique your work using the same criteria. Peer reviews can help you discover many ways to improve your own documents while making improvements in the documents of others. Figure 3.7 shows sample peer review questions.

As a college student, you may find that peer review is part of many of your writing assignments. Typically, your professor will ask you to bring into class a draft of your document shortly before the due date, and other members of the class will be required to critique your document using a critique sheet that includes pertinent criteria concerning the assignment. Usually, you are asked to check various elements of the document to see how well they fulfill the requirements of the assignment and the requirements of good writing and design. This kind of peer review has to be well prepared for and controlled by your professor to be as beneficial as it should be. Still, you will often find that your document will be much improved because other readers have pointed out shortcomings you failed to see.

As a corporate employee, you need to develop your own peer network, two or three people you can count on to look over and critique any essential communications you have to write. If the network is to be helpful to you, your peers must have good communication skills (if some members' writing skills are better than yours, then that's good news for you), and they must take the peer reviewing seriously. They have to be willing to sit down and carefully read your document from beginning to end, and they have to know how to offer constructive criticism. And, of course, for this kind of peer-review network to work in a corporate setting, you must be willing to return a favor with a favor. Be sure you devote as much time and care to reviewing the documents of others as they have devoted time and care to reviewing yours.

> Peer reviews can help you discover many ways to improve your own documents while making improvements in the documents of others.

Successful Collaboration in Peer Reviews

- Read the entire document first before making any comments on it.
- Make sure you know the document's purpose and intended audience. Two of the most important elements to scrutinize are how effectively the writing accomplishes the document's purpose and how well the document is suited for the intended reader. You should point out any problems that interfere with these basic goals.

(continued on p. 66)

FIGURE 3.7

Sample Peer Review Questions

Complaint Letter Assignment
Peer Review Sheet

Directions: Have one sheet of blank paper for each member of your group. Place your name and e-mail address at the top of each of these blank sheets. Please carefully read each complaint letter of each member of your group and then respond to the questions below for each member of your group. **Please provide the question number for each answer.** After the peer review is completed, each group member will take these comments home to make additional improvements.

Note: The questions below do not address all the requirements for this assignment. All the requirements are listed on the requirements sheet for the assignment.

1. Who is the audience for this letter? Does the writer address the letter to an individual within a business or organization?

2. Does the letter fulfill all the format requirements of a good letter in the heading, dateline, inside address, salutation, body, complimentary close, and signature block? Are the margins, line spacing within paragraphs, and line spacing between paragraphs correct? Note any suggested changes on the draft.

3. Does the writer effectively establish a common ground in the opening of the letter? Does he or she use a courteous tone and attempt to build rapport with the reader? If not, note suggested changes on the draft.

4. Does the writer effectively state the purpose for writing in the last sentence or two of the opening? If not, note suggested changes on the draft.

5. Does the middle of the letter discuss the reasons for the complaint? Is the writer specific about product names, serial numbers, invoices, dates and other details? If not, note any suggested changes on the draft.

6. Does the writer make a specific request for action toward the end of the middle of the letter? If not, note suggested changes on the draft.

7. Does the writer look to the future in the closing, and does the writer provide a courteous close? If not, suggest changes on the draft.

8. What persuasive strategies does the writer employ in the letter? Are they effective? Why or why not?

9. Is the overall tone (attitude toward the reader and the subject) professional and courteous? Does the writer avoid negative phrases and insults? If not, suggest areas on the draft where the writer might make improvements.

10. Are there any weaknesses in style (for example, word choice) or errors in grammar or mechanics (punctuation, spelling, capitalization, abbreviations, numbers)? Mark any suggested changes on the draft.

11. Does the letter carry out the specifications of the assignment? What could the writer do to better fulfill the assignment?

12. Record the grade you give the letter, based on your evaluation.

- Be thorough in the peer reviews. If a critique sheet is available for critiquing the document, make sure you understand every item on the critique sheet and what you are required to comment on.

- If no critique sheet is available, jot down your own 10- to 20-item checklist of things to look for, ranging from clarity of purpose to effectiveness of design. Continue to refine this checklist as you review the work of others. Soon you will have created your own reusable critique sheet.

- As you read the document, read it the way any careful reader would. If some point isn't clear, ask the writer if he or she can clarify the point. If you think a point is inaccurate, ask the writer to check the accuracy of the information. If you think an idea needs further discussion, ask the writer if he or she can elaborate.

- Note errors in the margins or attach a separate sheet of notes, handwritten or typed. These notes will be helpful to the writer of the document, especially if you have detailed suggestions for improvement. Be helpful by writing questions concerning points that are not clear or that need more elaboration.

- In addition to writing your comments and questions, also consider talking to your peers and asking them to clarify a point or to tell you what their concerns are. The discussion may simply be a five-minute overview or, depending on the complexity of the document and its importance, a critique that may take one or more days.

- Find something good to say about the document—and say it first—before launching into a list of what is wrong. People are often defensive when their work is criticized. The writer will be more receptive to your constructive suggestions if you can say something positive about the document first.

- As a reviewer, rank your suggestions for revisions. The writer may not have the time to make every change that you and others suggest, so a ranking by priority can be helpful. Also, if you are offering many suggestions for improvement, the writer may feel less overwhelmed if your major suggestions are ranked.

- Offer constructive criticism. Be truthful about weaknesses in the document, but point out the weaknesses tactfully and respectfully. Look for strengths, too. Remember that another writer's ego is at stake, and don't forget how you feel when others comment on shortcomings in your writing.

- Treat your team peers courteously and professionally at all times. Often peer reviews are assigned several days before a final version of a student's document is due. You must be prompt in your review of your peers' work so that they can make any necessary improvements before the assignment is due.

- Be helpful in the peer reviews. Take them seriously and expect your peers to take them seriously.

Benefiting from Reviews of Your Work

- Try to remember that the criticisms are about your document, not about you.
- Make sure you understand the criticisms. If you are uncertain, ask questions.
- Take your reviewer's comments seriously. Be receptive to helpful criticism. If you don't make the changes that the reviewer has suggested that you make, the reviewer may be reluctant to help you the next time and perhaps even completely unwilling to help the time after that.
- Learn from the reviews of others. Learn what you are doing wrong and avoid repeating the same mistakes. If your reviewer keeps calling attention to the same faults in punctuation, for example, make sure you learn how to avoid those mistakes in other documents.
- Reward your reviewers. Buy them coffee or lunch. Show them how much you appreciate their help, and, again, return their help in kind. You need these people to help you look good, and they need you. It's a mutually beneficial relationship.

IMPROVING COLLABORATIVE SKILLS

Regardless of the kind of collaboration model you are using or whether you are collaborating face-to-face or completely online, you will still face many interpersonal challenges. You'll need to know how to use a variety of strategies to help the group do the work it needs to do.

Enhancing Listening Skills

Just as many writers focus on what they want to say rather than on what the audience needs to know, many people are preoccupied with their own thoughts and not with what others have to say. Most people are poor listeners. They may listen intently for a few minutes, but they soon let their thoughts drift to something else. In their book *Effective Listening Skills,* Kratz and Kratz wrote, "Studies reveal that most people spend as much as 90 percent of their working days in one of four modes of communication: writing, reading, speaking, and listening. Of these four modes, however, we devote *more than half* our time to listening" (3).

While it's true that many people are difficult to listen to because of their voices or possibly because it takes them a long time to get to the point, you should still be able to enhance your listening skills nonetheless.

IT'S JUST THAT SIMPLE

How to work collaboratively? Make a list and divvy up the pieces.

—John M. Watts, Jr., fire safety consultant, Middlebury, Vermont

Improving Your Listening Skills

- Pay attention. When someone is talking to you, don't let your thoughts stray to some other topic.

- Maintain eye contact with the person or people talking to you.

- Try not to interrupt. Interrupt others only when a point needs to be clarified. Ask simply, "Do you mind repeating that point for me?"

- Be polite and sincere in your listening. Your listening should not be an act. It should be a genuine attempt to understand the other person's point of view.

- Don't rush the person you're listening to. Show that you value the conversation.

- Take notes only when necessary and try not to distract the speaker if you do take notes.

- Record a conversation only in special circumstances and only when you have the permission of the person or people you are recording.

- If you are having a conversation with more than one person at once, make sure you give equal attention to all those who speak.

- Listen to what is not said as well as what is said. In other words, learn how to read between the lines.

- Listen to body language as well as to what is spoken.

- Learn how to recognize qualities in the other party's voice. Listen to the person's words, but also pay attention to the tone of voice, how the person's voice is pitched, the facial expressions, and the person's stance. These are all clues to how the person actually feels about the situation you are both involved in.

- Learn how to figure out what the other person is trying to tell you. To be a good listener, you have to understand what the other person is trying to tell you instead of just trying to hear what you want to hear. You have to know how to read both verbal and nonverbal cues. Knowing how to read nonverbal cues can give you valuable information about the attitudes and emotions behind the words you are hearing.

> People can learn from genuine disagreements with each other, and considering the views of others can often make every team member more creative. Conflict can also motivate people to work harder on a project to make sure that the job is done well and that they are contributing their best effort.

Careful listening is not merely a matter of giving the other party a chance to speak. Careful listening is the best strategy for you to acquire all the information you need to know to collaborate and negotiate with the other person.

Handling Conflict

Even the best teams using the stratified model may encounter conflict. However, conflict can be both positive and negative. People can learn from genuine disagreements with each other, and considering the views of others can often make every team member more creative. Conflict can also motivate people to work harder on a project to make sure that the job is done well and that they are contributing their best effort. Conflict can also pressure team members to meet deadlines that they might otherwise miss.

Unfortunately, if a group is poorly managed—and at times even despite good management—members working on a project are sometimes just not able to get along. Some people may not be willing or able to do their fair share of the work. Some may fail their team by not delivering an essential part of a project when promised. Some team members may simply lack the interpersonal skills to communicate their views and their feelings effectively to other members.

There are no easy solutions for resolving conflict, but one step is to distinguish the positive kinds of conflict from the negative. Another step is to make sure there are a variety of ways to communicate concerns and opposing views.

Ways to Handle Conflict

- Accept the fact that differences of opinion will occur and often lead to good solutions.
- Give everyone on the team the opportunity to express ideas so that all members know they are contributing to the project.
- If you have to resolve conflict among members of a team, collect enough information from all sides of the disagreement. Focus on the current disagreement, and don't let team members digress from the subject at hand to the history of prior conflicts.
- Don't jump to conclusions about the views of any one side. Appearances can be deceptive.
- Don't assume that you know how each side feels about the matter.

- Assess the emotional state of those who are involved in the conflict. You may need to calm people who are highly agitated.
- Show sympathy toward all. Try to understand the situation from all points of view.
- Avoid blaming one person or one side in the conflict. Your goal should not be to alienate anyone but to resolve the conflict in the best interests of all involved.
- Be sincere and honest in your attempt to resolve the conflict. Treat both sides equitably.
- Make sure the conflict is resolved to everyone's satisfaction, or at least that the resolution is something everyone can accept.

Negotiating

Negotiating involves communicating with others in an attempt to resolve a conflict or some other matter. Successful negotiating is a difficult skill to master, but whether in life or in your work, negotiating is not something you have a choice about. You will have to negotiate often about all kinds of decisions and situations. You continually have to negotiate with your classmates, friends, dates, significant other, spouse, kids, colleagues, and others. So the issue is not whether you will negotiate. The issue is whether you will negotiate well or poorly.

Negotiating Skills

- Learn how to listen. (See the tip list, "Improving Your Listening Skills," earlier in this chapter.)

- Focus your attention on the other party. Maintain eye contact. Learn how to read what the eyes may be telling you. Your focus should not be on persuading but on perceiving. The better you understand what the other person is trying to say, the better you can respond.

- Be empathetic. Put yourself in the other person's shoes. As you listen, ask yourself why this person sees things that way, and ask yourself whether you would see things that way if you were that person.

- Let the other person completely explain his or her position. Don't interrupt. Now is the time to gather information that you can use later in the negotiating process.

- Explain your own position logically and clearly. Facts and a well-organized presentation will help your cause. Cover every pertinent point, and make sure that your facts are accurate. If necessary, modify your presentation to take into account points raised by the other person.

- Avoid arguing or shouting, expressing other hostility, or engaging in personal attacks. Keep the focus on the message. Nothing will be accomplished by other strategies. If you become angry, you give the other party an edge. Anger can be used to your advantage, but you need to know when and how to use it.

- Think win–win rather than win–lose. Many people believe that one person wins a negotiation and the other loses. However, if the negotiations are successful, both parties win. During your discussions focus not only on what you want to gain, but also on what the other party has to gain to feel good about the outcome.

- Be willing to compromise. There should always be a little room for flexibility in your negotiations. Even when big issues are at stake, compromise can usually be found. Negotiation often requires that you give something to get something. Think of what you can give in return for what you want.

- Expect compromise. Just as you should be willing to compromise, you have a right to expect the other party to compromise. Both sides must be flexible.

- Be willing to follow through with whatever you have agreed on.

- Be patient. After negotiations have been proceeding for a while, both sides may lose patience with each other. This is the time to be more patient than ever. Think of patience as a strategy to help you obtain what you want.

- Recognize negotiation as an ongoing process. If negotiations are particularly long and complex, it's a good idea to write everything down. Otherwise, you and the other party may later disagree about what you agreed on earlier.

CHOOSING THE ETHICAL PATH

Don't offer anything that you are not sincere about giving after the deal is finalized. You have to keep your word.

PARTICIPATING IN MEETINGS

Employees typically spend countless hours attending meetings in the workplace. Some are mandatory daily or weekly progress meetings. Some are informal; some are formal. Some are on pedestrian matters, and some are on matters of utmost importance or something in between the two. Many people dread meetings because they are too busy to attend them. And it is true that meetings can be a waste of time when they are poorly run, poorly organized, and too long. But only a little planning is required to run or to participate in much more efficient and productive meetings. When you invest time in a meeting, you should expect a sufficiently large payback to justify that investment.

Attending Meetings Productively

● Be on time. Be present only if you are needed.
● Be well prepared.
● Be attentive to the discussion so that your contribution does not repeat what was covered earlier by someone else.
● Be brief, relevant, focused, and courteous in your comments.

ON MEETINGS

Meetings are rarely as effective as they could be because most people who call them have no training in running effective meetings. Starting with a clear goal, making sure everyone comes prepared, and keeping to the topic would go a long way towards improving meetings.

—Geoff Hart, publications coordinator, Québec, Canada

One of the most effective ways to make a meeting more productive is to use and follow an agenda. The agenda of the meeting shows the aim of the meeting and points of discussion in priority order. In effect, it is a "to do" list for the meeting. Using an agenda helps to focus the meeting and keeps it from drifting off topic. Agendas should be composed and sent out in advance so that the participants know what is expected of them. If you circulate the agenda sufficiently far in advance, people have time to prepare fully for the meeting, and the meeting will not stall for lack of information. A well-written agenda minimizes the chance that a key member will show up unprepared for a crucial discussion. See Figure 3.8 for an example.

Writing and Using an Agenda

● Keep the agenda short. An agenda states the purpose, time, location, and goals of a meeting. It outlines each topic to be covered and often specifies the time allotted for each. Listing who is responsible for each topic and the type of action needed helps clarify the goals and direction of the meeting for the participants.
● List each item sequentially according to its order on the program. Include who is responsible for the presentation, what kind of action is needed, and the time allotted for the topic. Some items to consider for the agenda are approval of the minutes from the last meeting, committee reports, old business, new business, and guest speakers.

Planning and Running a Meeting

- Appoint someone to take the minutes for the meeting using the meeting agenda as a guide. (See "Minutes" section in Chapter 17.)
- Specify an ending time for the meeting.
- Set the time of the meeting carefully. If possible, ensure that the meeting starts on time. If it starts late, the time of all the attendees is being wasted. If latecomers are not critically needed, start without them.
- Change the timing of the meeting depending on the habits of the attendees. If people tend to waffle excessively, you can schedule the meeting just before lunch or going home. This gives people an incentive to be brief. If people tend to arrive late, start a meeting at an unusual time, such as nineteen minutes past the hour. This seems to improve punctuality.

- Invite only the minimum required number of attendees to a meeting. The more people present, the more who will want to air their views. Similarly, bringing people who are not needed to a meeting wastes their time.
- Before the meeting, ensure that decisions made at previous meetings have been acted on. This guarantees that the meeting will not be seen as just a time to discuss old issues once again.
- At the opening of the meeting, ask for additions to the agenda; get group approval for the agenda before you start the meeting.
- At the end of the meeting, summarize the points discussed and create an action plan from the decisions made. This ensures that everyone understands what has been decided and who will do what.

WAYS TO IMPROVE YOUR MEETINGS

- Clearly delineate the "Rules of Engagement." Agree on how the meeting will be run, topics that are out of bounds, and so forth.
- Respect the time: start on time and don't waste time. Finish a two-hour meeting in an hour and you have given the participants a gift they will thank you for.
- Provide refreshments. Food and drink are good.
- Plan, plan, plan.

—Bob Shapiro, senior program manager, Burlington, Massachusetts

---

FIGURE 3.8

Meeting Agenda

Meeting Agenda

1. General Announcements
   A. Awards
   B. New Employees
   C. Policy Changes

2. Team Reports
   A. Team 1
   B. Team 2
   C. Team 3
   D. Team 4

3. Old Business
   A. Contract with Oilco Company
   B. Contract with Netco Company

4. New Business
   A. New Product Line
   B. New Competitor

ACTING ETHICALLY

Ethical concerns will often come into play as you work collaboratively with others, largely because the others may support values that are either similar to or very different from yours. For example, you and your team members may share the values of dependability, efficiency, loyalty, and pride in your work. However, if you don't share these values, then difficulties in collaborating are likely to arise.

There are many kinds of ethical systems, ranging from those rooted in a religion to those that are completely secular. You have probably already decided which ethical system best suits you. Whatever you choose to adhere to, you are essentially choosing a system or hierarchy of values to live and act by. It's important to choose these values wisely and to adhere to them conscientiously.

But acting ethically is more complex than merely choosing your values wisely and adhering to them conscientiously. After all, many people choose negative values (for instance, greed, jealousy, hate) and adhere to those negative values conscientiously. Acting ethically, to have any meaning at all, must be based on positive values and lead to beneficial results. Over the centuries, most cultures have come to value respect for persons or others, and this value is a standard for ethical behavior in many cultures. We are judged in these cultures (and often these cultures are also judged) for how we demonstrate our respect for other people or how we fail to do so.

Resolving Ethical Issues

- Determine what your values are and be aware when actions or events conflict with those values. Determine, for example, whether values such as loyalty, friendship, or success are important to you. Once you determine which values are most important to you, it will be easier to decide whether, for instance, reporting a peer who is cheating on an exam is an action you should take.
- Be aware that others may have different values that are just important to them as your values are to you.
- Be aware that compromises don't necessarily undermine your values.
- Be aware that ethical dilemmas occur when you must choose between two strongly held values.
- Be aware that the challenges for you to behave ethically or at least to make decisions concerning your values will be constant.

Ethics provide restrictions—or obligations—on our behavior. We have many kinds of obligations ranging from personal obligations to professional obligations. Personal obligations may, for example, simply be keeping promises to family and friends. Professional obligations may be honoring a contract or working at our jobs as competently and professionally as possible.

From the workplace

Gregory D. Reed, Ph.D.

R. M. Condra Professor and Head, Department of Civil and Environmental Engineering, University of Tennessee Knoxville, Tennessee

Gregory has worked as an educator in the field of engineering for over 25 years. As chair of his department, he spends much of his time not only preparing written materials but also critiquing the writing of his students and other faculty members.

I am working in exactly the field I trained for—environmental engineering. Since earning my doctorate in 1976, I've worked in a university setting, first at the University of Missouri–Columbia and since 1981 at the University of Tennessee. I expect to stay in this field until I retire.

For my job, I write reports, proposals, letters, memos, e-mails, journal articles, and alumni-magazine articles. These are intended to keep our alumni and friends informed about the achievements and activities of the department. I also produce news releases for anything that occurs that we would like the community to recognize.

I supervise a variety of activities that require a review of communication instruments. I assign regular writing assignments in my classes, some of which are in an edit-and-resubmit mode for learning purposes and some for evaluation.

Another student supervision activity I perform is as a thesis and dissertation advisor for approximately two graduate students each year who are completing degree requirements. I review drafts the graduate students prepare and suggest improvements in their research and the organization of their written work. Often they need direction in organizing their procedures, analyzing their results, and writing up their findings in a way that will convey to their readers what they have accomplished.

I review all research proposals that faculty write prior to their submission in order to provide feedback on any unclear or missing information. And several journals have called on my expertise to provide peer review for articles submitted to them for publication. I evaluate both the content and presentation for correctness and consistency. My evaluations are then used to guide the authors as they refine their papers.

Most courses in our program include one or more communication activities as part of the assignments. Class writing assignments range from reflection papers on outside reading assignments to technical papers on specific topics to project reports of major activities. Some of these reports are also given to outside professionals for their feedback.

We expect our students to master technical report writing and oral presentation, business communications, public speaking and publication writing (for

Ethics also provide us with goals to strive for—ideals. For example, fairness and loyalty are common ideals. We may act one way or another depending on our ideal of being fair to everyone involved in a particular action.

Finally, ethics confront us with consequences—the positive or negative effects that result from our actions. Consequences may be obvious or subtle, direct or indirect, physical or emotional, immediate or long-term, intentional or unintentional. Determining whether or not an action is ethical depends a great deal on the nature of the consequence or consequences.

Acting ethically means showing a respect for others, honoring obligations, and living up to ideals to create good consequences. Determining when cer-

example, papers, manuals). Many students initially have trouble learning that they must write concisely. Since practice helps confidence, we ask our students to perform multiple times before they leave us. As a result, most graduates of the program are competent communicators—not perfect but effective.

Another part of my job is mentoring young faculty—meeting monthly and also on an as-needed basis. Most of the mentoring discussions are focused on activities and priorities, but the effective development of communications is an important part of the professional process.

I think these discussions have worked well because we do it in an improvement mode rather than in a punitive mode. The mentor is for positive gain, not negative criticism. This type of mentoring has made the tenure and promotion process smoother for the protégé, since knowing ahead of time what is acceptable and how to produce it creates a high probability of success. The department has a record of improved teaching. I think in every case, new faculty have improved their teaching effectiveness as a result of mentoring and evaluation feedback.

I never had a mentor myself (although I wish I had), but networking of other kinds has been very important to my career. It opened up opportunities that I was not aware of previously. While there have been many committee assignments that create relationships as a result of networking, I have also been able to participate in major impact activities such as helping to write policy/guidance documents for accreditation issues in both the American Society of Civil Engineers

(ASCE) and the American Academy of Environmental Engineers (AAEE).

It is my experience that people get new professional opportunities by making themselves known, principally by communication and networking activities. Regardless of the field or industry, there are always networking opportunities: professional organization memberships, attendance at local and national professional meetings, volunteering for committees, social and service club memberships such as Rotary or Kiwanis, Internet mailing lists and newsgroups, and family and church ties.

Insider Advice

Seek as many networking and learning experiences as possible and also interact with persons outside your area of expertise. Focus on the things of most value to your employer even if they are different from your personal priorities.

Write from the reader's need. Writers should know their audience well enough to write to their information need. If you don't know your audience, take the time to find out. Talk to them. Read about them. Find out their priorities and interests so you can address them appropriately in your communication (or at least avoid making them angry).

tain actions are ethical and acting ethically can be a challenge, but it is one you will need to face in your personal and professional life.

CHECKING WHAT YOU'VE LEARNED

Collaborating

- If you are part of a collaborative team, have you conscientiously worked on your particular responsibilities?
- Have you been helpful to your teammates and tried to accommodate their needs and requests?

- Have you treated your teammates courteously, respectfully, and professionally?
- Have you made an effort to resolve differences when they arise?
- Have you respected the opinions of others?
- Have you been fair when you were asked to evaluate the contributions of the other members of your team?

Peer Review

- Have you taken your peer-reviewing responsibilities seriously by providing helpful and constructive criticism, presented in a professional manner?
- If you have a review sheet to follow, have you answered all its questions?
- Have you promptly returned your feedback within the allotted time period?

Meetings

- Do you arrive at meetings promptly and are you prepared to participate?
- If you are asked to take minutes, are they complete and accurate?

Listening

- Do you listen attentively when you are in a meeting or having a conversation?
- If you disagree with someone, do you present your views calmly and avoid casting blame on others?
- Do you let others finish what they are saying and try to understand what they are trying to express?
- Do you pay attention not only to the words you hear but also to gestures and other body language?
- Are you willing to be flexible and to compromise in order to resolve disagreements?

Ethics

- Have you selected a set of values that enables you to make difficult decisions on ethical issues?
- Are you aware of the ethical code of your profession or discipline?

EXERCISES

 REVIEW

1. Write a paragraph discussing how you have experienced some of the advantages or the disadvantages common in collaborative work. Be prepared to discuss your views in class.
2. Write a paragraph discussing the difficulties you have experienced in face-to-face collaborations. Be prepared to discuss your views in class.
3. Create a bulleted list providing the ways you have shared information with others online in addition to using e-mail (for example, text, photo, audio, or video attachments).
4. Write a paragraph summarizing your strengths and weaknesses as a listener for either your personal or student or professional life. Be prepared to discuss your findings with the rest of the class.
5. Write a paragraph discussing how, based on your experience, insensitivity to cultural or gender differences in a group has created problems for the group. Be prepared to discuss your views with the rest of the class.

 THE INTERNET

1. You no doubt are increasingly being asked to collaborate online with others, whether they are peers in a college class or co-workers at your company. Make a list of some of the challenges you have faced in collaborating effectively with others online whether the difficulties are due to personalities or the tools you used (e-mail, attachments, Web bulletin boards, chat rooms), and be prepared to discuss this list in class.
2. Using several search engines, find information on at least two authoring tools that enable users to collaborate more effectively online. Write a brief paragraph discussing your findings.

 ETHICS/PROFESSIONALISM

Imagine that during the collaborative work you are doing on a project, you discover that one of your group member is plagiarizing his or her work for the project. Write a paragraph discussing how you would address this ethical problem. Be prepared to discuss your answer with the rest of the class.

 COLLABORATION

Working with at least two other students in class, make a list of your personality traits while your group members make a list of theirs. Compare your lists and be prepared to discuss any similarities and differences. Also be prepared to discuss whether or not you think these similarities and differences would present any special difficulties in group work.

 INTERNATIONAL COMMUNICATION

Corporate practices often differ from culture to culture. Some cultures encourage direct dealings with clients while others encourage a more indirect approach. American corporations, for example, typically are very straightforward in their dealings with clients while Japanese corporations concentrate more on context and relationship with clients. Write a paragraph discussing some of the difficulties you would expect to encounter in collaborating with others who are from a different culture from your own.

RESOURCES

Badaracco, Joseph L., Jr. *Defining Moments: When Managers Must Choose Between Right and Right.* Boston: Harvard Business School P, 1997.

Biederman, Patricia Ward. *Organizing Genius: The Secrets of Creative Collaboration.* Boston: Perseus, 1998.

Bishop, Sue. *The Complete Guide to People Skills.* Oxford: Gower, 1997.

Brown, William. *Interpersonal Skills for Leadership.* New York: Prentice Hall, 1998.

Chang, Richard Y. *Success through Teamwork: A Practical Guide to Interpersonal Team Dynamics.* Irvine: Chang, 1994.

Dombrowski, Paul. *Ethics in Technical Communication.* Boston: Allyn and Bacon, 2000.

Duarte, Deborah L., and Nancy Tennant Snyder. *Mastering Virtual Teams: Strategies, Tools, and Techniques That Succeed.* San Francisco: Jossey-Bass, 1999.

Hargrove, Robert. *Mastering the Art of Creative Collaboration.* New York: McGraw-Hill, 1998.

Humphrey, Watts S. *Managing Technical People: Innovation, Teamwork, and the Software Process.* Boston: Addison-Wesley, 1996.

Kratz, Dennis M., and Abby Robinson Kratz. *Effective Listening Skills.* Toronto: Irwin, 1995.

Lipnack, Jessica, and Jeffrey Stamps. *Virtual Teams: Reaching Across Space, Time, and Organizations with Technology.* New York: Wiley, 1997.

Rees, Fran. *Teamwork from Start to Finish: 10 Steps to Results.* San Diego: Pfeiffer, 1997.

Ruggiero, Vincent Ryan. *Thinking Critically About Ethical Issues.* 4th ed. Mountain View: Mayfield, 1997.

Schultz, Heidi. *The Elements of Electronic Communication.* Needham Heights: Allyn and Bacon, 2000.

Stark, Peter B. *It's Negotiable.* San Diego: Pfeiffer, 1994.

Syer, John. *How Teamwork Works: The Dynamics of Effective Team Development.* New York: McGraw-Hill, 1996.

Voss, Dan, and Lori Allen. *Ethics in Technical Communication: Shades of Grey.* New York: Wiley, 1997.

Wellins, Richard S. *Inside Teams: How 20 World-Class Organizations Are Winning through Teamwork.* San Diego: Jossey-Bass, 1994.

Yager, Dexter. *Dynamic People Skills.* Wheaton: Tyndale House, 1997.

4

Planning

Determining the Focus   80

Discovering Initial Ideas   85

Setting and Following Standards   91

Managing Your Document   96

From the Workplace   106

Planning can take time, but it undoubtedly also saves time and improves the quality of your work. In effect, you can't afford to avoid planning, and the larger the project the more essential the planning. Often, planning even short projects requires many of the same steps that a much longer document does. And, of course, the more complex the document, the more necessary planning becomes.

All the elements of planning, from determining your focus to creating a document plan, center on the audience for your document. Your reader should be the determining factor for what you cover in your document from the beginning, through the middle, and to the end. The information in this chapter will help you to plan the many kinds of documents you typically will write for a variety of audiences.

Some documentation projects are so massive that they require far more complex planning than this book can cover. If you are a documentation manager and find yourself responsible for a major project (for example, creating a series of software user manuals for a sophisticated software program), then you will benefit from a much more extensive discussion, such as JoAnn Hackos's *Managing Your Documentation Projects* (see the Resources section at the end of this chapter). Hackos's book is thorough, not only in addressing the planning phase but also in discussing the areas of content specification, implementation, production, and evaluation.

You will learn about:

- determining the focus of your communications: ascertaining the needs of your audience, narrowing your subject, stating your purpose, and defining your scope
- discovering initial ideas by brainstorming, mind mapping, and freewriting
- setting and following standards of style, mechanics, and design
- managing your documents by developing a schedule, planning the production, and creating a document plan
- using a variety of planning tools

DETERMINING THE FOCUS

When you take a photograph, you focus on your subject so that your picture will show exactly what you intend. Similarly, you refine your document's focus to maximize its effectiveness. How you focus your subject determines what information your audience will glean from your text. And just as in taking photographs, the decisions you make about what you are trying to express, who you expect will be viewing your work, how close you will be to your subject, and how broadly or narrowly you will frame your subject all contribute to the character and impact of the piece.

Determining the Informational Needs of Your Audience

Determining the focus of a document means understanding the audience and why its members need the information you are providing, narrowing the subject, stating the purpose, and limiting the scope or depth of detail in your document, whether it's correspondence, a report, instructions, policies and procedures, or a Web site. You will have properly determined your focus when you have done all these effectively.

You begin by determining what your audience's informational needs are and then by analyzing how you can best meet these needs in your document. (See Chapter 2 for a detailed discussion of understanding your audience and determining its informational needs.)

> " " You begin by determining what your audience's informational needs are and then by analyzing how you can best meet these needs in your document.

Narrowing the Subject

The subject of a document is its main area of concern or main topic. Initially, the subject is a broad area that requires further focusing. In a technical report, your subject may be deforestation, acid rain, laptop computers, modems, or fractals. In technical instructions, your subject may be how to install a new disk drive in a home computer or how to create a Web site. In a letter, your subject may be your qualifications for a job or a complaint about a company's products or services. All these are good subjects, but all lack a proper focus.

In academe, you are sometimes assigned a broad subject for a document, and then you are challenged to narrow your focus appropriately. Deforestation, for example, is a broad subject. Who is your audience? Do you have an audience other than the professor who gave you the assignment? Why does your audience need to know about the subject? What does your audience want to know about the subject? How much do you already know about the subject? How much more do you need to know to write the document? You must answer these questions and many others before you will have a valuable focus. See Figure 4.1 for more on broad versus focused subjects in college writing.

In college, you are sometimes given complete freedom to choose your subject. For example, in a typical introductory technical communication class, you may have to write both a proposal for and a technical report on a subject in your discipline. You also may have to write to a layperson or a peer about your subject. Of course, these requirements don't simplify matters completely. You still have thousands of subjects to choose from within your discipline. You may have to consider some new technology, issue, or trend, or a subject that you have recently studied in one of your other classes. The challenge lies in properly defining your focus for both yourself and your audience.

In industry, the subject is often more narrowly defined and a specific audience is often more readily apparent, but you still face the problem of achieving a focus or a statement of purpose. For example, you may have to write a letter in response to a customer's complaint or submit a status report to your

FIGURE 4.1

**Broad Versus Focused
Subjects in College Writing**

BROAD SUBJECTS	FOCUSED SUBJECTS	AUDIENCE
Discuss deforestation	Discuss the effects of deforestation on the economy in southern Brazil during the past ten years	College professor who requires current research on a topic concerning the economy in Brazil
Discuss a feature in Microsoft Word	Discuss how to create a watermark using Microsoft Word	Group of student peers who will test the instructions
Discuss political correctness	Define "political correctness" and outline its negative effects on college campuses	Students attending a forum concerning controversial campus issues
Discuss a significant event for the first semester of college	Discuss how you learned something new about your parents when they brought you to college at the beginning of your first semester	College graduate teaching assistant who requires a different perspective on the freshman experience
Discuss bias in prose	Discuss why the generic use of "he" persists as an issue	College professor who requires a paper discussing an issue in prose style

supervisor about the project you've been working on for the past few months. Or you might have to choose one kind of office equipment over another and recommend a course of action to your superiors. Typically, you will be required to respond to a great deal of pedestrian correspondence and e-mail asking you for updates, actions, favors, or information. Determining exactly what you want to write in your letter to the customer, status report to your supervisor, or routine correspondence is a matter of refining your subject in keeping with your intended focus. See Figure 4.2 for more on broad versus focused subjects in the workplace.

Stating the Purpose

Determining your focus also involves stating your purpose clearly and concisely. To establish your purpose for writing, you need to answer these questions: "Why am I writing this document?" "What do I want my readers to know, do, or accept?" "What do I want to accomplish with this document?"

For example, the subject of computers would be impossibly large and unmanageable for a technical report. However, an evaluation of the feasibility of converting from a PC-based shop to a Macintosh-based shop or deciding among several possible printers for your company is a narrow enough problem to allow for a meaningful report. Your purpose and your audience have given you a good focus for your document. If you decide that the structure of a recommendation report is the best approach for discussing advantages and disadvantages, then the choice of this kind of document further helps you to focus

BROAD SUBJECTS	FOCUSED SUBJECTS	AUDIENCE
Make a decision concerning purchasing new computers	Discuss the feasibility of converting a PC-based shop to a Macintosh-based shop	Owner of the small business Dynamic Consulting Services who needs reliable information before making a decision
Establish corporate style standards	Establish the format and style requirements for technical reports for the Systems Division of Oilco	Employees of the Systems Division of Oilco who have been required to follow standards
Provide an update on a project	Give a team presentation on the team progress on the Web project for the second quarter	Company CEO who has requested briefs from every major team for the second quarter
Respond to a customer complaint	Refuse to provide a refund for a company product	Customer who is upset about the quality of a product purchased from the company
Provide an update on a business trip	Provide a detailed report on the March 1–15 trip to Atlanta	Supervisor who requires the report for evaluation and reimbursement purposes

FIGURE 4.2

Broad Versus Focused Subjects in the Workplace

your subject: The structure of a recommendation report requires you to compare two or more courses of action and to recommend one of them or neither.

In a cover letter for a job, your purpose may be stated simply at the beginning of the letter: "I am writing to apply for the position as a traffic engineer that you advertised in the *Orlando Sentinel*." Your purpose is to let your reader know that you are applying for the job opening. In a progress report in brief memorandum format, you may write, "I am providing an update on the work completed so far and an overview of the work remaining to be done." In a complaint letter, you may state, "I am writing to call your attention to the poor service I received at your repair shop last Saturday." In a proposal, you may write, "I propose to write a report comparing Compaq and Toshiba laptop computers." In a technical report, you may state, "This report demonstrates how design engineers apply Hooke's Law to determine stresses on materials." See Figure 4.3 for more on purpose statements.

When and where you state your purpose depend on your purpose, your audience, and the kind of document you are writing. There are many kinds of openings, and many different strategies for making your purpose clear.

Often you should state your purpose as soon as you can in the opening of a brief document. However, many times you should not take such a direct approach. For example, you will often begin a complaint letter by establishing a common ground with your reader. Your specific purpose is to have the person act on your request, but in a complaint letter, you may not want to state the underlying purpose in the opening sentence of the letter. (See Chapter 14 for a

FIGURE 4.3

**Examples of
Purpose Statements**

From a background report: This background report will help educate computer operators regarding the health risks associated with computer use and the precautions they can take to diminish the effects.

From a co-authored recommendation report: This recommendation report presents a formal PC Maintenance Program to Integrated Marketing Company.

From a proposal: We are requesting permission to research, analyze, and compile information regarding the health problems related to computer operators.

From a complaint letter: I am writing to call your attention to the poor service I received at your repair shop last Saturday.

From a progress report: I am providing an update on the work completed so far and an overview of the work remaining to be done.

From a job application letter: I am applying for the position of Programmer/Analyst I in your Engineering Services Department in the Orlando printing facility.

From instructions: These instructions explain how to remove a defective alternator and install a new or rebuilt alternator in a 1990 Buick Regal equipped with a 3800 V-6 engine and air conditioning.

From a white paper: This paper discusses the types of middleware available, their strengths, and best applications. It then explains Talarian's SmartSockets in depth.

From a report: The report, written by the IITF Working Group on Intellectual Property Rights chaired by Assistant Secretary of Commerce and Commissioner of Patents and Trademarks Bruce A. Lehman, explains how intellectual property law applies to cyberspace and makes legislative recommendations to Congress to fine-tune the law for the digital age.

discussion of direct and indirect patterns in correspondence and some other examples.)

Defining your purpose and following through on it consistently are not simple tasks. Perhaps the two biggest problems many people face are determining their purpose for writing in the first place and controlling that purpose effectively throughout the document.

Limiting the Scope

Limiting your scope in a document is another essential step in establishing your focus. Scope is the depth of detail with which you are covering a subject. It is the specific range, limits, or boundaries of the subject you are discussing. Considering your scope helps you to narrow your subject so you can discuss it adequately.

Scope is in large part determined by audience. How much information does your audience need to know about your topic in order to do, know, or accept something? The answer helps you to determine the depth of detail. If you are writing a technical report on the disappearance of rain forests for a company bidding on the rights to harvest rubber in Brazil, you would save yourself a great deal of time by limiting your scope to rain forests in Brazil and not including rain forests elsewhere in South America and on other continents. In fact, your report would be even more manageable if you limited the scope to examining deforestation in Brazil over the past ten years.

Scope is determined by other factors as well. For example, time, budget, personnel, urgency, and ethics may be factors shaping scope. If you have only a few days to research a topic and write a document, you probably will have to narrow the scope considerably to finish on time. If you have a severely limited printing budget, you may be forced to write a short manual rather than a long one. If creating the document is a team project, the scope will be limited by the number of people available and their particular talents. If the document is needed urgently, you might have time to cover only the bare essentials. Finally, if a code of ethics prevents certain topics from being explored, this may limit your scope as well.

Scope Section from a Document

The scope of these instructions will not differentiate between the many types of softwoods available to the woodworker. Instead, it is assumed that you will use the most available type of softwood, pine. Since there are many different types of pine, it will also be assumed that you will have only the worst type of pine available at your local lumberyard: yellow and sappy pine.

DISCOVERING INITIAL IDEAS

Whether your writing task is a specific reaction to an urgent request or a response to an assignment allowing you to choose any topic that interests you, you still face the problem that all writers face: finding the best ideas for your purpose and audience. Discovery—or invention, as it is also called—plays just as important a role in technical communication as it does in other kinds of writing.

Knowing that you must write a particular kind of document does not solve your problem of discovery. You still need to find the topics and subtopics you will discuss. The structure of a formal set of instructions, for example, typically includes an introduction, a discussion of theory, a list of equipment or tools needed, a series of steps to be performed, troubleshooting, and warnings (see Chapter 19). The challenge lies in discovering and selecting the topics and subtopics you should discuss for the instructions, discovering

ON BRAINSTORMING

Initial brainstorming sessions are vital, during which answers are sought to such questions as "Why is the document being developed?" "What are the present or likely competing or comparable documents?" "Who are the intended readers and users?" "How are they expected to use it and for what purpose?" "What is the budget?" "What is the deadline?" "What is the document's expected 'shelf-life'?" "How will we know whether the document has been successful?" or "What are the criteria with which the document will be judged?" And so on. Such a session should precede any other discussion and especially any specific discussion about the document's appearance and content. This helps in arriving at more specific decisions and in choosing between alternatives. In general, communication is improved by being clear about the *why* rather than the *how*.

—Yateendra Joshi, director, information technology and services, New Delhi, India

**ON TOOLS FOR
SKETCHING**

Everyone at work teases me
about how I need to use a
whiteboard when I talk to a
group. I also use whiteboards
for my rough sketches. I use
paper and pencil in the early
parts of a project and then I
switch to Word and
PowerPoint for the actual
artifacts to be produced. I
keep wishing that the
whiteboard was another
input to my computer.

—George Johnston, software
development engineer,
Redmond, Washington

the best approach to your subject, narrowing your subject properly, and communicating with your audience effectively.

The phase of planning your document is not the outlining phase. The rigid structure of a topic or sentence outline is something that comes later in the planning process (see Chapter 6). In the outlining phase, you will more formally organize the ideas you acquire in the discovery phase of your planning. The emphasis in this part of the planning should be on creativity. Think of as many ideas, topics, approaches, or avenues as you (or a group) possibly can. You can use one or more of the common techniques of brainstorming, mind mapping, and freewriting to help generate valuable information.

Brainstorming

Brainstorming is used for everything from coming up with ideas for writing to developing creative solutions to problems. (See Figure 4.4.) If you are brainstorming about a topic for writing, then you need to think of as many ideas as you can that are associated with the topic. If you are brainstorming for a solution to a problem, then think of as many deliberately unusual solutions as possible and push the ideas as far as possible.

Sometimes you will do your brainstorming with a group of fellow students or co-workers. At other times, you will work alone.

FIGURE 4.4

Brainstorming

Brainstorming is a useful
technique for selecting and
developing a topic.

Brainstorming Alone

- Use whatever materials you prefer: self-stick notes, paper, note cards, a whiteboard, a blackboard, a flip chart, or any other device that will allow you to change, erase, connect, or move your ideas easily.

- Give yourself time just to think. Do nothing for the first ten minutes.

- Jot down ideas as quickly as you can. Use small self-stick notes, for example, one per idea. Use only a word, a symbol, or a phrase.

- Look for ways to piggyback ideas or to draw ideas out of other ideas.

- Don't try to evaluate or criticize your ideas.

- Stress quantity, not quality. Try to think of as many ideas as possible.

- List practical and impractical topics or solutions. Have fun.

- Limit the time of the session if you are tired; otherwise, continue for as long as you can think of new ideas.

- Set aside the work and do some other activity for a while.

- Challenge yourself to be even more creative when you return to your brainstorming.

Brainstorming in a Group

- Reach an agreement about which tools to use to record the group's ideas. You may choose simply to use a chalkboard or a flip chart. Let everyone see all the ideas that are being developed.

- Appoint someone to lead the brainstorming session. The person should encourage everyone to participate, to be enthusiastic, and to be uncritical. The leader should also keep the group from focusing on one topic for too long.

- Set a definite period of time for the brainstorming session.

- Participants should try to think of as many ideas as possible.

- Participants should also use the ideas of others to come up with new ideas or topics.

- Allow time for people to brainstorm individually.

- Avoid letting a few members of the group dominate the session. Encourage those who are less active to jump in, and monitor the more active ones to make sure they are not interrupting others who may want to contribute but are unable to get their contributions heard.

- Avoid any criticism of ideas or topics. Criticizing ideas can stifle the creativity. During brainstorming, no idea is wrong.

- Enjoy the brainstorming experience. Brainstorming should be a fun experience. Try to think both of topics that are practical and of others that are impractical.

Mind Mapping

The major difference between brainstorming and mind mapping is that in brainstorming you start with a clean slate, and in mind mapping you begin with a core topic or idea and use strategies to generate ideas that branch out from the core idea. Of course, some mind mapping occurs during the brainstorming session as well. In mind mapping, you typically place your central idea on a page, poster, or self-stick note and then branch other ideas off the central idea. Mind mapping is also commonly referred to as *clustering* because you cluster related ideas together using this approach.

You can mind map in any way you choose. Use the materials and the approach that are best for you. See Figure 4.5 for an example of mind mapping.

Effective Mind Mapping

- Use whatever material you prefer—a page, poster, whiteboard, blackboard, flip chart, self-stick notes, or blank note cards—and write the major idea or topic in the center.

- Draw lines or branches from the major idea or topic to show topics that are related to your main idea or topic.

- To begin, ask who, what, why, where, when, and how about your topic.

- As you begin to list topics, branch off into smaller related topics.

- Don't worry for now about the organization of the topics.

- Try different colors of paper, cards, or pens to show related ideas.

- After you have finished brainstorming, organize and evaluate your ideas or topics. Put the notes into groups of related ideas. Try different combinations.

- Erase the topics that are too far afield from your topic. Throw away what you don't want.

- Draw lines to connect related ideas.

- If necessary, move ideas from one area to another until the placement of your ideas begins to make more sense.

- Don't hesitate to add ideas if you have missed something.

- Continue to work until you have mapped your entire document.

- Step back and look at what you have created.

- After evaluating your mind map, decide what your main topics are and which ideas fit under them.

- Construct a tentative table of contents using your final mind map.

- Share the tentative table of contents with others who can help you spot problems in your approach to the topic.

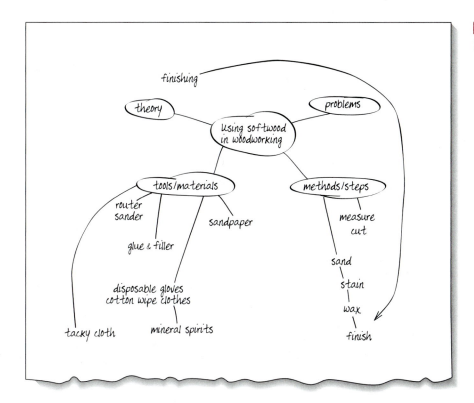

FIGURE 4.5
Mind Mapping

Freewriting

Like brainstorming and mind mapping, freewriting is a useful technique for generating ideas in the planning stage. It's also a helpful technique later in the writing stage of your project. The key to freewriting is to avoid editing or revising your work as you write. Ignore the rules and guidelines on punctuation, spelling, grammar, organization, and so on. Just start writing and keep writing without correcting your prose in any way. See Figure 4.6 for an example of freewriting.

Think of freewriting as brainstorming in prose. You continue to write on your topic or any topic that comes to mind. Later you'll review what you've written and start looking for key ideas. You can, for example, use freewriting to generate ideas about your topic and then use mind mapping to give more structure to your ideas and to find connections.

You can also use freewriting after you've brainstormed or used mind mapping. Use the topics you've generated with those techniques to create topic sentences and rough paragraphs.

FIGURE 4.6

Freewriting

Woodworking may be a good topic for the instructions assignment but it's a broad topic and will need focusing. I've done woodworking of all kinds for many years, so deciding what kind of woodworking might be hard to do. Maybe I should write about how to build a simple bookcase. Maybe I should write about working with a particular kind of wood. I know more about working with softwoods than other kinds of woods. Perhaps this is the best way to go for my focus. I think I'll write about working with softwood in woodworking since I recently completed a woodworking project using this kind of wood. Will have to think about the rationale or theory behind working with this kind of wood and then come up with tools and materials needed. Lots of tools and materials needed but not too many for the assignment. Need to sketch out all of the steps involved from selecting the softwood to finishing. Should take photos of the major steps involved. And will need to think of various kinds of troubleshooting to help anyone in a jam.

Later, when you are writing the first draft of your document, you may want to use freewriting to overcome writer's block. Just start writing. Then when you have something written, you'll find it easier to write more because you will be looking for ways to revise.

Effective Freewriting

- Write without stopping.
- Write without editing.
- If you're writing at the computer, turn off your monitor while you're freewriting so that you are not tempted to edit or revise too soon.
- Don't criticize your own freewriting or allow others to criticize it.

(continued)

- Let the freewriting you've done sit for a while. Come back to it later.

- Look over what you've written to see whether any topics stand out.

- Look for any connections among topics and possible subtopics.

- Remember that the purpose of freewriting is to help you discover ideas. What you've written is not a rough draft or first draft of your document. However, don't discard what you've written either. Some of the material you have written may be useful later.

SETTING AND FOLLOWING STANDARDS

While you are in school, professors constantly set standards for the kinds of documents you create. They may require, for example, that your major research paper be double-spaced and have one-inch margins and numbered pages. Your professor may require you to use a particular documentation style such as the style of the Modern Language Association (MLA) or the American Psychological Association (APA). (See "Documentation Styles" in Appendix C.) Your professor also may require you to write in a particular academic style and to use a serious or professional tone. The professor may be particularly demanding about proper grammar and mechanics—punctuation, spelling, numbers, capitalization, and abbreviations. All these requirements are common for documents written for college courses.

Professionals in the workplace often have very specific standards for the kinds of documents they write, too. Many companies have a style guide and standards manual specifying everything from preferred spellings for various words to the overall design and layout of memos, letters, manuals, and other documents.

Style guides are documents that tell members of an organization or employees of a company the rules or guidelines they should or must use for internal and external communications. When you create a style guide, you may be trying to ensure internal consistency for one document or for a whole suite of documents. Therefore, many style guides are only a few pages long, while others take up an entire volume. Bear in mind that style guides are subject to frequent revision. Even such respected style guides as the *MLA Handbook* began many years ago as a few pages stapled together.

Typically, style guides contain rules or guidelines pertaining to conventions in design or format, mechanics, style, and graphics. Procedures concerning editing and editing cycles, printing, and other matters may also be covered. Design topics might include the format of formal reports and manuals (the format of front matter such as the cover, title page, copyright page, table of contents, and introduction), the elements of page design for the body of

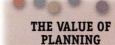

THE VALUE OF PLANNING

On a project that included internationalization and localization of the product, a plan to create a glossary that ensured terminology consistency made a tremendously positive impact on the overall product—not just on the documentation. It added a level of "fit and finish" that would otherwise not have been there for a first release. Similar planning resulted in huge savings in the translation phase of the project; the translation vendor was able to get as much as 75 percent leverage from one document to another and from one medium (printed docs) to another (help files).

—Sharon Hopkins, documentation specialist, Burlington, Massachusetts

the report or manual (page size, margins, headers and footers, headings, pagination, fonts), and the order and content of back matter (appendixes, glossary, index, works cited).

A style manual may also specify the format for internal memos and external letters. If guidelines for mechanics are offered, topics such as grammar, punctuation, spelling, and numbers may be treated. For style, numerous topics may be covered, including tone, diction, technical terms, sentence length and variety, and active and passive voice. Guidelines for graphics might cover tips for preparing your own graphics, placement of graphics, and guidelines concerning the kinds of graphics to include. A section on editing may clarify distinctions among substantive editing, copyediting, and proofreading, and may spell out how the editing cycle is done so that work is reviewed and edited properly by peers or an editor. Procedures for preparing a document for printing, methods for printing, and other print issues are typically covered as well. See Figure 4.7 for an example of a corporate style guide table of contents.

Creating Style Guides

- If your organization or company does not have a style guide, determine the need for one by polling people within the company. If your organization or company already has a style guide, evaluate how effectively it meets current needs.

- Before beginning any writing on your style guide, go through the necessary steps of planning and researching the topic.

- Make creating a style guide a collaborative effort. Even if you are solely responsible for creating the guide, you should consult those who will use it about the topics to include. With their help, you can create a thorough document plan describing the purpose, scope, content, organization, style, and design of your proposed style guide.

- Focus on making your style guide a document that people will want to use. You may have to determine whether it will be more effective in print, online, or both.

- Cover only the essential topics. Wherever possible, refer your readers to more established or authoritative sources for some topics. Different style guides are suitable for different fields of knowledge or discourse communities. Choose a style guide from among the established ones in your field and use it as a foundation for your own style guide. See the Resources section at the end of this chapter and Appendix C for information about particular style guides.

- Follow the principles of good writing and design in your style guide. Your style guide should be a good example of a product that adheres to the guidelines you establish.

(continued)

FIGURE 4.7

**Corporate Style Guide
Table of Contents**

TABLE OF CONTENTS

Page

INTRODUCTION **9**

Purpose 9
Scope and Authority 9
Organization of This Manual 10

REPORT COMPONENTS AND ORGANIZATION **11**

General Principles 11

    The Technical Report (TR) 11
    The Special Report (SR) 11
    Use of Terms "Study" or "Research" 11

Report Numbers 12
Report Dates 12
Report Titles 12
Report Elements 12
Front Cover 13
Title Pages 13

    NAVAIRWARCENTRASYSDIV – Prepared Unclassified Reports 13
    Contractor-Prepared Unclassified Reports 15
    Back of Title Page 17

Report Documentation Page (SF 298) 17
Foreword or Acknowledgments 17
Executive Summary 21

    Problem 21
    Objective 21
    Approach 21
    Findings ....
    Conclusions 21
    Recommendations 21

Table of Contents 23

    List of Figures 23
    List of Tables 23

- Provide reader aids: a table of contents, tabs, sectional tables of contents, a glossary, and an index. Make your style guide as easy to use as possible. Try to anticipate how your readers will use it and provide the information where it easily can be found.
- Choose a paper quality and a binding method suited to the constant use your manual will have. Make it easy to add new pages without having to replace the entire volume. For an online manual, follow the guidelines for creating effective online information (see Chapter 8).
- Make sure your style guide is thoroughly reviewed and evaluated by others so that it will be more usable.
- When the style guide is printed or made available online, make sure it is used. Don't let your peers and others slip back into their practice of ignoring established conventions concerning format, mechanics, style, editing, and design.

Determining the Style

Tone and style are complex topics that are covered in more detail in Chapter 7. However, it's important to keep in mind that tone—your attitude toward your reader, your subject, and yourself—and style—your manner of expressing yourself in your prose—need to be planned to some degree even before you begin writing.

Achieving the proper tone is, of course, closely related to your focus, purpose, and audience. You should give some thought before you write to the primary attitude you want to convey—whether, for example, you want to be serious and professional, humorous, or especially tactful. Tone is also a matter of distance, so you need to consider how personal or impersonal you're going to be. Are you going to address the reader as "you," for example, or are you going to use a third-person point of view?

> " In part, the kind of person you are defines your writing.

Your writing style for a particular document can be planned to a degree. You need to decide in advance whether you are going to discuss your subject in a plain style or a more complex prose style. Consider the types of sentences and paragraphs you will be using and the variety and nature of the arguments that will make up the development of your document. You need to give some thought to your ethos—character, credibility, authority—and how you can strengthen this ethos in your document (see "Credibility" in Chapter 2). You can plan these and other elements of your style somewhat, but there's also a quality in your style that's beyond your control. In part, the kind of person you are defines your writing.

Determining the Mechanics

Grammar is the system of conventional relationships between words and their functions in a language. Mechanics are the spelling, punctuation, numbers, capitalization, and abbreviations you use in your writing. (Appendixes A and B will give you detailed information on these issues.) Although you cannot create your own grammar rules to follow in your document, you can decide the spellings you prefer, the punctuation marks you will use to indicate various elements, and the abbreviations, if any, you will use. Any problems in mechanics will ultimately be dealt with during the revising stage, but you can avoid some basic problems by ensuring some consistency during the planning stage.

Determining the Design

Design deals with arrangement and appearance rather than content. It concerns everything from margins to fonts and illustrations. Increasingly, writers of even the most basic memos and letters face many design choices before they begin writing. Chapters 8 and 9 provide a thorough discussion of the many design and illustration considerations you must take into account for the different kinds of documents you will write.

Unfortunately, many writers give little consideration to how even their briefest documents look. Often, the font is too small, there are too many kinds of fonts on a page, headings are nonexistent or confusing, margins are crowded, too much text is on the page, the paragraphs are too long, and so on. Such faults show that many writers are more concerned with what they want to write than with the visual appeal of their documents. And these symptoms and others show that some writers are more preoccupied with themselves than they are with their readers. See Figure 4.8 for an example of a poorly designed document.

Perhaps it's overstating the matter, but in many respects the visual appeal of your document can be as important as the text. The design, illustrations, and white space are, like the text on the page, active participants in your efforts to communicate with the reader.

Most writers use a full-featured word-processing program such as Word or WordPerfect, a modest publishing program such as Publisher, or a sophisticated desktop-publishing program such as PageMaker or FrameMaker. These programs and others enable writers to make decisions about the formats of their documents even before they begin writing. Some of the programs offer templates, which are essentially predesigned documents. The writer provides the text, and the program helps to create or automatically creates a new memo, for example, in a contemporary, elegant, or professional style. The style that is created may automatically set up the document's margins, headings, heading hierarchy, pagination, and fonts, among many other elements. See Figure 4.9 for an example of a document template.

FIGURE 4.8

Sample Overcrowded
Document

Memorandum

To:	Jack Jason
From:	Ken Smith
Date:	March 13, 2____
Subject:	Print Room Improvements

I have noticed several wasteful activities while working in the print room, and I have solutions to save the company money.

First, there is a large amount of paper that is wasted during the printing of daily reports. The reason for such a waste is the header and footer pages attached to each individual report. There are two pages at the beginning and two pages at the end. This means a single-page report results in 5 printed pages—4 of which are thrown away. I understand that these pages were originally attached so that the reports could be easily separated and identified, but they are not necessary now. The print operators are familiar with every report and can easily identify each without needing cover sheets.

Taking away these cover sheets would save the company supplies. Consider the 30 reports that the second shift prints. Using no cover pages would result in 120 saved sheets a night. That is over 1.5 boxes a week for one shift alone!

Next, screen prints from the Daily Sales floor are printed on the 08E. These pages are given a lower priority than other reports and are thus printed hours after they were actually created. When they are finally delivered to the appropriate person, the screen prints are usually out of date and unusable.

A way to alleviate this is to send the screen prints to a less expensive printer, such as a bubble jet printer, that can be placed on the Daily Sales floor. This printer can be dedicated solely to screen prints. This way the screen prints would be timely, and the bigger printers can stay focused on the higher priority and time-consuming jobs.

Finally, printer ribbons are being wasted. Current policy requires the print operator to change the ribbons on printers PRT020700 and PRT020701 before printing AP checks. By doing so, the operator throws away ribbons that usually have very little use. These ribbons are being wasted since they could still print another 500 pages.

I propose we do not print the AP checks at a set time each night. Instead, AP checks should be printed after the ribbons **need** to be changed on the printers. This way the checks would be printed with a fresh ribbon, and the old ribbons would be completely used. This method will not create any problems with delivery of the checks since the checks are normally placed in the AP box, where they are picked up 8 hours later.

These improvements will help cut down waste in the print room and will help save the company money in supplies.

MANAGING YOUR DOCUMENT

Managing your document means planning for all of the details necessary to make sure it is completed, submitted on time, produced appropriately, and, if applicable, produced within budget. The level of management a document

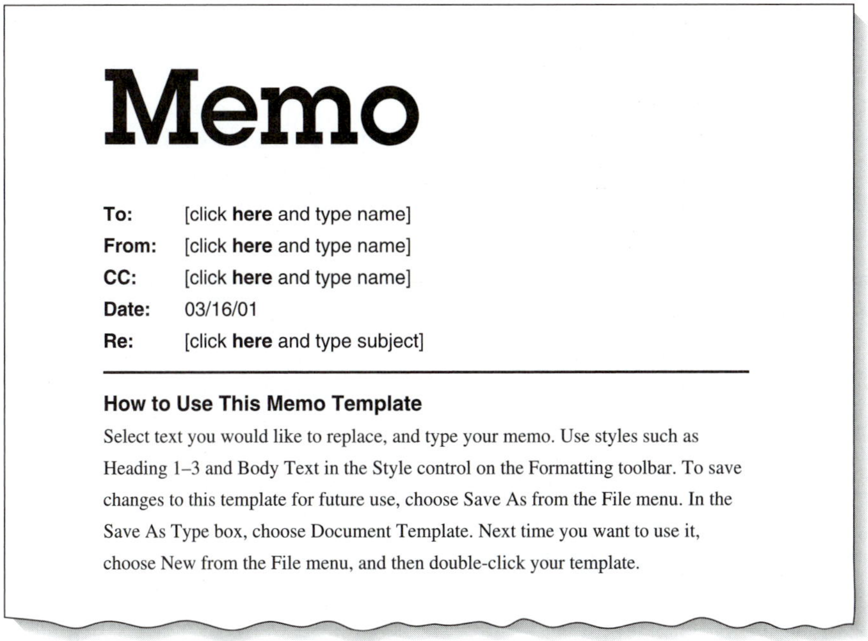

Memo

To: [click **here** and type name]
From: [click **here** and type name]
CC: [click **here** and type name]
Date: 03/16/01
Re: [click **here** and type subject]

How to Use This Memo Template

Select text you would like to replace, and type your memo. Use styles such as
Heading 1–3 and Body Text in the Style control on the Formatting toolbar. To save
changes to this template for future use, choose Save As from the File menu. In the
Save As Type box, choose Document Template. Next time you want to use it,
choose New from the File menu, and then double-click your template.

FIGURE 4.9

Sample Document Template

requires varies with the kind of document and its length. For many brief documents—such as letters, memos, and e-mail—little management is involved. For longer projects, the management required typically is extensive.

If you are the sole author of a document, you still need to divide the writing process into smaller tasks before you can begin work on it and then finish it appropriately. If you are collaborating with others, you need to make many decisions on almost everything from assigning tasks to determining a complicated production budget.

Estimating Time and Scheduling

Whether you are writing a brief memo or collaborating on a large multivolume user guide for a new software program, estimating and scheduling are essential tasks. For example, for the memo, you might estimate that writing and distributing it will take 15 minutes; for the multivolume user guide, you might estimate it will take you and three other writers six months to complete the project.

In a typical junior- or senior-level technical writing course, students must estimate how long it will take to complete all the course's various assignments, such as an application letter and résumé, a letter of adjustment, a set of instructions, a proposal, a technical report, and an oral presentation. Some of the assignments can be done in much less time than others. Sometimes you may be asked to create a schedule providing proposed completion dates and tasks. This schedule may take many forms, ranging from an informal table to a Gantt chart (see Chapter 9).

In college or in industry, you often will find yourself working with others on a writing project. If you are collaborating with several others to complete a document, you need to manage the document early in the process rather than waiting until later.

Evaluating the Complexity of a Project

- Research the scope of the project. Make sure you find out as much about the project as you can. If possible, talk to others who have worked on similar projects.
- Consider how much planning, researching, writing, editing, revising, designing, illustrating, reviewing, and evaluating the project will require.
- Estimate the production time
- Establish specific goals or objectives for the project.
- Create a document or project plan. See "Creating the Document Plan" later in this chapter.

Breaking a Project into Smaller Units

- Divide the project into tasks. Write down the tasks that you need to accomplish; if they are large, break them into their component elements. If these still seem large, break them down again. Do this until everything that you have to do is listed.
- Create or assign a team member to write detailed "to do" lists that show the tasks that must be carried out to achieve your team's project or document goals. Assign a priority to each task, for example, from A (very important) to F (unimportant). If necessary, reassess the priorities, demote the less important high-priority items, and rewrite the list in priority order.

Establishing a Schedule

- Become familiar with various published estimates of time for tasks. Interview others about the time a particular task might require.
- Work in "downtime" to allow for unexpected delays or risks. When you have to guess time, particularly when you will be held to a deadline, be

(continued)

sure that you allow time for other factors, such as higher-priority tasks, emergencies, client meetings, vacations and sicknesses, and supply interruptions.

● Use a log or time-tracking software to track the time for the various documents you write. A log may simply be a listing of the dates, tasks, and the amount of time you devote to each of the tasks. Keep track of every task in quarter-hour increments. (See Figure 4.10.)

● Stick to your schedule, deviating from it only for a good reason, but be prepared to make adjustments when necessary.

● Use progress or status reports to review compliance with your schedule.

Date	Task	Start Time	Stop Time	Total (in hours)
1/18/01	Met with David Johnson	4:00 p.m.	5:15 p.m.	1.25
	Refined group directory; perused EMA documents;	6:00 p.m.	6:30 p.m.	0.50
	e-mailed teammates			
1/22/01	Read e-mail from David Johnson; forwarded message to teammates	11:10 a.m.	11:15 a.m.	0.25
1/24/01	Attempted to create templates for EMA (failed)	6:30 p.m.	8:30 p.m.	2.00
1/25/01	Discussed project with teammates	4:00 p.m.	5:15 p.m.	1.25
	E-mailed David Johnson to request visitation	5:15 p.m.	5:20 p.m.	0.25
1/29/01	Read e-mail from David Johnson; informed teammates of message	2:15 p.m.	2:20 p.m.	0.25
1/30/01	Visited EMA (45-minute drive, one way)	3:30 p.m.	5:30 p.m.	2.00
	E-mailed documents to teammates	6:40 p.m.	6:45 p.m.	0.25
2/1/01	Worked on project in class	4:00 p.m.	5:15 p.m.	1.25
2/6/01	Finalized project proposal assignments; divided team	5:15 p.m.	5:45 p.m.	0.50
	into subgroups			
	Divided PDs among subgroups	6:00 p.m.	8:30 p.m.	2.50
2/7/01	Began writing project proposal	3:30 p.m.	5:15 p.m.	1.75
2/8/01	Worked on project in class	4:00 p.m.	5:00 p.m.	1.00
2/12/01	Read e-mail and sent e-mail to David Johnson	12:00 p.m.	12:05 p.m.	0.25
2/13/01	Peer-edited project proposal; e-mailed teammates	4:15 p.m.	5:15 p.m.	1.00
	E-mailed David Johnson; further work on project proposal;	6:00 p.m.	8:30 p.m.	2.50
	updated task sheet			
2/14/01	Received proposal sections; collated and edited proposal	12:30 p.m.	2:30 p.m.	2.00
	Wrote progress report	5:45 p.m.	6:30 p.m.	0.75
	Further work on proposal	8:00 p.m.	8:30 p.m.	0.50
2/15/01	Worked on progress report	12:30 p.m.	1:00 p.m.	0.50
	Finished project proposal	4:15 p.m.	5:15 p.m.	1.00
	Finished progress report; made log entries	5:15 p.m.	5:45 p.m.	0.50
				24.0

FIGURE 4.10

Time Log

Planning the Production

Part of managing your document requires you to plan how to produce it. Will you simply use a word-processing program or desktop-publishing program and print it using an inkjet or laser printer? Will you require so few copies that you can print them on your home printer? Is the printing job so large that your company requires you to contract the job with a commercial printer? Will you use color? Expensive paper? Provide a cover? How will you distribute the document? These and many other questions must be considered during the planning phase.

Planning your printing at the beginning of the project will help prevent production problems. Make a detailed list of the printing you have done over the past few months and project how much printing you expect to do over the next six months. Consider many factors, including how quickly you will need some print jobs, how large the print jobs might be, and whether or not you will need color, illustrations, and so on. Review each job to determine what needs to be printed, how the information should be printed, and what kind of materials should be used. Good planning for your printing jobs will save you time, materials, and money.

> " "
> Good planning for your printing jobs will save you time, materials, and money.

When reviewing each print job, your first priority should be to gather all the information you can about the document you plan to print. Make sure the printed document really is needed. You should ask what the consequences would be if the document were not printed, whether the document serves its stated purpose, whether the cost of printing and processing justifies the printing, and whether other related documents already exist. Sometimes you will discover that it isn't necessary to print the document after all.

Once you have determined that the document should be produced, you should ask who, what, why, where, when, and how: Who will use it? What is the purpose? What quality of printing is necessary? Why is the document used? Where is it used? When is it used? How is it used? How many copies are needed?

In general, you will want to produce your document at the highest quality you can afford. But quality in printing is closely tied to purpose. The quality of the document depends on how well the document fulfills its purpose, and that depends on its use. For example, if the document is to become part of a permanent record, you will want to ensure that the document is durable. Other factors determining how a document must be printed include whether its users will write on it, whether it is intended for interoffice use, whether it will be used many times or only once. Answering such questions will help you decide on the essential quality.

For many documents, photocopy quality is adequate and can be produced quickly and inexpensively. When high-quality, large-quantity, or multicolor printing is needed, the job may require more traditional printing methods, such as negatives and aluminum plates.

Creating the Document Plan

Some documents require a document plan and some do not. If you are writing a brief memo or letter, you don't usually need to create a document plan. However, if you are in a college course and you are required to collaborate with others to create, for example, a software user's guide, you'll need to plan this guide extensively. You'll need to go through all the steps discussed so far: determining the focus, generating ideas for topics, organizing, setting standards, and managing your document. If you are required to submit a formal document plan, you most likely will provide a detailed discussion of your subject, purpose, scope, audience, outline, standards, schedule, responsibilities, and qualifications.

Some people consider the steps you need to perform in the planning phase as creating a document plan. Others refer to the steps as creating a kind of proposal for a document. Still others refer to this part of the process as creating the document blueprint. Whatever you call the planning stage, it's essential even though it may be time consuming. By some estimates, by the end of this planning phase, you will have completed 60 percent of the work required for your document. A thorough document plan written at the beginning of the project will save you and your team time and effort later and will help you and your team stick to the schedule.

In industry a document plan is essentially a blueprint for the entire project—from the research to the plan for distributing the document after it is completed. You might be required to complete a detailed formal document plan form, typically covering subject, purpose, scope, assumed audiences, audience use of the document, elements needed for the document (from title page to index and from letter of transmittal to warnings or notes), graphical elements, style, reviews needed (for example, legal, marketing, and research), production (including budget details), timetable for the project, outline for the project, and project distribution date.

With a detailed document plan, all the team members know their tasks and deadlines and can plan accordingly. Creating such a detailed document plan requires a great deal of time, but it is time that is well invested. If done effectively and thoroughly, such detailed planning gives the project a clear purpose and a clear priority. See Figure 4.11 for a list of items in a typical document plan.

Using Planning Tools

Software programs available today offer a sophisticated array of features for helping college students and professionals accomplish much more work in much less time. Keep in mind, however, that even the best software won't make you a better writer, planner, or designer if you don't already know a great deal about writing, planning, and designing. Planning tools don't guarantee quality,

FIGURE 4.11
Document Plan Contents

Document Plan

Date Assigned: _____

Author (s): _____

Tentative Title: _____

Subject: _____

Purpose: _____

Scope: _____

Audience: _____

How Audience Will Use the Information: _____
_____

Other Audience Considerations (environment in which document will be used,
document format preferences, special needs): _____
_____

Elements Needed for Document: _____
_____

Illustrations Needed for Document: _____
_____

Style for Document: _____

Reviews Needed: _____

Production (type, time, cost): _____

Timetable for Project: _____

Outline for Project: _____

Project Distribution Date: _____

and they don't, by themselves, create quality. The planning tools briefly summarized here concern project scheduling, personal information management,
outlining, creativity, flowcharts, storyboarding, database management, presentations, and cost estimating.

Project-scheduling software helps you to plan a project more carefully and
efficiently. These programs take as input dates, resources, deliverables, milestones, critical paths, dependencies, and due dates. They display graphically
the progress of your project and can provide regular printed reports on what is
happening and how the team is doing. Project, FastTrack Schedule, and ivan
are three well-known, widely used programs of this type. See Figure 4.12 for a
look at a schedule created by a scheduling program.

Personal information management programs and their hardware equivalents, personal digital assistants, help you organize both your personal and

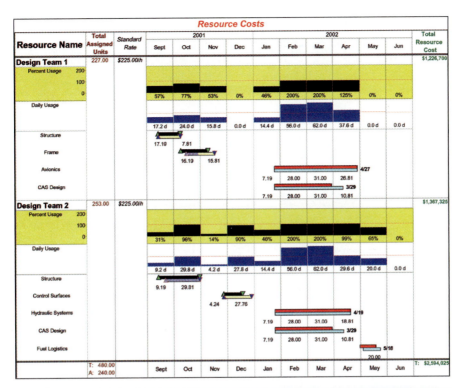

FIGURE 4.12

**Project Scheduling
Software**

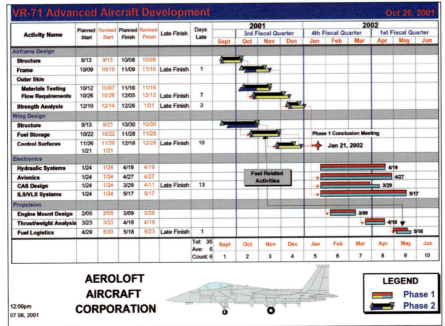

FIGURE 4.13

Personal Information Management Software

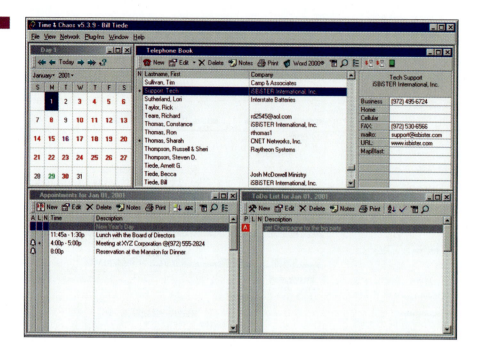

business schedules effectively. Software programs—such as Sidekick, DayTimer, Outlook, and Time and Chaos—and print versions of personal organizers—such as DayRunner and DayTimer—offer effective ways to prioritize daily tasks, note appointments, keep track of contacts, provide reminders, and so on. See Figure 4.13 for an example of this type of tool.

Outlining programs may be built into a full-featured word-processing program or come as a separate program. An outlining feature can help you easily list your major thoughts and quickly rearrange them with a few keystrokes or clicks of a mouse. You can use a stand-alone program, such as Grandview (a DOS-based outliner), Ecco, AmiPro, or WordPro (a much slower replacement for AmiPro); a combination outliner and word processor, such as Word; or an outliner and flowchart program, such as Inspiration.

Creativity programs work with you to enhance your creative output. One such program is IdeaFisher, which consists of an interactive database of questions and idea words and phrases. Questions provided by the program help you define, clarify, modify, and evaluate your needs. You can even add your own questions to the thousands already supplied. Another creativity program is Inspiration, which facilitates mind mapping. Instead of listing your ideas from top to bottom, mind mapping and Inspiration work from the center out.

You can do this on paper by starting with a central idea and adding your thoughts, connecting them like spokes from an axle.

Flowchart programs enable you to document a process. Some word-processing programs help you create basic flowcharts, but many programs are available that specialize in creating flowcharts of all kinds. The Visio products are some of the most widely used programs for creating flowcharts, work-flow diagrams, organizational charts, project timelines, geographic maps, mind-mapping diagrams, network diagrams of various sorts, Web site and software diagrams, and user interface designs. RFFlow and SmartDraw are two other programs you might try.

Storyboard programs enable you to plan or brainstorm. A variety of tools are available to help you create mock-ups of your multimedia projects. Some are created specifically for the storyboarding process; others, such as Apple HyperCard, Adobe Persuasion, and Microsoft PowerPoint, are presentation tools that can be readily adapted to this use.

Database management programs enable you to handle large amounts of interrelated information. These programs are very powerful, but their complexity often makes them difficult to master. However, during the information-gathering stage of your research, the information management stage, and even into the information-presentation stage, you may find that the volume and complexity of your findings resist simpler or more direct methods. Microsoft Access and FileMaker Pro are two well-regarded general tools, but there are many others. Some are Web-based, such as Intuit QuickBase, which can be used at no charge for smaller applications. In addition to these general database programs, bibliographic software will help you keep track of your research notes and sources. See Chapter 6 for a more detailed discussion of databases.

Presentation programs enable you to plan, prepare, and present effective presentations for a group. Programs such as PowerPoint and Presentations are just two of the many programs that can help you create slides, transparencies, handouts, and more for your technical presentations. More specific information about some of these programs is discussed in Chapter 13. These programs are mentioned briefly here because they can also be helpful when you are in the planning stage of a project. Microsoft PowerPoint can be adapted for use as a brainstorming, mind mapping, or organizing tool to help develop your ideas. You can easily add, import, and rearrange slides until you have a complete visual map for your document.

Cost-estimating software offers quick and convenient ways to determine your costs before you begin a project. Cost-estimating software can drastically cut your estimating time as well as save you money. CNC Concepts Profit Planner and other programs can help you determine exactly what the costs will be before you submit your proposal for a particular job.

Find these and similar programs online, download demos where available, and experiment. See what works best for you.

From the workplace

Ann Vogt

Technical Writer/Web Developer
FORTEL Inc.
Longwood, Florida

Ann has what many people would consider the perfect job: she develops documentation and Web sites in the comfort of her own home office. Ann is a telecommuter, and, as such, she enjoys all the advantages and benefits of being a full-time employee without many of the disadvantages.

In my current job, I design, develop, and implement online documentation for various software applications. The best part is that I can do this as a telecommuter. All of my work is conducted online or by telephone. I live in Florida and I maintain a virtual office out of my home for FORTEL Inc. located in Fairfax, Virginia. My company provides me with a desktop PC, cable modem, and business telephone line, and I own a personal laptop for traveling. I gain access to the company's network through a Virtual Private Network (VPN).

Working this way, I don't have to put up with office politics on a day-to-day basis. I count my blessings that I have such a good job when I hear what nightmares other people endure with theirs.

What I miss, though, is the actual physical meetings between my colleagues. It is always easier to get information from a person who is physically talking to you, rather than corresponding through e-mail. And you can't see body language over e-mail either. Additionally, the nonsynchronous nature of e-mail has both an upside and a downside: you don't have to be on the same time schedule as the other person, but through e-mail you can't get a feel for what the other person is thinking until you receive the reply.

Working with computers comes very naturally to me. Years ago, I taught myself how to work with computers. In 1988, I acquired an 8088 IBM PC with two 5.25-inch floppy disk drives. I read books and taught myself DOS. From there I moved up to a 486 MHz processor with Windows 3.1 and now I am working on a fast Pentium-processor computer. I can also work on Macintosh or Apple computers. The Tech-Writing Lab at college had both PCs and Macs.

I write a variety of documents on the job: status reports, e-mails, memos, letters, software user manuals, and online software user manuals. Without a computer, I couldn't do my job, at least not efficiently.

CHECKING WHAT YOU'VE LEARNED

- Have you planned effectively by analyzing your audience and understanding its informational needs?
- Have you further determined the focus of your document by narrowing the subject?
- Have you determined the purpose or objectives of your document?
- Have you limited the scope appropriately?
- Have you successfully used various techniques—brainstorming, mind mapping, and freewriting—to help you discover initial ideas?
- Have you established the standards for the style, mechanics, and design of your document?

I use my computer:

- to make telephone calls
- to conduct netmeetings
- for e-mail
- to create business cards
- for correspondence and to address envelopes
- to create, resize, reshape, and recolor images
- to create online help
- to write and edit documents
- to create Web pages
- as a stereo system to play CDs
- to access the Web for researching various subjects
- for creating presentations
- for doing process flows
- to receive the daily news and stock reports
- to create expense reports

What I've noticed is that when I write and design for Web documents, I plan and write differently from how I would if I were working on paper. For example, I do a lot of drawing, grouping, and storyboarding when I develop a Web site. I especially have to consider navigation and information design. If a person can't get to or find the needed information, then what good is the information or the site?

I also have to be careful about legalities for my company and the information contained within my sites. Legal disclaimers are always necessary on any Web site, since the distribution of the material is so un-predictable. I am especially concerned about copyrights of source code, information, images, and site design. I create my own graphics, site design, and source code because my company could be held liable if I post someone else's work to the site.

In addition to my Web work, I prepare a good bit of online documentation. Here, too, special considerations apply. Paper documentation is written in formal grammar and follows a linear format; online documentation has a conversational style and an interactive aspect not possible with paper documents. With online documentation, users can go directly to the subject matter they need by the click of a button, but with paper documentation they must page sequentially through.

Insider Advice

- Keep an open mind and be a good listener. It is amazing what information you can compile from listening to other people talk about their positions and their daily work tasks.
- Learn assertiveness, be persistent, and don't be afraid to suggest new ways of doing things.
- Ask a lot of questions. You may find a lot of resistance to your suggestions or questions at first, but someday your persistence will pay off.
- Keep in touch with people you meet, because those people may just keep you in mind when promotions or raises come due.

- Have you effectively managed your document by estimating the time and scheduling, planning the production, creating the document plan, and, when necessary, effectively using one or more planning tools?

EXERCISES

 REVIEW

1. Review Figure 4.1 and Figure 4.2, which show broad subjects versus focused subjects in college writing and in industry. Create your own sample chart showing broad subjects versus focused subjects in college writing or in industry writing.

2. Review Figure 4.3, which shows sample purpose statements from various documents. Create your

own chart listing at least six purpose statements you might use for correspondence (letters, memos, e-mail), reports, instructions, or policies and procedures.

3. Using the techniques discussed in this chapter for brainstorming alone, create a list of topics you would possibly like to research further for a technical report.

4. Write a paragraph discussing the key differences between brainstorming and mind mapping for discovering initial ideas.

5. Use 10 to 20 minutes of class time to try freewriting about a topic of interest to you for a possible Web site, a set of instructions, or a report. Be prepared to discuss whether or not the freewriting exercise helped you to discover any potential topics.

 ### THE INTERNET

Find and look at the main pages of three different corporate or organization Web sites. Discuss how effectively you think the prose on each site makes the site's purpose clear. Write down the purposes of the sites and be prepared to discuss them in class.

 ### ETHICS/PROFESSIONALISM

Suppose you are required to complete a document or a project without enough time to create a quality product. Write a paragraph discussing the ethical and professional issues that potentially arise when you are required to create a document or project with too little time to assure quality.

 ### COLLABORATION

Working together in groups of two or more students, use the techniques for brainstorming in a group discussed earlier in this chapter. Create a list of ways planning has proved useful in the past to members of the group.

 ### INTERNATIONAL COMMUNICATION

As you would expect, different cultures have different expectations concerning planning, time management, and scheduling. Write a paragraph discussing some potential problems in dealing with a client from a culture that has a more relaxed view than American culture of keeping appointments.

RESOURCES

American Political Science Association. *Style Manual for Political Science.* Rev. ed. Washington: American Political Science Association, 2001.

American Psychological Association. *Publication Manual of the American Psychological Association.* 5th ed. Washington: American Psychological Association, 2001.

Buzan, Tony. *The Mind Map Book: How to Use Radiant Thinking to Maximize Your Brain's Untapped Potential.* New York: Dutton, 1994.

Chicago Manual of Style. 14th ed. Chicago: U of Chicago P, 1993.

Council of Biology Editors. *Scientific Style and Format: The CBE Manual for Authors, Editors, and Publishers.* 6th ed. Cambridge: Cambridge UP, 1994.

de Bono, Edward. *Serious Creativity: Using the Power of Lateral Thinking to Create New Ideas.* New York: HarperBusiness, 1992.

Gibaldi, Joseph. *MLA Handbook for Writers of Research Papers.* 5th ed. New York: Modern Language Association, 1999.

———. *MLA Style Manual and Guide to Scholarly Publishing.* 2nd ed. New York: Modern Language Association, 1998.

Hackos, JoAnn T. *Managing Your Documentation Projects.* New York: Wiley, 1994.

Microsoft Corporation. *The Microsoft Manual of Style for Technical Publications.* 2nd ed. Redmond: Microsoft, 1998.

New York Public Library. *Writer's Guide to Style and Usage.* New York: HarperCollins, 1994.

Skillin, Marjorie E., and Robert M. Gay. *Words into Type.* 3rd ed. Englewood Cliffs: Prentice Hall, 1974.

5

Gathering Information

Research   111

Personal Knowledge   113

Interviewing   113

Questionnaires and Surveys   118

Focus Groups   121

Experimentation   122

Written or Recorded Information   124

Using the Library—Print Sources   125

Using the Library—Electronic Sources   142

From the Workplace   166

IN THIS CHAPTER

When you begin your research, the sources of information may seem either overwhelmingly abundant or frighteningly sparse. Learning about the resources available can cut the task down to size. Once you have some experience in using the library and its online connections, you will find the task of finding information to be quite a manageable one.

Many sources are available to you; no one source will provide everything you need. You can use a variety of references when you do research.

You will learn about:

- people, an often overlooked source of information. You can use knowledge you already possess; ask your professors, colleagues, and classmates for information; and obtain data from interviewing others.

- surveys, questionnaires, and focus groups. Carefully selected readers, customers, and other subsets of your target audience can provide useful information.

- the scientific method. In the laboratory and out in the world, scientists use this method to discover and confirm information through experimentation.

- libraries. Collections of print, electronic, and online information and links to catalogued and organized information located elsewhere provide vast amounts of knowledge once you know how to access it.

- online databases and Internet search engines. Search these to locate printed and nonprint information.

- critically viewing information. Interpret and evaluate the information you have found.

RESEARCH

Some people love to do research and others are a bit overwhelmed when faced with a project that requires it. Research may sound challenging and interesting, or it may sound boring and tedious. Perhaps to you it combines both characteristics at the same time. If you are a science major, you may believe that research should be confined to the work you do in a laboratory. And if you're a math or engineering major, you may think that research is something other students have to do, but something that doesn't really concern you.

Other people find research a rich and rewarding challenge. Searching out information from a variety of sources and putting it together into a coherent whole is a very satisfying activity for many people.

No matter which category you fall into, the fact is that research plays a large role in many types of careers. So learning how to conduct research is

> If you have mastered good research skills, you will be better equipped to conduct your life as an informed participant.

giving yourself a skill that you will use not only in college but also possibly throughout your working life. Furthermore, if you have mastered good research skills, you will be better equipped to conduct your life as an informed participant in many other arenas: politics, consumerism, and hobbies, to name a few. If you know how to do research, you know how to ferret out information, how to organize and evaluate it, and how to present it to others or use it yourself.

Students are often overwhelmed when they are faced with researching a topic. You may have been told that the first place to look for information when you are doing research is in the library. The good thing about that claim is that a library is a fairly self-contained place, so the search for information should theoretically be manageable within the walls of the library system. The not-so-good thing about the claim is that it is only somewhat true, and the library's resources don't stop at its four walls any more.

Then there are those who believe that anything they need to know can be found somewhere on the Internet, so the search for information can begin and end there. This belief is becoming more widespread as students have easier and quicker access to online resources. As in the case of libraries, the Internet can be a fine source of information, but it is unlikely to yield all the information you need either, since by one estimate less than 10 percent of catalogued human knowledge is currently available electronically.

You may be surprised to learn that no matter how extensive your school's library and no matter how enormous the Internet, those two resources do not come close to accounting for all the information at your disposal during the research process. The challenge when you do research is to amass good information without being overwhelmed by facts you cannot use, either because they are not central to your search or because they are unreliable or of questionable quality. (See Figure 5.1.)

When you are doing research, basically you are gathering and processing information. To start with, you have to decide what your audience needs to

FIGURE 5.1

Research Resources

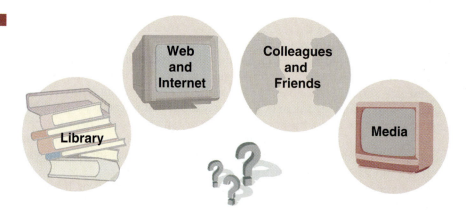

know. Recall that in Chapter 2, you learned that considering the audience's needs requires a careful look at your purpose, scope, and context. Once you have identified what your audience needs to know, you can continue with your planning. And as you have already seen in Chapter 4, you consider many issues as part of your planning—subject, purpose, scope, audience, mechanics, style, and others—before you write a single word. Part of the planning process is developing your approach: deciding what kinds of information you need and thinking about where you will find them. An important source for information of this kind can be developed without leaving your desk. Brainstorming, mind mapping, and freewriting were discussed in Chapter 4; review those sections, since they explain what are often the earliest steps on your research path.

PERSONAL KNOWLEDGE

Knowledge is what you have learned from observation and research. Sometimes the best place to start your research is with yourself. Perhaps through previous or current personal experience you acquired firsthand knowledge about your topic. You learned or are learning about your topic by reading, seeing, listening, or doing.

Many people don't realize how much they already know about a topic. They often are surprised at how much information they come up with through extensive self-analysis and use of a listing or visualization technique such as brainstorming and freewriting. Start with what you already know and use that information to identify what is still to be obtained elsewhere.

INTERVIEWING

Once you have considered the information you already have about your topic, it is time to branch out and seek information held by others.

Informational interviews are one-on-one meetings with other people who have information you want. Often, if you want to know something, the easiest and most direct way to find out about it is to ask others. You can ask your friends, colleagues, professors, or mentors. But often the person who you think has information of use to you is someone you don't interact with in the course of your normal schedule.

People who are knowledgeable about your topic are often called *subject matter experts,* or SMEs. Interviews with SMEs can provide valuable information in almost any discipline. You may even find yourself in a situation in which you must talk to several subject matter experts to acquire the information you need. One area in which you may find yourself in need of information is when you are preparing to enter the workforce. Job information interviews are discussed in Chapter 11.

ASKING QUESTIONS

Ask questions. Other people have a lot of information they are willing to share with you if you just ask. It also keeps you from pretending you know what you don't.

—Lisa Mezzatesta, director of learning and development, Atlanta, Georgia

The informational interview has four phases: researching for the interview, preparing for the interview, conducting the interview, and following up on the interview.

Researching for the Interview

In this phase you decide whom you will contact. You are looking for subject matter experts—people who are knowledgeable about your subject. You will need to research the credentials of these experts. If they work in a university or other school setting, find out what they have published. If they are in industry, find out what their achievements have been. A professor who is well published in a field is generally more knowledgeable than someone who is not as well published. A person who has accomplished a great deal in industry is often more credible than someone who has not. In addition to doing research about the SME, before the interview you'll have to do some research about the subject itself. You need to find out what the important issues are, who the important players are, and what changes or trends are taking place.

Sometimes you also have to research the company that employs the SME. Look for information about the company, its products, its position in the industry, its primary competitors, its size and location, number of employees, and international presence. You can find out about a company through various print and electronic sources in the library, from the company's World Wide Web site, from your campus or local placement office, from an on-site visit or tour if the company is local, and from professional organizations in the field or industry.

Preparing for the Interview

In addition to finding out more about the subject matter expert, the subject in question, and the company and its products, you need to prepare for the actual interview.

After making the preparations, plan how long the initial interview will be. Decide whether one long interview will suffice or if a series of shorter interviews would be better. Make the actual physical arrangements for seeing the interviewee—scheduling the meeting, reserving the meeting room, providing for any travel, brewing of coffee or chilling of other beverages, and so on.

Prepare for the interview by creating a list of questions. Of course, the questions you ask depend on the subject you are researching. Don't waste your interviewee's time by scheduling an interview and then having only a vague idea of what questions you want answered. Figure 5.2 shows some typical questions from an informational interview.

Getting Ready for the Interview

- Decide in advance how you will keep track of the information you obtain: by taking notes, by audio or video recording, or by a combination of these. Obtain any necessary recording permissions in advance of the interview.

- Check if you will need security clearances to go onto the premises of your subject's place of employment. Allow enough time for paperwork, obtaining a badge, and other security matters. Make sure you have any required documents or identification cards with you. If you will not be able to bring them, find out whether you can substitute other documents.

- Make any arrangements necessary for an on-site visit at your own workplace, if the interview will be on your own turf. Arrange for clearances if necessary, and plan how you will make your subject feel comfortable and welcome.

- Consider what you're going to wear: business-appropriate clothing for some situations or possibly safety gear for a construction-site interview, for example.

Can you tell me something about the company? When was it founded? Is this facility one of many? If so, what does this facility specialize in?

What is the company's primary purpose? What are its corporate values? What is its future direction, in your view?

What is your division called? What are its responsibilities? How does this division (or department) fit into the larger organizational chart?

What is your position here? What are you responsible for providing? Are there others who are doing work similar to yours here? What kind of educational background led you to this job?

What type of projects do you work on? Would you describe something about them? How did you prepare for this project: school, other training, previous experience?

Can you recommend any further sources I can pursue for information on your subject? Is my background, education, and experience suitable for this type of work?

FIGURE 5.2

Informational Interview Questions

Planning the Interview

- Think of the topics you want to cover in the interview and organize them in a logical order.
- Formulate questions that will elicit answers on your topics.
- Organize the questions in a logical order, but be prepared to be flexible if the answers you receive lead to a topic not on your original list.
- Focus carefully on the list of questions. Limit the number of questions to between 10 and 30 questions depending on the subject.
- Study your final list carefully, so that as the interview progresses you can ask the right questions at the right time.

Finally, in your preparation for an important interview, it's a good idea to practice the interview.

Practicing the Interview

- Invite a friend to play the role of the interviewee and then go through your list of questions.
- Practice your questions and work on your body language in front of a mirror. Find those poses that show that you are confident and poised, that you are eager to learn from this person, and that you understand what you are told.
- Ask follow-up questions on any points that you don't fully understand.

Conducting the Interview

Now that you have done your research and otherwise prepared for the interview, you should be ready to conduct the interview and be confident that it will go well. Remember that there is an art to interviewing. You want to make the person you are interviewing relax and feel comfortable with you. Be aware of first impressions, both the ones you receive and the ones you provide. From the handshake to small talk to any offer to provide refreshments, you show the other person that you are concerned with creating and maintaining a friendly, yet businesslike, atmosphere.

When the interview part of the encounter begins, remember to focus on why you set up the interview in the first place. You are trying to obtain information, so ask your questions clearly and listen to the answers carefully to make sure you're given the answers that will be useful to you. Your attentive listening helps ensure that you will understand the information provided to you.

In addition to listening effectively, focus on taking effective notes, whether you do so with a pencil and pad, a laptop computer, an audio recorder, or a video recorder. Keep in mind that many people are uncomfortable about having their voice recorded and even more uncomfortable about video recording.

Even after the interview is over, you still have a lot of work to do. If you're going to use or publish any direct quotations, make sure you obtain the necessary permissions in writing from the interview subject, the subject's employer, or both. Before you leave be sure to thank the interviewee for spending time with you and providing useful information.

Following Up on the Interview

When you return from the interview, take a few minutes to send a written thank-you letter to the person you interviewed. And don't wait long before carefully reviewing your notes; do it while your memories of the interview are fresh. You may be able to add helpful comments throughout your notes. Consider working your notes into an outline to organize them.

As you review your notes you may also think of questions you should have asked. A telephone or e-mail follow-up asking for clarification or elaboration will help you make the report of the interview more complete, should that be necessary. If you have to prepare your notes for someone else to see, be sure to follow all of the necessary style requirements and meet the deadlines for providing the notes. The steps that you take after the interview is over are just as important as the other parts of the interview.

Telephone and Mail Interviews

Sometimes meeting with the subject matter expert in person is not practical or feasible. In that case you may be able to conduct your interview by telephone or by mail or e-mail. Mail interviews have a lot in common with questionnaires, which you will learn about in the next section.

CHOOSING THE ETHICAL PATH

Even if the interviewee is not disturbed by recording devices, making a taped record of an interview without written permission from the interviewee's employer is an ethical issue and also may expose you to legal issues later on. So if you're doing any recording, you'll need to obtain all of the necessary permissions in advance.

" "

The steps that you take after the interview is over are just as important as the other parts of the interview.

Conducting a Telephone Interview

- Contact the interview subject and make an appointment for the interview. Tell the subject how long the interview will last, ask if that time is available and acceptable, and stick to your schedule.
- Prepare for the telephone interview the same way you would for the in-person interview: prepare a list of questions, and practice—perhaps with your friends or co-workers—delivering them so you can move smoothly from one question and response to the next.
- Telephone the subject promptly at the appointed time.

(continued)

- If the interview subject is unavailable at the agreed-upon time, respond professionally and pleasantly and try to reschedule the interview.
- After a short courtesy introduction, begin the interview without unnecessary delay. The person whom you are interviewing is doing you a favor, so conduct the interview accordingly.
- Listen carefully to the replies to your questions, ask follow-up questions for elaboration or clarification, and then move on. Take notes as you go along.

- Do not tape record the interview unless you have received prior permission to do so from your interview subject. If you have permission and are recording the interview, begin the recording by stating the name of the interviewee, your name, and the date.
- When the interview is over, at or before the agreed-upon time, thank your subject and bring the interview to a cordial, yet professional, close.
- Send a thank-you note after the interview.

QUESTIONNAIRES AND SURVEYS

Questionnaires and surveys are useful ways to gather material and research information. Along with interviews they allow for a more personal response and are often used when opinions and attitudes are required. Questionnaires can be administered face-to-face, over the telephone, by mail, or on the Internet.

Questionnaires are valuable, but only if they ask appropriate questions that people can understand and only if they are written in a format that people can answer easily. When you are designing a questionnaire, you must give it a lot of thought, prepare it carefully, and test it thoroughly. As with all writing, you should think through the process in depth. What do you want to find out, how will you go about finding it, what kind of questions will be in the questionnaire, and how will you analyze the data?

You must consider the two important concepts in survey research: validity and reliability. *Validity* considers whether you are measuring what you are setting out to measure; *reliability* looks at whether the results you obtain are stable, that is, whether you will get the same results each time you administer the test instrument.

Start by determining whether a questionnaire is the best method for gathering the data you need. Why do you want to use a questionnaire? Clearly define your focus and purpose. When you decide to gather information using a questionnaire, you may be looking for either qualitative information (considering the nature or type of responses) or quantitative information (considering the prevalence or numerical totals of the responses). Prepare a draft set of questions and a draft format. Test the questions on several subjects and then modify the questionnaire. Creating a questionnaire is a process. When the questionnaire is as good as you can make it, distribute it, collect it, and then analyze the data. See Figure 5.3 for an example of a survey.

FIGURE 5.3

Excerpt from a Survey

SOURCE: Don Zimmerman

50a. Do you access the WWW from campus? _____ Yes _____ No

50b. If yes, what type of computer do you use? Check all that apply.

_____ IBM & IBM clones _____ Workstation (Sun, HP, DEC, etc.)

_____ Apple/Macintosh _____ Other (specify): _____

50c. If yes, which Web browser do you use on campus? Circle your response.

    a. Netscape Navigator (What version? _____)

    b. Lynx (What version? _____)

    c. Microsoft Explorer (What version? _____)

    d. Mosaic (What version? _____)

    e. Other (specify): _____

    f. Don't know

51a. Do you recall how you learned about the WWW?

_____ Yes _____ No

51b. If yes, how did you learn about it? Check one.

_____ Friend	_____ Magazine
_____ Newspaper	_____ Television
_____ Instructor/teacher	_____ Coworker

Other (specify): _____

_____

52. Who introduced you to using a WWW browser? Circle your response.

    a. Self   **b.** Professor   **c.** Supervisor   **d.** Friend or coworker   **e.** Other

53. Who set up the computer you use to access the WWW? Circle your response.

    a. Self   **b.** Friend or coworker   **c.** Computer professional   **d.** Other

For questions 54–61, indicate the importance of each when accessing the WWW.

	Not Important			Very Important	
54. Access speed	1	2	3	4	5
55. Graphics/visual interest	1	2	3	4	5
56. Information currentness	1	2	3	4	5
57. Information specificity	1	2	3	4	5
58. Information range	1	2	3	4	5
59. Ease of finding information	1	2	3	4	5
60. Information quality	1	2	3	4	5
61. How many screens it takes to find the information	1	2	3	4	5

62. How many links (underlined words, hot buttons, etc.) will you click on before you abandon a search?

    a. 1–5   **b.** 6–10   **c.** 11–15   **d.** 16–20   **e.** 21 or more

Creating a Questionnaire

- Use specific, concrete words instead of general, vague ones. Use questions that require yes or no answers or ones that give a choice of several possible responses.

- Give your readers enough choices. For example, when a multiple-choice question doesn't cover all of the possible answers, provide the possible answer of "other" and allow readers to explain their unlisted choice in more detail.

- Phrase your questions as simply as possible to avoid confusion. For example, rephrase the question "Should the purchasing department deny requests for duplicate items without checking first with the originating department?" as "Should the purchasing department verify duplicate orders with the originating department?"

- Avoid asking two questions in one. Consider for example: "Do you believe the school should require students to provide their own computers, and should they be PCs?" Readers may agree with the first question but differ on the second, or they might disagree with the first question but feel pressured to change their mind by the second question.

- Avoid overuse of styles for emphasis. Styles concern your use of italics, bold, or underlining. Italics, bold, or underlining can help call attention to various keywords, but if your questionnaire has too many words in boldface type, for example, readers can lose track of what needs emphasis and what does not.

- Help your readers to make effective comparisons. Avoid asking questions such as "Do you think your computer lab is a better equipped lab?" Instead, rephrase the question as "Do you think your computer lab is better equipped than the computer lab in the library?"

- Avoid mistaken assumptions. The question, "Would a workshop on PowerPoint be more valuable to you than a workshop on FrontPage?" assumes that the two programs are comparable and asks readers to guess what you meant by "valuable." Rephrase as: "Which software program training do you need most—creating presentations or creating Web pages?"

- Phrase your questions so your readers will provide useful information in their responses. The question: "Do you think the department will need to hire more faculty over the next two years?" requires you to ask several follow-up questions. Rephrase as "List the areas in which you think the department should hire faculty over the next two years."

- Make the length of the questionnaire appropriate to the purpose. Determine carefully what kind of information you need, and ask questions concerning only this information. If you fail to ask key questions, you might have to send out a revised questionnaire to obtain the information you should have obtained the first time.

(continued)

- Ask sensitive questions—such as age or income—last if you must collect this information in order to validate or categorize the responses. Once they have spent time answering your other, non-sensitive questions, readers may feel they have time invested in the process and will go ahead and complete the form.

- Increase the response rate to your survey or questionnaire by contacting the subjects at least three times: before you send out your document, while it is out, and when it is due back.

FOCUS GROUPS

When you are writing for an audience, you want to make sure that the information you will be presenting is the information your audience wants and needs. Sometimes knowing which information to present can be elusive. At times, the best way to discern your audience's needs is to go directly to representatives of that audience.

Focus groups can be used both to develop information for your documents (including Web sites) and test the effectiveness of existing or in-progress documents. For a typical focus group, you assemble a small group of potential users of your information along with a moderator to focus the discussion. The key to successful focus groups is maintaining a good flow of conversation fairly evenly among the participants. If instead one or two people dominate the conversation, you are losing potentially valuable information the other participants might have contributed. In addition to maintaining the conversation flow, the moderator is responsible for keeping the group on topic, without digressions. When the focus-group session is over, the moderator writes up the results. Often the focus group has observers, who also may take notes or audio- or videotape the session.

One useful method for running a focus group is called the *nominal group technique.* It is a structured plan that moderators (also called facilitators) use to manage individual participation within the group. With this method, all members have the opportunity to contribute and help form a consensus. Each person offers as many ideas as possible, either orally one person at a time or anonymously on index cards. Then all the responses are discussed and participants rank them from best to worst.

Focus groups can be useful when you want to know people's reactions and ideas, but they are usually expensive to run and don't always produce useful data. When you ask people for their opinions or to report how they use a particular product, you are getting data passed through a very subjective sieve. You will learn about what people think they want, rather than what they may actually need. Usability testing—direct observation of how people use products—will show you a much more accurate picture. (Usability testing is a form of evaluation discussed in Chapter 10.) But often the product is not yet available to be sampled, and knowing what people want in a product can be helpful in its development and in the development of the documents that accompany the product.

EXPERIMENTATION

There are many ways of learning about a subject. You can read books and journal articles, attend classes and lectures, or perform a variety of activities to discover information yourself. In general, these are also the steps that scientists use to advance their own knowledge and that of society. Books, journal articles, classes, and lectures will bring you up-to-date information in your field. But knowledge in a field is not immutable; that is, it can change over time. If you are wondering how knowledge—awareness and understanding—can change, you have only to look at what kinds of things can be "known."

Basic Terms

Fact: A fact is a report of something seen, heard, smelled, tasted, or felt. Only through the senses do we gain any knowledge of the world outside the mind.

Concrete Term: A concrete term designates something that exists in the physical world.

Abstract Term: An abstract term designates a concept that does not exist in the physical world: *justice, truth, heroism.*

Hypothesis: A hypothesis is a tentative generalization made after observation of only a few particulars; further observation may prove it to be untenable.

Theory: A theory is a hypothesis that has been thoroughly tested and generally is accepted unless and until it is superseded by another.

Law: A law is a general statement that has been widely tested and that has an overwhelming amount of evidence to support it.

Opinions and **Judgments:** Opinions and judgments are particular or general statements of varying degrees of validity. *Facts* are verifiable; they are supported by objective evidence. *Opinions* and *judgments,* though they may be supported by objective evidence, are not verifiable in the same objective way. Often they are based on emotion, prejudice, or personal taste.

In science, various terms are used to refer to information about a topic, depending on where it falls in the verification process. Familiarize yourself with the basic terms used to denote information gathered in the sciences.

What Is a Scientific Theory?

Calling something a theory is not the same as saying it is a guess or an opinion. The term *theory* is used in science to refer to an explanation that is a good fit for the data we have at this time. When new data are discovered, perhaps calling the theory into question, a new theory can be proposed and tested to see if it explains the observed data better than the old theory. This process of testing, accepting, and replacing theories is a cornerstone of the scientific method and of scientific progress.

Most students already have had some exposure to the scientific method. The physical, life, and social sciences rely on experimentation as an important method of gathering information on a subject. Successful experimentation depends on your ability to follow the steps of the scientific method.

The major steps of the scientific method generally follow this path:

- Define the problem as specifically as existing knowledge will permit.
- Summarize the work already done. Make sure that the problem has not already been solved. Compare similar phenomena. The solution to one problem may be useful in finding the solution to another problem of the same kind.
- Formulate a hypothesis. Propose a tentative answer to the problem.
- Test the hypothesis. By observation and experiment, try to establish the falsity or the truth of the hypothesis.
- Modify the hypothesis. You may verify your hypothesis, disprove it, extend its original scope, or modify or restrict it.
- Publish the results. After you have thoroughly tested your hypothesis and have verified it through further observation and experimentation, publish your results.
- Submit the final hypothesis for verification. When your results are published or privately submitted, you should expect others to test your hypothesis by repeating your experiments and devising new experiments.
- Establish a theory. After a published hypothesis has been thoroughly rechecked and retested and has been verified to the satisfaction of many researchers in the area, then the hypothesis becomes a theory. See Figure 5.4 for an example.

CHOOSING THE ETHICAL PATH

Every discipline has a code of ethics and standards, and you are responsible for adhering to the standards of your discipline. Many professions have review boards to enforce their ethical and professional standards. Experimentation—especially on humans—carries with it a great responsibility. When you engage in activities that have the potential to affect the lives and well-being of other human beings, you must be especially careful that you are treating those people in an ethical way in keeping with the highest standards of your discipline.

FIGURE 5.4

The Scientific Method

SOURCE: http://prime.jsc.nasa.gov/Rov/
method.html

STEP	EXAMPLE
Step 1: State the problem.	"I need to build a robot to accomplish my mission."
Step 2: Research the problem.	What will it take to solve my problem What do I know, and need to know, about my problem? To solve my problem, "I need to know *how* to build a robot." How do I do that? ■ Examine the possibilities. ■ Eliminate poor choices. ■ Consider likely choices.
Step 3: Form a hypothesis.	A possible solution to my problem. The simplest solution is often the best solution! "Based on my research, I will build a robot called GoBot."
Step 4: Test the hypothesis.	Perform an experiment to see if your hypothesis works. "Put GoBot in the simulator."
Step 5: Draw conclusions from the data.	Data are the results of an experiment. Simply put, there are only two possibilities: (1) If your hypothesis was correct, you now have a successful robot. (2) If your hypothesis was incorrect, the experiment failed. Don't give up! Do more research! ■ What was wrong with the original hypothesis? ■ Did you make a poor selection? ■ Was your experiment flawed? ■ Form another hypothesis based on additional research. ■ Test your new hypothesis.

WRITTEN OR RECORDED INFORMATION

Today's libraries offer a wide variety of print and nonprint sources. You already know that college and university libraries are not the only kind of libraries in which you can conduct your research. Most communities have good public libraries, and many companies have extensive corporate libraries. There are also numerous government libraries and other kinds of special libraries. Whatever kind of library or libraries you decide to use, you need to have a basic familiarity with how to find what you need.

Libraries comprise more than just books and journals. They also have catalogs, bibliographies, databases, and recordings in a variety of media: paper, online, film, tape, microfilm, microfiche. Libraries also offer many services that can save valuable time in your research efforts. For example, inexperienced researchers often make the mistake of thinking that if a book, journal article, or other source is not available in their library, then they are out of luck or will have to travel to another library. But most libraries have interlibrary loan services, which can locate almost any book or article in relatively little time for little or no expense.

Librarians are the specialists who are trained to know which resources provide what data, so for many library searches, consulting the librarians should be your first step. In addition to the printed and online sources available to you as a library patron, you also have resources around the world that you probably would not know about unless you were trained in library science.

Many university libraries offer a search service to students and faculty members who are beginning complex research projects. If your project might be one that could benefit from such a search, make an appointment with the reference or research librarian at your library. Often, the initial steps of these searches can be performed at no cost to you. And even if you do have to pay a fee for some of the research, it will usually be a very small investment relative to the value you will receive.

> " "
> For many library searches, consulting the librarians should be your first step.

USING THE LIBRARY—PRINT SOURCES

Your local college or community library is typically the largest depository of printed material of all kinds—books, journals, magazines, newsletters, pamphlets, government documents, and so on. By becoming familiar with a few basic resources, you can learn how to navigate through all this material to find the information you need.

Planning Your Research

- Allow enough time. All phases of the process take a lot of time, from planning to writing and revising the paper. It is all too easy to procrastinate. If you wait too long before beginning the necessary work, you risk running out of time before you have found all the information you need.

- Define the topic as precisely as possible early in the research process. Use whatever strategies you prefer for helping you to focus your topic. For example, state your topic as a question and then identify the main concepts or keywords in your question. Consult a librarian to design research strategies.

- Decide how you will document your research steps. You can put notes on index cards, in a notebook, into a laptop computer, or on a network site. Document not only the sources of direct quotations and paraphrases, but also sources you consulted but did not use. Write a complete citation for each source; you may need it later. Also write down where you found the source.

Figures 5.5 and 5.6 are examples of the types of notes you will take as you consult your sources.

Locating Information

● Translate your topic into the subject language of the indexes and catalogs you use. The librarian can help you find where to locate keywords relating to your search. The Library of Congress subject headings, for example, are a good beginning when you need a controlled vocabulary to focus your search.

● Work from the general to the specific. Get general information on the subject and related areas. Look up your keywords in the indexes to subject encyclopedias. Read articles in the encyclopedias to set the context for your research. Note any relevant items in the bibliographies at the end of the encyclopedia articles.

● As you read articles, note significant names, dates, events, organizations, and issues. You may want to consult other reference sources, such as annuals for current research on a topic, handbooks that outline all aspects of a specific subject, or a statistical source.

● Check for additional background information in your lecture notes, textbooks, and reserve readings.

● Ask questions. When you don't know how to find information you're looking for, ask a librarian for help.

Find a good variety of appropriate sources. Most professors who assign research papers expect you to use a variety of sources, including books, journal articles, and databases. Don't rely exclusively on one medium, such as the World Wide Web, for your sources.

FIGURE 5.5

Paraphrase Card

| Author   Topic |

| Page number (or other source information) |

| Paraphrase of original source (rewording of original into your words and style) |

FIGURE 5.6

Bibliography Card

```
Author's name
Title of work
Publication information

Other publication items (for example,
editor, edition, journal issue)

Library call number (if applicable)

Your notes about content (if any)
```

Types of Sources

- For books, find your subject in the Library of Congress Subject Headings Search in the online catalog. If you know of a good book on your topic, look up the subject headings listed for that book and search for other books using the new subject headings. Check bibliographies in articles, books, encyclopedias, and other sources.

- Investigate current research and information on a topic in periodical articles. You may be required to use scholarly journals rather than magazines and other types of periodicals. Learn the difference between a scholarly journal and other types of periodicals. Use print periodical indexes and abstracts. Use electronic indexes.

- Ask a librarian about online database searches.

- Check bibliographies in articles, books, encyclopedias, and other sources.

- Look for current research and information on the Internet. Further information on Internet sources is provided later in this chapter.

See Figure 5.7 for a list of print and electronic indexes.

Finding Material in Other Libraries

- Interlibrary loan: You can request a book or journal article from another library through interlibrary loan. Start your research early, since interlibrary loans take time.

- Online catalogs: Ask a librarian how to connect to another library's catalog on the Internet. If you are short on time, you may need to go to the

(continued)

library and photocopy the article yourself. See Figure 5.8a and b for a sample online search.

● Reciprocal privileges: Many university libraries allow you to use the library, but will not allow you to check out books if you are not a student, faculty member, or staff employee there. Others will.

FIGURE 5.7

Library Sources: Print and Electronic Indexes

Academic Index and Fulltext: Indexes articles in approximately 1,000 scholarly journals and popular magazines in the arts, humanities, social sciences, science, and technology. Abstracts are included for some articles. Provides access to ASCII full text of some articles.

Books in Print/Out of Print—with Reviews: Provides complete, publisher-verified information on all U.S. books in print. Includes more than 900,000 new or revised records each year and covers scholarly, technical, popular, adult, juvenile, and reprint titles. Includes full-text reviews.

Business Index and Fulltext: Contains citations to articles in more than 800 journal titles including business, management, and trade journals; some 80 regional and local journals and newspapers; and business-related articles from more than 3,000 other publications. Includes topics such as business, management, industry, world affairs, case studies, technology, and industry profiles. Provides access to ASCII full text of some articles.

Center for Research Libraries Catalog: The Center for Research Libraries (CRL) is an international not-for-profit consortium of colleges, universities, and libraries that makes available scholarly research resources to users everywhere.

Engineering Index: Engineering Index covers significant engineering and technical literature from journals (more than 1,500), technical reports, engineering society publications, books, and conference proceedings and papers (more than 600).

ERIC: Education Resources Information Center has represented the most complete bibliography of educational materials available since 1966. The ERIC database is a guide to published and unpublished sources on thousands of educational topics, with information from RIE (Resources in Education) and CIJE (Current Index to Journals in Education).

Index to Legal Periodicals and Books: Provides thorough, reliable indexing of more than 570 journals, yearbooks, law reviews, and bar

(continued)

FIGURE 5.7

(continued)

association publications. Covers all areas of jurisprudence, including court decisions, legislation, and original scholarship.

Legal Trac: LegalTrac provides indexing for approximately 800 of the most highly regarded legal publications: major law reviews, legal newspapers, law specialty publications, bar association journals, and international legal journals. Each title is selected on the basis of criteria provided by a special advisory committee of the American Association of Law Libraries. LegalTrac also contains law-related articles from more than 1,000 additional business and general interest titles.

PsycINFO: Covers scholarly literature in experimental psychology (human, animal, and comparative), psychosexual behavior, educational psychology, applied psychology, sports psychology, and other subjects. Includes original research and journal articles, literature reviews, reports of surveys, case studies, theoretical discussions, bibliographies, and descriptions of tests and apparatus. Indexed materials are selected from more than 1,300 journals published in 50 countries and 28 languages. Most records have abstracts.

Ulrich's International Periodicals Directory: Provides information on prices, frequency of publication, addresses, publishers' phone and fax numbers, e-mail and Web site addresses for more than 270,000 journals, magazines, annuals, series, newspapers, and other periodicals published worldwide. Indicates whether periodicals are available in print, microform, online, CD-ROM, or other formats. Identifies audience, such as scholarly or trade. Identifies special features, such as the presence of reviews or indexes, whether a journal is refereed, and which indexing/abstracting services cover the periodical.

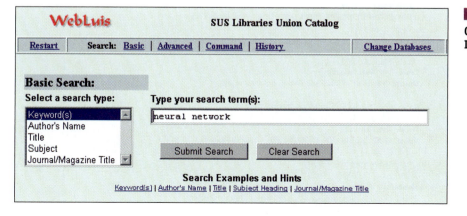

FIGURE 5.8a

Online Library Search: Library Search Screen

FIGURE 5.8b

**Online Library Search:
Search Results Screen**

| Restart | **Search:** Basic | Advanced | Command | History | Change Databases |

Search: k=neural network
Hit Count: 863
Records: 1 to 25

➡

Marked Records: 0

☐ **1** neural network applications in detecting metal casting defects in manufacturing using the cascade correlation algorithm
  Florida A&M University
  COLEMAN LIBRARY No call number available -- Check Shelf
    FAMU Master's Thesishoused in Special Collection

☐ **2** Adaptive antennas for wireless communications
  2001
  Florida State University
  DIRAC SCIENCE LIBRARY TK7871.67 .A33 A33 2001 -- AT THE BINDERY. DUE 05/08/01

☐ **3** Antigen processing and presentation protocols
  2001
  UF Health Science Ctr (HC)
  HEALTH SCIENCE CENTER LIBRARY QH 506 M5922 v.156 2001 -- Not checked out

☐ **4** Antigen processing and presentation protocols
  2001
  USF SHIMBERG HEALTH SCI LIB.
  HEALTH SCIENCES Circulation WO 680 A629 2001 -- Not checked out

☐ **5** Antigen processing and presentation protocols
  2001
  USF-TAMPA/ST. PETE/FMHI/LAKE
  TAMPA circulating collection QR184.34 .A55 2001 -- Not checked out

☐ **6** Gateway to memory : an introduction to neural network modeling of the hippocampus and learning
  Gluck, Mark A.; 2001
  UF Health Science Ctr (HC)
  HEALTH SCIENCE CENTER LIBRARY WL 314 G567g 2001 -- Not checked out

☐ **7** Gateway to memory : an introduction to neural network modeling of the hippocampus and learning
  Gluck, Mark A.; 2001
  Florida State University
  DIRAC SCIENCE LIBRARY QP383.25 .G58 2001 -- Not checked out

☐ **8** Gateway to memory : an introduction to neural network modeling of the hippocampus and learning
  Gluck, Mark A.; 2001
  Florida Gulf Coast University
  General Collection QP383.25 .G58 2001 -- Not checked out

☐ **9** Operations research : a practical introduction
  Carter, Michael W.; 2001
  Florida State University
  DIRAC SCIENCE LIBRARY T57.6 .C367 2001 -- Not checked out

☐ **10** Quantitative approximations
  Anastassiou, George A., 1952-; 2001
  Florida State University
  DIRAC SCIENCE LIBRARY QA221 .A5365 2001 -- Not checked out

Working with Your Information

- Make sure you don't have too many or too few sources. If you are doing research for a class project or paper, ask your instructor for guidelines on the appropriate number of sources. If you are doing research for your job, solicit this information from your colleagues or supervisor.

- Evaluate what you have found. Screen your information for authority, accuracy, honesty, and completeness. If you have found too many or too few sources, you may need to narrow or broaden your topic. Check with a reference librarian, your instructor, or your supervisor.

- Use a standard format for your bibliography. Ask which citation style is required. In some sciences, the CBE (Council of Biology Editors, now the Council of Science Editors) style is used. In other areas, the APA (American Psychological Association), the *Chicago Manual of Style* or Turabian, or the MLA (Modern Language Association) style is preferred.

See Chapter 6 on organizing and managing information for more on working with your information. Also, additional information on citation styles can be found in Appendix C.

Card Catalogs

Most libraries have converted their traditional card catalogs into online catalogs. Some libraries maintain the card catalog while making the conversion. Few libraries have retained card catalogs, but it's still a good idea to be familiar with a card catalog system in case you find yourself doing research in such a library.

Traditional card catalogs are large filing cabinets of index cards organized by subject, title, or author. Some libraries combine organization of these categories in various ways. See Figure 5.9 for an example of a card catalog card.

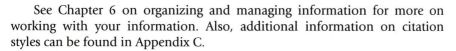

```
UA
23       National security and the U.S.
.N2483     Constitution : the impact of the
1088       political system / edited by George
           C. Edwards III and Wallace Earl
           Walker. -- Baltimore : Johns Hopkins
           University Press, c1988.
           xii. 340 p. ; 24 c.
           Includes bibliographies and index.
           ISBN 0-8018-3684-0 (alk. paper)
           1. United States--National security.
         2. Civil-military relations--United
         States.  3. United States--
         Constitutional history. I. Edwards,
         George C.  II. Walker, Wallace Earl,
         1844-     III. Title: National
         security and the US Constitution.

FOFT  07 FEB 89   17551847  FTUUsl      88-655
```

FIGURE 5.9

Library Card Catalog Card

Reference Works

Most libraries have one central area for their reference holdings, which include everything from abstracts, encyclopedias, statistical sources, government documents, and dictionaries to biographical publications, print databases, guides to other reference materials, and general reference materials. In a big library you'll find thousands of reference works of all kinds. Widely used reference works include *Books in Print, Information Sources in Science and Technology,*

FIGURE 5.10a

Sample Page from the Online *Applied Science and Technology Abstracts*: Information Page

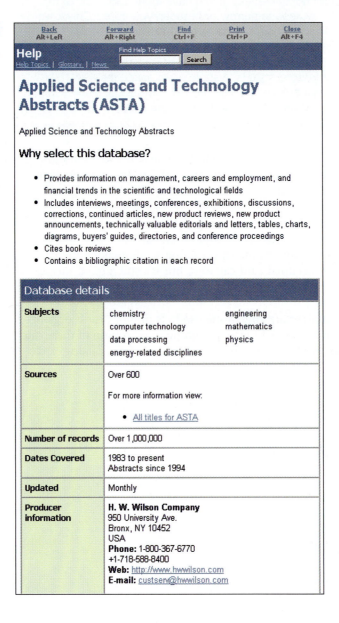

Reference Books Annual, Ulrich's International Periodicals Directory, and *Library of Congress Subject Headings.* Looking carefully through the sources pertaining to your topic will give you a good sense of what may be available. Unlike working your way through electronic sources, checking through printed matter can often yield unexpected benefits in the form of nearby materials that are useful to your research. As you browse through the shelves, you may see a volume that contains just the information you need, even though you didn't know about this source beforehand.

Print Abstracts and Indexes

Print abstracts and indexes identify published research articles on your topic. An abstract is a type of index for scholarly journals, usually arranged by subject. In addition to the journal citation, a descriptive paragraph is also included. Online services are increasingly providing this same information. Some typical print abstracts are *Biological Abstracts, Chemical Abstracts, Dissertation Abstracts, Engineering Index,* and *Applied Science and Technology Index.* Useful indexes for medicine and science include *Index Medicus* and *General Science Index.* Most online databases began indexing journals in the mid-1980s. To locate older articles, use print indexes, some of which date to the 1800s. See Figure 5.10a–d for an example of an online index.

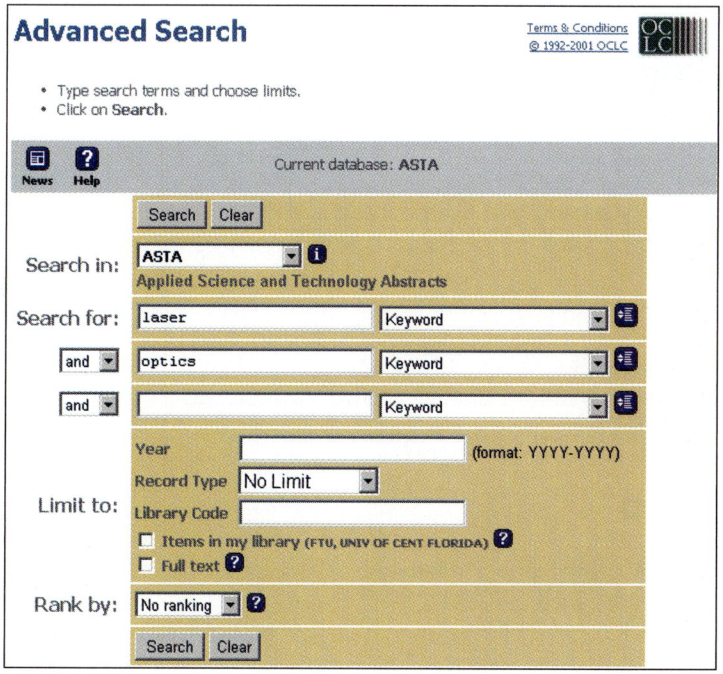

> Unlike working your way through electronic sources, checking through printed matter can often yield unexpected benefits in the form of nearby materials that are useful to your research.

FIGURE 5.10b

Sample Page from the Online *Applied Science and Technology Abstracts*: Search Page

FIGURE 5.10c

Sample Page from the Online *Applied Science and Technology Abstracts*: Search Results

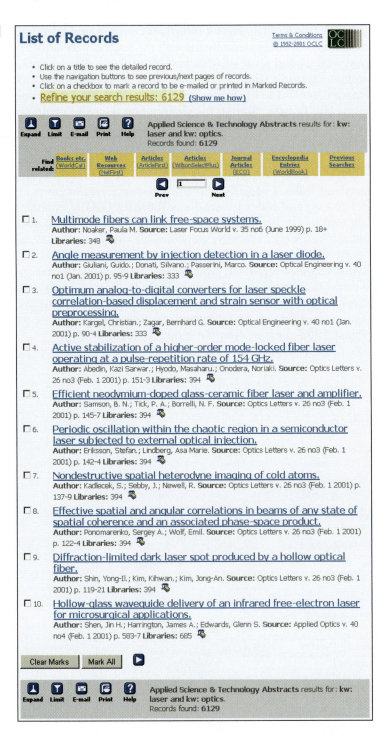

Database:	ASTA
Copyright:	Database Producer Copyright © the H.W. Wilson Company. All rights reserved.
Ownership:	**FirstSearch indicates your institution subscribes to this publication.**
	• Libraries that Own Item: 333
	• Search the catalog at University of Central Florida
Author(s):	Giuliani, Guido. ; Donati, Silvano. ; Passerini, Marco.
Title:	**Angle measurement by injection detection in a laser diode.**
Source:	*Optical Engineering* v. 40 no1 (Jan. 2001) p. 95-9 **Journal Code:** Opt Eng
	Additional Info: United States
Standard No:	**ISSN:** 0091-3286
Details:	bibl il.
Language:	English
Review:	Peer-reviewed journal
	SUBJECT(S)
Descriptor:	Angles -- Measurement.
	Semiconductor lasers -- Measurement uses.
	Retroreflection (Optics).
Record Type:	article
Article Type:	feature article
Accession No:	BAST01010681

FIGURE 5.10d

Sample Page from the Online *Applied Science and Technology Abstracts*: Detailed Record

Periodicals

Periodicals are the journals, magazines, newspapers, and newsletters in a library. Most disciplines have at least one major journal, and many have numerous journals in which research findings are reported. Magazines include trade and special interest publications. Trade magazines are typically for professionals in a field; special interest publications may be for hobbyists or professionals in fields such as computers or photography. Newsletters are brief publications (four to twelve pages) focusing on the current events in a company or discipline. Finally, most libraries carry a variety of local, state, national, and international newspapers. If you don't know which periodicals might be helpful to you in your search, consult a periodical index, such as *Readers' Guide to Periodical Literature* for general periodicals, the *Applied Science and Technology Index* for technical subjects, or any of the other useful indexes suggested by your librarian.

Books and Monographs

Books may be on a variety of special interest topics or may be textbooks, monographs, or trade books. A library that uses the Library of Congress Classification System will have books in 21 classes. See Figure 5.11 for a list of Library of Congress classifications. A library that uses the Dewey Decimal System organizes its titles in a different way. See Figure 5.12 for a list of Dewey Decimal classifications.

FIGURE 5.11
Library of Congress Classifications

A—General Works
B—Philosophy. Psychology. Religion
C—Auxiliary Sciences of History
D—History (includes Travel)
E—America
F—United States. Canada. Latin America
G—Geography
H—Social Sciences
J—Political Science
K—Law

L—Education
M—Music
N—Fine Arts
P—Language and Literature
Q—Science
R—Medicine
S—Agriculture
T—Technology
U—Military Science
V—Naval Science
Z—Books in General

FIGURE 5.12
Dewey Decimal Classifications

000—Generalities
100—Philosophy and Psychology
200—Religion
300—Social Sciences
400—Language
500—Natural Sciences and Mathematics

600—Technology (applied sciences)
700—The Arts
800—Literature and Rhetoric
900—Geography and History

Some libraries use a combination of these two major methods, but with either system you will find that books on the same topic usually have similar call letters (classification numbers) and usually will be shelved near each other. Exceptions may be oversized books, which often are shelved by size; reference books, which may be grouped with other reference materials; rare books, which usually are kept in a separate part of the library; and special collections, which also are found in a separate area of the library. In some cases you will need special permission to examine rare sources or those in a special-collections area.

Government Publications

Many libraries are depositories for federal, state, and local government publications and usually have a dedicated area presided over by one or more staff members who specialize in archiving material and assisting people with the holdings. Typical government publications range from books, periodi-

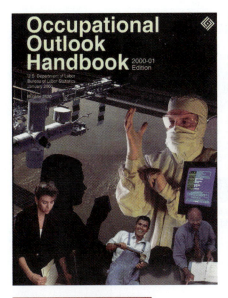
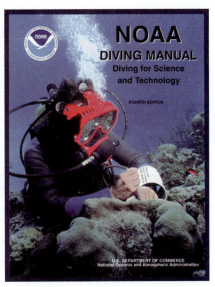

FIGURE 5.13

Government Publications

cals, and special reports to all kinds of technical reports. Increasingly, much of the material is available in electronic format and microform (microfilm and microfiche). See Figure 5.13 for examples of government publications.

Special Collections, Maps, and Archives

Special collections are the papers and personal documents of the people who are important in a particular field. Map collections may consist of every kind of world, country, state, and local map. Archives are groupings of scholarly and rare collections, local history collections, and university documents, including faculty and staff publications, master's theses, doctoral dissertations, graduate research reports, official university documents, university press publications, and memorabilia such as drawings of the campus, catalogs, directories, yearbooks, and the student newspaper.

Evaluating Print Sources

Many people tend to trust the printed word over other forms of information. Perhaps it is because we were taught from the time we began school that books were the resources to turn to if we needed to "get the facts." The impression we have that books, magazines, and newspapers hold authoritative information probably subtly reinforces this assumption. But as we all eventually should have learned, just because something appears in print doesn't mean it is true or correct.

FIGURE 5.14a

Sample Page from Online
Book Review Digest:
Information Page

Book Review Digest (BookReview)

Reviews of current English-language fiction and nonfiction books

Why select this database?

- Cites and excerpts reviews of current English-language fiction and nonfiction books for adults and children
- Covers periodicals published in the United States, Canada, and Great Britain
- Includes only reviews that have appeared within 18 months of the book's publication

Database details

Subjects	English-language fiction and non-fiction books excluding reviews of textbooks, government publications, and technical books in law and the sciences
Sources	Over 7,000 books each year For more information view: • All titles for Book Review Digest
Number of records	Over 422,000
Dates covered	1983 to present
Updated	Monthly
Producer information	**H. W. Wilson Company** 950 University Ave. Bronx, NY 10452 USA **Phone:** 1-800-367-6770 +1-718-588-8400 **Web:** http://www.hwwilson.com **E-mail:** custserv@hwwilson.com

As Internet use becomes widespread, we have to stop and remind ourselves that many so-called facts we read are only opinion. The here-today, gone-tomorrow nature of online information helps us to remember the ephemeral nature of what passes for solid data in some contexts.

Print sources, because they don't change until updated in new editions (and even then the original edition often is still available even years later), tempt us to give them more authority than they warrant. After all, they are the same today as they were yesterday, and tomorrow will be no different. Print sources, however, are as prone to error and misstatement as any other information medium. Therefore we have to learn how to evaluate what we are reading, regardless of where we read it.

See Figure 5.14a–d for an example of an online book-review index.

Advanced Search

Terms & Conditions
© 1992-2001 OCLC

OCLC

- Type search terms and choose limits.
- Click on **Search**.

News   Help

Current database: **BookReview**

| Search | Clear |

Search in: BookReview
Reviews of current English-language fiction and nonfiction books

Search for: microchip   Keyword

and   [   ] Keyword

and   [   ] Keyword

Limit to:
Year [   ] (format: YYYY-YYYY)
Record Type No Limit
Library Code [   ]
☐ Items in my library (FTU, UNIV OF CENT FLORIDA) ?
☐ Full text ?

Rank by: No ranking ?

| Search | Clear |

FIGURE 5.14b

Sample Page from Online
Book Review Digest:
Search Page

Assessing Print Sources

- What are the author's educational background, academic or industry affiliation, previous writings, and experience in this area? Is this book or topic in the author's area of expertise? Have you seen the author's name cited in other sources or bibliographies? Respected authors are cited frequently by other scholars.

- When was the source published? Is it current or out of date? Topic areas of continuing and rapid development, such as those in the sciences, demand more current information. On the other hand, topics in the humanities often require material that was written many years ago.

- Is it a first edition? The existence of later editions indicates that a source has been revised to reflect changes in knowledge. Also, a work that has had many printings or editions is likely to be a standard source in the field and has a higher chance of being reliable.

- Who is the publisher? A source that is published by a university press, for example, is likely to be scholarly. The fact that a publisher is reputable does not necessarily guarantee quality, but it does show that the publisher may have high regard for the source being published.

- Is it a scholarly or a popular journal? The distinction is important because it indicates different levels of complexity in conveying ideas and different standards of peer review. A peer-reviewed

(continued)

FIGURE 5.14c

**Sample Page from Online
Book Review Digest:
Search Results**

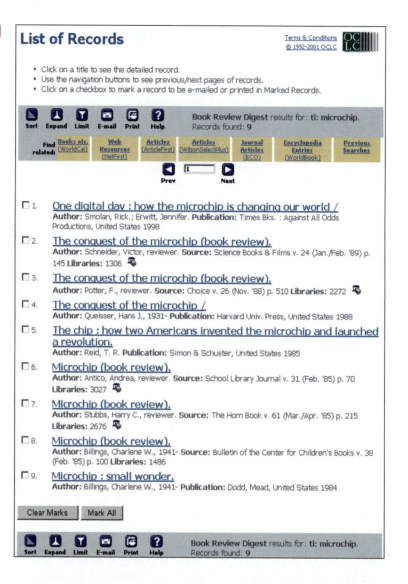

List of Records

Terms & Conditions
© 1992-2001 OCLC

- Click on a title to see the detailed record.
- Use the navigation buttons to see previous/next pages of records.
- Click on a checkbox to mark a record to be e-mailed or printed in Marked Records.

Sort Expand Limit E-mail Print Help   Book Review Digest results for: **ti: microchip.**
                                             Records found: 9

Find related: **Books etc.** (WorldCat) **Web Resources** (NetFirst) **Articles** (ArticleFirst) **Articles** (WilsonSelectPlus) **Journal Articles** (ECO) **Encyclopedia Entries** (WorldBook) **Previous Searches**

◄ Prev   [1]   ► Next

☐ 1. One digital day : how the microchip is changing our world /
Author: Smolan, Rick.; Erwitt, Jennifer. **Publication:** Times Bks. : Against All Odds Productions, United States 1998

☐ 2. The conquest of the microchip (book review).
Author: Schneider, Victor, reviewer. **Source:** Science Books & Films v. 24 (Jan./Feb. '89) p. 145 **Libraries:** 1306

☐ 3. The conquest of the microchip (book review).
Author: Potter, F., reviewer. **Source:** Choice v. 26 (Nov. '88) p. 510 **Libraries:** 2272

☐ 4. The conquest of the microchip /
Author: Queisser, Hans J., 1931- **Publication:** Harvard Univ. Press, United States 1988

☐ 5. The chip : how two Americans invented the microchip and launched a revolution.
Author: Reid, T. R. **Publication:** Simon & Schuster, United States 1985

☐ 6. Microchip (book review).
Author: Antico, Andrea, reviewer. **Source:** School Library Journal v. 31 (Feb. '85) p. 70 **Libraries:** 3027

☐ 7. Microchip (book review).
Author: Stubbs, Harry C., reviewer. **Source:** The Horn Book v. 61 (Mar./Apr. '85) p. 215 **Libraries:** 2676

☐ 8. Microchip (book review).
Author: Billings, Charlene W., 1941- **Source:** Bulletin of the Center for Children's Books v. 38 (Feb. '85) p. 100 **Libraries:** 1486

☐ 9. Microchip : small wonder.
Author: Billings, Charlene W., 1941- **Publication:** Dodd, Mead, United States 1984

[Clear Marks]   [Mark All]

Sort Expand Limit E-mail Print Help   Book Review Digest results for: **ti: microchip.**
                                             Records found: 9

journal article has been evaluated and accepted by acknowledged authorities in the field.

● Who is the audience? Is the publication aimed at a specialized or a general audience? Is the source too elementary, too technical, too advanced, or just right for your needs? Has the topic been over-simplified to suit a lay audience, with the possible loss of detail or precision that a professional audience requires?

● Is the information fact, opinion, or propaganda? It is not always easy to separate fact from opinion. Facts can usually be verified; opinions, though they may be

(continued)

FIGURE 5.14d

Sample Page from Online
Book Review Digest:
Detailed Record

Database:	BookReview
Copyright:	Database Producer Copyright © the H.W. Wilson Company. All rights reserved.
Ownership:	• Search the catalog at University of Central Florida
Title:	**One digital day : how the microchip is changing our world** /
Author(s):	Smolan, Rick. ; Erwitt, Jennifer.
Publication:	Times Bks. : Against All Odds Productions,; United States
Year:	1998
Description:	223 p. : il col il.
Language:	English
Standard No:	**ISBN:** 0812930312 (Times Bks.) :
Abstract:	"According to the introduction, 'Today there are nearly 15 billion microchips of some kind in use--the equivalent of 2 powerful computers for every man, woman and child on the planet.' Photos illustrate their uses in . . . (things) from laptop computers to automobiles, from telephones to refrigerators." (SLJ).
	SUBJECT(S)
Descriptor:	Microprocessors. Technology -- Social aspects.
Class Descrpt:	**LC:** TK7819; **Dewey:** 303.48
Responsibility:	created by Rick Smolan and Jennifer Erwitt; designed by Tom Walker.
Record Type:	monograph
Accession No:	BBRD99326400

based on factual information, evolve from interpretation of facts. Skilled writers can make you think that their interpretations are facts.

- Does the information appear to be valid and well researched, or is it questionable and unsupported by evidence? Assumptions should be reasonable. Be on the lookout for errors or omissions.

- Is the author's point of view objective and impartial? Is the language free of emotion and bias? Can you identify any biases inherent in the language used by the author?

- Does the work update other sources, substantiate other materials, or add new information? Does it extensively or marginally cover your topic? You should explore enough sources to obtain a variety of viewpoints.

- Is the material primary or secondary? Primary sources are the raw material of the research process. Secondary sources are interpretive or extrapolative and are based on primary or other secondary sources.

- Is the publication organized logically? Are the main points clearly presented? Do you find the text easy to read, or is it stilted or choppy? Is the author repetitive?

- Has the book or article been reviewed elsewhere? Locate critical reviews of books in a reviewing source, such as *Book Review Index* or *Book Review Digest*. Is the book under review considered a valuable contribution to the field? Do the various reviewers agree on the value or attributes of the book?

USING THE LIBRARY—ELECTRONIC SOURCES

Today's college, community, corporate, government, and special libraries are nothing like libraries of even just a few years ago. Libraries now offer a wide variety of electronic sources and services, both within the library and through online access to other sites.

Electronic sources have several advantages over print sources. They can more easily be kept up to date and are searchable using combinations of Boolean operators for searches of keywords, subject, and other fields. (See Figure 5.15.) Electronic sources can be accessed at a computer workstation and printed out wherever you are. They also can easily be saved for future use or reference, can be e-mailed to you or a colleague, and can be reprinted as needed.

Online Catalogs

Most university libraries and many major city libraries now make their holdings available through online catalogs. These catalogs offer far more than just a listing of holdings of books, periodicals, indexes, and so on. Many provide search capabilities and databases as well as access to sophisticated research services. See Figure 5.16a and b for an example of a typical library online catalog.

Online catalogs provide the same information available from card catalogs, with some significant advantages. Online catalogs can be searched by keyword, author, title, catalog, and number, using Boolean search terms (AND, OR, NOT). They can provide full-text access in some cases, and can link to services that provide text via fax or e-mail at little or no charge to you. Online catalogs also can be accessed remotely from your own computer via telephone or the World Wide Web using any graphical browser. Check the "Help" section of

FIGURE 5.15

Boolean Operators

OPERATOR	USE	EXAMPLE	RESULT
AND	Searches for results that contain both requested terms	mining AND uranium	uranium mining, mining uranium, and other results that contain both terms
OR	Searches for results that contain either requested term	mining OR uranium	mining (e.g., coal, silver, gold, uranium) and uranium (e.g., refining, weapons, mining)
NOT	Searches for results that exclude the term	mining NOT uranium	"mining" but not "uranium mining"
ADJ	Searches for adjacent terms in the specific order presented	uranium ADJ mining	"uranium mining" (but not "mining uranium")

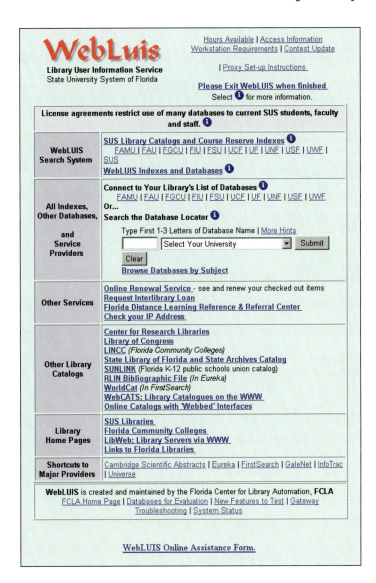

FIGURE 5.16a

Library Online Catalog: Library Services Screen

the online catalog for tips on maximizing the effectiveness of your search. And ask the reference librarian for help in using online catalogs.

Electronic Reference Sources

Many libraries have extensive electronic reference sources available for their patrons, and many of these can be searched through CD-ROMs or online databases.

FIGURE 5.16b

Library Online Catalog: Library Book Information Screen

Title:
    The Chicago manual of style.
Edition:
    14th ed.
Published:
    Chicago : University of Chicago Press, 1993.
Description:
    ix, 921 p. : ill. ; 24 cm.
Notes:
    Includes bibliographical references (p. 861-869) and index.
ISBN:
    0226103897 (cloth : alk. paper)
Subjects, general:
    Printing, practical--United States--Style manuals.
    Authorship--Handbooks, manuals, etc.
    Publishers and publishing--United States--Handbooks, manuals, etc.
Subjects, medical:
    Authorship--handbooks
    Printing--handbooks
    Publishing--handbooks
    Writing--handbooks

Sample of databases that may be available electronically:

America: History and Life

Business Abstracts

Government Printing Office Catalog of Government Publications (GPO)

Criminal Justice Abstracts

MLA International Bibliography

General Science Abstracts

Historical Abstracts

Humanities Abstracts

Mergent (formerly Moody) Company Data

National Trade Data Bank (NTDB)

National Technical Information Service (NTIS)

Oxford English Dictionary

Social Sciences Abstracts

Many databases and reference sources are to be found on the World Wide Web, often linked to the library's Web site or information system. Others can be accessed independently of the library. See Figure 5.17a and b for an example of an online reference source.

FIGURE 5.17a

Onelook Dictionaries: Dictionary Search Screen

FIGURE 5.17b

Onelook Dictionaries: Search Results Screen

Take our Survey. INSIGHT EXPRESS
click this banner to visit our sponsor

Search Results

Jump to: Arts and Humanities, Business, Computer/Internet, Medical, Miscellaneous, Religion, Science, Sports, Technological, General, Slang

General

1. Cambridge International Dictionary of English -includes definition (English), phonic pronunciation (indexed 20.01.2001)
    1. hologram
    To home page of this dictionary(12KB)
2. Comprehensive English to Turkish Dictionary -includes translation (English, Turkish), definition (Turkish) (indexed 03.02.2001)

    1. hologram

    To home page of this dictionary(141B)
3. WordNet Vocabulary Helper (NotreDame) -includes definition (English), synonym (indexed Jul 5 1997)
    1. hologram
    To home page of this dictionary(949B)
4. AllWords.com - English with Multi-Lingual Search -includes translation (English, German, Dutch, French, Italian, Spanish), definition (English), sound pronunciation, synonym, example phrase (indexed 15.01.2001)
    1. hologram
    To home page of this dictionary(28KB)
5. Cambridge Dictionary of American English -includes definition (English), phonic pronunciation, example phrase (indexed 25.02.2001)
    1. hologram
    To home page of this dictionary(12KB)

FIGURE 5.17b

(continued)

6. Dictionary of Difficult Words -includes definition (English) (indexed 03.02.2001)
   1. hologram
   To home page of this dictionary(12KB)
7. Dictionary.com -includes definition (English), antonym, phonic pronunciation (indexed 27.01.2001)
   1. hologram
   To home page of this dictionary(7KB)
8. General English-Spanish -includes translation (English, Spanish) (80KB, indexed 27.01.2001)
   1. hologram
   To home page of this dictionary(9KB)
9. German - English -includes translation (English, German) (indexed 28.01.2001)
   1. hologram
   To home page of this dictionary(740B)
10. Merriam-Webster's WWWebster Dictionary -includes definition (English), illustration, phonic pronunciation, origin, thesaurus (indexed Oct 10 1997)
    1. hologram
    To home page of this dictionary(3KB)
11. The American Heritage® Dictionary of the English Language -includes definition (English), illustration, phonic pronunciation, sound pronunciation, origin, example phrase, reverse lookup (indexed 25.02.2001)
    1. hologram
    To home page of this dictionary(84KB)
12. The Wordsmyth English Dictionary-Thesaurus -includes definition (English), synonym, phonic pronunciation, example phrase (indexed 09.01.2001)
    1. hologram
    To home page of this dictionary(13KB)
13. Ultra Lingua English Dictionary -includes definition (English), synonym, reverse lookup (indexed 25.02.2001)
    1. hologram
    To home page of this dictionary(10KB)
14. CMU Pronouncing -includes phonic pronunciation (indexed 25.02.2001)
    1. HOLOGRAM
    To home page of this dictionary(4KB)
15. Lexical FreeNet (shows word connections) -includes synonym, antonym, phonic pronunciation, rhyme (indexed 09.02.2001)
    1. hologram
    To home page of this dictionary(17KB)

Sample of online reference sources:

Encyclopedia Britannica <http://www.britannica.com/>

OneLook Dictionaries <http://www.onelook.com/>

Best Information on the Net (BIOTN) <http://library.sau.edu/bestinfo/>

Needle in a CyberStack—the InfoFinder <http://members.home.net/albeej/>

CHOOSING THE ETHICAL PATH

When non-authorized users have access to a restricted database, the library is in violation of its agreement with the provider and may lose its contract. When in doubt, ask a librarian.

Commercial Databases

Many other databases can be searched through a library's online catalog or via gateways (Web interfaces to remotely accessible resources). Other electronic resources are available only in the government documents area of a library, such as U.S. Census Databases (various databases for searching detailed demographic social and economic data from the latest census).

Many libraries offer access to invaluable research services such as Ingenta, EBSCOhost, EUREKA, Global Legal Information Network, LEXIS-NEXIS, Dialog, FirstSearch, and WESTLAW. (See Figure 5.18.) These usually are provided to the libraries through subscription, and that fee entitles library patrons to read and use these services. Some databases carry restrictions for off-campus use, and their use is limited to university students, faculty, and staff.

FIGURE 5.18

Research Services

RESEARCH SERVICE	DESCRIPTION/FEATURES
Ingenta (formerly UnCover)	delivers millions of articles from more than 18,000 multidisciplinary journals online. It contains brief descriptive information about more than 8 million articles published since late 1988 and includes current issues of journals. Once you specify your area of interest, the service can e-mail notification of new articles that fit your requirements. You or your library may have to pay an added fee for this service.
EBSCOhost	is a full-text database that enables users to search titles of more than 15,000 journals. It also provides access to newspapers, pamphlets, brochures, and company information.
EUREKA	is a software system that is used to search a variety of databases. The bibliographic file available through EUREKA contains information about more than 30 million titles drawn from books, periodicals, recordings, scores, archival collections, and other kinds of material held in major research institutions.
Global Legal Information Network	is a database of laws, regulations, and other complementary legal sources in a variety of languages. The documents included in the database are contributed by the governments of the member nations from original official texts.
LEXIS-NEXIS	collects and provides legal news and information under the LEXIS trademark and general, business, and trade news under the NEXIS trademark. The database provides access to more than 7,000 newspapers, newsletters, magazines, trade journals, wire services, and broadcast transcripts. The legal part of the database, LEXIS, consists of federal and state case law, statutes, secondary sources such as law reviews, and state legal materials. Many of the documents provide the full text of the original.
Dialog	is one of the major vendors of online databases. It provides access to more than 500 databases. Databases may contain citations, full text, or tabular data. The Knight-Ridder–owned newspapers and many news services articles are available in full-text format.
OCLC's FirstSearch	is a database that is available through a library's information system. It offers many kinds of other databases, including *World Book Encyclopedia,* a full-text academic and professional journal collection, a health reference center, and a religion database. FirstSearch also offers online full text for *General Science Abstracts, Humanities Abstracts*, and *Social Sciences Abstracts*. Databases available through FirstSearch vary from library to library.
WESTLAW	is a service of West Publishing Company and a vast online source of legal and business information accessing more than 10,000 databases that cover a variety of jurisdictions and disciplines, including statutes, codes, federal regulations, public records, insurance materials, securities law information, rules, judicial and administrative decisions, and legal articles and periodicals. News, business, and financial information are also covered.

Using these services effectively is more than a matter of just accessing them. You should be familiar with a few strategies for successful searching before you go online.

Planning an Online Search

- Planning a search takes time at the beginning, but it will save time later. First decide on a search keyword or phrase. Some sources of search terms are words or phrases describing the topic, words or phrases that are used in discussing the topic, and names of people who are likely to be mentioned when discussing the topic.

- Refine your search. If your search doesn't produce the results you want, refine the terms. Your search may produce many pages that aren't of interest to you because the search term has meanings other than the one you intended or can be used in contexts other than the ones you anticipated.

- Consider replacing the search term with a synonym. Unfortunately, the synonym may bring up its own set of irrelevant pages, so you may not want to use this approach often.

- Add another search term (using the AND operator if the search engine supports it or putting the terms in quotation marks if they form a meaningful phrase). The additional word can be another term selected to get articles related to the topic, or it can be a search term for a broader topic that includes your topic.

- Exclude the unwanted articles directly by devising a search to match the articles you don't want and using the NOT operator to exclude them.

- Determine why some searches fail to turn up helpful links. In addition to selecting Web pages you are not interested in, searches can fail by overlooking articles that you are interested in. Examine unwanted pages to learn why a search didn't work as intended. But unfortunately you have no way of knowing if or why your search missed pages you would have wanted.

- Follow other relevant links. If you find one relevant page, you can use it to find other useful pages. The usual way to do this is to go to the relevant page and follow links to other pages. Or you can use the "find related pages" feature provided by some search engines and newer versions of the major browsers.

- If your search engine offers advanced features, use them to control your search in a variety of ways. AltaVista's advanced search capabilities, for example, enable you to control the search by dates, by your own rankings, and by variations of complicated search strings.

Figure 5.19 shows the result of a less successful online search. Figure 5.20 shows the result of a second try.

Home > **Web Pages Search**

| | **Web Pages** | **Products** | **Directories** | **Images** | **Video** | **MP3/Audio** | **News** |
| 710,870 pages found. | | | | | | | |

Search for: Help | Customize Settings | Family Filter is off

`astro`   any language ▼   **Search**

☐ Search within these results   Tip: hotels Paris -"bed and breakfast"   Advanced Search

Related Searches: - astro abby   - +houston +astros   - chevrolet astro
- astro boy   - astro van   - astro world   - astro turf

See reviewed sites in: Chevrolet Astro | Kurt Busiek's Astro City | Man o Astro-man? | Man or Astro-Man? Audio and Video | Scientific Photography Techniques | Smash Mouth, Astro Lounge

Featured Site:
- **PriceQuotes.com: Fill Out New Chevrolet**
request form. Compare local dealer prices.

Computers
uBid.com
Come see what a
$9 Bid buys you!
SONY, HP, COMPAQ

astro - Click here for a list of Internet Keywords related to **astro**.

1. *Astro* **Abby**
Astroabby offers free daily, weekly, monthly horoscopes (astrological forecasts). Message boards, feng shui, free relationship and job advice,...
URL: http://www.astroabby.com/
Translate More pages from this site Related pages

FreeMerchant.com
Build A
Web Site for
Your Business

2. *Astro-***Space Web Hosting!**
MEMBER LOGIN: Member ID: Password: Forgot your password? Enter your email and we'll mail it to you. From the world's Most Popular Associates...
URL: http://www.astro-space.com/link/
Translate More pages from this site Related pages

3. The Munich *Astro* **Archive**
Current events: Some minor meteor showers in February. This project has been started for all people interested in Astronomy and Astrophysics. You do...
URL: http://www.maa.mhn.de/
Translate More pages from this site Related pages

4. Astronomie im Cyberspace - *astro***Info**
astroInfo is a service of the Swiss Astronomical Society. It offers lots of helpful Informations, mostly written in German and English
URL: http://www.astroinfo.org/deutsch.html
Translate More pages from this site Related pages

5. *Astro-***link**
Astro-link. Esplora il cielo con noi. Click here for the light international version. Unisciti al gruppo Seti@mclink.it. Solo qui trovi. L'immagine...
URL: http://www.mclink.it/mclink/astro/astro.htm
Translate More pages from this site Related pages

6. Frequently Asked Questions for sci.*astro* **[Astronomy]**
sci.**astro** is a newsgroup devoted to the discussion of the science of astronomy. Its content ranges from the Earth to the farthest reaches of the...
URL: http://sciastro.astronomy.net/
Translate More pages from this site Related pages

7. *Astro* **Star Online Shop**
Horoskope - Astrologie - AstroStar - Erstellen Sie Ihr Horoskop selbst - Horoskope für Laien und Profis. Home. Service. Registrierung. Warenkorb....
URL: http://www.astrostar.de/
Translate More pages from this site Related pages

8. The *Astro-***List Home Page**
Welcome to the **Astro**-List Home Page. About The **Astro**-List. (the discussion list) About **Astro**-Update. (an announce-only list) *** The **Astro**-List FAQ...
URL: http://www.grantbob.com/moam/astro.html
Translate More pages from this site Related pages

9. CyberAstro: Vedic Astrology for the new Millennium
Free predictions & personalized horoscopes using ancient Vedic principles. Unique & precise predictions making ancient principles applicable for...
URL: http://www.cyberastro.com/
Translate More pages from this site Related pages

10. Welcome To *ASTRO*
Contact **ASTRO** | Programme Search | Programme Listings | Sitemap | Subscribe Now. Privacy Policy | Terms & Conditions.
URL: http://www.astro.com.my/
Translate More pages from this site Related pages

FIGURE 5.19

Online Search—First Try

The search term ("astro") is too general so the results are too numerous. (See "pages found," upper left.)

FIGURE 5.20

Online Search—Second Try

The search term is specific enough that a manageable number of citations are returned. (See "pages found," upper left.)

Home

| 108 pages found. | Advanced Web Pages | Advanced Images | Advanced MP3/Audio |

Boolean query: Help | Customize S

astro and (ultraviolet near observatory) and domain:gov

Sort by: [Search]

Show me: Language: [any language ▾]

From: [   ] To: [   ] dd/mm/yy One result per Web site ☐

Drive traffic to your site. Submit a Site

1. No Title
Astro-2 Public Affairs Status Report #1 6:00 a.m. CST (0/5:22 MET), March 2, 1995 Spacelab Mission Operations Control Marshall Space Flight Center...
URL: science.ksc.nasa.gov/shuttle/missions/st...-67-poco-01.txt
Translate Related pages

2. Spacelink - Astro Observatory
Learn about the Shuttle-borne Ultraviolet Observatory called Astro. This facility was used by many scientists to investigate a variety of...
URL: spacelink.msfc.nasa.gov/NASA.Projects/Sp...index-text.html
Translate Related pages

3. Spacelink - Flight 068 STS-67
The STS-67 mission described in this area was the second flight for astro telescopes (ASTRO-2)that will give astronomers a view of the universe...
URL: spacelink.msfc.nasa.gov/NASA.Projects/Hu...index-text.html
Translate Related pages

4. Astrophysics Missions
Astrophysics Missions. NASA Headquarters keeps on-line short descriptions of Astrophysics Missions currently operating, missions under development...
URL: www.hq.nasa.gov/office/astrophysics/asph-miss.html
Translate Related pages

5. Dr. Ben Dorman
Archive Interfaces ... Argus. Astrobrowse. Browse. SkyView. Resources/Education ... Address. APOD: Pict of the Day. Ask an Astronomer. Bibliography....
URL: astroe.gsfc.nasa.gov/docs/bios/dorman.html
Translate Related pages

6. Mission Communication Services
SCIENCE, AERONAUTICS, AND TECHNOLOGY FISCAL YEAR 1996 ESTIMATES BUDGET SUMMARY OFFICE OF SPACE COMMUNICATIONS MISSION COMMUNICATION SERVICES SUMMARY...
URL: www.hq.nasa.gov/office/budget/fy96/sat_5.html
Translate Related pages

7. Resource Center
Resource Center. Description. The resource center will provide informationon aeronautics, astronomy, weather and remote sensing with the use of...
URL: www.grc.nasa.gov/WWW/MAEL/resource.html
Translate Related pages

8. JSC Digital Image Collection - S89-41412
JSC Digital Image Collection Press Release Images. NASA Photo ID: S89-41412 File Name: 10063886.jpg Film Type: 4x5 Date Taken: 08/10/89 Title: STS-35...
URL: images.jsc.nasa.gov/images/pao/STS35/10063886.htm
Translate Related pages

9. Astro-2 Flight Day 8 Status Reports
Flight Day 8 Status. ASTRO-2. Orbiter Status Mission Control Center Johnson Space Center Houston, Tx. STS-67 Status Report #14 Thursday, March 9,...
URL: astro-2.msfc.nasa.gov/Shuttle/astro2/log/fd8.html
Translate Related pages

10. NASA Video Catalog 1995
19 SPACECRAFT INSTRUMENTATION. N94-18956* National Aeronautics and Space Administration. Marshall Space Flight Center, Huntsville, AL. ASTRO-1 TO...
URL: www.sti.nasa.gov/videocat/CAT19.htm
Translate Related pages

Result Pages: **1** 2 3 4 5 6 7 8 9 10 11 [Next >>]

Successful Online Searching

- Be aware of the different kinds of databases. Bibliographic databases: author, title, and source of full texts that are located elsewhere. Numeric databases: tables of statistical data. Directory or dictionary databases: factual information about products, institutions, and subjects. Full-text databases: complete text of magazine articles, newswire articles, encyclopedia entries, and other items.

- Familiarize yourself with other key differences in databases. Databases vary in subject content (business, medical, technical), amount of data (brief citation, abstract, full text), manner of data presentation (text, image, table), technical level (general interest, research reports, scientific data), and currency or recency (from newswires updated hourly to encyclopedias updated annually).

- Select the appropriate database(s) on the basis of your research needs. How many sources are collected? How are they selected? Do they cover the relevant journals for your topic? How many results do you need? How technical should they be? How current?

- Be prepared to conduct sequential searches. You may think of new ways to ask your question based on the results of your initial searches.

- Refine the key concepts in your topic. Select words and phrases that express each concept and are appropriate for the database(s) chosen.

- Vary your strategy to match the database type. For example, in partial databases (citations, abstracts) think of all possible search terms. In full-text databases, use proximity connectors (*near, adjacent to*) to link terms closely.

- Use database and software features: truncation (abbreviated search term endings); logical (*and, or, not*) and proximity (*near, same, within*) connectors; and controlled vocabulary (found in specialized thesauri and headings lists such as the Library of Congress Subject Headings) as keywords to create effective search statements.

- Use online help instructions for each database to help fashion your search most efficiently for the particular databases you are using.

- Ask a reference librarian to help design a search strategy and to select appropriate databases and other resources.

See Figure 5.21a–d for examples of online databases.

The Internet and the Web

One simple description of the Internet is "everyone's computer hooked up to everyone else's computer." Thus, if you have an Internet connection for

FIGURE 5.21a
Online Databases: Bibliographic Database

Title:	Laser beam shaping : theory and techniques / edited by Fred M. Dickey, Scott C. Holswade.
Published:	New York : Marcel Dekker, c2000.
Physical Details:	xi, 428 p. : ill. ; 24 cm.
Version:	Blackwell North America, enhanced CIP records - XBCP
Series:	Optical engineering ; 70.
Other Authors:	Dickey, Fred M., 1941- Holswade, Scott C., 1963-
Subjects:	Laser beams. Beam optics.
Notes:	Includes bibliographical references and index.
LC Call Number:	TA1677 .L3622 2000
DDC:	621.36/6
LCCN:	00-31598
ISBN:	0-8247-0398-7 (alk. paper)
Record ID:	XBCP0031598-B

your computer at home, at a university, or at work, you have access to any other computer hooked up to the Internet and any other library in the world that has an Internet connection. Of course, some of the libraries are more accessible than others, and for some you have to provide appropriate identification as an authorized user to access them.

Most library catalogs are available on the World Wide Web, enabling you to access the library catalog from your own computer as if your computer were a terminal in the library. There are several main places to start when you want to access a particular library and you do not know its URL (Uniform Resource Locator) Web address. One is the master index of libraries maintained at Yale and other sites. The Yale catalog of libraries <http://www.library.yale.edu/pubstation/libcats.html> is a good place to start when you know which library you want to find but don't know how to find it. Another is <http://www.libdex.com/>. And for a look at a really comprehensive library catalog, check out the Library of Congress <http://lcweb.loc.gov/>.

Many of the electronic sources available in your local university or community library are the same sources that you can now access via the Internet. Web pages provided by many libraries can link to Internet reference sources including biographies, citation guides, city directories, dictionaries, handbooks, maps, news distributors, quotations, science data, statistics and demographics, zip-code guides, and general information.

FIGURE 5.21b

Online Databases:
Numeric/Statistical
Database

No. 926. Cable and Pay TV—Revenue and Expenses: 1990 to 1998

[In millions of dollars (22,165 represents $22,165,000,000), except percent. Based on a sample of taxable employer firms with one or more establishments that are primarily engaged in the dissemination of visual and textual television programs on a subscription or fee basis. For SIC 4841. Based on the 1987 Standard Industrial Classification code; see text, Section 17, Business]

Item	Total					Percent distribution		
	1990	1995	1996	1997	1998	1990	1995	1998
Total and other pay TV revenue	22,165	32,541	37,027	41,499	46,945	100.0	100.0	100.0
Advertising	1,882	4,466	5,007	5,627	6,643	8.5	13.7	14.2
Program revenue	3,816	4,843	5,438	6,313	7,473	17.2	14.9	15.9
Basic service	10,933	16,310	18,621	21,134	24,255	49.3	50.1	51.7
Pay-per-view and other premium service	4,351	5,068	5,696	5,906	5,994	19.6	15.6	12.8
Installation fees	302	445	508	555	619	1.4	1.4	1.3
Other cable and pay TV revenue.	881	1,409	1,757	1,964	1,960	4.0	4.3	4.2
Total operating expenses	19,354	26,428	30,471	35,060	41,606	100.0	100.0	100.0
Annual payroll	2,816	4,519	5,061	6,027	7,337	14.5	17.1	17.6
Employer contributions to Social Security								
and other supplemental benefits	588	1,000	1,150	1,293	1,581	3.0	3.8	3.8
Program and production costs [1]	5,926	9,442	11,239	12,839	14,920	30.6	35.7	35.9
Depreciation	3,611	4,433	4,990	6,117	7,246	18.7	16.8	17.4
Lease and rental payments	513	682	764	836	998	2.7	2.6	2.4
Purchased repairs	343	555	615	648	740	1.8	2.1	1.8
Insurance	110	175	190	213	236	0.6	0.7	0.6
Telephone, other purchased communications . .	133	283	321	350	389	0.7	1.1	0.9
Purchased utilities	188	215	241	265	318	1.0	0.8	0.8
Purchased advertising.	467	891	1,062	1,153	1,402	2.4	3.4	3.4
Taxes.	310	429	436	470	499	1.6	1.6	1.2
Other operating expenses	4,349	3,804	4,402	4,849	5,941	22.5	14.4	14.3

[1] Includes costs from basic cable, pay-per-view, premium services, in-house programs, and other program and production costs.

Source: U.S. Census Bureau, *Annual Survey of Communication Services.*

FIGURE 5.21c

Online Databases:
Directory Database

Information Technology Systems Inc

DB Dun & Bradstreet

Address:	95 Wells Ave Newton, MA 02459-3299
County:	MIDDLESEX
Country:	United States
Telephone:	(617) 964-6250
Line of Business:	Web Development Service Package Software Development Internet Service Provider and An Adv Serv For Casino Ind On The Web
Employee Range:	20-49
Sales Range:	$5,000,000-9,999,999
D-U-N-S ® Number:	62-575-2969

Report: D&B Business and Credit Report

Dun & Bradstreet Business and Credit Reports help you establish credit terms, leverage your customer and supplier relationships, and better manage the risk of doing business. Please click the button below to purchase a D&B report. View report samples and descriptions.

FIGURE 5.21d

**Online Databases:
Full-Text Database**

Result 1 of 596 ▶ | Refine Search | Result List | Find More | Print/Email/Save | [Go To Full Text] [Tips]

Title: Macrodoctor, come meet the nanodoctors.

Subject(s): NANOTECHNOLOGY; MEDICINE -- Research; ROBOTICS; THERAPEUTICS

Source: Lancet, 03/10/2001, Vol. 357 Issue 9258, p778, 1p, 1c

Author(s): Morris, Kelly

Abstract: Focuses on research into the creation of nanorobots that will perform diagnostic and treatment actions within the body. Creation of a virus-sized biomolecular motor fueled by ATP; Development of branched DNA molecules that can self-assemble into geometrical objects and nanodevices; Research into dendrimer structures; Obstacles to such devices, including navigation and recognition; Information on PEBBLEs, or probes encapsulated by biological localised embedding; Question as to the safety of such devices and how soon they might be available.

AN: 4170287

ISSN: 0099-5355

Note: We subscribe to this magazine.

Database: Academic Search Elite

Print: ☐ Click here to mark for print.

Text Available: 📄 Full Page Image

_____

[Go To Citation]

Select Language ▼ | Translate

Section: Feature

MACRODOCTOR, COME MEET THE NANODOCTORS

In the 1966 film Fantastic Voyage, a mini-submarine of medics travels from vein to brain to laser a clot. That scenario remains science fiction. But if the emerging field of nanomedicine fulfils its early promise, such voyages could become science fact. Robert Freitas (Zyvex, Richardson, TX, USA) envisages billions of minute, self-assembling, computerised, bioelectromechanical systems--"nanobots"--swarming to the injury site, sensing, diagnosing, then activating therapeutic systems and even cellular repair. The microbe-sized robot would then transmit collected data to the "macrodoctor". In Nanomedicine (www.nanomedicine.com), Freitas presents nanobots that may one day be made with molecular nanotechnology.

Sheer speculation? Not quite. On Nov 24, 2000, Carlo Montemagno's team at Cornell University (Ithaca, NY, USA) reported a creation that suddenly brought the nanobot nearer to the clinic. The team encouraged tiny nickel nanopropellors to link with molecules of the enzyme F1-adenosine triphosphatase (ATPase) mounted on pedestals. The g subunit of this protein can rotate in response to ATP synthesis/hydrolysis with almost 100% efficiency. When the group added ATP, the propellors that remained attached spun at eight revolutions a second, a virus-sized biomolecular motor (Science 2000; 290: 1555-58). The team is now investigating ways to turn light energy into ATP, generating recyclable fuel that would render such devices autonomous.

DNA is another molecule with exploitable nanoscale properties. Nadrian Seeman's team at New York University (NY, USA) has developed branched DNA molecules with "sticky ends" that can self-assemble into geometrical objects and nanodevices. Via a chemically induced conformational change of DNA, current devices can adopt two states. Once devices linked in an array can be targeted individually, many more states will be possible, explains Seeman, who expects to generate complex states within 3-5 years.

Other biocompatible molecules are good candidates for nanobot building blocks. University of Michigan researchers (UM, Ann Arbor, MI, USA), led by James Baker, were recently granted one of the National Cancer Institute's Unconventional Innovations Program (UIP) awards to study tree-like polymers called dendrimers. Research so far is on cultured cancer cells, but the hope is that dendrimer structures could deliver gene therapy or intracranial implants without eliciting an immune response.

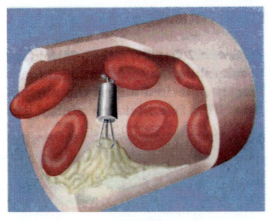

Mission possible?

These earliest nanostructures for in-vivo use could be in prototype within a decade, says Tejal Desai (University of Illinois, Chicago, IL, USA). With Mauro Ferrari (Ohio University, OH), she has developed silicon-based microcapsules with nanopores to deliver cells, drugs, proteins, peptides, and nucleic acids. "These can be implanted to release cell-secreted hormones or help to provide needed growth factors or nutrients to repair damaged tissue." They have shown that encapsulation improves insulin secretion from neonatal rat pancreatic islet cell xenografts. This is far from Freitas' nanobots, but, says Desai, "one can think about similar type capsules being able to travel through the bloodstream and release their contents at desired locations based on binding to cell-specific receptors".

Back in the future, navigation is not easy. In Fantastic Voyage, doctors viewed the journey from inside and out, and the vision of Raoul Kopelman (UM) sounds like the sequel. "The principle is that the nanosubs--called dynamic nanoplatforms--find cancer cells and adhere to them with the help of molecular recognition elements that are located on their external surface." Until the hypothesised autonomous motors and onboard nanoelectronic guidance systems are available, one possibility is to use external magnetic fields. Recognition is the next step, but when Kopelman began developing fibre-optic sensors, he realised that a different technology was needed to reduce interference with cells.

Along came PEBBLEs--probes encapsulated by biological localised embedding-- nanospheres 20-200 nm wide, delivered into cells with 99% viability, via liposomes, a gene gun, or even macrophage ingestion. There, an individual PEBBLE can measure pH, oxygen, electrolytes, nitric oxide, or early changes of apoptosis. Currently, the team uses fluorescence to read their intracellular analysis.

The future is more difficult to read, says co-worker Eric Monson. So far, the team has also received a UIP award to develop nanoplatforms with added features: magnetic contrast particles to enhance magnetic-resonance imaging, luminescent bodies to assist optical imaging, and specialised photosensitisers. When lit by a laser, the latter would produce reactive oxygen species to kill neighbouring cancer cells. This means, says Kopelman, a supply of "killer radicals" produced from ever-available water and oxygen.

Swarming lethal nanobots do not sound comfortable. But Kopelman reassures that these nanoplatforms are lethal only under laser illumination, which would be controlled by a macrodoctor. Since safety requirements will be built into systems, Freitas believes that adverse effects of nanostructures are likely to be as mundane as "nanopyrexia", where components act as unexpected pyrogens. Indeed, the Foresight Institute has already drafted safety guidelines (http://www.foresight.org/guidelines/).

The big question is "how long?". Zyvex's planned molecular assembler will be 10 years at least, and the Star Trek "Borg nanoprobe" scenario seems decades away. The first question, says Seeman, "is whether we want to make it a reality. What problems does nanorobotics solve, and is this the best solution to those problems?" Freitas points to several potential advantages, including speed, strength, and reliability: "An injection of a large number of nanorobots could completely clear a stroke clot in a time that is in the order of one blood circulation time". Such treatment will need to prove itself superior to available therapy, such as thrombolysis. For cancer therapy, Martin Philbert (UM) highlights situations in which tumours are deep-seated, otherwise inoperable, and/or below the resolution of conventional imaging techniques. But, the beauty of nanomedicine is that systems will be specifically designed then self-built, molecule by molecule, for any function, at any level down to the atom. Perhaps this is why the forward-thinking chair of Foresight, Eric Drexler, predicts that nanomedicine will dominate medical technology research for at least half this century.

~~~~~~~

By Kelly Morris CS, Queen Victoria Hospital, East Grinstead, West Sussex, UK; Sanjay Varma, FRCS, Queen Victoria Hospital, East Grinstead, West Sussex, UK and Caroline Mackie Ogilvie, Dphil, Cytogenetics Department, Division of Medical and Molecular Genetics, Guy's and St Thomas' Hospital Trust, London SE1 9RT, UK , Brisbane, Queensland, Australia; Jeff Hall, PhD, PPGx Inc, La Jolla, California, USA; Masataka Kudo, PhD, Division of Reproductive Biology, Department of Gynecology and Obstetrics, Stanford University Medical Center, Stanford, California, USA; Nicholas G Martin, PhD, Genetic Epidemiology Unit, Queensland Institute of Medical Research and Joint Genetics Program, University of Queensland, Brisbane, Queensland, Australia and Aaron J Hsueh, PhD, Division of Reproductive Biology, Department of Gynecology and Obstetrics, Stanford University Medical Center, Stanford, California, USA ney

Copyright of **Lancet** is the property of Lancet and its content may not be copied or emailed to multiple sites or posted to a listserv without the copyright holder's express written permission. However, users may print, download, or email articles for individual use.
Source: Lancet, 03/10/2001, Vol. 357 Issue 9258, p778, 1p, 1c.
Item Number: 4170287

◄ Result 1 of 596 ► | Refine Search | Result List | Find More | Print/Email/Save | [Go To Full Text] [Tips]

FIGURE 5.21d
(continued)

An incredibly vast range of resources is at your fingertips, and knowing the best ways to find and access all of the available information databases is a formidable task. Of course, just finding information is not enough; you also need to know how to evaluate what you have found. As with print sources and other media, you need to gauge the authority, accuracy, honesty, and completeness of Internet sources. See the "Evaluating Online Sources" section later in this chapter for a discussion of evaluation strategies and management strategies concerning information you find in the course of your research.

Older Programs

With the increasing volume and breadth of information available on the World Wide Web, older methods of Internet research are going the way of the rotary-dial telephone. Just as the rotary-dial telephone can still place a call for you, these other programs, such as gopher, still exist and can provide useful information. In fact, some information available online can be accessed most directly using these older methods. But entering numeric codes to view nested menus of information is a tedious process when you are used to clicking on hyperlinks to view a wide variety of text and multimedia content.

Gopher is a type of Internet search program, providing a menu-driven search function to find information. A selection of menu options leads to other menus and perhaps even other menus, until you finally reach the information you are seeking.

Gopher on the Telephone

If you think Gopher sounds familiar, you are right. Gopher searching may remind you of some telephone calls you have made recently. More and more often, when you try to reach someone at a business you first must negotiate a seemingly endless series of menu choices until finally you are either disconnected, lost in the menu equivalent of a dead end, or—if you are fortunate—transferred at last to the department or person you are seeking.

Search Engines

With the rapidly growing number of sites on the Internet, especially Web sites, it can be very difficult to locate what you are looking for. Fortunately, many powerful and flexible search engines are available to help you locate specific information resources. Search engines are computer programs that enable you to type in a search word or phrase, which the program uses to search the Internet for documents (and, depending on the search engine, graphics and audio files) that contain that term.

To use a search engine, you enter keywords, which the search engine software uses to hunt through its database to locate Internet references. As language-processing algorithms become more sophisticated, search engines become more and more user friendly. In many search engines, you can frame your search in the form of phrases or even sentences, and the program will "parse" (interpret) your question and determine—often very accurately—what you are requesting. These algorithms are not perfect, but they are improving every day. A summary of the files containing the keywords or concepts is presented in a list of URLs (Uniform Resource Locators—addresses on the World Wide Web) that link to Internet sites. Search engines are a public service offered by numerous companies, and they frequently display paid advertisements to cover their costs. (See Figure 5.22.)

FIGURE 5.22

Major Search Engines

SEARCH ENGINE	DESCRIPTION/FEATURES
AltaVista http://www.altavista.com/	Conducts full-text search, displays pages in multiple source languages.
AOL Search http://search.aol.com/	Uses Open Directory Project and thousands of additional sites.
Ask Jeeves http://www.ask.com/	Performs natural-language search.
CNET Search.com http://www.search.com/	Sends search query to several search engines at one time and integrates the results into one list.
Direct Hit http://www.directhit.com/	Organizes search results according to their relevancy to users who were looking for similar information.
Excite http://www.excite.com/	Analyzes search index; reviews the information content of the Web pages, their meta-tags, referring anchor text, and link popularity.
FAST Search http://www.alltheweb.com/	Searches large index of sites for fast retrieval of information.
Google http://www.google.com/	Performs targeted searches by treating multi-word searches as Boolean AND searches.
GoTo http://www.goto.com/	Allows advertisers to bid for placement in search results on keywords that are relevant to their Web sites.
HotBot http://hotbot.lycos.com/	Allows full-text searches that can be modified or refined.
IWon http://www.iwon.com/	Combines search engine with daily sweepstakes.
Looksmart http://www.looksmart.com/	Provides category searches, keyword searches, and chat-based searches.
Lycos http://www.lycos.com/	Provides results from indexed directory, most popular sites first; also provides results from Open Directory search.
MetaCrawler http://www.metacrawler.com/	Queries many search engines, retrieving results across the Internet; organizes them in a uniform format, ranked by relevance.

(continued)

FIGURE 5.22

(continued)

SEARCH ENGINE	DESCRIPTION/FEATURES
MSN Search http://search.msn.com/	Provides directory of Web sites, with secondary results from Inktomi, RealNames, and Direct Hit.
NBCi http://www.nbci.com/	Uses directory of Web sites, organized topically into categories and organized hierarchically (general topics to more specific topics); categories also available alphabetically.
Netscape Search http://search.netscape.com/	Provides results in several categories: partner search results, official Web sites, Netcenter pages, Web site categories, reviewed Web sites, and sometimes Google.
Northern Light http://www.northernlight.com/	Searches Web and non-Web sites; provides sorted results.
Open Directory http://dmoz.org/	Provides sites indexed by categories managed by volunteer editors.
Prime Search http://www.primecomputing.com/search.htm	Submits search to many search engines and presents results for each.
Raging Search http://ragingsearch.altavista.com/	Uses full-text indexing, evaluated by text relevance and link analysis.
RealNames http://web.realnames.com/	Provides company Web sites through name searches; allows browsing on preregistered keywords.
Yahoo http://www.yahoo.com/	Evaluates sites in human-compiled categories.
W3 Search Engines http://cuiwww.unige.ch/meta-index.html	Provides extensive lists of search engines.
WebFerret http://www.ferretsoft.com/	Searches through many engines and eliminates duplicate responses.
WebTop http://www.webtop.com/	Uses "Information Zones" to aid searches.

Major Search Engines

Generally, each search engine has unique characteristics. Each uses slightly different methods to collect, index, search, and display the information it finds. Some categorize sites by general topic, some specialize in names or titles, and still others are organized by qualities or characteristics. It is valuable to read the help sections that accompany the different search engines. The trick is to find a search engine that works best for the kinds of searches you do and learn how to compose efficient searches.

If you don't find what you're looking for on one search engine, try the same search on a different search engine. Some programs, such as WebFerret <http://www.ferretsoft.com/> and Ask Jeeves <http://www.ask.com>, enable you to have several search engines work for you at the same time. See Figure 5.23a and b for examples of search engine screens.

Meta Search Engines

The meta search engines, which combine searches of a number of the individual engines, have distinct limitations. They generally use the most basic searches of each of the major engines and do not handle complex search constructs well. If you are looking for a one-of-a-kind item that can be uniquely defined with a few choice words, they may serve well. If you are looking for the best of many items, they are not likely to be appropriate. However, they are gaining the ability to use the more sophisticated search modes of each platform.

Meta search engines don't actually do any searching; they take a query, submit it to various search engines, and present the results. Their disadvantages include that submitting to multiple search engines is likely to be a waste of resources. There are enough pages out on the Web that a single search engine will

FIGURE 5.23a

Search Engine Screens: Advanced Google Search

FIGURE 5.23b

Search Engine Screens: Results of Search

usually produce a large number of results. Additionally, if you really do need to search every possible page, you probably have to use queries that contain features (for example, phrases) that many search engines don't support. Look for meta searchers at <http://searchenginewatch.internet.com/links/Metacrawlers/>.

Evaluating and Using Search Engines

Although many people have a favorite search engine, there is no best search engine. Some are simply more useful than others for helping you find the kind of information you need. Spend the necessary time carefully reading the help screens for the various search engines and doing test searches with them. Call up a Web search on *search engine reviews* and compare search-engine features.

Search Engine Reviews

Search Engine Watch <http://searchenginewatch.com/resources/reviews.html>

ZDNet Search IQ <http://www.searchiq.com/>

Consumer Search <http://www.consumersearch.com/>

The following criteria will help you decide which search engine to use.

Evaluating Search Engines

- Know what you are looking for. For each type of information there will be a search engine that will be more helpful than others, although there is quite a bit of overlap. A subject list such as Yahoo, rather than a search engine, may be what you really need.

- Find out what part of the Internet the search engine accesses and how it performs its searches. You can usually learn about these abilities by reading the search engine's help file. Sometimes you will have to consult reviews of various search engines to see what each search engine can do.

- Evaluate the quality of the search engine by determining how you can search it. Can you perform only simple keyword searches, or can you search in more advanced modes? Can you revise and edit a completed search using the search engine, or must you retype the search each time?

- Find out how the search results are ranked and displayed. In most cases the ranking is based on the number of times your search words appear in the document, how close your search terms are to each other within the document, how close your terms are to the top of the document, or a combination of all three.

- Determine whether the search finds truly relevant information. Try some "typical" searches at a variety of search engines. Develop a few sample searches around your interests, and test them with a few search engines. See which search engines seem to find the information that you are looking for, and use them often.

- Be prepared to repeat your search with other search engines, refine your search with different, related terms, or both. Don't settle for the first links your search engine turns up. Some search engines "sell" prime spots on results lists. In other cases, changing your search terms will bring up different results. Be persistent.

Search Indexes or Catalogs

One major difference between a search engine and a general index (also called a directory or catalog) is that an index will not list your URL if you do not register it with that particular service. Another major difference is that indexes do not use the software programs (for example, spiders, robots, and scooters) that search engines use to find what is available on the Web. Indexes usually are subdivided into categories, and you have to submit your URL under the most appropriate heading.

Basic Terms

Spiders, Robots, and Scooters: Software that looks for information based on programmed criteria and gathers and indexes lists of Web sites for search engines.

Most indexes organize their listings into subject search trees. At the top of the search tree, you select a general topic, which takes you to a list of subtopics. You then select the appropriate subtopic. Repeat until you reach a list of sites for the topic you are interested in. Subject trees are easy to use and give good results if the topic you are interested in happens to appear in the subject tree.

Yahoo <http://www.yahoo.com> is the biggest of the directories organized by subject matter, and it is probably the best. It is very useful for finding good collections of resources for a topic. It has an advanced search mode, too. Yahoo is like an Internet yellow pages. The Web sites are provided by people who have found an interesting or useful site and have completed a form suggesting where the link should be placed in the Yahoo directory. You can search by browsing this hierarchical directory or by entering names or keywords. The directory and classification system are both very good, and Yahoo is a good place to start for almost any kind of Internet or Web search. (See Figure 5.24a and b.)

Weaknesses of the Internet for Research

Although information on the Internet is increasing at a phenomenal rate, be aware that some kinds of information are not yet available. Such information includes many kinds of historical information before 1990, information about many small companies (even though many companies are on the Web, many are not), many kinds of dictionaries or business handbooks for specific industries, and so on.

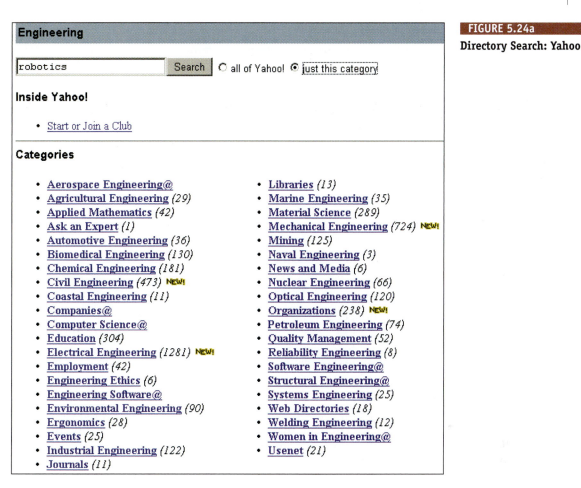

FIGURE 5.24a
Directory Search: Yahoo

Also, the Internet is nothing like a library when it comes to authenticating information. Information is not stable on the Internet; it can appear and disappear from one moment to the next. Even if the URL doesn't change—and it often does—documents can be pulled or changed without leaving a trace of what was formerly there. And although browser companies will tell you otherwise, a determined hacker can break into an Internet location and change the information, so even supposedly reliable sites should be reviewed carefully.

Evaluating Online Sources

In the case of Internet files and documents, some of the questions for evaluating print sources cannot be easily answered, but the print guidelines should help you approach information with some measure of critical analysis.

FIGURE 5.24b
Directory Search Results

Yahoo! Site Matches (1 - 13 of 230)

Science > Engineering > Mechanical Engineering > **Robotics** > Competitions
- BattleBots - the ultimate competition of extreme robotic sports, utilizing destructive weapons such as saws, hammers, and spikes.

Science > Engineering > Mechanical Engineering > **Robotics** > Institutes > Carnegie Mellon University@
- **Robotics** Institute

Science > Engineering > Mechanical Engineering > **Robotics** > Companies@
- Sarcos - designing and building robotic systems, medical devices, and micro-systems for practical applications.
- ActivMedia's Professional Mobile **Robotics** - moderately priced, sophisticated mobile robots for education, research and applications.
- GreyPilgrim - developers of EMMA, a flexible robotic arm. Applications include nuclear storage tank waste retrieval, telepresence camera deployment, and fire suppression monitors.

Science > Engineering > Electrical Engineering > Organizations > Professional > Institute of Electrical and Electronics Engineers (IEEE) > IEEE **Robotics** & Automation Society
- IEEE **Robotics** & Automation Society

Science > Engineering > Mechanical Engineering > **Robotics** > Institutes
- Stanford **Robotics** Laboratory
- JPL **Robotics** - rover and telerobotics program overview, robotic vehicles, NASA research tasks.
- NASA Ames Research Center - Intelligent Mechanisms Group - responsible for developing planetary and space-based robotic systems.
- Oak Ridge National Laboratory - **Robotics** and Process Systems Division - developing robotic and telerobotic solutions to real-world problems in environmental remediation, waste management, and military applications.
- Cambridge University Speech Vision **Robotics** Group
- Brown University **Robotics** Group

Science > Engineering > Mechanical Engineering > **Robotics** > Institutes > University of Southern California@
- **Robotics** Research Lab - autonomous/mobile **robotics**, robot colonies, neural networks, machine learning, motor control, assembly planning, robot hands, robot helicopters.

It is important that you apply critical standards to the information you find on the Internet. Keep in mind that the Internet is a network of networks that have widely different goals and origins. No central authority governs the information you find on the Internet. You need to consider what you want from your Internet research. Are you looking for facts, opinions (anyone's or an expert's opinion), strong arguments, statistics, eyewitness reports? Are you trying to find new ideas, more support for a position? When you have established what you are looking for, then you can screen your Internet sources by testing them against your research goal.

Evaluating Internet Sources

● Bear in mind that many sources published on the Internet have not been reviewed by a refereeing process, by peers or other authority, by an editor, or by libraries. Anyone can put up a Web site whether the information is reliable or not.

● Evaluate the author's reliability and credibility. Who is the author? What are the author's occupation, position, education, and experience? What are the author's credentials? How well has the author documented the sources of the information presented?

(continued)

- Try to ascertain the material's accuracy. Are the facts correct? How does this information compare with other sources in the field?

- Identify the author's perspective. Does the author have a bias or express a particular point of view? Is the author affiliated with particular organizations, institutions, associations? Is the author's perspective directed toward a specific audience? Is it culturally diverse or narrowly focused?

- Evaluate the author's purpose. For what audience is the author writing? Is this reflected in the writing style, vocabulary, and tone? Does the material inform? Explain? Persuade? What conclusions are drawn? Is there sufficient evidence for those conclusions?

- Look for evidence of quality control. Is the information presented on an organizational Web site or a home page? If the site is an online journal, is it peer reviewed? Is the information taken from authoritative books and journal articles?

- Critically view the quality of the content. What kind of information is it? Is it fact or opinion? Is there any documentation? Bibliography? Footnotes? Credits? Quotations? Are any major findings presented? How does the information compare to other related sources?

- Evaluate the quality of the format. Can you clearly identify what type of information it is? Is it a Web home page? Is it a newsgroup posting? Is it a file or downloadable software? Is it a government report? Is it an advertisement?

- Check the material for completeness. Does it have the features you need: graphs, charts, illustrations, glossaries, maps?

- Analyze the content for balance, objectivity, bias, and accuracy. What is the intended purpose of the information? Why is the information being offered? What is the perspective of the publication? Is the information presented accurately and objectively? How can you tell? What clues are present to help you judge?

- Check for timeliness. When was the information produced? Is it too old or too new for the needs of your research?

- Ascertain originality. Is it primary information or secondary information? Is the originality of the information important for your research?

- Review accessibility. How accessible is the information? How easy is it to find and use? How much time does it take to access the resource? How stable is the information resource or its provider? Will it be available if you need it later? Be aware that some Internet information is transitory.

- Consider cost. Is the information free, or is there a fee? It can be beneficial to pay for information if, for example, paying for it saves you time, you will make or save money by having the information, or it is the only known source of the information.

- Look for documentation. Are any sources provided for the information at the site? What kind of support is given for the information? How does the author know this information?

From the workplace

Jean Weber

Consultant and Independent Contractor:
Scientific and Technical Writer and Editor
Airlie Beach, Queensland, Australia

Jean has found over the course of her career that part of her work as a consultant involves educating her clients about how best to benefit from her expertise. Not all clients are receptive to that information, but when they are, they find they have received more value from her input than they anticipated.

I have a bachelor's degree in botany and a master's in plant ecology, but I work in neither of those fields right now. I've changed jobs several times since earning my degrees: first from research into science editing, then into technical writing and editing. I also moved several times, including from the United States to Australia and then within Australia, partly to improve my prospects for promotion but also because I like variety and learning new things.

After more than 20 years as an employee, in 1988 I began working as a contractor and later as a consultant. Most of those jobs have been fairly short (by my preference). At this time I am officially "retired," but I continue to write and edit. I find myself very inter-

ested in Web-based communication and am pursuing that interest. Now I mainly write Web pages and the occasional grant application, and edit business planning documents.

Remaining in the Loop

Working as a consultant has taught me something about information flow. When I work for clients that don't have well-defined processes in place to assure that I am "in the loop" for needed data, I make sure my contract states my dependencies, including access to the necessary people. I make it quite clear to the relevant managers that I cannot do my job without certain inputs and explain that they are wasting their money if I don't get the access and information I need. Usually the situation improves, but if it doesn't, I bombard the manager or other relevant people with my best efforts and ask for comments and corrections. I've had several managers thank me profusely for nagging them so effectively.

In extreme cases, when nothing I do improves the situation, I tell them they are in breach of contract

With so much Internet information available, it is easy to suffer from information anxiety or information glut. Use the evaluation criteria just listed to help you decide what information you really want to look for, save, and use for your research.

CHECKING WHAT YOU'VE LEARNED

Personal Information

- Have you brainstormed or used other information-gathering techniques to uncover information and ideas you already have?
- Have you spoken with your instructors and classmates about your topic to find out if they have ideas or information you can use?

and quit (having left a paper trail of memos to cover myself).

Usually the problem is with management, which often has no idea what I do or can contribute to a project. In these cases, I try to educate the appropriate people. I've found that if I'm seen as a consultant, usually I am listened to and get results. If I'm seen as just another contractor, they may consider me little more than a glorified secretary and pay no attention at all. So I try to ensure, from the start, that I'm seen as a consultant. I always take the approach of "what can I do for you—how I can save you money and add value to your project, thus justifying my relatively high pay."

Sometimes the problem isn't that people are being difficult, but that there is no mechanism for information flow. I often suggest ways to improve this. Writers and editors can and should contribute to development much earlier in the product life cycle, for example in the design stage. Sometimes it's as simple as adding me to the development team's distribution list or having me sit in on team meetings.

Insider Advice

My advice to newcomers would be: read as widely as possible; join Internet discussion groups; get on relevant e-mail newsletter lists. Learn people skills, including active listening, negotiation, and persuasion.

Keep an open mind and don't be dogmatic; try to learn as much as you can from every situation.

Without making a pest of yourself, ask lots of questions or do as much self-study as possible to learn more about the subject matter you're working with, the publication process, your employer's business, business processes in general (many scientific and technical communicators know a lot about science or technology, but woefully little about business realities), and related subjects. For example, if you're working with Web pages, you don't need to be an expert in HTML or Java or Perl, but you do need to know enough to ask intelligent questions and understand the answers so you can deal with people who are expert in those subjects.

In my experience, group projects work best when everyone can contribute to the planning and "buy into" the process, so everyone feels partial ownership and accepts responsibility for the success of the project. You need someone to coordinate or facilitate the group, but not to tell everyone what to do. What works depends almost entirely on the people involved: their skills, expertise, and interests, but most importantly their attitude. If the team members want the project to succeed, they will find a way, but if someone doesn't want to be involved, any process has problems.

Interviews

- Have you prepared your questions, researched the company and the person you are interviewing, and practiced your delivery?
- Have you arranged for any security clearances and recording permissions beforehand?
- Have you taken notes and reviewed them immediately after the interview?
- If you had follow-up questions, did you present them in a timely way after the interview?
- Did you send a thank-you note to the person you interviewed?

Questionnaires and Surveys

- Did you construct your questions to provide adequate choices and clear language?

- Have you avoided asking leading questions that steer your subjects into answers that do not reflect their actual views?
- Have you pretested the questionnaires or surveys and revised the wording when necessary?
- Have you validated the responses you received and analyzed them according to accepted practice in your field?

Focus Groups

- Have you provided a facilitator to keep the discussion on target and ensure that each participant has an equal opportunity to give views?
- Have you written up the results of the session promptly and accurately?

Experimentation

- Have you followed the steps of the scientific method?
- Is your question formulated clearly and unambiguously?
- Have you researched work that preceded yours and made yourself knowledgeable about the work of others and the state of research in your field?
- Have you formulated a testable hypothesis?
- Have you designed your experiment in conformity with the ethical standards of your discipline?
- Does your experiment test exactly the hypothesis you are proposing?
- Have you analyzed your results and reported them fully and ethically?

Library

- Have you consulted the librarian to help plan your research?
- Have you reviewed reference works on your topic?
- Have you used keyword searches in catalogs and databases to track down sources and bibliographic information?
- Have you followed the sources to other sources and refined your search as you went along?
- If you needed sources not found in your own library, have you investigated interlibrary loan, fax-on-demand, or electronic database sources?
- Have you used several search engines and search strategies to refine your search and discover subject headings and keywords suggested by earlier sources?
- Are your sources peer reviewed?
- Have you viewed critically the sources of your information?

EXERCISES

 REVIEW

1. Select someone who is knowledgeable about your field, perhaps a professor or a graduate student. Conduct an informational interview with that person to find out what a career in your field might offer you.
2. Find one full-text database in your library and print out an article from a journal published in the last 12 months.
3. List three databases available in your school's library that require users to be members of the school community—faculty, students, or staff.
4. Log into the library at your school, either from a computer lab on campus or from your own computer. Find a list of the available online databases, and bring to class a list of ten of them. Note which ones provide full-text articles and which require a school authorization code (student number) for access.
5. Compare the tip list for evaluating print sources with the tip list for evaluating Internet sources. Make a bulleted list of the elements the two lists have in common and of the elements that are different on the two lists.

 THE INTERNET

1. Select a specific question and submit it to five different search engines. Bring to class the first ten listings returned by each engine.
2. Follow the first three links you found for each search engine. Does the site contain the information you were looking for? For each site, be prepared to say how the search engine did or didn't provide useful results.
3. Refine your search from question 1, using AND or NOT operators to narrow the focus. Now check those same five search engines. Visit the first three sites for each. Are they the same as in question 2? Are the results better or worse for each search engine?

 ETHICS/PROFESSIONALISM

Review the tip list near the end of this chapter concerning evaluating Internet sources. Find one Web site that contains inaccurate information, biases of any kind, evidence of poor quality control, evidence of heavily opinionated content, or evidence of poor quality in the content or design. Discuss what, if any, ethical or professionalism issues are raised by these weaknesses.

 COLLABORATION

Your instructor will place you in small groups of four or five students for this exercise concerning focus groups. Each group in the class will be a mock focus group. Each group should select one member to be the group facilitator and another to be the group observer. The facilitator will help keep the discussion going concerning the chosen topic and will make sure everyone has a chance to contribute. The observer will both participate as a group member and take notes on what is discussed. Each group will spend about 20 minutes discussing a topic provided by your instructor. After the mock focus-group discussion is complete, the facilitator of each group should be prepared to discuss the conclusions of the group with the class.

 INTERNATIONAL COMMUNICATION

Using a Web browser, go to the English version of the Web site for Yahoo at Yahoo.com. Scroll down the first page to find the listing of the Web sites for Yahoo in Europe, Asia Pacific, and the Americas. Review at least six of these sites noting any biases in the way the information or design is presented for one culture compared to how the information or design is presented to another culture. Make a bulleted list of the biases you have noted, and be prepared to share this list with the class.

RESOURCES

Booth, Wayne C., Gregory G. Colomb, and Joseph M. Williams. *The Craft of Research.* Chicago: U of Chicago P, 1995.

Dillman, Don A. *Mail and Internet Surveys.* New York: Wiley, 2000.

Lester, James D. *Writing Research Papers: A Complete Guide.* 9th ed. New York: Longman, 1999.

MacNealy, Mary Sue. *Strategies for Empirical Research in Writing.* Needham Heights: Allyn and Bacon, 1998.

New York Public Library. *Writer's Guide to Style and Usage.* New York: HarperCollins, 1994.

Porter, Lynnette, and William Coggin. *Research Strategies in Technical Communication.* New York: Wiley, 1995.

Pyrczak, Fred. *Writing Empirical Research Reports: A Basic Guide for Students of the Social and Behavioral Sciences.* Los Angeles: Pyrczak, 1992.

Salant, Priscilla, and Don A. Dillman. *How to Conduct Your Own Survey.* New York: Wiley, 1994.

Skillin, Marjorie E., and Robert M. Gay. *Words into Type.* 3rd ed. Englewood Cliffs: Prentice Hall, 1974.

Turabian, Kate L. *A Manual for Writers of Term Papers, Theses, and Dissertations.* 6th ed. Chicago: U of Chicago P, 1996.

Zimmerman, Donald E., and Michel Lynn Muraski. *The Elements of Information Gathering: A Guide for Technical Communicators, Scientists, and Engineers.* Phoenix: Oryx, 1995.

Zimmerman, Donald E., and Dawn Rodrigues. *Research and Writing in the Disciplines.* Fort Worth: Harcourt, 1992.

6

Organizing and Managing Information

Organizing Information   172

Evaluating Information   181

Reporting Information Ethically   182

From the Workplace   188

IN THIS CHAPTER

When you do research, you find and collect information so you can use it in some other form. Once you have gathered and evaluated the information using the research techniques discussed in Chapter 5, you are faced with the task of taming that information so that you can present it in the most effective manner. You will need to figure out what you have, decide which information is useful for your purpose, and put it into usable form. Organizing and managing information can be a challenge, but if you develop a systematic approach, you will find both of these will be easier tasks.

You will learn about:

- techniques for organizing and arranging information in a variety of media and formats: note cards, electronic and paper-based databases, outlines, trees, flowcharts, and storyboards

- the different ways of conveying other people's ideas by quoting, paraphrasing, and summarizing

- the importance of avoiding plagiarism—the representing of someone else's work as your own

- the ins and outs of copyright—its uses and applications, both to works you use and works you create

ORGANIZING INFORMATION

There are many ways to organize the information you find as you do research, but the first thing you will probably do is take notes as you read through the various sources you find on your topic.

Note Cards, Notebooks, and Computers

Many researchers use 3×5 or 4×6 cards to store information during their research. They create bibliography cards for sources they want to look at or have already consulted. They also create a variety of note cards with comments about the sources they read. Some researchers prefer to use bound notebooks for writing down source information and material collected from their sources. In an age of laptop and notebook computers, however, many researchers are storing information electronically.

Often, students are reluctant to use bibliography cards for research. They question the need to organize their research so formally and so tediously. Who wants to write down all that information on a lot of cards? Isn't it easier to photocopy everything? Why is it necessary to keep track of research with cards, a notebook, or a laptop computer?

In fact, whether you use 3 × 5 or 4 × 6 cards for your sources or use a computer program to keep track of them, you need a system to record complete documentation of all the sources you are consulting. Keep an accurate record of your sources so that you can fully document them later without having to track them down again for missing information. Some sources will be difficult or even impossible for you to obtain a second time, so make sure you get all the information you need the first time out. Keeping an accurate record is important so that you can give credit to others where credit is due, and so your readers can see how you have supported your views with the authority of others. (See Appendix C for information on how to format citations of outside sources.)

Good notes are the core of good research, whether you're gathering information from personal experience, using a variety of libraries, or surfing online. For the sake of time, keep your comments—your own, a paraphrase, an indirect quotation, or a direct quotation—brief. However, be sure to write down as much as you need to.

Whichever method you prefer—paper notes or computer notes—the important point is to have a method. Inexperienced researchers typically have no system or method, loosely keep track of the sources they consult, carelessly use material from various sources, and thus often waste time later trying to determine which sources they used in their work.

> ❝ ❞
> Whichever method you prefer, the important point is to have a method.

Databases

Databases enable you to put large amounts of information into an organized form. The telephone book is a database and so is the dictionary. Databases do not necessarily require the use of a computer. You probably already maintain several databases without even knowing it. Any time you keep track of information with some type of organized system, even a list, you are managing a database. Your calendar, personal phone book, and "to do" list are all databases, even if you commonly write them in pencil.

Managing your information is the key to using it efficiently. Many computer programs help you manage your databases. The choice of software depends on the kind of database and the type of manipulation you have to perform. Read-only databases, predefined databases, flat-file databases, and relational databases are types of computer databases. Figure 6.1 shows a relational database.

As a practical matter, if you want to use computerized databases to collect and organize information you gather from your research, you will have to use specialized software designed for this task, such as ProCite, Citation, or EndNote, or you will have to set up your own database using a more general database program such as Access. See Figure 6.2 for a look at a ProCite record.

FIGURE 6.1

Relational Database

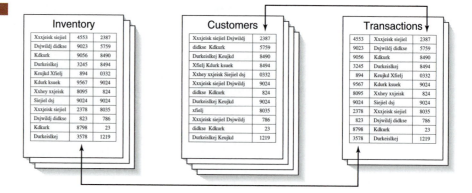

Inventory		
Xxxjeisk siejiel	4553	2387
Dsjwildj didkse	9023	5759
Kdkurk	9056	8490
Durkeislkej	3245	8494
Keujkd Xfielj	894	0332
Kdurk ksuek	9567	9024
Xxhey xxjeisk	8095	824
Siejiel dsj	9024	9024
Xxxjeisk siejiel	2378	8035
Dsjwildj didkse	823	786
Kdkurk	8798	23
Durkeislkej	3578	1219

Customers	
Xxxjeisk siejiel Dsjwildj	2387
didkse Kdkurk	5759
Durkeislkej Keujkd	8490
Xfielj Kdurk ksuek	8494
Xxhey xxjeisk Siejiel dsj	0332
Xxxjeisk siejiel Dsjwildj	9024
didkse Kdkurk	824
Durkeislkej Keujkd	9024
xfielj	8035
Xxxjeisk siejiel Dsjwildj	786
didkse Kdkurk	23
Durkeislkej Keujkd	1219

Transactions		
4553	Xxxjeisk siejiel	2387
9023	Dsjwildj didkse	5759
9056	Kdkurk	8490
3245	Durkeislkej	8494
894	Keujkd Xfielj	0332
9567	Kdurk ksuek	9024
8095	Xxhey xxjeisk	824
9024	Siejiel dsj	9024
2378	Xxxjeisk siejiel	8035
823	Dsjwildj didkse	786
8798	Kdkurk	23
3578	Durkeislkej	1219

Basic Terms

Read-only databases: These already have been developed for you, usually by a professional programmer or team. Some examples are various Internet search engines, online card catalogs, and airline reservation systems.

Predefined databases: These are commercially available databases for people who want to manage a database but don't want to build it themselves. Often they focus on a specific topic in the business or home market, such as wedding preparation, video-library management, invoice handling, inventory, or payroll.

Flat-file database: These are capable of handling only one table (or data set) at a time. For home use, this is often just fine. You usually don't need any more than this to deal with your holiday-card list or stamp-collection inventory.

Relational database: These are perhaps the most useful database—and certainly the most powerful—in the corporate world. They are much like flat-file databases, except they allow the use of multiple tables. For example, you can keep track of inventory, customers, and transactions in three distinct tables that share some fields. The tables are separate but related, so the database is called a relational database. Big database management systems such as Oracle, Paradox, and Access help you create and manipulate relational databases.

Suppose you are researching a topic and want to use databases to manage the information you find. A database can keep track of all the bibliographic information for each source. If you use a laptop computer, you enter information into the database as you read each source, bypassing paper notes entirely. You can take notes in the database and enter keywords into each record. Later

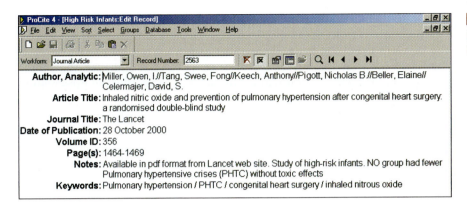

FIGURE 6.2
Bibliographic Database Record

you can do sophisticated searches through your database to locate records with specific combinations of information. When you are ready to write up your research, you can have the software generate your bibliography in any of a number of preset citation styles or you can specify a custom style and your entries will be formatted according to those specifications.

Outlines

You've no doubt been told by writing instructors to outline your ideas before you begin writing. But since you know that outlining requires time, you may not feel that it is worth the effort. You may prefer just to begin writing and shape your thoughts as you proceed. But devoting even a few minutes to deciding what you want to write (on the basis of what your audience needs to know) before you begin writing will save you time, lots of time. Outlining, like most planning, is a time saver.

Massive amounts of information require taming. You need to have some way to represent the large volume of information in a shorthand way so you can work with it structurally before dealing with it as a large number of details. Experienced writers create an outline of what they want to write about. The benefit of creating an outline of your material is that you can visualize the structure of the information and arrange topics so they flow logically from one topic to the next. By looking at the topics and subtopics instead of at the text itself, you can more easily discern problems of organization, problems that the full text might have distracted you from seeing. The outline may be a quick, informal list of topics and subtopics on the back of an envelope, or it may be a more formal outline using the outline feature of a full-featured word processing program such as Word or WordPerfect. Some projects require an outline as a deliverable, for example information plans and content specification. In these cases, your outline is not only a tool to organize your information but also a presentation of how you will proceed or what your document will contain.

One of the most successful strategies you can use for communicating with your audience is to set up a logical, effective organization for your document. The keyword here is audience. Remember, you want to organize and present your ideas in a way that makes the most sense to your audience, the people who will be using your information. In fact, the most effective presentation for one audience may turn out to be only mediocre for another.

Many writers who know their subject well think primarily of how they would like to present the information. They think of the key topics they want to cover and the points they want to use to support each key topic. The problem with this approach is that these writers are thinking only about what they want to cover, not about what the audience needs to know. For your document to be effective, organize it so that your readers are able to follow the flow of information in a way that seems natural to them.

Informal Outlines

An informal outline may be simply a listing of topics you choose to cover in a memo, letter, report, or other document. The listing allows you to see your topics on screen or paper. For many kinds of writing tasks, especially brief documents, the informal outline will be the most common. Figure 6.3 is an example of an informal outline.

Formal Outlines

The formal topic outline is a common type of outline in which you use keywords or phrases for major headings and subheadings. Each key topic should represent one main idea, and the subtopics should represent supporting topics for each key topic. In a brief document, each key topic may repre-

---

FIGURE 6.3

Informal Outline

An informal outline for a typical lab guide

How to Use This Manual

Lab Access

Lab Hardware

Lab Software

Lab Manuals

Lab Procedures

Policies for Lab Assistants

Policies for Students Using the Lab

FIGURE 6.4
Formal Topic Outline
A topic outline for a Web style guide for instructors of distance learning classes

I. Instructional Issues
    A. Course Descriptions
    B. University Process of Course Delivery
    C. Copyright Issues

II. Aesthetics Issues
    A. Web Page Layout
    B. Web Page Length
    C. Graphics
    D. Types of Graphics
    E. Color in Graphics

III. Technical Issues
    A. Hypertext Markup Language
    B. Ordered Lists
    C. Unordered Lists
    D. Definition Lists
    E. List Attributes
    F. Tables
    G. Frames
    H. Footers

IV. Accessibility Issues
    A. Accessibility
    B. Blindness
    C. Impaired Vision
    D. Hearing Impairments
    E. Sensitivity Issues
    F. Multicultures
    G. Gender
    H. Disabilities

sent one paragraph, and each subtopic may represent a supporting idea in that paragraph. In a longer document, each key topic may represent a main idea, and each subtopic may represent a separate supporting paragraph for that topic. Figure 6.4 is an example of a formal outline.

The formal sentence outline is another common strategy. At its simplest, each key topic sentence may be the main topic sentence of the paragraph, and each subtopic sentence may be a supporting idea for that main topic sentence. A more complex sentence outline may show key ideas in each topic sentence on the outline, and each supporting sentence is typically a topic sentence for a supporting paragraph.

Outlining

- Think about your topic and how it falls into different areas or subtopics. Each one of the areas or subtopics will be a separate paragraph or section. Those major areas are your first-level outline entries.

(continued)

- Go through each first-level heading, put it in its logical place in the outline, and place second-level topics in appropriate order below each. Repeat the process with more detailed information in the third and lower levels. You don't have to follow a particular order when adding your lower levels, as long as you build a logical and useful structure.
- Look at the outline and check that all the lower-level items fit within the appropriate higher levels. If not, move them around. An outline is a tool—it serves you, not the other way around. By the time you finish your outline, you should have a solid framework on which to build your document.
- View the outline you have created as your audience will view it. Do your ideas go from the simple and familiar to the complex and less familiar? Is the progression steady, without obvious jumps? Have you fulfilled your readers' needs and expectations?

Trees

The outline is primarily a word-based organizer for your document. Many experienced writers prefer to organize their topics in a different fashion. Other, more visual methods may be more suitable for your needs. If you are primarily a visual thinker or if you are working on a project with more of a visual component (such as a video script), more graphical organizing techniques may work better for you.

Tree diagrams show relationships among topics and subtopics. See Figure 6.5 for an example of a tree diagram. Using a tree to outline your document has several advantages over more traditional word-based outlining. With the outline, structure is invisible and has to be imagined. Relationships in an outline are represented indirectly, in numbers and letters such as I.C.2.b, so you have to infer structure by interpreting the numbers and letters.

FIGURE 6.5

Tree Diagram

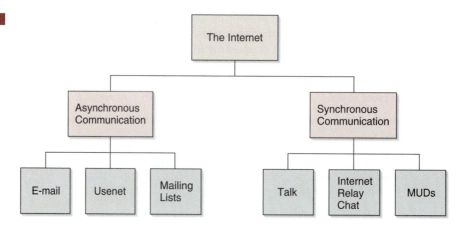

One advantage of a tree is that you can see relationships immediately, since the structure is represented visually. You can see where a point fits in, see corresponding points on the same level, and see which points are logically above or below one another. You can also step back and see the document as a whole, noting proportion and balance among its various parts.

A second advantage of a tree is that it helps you keep the big picture in mind. The outline form encourages you to go to the deepest level of detail almost immediately, for example, I.A.1.a. It's easy to get lost and forget the larger point you are trying to make. By contrast, the top-down approach in which you fill out a tree one level at a time helps you keep your sense of context and direction.

A third advantage is that a tree helps you to manage your thinking. Constructing a large, coherent, conceptual structure is not a natural mental act. You can't hold all the details and relationships in memory. You need to get the details and relationships out in front of you so that you can see and work with them. The tree, particularly when done with self-stick notes, provides a flexible, efficient medium around which to think and in which to organize your ideas.

To help you manage your thinking during this step, use a tree diagram that looks like a family tree or an organization chart. This kind of tree differs from its real-world counterparts in that the tree diagram is drawn upside down, with its "root" at the top and its "leaves" at the bottom.

Using a Tree Diagram

- Put the one overriding point you want to make at the top (root) of the tree.
- Use self-stick notes and write one point per note. Transfer some self-stick notes from the brainstorming or mind-mapping steps you performed, as described in Chapter 4.
- Divide your focus into its three or four (or however many) largest, most important points.
- Place the main points under the top point, left to right in some logical order.
- Focus on each of these points in turn. Divide each into its largest component points.
- Place subpoints under the appropriate main point, left to right.
- Repeat the process, one level of the tree at a time.
- Stop when the bottom points correspond to manageable blocks of ideas or information that you can easily write about, for example, a paragraph for unfamiliar material or a page for material that you know well.

Flowcharts

Flowcharts are widely used in many disciplines and professions for all kinds of planning and problem-solving purposes. Like trees, flowcharts show immediate relationships, but flowcharts are specifically designed to show

FIGURE 6.6
Flowchart

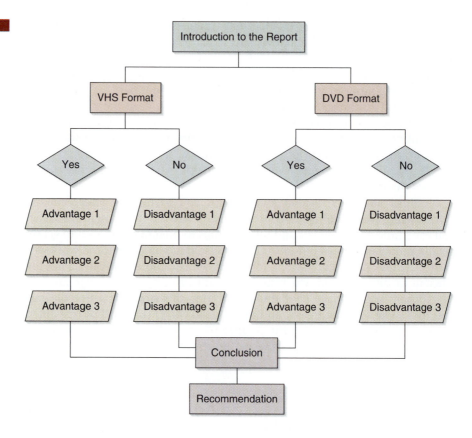

processes and procedures. They help you to visualize the organization of your document as well as your transition from one key concept to another. Unlike trees, flowcharts enable you to follow a sequence of steps or ideas; trees emphasize relationships and a hierarchy. See Figure 6.6 for an example of a flowchart.

When you use a flowchart, you break down a process or procedure into steps. The steps can be quite broad in the case of a large project or quite detailed in the case of a smaller procedure. Often you will use a flowchart to define the major steps you will cover, and then you will create a separate flowchart for each part of the larger process. For a computer-science project, for example, the levels of flowcharting might correspond to the steps in a project, a computer program, a subroutine, and a function call or macro, progressively fine-tuning the procedure until it is finished.

Storyboards

Storyboarding is another widely used planning technique. In the film and television industries, storyboarding is used to plan practically every shot for a

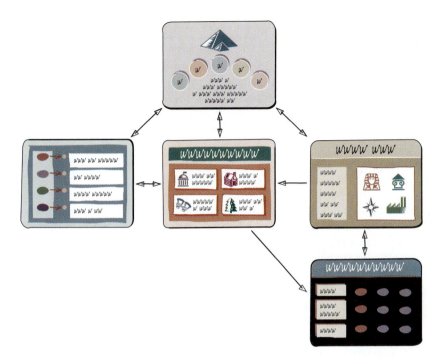

FIGURE 6.7

Thumbnail Sketch for a Web Site

film or television show. Storyboarding can also be used effectively to organize the structure of a short story or novel or to plan a Web site. Information may be represented hierarchically or linearly or both. In storyboarding a Web site, for example, you would sketch and rough out each Web page. Start with your main or home page. Give each Web page a title and a rough description of the content and kinds of images you will provide. Then sketch out the links between the Web pages, and use arrows or lines to show the direction of the link. Figure 6.7 shows what a thumbnail sketch looks like. You can use the thumbnailing feature available with some computer software to create and manage your storyboards.

EVALUATING INFORMATION

While you are researching your topic, you must give careful attention to the quality of the information you find. Whether the source is in print, on the Internet, or available in some other medium, you need to determine how authoritative, reliable, accurate, and complete it is. There is no easy solution to determine the quality of the information you find, and this is especially true of information you find on the Internet. See the "Gathering Information" section in Chapter 5 for tips on evaluating print sources and online sources.

REPORTING INFORMATION ETHICALLY

**CHOOSING THE
ETHICAL PATH**

Make a commitment to be honest about properly attributing the work and ideas of others.

When you do research, you typically deal with information found in a number of places, put there by a number of people before you. This information has a connection to the people who put it there, and you have a responsibility to treat the information not as free for the taking but as the intellectual output of others.

Plagiarism

Plagiarism is representing the work or ideas of someone else as your own. Unlike fraud—falsifying data and conclusions based on those data—plagiarism is based solely on representing someone else's work or ideas as your own.

In the college community, plagiarism takes many forms. When students copy someone else's answers during an exam, this action constitutes plagiarism. When students turn in papers written by someone else and claim that they wrote the paper, they are committing plagiarism. When students use material (for example, prose or illustrations) from other sources—such as Web sites— and fail to acknowledge the sources appropriately, they are plagiarizing. In sum, plagiarism is stealing the work or ideas of others.

Of course, college students aren't the only ones who plagiarize. College professors have been known to steal the work of their graduate students or colleagues, employees have been known to steal the work of their fellow employees or that of employees at other companies, novelists have been known to lift entire passages from the works of other novelists, and so on. Plagiarism and copyright infringement overlap to an extent (see "Copyright" later in this chapter), but they can and often do occur independently of each other.

Plagiarism is an ethical issue. You have an obligation to represent accurately and honestly any sources you use. Because plagiarism is unethical and may have serious consequences, it's important to know how to avoid plagiarizing.

Avoiding Plagiarism

- Keep careful track of what work and ideas are yours and what work and ideas belong to someone else.

- Make sure you know the difference between an idea that is general knowledge and one that must be credited to someone in particular. General knowledge is information that can be found in general reference works and that anyone in a specific discipline would know. Other information must be credited to its source.

- Keep in mind that material you find on the Web, while easy to copy, is actually the property of its author. The fact that the material—

(continued)

text, graphics, sound, or video—is readily available does not mean you are free to appropriate it. If you use someone's work, you must have permission and you must credit the source.

- Learn and use a careful system for researching and keeping track of the work and ideas of others. Always write down the complete bibliographic data for all sources you consult. Review the earlier discussion on how to use note cards and bibliographic database software.

- When in doubt about how much of what you are writing actually derives from the work of another, provide credit.

- Work on the art of paraphrasing. When you want to use someone else's idea but not the exact quo-

tation, reword the idea in several ways. Choose the rewording that best suits your purpose, subject, audience, and context. Document the paraphrase properly; even if you reword the idea, you still must give proper attribution.

- Give proper acknowledgment even for works that you adapt for your own purposes. For example, if you take someone else's technical illustration and modify it, you must acknowledge the original author or artist and source. Obtain permission from the author or artist to use works you have modified or adapted. Creating a derivative work from someone else's copyrighted material can be an infringement of copyright unless you have obtained permission.

Paraphrasing Versus Direct Quotations

Paraphrase

A paraphrase is a careful rewording of the ideas and sentences of another author in your own words. Creating a good paraphrase takes time. You have to read carefully and have a good understanding of the original quotation. Then you must have the ability to rewrite the information in your own words. Taking the time at the beginning to paraphrase will save time later in the writing phase of your project. When you take extra care during this phase of your research, you avoid inadvertent plagiarism later. A typical paraphrase card consists of author, source, page number (if available), the paraphrase, and a note indicating that what you have provided is a paraphrase.

Summarizing

Summarizing is a more polished kind of paraphrasing. In paraphrasing, you go through the source material and reword it to provide the gist of individual sentences or paragraphs. When you summarize, you abstract the meaning of the whole paragraph or larger unit, normally in more general terms. The summary you prepare for your notes will probably be a two- or three-sentence overview of the kind of information (and perhaps the general conclusions) to be found in the source. You will use the summary you prepare in this way to refer in a broad way to the source when you write your paper or other type of document. This type of summary is typical in literature reviews (see Appendix D for more on this form).

Do not confuse a summary you might prepare for your own note-taking or your literature review with a summary or abstract you might write for a report. (See the "Abstract" and "Executive Summary" sections in Chapter 18.) A summary or abstract you write for a report will be more comprehensive, since it will sum up all that you have learned and provided in the report. The purpose for the summary or abstract is different from your purpose when you take notes. The note-taking summary will be a useful early stage in your data collection. The report summary typically will be the overview of your report, once it is completely written. Figure D.1 in Appendix D shows a typical use for summary notes.

Quotation

The two types of quotations are direct, which repeats the exact words used, and indirect, which describes the information conveyed. For a direct quotation, be sure to copy the quoted material verbatim, even including any errors that are part of the original text. An indirect quotation differs from a paraphrase in that a paraphrase rewords the concept being described. An indirect quotation is more like a direct quotation except it refers to what was said instead of quoting it exactly.

Basic Terms

Direct Quote: The style guide advises, "Use en dashes when you want to express ranges of numbers, sports scores, or two partners in a noun pair."

Indirect Quote: The style guide says to use en dashes for ranges of numbers, sports scores, and noun pairs.

Paraphrase: The style guide suggests several uses for the en dash (number ranges, sports scores, noun pairs).

Even after just a few hours of intensive research, you may find that you've accumulated a good number of bibliography and note cards or database entries. Because this approach can be time-consuming, you'll need to be careful about the sources you use. As you work, try to determine whether the comments you are paraphrasing or quoting are valuable, insightful, or interesting. You'll need to be a discriminating reader and a highly selective note taker, lest you allow the important information to be overwhelmed by a sea of inconsequential facts.

Copyright

Perhaps no topic is as misunderstood as copyright. Copyright is something you have probably heard about and perhaps thought about, and you may have an idea that it also has something to do with plagiarism, but the details may be fuzzy.

Copyright is the right of authors to have control over the use of their writings or other works. It is a right protected by the United States Constitution and by laws designed to clarify the type and duration of this control. A work is copyrighted as soon as it is fixed in a tangible medium of expression—that is, as soon as it is recorded: on paper, on magnetic tape, on CD-ROM, on the Web, and so on. Some people have the mistaken impression that works—text, audio, video, graphics—found on the Web are free for the taking. But use of these works is subject to copyright laws too.

Copyright is one of those topics that have legal consequences: What you don't know can hurt you. Perhaps you think that if you are a student, copyright issues don't apply to you. You may have heard that educational uses of copyrighted materials are considered "fair use," and you don't have to concern yourself with them. (See "Fair Use Doctrine" later in this section.) Or you might have seen someone's list of rules and believed that as long as you follow them, you will be fine. Unfortunately, copyright is much more complicated than that.

Why is copyright important? It's important because it is a legal concept that you must deal with every day. In school or in the workplace, you face copyright issues whenever you use the wording or graphics in someone else's document and whenever you create a document of your own.

Using Copyrighted Material

If you have ever read a book, viewed a film, listened to a song, watched television, or surfed the World Wide Web, you have used copyrighted materials. What do reading, viewing, listening, watching, or surfing have to do with copyright? And why should you know about copyright to perform these activities? You should know about copyright because you have certain rights as a user of copyrighted materials. These rights don't depend on your being a student or a nonprofit organization, nor do they depend on your using a small or large amount of the original work.

You are using the copyrighted work if you read, view, listen, watch, or surf the work as an individual. You may have purchased your copy, or you may have borrowed it from someone else. As long as you have acquired it legally, you are entitled to use it. Using it means enjoying it in the manner intended by the work's creator.

Computer software is a difficult issue for consumers, because most software is licensed, not sold. You may think you are buying the software you see in the store, but you are not: you are buying the license to use it. Under the terms of the license, you are permitted certain uses and forbidden others. For example, the license spells out the conditions under which you can sell the software. Once you've bought a book or audio recording, you can sell it as you wish. With software, you own the license—not the product—so the software itself is not yours to sell. Read the license when you buy software and be aware of your rights and responsibilities.

Incorporating Copyrighted Material into Your Work

A compiler is someone who puts together preexisting material, perhaps combined with original material, to form a new work. You are a compiler if you create a brochure that uses some of the promotional material created by your company for its other advertisements. You are a compiler if you write computer documentation and use screen shots as graphics. You are a compiler if you put together a multimedia presentation made up of music and video clips that someone else created. You are a compiler if you write a literature review for one of your classes.

When you combine previously written or recorded information into your new work, you will be concerned about the copyright issue. What material are you entitled to use? How do you find out?

BASIC TERM

Boilerplate: Material that is designed to be reused, perhaps in combination with other reusable or original material, is called boilerplate.

If you are writing a paper for a class and want to cite someone else's work to support your argument, you can do so, even quoting the other person's exact words, provided that you credit your source (an ethical requirement) and take only enough of the source material to make your point and no more. In this case, you do not have the copyright owner's permission to use the copyrighted material, but you are taking advantage of the "doctrine of fair use" to stay within the law.

If your employer asks you to write a manual or a brochure using previous versions of the manual or other promotional materials developed by your company, you can be fairly certain that you are entitled to use and reuse the materials you're given. In this case, your employer owns the copyright to the material and has given you permission to use it.

The two situations, the classroom and the workplace, both permit reuse of copyrighted materials, but for different reasons. In the classroom, you are reusing the material of others under the doctrine of fair use. If your use qualifies, you do not have to ask permission to use small amounts of the works of others for educational purposes. (See the next section for more information on fair use.) In the workplace, you must have permission of the copyright owner before you can use copyrighted works to form a new work. Your employer can give you permission for works owned by the company. For works that are under copyright to others, you must request permission and perhaps pay a licensing fee. It can be very difficult to ascertain who owns the copyright to some works, especially multimedia works that involve many rights (text, video, and music, to name a few). In some cases, notably music, agencies that specialize in licensing copyrighted works can handle the arrangements for you, collecting the fee from you and crediting it to the copyright holder. In other cases, finding out who owns the copyright can be difficult, and it is best to consult an attorney who specializes in intellectual property rights (such as copyrights, patents, and trademarks) to make sure you have not infringed, however inadvertently, on someone else's copyright.

Copyright information for printed material (and in some cases for online material) is often available somewhere in the work itself. The reverse of the title page in a book usually is used to present copyright and other information for that book. Figure 6.8 (page 190) shows a typical copyright page. In journals, the information is found in the masthead (list of important information about its editorial and publication information) and sometimes somewhere in each article (usually either at the foot of the first page, the foot of every page, or at the end of the article). You can learn quite a lot from looking at the copyright information in these sources.

Fair Use Doctrine

When you use copyrighted materials in a school or other setting and don't obtain permission from the copyright owner, you are relying on the doctrine of fair use to excuse you from what would otherwise be an infringement of copyright. Fair use is a provision of the copyright law that exempts you from having to get the copyright holder's permission under certain circumstances. If you claim that your use is fair and the copyright holder takes you to court, the court will determine the case based on how your use fits into the four provisions of the fair-use exemption. According to the Copyright Act of 1976, the court will consider:

- The purpose and character of the use, including whether such use is of a commercial nature or is for nonprofit educational purposes;
- The nature of the copyrighted work;
- The amount and substantiality of the portion used in relation to the copyrighted work as a whole; and
- The effect of the use on the potential market for the copyrighted work.

You will notice that no specific numbers of words are mentioned in these tests. Some people will tell you that you can borrow others' words if you haven't used more than 250 words, or 500 words, or 1,000 words. Or others will say that you are entitled to use up to some percentage of the work. Many

From the workplace

Paul Lockwood
Team Leader, TransUnion LLC
Chicago, Illinois

Paul has years of experience working in the communication field, but rather than limiting his career to one area, he has moved among several, finally landing in management where he oversees a team of writers. He finds that teamwork, using brainstorming and other techniques, creates a much better document, spurring on the team members to improve the final product together.

I am not working in the field I trained for (radio/TV/film), because my life has taken some unexpected twists and turns, and I've been able, fortunately, to twist and turn along with it. My classes in journalism, radio, and TV production at Northwestern University—combined with my work and internships at radio stations during high school and college—helped me land two radio news job offers in Rockford, Illinois, within a month of graduation. I accepted one, allowing me to live at home for a while (until I could get on my feet).

I stayed at that first job for more than five years, moving up to be the sole news director for two radio stations. I probably would have stayed longer if new owners hadn't asked the old owners to lay off several employees in various departments, sending me to the unemployment line.

I've changed professions a *little* less frequently than Imelda Marcos changed shoes, but in the almost 20 years since college, I've worked in broadcast journalism (AM/FM radio station), public relations (residential facility for developmentally disabled children), marketing (architectural/interior design firm), technical writing/editing (financial software and credit services companies), proposal writing, and now management. I'm hoping that I'll succeed in management and stay in that arena until I retire, but I trust that my communication skills will serve me in good stead whether that's the case or not.

A large percentage of my work is conducted online. I've been using a PC since 1988 when I started doing marketing work for an architectural/interior design firm and needed to generate marketing letters, mass mailings, etc. That was a stand-alone PC. Now, I use a networked PC with Internet access for e-mail, document creation, presentation development, time tracking, spreadsheet record keeping, online document editing, newsletter creation, and research.

I find myself conducting a lot of interpersonal communication via e-mail instead of picking up the phone or walking over to a co-worker's desk. I don't want to lose personal contact and the chance to see or hear the reaction of the person I'm communicating

universities publish guidelines they suggest you follow. *These rules of thumb have no basis in law.* They are suggestions for keeping within reasonable limits for the third test, that of "amount and substantiality." Remember that the amount and substantiality clause is just one of four tests.

Copyrighting Your Work

If you are a writer, student, webmaster, illustrator, multimedia specialist, computer programmer, or other content developer, you are creating copyrightable material. Who then owns that copyright depends on your particular situation. If you are a student and have written a paper for a class, the copy-with, but sending off an e-mail is so easy that I have to stop and ask myself, "Isn't this important enough that I should really discuss this matter in person or on the phone?"

When I was writing on paper (e.g., typing), I also had to be more conscious of my typing. Backspacing over a word—or deleting a phrase—wasn't as simple as today's word processors make it. That fact alone makes the composition of an e-mail even more attractive. I can reword a sentence to my heart's content and not have to destroy a notepad full of paper writing, rewriting, and tossing out my first drafts.

Part of my job is to supervise others who prepare written communications. I think one area that gives many people trouble is flow and organization. Figuring out what the reader needs to know and putting all of the necessary information into a logical order—not individual procedures so much, but the entire series of processes—can be challenging, especially if your assistance is requested after most work on the project has already been done. I also think it's difficult for some people—me included—to be succinct without leaving out important details or examples that the average reader would need for understanding.

At my current job, most documents are created as an individual effort, with other team members helping only with peer edits. However, as a team leader, I'm always looking for projects that allow for collaboration. When my team was asked to provide intranet pages about our area, I asked three of my associates to work together on developing those pages and I asked one of them to take the lead on the project. Beyond that, I left it up to the team on how the work should be divvied up.

The only disadvantage to working collaboratively is the need to rely on other team members to complete their portions of a project before it's entirely finished. If any individual team member doesn't do a fair share of the work, or doesn't do it in a timely fashion, the other members of the team can feel resentful.

Advantages to working on a project as a team typically outweigh the disadvantages, in my opinion. The biggest advantage: more ideas. When one person brainstorms, you get X number of ideas; when more people brainstorm, not only do you get X plus Y plus Z number of ideas—the ideas each might come up with separately—but you also get ideas that spring from the other team members' suggestions. It's kind of like getting compound interest on the "brain bank accounts" that have been pooled together.

Not all large projects lend themselves to a collaborative effort. To some degree, it may depend on the amount of time needed to bring an associate up to speed on the details surrounding a project versus the time available. It may be easier to have just one contact person for the internal customer to deal with. However, if a project can be broken up in pieces and if available resources make collaboration possible, a team approach can benefit both the employer (more ideas) and the associate (less isolation, more working relationships being built).

right is yours. No one else can reprint your paper without your permission. If you write computer documentation for a company that employs you to do that writing, your employer owns the copyright for your work. In this situation, the work is considered a "work for hire." You hold no rights to the finished work, even though you wrote it. For the purposes of copyright law, your employer would be considered the author of the work. If you are an independent contractor who is hired to create a particular project, Web site, book, brochure, computer-based training module, or multimedia compilation, you may own the copyright or it may be owned by the person or firm that contracted with you to create the work. Your contract should spell out who is to own the copyright for the finished work.

FIGURE 6.8

Book Copyright Page

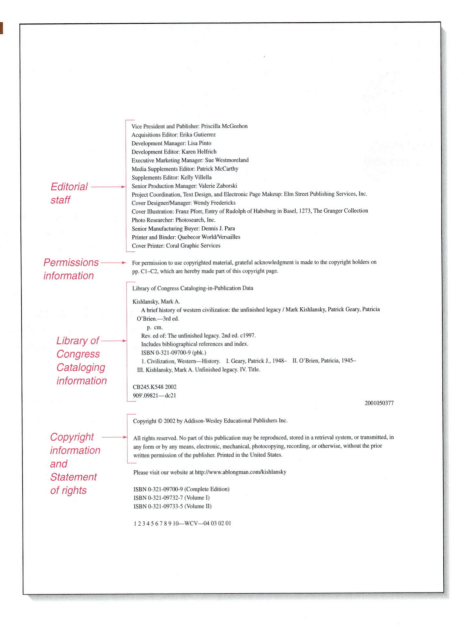

Vice President and Publisher: Priscilla McGeehon
Acquisitions Editor: Erika Gutierrez
Development Manager: Lisa Pinto
Development Editor: Karen Helfrich
Executive Marketing Manager: Sue Westmoreland
Media Supplements Editor: Patrick McCarthy
Supplements Editor: Kelly Villella
Senior Production Manager: Valerie Zaborski
Project Coordination, Text Design, and Electronic Page Makeup: Elm Street Publishing Services, Inc.
Cover Designer/Manager: Wendy Fredericks
Cover Illustration: Franz Pforr, Entry of Rudolph of Habsburg in Basel, 1273, The Granger Collection
Photo Researcher: Photosearch, Inc.
Senior Manufacturing Buyer: Dennis J. Para
Printer and Binder: Quebecor World/Versailles
Cover Printer: Coral Graphic Services

Editorial staff →

For permission to use copyrighted material, grateful acknowledgment is made to the copyright holders on pp. C1–C2, which are hereby made part of this copyright page.

Permissions information →

Library of Congress Cataloging-in-Publication Data

Kishlansky, Mark A.
    A brief history of western civilization: the unfinished legacy / Mark Kishlansky, Patrick Geary, Patricia O'Brien.—3rd ed.
        p. cm.
    Rev. ed of: The unfinished legacy. 2nd ed. c1997.
    Includes bibliographical references and index.
    ISBN 0-321-09700-9 (pbk.)
    1. Civilization, Western—History. I. Geary, Patrick J., 1948– II. O'Brien, Patricia, 1945–
III. Kishlansky, Mark A. Unfinished legacy. IV. Title.

CB245.K548 2002
909'.09821—dc21

                                                                                    2001050377

Library of Congress Cataloging information →

Copyright © 2002 by Addison-Wesley Educational Publishers Inc.

All rights reserved. No part of this publication may be reproduced, stored in a retrieval system, or transmitted, in any form or by any means, electronic, mechanical, photocopying, recording, or otherwise, without the prior written permission of the publisher. Printed in the United States.

Please visit our website at http://www.ablongman.com/kishlansky

ISBN 0-321-09700-9 (Complete Edition)
ISBN 0-321-09732-7 (Volume I)
ISBN 0-321-09733-5 (Volume II)

1 2 3 4 5 6 7 8 9 10—WCV—04 03 02 01

Copyright information and Statement of rights →

Copyright Protection

The requirements for registering a copyright have changed over the years, but contrary to popular belief, a work does not have to show a copyright sign or notice, nor does it have to be registered, to have copyright protection. The U.S. Copyright Office still registers copyrights, however, and your copyrights can be registered by sending in the appropriate form for the type of work, a small filing fee, and two copies of the work. Your ability to recover maximum damages from infringers depends on prior registration of your work. You can request the forms you need from the Copyright Office by calling the Copyright Hotline at (202) 707-3000. These forms are also available on the World Wide Web at <http://www.loc.gov/copyright/forms/>.

CHECKING WHAT YOU'VE LEARNED

Organizing Your Information—Taking Notes

- Are your notes accurate, complete, and well documented?
- Have you recorded the information you found in a consistent format, using notebook, cards, or a database?

Documenting Your Sources

- Have you included complete bibliographic details identifying your sources?
- If you have quoted verbatim sections of text, have you noted that in your notes?

Using Organizing Structures

- Have you constructed a logical structure for your writing using an outline, tree, flowchart, or storyboard?
- If you are using an outline, is your outline well organized and complete?
- If you are using an outline, are the first-level headings appropriately broad, parallel, and logically ordered?
- Does each lower-level heading appear below the appropriate higher-level heading?
- Does the structure you have created support the points you are trying to convey?

Avoiding Plagiarism

- For each and every fact or opinion you collect for your research, have you documented its source or showed how you derived it?
- Have you given credit for all work that is not your own?
- If you have paraphrased or modified someone else's work, have you given credit to your source?

Copyright

- If you are using material created by others, do you have permission to do so?
- If you intend your use of material created by others to be a fair use, do you have good reason to think that your use qualifies as such?
- If you are using copyrighted material and that use does not fall under the fair use guidelines, have you obtained permission to use the material from the copyright owner?

EXERCISES

 REVIEW

1. Choose a topic you are very familiar with, perhaps one of your hobbies. Jot down some things you would like to tell an audience about your topic, and organize those ideas into a formal outline with at least four main topics, each having at least two subtopics. Bring your outline to class for discussion.

2. Change the formal outline you created in Exercise 1 into a tree outline. Start by placing the broad topic at the top. Then begin placing subtopics below this topic in the manner discussed earlier in this chapter concerning tree outlines. Be prepared to discuss any advantages in organizing the information this way.

3. Consider a simple process you know well (for example, registering for classes, hunting for an apartment, finding a book or journal in the campus library) and create a flowchart for your topic following the guidelines discussed in this chapter.

 THE INTERNET

1. Find a Web site that has no more than 20 separate pages including the welcome or home page. Using a pencil and paper, sketch a storyboard showing how the Web site is organized.

2. Find five different Web sites that display information establishing that the site is copyrighted. Discuss any differences in the approaches for establishing the copyright on these pages.

 ETHICS/PROFESSIONALISM

1. Review the discussion of plagiarism in this chapter. Create a brief (one- or two-paragraph) scenario showing a student facing a difficult ethical decision concerning plagiarism. Discuss what you would tell the student to help him or her resolve the problem in an ethical and professional manner.

2. Review the discussion of copyright in this chapter. Provide a one-paragraph example of what

you would consider a violation of copyright based on what you have read.

COLLABORATION

Working in small groups of three students, effectively paraphrase the following two-paragraph direct quotation:

> Every page on the World Wide Web has an address, just like we have addresses for our homes and businesses. This address is called the Uniform Resource Locator, or URL (you can go ahead and forget the term "uniform resource locator"). The abbreviation URL is usually pronounced as its initials: you–are–ell.
>
> When you finish your Web site, you will post it on a server, which is a special computer directly connected to the Internet 24 hours a day. Every page on the World Wide Web is stored on a server; there are millions of servers. (Unless you are a big company, you usually don't own your own server.) Whoever does own the server and is hosting your site will work with you to determine what your personal URL will be. Once you know the URL for your site, you can tell everyone and they can visit your fun and enchanting pages.

Robin Williams and John Tollett, *The Non-Designer's Web Book: An Easy Guide to Creating, Designing, and Posting Your Own Web Site.* (Berkeley: Peachpit, 1998), 25.

Discuss what makes your paraphrase an effective paraphrase. Then create an example of an ineffective paraphrase, one that might be considered plagiarism. Discuss why that example might be considered plagiarism.

INTERNATIONAL COMMUNICATION

Many countries recognize copyright laws; however, many countries still do not. Find an example of a country that does not observe copyright law and discuss an example of how at least one business in the country has violated copyright law. Also briefly discuss the consequences of the copyright violation.

RESOURCES

Booth, Wayne C., Gregory G. Colomb, and Joseph M. Williams. *The Craft of Research.* Chicago: U of Chicago P, 1995.

Fishman, Stephen. *The Copyright Handbook: How to Protect and Use Written Works.* 5th ed. Berkeley: Nolo, 2000.

Hackos, JoAnn T. *Managing Your Documentation Projects.* New York: Wiley, 1994.

Kirsch, Jonathan. *Kirsch's Handbook of Publishing Law.* Los Angeles: Acrobat, 1995.

Lester, James D. *Writing Research Papers: A Complete Guide.* 9th ed. New York: Longman, 1999.

Porter, Lynnette, and William Coggin. *Research Strategies in Technical Communication.* New York: Wiley, 1995.

Smedinghoff, Thomas J. *The Software Publishers Association Legal Guide to Multimedia.* Reading: Addison-Wesley, 1994.

Zimmerman, Donald E., and Michel Lynn Muraski. *The Elements of Information Gathering: A Guide for Technical Communicators, Scientists, and Engineers.* Phoenix: Oryx, 1995.

Zimmerman, Donald E., and Dawn Rodrigues. *Research and Writing in the Disciplines.* Fort Worth: Harcourt, 1992.

PART TWO

Writing, Designing, Illustrating, and Editing

Chapter 7
Achieving an Effective Style   197

Chapter 8
Designing Pages and Screens   234

Chapter 9
Illustrations   294

Chapter 10
Editing, Revising, and Evaluating   328

7

Achieving an Effective Style

Style and Discourse Communities   198

Style and Genre   199

Kinds of Styles   201

Improving Your Writing Style at the
   Word Level   203

Improving Your Writing Style at the
   Sentence Level   215

Improving Your Writing Style at the
   Paragraph Level   216

Improving Your Writing Style in
   Larger Segments   221

Developing an Appropriate Tone   222

Avoiding Bias   225

Understanding Cultural Contexts   227

From the Workplace   226

IN THIS CHAPTER

Style, simply defined, is your manner of writing in your prose. An effective prose style develops from many areas—the discourse community for which you are writing; the genre you select to write; the subject, purpose, and scope of your document; your choice of words; your sentences and how you connect the sentences within paragraphs and from paragraph to paragraph; your tone; your ability to avoid bias; and various cultural contexts. As you continue to improve your understanding of how these elements constitute style, you will have better control over them and thus improve your own style.

You will learn about:

- style and discourse communities: how your audience affects the way you write
- style and genre: the ways various document types influence your decisions about writing style
- kinds of styles: plain and complex, formal and informal, noun and verb styles
- how to improve your writing style at the word, sentence, and paragraph levels as well as in larger segments through control of diction, usage, level of technicality and detail, jargon, nouns and verbs, voice, and other aspects
- how to develop an appropriate tone for your documents: how your attitudes toward your subject, your audience, and yourself guide you in selecting the way you will write—familiar or distant, serious or humorous, conversational or instructive, formal or relaxed
- how to avoid many kinds of bias: gender, religious, racial, cultural
- how to understand the cultural contexts for your documents: identifying culturally sensitive topics and conventions

UNEXPECTED BENEFITS

The course that helped me with my career was the English course that I didn't really want to take. Since taking the course, my written communications have become much clearer.

—George Johnston, software development engineer, Redmond, Washington

STYLE AND DISCOURSE COMMUNITIES

Some of your choices about how you write depend on the purpose of your writing. Others are just part of your personal style regardless of the situation. But many of your choices depend on whom you're writing for. Thus, style is directly tied to audience. Every audience represents a discourse community, and often each audience represents many discourse communities. (Discourse communities are discussed in more depth in Chapter 2.) Typical discourse communities are students in the same major, members of a profession, and practitioners of a hobby. Computer science students, lawyers, engineers, and gardeners each have a specialized language, experiences, basic knowledge, expectations, values, methodologies, idiosyncrasies, and goals.

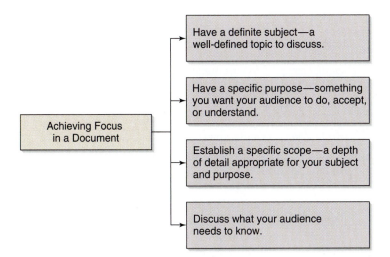

FIGURE 7.1

Focus in a Document

As much as possible, your decisions about what to write and how to write about it must be directly tied to your readers and their interests. Realize that your document may fail if you don't take into account many considerations concerning the discourse community for which you are writing. The point here is more complex than to suggest merely that you write differently to lay people, paraprofessionals, professionals, executives, technicians, or experts. Rather the point here is that all these audience levels are present in almost any discourse community. Chapter 4 discusses ways to help you narrow the focus of your subject according to what your readers need to know; also see the discussion of audience analysis in Chapter 2 for ideas on how to consider the interests of the discourse community for which you are writing.

If you have planned your document well, you will have a focus—a definite subject, purpose, and scope for your intended audience. You will have appropriately narrowed the discussion of your subject, and you will be telling your audience what it needs to know. (See Figure 7.1.)

STYLE AND GENRE

Just as the discourse community directly shapes the style, so does the genre or the kind of document you are writing. Typical genres in the technical professions are correspondence (letters, memos, e-mail), instructions, informal reports, formal reports, policies, procedures, and proposals. Some genres require a more formal style; others allow a wide range of styles.

For example, a job application letter requires a serious tone and, in general, a more formal diction than a personal letter to a friend. An abstract for an article in a chemistry journal will usually be more formal than an executive summary for a technical report. A software user guide for a novice audience

FIGURE 7.2
Types of Documents

TYPE OF DOCUMENT	APPROPRIATENESS	STYLE
Letter	For communicating formally from one company or organization to another company or organization For applying for a job and for other kinds of job correspondence	Style is often more formal than informal
Memo	For internal communications within a company or organization	Style is often more formal than informal but may be informal
E-mail	For informal communications within a company or organization For informal communications with friends or associates	Style is often informal but may be formal
Proposal	For internal communication within a company or organization or external communication between one company or organization and another	Style may be informal (in letter, memo, or e-mail format) or formal (in book format)
Instructions	Internal or external communication For personal or private communications	Style may range from very informal to formal
Policies and Procedures	For internal communication within a company or organization	Style may range from informal to formal
Informal Report	Internal or external communication	Style is often more informal than formal but may be formal. May be in letter, memo, or e-mail format
Formal Report	Internal or external communication	Style is often formal and is typically in book format

will generally be more informal and conversational than a technical reference guide for the same product. And an official government report on the space shuttle *Challenger* disaster requires a more serious tone than an instruction manual on how to build toy rockets.

Sometimes it is difficult to determine the best genre to use in a particular situation. For example, for some kinds of business correspondence, it may make a better impression to correspond by letter than by informal e-mail message, since e-mail is generally a more informal medium than print correspondence. It is still more widely accepted to apply for a job by mailing a cover letter and résumé to the prospective employer. Yet many companies are encouraging applicants to send initial inquiries and résumés by e-mail or fax.

And what is usual practice in one industry or geographical location may be quite different from usual practice in another. (See Figure 7.2.)

KINDS OF STYLES

Before they write, many writers don't give a lot of thought to the kinds of styles that are available to them. If they have a habit of writing in a plain style (clear, straightforward prose), then they will typically write just about everything in a plain style. However, skillful writers will use the style that best suits the subject, purpose, scope, audience (including discourse community), genre, and context.

For example, if you are writing a simple training manual to help soldiers learn the basics of a new weapon, you may choose to use a simple primer style for every sentence you write. (A primer—pronounced "primmer"—is a beginning reading book for children.) If you are writing a scientific article for the *New England Journal of Medicine,* you will cultivate a complex style (a more intricate or involved prose style) to impress on your expert readers the sophistication of your argument and your command of the subject. If you are writing a software manual for novices and trying to teach them how to use a new software program, you will use a plain style throughout to make sure your readers can understand the necessary tasks they must perform to use the program.

You have many choices when you select a dominant or major style for your document: plain or complex style, noun style, verb style, affected or pretentious style, formal or informal style. These styles may be combined. For example, many people write in both a verb style and a noun style (using many verbs and nouns throughout). Often, writers whose chief style is complex make their style more difficult by combining it with an affected style (a style that is pretentious). And, of course, there are a wide variety of levels of formality, ranging from the formal to the informal, for each style. By becoming familiar with these styles, you will give yourself the freedom to express your ideas more effectively in your technical documents.

You may use many styles in your writing, but by far the two most usual styles you will use and read are the plain style and the complex style.

Plain Style

A plain style, one that is straightforward and easy to understand, is the dominant style in technical prose. Also referred to as a reader-friendly style, this style is common in technical prose because readers want prose that enables them to read quickly and to apply the information correctly. The plain style seeks simplicity over complexity. In the plain style, language is generally simple and straightforward. Short, commonly used words combined into simple, short sentences, often written in the second-person "you" style, invite the reader into the text. The tone is friendly rather than impersonal. The strategies for a plain style are almost endless.

An Example of a Plain Style

Many years ago I received a tree identification book for Christmas. I was at my parents' home, and after all the gifts had been opened I decided to go out and identify the trees in the neighborhood. Before I went out, I read through part of the book. The first tree in the book was the Joshua tree because it only took two clues to identify it. Now the Joshua tree is a really weird-looking tree and I looked at that picture and said to myself, "Oh, we don't have that kind of tree in Northern California. That is a weird-looking tree. I would know if I saw that tree, and I've never seen one before." So I took my book and went outside. My parents lived in a cul-de-sac of six homes. Four of those homes had Joshua trees in the front yard. I had lived in that house for thirteen years and I had never seen a Joshua tree. I took a walk around the block, and there must have been a sale at the nursery when everyone was landscaping their new homes—at least 80 percent of the homes had Joshua trees in the front yards. *And I had never seen one before!* Once I was conscious of the tree, once I could name it, I saw it everywhere. Which is exactly my point. Once you can name something, you're conscious of it. You have power over it. You own it. You're in control.

So now you're going to learn the names of several design principles. And you are going to be in control of your pages.

Robin Williams, *The Non-Designer's Design Book* (Berkeley: Peachpit, 1994) 13.

Complex Style

A complex style is characterized by a technical vocabulary and complex or compound–complex sentence structure, with perhaps long paragraphs exposing complex concepts. Complex styles can seem more distant and less personal than the plain style through use of a less friendly tone, but depending on the genre, audience, subject, purpose, and scope of your writing, a complex style may be just the approach you need to convey your information effectively. Complex styles can be difficult to read, however, and one reason is that style and content are so closely related. A complex style often accompanies complex material. If a subject is only slightly technical, it is easier for a reader to understand than a subject that is moderately or highly technical. Highly technical material is often difficult to read because the language is formal and because the topic is advanced. Many subjects are more technical, abstract, theoretical, or difficult than others. Still, a complex style, handled competently, can clarify a technical subject even to a novice audience.

Example of a Complex Style

The Promethean theft of fire has become a familiar symbol for the scientific endeavor—the wrestling of the secrets of nature from the gods and conveying them to humankind to ease its lot. But the traditional image of the scientist-as-writer, an image common both within science and without, is, in contrast, a peculiarly humble and constricted one. Gone are the creativity and daring of the Titan. In their place is the self-effacing toil of the amanuensis, for, unlike poets, who are free to create the world anew as they write of it, scientists must be totally circumspect, must expunge every trace of their own personalities from their work, as they record only what is there. The scientist must view the world through some impersonal ocular device, the spectacles of objectivity, rather than through the eyes of a person. The scientist must weigh the world not in a hand but in a balance; must measure it not with a stride but with a calipers. The Promethean scientist may uncover the secrets of the gods but must whisper them—like someone with an artificial larynx—in a voice devoid of emotion so as not, as the Fiesers put it for fellow chemists, to "divert attention from the story we are trying to tell." Above all, scientists dare not run naked through the streets shrieking "Eureka!" or they will, as the Fiesers say, "violat[e] principles of good usage."

This view of the discourse of the scientist cannot be allowed to stand. Rather, the scientist–writer must be untrammeled and encouraged to express individuality.

David Locke, *Science as Writing* (New Haven: Yale UP, 1992) 57.

IMPROVING YOUR WRITING STYLE AT THE WORD LEVEL

Achieving an effective style consists of making every improvement you can at the word, sentence, and paragraph levels. Keep all of these levels in mind as you write, and concentrate on improving your writing on all of these levels. One key to improving your writing at the sentence, paragraph, and higher levels is to make sure you have a good command of your writing at the word level.

Levels of Diction

Diction is your choice of words. You tend to make certain word choices, even if unconsciously, according to your writing habits, the needs of your audience, your purpose, your scope, and the genre. Perhaps you normally favor concrete terms, simple words, and a nontechnical vocabulary. Or perhaps you normally choose more abstract words, more literary images, and more emotionally expressive prose. Along with your personal preferences, you will certainly modify your diction according to the particular needs of the document you are working on. And in technical prose, you will have to deal with subject matter and audience considerations that may require a vocabulary that is quite different from everyday language.

Just as there are many levels of formality in style—from highly formal to highly informal—there are many levels of diction. The four generally accepted

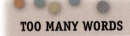

TOO MANY WORDS

I find that inexperienced writers (especially in science) use too many words and they are afraid to use the active voice. Their writing conveys a lack of confidence in their own work.

—Rochelle Schwartz-Bloom, Ph.D., associate professor, Durham, North Carolina

levels of diction are formal, informal, colloquial, and slang. Any of these four levels may be correct in a particular context but incorrect in another.

Formal

Formal diction is the language that is appropriate for a formal context. You would expect to hear formal speech at a commencement address or a State of the Union speech, and you would expect to read formal prose in a contract, government document, document abstract, or academic journal article. The choice to use formal diction is determined by the context, and the context is determined by your purpose, the genre of the technical document, the audience, and other factors. Sometimes you will be able to choose your diction, and sometimes the genre will determine the diction you must use. Some genres tolerate a range of diction. For example, you may find that rather than keeping to a highly formal diction in a documentation set, you can use an informal approach quite appropriately.

An Example of Formal Diction

Creativity is manifested in virtually every significant aspect of the human experience, among which technology stands out for a number of reasons.

First, because it is intimately woven into the fabric of human existence across so many dimensions—personal, societal, economic, national, and international—it provokes strong emotions—exhilaration, admiration, wonder, distaste, fear, and loathing depending on one's view. Second, unlike many other domains of the creative spirit, but in common with the scientific endeavor, its fruits are exposed to the fiercest and hardiest tests of survivability: only those artifactual forms that withstand the storm and stress of the real world are acknowledged and accepted as acts of true invention. But whereas science deals to some extent with idealized and approximate models of the real world, technology (like organisms) must cope with raw nature. Scientific laws at best approximate nature's behavior. But artifacts are far from idealized forms. There is something dramatically substantial about steam engines, cathedrals, skyscrapers, computers, aircrafts, automobiles, bridges, and blast furnaces. A scientific theory that fails will at best be revised or modified and at worst be consigned to the scrapheap of history. If an artifact fails, its consequences are felt in tangible, poignant, and sometimes, terrible ways. As the failures of nuclear power plants, chemical plants, aircraft, bridges, and pharmaceutical products have shown, consequences reverberate within and across nations. Unlike the artist, writer, or scientists, the technologist must be creative in a responsible way.

Third, though now firmly paired with science, technology is as old as mankind, whereas science, or what was formerly called natural philosophy, is scarcely five hundred years old. Thus, invention, design, and the making of artifacts is fundamentally independent of science and, indeed, as independent a human endeavor as are the practices of art, science, and literature.

Subrata Desgupta, *Technology and Creativity* (New York: Oxford UP, 1996) 185–186.

Informal

Informal refers to ordinary, casual, or familiar use. Traditionally, technical documents have been formal and, in fact, rather stuffy. To some people, "technical document" is just another way of saying "unreadable." But technical documents have evolved from the stilted works of years ago, and many of the most effective examples today are written in an informal prose style. And an informal prose style can now be appropriate for a good many technical genres, such as letters, memos, and e-mail.

Example of Informal Diction

Content Is King: Notes About Writing

Most of the hubbub and hoopla surrounding the Web these days focuses on gorgeous graphics, fancy fonts, and other stylistic considerations. And, as you've read in several places in the book, we're just now starting to see new innovations that make Web pages truly interactive. But to the people who lust for flashy images and other eye candy, and to the pie-in-the-sky types who yearn for the Web's hands-on future, I have one thing to say: It's the content, stupid! For now and the foreseeable future, at least, this is the central fact of Web page publishing, and it often gets obscured behind all the hype.

And, unless you're an artist or a musician or some other right-brain type, content means text. The vast majority of Web pages are written documents that rely on words and phrases for impact. It makes sense, then, to put most of your page-production efforts into your writing. Sure, you spend lots of time fine-tuning your HTML codes to get things laid out just so, or tweaking your images, or scouring the Web for "hot links" to put on your page, but you should direct the majority of your publishing time towards polishing your prose.

Paul McFedries, *The Complete Idiot's Guide to Creating a Web Page* (Indianapolis: Macmillan, 2000) 332.

Colloquial

Colloquial refers to conversation or diction that is used to achieve conversational prose. It may also mean everyday speech and slang. In many situations, colloquial prose will not be appropriate as a workplace diction choice. Occasionally, as in certain e-mail correspondences, it may be acceptable. The "Dummies" series of computer books is an example of colloquial diction used successfully to document computer software and operating systems.

Example of Colloquial Diction

June 4

Major brainstorm last night! Woke up in a babbling frenzy. Images of gears, motors, fan belts, generators, all sorts of gizmos and gadgets buzzing through my brain. I'm jotting down what I can remember in this journal. These notes will record my progress as I undertake construction. The basic concept is this: the world is in danger of becoming boring and brain-dead and what we all need is some kind of major outrageous mind-blowing challenge! I'm talking about BIG TIME challenge. Something that will really make you wrack your brain and THINK. But it's gotta be fun! It's gotta be wild and intense and full of weird twists and tricks. And that's when it hit me: a machine! An incredible machine! A machine that changes into a hundred different puzzles, games, and gadgets! and so . . . I'm taking on this outrageous task of inventing this machine. What will it do? How will it work? The possibilities are endless!

July 16

Another major eureka today! Found a totally wild way of producing mechanical energy via critter power: the hamster and the monkey bike. Low overhead, too: a few hunks of moldy cheese and a crate of bananas, and I'm in business.

It won't be long now! The even more Incredible Machine is almost ready . . .

The Even More Incredible Machine: Journal Entries June thru August (Coarsegold: Sierra On-line, n.d.) 26.

Slang

Slang and colloquial language overlap. Slang is sometimes thought of as a synonym for colloquial language, but in fact it has its own distinctive features. Slang is colloquial language with an attitude. It consists of a vocabulary shared by a particular group, often with the purpose of excluding others. You would not use slang in a document unless you knew that it was expected by the discourse community you were writing for.

An Example of Slang

Apple Computer is taking the pipe and there is nothing, no force in the universe, that can stop it. Their products are being dropped like hot potatoes by nearly every big corporation and being relegated to a few—very minor—roles in the departments where the weenies and air-heads work. Every day, fewer and fewer software vendors support this platform and increasing numbers of THEM announce their first or only releases for Windows/PC. Sales fall, Apple's prices and, as a result, margins slip downward—this MUST affect R&D spending. And, virtually nobody else is spending R&D money on this platform, at least as far as hardware is concerned.

<newsgroup alt.binaries.warex.ibm-pc> May 6, 1996, 21:21:55 GMT.

Denotation and Connotation

The denotative meanings of a word are the dictionary meanings of the word. The connotative meanings of a word are the additional meanings that we associate with the word. Connotations are the hidden agendas our words carry along with them. The words you choose may be absolutely correct denotatively, but their connotations can either sabotage or strengthen the effectiveness of your prose. You are responsible for the effects your words create, so be

WORD	DENOTATION	CONNOTATION
Red	a color, blood	anger, irritation
White	a color, snow	purity, innocence
Green	a color, grass, money	inexperience, envy
Blue	a color, sky	sadness, depression
Wind	air in natural motion	sudden force
Home	a dwelling	warmth, comfort, affection
Mountain	a natural elevation of the earth's surface	calm, quiet, peacefulness, difficult-to-attain goal

FIGURE 7.3

Denotation and Connotation

sure you take into account the sometimes subtle messages they carry along. See Figure 7.3 for denotation and connotation examples.

Usage

Usage, simply defined, concerns appropriate and accurate word choice. (Also see the discussion of jargon below for the problems a specialized vocabulary presents to writers of technical prose.) It's important to realize that writers of technical prose have as many problems with words in the general vocabulary as other writers do. Writers of technical prose, as do other writers, often confuse *affect* and *effect, bring* and *take, can* and *may, shall* and *will, comprise* and *constitute,* and so on.

Common mistakes in usage include archaic expressions (words that are old-fashioned and no longer used naturally) such as *amongst;* barbarisms (word distortions) such as *disremember* and *irregardless;* and improprieties (good words used inappropriately) such as *set* for *sit, most* for *almost, accept* for *except.* Writers may also misuse idiomatic expressions (expressions that are particular to every language and often not governed by the rules of grammar) such as *get into hot water* or *with a grain of salt.* See Figure 7.4 for examples of archaisms, barbarisms, and improprieties.

Long Words

Most often, a simple or plain style should be your objective in writing technical documents. The strategy of simplicity does not mean you should patronize your audience or unnecessarily simplify your prose. After all, you are often writing about a complex subject. However, it does mean that as much as possible and as often as it suits your purpose, you should prefer the familiar word to the unfamiliar word, the simpler word to the more complex word,

FIGURE 7.4

Archaisms, Barbarisms, and Improprieties

Archaisms—words that are old-fashioned and no longer used naturally

albeit (although)

amongst (among)

aught (anything)

methinks (I think)

nigh (near)

Barbarisms—word distortions

source (as a verb)

gift (as a verb)

input (as a verb)

disremember

irregardless

Improprieties—good words used inappropriately

set *for* sit

accept *for* except

most *for* almost

lay *for* lie

affect *for* effect

disinterested *for* uninterested

and a plain style to an affected or pretentious style. Many writers of technical prose use language that is more complex than it needs to be. And many needlessly use jargon, in the sense of unnecessarily technical language, that is totally unsuited to their audience. You will read more about jargon later in this chapter. See Figure 7.5 for examples of pretentious and simpler words.

Abbreviations, Acronyms, Initialisms

In general, abbreviations are shortened versions of words or phrases and are formed by the first letters of words: *co.* for *company* or *c.o.d.* for *cash on delivery.* Abbreviations save space in technical prose, but abbreviations may also present problems for your readers. There is no guarantee that all your readers will understand your abbreviations, so you have to analyze your audience when you are deciding whether to use abbreviations. If you do choose

PRETENTIOUS	SIMPLER
utilize	use
prioritize	rank
finalize	complete, finish
strategize	plan
feedback	response
interface	communicate, interact
dialog (as a verb)	discuss
output	results
factoid	fact
obsoleted	made obsolete

FIGURE 7.5

Pretentious Words and Simpler Words

to abbreviate, identifying the abbreviations first will aid your reader. Also, in longer documents, it's common practice to include a list of abbreviations or acronyms or both.

Example

According to the Drug Abuse Warning Network (DAWN), drug-related emergency admissions are at an all-time high. DAWN has completed a new questionnaire to widen its research to include ages and ethnic background.

Acronyms are abbreviations formed by combining the first letter or letters of several words. An acronym is pronounced as a word and should be written in capital letters without periods: *NASA* for National Aeronautics and Space Administration; *RAM* for random-access memory. Acronyms that have become accepted as nouns are the only exception to the capitalization rule. These acronyms are written with lowercase letters without periods: *scuba* (self-contained underwater breathing apparatus); *sonar* (sound navigation ranging).

Initialisms are abbreviations that are formed by combining the first letter of each word in a phrase consisting of many words. An initialism is pronounced as separate letters: *STC* (Society for Technical Communication); *p.m.* (post meridian). Initialisms are written using both uppercase and lowercase letters. Use periods for only lowercase initialisms. The two exceptions to this rule are geographic names and academic degrees: *U.S.A.* (United States of America); *A.A.* (Associate of Arts). The common rule for plural acronyms and initialisms is to add an *s*, without an apostrophe: *ATMs; CRTs*.

Consider your reader's knowledge concerning acronyms and initialisms. What might be familiar to you will not necessarily be familiar to your reader. When you first use an acronym or initialism, spell out the entire phrase with the acronym or initialism in parentheses. Spelling out the acronym or initialism when it is first used will guarantee that your reader will know what the abbreviation means.

Often, readers will not read long documents sequentially. When writing a long document, you should periodically write out the acronym or initialism in parentheses after the abbreviation. Using this technique will ensure that your reader will not have to refer elsewhere continually to find the meaning of the acronym or initialism. Acronyms and initialisms should also be placed in the glossary of your document.

Filling your prose with abbreviations, acronyms, and initialisms has many names, including abbrevomania and agglomerese.

Action Verbs

Verbs express the action in a sentence. Action verbs are specific verbs that descriptively tell the audience what was or will be done. When you use passive voice and weak, colorless verbs, you deprive your prose of a simple yet powerful tool for carrying your message effectively. Choose verbs that express action and use the active voice. Often writers bury the action of a sentence in nouns, adjectives, or other parts of speech.

Original: The chemist completed the dilution of the solution and performed the transference of the diluted solution to the beaker.

Revision: The chemist diluted the solution and transferred it to the beaker.

Good writers make abundant use of action verbs. Verbs make your writing more direct and forceful. Action verbs in an employment letter or résumé may include *designed, collaborated, edited, wrote, accomplished, organized, directed, polished, reworked, networked, pioneered, supervised,* and *advanced.* The list of possible action verbs for a résumé or employment letter is almost endless. In instructions, simple imperative statements use action verbs to tell readers exactly what needs to be done: *Insert* the cable into socket A; *press* the Enter key; *right click* on the desktop and *select* Properties from the menu; or *Cut* the blue wire ¼ inch from its base.

Active Voice

Active voice, like action verbs, is another strategy for helping your readers recognize the agent or doer of an action, and, like action verbs, active voice helps to make your writing more direct and forceful. Active-voice prose tells your readers quite clearly who is doing what to whom. To write in the active voice, place the actor in the subject position of the sentence. Active voice helps readers to recognize more quickly who is doing what action, helps to make sentences shorter, and helps to avoid the ambiguity created by using passive voice.

Original: The Novell Netware network was set up in the lab by the systems administrator so 20 workstations could share programs and printers.

Revision: The systems administrator set up the Novell Netware network in the lab so 20 workstations could share programs and printers.

Passive Voice

Passive voice makes the agent of the action less clear. Sometimes passive voice weakens a sentence because it increases the ambiguity.

Original: Every evening the lab must be cleaned and the computers checked for viruses.

Revision: Every evening you must clean the lab and check the computers for viruses.

Depending on your purpose, you may need to use passive voice at times:

- to deemphasize or obscure the person who is doing the action. In the workplace, it can be more appropriate to write "a decision was made to require more overtime" than to write "John Smith decided to require more overtime." John Smith may prefer to remain anonymous concerning this unpopular decision.
- to emphasize action performed rather than the agent that performed it.
- to avoid repetitions of "I" or "We" at the beginning of each sentence, alternating active verbs with passive ones.
- to conform to the expectations and conventions of the discourse community for which you are writing.
- to emphasize the grammatical subject in order to show the positive cause of an action. For example, compare *Marion was promoted by her boss after only six months on the job* to *Marion's boss promoted her after only six months on the job.* The first emphasizes Marion's responsibility for gaining a quick promotion; the second emphasizes the boss's responsibility in promoting Marion.

Since passive voice weakens the impact of your verb, you will want to ensure that when you use it, you are using it for a good reason.

Noun Strings

Noun strings are formed by stringing together two or more noun phrases. Noun strings are often a problem in technical prose if there are too many modifiers for the nouns.

Original: Place a disk in the A: drive of your multimedia Pentium office computer.

Revision: Place a disk in the A: drive of your office computer.

Nominalizations

A nominalization occurs when you turn a verb into a noun or when nouns do the work of other parts of speech. Nominalizations may be created by turning a verb into a noun (*nominalize* into *nominalization*), by nominalizing adjectives (*careless* into *carelessness*), or by adding -ing to a verb (*The naming of the boat*). Nominalizing verbs or adjectives is a common practice, but overuse of nominalization often creates a passive style. And nominalizing often requires using more words to say the same thing: for example, *He was guilty of carelessness* instead of *He was careless*.

Jargon

Technical prose style consists, in part, of a specialized vocabulary or, more broadly, a specialized language. Every discipline, profession, trade, or hobby has its special vocabulary, and using this special vocabulary appropriately requires careful attention. However, this necessary specialized language is often misused, abused, or used pretentiously, and you must understand what the misuses are to know how to avoid them. See Figure 7.6 for examples of jargon as pretentious language.

Like technical terms, the term *jargon* applies to the specialized vocabulary of a trade, profession, hobby, or science. When used within the trade or profession, it serves as a verbal shorthand to convey exact information in an abbreviated form. But when it is used outside its own discourse community, it can confuse and confound. Since this is sometimes the intent, jargon is often correctly perceived as pretentious or hostile in those contexts. Jargon is known by other names as well: computerese, engineerese, bureaucratese, governmentese, academese, officialese, tech speak, technospeak, newspeak, doublespeak, doubletalk, and pentagonese.

Unless you are writing within a discourse community that is familiar with the jargon, you will better serve your audience by avoiding its use. Whether the

CHOOSING THE ETHICAL PATH

If creating a verbal smokescreen is your intent, then perhaps you need to reexamine your purpose in writing.

FIGURE 7.6

Pretentious Jargon

PRETENTIOUS JARGON	SIMPLER ALTERNATIVES
peripheral	disk, printer, modem, scanner
configure	set up
functionality	functions (noun)
methodology	method
price point	price
end-user	user
data warehousing	collecting and analyzing customer information

jargon is simply incomprehensible vocabulary or gobbledygook designed to obscure your meaning or absence of meaning, you are not communicating by using it. If your use of jargon unintentionally confuses, then have others review your work for clarity and revise your work where necessary.

Of course, there are specialized languages that are similar to jargon. These include shop talk, computerese, and technobabble. Shop talk is jargon that has become so specialized that it applies only to one company or subgroup of an occupation. For example, shop talk at the Kennedy Space Center in Florida includes words or phrases such as *stand by* (please wait), *Roger* (okay), *under-volt* (low electrical gauge reading), *full-scale high* (gauge needle off the scale to the high side), and *showing zip* (no reading).

Computerese is the use of computer jargon in your writing. Technobabble is an offshoot of computerese. Computerese or computer jargon devolves into babble when it is used as filler or decoration, when it is employed intentionally for obfuscatory purposes, when it is employed gratuitously, when it is used obsessively, and when it is used by people who are unfamiliar with its meanings in an attempt to sound as if they know what they are talking about.

Unfortunately, writers who have become accustomed to hearing and using computerese in appropriate contexts often slide into its use even when it's not appropriate. In-house terms, common at your company, can appear in your writing even when you are writing for an audience that would not be familiar with the expressions. Guard against letting your usual work vocabulary spill into documents that are intended for others.

People as Machines

Personification means using terms of human characteristics and applying them to inanimate objects: *That car is just being stubborn.* The opposite process—perhaps we should call it *mechanization*—uses inanimate descriptors to refer to people.

One author warns that this process is already active and spreading. The nonvirtual (noncomputer) world is called the *carbon community* or *meatspace*; to be fired is to be *uninstalled*; a new employee who does not need to be trained is *plug-and-play* (Kakutani).

Of course, clear technical language consists of more than just using technical terms your audience understands. An ill-defined purpose, a confusing organization, poorly written sentences, overly long paragraphs, and many other faults contribute to an ineffective document. Yet there are many factors you can consider to make your use of technical terms more appropriate.

Achieving Clarity with Technical Terms

● Understand the meanings of jargon—necessary technical terms you must use for many occasions within a discourse community, inappropriate technical terms used for the wrong audience, and technical terms used pretentiously.

● Use jargon and other types of specialized language appropriately. Define jargon when it's necessary to use it; avoid it when it's not necessary. If you must use jargon for an audience that is unfamiliar with it, provide a glossary or define terms when you introduce them for the first time in the text.

● Provide an analogy or some other kind of comparison, anecdote, concrete example, illustration, or nontechnical explanation to help explain your point.

● Omit unnecessary modifiers and qualifiers and excessive wordiness.

● Use terminology consistently.

Ambiguous Modifiers

A modifier is any word or group of words that restricts, limits, or makes more exact the meaning of other words. The modifiers of nouns and pronouns are usually adjectives, participles, adjective phrases, and adjective clauses. The modifiers of verbs, adjectives, and adverbs are adverbs, adverb phrases, and adverb clauses: *a nervous, high-pitched* giggle; *the* boy *in the first row; royal* purple; *sickeningly* sweet; *scorching* hot.

Meaningless (ambiguous) modifiers are modifiers that neither restrict nor make clear the meaning of other words. These modifiers are often used to make the prose sound more important or impressive: She was *quite* happy to see her boyfriend again; He was *very* excited to be at the concert; The audience talked about how *extremely* hot the theater was. While such modifiers or intensifiers are not always meaningless, many writers have a tendency to overuse them in their writing.

Trite Phrases or Clichés

A cliché is a trite phrase or expression, something that has become overly familiar or commonplace. The term comes from a French word for stereotype plate, a block for printing. The reader pays little attention to the words because they have been so overused. Examples include *a crying shame, slept like a dog, stick to your guns,* and *in this day and age.*

IMPROVING YOUR WRITING STYLE AT THE SENTENCE LEVEL

The ability to construct clear, concise, and accurate sentences in technical prose is an invaluable skill. In early drafts of the writing process, many of your sentences may be ambiguous, longer than they need to be, and somewhat inaccurate in content. Effective sentences require a lot of editing and revising. Often you may have to abandon the sentence you've been struggling with and just start over. And, of course, it helps to have a thorough understanding of the components of a good sentence, from forms to sentence length to variety.

Sentences and Technical Terms

When readers see a technical term for the first time, particularly a term that they will not instantly recognize, they can best grasp that term if it appears not at the beginning of a sentence, in its topic, but at the end.

Original: Standard protocols are used by programmers when they write their programs to ensure that different types of computers can work together.

Revision: To ensure that different types of computers can work together, programmers write their programs using standard protocols.

Technical term defined toward the end: The incubation of peripheral-blood lymphocytes with a lymphokine, interleukin-2, generates lymphoid cells that can lose fresh, noncultured, natural-killer-cell-resistant tumor cells but not normal cells. We term these cells lymphokine-activated killer (LAK) cells.

> **ADJUST THE TECHNICALITY**
>
> Know your audience and adjust the technical level of the material accordingly.
>
> —John M. Watts, Jr., fire safety consultant, Middlebury, Vermont

Emphasis

Sentence emphasis is the art of ending a sentence well. Strategies for achieving sentence emphasis include the following:

1. Trimming the end of the sentence:

Original: Many major computer manufacturers now have Web sites listing a complete product line offering the opportunity for consumers to choose online the exact features they want for their computer and, once the order is placed, offering the opportunity to track their computer from production to shipping.

Revision: Many major computer manufacturers now have Web sites listing a complete product line offering the opportunity for consumers to choose online the exact features they want for their computer and the opportunity to track their order from production to shipping.

2. Shifting less important ideas to the front of the sentence:

Original: The major computer manufacturers are marketing their products much more effectively than they were just a few years ago, according to the experts.

Revision: According to the experts, the major computer manufacturers are marketing their products much more effectively than they were just a few years ago.

3. Shifting more important ideas toward the end of the sentence:

Original: You will see that the major computer manufacturers offer better deals to those consumers who order directly from the manufacturer than the deals consumers often receive when they buy a computer from a major retailer.

Revision: If you compare the deals that consumers receive by ordering their computers directly from a major computer manufacturer with the deals they receive by buying their computer from a major retailer, consumers almost always receive a better deal ordering direct.

Variety

> Sentence variety is a matter not only of sentence form, but also of sentence function, style, combining techniques, and length.

Sentence variety is essential for achieving an effective style. Using too many simple sentences together may create a primer style; using too many compound–complex sentences may create a turgid or inflated style. Sentence variety is a matter not only of sentence form, but also of sentence function, style, combining techniques, and length. Varying sentence length is especially important. Place too many short sentences together and you create a choppy style; place too many long sentences together and you create a wordy style.

It's impossible to set a limit on the length of a sentence. The average length of a sentence is eighteen words, but many longer sentences are often necessary. The complexity of the information is also a factor in determining sentence length. A long sentence may have too much complex information and would be better rewritten into several shorter sentences. Consider also your readers' familiarity with the material, the importance of the material, whether the sentence is offering new or repetitive information, and the method you will use to achieve a logical flow of ideas.

IMPROVING YOUR WRITING STYLE AT THE PARAGRAPH LEVEL

Good writers give as much careful attention to paragraphs as they do to words, clauses, phrases, and sentences. On the paragraph level, technical prose differs from nontechnical prose in its use of section headings or summaries to alert readers to the topic of the succeeding or preceding paragraphs. Thus, paragraphs in some technical documents may not have a typical topic sentence. Headings, headers, footers, and other aids guide readers and add to the message that is conveyed in the body text. At the same time, the rules for writing effective technical paragraphs are not so different from those for writing any other kind of paragraph:

- Limit yourself to one major topic per paragraph.
- Develop your topic using an appropriate paragraph pattern.
- Control the flow.
- Provide adequate details.

Writing on One Topic

Each paragraph should focus on one key idea or complete thought. One of the major reasons for ambiguity in writing is that many writers combine several different topics into one paragraph. A carefully constructed outline will help you to determine what your key ideas are. See Chapter 6 for a discussion of outlining and organizing information.

An Example of a Paragraph on One Topic

The Web represents the same unlimited potential to people in rural communities as it does to people in big cities. Remember when designers ran across town to show a client a layout for an ad, a brochure, or a flyer? As a Web designer you can upload files to the "server" (the computer where the Web pages are stored so the world can see them) right from your home or office, go online to test the files, make any necessary corrections, and re-upload the files—all without leaving your desk. The clients can view the changes from their own offices, make suggestions, approve or disapprove, all without anyone having to physically meet in the same space. The client may be on the other side of town or on the other side of the world—it doesn't matter. A client in California may hire a designer in Mississippi to design a Web site that will be hosted on a server in Florida. The server storing the Web site doesn't care if the designer is uploading from Los Cerrillos, New Mexico, or New York City, New York.

Robin Williams and John Tollett, *The Non-Designer's Web Book* (Berkeley: Peachpit, 1998) 100.

Developing the Paragraph Topic

Good paragraphs have an appropriate pattern or order. You must decide how you will go about developing your topic. Will you begin with your topic sentence? pose a question? contrast or define? As you gain experience in writing effective paragraphs, you will find that even though paragraphs can follow certain patterns, they don't necessarily follow them in exactly the same way. You may use a topic sentence to start your paragraph, carry the middle, or end it. In fact, your paragraph may express one topic and still not have one particular sentence embody that topic.

Common paragraph patterns include the following:

- **Example paragraphs**—Example paragraphs make a statement and support it with specific examples.

- **General-to-specific paragraphs**—General-to-specific paragraphs begin with a broad statement of the paragraph topic and progress to more and more specific points to support the topic.
- **Specific-to-general paragraphs**—Specific-to-general paragraphs build the topic from the ground up, going from detail to detail until the whole idea is complete.
- **Question-to-answer paragraphs**—Question-to-answer paragraphs pose a question, sometimes rhetorically or theoretically, sometimes specifically or realistically, then proceed to provide the answer.
- **Definition paragraphs**—Definition paragraphs define a term or concept.
- **Description paragraphs**—Description paragraphs offer a vivid impression of a person, place, or object.
- **Narration paragraphs**—Narration paragraphs relate an event.
- **Comparison paragraphs**—Comparison paragraphs compare topic A with topic B.
- **Contrast paragraphs**—Contrast paragraphs contrast topic A with topic B.
- **Analogy paragraphs**—Analogy paragraphs compare an unfamiliar topic to a familiar topic.
- **Classification paragraphs**—Classification paragraphs divide a topic into categories.
- **Enumerative paragraphs**—Enumerative paragraphs number the points they will cover as first, second, and third.
- **Cause-and-effect paragraphs**—Cause-and-effect paragraphs discuss the effects of a particular cause.

Common Paragraph Patterns

Example paragraphs

General-to-specific paragraphs

Specific-to-general paragraphs

Question-to-answer paragraphs

Definition paragraphs

Description paragraphs

Narration paragraphs

Comparison paragraphs

Contrast paragraphs

Analogy paragraphs

Classification paragraphs

Enumerative paragraphs

Cause-and-effect paragraphs

Look at the following sample paragraphs to see how they illustrate paragraph patterns.

Definition Paragraphs

If you have done much surfing on the Web, you have probably noticed that some images seem to be painted in from top to bottom while others come slowly into focus. GIFs that slowly come into focus are *interlaced*—the ones that appear from top to bottom are not. If you're like most people, you probably prefer to watch an interlaced image develop instead of a noninterlaced one.

With a *noninterlaced* image, the data is stored in the file in regular sequential order, row 1 followed by row 2 followed by row 3, and so on. Thus, the image appears on the screen from top to bottom. An interlaced image stores every eighth row (row 1, row 9, row 17, and so on), followed by every fourth row (row 2, row 6, row 10, and so on), followed by every other row (row 3, row 5, row 7, and so on), followed by the remaining rows. The effect is that the GIF materializes on the screen as if Scotty himself had beamed it there.

Judi N. Fernandez, *GIFs, JPEGs, & BMPs: Handling Internet Graphics* (New York: MIS, 1997) 13–14.

A Question-to-Answer Paragraph

How do you learn about your users' views of the information world you need to design? Formal market research methods such as surveys and focus groups may corroborate your initial design ideas, but the first sources of information must be closer to the user communities. Begin by studying how the users are supported by information today, focusing especially on cases where possibly inadequate sources of information exist. Study your users by observing them at work and asking them about the challenges and problems that occur when they try to perform tasks, solve problems, or otherwise strive to work effectively.

JoAnn T. Hackos and Dawn M. Stevens, *Standards for Online Information: Publishing Information for the Internet/World Wide Web/Help Systems/Corporate Intranets* (New York: John Wiley & Sons, 1997) 20.

Achieving an Effective Flow

The sentences in an effective paragraph should flow smoothly from the first to the last. The smooth flow is achieved mainly by the two principles of cohesion and coherence. You create cohesion from sentence to sentence in a paragraph by including information that is old and information that is new in each sentence. Each sentence thus links to the previous and following sentences, bringing the paragraph together into a cohesive whole.

Example of cohesion

Develop the presentation using a *flowline* metaphor. The *flowline* contains icons that represent the various *steps* in your procedure. The *steps* can be *multimedia* elements or *interactive* points. *Multimedia* and *interaction* can be combined to create an effective learning module.

You create coherence in a paragraph by using transitional words and phrases, repeating key words, and repeating key ideas. The transitional words, repeated words, and emphasis on key ideas join the sentences together by showing how the idea flows from the first sentence through until the last.

Example of coherence

Multimedia can be a tremendous teaching tool. *For example,* students can learn about the Egyptian pyramids by reading text about the pyramids while also viewing photographs, watching video, and listening to audio. *Multimedia has already proven its value as a teaching tool* through the hundreds of multimedia CD-ROMs available to high schools and colleges on numerous topics. *In addition,* multimedia programs are becoming less expensive every year, enabling more schools and colleges to purchase more programs.

Providing Adequate Details

Controlling the level of detail in a technical document can be a challenge even to the experienced writer. The difficulty lies in finding the correct level without either confusing your readers by vagueness or drowning them in information they do not need. Unsurprisingly, the appropriate level of detail will depend on your purpose and scope. If you are preparing assembly instructions for a piece of machinery, for example, appropriate detail would include explaining what to do with the various parts. You wouldn't want to include details of the design of the individual circuit boards or the composition of the metallic alloys used in the device. On the other hand, an instruction manual on how to use the device probably would not cover details necessary for its assembly.

Aside from purpose and scope, you must consider your audience when planning detail. Are your readers engineers who are very familiar with the constituent parts of the item being described? If so, you can refer to the individual parts by their standard names and expect your audience to follow you. If your audience is inexperienced with the material, you may have to increase the level of detail you supply to ensure that your descriptions and explanations do not assume too much prior knowledge. Or, conversely, you may want to reduce the level of detail for your novice audience and present only the material that it specifically needs to know.

Consider your genre when you plan your details. What is the appropriate level of detail in a job application cover letter, for example? Should you include as much detail as you would in a résumé? Too much detail can be as ineffective as too little.

Handling New Information

Readers can best understand long and complex units of information when that information falls at the ends of sentences. In addition, readers understand new information—particularly unfamiliar technical information—more easily at the ends of sentences. Putting new information at the ends of sentences, rather than at the beginning, signals to readers that these are the important concepts you will be developing in the sentences that follow.

In general, readers best comprehend long complex units after they have read a relatively short and clear subject-plus-verb sequence. Don't start a sentence by forcing them to struggle through a list of items, a complex set of conditions, or long abstract clumps of nominalizations.

Original: The suggestion by the committee that more multimedia be used in Freshman English classes as an additional way of teaching the fundamentals of composition more effectively is controversial.

Revision: The committee suggests that more multimedia be used in Freshman English classes as a an additional way to teach composition. Of course, the suggestion is controversial.

Avoiding Ambiguous Reference

Ambiguous references occur in paragraphs when it is difficult to tell what the reference is in one or more sentences. The ambiguity leads to at least several different interpretations.

Original: Several companies are competing for the contract with our company to provide in-house seminars to our employees. These can be helpful to improving customer relations. They can also boost employee morale.

It's not clear in this example what the "These" in the second sentence refers to from the first sentence. And it's not clear in the third sentence what "They" refers to from the second sentence.

Revision: Several companies are competing for the contract with our company to provide in-house seminars to our employees. These seminars can help improve customer relations and boost employee morale.

IMPROVING YOUR WRITING STYLE IN LARGER SEGMENTS

Larger segments of your technical documents deserve as much attention as the smaller segments of paragraphs, sentences, and words. Unity, flow, order, and depth of detail—qualities that are essential to good paragraphs—are equally essential for effective larger segments. Improve your larger segments by ensuring that:

- each segment covers one topic
- the paragraphs within the larger segment flow smoothly from one to the next
- the paragraphs occur in logical order within the segment
- each segment is adequately detailed

Effective organization is the key to creating larger segments:

- Place the most important information first within each segment.
- Avoid too much complexity.
- Present the information you are discussing in small, simple chunks and short sections.

See Chapter 8 for ways to use headings and lists to help your readers recognize the organization of your documents.

DEVELOPING AN APPROPRIATE TONE

Tone is usually defined as your attitude toward your subject and your audience. However, tone is more accurately defined as your attitude toward your subject, your audience, and yourself. You must carefully consider all three to convey the desired attitude in your documents. Your writing may have a clear purpose, be well organized, and be free of errors in grammar, spelling, and punctuation, but unless you also convey an appropriate tone, your document may fail to communicate your message to your intended audience.

Planning is just as appropriate for tone as it is for content and organization. It is up to you to plan the attitude you want to convey. Will it be angry, conciliatory, deferential, authoritative, humorous, sarcastic, pedantic, apologetic, exasperated, or something else? Conveying attitude effectively takes a great deal of skill. You must aim for consistency and appropriateness. Your readers follow your attitude toward the subject, themselves, and yourself through your handling of the vocabulary and sentence structure appropriate to the attitude.

You establish a tone in your writing by controlling your perceived distance from your readers, conveying your attitude and emotion, and showing your character. Distance is achieved through formality and impersonality; closeness occurs through informality and personability. You personalize your prose through the use of personal pronouns that bring you and your readers closer: *you, we, us*. Use an informal manner of address: *Let's look at the next message box and see what we can do here* instead of *The next step is to open the message box and read the menu items*. Depending on the context, you may need a more personal or a more impersonal approach. The key is to decide which will work more effectively in the context and use that tone consistently throughout the document.

Tone is, in part, a matter of the attitudes and emotions you want to convey about your subject and to your audience. Examples of attitudes are trust, distrust, sincerity, insincerity, seriousness, lightheartedness, hope, despair, belief, incredulity, acceptance, denial, desire, repulsion, attraction, and rejection. Examples of emotion are anger, love, hate, desire, envy, lust, joy, excitement, disgust, contempt, revulsion, obsession, and indifference. As you can see, attitudes and emotions overlap. What's important is to realize that all of these attitudes and emotions (and many more) can be the basis of an appropriate tone in a piece of writing. The emotion and attitude that you convey in your writing should never be the accidental result of your feelings of the moment.

Before you write, decide how you want to treat both your subject and your audience. For example, do you want to treat the subject seriously and convey this seriousness to your audience? Or do you want to treat your subject with anger and convey the anger to your audience? To convey a serious tone, you have to show your readers that you respect and take them seriously, that you take the subject matter seriously, and that you also take yourself seriously. To convey this serious tone, you have to choose your words carefully, phrase your sentences and paragraphs with skill, and organize the document so that it will achieve the desired effect. To convey anger about a subject, all of your style choices must help you suggest this anger appropriately.

Finally, you establish a tone by showing your readers your character. After all, your credibility depends on your establishing a relationship with your readers, and to do that, you have to show them that they can rely on your competence. (See "Credibility" in Chapter 2.) So tone is a matter of ethos (*ethos* is a Greek word meaning *custom* or *character*) and how you establish ethos with your audience.

Decide what kind of relationship you want to have with your audience. Do you want your audience to regard you as a friend? Do you want your audience to regard you as highly informed and knowledgeable? As trustworthy? As a guide? As a fellow traveler? As a victim? As all-knowing? State the ideas and thoughts that show clearly what kind of relationship you want with your audience. For example, if you have reservations, state that you have reservations. If you have confidence in the situation, state that you have confidence. Remember before you begin to write that you can add all kinds of phrases and sentences to influence the way your readers will perceive you.

After you decide what tone you want to convey and after you have reviewed the possible effect of the situation on your communication, you need to choose the appropriate words for your message. If you want to establish a friendly tone, for example, avoid accusatory words and phrases. Also remember that readers can recognize and appreciate your efforts to be friendly, courteous, concerned, or insistent without being too angry.

There are many occasions for being brief, but there are also times when careful attention to detail is necessary. To make your tone convincing, it is sometimes necessary to write richly detailed paragraphs. For example, one effective way to write an angry letter is to provide lots of details to make your points convincingly and, of course, to avoid any personal attacks on the reader's abilities or integrity. Often the reader will see that your anger is well justified.

> The emotion and attitude that you convey in your writing should never be the accidental result of your feelings of the moment.

Humor is an area where you can have an immediate effect on readers' perceptions of you as a person.

Using Humor

- Consider your audience. What does your audience expect from the document? Will humor enhance or hinder the message?

- Consider the genre of your document. Some genres—e-mail, letters, memos, and others—readily lend themselves to a humorous approach, while others—such as abstracts, summaries, reference manuals, and feasibility reports—do not.

- Consider the purpose of the document. If your purpose is to explain something serious or of a delicate nature, resist the urge to use humor. But if your purpose is to put your audience at ease when introducing new and perhaps intimidating material, then you might well consider using humor to achieve your goals.

- Consider the subject matter. Some subjects just do not lend themselves to humor: injury, illness, and death should be treated respectfully and seriously unless some unusual circumstance warrants the exceptional humorous treatment.

- Be cautious when using humor to make sure that you have not relied on a culturally dependent point of view to generate humorous effect. Keep in mind that humor depends on a shared point of view. What seems funny to you may not amuse your readers if their background or outlook is different from yours.

- Use humor for a reason. Gratuitous humor will seem out of place if it is dropped into a document for no apparent reason.

- Balance humor with the rest of your prose. Even when humor is appropriate for the context, too much humor can defeat your purpose. After all, unless you are writing a joke book, your document has some other purpose besides entertainment.

- Be alert for possible offensive interpretations to your humor. Humor that is derived from negative sexual, social, cultural, national, religious, or racial stereotypes has no place in documents produced in school or on the job. Even sarcasm may be misinterpreted by your audience, so avoid it unless you have a very good reason for using it.

- If you use humor, be consistent. If humor is part of your approach in a document, make it an integral element of the document, well absorbed into the text. The sudden appearance of humor in a serious document can be very jarring.

- When your document can benefit from a lighter touch, don't shy away from humor. In the right setting and with the right treatment, an overly drab subject can be made more palatable with a sprinkling of humor to spice it up.

Don't forget that the page layout and design of your letter, memo, or report also help to establish tone. Hard-to-read fonts, too many fonts, fonts that are too small, a poor choice of paper color, poor margins and spacing, the wrong binder, and many other physical properties of your document can make a negative impression on the reader. You can make careful decisions about your tone, diction, opening, middle, and ending, but unless you also give careful attention to the appearance of your document, you are not doing all you can to communicate well. See Chapter 8 and Chapter 9 for more information about enhancing the effectiveness of a document through managing its appearance.

AVOIDING BIAS

Bias is an inclination or personal judgment, a prejudice, a preconceived judgment or opinion. Essentially, to have a bias is to favor someone, something, or some idea. If you have a bias, you are not usually being fair, impartial, or objective. Of course, it's difficult to be free of bias. All of us have feelings, opinions, beliefs, and attitudes about all kinds of issues, people, and things. However, you don't have to be an automaton to be mostly free of bias. Ultimately, bias is about degrees or levels. Bias may range from a slight inclination or disposition to a blatant prejudice. When you write, you need to be aware of potential biases that can shape your writing.

Writers may reflect all types of bias in their writing. Kinds of bias include gender, corporate, philosophical or religious, political, racial, cultural, age, size, and bias against people who are physically and mentally challenged.

Gender bias is bias in attitudes, language, and actions by members of one sex against the other or against one's own sex. Many people, of course, have biased attitudes toward one sex but don't necessarily express their attitudes in language or directly in action. Others use sexist language, language that expresses stereotyped views or assumes that one sex is superior to another. Still others express their bias toward one sex through physical acts ranging from sneers to violence.

Gender bias is a particular problem in writing, since over the centuries the English language has developed into patterns that follow the assumptions of those who have committed their ideas to paper. These assumptions have often made men the model or placeholder both in cases in which men were the usual subjects of the action and in cases in which a "generic" person was intended. Today, these language patterns are considered exclusionary and should be avoided.

Unless your purpose for writing is to reveal a bias or to write propaganda, you must always be aware of how your reader will perceive the words you use in order to make sure you avoid biased language.

From the workplace

John M. Watts, Jr., Ph.D.

Director
Fire Safety Institute
Middlebury, Vermont

Early in his career, "Jack" faced a choice between developing his management skills and increasing his engineering expertise. He chose engineering but soon discovered that much of his work would require him to develop his writing, editing, and presentation abilities. This aspect of his job became dominant, and now he credits his career success and the enjoyment he experiences in his work to his strong communication skills.

I function in a small arcane discipline, fire safety science and engineering, that is rapidly evolving technologically, largely due to international communication and cooperation. Basically what I do is apply the principles of industrial engineering and operations research to fire protection engineering. We interface with many related technical disciplines such as architecture, human factors and ergonomics, and physics and chemistry of combustion, as well as with fire departments and building code officials around the world.

My role is to try to bring all this together, a large part of which I do as editor of *Fire Technology* (a part-time position that I fulfill remotely from my home) and as director of my own fire safety engineering education, research, and information organization that focuses on innovative approaches to technical aspects of fire. I am sure that this is the work I will continue to do until I retire.

I reached my current career by passing through several other fields along the way. In college I majored in fire protection engineering. Unfortunately, my school courses prepared me quite poorly for my first job after graduation, which involved training people on adding machines. It quickly evolved into personnel management, for which I had no formal training except trial and error. The situation was one of the most uncomfortable I have ever faced.

As a recent engineering graduate with no training in personnel management (and limited experiential knowledge to fall back on) I was in charge of 15 persons older than I. The decisions I was forced to make

Avoiding Gender Bias

- Unless a specific male person is referred to, do not use the so-called generic he. Substitute plural forms—*they, their, theirs*—or second-person forms—*you, your, yours*—whenever possible. If you can't avoid third-person singular forms, include both genders joined with *or—he or she, him or her, his or hers.*

- Do not use modifiers or suffixes that can be regarded as belittling or less than their unmodified counterparts. Use *actor, waiter,* and *doctor,* regardless of the sex of the person; use *flight attendant* rather than *stewardess.*

- Avoid gender-stereotyped or demeaning characterizations.

- Whenever possible, use examples drawn from both sexes.

- Vary the order by which you refer to people so that you're not always mentioning the men first or the women first.

- Be sensitive to possible sexism in assigning roles in examples.

regarding performance evaluations—and hence the lives of people—were completely ad hoc. I enjoyed the challenge but I didn't think I could be both a manager and an engineer. I stuck it out for two years but realized that I needed to either pursue a degree in management or find a different position. I chose the latter and went to graduate school in industrial engineering and operations research—this was before computer science was anything but crossing wires.

Interestingly, although I work as an "engineer," probably 90 percent of my time is devoted to communication, mostly written. I prepare a variety of written materials: reports, proposals, letters, memos, e-mails, instruction and procedures manuals, newsletters, and press releases.

Additionally, as editor of the peer-reviewed journal *Fire Technology,* I am responsible for the scientific accuracy of the content. One or two days of my work week therefore involve technical editing. Part of what I do involves reading works of other engineers—an often painful task. I think U.S. engineering schools are remiss in their attention to communication. Perhaps this will change, as we seem to be placing more emphasis on communication skills. At least I hope so.

My change to writing on the computer from writing on paper corresponded with a major change in employment. I never learned to type in college, with the rationalization that in the future I would always have a secretary. But when I became essentially self-employed, I became my own secretary. Thanks to Mavis Beacon (a typing course) I learned to type well enough to get along with a computer keyboard.

Writing on the computer is definitely different from writing on paper. I make more use of outlines and go through many more drafts. The end result is a much better document, in my opinion. Drafts can be produced quickly and printed and changed easily. Cut and paste is keystrokes rather than scissors and tape. Yet, for about 15 years, I was still editing offline, on hard copy. It is only within the past five years that I have gotten comfortable reading and editing on-screen. I think the advancements in word processors have something to do with that.

I still do some teaching. When I teach, I try to raise the level of communication skills of my students as much as possible. What many people still need to learn is that there is so much more to communication than grammar. I cannot require that my students take courses in communication skills, but I always strongly recommend it. In the sciences, if you cannot communicate what you did, it is all but worthless.

UNDERSTANDING CULTURAL CONTEXTS

International technical communication presents many special challenges concerning style and tone. Mastering the intricacies of international technical communication requires a great deal of knowledge, but a few key areas can be covered here. Most mistakes in international communication involve the following areas.

1. Many writers are not specific enough in their documents. They fail to use simple, straightforward language to state exactly what they mean.
2. Many writers use metaphors, clichés, jargon, idioms, slang, and other language variations that foreign readers have difficulty understanding.
3. Many writers use too many big words and long sentences. They should use simpler, shorter words and shorter sentences.
4. Much international communication requires documents to be punctuated carefully, even heavily, and many writers fail to adhere to this requirement.

5. Many writers fail to respect the customs of their audience's country or culture. They fail, for example, to consider how they may be violating various social customs concerning proper address for other people, using inappropriately informal tones, or ignoring certain religious taboos. An effective tone is especially difficult to master in international communication. For example, you must often be direct and straightforward in cultures such as those of the United States, Switzerland, and Germany, whereas in cultures such as those of Japan, Arabia, and Latin America, you often need to be or should be less direct.

CHECKING WHAT YOU'VE LEARNED

- Does your document show that you understand and have met the expectations of the discourse community for which you are writing?
- Is the level of formality in your document appropriate for the audience, subject, purpose, scope, genre, and context?
- Have you worked on improving the style at the word level throughout the document?
- Have you worked on improving the style at the sentence level throughout your document?
- Have you worked on improving the style at the paragraph level (and larger sections) throughout your document?
- Have you established the most appropriate tone—your attitude toward yourself, your subject, and your audience—throughout your document?
- Have you been sensitive to the many kinds of bias and avoided them throughout your document?
- Have you been careful about the cultural contexts of your document?

EXERCISES

 REVIEW

1. The following sentences or groups of sentences contain unnecessary words and other problems of wordiness. Rewrite them to make them more concise.

   A. As you browse through this work in progress, please take a moment to give feedback on any errors, problems, or suggestions you may have.

   B. A physical model is a model whose physical characteristics resemble the physical characteristics of the system being modeled.

   C. For example, the buoyancy and ship handling characteristics of a ship are typically modeled using math and physics equations. Similarly, the ship's rate of turn at a given surface speed and the effects of current and wind on the ship's relative movement and position are modeled using complex math formulas.

D. For example, math models of traffic flow are regularly used by city planning officials to relieve congestion by determining the optimal timing and length of traffic lights under certain conditions. As drivers, we all know that these traffic flow models become less effective when the underlying conditions or assumptions upon which the model is based are incorrect.

E. For example, say that you are interested in studying the relationship between a specific population of predator and prey given that the available amount of space available to both populations is shrinking. By producing a graph of these three factors over time, one could gain a greater understanding of the nature of this complex relationship.

2. The following sentences contain pretentious words. Rewrite them to make them more clear. Where necessary, use a dictionary or thesaurus to help you provide simpler words.

A. To optimize the performance of your computer, schedule various maintenance programs to run at least once a week.

B. Bill prioritized his options to determine which option was the most important.

C. The utilization of cell phones has increased on college campuses nationwide.

D. To accelerate the growth potential of the company's client base, we decided to explicate the strengths of our company's products in on-site presentations.

E. Before installing this peripheral device, be sure your computer is not in a performance mode.

3. The following sentences are written in passive voice. Rewrite them using the active voice.

A. We were captivated by today's speaker as many of his exploits were related by him.

B. Professor Smith was known by many students and liked by everybody.

C. The policies of the company must be understood and followed by every employee.

D. Since the final project was completed by Gail and Susan, the project was mailed to the professor by the two other group members, Phil and Tom.

E. After the computer was repaired, it was checked for viruses by the lab manager.

F. It was concluded by John that he had been placed in the best peer review group.

G. Although the employees were delighted by the presentation, there were so many slides that they could not be fully appreciated by everyone.

H. We were invited by the company president to see her office.

I. It was revealed by the group members that no one was prepared for class that day.

J. It was decided by the professor to place Phil and Ann in different groups.

4. The following sentences contain trite expressions or clichés. Revise them to make them more effective sentences.

A. It's time to get down to business and put our noses to the grindstone.

B. The success of our team is largely due to every member's willingness to go the extra mile.

C. To understand our clients, we need to walk a mile in their shoes.

D. For this team to complete its project on time, everyone will have to bite the bullet.

E. When the chips are down, the best leaders take decisive action.

5. Look at the poorly detailed job application letter in Figure 7.7 and the adequately detailed job application letter in Figure 7.8. Write a paragraph discussing how much more effective the second letter would be in helping the applicant get the job.

6. Find a complex prose example (three to five paragraphs) discussing some topic in your discipline. If you have a technical hobby or interest, you may also choose a prose example from one of these areas. This example should be from a published source. To qualify as complex prose, the example should have some undefined technical

FIGURE 7.7
Poorly Detailed Job Application Letter

1800 Temple Street
Apartment 50
New York, New York 10026

April 11, 2____

Mr. Phil Ramirez, Manager
Human Resources
Marquis Company
7501 Jefferson Street
Princeton, NJ 08543

Dear Mr. Ramirez:

I am applying for the position of Programmer/Analyst I in your Engineering Services Department in the Atlanta printing facility.

I am currently a junior at State University of New York and will graduate in December 2____ with a Bachelor of Science degree in Computer Science. In addition to taking many programming courses, I have excelled in the setup, maintenance, and theory of computer networking and operating systems.

As outlined in my résumé, my previous experience has required my working in a team environment as well as independently.

I would appreciate the opportunity of an interview, at your convenience, to further discuss my qualifications and strong desire to work with your company. I can be reached at (212) 555-5555.

Sincerely,

John Jacobs

John Jacobs

terminology, fairly long sentences, some difficult content, and perhaps an impersonal tone. Also, most of the paragraphs should be long rather than just a few sentences each. Rewrite this complex prose example into a plain, reader-friendly style for a novice. Then provide a brief memo (one page) discussing the changes you made to create your example of a simpler prose style. Turn in a photocopy of the original complex prose example, your revision, and your memo.

FIGURE 7.8

Adequately Detailed Job Application Letter

1800 Temple Street
Apartment 50
New York, New York 10026

April 11, 2___

Mr. Phil Ramirez, Manager
Human Resources
Marquis Company
7501 Jefferson Street
Princeton, NJ 08543

Dear Mr. Ramirez:

I am applying for the position of Programmer/Analyst I in your Engineering Services Department in the Atlanta printing facility. I am well aware of the worldwide respect that the company has earned since its beginning in 1882, and if given the opportunity, I would strive toward maintaining that reputation.

I am currently a junior at the State University of New York and will graduate in December 2___ with a Bachelor of Science degree in Computer Science. As part of my coursework, I received a thorough and in-depth education in C, C++ and JAVA programming languages. In addition to taking many programming courses, I have excelled in the setup, maintenance, and theory of computer networking and operating systems. I am also a member of the ACM (Association of Computing Machines) and attend local meetings on the future of computing. I enjoy the challenge of staying on the cutting edge of technology and have attended several company-sponsored training classes. In fact, my desire to maintain skills, knowledge, and experience in a competitive and dynamic environment was the driving force for pursuing a degree in the rapidly changing field of computers.

As outlined in my résumé, my previous experience has required my working in a team environment as well as independently. These skills are vitally important in the position of Programmer/Analyst as one must understand the problem and interface effectively with people and computers in order to ensure that the most efficient solution is achieved.

I would appreciate the opportunity of an interview, at your convenience, to further discuss my qualifications and strong desire to work with your company. I can be reached at (212) 555-5555.

Sincerely,

John Jacobs
John Jacobs

THE INTERNET

1. Find a Web site that contains effective conversational text and discuss why you think the text is so effective.

2. Find a Web site that contains a lot of jargon or specialized language. Make a list of the terms you think are jargon, and bring this list to class for discussion.

ETHICS/PROFESSIONALISM

Jargon is the specialized terms of a trade, profession, or hobby. However, jargon may also be pretentious terms used merely to impress an audience. Find an example of a brief document (e-mail, memo, letter, report, proposal) that contains pretentious language. Identify the specific audience for the document, and then write a paragraph discussing the ethics and the professionalism of using the pretentious language for the intended audience.

 COLLABORATION

1. Working with two other students in the class, compile a list of words all of you commonly confuse (for example, *affect* and *effect*). Be prepared to share your lists with the class.
2. Working with two other students in the class, first discuss and then make a list of all the personal and professional discourse communities you belong to. Then each of you choose one of the discourse communities and make a list of the values, expectations, and some of the typical terms or jargon used in the discourse community. Be prepared to share the list with the class.

 INTERNATIONAL COMMUNICATION

1. Review the tip list concerning achieving clarity with technical terms. Write a paragraph discussing what changes, if any, you would make to this list to have it apply to using technical terms for an international audience.
2. Review the discussion of five areas of common mistakes in communicating with international audiences in the "Understanding Cultural Contexts" section. Find a brief sample document that contains one of these mistakes. Write a paragraph discussing what the writer could have done to avoid the mistake or mistakes.

RESOURCES

Andrews, Deborah, ed. *International Dimensions of Technical Communication.* Arlington: Society for Technical Communication, 1996.

Bosley, Deborah S. *Global Contexts: Case Studies in International Technical Communication.* Needham Heights: Allyn and Bacon, 2001.

Cook, Claire Kehrwald. *Line by Line: How to Improve Your Own Writing.* Boston: Houghton Mifflin, 1985.

De Vries, Mary A. *Internationally Yours: Writing and Communicating Successfully in Today's Global Marketplace.* New York: Houghton Mifflin, 1994.

Ewing, David. *Writing for Results in Business, Government, the Sciences, and the Professions.* 2nd ed. New York: Wiley, 1985.

Fahey, Tom. *The Joys of Jargon.* New York: Barron's, 1990.

Frank, Francine Wattman, and Paula A. Treichler. *Language, Gender, and Professional Writing: Theoretical Approaches and Guidelines for Nonsexist Usage.* New York: Modern Language Association, 1989.

Hoft, Nancy L. *International Technical Communication: How to Export Information About High Technology.* New York: Wiley, 1995.

Jones, Dan. *Technical Writing Style.* Boston: Allyn and Bacon, 1998.

Kakutani, Michiko. "When the Geeks Get Snide: Computer Slang Scoffs at Wetware (the Humans)." *New York Times.* 27 June 2000. Online. <http://www.nytimes.com/library/tech/00/06/biztech/articles/27note.html>.

Lanham, Richard A. *Analyzing Prose.* New York: Scribner's, 1983.

———. Revising Prose. 3rd ed. New York: Macmillan, 1992.

Lutz, William. *Doublespeak: From "Revenue Enhancement" to "Terminal Living": How Government, Business, Advertisers, and Others Use Language to Deceive You.* New York: Harper, 1989.

———. *The New Doublespeak: Why No One Knows What Anyone's Saying Anymore.* New York: HarperCollins, 1996.

Miller, Casey, and Kate Swift. *The Handbook of Nonsexist Writing.* 2nd ed. New York: Harper, 1988.

Rubens, Philip, ed. *Science and Technical Writing: A Manual of Style.* New York: Holt, 1992.

Smith, Edward L., and Stephen A. Bernhardt. *Writing at Work: Professional Writing Skills for People on the Job.* Lincolnwood: NTC, 1997.

Varner, Iris, and Linda Beamer. *Intercultural Communication in the Global Workplace.* Chicago: Irwin, 1995.

Williams, Joseph M. *Style: Ten Lessons in Clarity and Grace.* 5th ed. New York: Longman, 1997.

8

Designing Pages and Screens

Conventions and Expectations   235

Principles of Design   240

Ways to Organize Space   247

Typography   253

Using Color   265

Additional Design Principles for Screen and
    Web   270

First Aid for Your Document Design   289

From the Workplace   290

IN THIS CHAPTER

Designing pages and screens requires a different set of skills from those you use when you craft text. When you create a document, you are concerned with both the words you will use and the appearance of the page or screen or, in other words, both the *text* (sometimes called the *content*) and the *design*. Design concerns the appearance and placement of text, text art or line art, illustrations, and white (or blank) space on a page or screen. And design also concerns some of the production choices you make for a technical document—whether it's online or printed, for example, what kind of binding and paper you will use for a print document, and what kind of screens and resolutions you have available for an online document.

Design elements are part of your message. Used well, they can help readers to find, understand, and remember the information more effectively. Used poorly, they can impede your readers' journey through the material and send them away without delivering your message. Effective design attracts readers to the content and adds credibility to the document and thus to your message. It makes people want to read what you have written and makes your documents easier to use.

You will learn about:

- following patterns and conventions suitable for your purpose
- forming design goals: how to decide what effects you want to achieve and how to go about accomplishing them
- the manipulation of space on your page or screen: how various patterns can provide pleasing and effective outcomes
- letterforms or typefaces and how they can be manipulated, spaced, and combined on a page or screen, yielding the most effective, usable result
- color: making it work for you
- online conventions: what people expect and how to use those expectations to your advantage
- organizing on-screen space to take best advantage of the special characteristics of screens and browsers

CONVENTIONS AND EXPECTATIONS

Readers come to a document, whether on paper or on screen, with certain expectations. Depending on the sort of document, they expect that certain conventions will be followed. If you want your documents to present your message effectively, you will have to be aware of those expectations and make sure you either satisfy them or have a good reason for not satisfying them.

ON APPEARANCE

The way something looks says almost as much as what the content contains.

—Helen Cygnarowicz, VP operations, Santa Clara, California

You are probably already familiar with many conventions of print documents. And later in this chapter you will learn about readers' expectations concerning Web pages.

As an example, in a book you would expect that the pages making up the individual chapters will be printed on both sides and bound or arranged in succession. The pages will probably be numbered to make it easier to jump to a specific subject. The chapters will be numbered, too, and the chapter information is likely to be listed in a table of contents. The book may have a cover with information about the title, author, and publisher. There will be a title page, a copyright page, and perhaps a dedications or acknowledgments section. At the end of the book there might be appendixes, a glossary, and an index.

A newsletter will be arranged quite differently. Its various articles will share space with other articles on the same page, and if the entire article does not fit into the space allotted on the page, it may be continued on another, perhaps distant, page. The continuation section on the distant page may be in the company of other continuation sections from other articles. The pages of

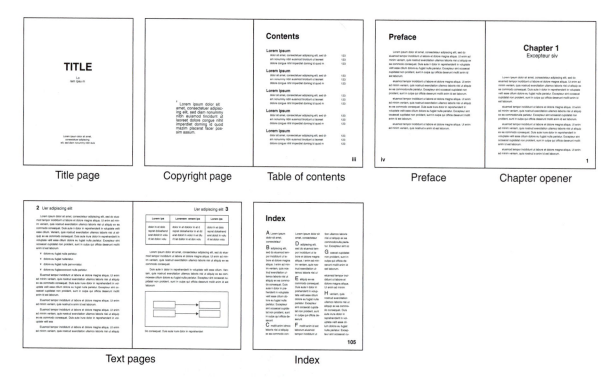

Title page   Copyright page   Table of contents   Preface   Chapter opener

Text pages   Index

FIGURE 8.1a

Layouts for Printed Matter: Book Layout

Title page — Contents masthead and copyright notice — Text page with articles and graphics — Back page with mailer and postage indicia

FIGURE 8.1b

Layouts for Printed Matter: Newsletter Layout

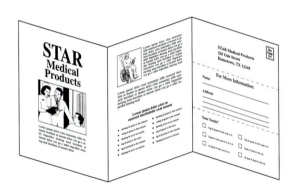

FIGURE 8.1c

Layouts for Printed Matter: Brochure Layout

the newsletter may also share space with advertisements, a table of contents, and a masthead (containing information about the organization that publishes the newsletter and the people who worked on it).

A brochure will have another type of arrangement. If it folds into three sections, each of the sections will contain marketing-type material, and probably both sides of the page will be used, making six sections in all. One of the sections might be reserved for mailing information, if the brochure will be stapled and mailed without an envelope. See Figure 8.1a, b, and c for examples of document arrangements.

Similarly, when you write a paper for one of your classes, many of the decisions about its design will be made for you: your instructor will specify the required page margins, the between-line spacing, and the documentation style (for example, MLA, APA, CBE) of your discipline. You will probably use

FIGURE 8.2

Considering Design

DOCUMENT	FEATURES
Software manual	▪ table of contents and index ▪ numbered lists of instructions ▪ headings, headers, footers
Assembly manual	▪ table of contents and index ▪ exploded diagrams with callouts ▪ lists of parts ▪ numbered lists of instructions
Newsletter	▪ stapled or folded pages ▪ multiple columns per page ▪ table of contents ▪ masthead (publication schedule and editorial staff listing) ▪ articles continued on later pages ▪ mailing information on outside
Technical report	▪ table of contents ▪ title page ▪ executive summary or abstract ▪ appendixes ▪ standardized headings ▪ multiple volumes possible
Proposal	▪ memo format or book format ▪ standardized headings ▪ appendixes
Memo	▪ limited length ▪ standardized header block ▪ headings possible but not standardized
Business letter	▪ choice of standard formats ▪ letterhead stationery ▪ length normally limited ▪ headings possible but not usual

FIGURE 8.2

(continued)

DOCUMENT	FEATURES
Résumé	■ length very limited ■ standardized headings ■ bulleted lists
Web site	■ headers ■ navigation buttons and bars ■ underlined link indicators ■ color and graphics
Lab report	■ standardized headings ■ standardized format ■ sketches, tables, and figures ■ appendixes possible
Journal article	■ single or double columns ■ graphics and figures common ■ headers and footers usual ■ headings usual ■ references at end ■ author biography

$8\frac{1}{2}$-by-11 inch white paper, double-space the text, use a ten-point or larger fairly traditional font, print on one side only, and perhaps provide a cover.

On the other hand, suppose you are designing a document and you don't have an instructor or a style guide to follow. How will you decide on the optimal choices? Here is where a solid knowledge of good design principles will carry the day. You don't have to reinvent the wheel when talented and well-informed practitioners before you have grappled with these issues and experimented with a variety of settings to help you.

Your first step should be to familiarize yourself with the look of publications like the one you will be designing. See how others have solved the same problems you are facing. See Figure 8.2 about considering design.

The more you look at examples of both good design and mediocre design, the more you will train your eye to know what to look for. You will be able to look at a design—yours or someone else's—and analyze what works and what doesn't. See Figure 8.3a and b for design examples.

FIGURE 8.3a

Effective Design: A Poorly Designed Page, with Elements Unbalanced

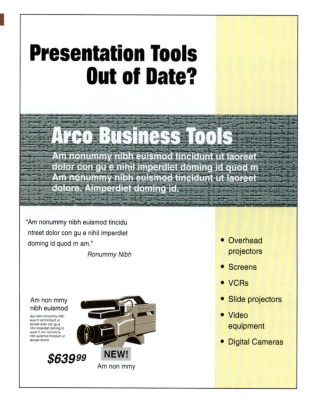

PRINCIPLES OF DESIGN

Several basic guidelines will help you to make design decisions. Mastering the principles of simplicity, symmetry, consistency, readability, and usability will help you reach your audience and achieve your communication goals. Read about these principles and think about how they apply to a document or project you are working on. See Figure 8.4 on applying principles of design.

Simplicity

Simplicity is a matter of restraint. A complicated page or screen is a confusing page or screen.

- Choose fewer elements rather than many. Your document will look better and function more effectively if you present a few elements in

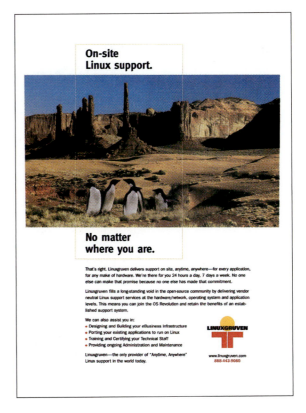

FIGURE 8.3b

Effective Design: Two Well-Designed Pages, with Elements Balanced to Achieve a Striking, Arresting Image

harmony rather than many elements in discord. If there are too many elements on a page, they compete for attention.

■ Don't provide too many combinations of text, text art, and graphics. You will know you have too many combinations when your page or screen is cluttered and unruly looking. One or two graphics per page or screen; one or two typefaces per page or screen; one or two examples of text art (curved text or other effects) are plenty. And the smaller the space, the more potentially cluttered the look.

■ Unclutter your display space: use blank space to punctuate your design and separate items of text and graphics. Group related items together, but leave plenty of space between the page edge and the text or graphics, leave room around the graphics, and keep paragraphs spaced apart so the eye can discern where one ends and the next one begins.

FIGURE 8.4

Applying Principles of Design

	PAGE	SCREEN
Simplicity	■ few fonts ■ few graphics ■ up to two or three columns ■ few textboxes ■ few marginal notes	■ few if any frames or delimited areas
Symmetry	■ balance within and between pages	■ screen elements balanced
Consistency	■ headers and footers ■ headings and heading styles	■ navigation aids ■ headings ■ color
Usability	■ table of contents, index ■ obvious hierarchies provided by headings	■ easy and obvious navigation ■ standard navigation elements
Readability	■ generous use of white space ■ adequate font sizes ■ readable, legible typefaces ■ paragraph spacing controlled ■ line length controlled	■ generous use of blank space ■ adequate resolution ■ readable, legible typefaces ■ absence of distracting animations

■ Plan the way the user will access the material. How does it flow? What path does the eye follow through the page or screen? What type of motion are you setting up for the reader? A simpler design provides an easier navigation task.

See Figure 8.5a and b for simplicity examples.

Symmetry

Symmetry concerns how you balance or contrast design elements on a page or screen. Work on keeping elements balanced visually. Try to arrange items so that busier areas have a counterbalancing section of similar weight opposing them. Step back from the page or screen and view it as an arrangement of objects rather than as words and pictures. Do all the elements fall on the same half of the page or screen—upper, lower, left, or right? Shuffle them around to see whether another arrangement would be more pleasing.

Not all design has to be symmetrical around a center line, and in fact it is often more effective and visually pleasing not to have complete symmetry. Sometimes you may want to organize your text and graphical elements around a guide. You can line up several elements flush to a vertical line, either present or implied, and provide a pleasing effect of alignment. If you create an asym-

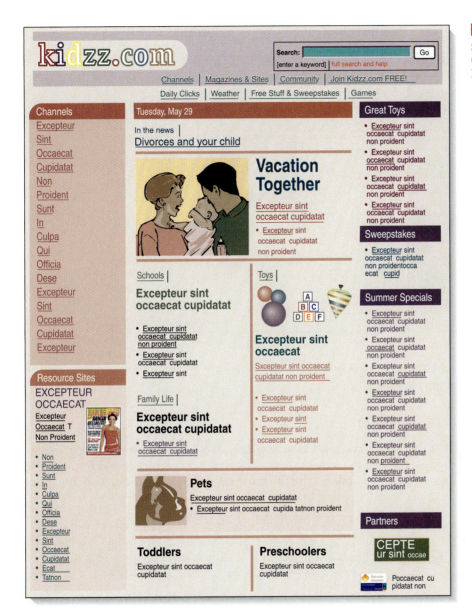

FIGURE 8.5a

Simplicity in Design: A Cluttered Web Page, with Hard-to-Read Information

metrical design, try to provide for balance. The effect you are striving for is the one that uses the tension between opposing elements in a positive way. Think about the overall view the reader will see. If you are preparing a document with facing pages such as a book or newsletter, you must consider how the opposing

FIGURE 8.5b

Simplicity in Design: Web Page Showing Clean, Simple Design

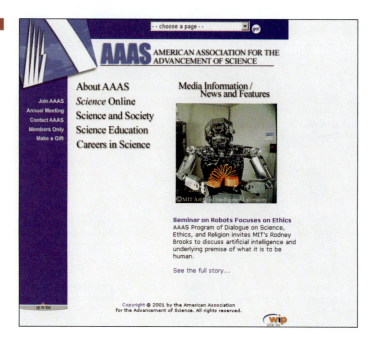

pages balance each other, too. See Figure 8.6 for examples of symmetry and asymmetry in design.

Consistency

Consistency concerns how you use repetition effectively in your design choices. Use design elements with consistency on each page and from page to page within a document. Use the same screen elements for each Web page or

Symmetrical

Symmetrical

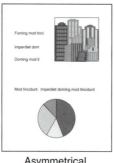

Asymmetrical

Asymmetrical

FIGURE 8.6

Symmetry in Design

FIGURE 8.7

Consistency in Design

Although the text and graphics vary from page to page, the consistent design elements—header, page number, headings, and color bar at the foot of the page—create a unified look throughout the document.

other online page. A ruled line at the top or bottom of each page can unify the look of your print document. A navigation bar or company logo can unify the look of each page of an online document. Consistent headings, fonts, margins, white space, and other elements contribute to an effective design. Color can be another strongly unifying element when it is used carefully. Of course, your margins and paragraph styles also lend a consistent look to your page. See Figure 8.7 for a consistency example.

Readability

Elements on a page or screen should not be difficult to read. More than that, they should be appealing to read. Present your text in an appropriate size and style based on its intended use—standard and traditional typefaces for academic and business use, more casual typefaces and sizes for informal use in club newsletters or advertisements—and make sure all graphics are easy to read. Your text should not be written so densely as to be incomprehensible. Avoid using all uppercase letters, which are harder to read in long lines of text. Use the principles of good typography to make text easily readable (see the typography section later in this chapter). Group related ideas or concepts together on the page or screen to aid the reader in following connections. In designing a résumé, for example, you should group your name and contact information (address, telephone number) together, and group career information under major headings (for example, Objective, Education, Work Experience). See Figure 8.8 for a readability example.

Usability

Usability refers to how easily the reader can access and apply the information provided in your document. The key information should be easily identifiable with headings, subheadings, and rules, if appropriate. Test the usability of your document in conditions that are as similar as possible to those your

WRITING ONLINE

Working online makes it easier to try out different layouts and typefaces. One now sees a greater variety in design all round. But again, communicators must resist the urge to play with the design at the cost of the time that ought to be spent on working on text to make it simpler, more lucid, and more euphonious (to list the hallmarks of good prose as enunciated by one of its foremost exponents, namely Somerset Maugham).

—Yateendra Joshi, director, information technology and services, New Delhi, India

FIGURE 8.8
Readability in Design

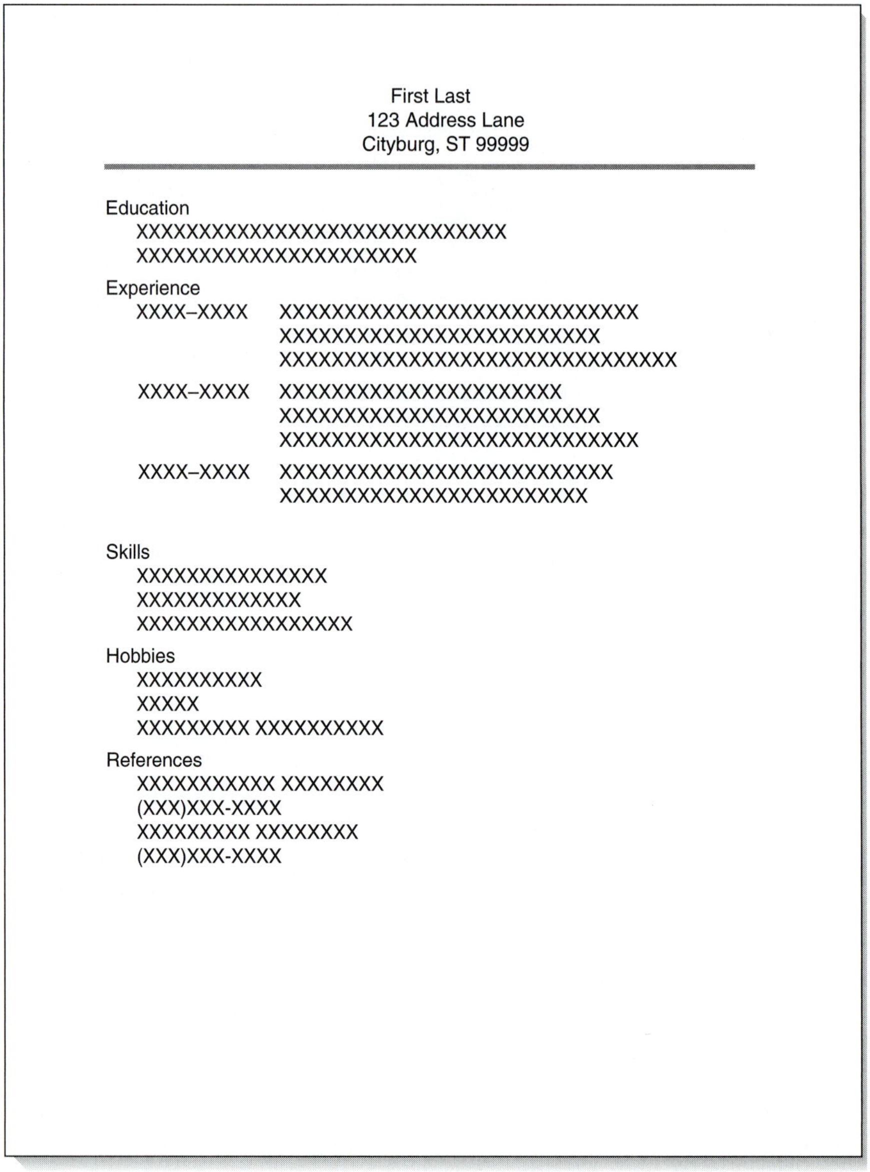

First Last
123 Address Lane
Cityburg, ST 99999

Education
XXXXXXXXXXXXXXXXXXXXXXXXXXXX
XXXXXXXXXXXXXXXXXXXXXX

Experience
XXXX–XXXX   XXXXXXXXXXXXXXXXXXXXXXXXXXXX
XXXXXXXXXXXXXXXXXXXXXXXX
XXXXXXXXXXXXXXXXXXXXXXXXXXXXXX

XXXX–XXXX   XXXXXXXXXXXXXXXXXXXXX
XXXXXXXXXXXXXXXXXXXXXXX
XXXXXXXXXXXXXXXXXXXXXXXXXX

XXXX–XXXX   XXXXXXXXXXXXXXXXXXXXXXXX
XXXXXXXXXXXXXXXXXXXXXXX

Skills
XXXXXXXXXXXXXX
XXXXXXXXXXXX
XXXXXXXXXXXXXXXX

Hobbies
XXXXXXXXXX
XXXXX
XXXXXXXXX XXXXXXXXXX

References
XXXXXXXXXX XXXXXXXX
(XXX)XXX-XXXX
XXXXXXXX XXXXXXXX
(XXX)XXX-XXXX

readers will encounter. For example, if they will be using the document in dim light, the print will have to be bigger, and you will need to provide even more white space than usual. Verify your design's usability by having typical readers try to use it to accomplish a task—following instructions, navigating a Web site, or understanding a description or other text.

Design Principles

- Treat your text and visuals as elements to arrange on the page or screen.
- Stand back and see how the various elements look together as blocks of light, dark, and color. Move far enough away so that you can't read the actual text. Appearance is your concern. You can tell quite a lot about how successfully you have incorporated the principles of simplicity, symmetry, and consistency this way.
- Try different arrangements of the various page elements. Rearrange several times until you find a balanced layout. No one element should overpower the others.

- If you have one very strong element, balance it on the page or screen with several lesser elements on the opposite side of the page or screen.
- View the page or screen in the same type of setting as your readers will. Is the text large enough to be seen and read easily? Are captions or other information too small or too close to the items they are describing?
- Have someone else look at your design to see if it embodies the principles of design: simplicity, symmetry, consistency, readability, and usability.

WAYS TO ORGANIZE SPACE

Your first consideration when you start figuring out how you will break up your page or screen into areas of text, graphics, dividers, and white space will probably be to decide how you want to separate the page or screen content from the background or frame. You know that the text and graphics will not cover the entire surface, so what will you use to divide the used space from the unused space?

White Space

White space (also called blank space) is something you may not be used to thinking about. After all, in some sense it's something that isn't there. But white space is a critical element in the design of a document.

White space is your margins, the space between paragraphs and lines, the space between words and letters. In an illustration or other graphic, white space is the background behind the graph or chart, the space between elements, the area around captions and callouts. See Figure 8.9 for an example of white space.

If you don't plan for enough white space in your document, you will give your readers a reading chore that they may abandon without finishing. Ample

TOO MUCH OF A GOOD THING?

Although white space (or for online documents, blank space) is crucial to the design of most documents, it can be overused. Excessive blank space can separate items that belong together, making their connection less obvious. And for online applications, if you have too much blank space, readers may have to scroll down to see your whole page, making the page less attractive and less usable.

FIGURE 8.9
**White Space on the Facing
Pages of a Book**

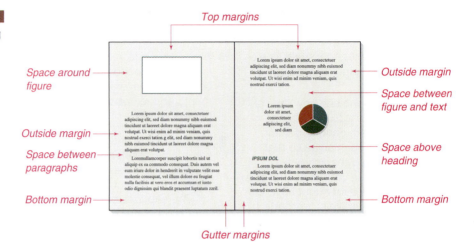

use of white space prevents your document from looking cramped, crowded, messy, and unreadable. White space increases the usability of your document. And if your document is more usable, its message will be more persuasive and effective. See Figure 8.10 for examples of the effects of different amounts of white space.

FIGURE 8.10
Using White Space

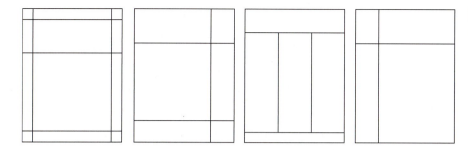

FIGURE 8.11
Newsletter Grids

Grids

When you are ready to lay out your text and visuals on the page or screen, you will discover that there are many ways to lay out your page and no one correct way will work for all documents. But there is a method you can use to assure that your document is arranged in a pleasing and effective way, and that is by using grids.

Graphic designers often use grids to balance text, headings and titles, visual aids, and white space on a page. A grid is a division of your page or screen into a combination of vertical and horizontal lines used to guide the placement of other elements such as text, graphics, and white (or blank) space. See Figure 8.11 for examples of various grid patterns. The grid lines are not visible to your reader; they are lines that you use during the design process to arrange elements on the page or screen.

Why Use Grids?

- Grids can indicate top and bottom margins, side margins, paragraph indention, and any other planned layout elements.
- Grids help you determine—and your reader discern—the appropriate relationships among your text, headings and titles, and visual aids.
- Grids help you show a visual connection between elements.
- Grids in complex configurations, such as columns, give you even more creative flexibility.
- Grids aid you in experimenting with headings and titles, text, visual aids, and white space in various configurations to determine the design that you think will emphasize your message and appeal to your readers.

Rules and Border Graphics

You have seen that you can use invisible gridlines to separate elements on the page or screen, but you can also use more explicit and visible divisions, such as rules (straight lines) and decorative or border graphics. Rules and border graphics can lend consistency to your documents by separating sections or other elements in a predictable way. For example, if you are writing a report, you can begin each of its major sections with a ruled line. You can use flourishes to mark off the ends of sections or chapters. Flourishes are small graphics that are used to end sections in some older printed works. They serve as a signal to the reader that something is about to change. On Web pages, forward and back buttons serve the same purpose—they indicate the end of the current page and the possibility of moving sequentially to another page. See Figure 8.12 for examples of border graphics.

Headers and Footers

Another type of page or screen division that separates background from foreground is the header and footer. Headers and footers serve to unify the look of a document by giving each page or screen the same frame, and they also serve as navigation aids, helping readers orient to where they are in the document. Headers (also called running heads) have the name of the chapter or Web page, the name of the section, or simply the name of the book or Web site at the top of each page or just at the top of each even or odd page. You can set up running heads in your word-processing program or your page-layout program. Footers are also very common in documents and can provide information similar to the information in headers. Often, footers have page and section numbers, although these can also appear in headers. Some pages have both a header and a footer, some just one or the other. Only rarely will you see a printed page without either.

A seeming exception to the rule of having a consistent page design throughout the document is the chapter page. A chapter page is the first page of a section or chapter. Usually these are designed to look a little different from the average page, and often the difference means no page number or a page number located differently from those on other pages. Look at a sample of books to see how various book designers have handled the challenges of headers, footers, and chapter pages. Figure 8.13 illustrates a treatment of headers and footers on chapter pages and interior pages.

Text Lists

Text as a design element is discussed later in this chapter. The section on typography covers letterforms, size, weight, spacing, and alignment. But on a more basic level, you have to think about text design as soon as you think

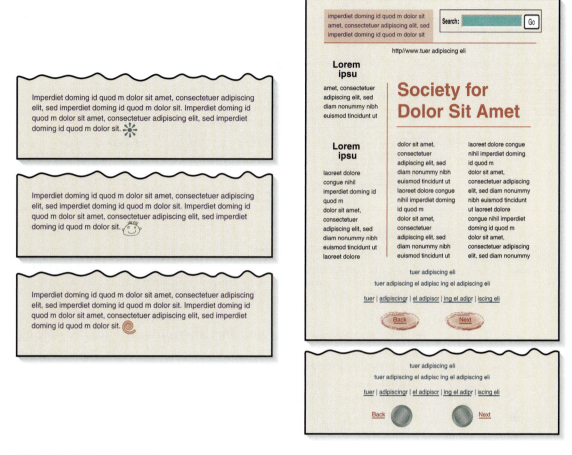

FIGURE 8.12

Border Graphics

Distinctive graphics can be used to end a printed section or as decorative navigation buttons on a Web page.

about how you are going to organize the space on your page or screen. After all, text is one of the important items that you will be working with. And lists are a time-honored method of organizing and managing textual information.

Lists have several advantages over narrative text in technical prose:

- Lists are easy to scan. The reader can easily pick out individual items when items are lined up in a list.
- Lists can be numbered to indicate sequence.
- Lists can be more succinct than narrative prose because list items do not have to be complete sentences.

(a)   (b)

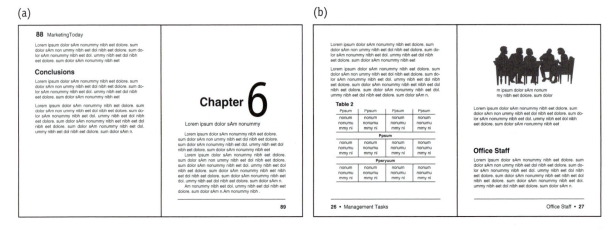

FIGURE 8.13

Headers and Footers on Printed Pages

(a) On the chapter-opening page, the page number is at the bottom and there is no header (running head); (b) The footer (running foot) on the left gives the chapter title, and the one on the right gives the section title.

- Lists can show hierarchy, since they always display text as an ordering of items.
- Lists can be formatted to indicate the importance or non-importance of order. If a list is *bulleted,* the order doesn't matter. If a list is *lettered,* the order is somewhat important, but there may be some flexibility in the order or the items may be considered equivalent. If a list is *numbered,* the items occur or should be performed in the indicated order.
- Lists can provide visual variety to a page that is otherwise "text heavy."

The above list is a bulleted list and could not reasonably have been either a numbered or lettered list. Figure 8.14 shows a different type of list, one in which the order is significant and important.

FIGURE 8.14

Numbered Instructions

Replacing Memory Module on Your Laptop

1. Remove battery or other power source.
2. Unscrew and remove back panel.
3. Gently but firmly lift out memory module.
4. Snap new memory module into place.
5. Replace back panel.
6. Restore battery or other power source.
7. Reboot device to verify proper functioning.

What you can see in both types of lists is that list items must be parallel. They are either all sentences or all phrases. If they are sentences, they are usually either imperative sentences or declarative sentences, and they are capitalized and punctuated just like any other sentence. See Appendix B for more on sentences and phrases. See Appendix A for additional information about lists.

TYPOGRAPHY

Typography is the visual image of your text: the forms of the letters and how they're put together into words, sentences, and paragraphs. It is a vital element in the design of your document, because typography is what your readers see when they look at your text. Depending on your purpose, you may want the typography to go relatively unnoticed by your readers, or you may want the typography to be a significant design feature. Typography can call attention to itself and distract the reader from your prose, or it can enhance your document's effectiveness and subtly reinforce your message.

You may be familiar with the terms *legibility* and *readability.* These are not the same things. Legibility concerns the presence of easily recognizable letter forms; readability refers to the easy accessibility of the message. Make your documents legible by paying attention to typefaces, type sizes, and spacing. Make them readable by using the best practices of document design and good writing. Unless you are aiming to make your writing difficult or daunting to read, your goal should be to obtain the highest legibility and readability possible through your typographic and other design choices. Test both legibility and readability by having others, preferably those who will actually be using your documents, try them out.

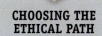

Legibility concerns the presence of easily recognizable letter forms; readability refers to the easy accessibility of the message.

Typefaces and Fonts

Font—or more correctly, typeface—refers to the characteristics of the letterforms themselves. The term *font* actually means the specific combination of typeface and size that together form a typographic element. For convenience, typefaces are grouped into various categories according to their appearance and typical use. See Figure 8.15 for examples of typefaces. You will find it helpful to familiarize yourself with the general characteristics and uses of these categories so that you can make informed decisions about which ones you will use. Often typefaces in the same categories may be substituted for one another for a pleasing outcome.

Typefaces developed from the handwriting styles that were in use before the invention of the printing press. Because they derive from penned letterforms, many typefaces retain some of the features of handwritten lettering. You will often see little bars on the ends of letters, particularly in the body text of books. These terminating lines, called *serifs,* point back to the time when

CHOOSING THE ETHICAL PATH

Why do some product warranties feature tiny-sized print, often in all capital letters? Because these are difficult to read.

FIGURE 8.15

Categories of Typefaces

Type Group	Example
Oldstyle	Bookman Old Style Garamond Times New Roman
Modern	Ellington Bernhard Modern
Slab serif	Courier **Rockwell**
Sans serif	Arial Helvetica Gill Sans
Script	*Caliban* *Viner Hand*
Decorative (novelty and symbols)	Quake Gikkyag Greymantle

scribes would end their letters and words with these finishing strokes. Even texts chiseled in stone often show serifs. Times New Roman and Garamond are typefaces with serifs. Serif typefaces are generally thought to be easy to read, perhaps because the combined effect of the serifs along the base of the written line guides the reader's eyes forward. See Figure 8.16 for examples of serif typefaces.

Another major category of typefaces is the *sans serif* typeface. *Sans* means "without," and sans serif typefaces, of course, have no serifs. Arial and Helvetica are popular sans serif typefaces. Very often, you will see sans serif typefaces in headlines, on computer screens, and on road signs. Sans serif typefaces present a very clean, uncluttered appearance. They are thought to be more difficult to

FIGURE 8.16

Examples of Serif Typefaces

Times Roman
Lorem ipsum dolor sit amet, consectetuer adipiscing elit, sed diam nonummy nibh euismod tincidunt ut laoreet dolore congue nihil imperdiet doming id quod mazim placerat facer possim assum.

Century Old Style
Lorem ipsum dolor sit amet, consectetuer adipiscing elit, sed diam nonummy nibh euismod tincidunt ut laoreet dolore congue nihil imperdiet doming id quod mazim placerat facer possim assum.

New Baskerville
Lorem ipsum dolor sit amet, consectetuer adipiscing elit, sed diam nonummy nibh euismod tincidunt ut laoreet dolore congue nihil imperdiet doming id quod mazim placerat facer possim assum.

read in body text than serif typefaces, but some studies suggest that in fact the easiest typeface to read is the one you have become accustomed to reading, be it serif or sans serif. See Figure 8.17 for an example of a sans serif typeface.

Within each category of typeface, there are various families of type. A type family comprises all the sizes of a particular typeface, along with their associated italic, bold, and specialty forms. Specialty forms may include ligatures, that is, pairs of letters that are specially modified to fit together well, such as "fi" or "fl"; extended character sets, such as accented letters that are useful in non-English prose; and mathematical symbols.

As Figure 8.15 shows, serif typefaces fall broadly into categories such as Old Style, Modern, and Slab Serif, based on differences in the style of the serifs, the angle at which the serifs terminate, and the relative thinness or thickness of the letter strokes. Examples of some popular and useful serif typefaces are Times New Roman, Caslon, Palatino, Baskerville, and Garamond. (See Figure 8.18 for examples of serif typefaces.) The sans serif typeface families are not normally divided into groups, since they have no serifs and, for the most part, they do not feature varying stroke widths. Some well-known examples of sans serif typefaces are Helvetica, Univers, Gill Sans, and Frutiger. See Figure 8.19 to see several examples of sans serif typefaces.

This typeface has no serifs.

FIGURE 8.17

Typical Sans Serif Typeface

FIGURE 8.18

Sample Alphabets in Common Serif Typefaces

Times Roman
ABCDEFGHIJKLMNOPQRSTUVWXYZ
abcdefghijklmnopqrstuvwxyz

Caslon
ABCDEFGHIJKLMNOPQRSTUVWXYZ
abcdefghijklmnopqrstuvwxyz

Palatino
ABCDEFGHIJKLMNOPQRSTUVWXYZ
abcdefghijklmnopqrstuvwxyz

New Baskerville
ABCDEFGHIJKLMNOPQRSTUVWXYZ
abcdefghijklmnopqrstuvwxyz

Garamond
ABCDEFGHIJKLMNOPQRSTUVWXYZ
abcdefghijklmnopqrstuvwxyz

FIGURE 8.19

Examples of Sans Serif Typefaces

Helvetica
Lorem ipsum dolor sit amet, consectetuer adipiscing elit, sed diam nonummy nibh euismod tincidunt ut laoreet dolore congue nihil imperdiet doming id quod mazim placerat facer possim assum.

Frutiger
Lorem ipsum dolor sit amet, consectetuer adipiscing elit, sed diam nonummy nibh euismod tincidunt ut laoreet dolore congue nihil imperdiet doming id quod mazim placerat facer possim assum.

Gill Sans
Lorem ipsum dolor sit amet, consectetuer adipiscing elit, sed diam nonummy nibh euismod tincidunt ut laoreet dolore congue nihil imperdiet doming id quod mazim placerat facer possim assum.

In addition to the categories of serif and sans serif, you will see many novelty typefaces. Of great interest to would-be desktop publishers, novelty typefaces have become the toy of the home and small-business computer owner. Novelty typefaces must be used sparingly, if at all, for technical prose. They can add a touch of humor to an otherwise dry document, but they are visually distracting and may lessen the effectiveness of your document.

Still another category of typeface, one that has attained great popularity in recent years, is the symbols typeface. Wingdings, dingbats, musical symbols, funny faces, and hundreds of other nonalphabetic typefaces help the text designer bring a graphical presence to a document as easily as typing words. Putting illustrations on your page or screen can be as easy as clicking your mouse and typing a few keystrokes. See Figure 8.20 for examples of novelty and symbols typefaces.

FIGURE 8.20

Novelty and Symbols Typefaces

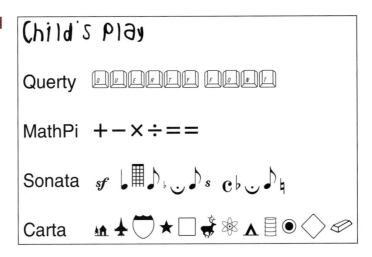

When you are choosing typefaces for your document, bear in mind that your goal is to get your readers to assimilate the information it contains. If the typeface you have chosen cannot be read easily by your audience, you will not have achieved your goal.

Choosing Typefaces

- Select typefaces that are easy to read and do not detract from your message.
- Choose typefaces that go together if you use more than one. For simplicity, stick with at most two typefaces—a serif typeface for body text and a coordinating sans serif typeface for the headings. Choose typefaces that have similar size and shape for the letterforms and that seem to go well together.
- Stick to so-called *normal*—also called *roman*—type when possible. Normal type is the unstyled, plain version of the typeface. In other words, avoid extensive use of italics or boldface type.
- Avoid using all capital letters, even for headings, unless the style guide you are following requires them.

TIPS

Size

Since your document usually must fit into certain page or screen size limits, you will have to consider how large your type will be. Type height is measured in points (pt), with 72 points equaling approximately one inch. So a font that is 12 pt is about one-sixth of an inch in height. The height itself refers to the size of the body of metal the type would have been cast onto back before type became software. The term is still used, and it is a convenient, although approximate, guide to how big your letters are likely to be.

Standard body text normally falls in the range of 10 to 12 points. Headlines can be 18-point, 24-point, 36-point, or larger. Some fonts are slightly larger than others, even when they are compared at the same point size. This difference in size is an artifact of the way type size is measured, and it becomes important when you want to figure out how much space your text will take up. Try substituting different fonts in the same size, and you will see a noticeable difference between them. Figure 8.21 shows how different several typefaces can be, even when they are all the same nominal size.

In addition to the size of the letters, you should pay attention to line length. The rule of thumb for line length is to provide enough room on the line for two-and-a-half alphabets' worth of letters. Longer than that, and the eye has trouble following the text back down to the beginning of the next line. Shorter than that, and the message is too choppy and broken up. See Figure 8.22 for an example of line length.

FIGURE 8.21

Typefaces and Sizes

These typefaces are shown in the same size, but because of their designs, they look as if they are different sizes.

Serif Typefaces

New Baskerville
Standard body text normally falls in the range of 10 to 12 points. Headlines can be 18-point, 24-point, 36-point, or larger. Some fonts are larger than others, even when they are compared at the same point size.

Clarendon
Standard body text normally falls in the range of 10 to 12 points. Headlines can be 18-point, 24-point, 36-point, or larger. Some fonts are larger than others, even when they are compared at the same point size.

Garamond
Standard body text normally falls in the range of 10 to 12 points. Headlines can be 18-point, 24-point, 36-point, or larger. Some fonts are larger than others, even when they are compared at the same point size.

Sans Serif Typefaces

Folio
Standard body text normally falls in the range of 10 to 12 points. Headlines can be 18-point, 24-point, 36-point, or larger. Some fonts are larger than others, even when they are compared at the same point size.

Helvetica
Standard body text normally falls in the range of 10 to 12 points. Headlines can be 18-point, 24-point, 36-point, or larger. Some fonts are larger than others, even when they are compared at the same point size.

Weight and Color

Weight and *color* are terms that relate to the effect of type on the page or screen. The weight of a typeface refers to the heaviness of its letterforms. Try to select a typeface that will do the job without weighing down the page with its darkness or failing to carry its message because of its lightness. Discrepancies of weight can sometimes be adjusted by changing the size of your font and its spacing, but selecting the right font in the first place will save you much trouble later on.

Color is the impression the text makes on the reader with its overall density. See Figure 8.23 on page 260 for examples of the differences in weight and color among typefaces. When color is used in this way, it does not refer to what we usually mean by color—red, blue, green, and the like. Instead, here color means the darkness or lightness that a page of text seems to have for a given typeface. You will want to have your text display an evenness of color by

Line Length and Font Size

Look at Figure 8.22 as you read the following discussion.

If you use 12-pt Times New Roman and want the line to be approximately 65 characters (two-and-a-half alphabets' worth) in length, your text line will span 5 inches, so you might set your left and right margins at 1.75 inches each. If instead you use 12-pt Bookman Old Style, 65 characters would take up about 6 inches and you might then set your margins at 1.25 inches. Courier New takes up 6.5 inches for 65 characters, so your margins would be set at 1 inch each.

Typefaces that are relatively small for their point sizes—Garamond, for example, at 4.75 inches for 65 characters—should be used in larger sizes to fit the page more proportionately. For example, 15-pt Garamond would take up an equivalent space on the line as 12-pt Bookman Old Style.

The converse of trying to arrange your line length to accommodate two-and-a-half alphabets is adjusting your type size to fit proportionately to your page size. In the example shown in Figure 8.22, if your page size was $8\frac{1}{2}$ by 11 inches and you wanted to use Garamond type, you might move up from 12 point to 15 point in order to fill the space more comfortably and keep more standard margin sizes. You can experiment with different typefaces, sizes, and margins for the most pleasing results.

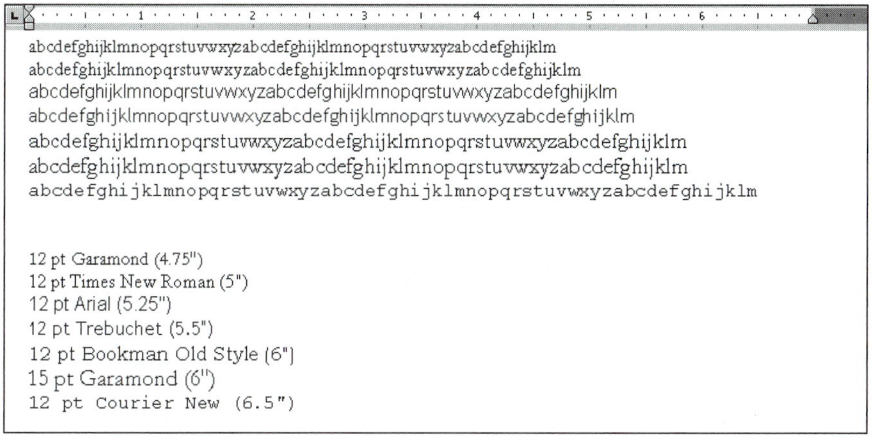

abcdefghijklmnopqrstuvwxyzabcdefghijklmnopqrstuvwxyzabcdefghijklm
abcdefghijklmnopqrstuvwxyzabcdefghijklmnopqrstuvwxyzabcdefghijklm
abcdefghijklmnopqrstuvwxyzabcdefghijklmnopqrstuvwxyzabcdefghijklm
abcdefghijklmnopqrstuvwxyzabcdefghijklmnopqrstuvwxyzabcdefghijklm
abcdefghijklmnopqrstuvwxyzabcdefghijklmnopqrstuvwxyzabcdefghijklm
abcdefghijklmnopqrstuvwxyzabcdefghijklmnopqrstuvwxyzabcdefghijklm
abcdefghijklmnopqrstuvwxyzabcdefghijklmnopqrstuvwxyzabcdefghijklm

12 pt Garamond (4.75")
12 pt Times New Roman (5")
12 pt Arial (5.25")
12 pt Trebuchet (5.5")
12 pt Bookman Old Style (6")
15 pt Garamond (6")
12 pt Courier New (6.5")

FIGURE 8.22

Line Length

These typefaces yield different line widths for the same amount of text.

FIGURE 8.23

Weight and Color in Text

Typefaces have different densities: some are darker, some are lighter.

Century Lorem ipsum dolor sit amet, consectetuer adipiscing elit, sed diam nonummy nibh euismod tincidunt ut laoreet dolore magna aliquam erat volutpat. Ut wisi enim ad minim veniam, quis nostrud exerci tation ullamcorper suscipit lobortis nisl ut aliquip ex ea commodo consequat. Duis autem vel eum iriure dolor in hendrerit in vulputate velit esse molestie consequat, vel illum dolore eu feugiat nulla facilisis at vero eros et accumsan et iusto odio dignissim qui blandit praesent luptatum zzril delenit augue duis dolore te feugait nulla facilisi.

Helvetica Lorem ipsum dolor sit amet, consectetuer adipiscing elit, sed diam nonummy nibh euismod tincidunt ut laoreet dolore magna aliquam erat volutpat. Ut wisi enim ad minim veniam, quis nostrud exerci tation ullamcorper suscipit lobortis nisl ut aliquip ex ea commodo consequat. Duis autem vel eum iriure dolor in hendrerit in vulputate velit esse molestie consequat, vel illum dolore eu feugiat nulla facilisis at vero eros et accumsan et iusto odio dignissim qui blandit praesent luptatum zzril delenit augue duis dolore te feugait nulla facilisi.

Frutiger Lorem ipsum dolor sit amet, consectetuer adipiscing elit, sed diam nonummy nibh euismod tincidunt ut laoreet dolore magna aliquam erat volutpat. Ut wisi enim ad minim veniam, quis nostrud exerci tation ullamcorper suscipit lobortis nisl ut aliquip ex ea commodo consequat. Duis autem vel eum iriure dolor in hendrerit in vulputate velit esse molestie consequat, vel illum dolore eu feugiat nulla facilisis at vero eros et accumsan et iusto odio dignissim qui blandit praesent luptatum zzril delenit augue duis dolore te feugait nulla facilisi.

New Baskerville Lorem ipsum dolor sit amet, consectetuer adipiscing elit, sed diam nonummy nibh euismod tincidunt ut laoreet dolore magna aliquam erat volutpat. Ut wisi enim ad minim veniam, quis nostrud exerci tation ullamcorper suscipit lobortis nisl ut aliquip ex ea commodo consequat. Duis autem vel eum iriure dolor in hendrerit in vulputate velit esse molestie consequat, vel illum dolore eu feugiat nulla facilisis at vero eros et accumsan et iusto odio dignissim qui blandit praesent luptatum zzril delenit augue duis dolore te feugait nulla facilisi.

selecting appropriate typefaces, using capital letters sparingly, and controlling the spaces between letters, words, lines, and paragraphs.

Spacing: Letter, Word, Line, Paragraph

You may not have had to adjust the spacing between letters in a word or words in a line. But you have almost certainly had to think about spacing between lines in a paragraph during your school years. Whenever you typed a paper for a class, your instructor had to tell you whether single or double spacing was required. What you may not have realized is that there are many other possibilities to consider when you are talking about spacing.

You will have to plan how much spacing you will allow

- between paragraphs
- between sections
- between a heading and the following paragraph
- between the headers found at the top of every page and the beginning lines of that page
- between the edge of the type and the edge of the page
- between the binding of the paper or book and the beginning of each line of type

These and many other issues are all examples of the use of white space interspersed in your text.

Letter Spacing

Most of the time, you will not have to concern yourself with the spacing between letters in a word, although if you use a monospaced (uniform width per letter) typeface—in e-mail, for example—you may have found yourself experimenting with extra spaces between letters (`emphasize` versus `e m p h a s i z e`). Adjusting space between letters is called kerning, and it can be done using word-processing software or page-layout software. Also, as you already learned in the section on typefaces and fonts, joined characters, called ligatures (such as "ff" or "fl"), are often provided for those pairs of letters that need to be set especially close together. You don't need to worry about letter spacing because the designers of the font you are using have worried about it for you. They have adjusted the spacing between various specific pairs of letters to ensure that the result is pleasing and easy to read. Some letters need to be closer than the average distance; others need to be farther apart. But unless you are working with an unusual typeface or an unusual size for that typeface, it's best to leave the kerning to the experts.

Word Spacing

The spacing between words on a line is controlled by several factors, some of which you may want to change at times. In general, the spacing depends on your choice of alignment and justification (see next section). Lines that have smooth margins both left and right will have extra space added automatically between words to make the ends of the lines fall out at the same place. Sometimes that creates problems when the extra spaces accidentally line up with each other from one line to the next, forming so-called rivers of white space. See Figure 8.24 for an example.

Even if you are not using straight-edge margins, you may want to modify the spacing between words. For example, you may want to modify the spacing

---

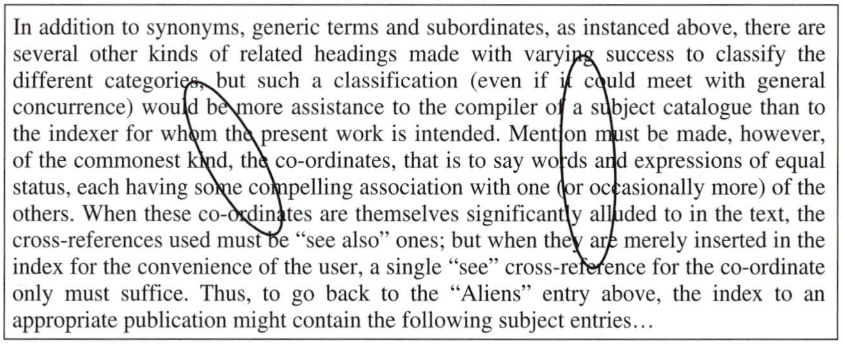

In addition to synonyms, generic terms and subordinates, as instanced above, there are several other kinds of related headings made with varying success to classify the different categories, but such a classification (even if it could meet with general concurrence) would be more assistance to the compiler of a subject catalogue than to the indexer for whom the present work is intended. Mention must be made, however, of the commonest kind, the co-ordinates, that is to say words and expressions of equal status, each having some compelling association with one (or occasionally more) of the others. When these co-ordinates are themselves significantly alluded to in the text, the cross-references used must be "see also" ones; but when they are merely inserted in the index for the convenience of the user, a single "see" cross-reference for the co-ordinate only must suffice. Thus, to go back to the "Aliens" entry above, the index to an appropriate publication might contain the following subject entries…

FIGURE 8.24
Rivers of White Space

if you are trying to squeeze more words onto a line than the default spacing allows, or if you are writing a headline or other header and need the words to stretch out to fill a line. Here again, you can make changes to between-word spacing using a word processor or layout program. See Figure 8.25 on letter spacing and word spacing.

FIGURE 8.25

Letter Spacing and Word Spacing

Expanded Letter Spacing
Lorem ipsum dolor sit amet, consectetaur adipiscing elit, sed do eiusmod tempor incididunt ut labore et dolore magna aliqua. Ut enim ad minim veniam, quis nostrud exercitation ullamco laboris nisi ut aliquip ex ea commodo consequat. Duis aute irure dolor in reprehenderit in voluptate velit esse cillum dolore eu fugiat nulla pariatur. Excepteur sint occaecat cupidatat non proident, sunt in culpa qui officia deserunt mollit anim id est laborum.

Compressed Letter Spacing
Lorem ipsum dolor sit amet, consectetaur adipiscing elit, sed do eiusmod tempor incididunt ut labore et dolore magna aliqua. Ut enim ad minim veniam, quis nostrud exercitation ullamco laboris nisi ut aliquip ex ea commodo consequat. Duis aute irure dolor in reprehenderit in voluptate velit esse cillum dolore eu fugiat nulla pariatur. Excepteur sint occaecat cupidatat non proident, sunt in culpa qui officia deserunt mollit anim id est laborum.

Normal Letter Spacing
Lorem ipsum dolor sit amet, consectetaur adipiscing elit, sed do eiusmod tempor incididunt ut labore et dolore magna aliqua. Ut enim ad minim veniam, quis nostrud exercitation ullamco laboris nisi ut aliquip ex ea commodo consequat. Duis aute irure dolor in reprehenderit in voluptate velit esse cillum dolore eu fugiat nulla pariatur. Excepteur sint occaecat cupidatat non proident, sunt in culpa qui officia deserunt mollit anim id est laborum.

Increased Word Spacing
Lorem ipsum dolor sit amet, consectetaur adipiscing elit, sed do eiusmod tempor incididunt ut labore et dolore magna aliqua. Ut enim ad minim veniam, quis nostrud exercitation ullamco laboris nisi ut aliquip ex ea commodo consequat. Duis aute irure dolor in reprehenderit in voluptate velit esse cillum dolore eu fugiat nulla pariatur. Excepteur sint occaecat cupidatat non proident, sunt in culpa qui officia deserunt mollit anim id est laborum.

Decreased Word Spacing
Lorem ipsum dolor sit amet, consectetaur adipiscing elit, sed do eiusmod tempor incididunt ut labore et dolore magna aliqua. Ut enim ad minim veniam, quis nostrud exercitation ullamco laboris nisi ut aliquip ex ea commodo consequat. Duis aute irure dolor in reprehenderit in voluptate velit esse cillum dolore eu fugiat nulla pariatur. Excepteur sint occaecat cupidatat non proident, sunt in culpa qui officia deserunt mollit anim id est laborum.

Normal Word Spacing
Lorem ipsum dolor sit amet, consectetaur adipiscing elit, sed do eiusmod tempor incididunt ut labore et dolore magna aliqua. Ut enim ad minim veniam, quis nostrud exercitation ullamco laboris nisi ut aliquip ex ea commodo consequat. Duis aute irure dolor in reprehenderit in voluptate velit esse cillum dolore eu fugiat nulla pariatur. Excepteur sint occaecat cupidatat non proident, sunt in culpa qui officia deserunt mollit anim id est laborum.

Leading

The two types of spacing you have just read about—letter spacing and word spacing—are elements you may never have to deal with yourself. But when it comes to between-line spacing you may very well be called on to change the settings that your word processor or layout program suggests.

One way to think of between-line spacing is as single spacing, double spacing, and so on. Any word processor can do this spacing for you. Layout programs will give you more flexibility and control over the spacing between lines by letting you control the distance—called *leading* and pronounced "ledding"—directly. Although for most applications you will not need to modify the default leading, occasionally you will, particularly if you deal with extra-large type (as in headlines) or extra-small type (as in footnotes or legal "fine print"). Check your word processor or layout program for information on how to modify the leading of paragraphs or individual lines. Figure 8.26 shows examples of how leading can change the appearance of your text.

Alignment and Justification

When you design how your text will look on the page or screen, one of the important decisions you make is how to align and justify your text. If your instructor requires that you follow a particular style guide, follow its alignment and justification requirements.

Alignment describes how the text fits within its space. Text can be left aligned, center aligned (or centered), or right aligned. Justification describes

No Leading
Lorem ipsum dolor sit amet, consectetaur adipiscing elit, sed do eiusmod tempor incididunt ut labore et dolore magna aliqua. Ut enim ad minim veniam, quis nostrud exercitation ullamco laboris nisi ut aliquip ex ea commodo consequat. Duis aute irure dolor in reprehenderit in voluptate velit esse cillum dolore eu fugiat nulla pariatur. Excepteur sint occaecat cupidatat non proident, sunt in culpa qui officia deserunt mollit anim id est laborum.

1-point Leading
Lorem ipsum dolor sit amet, consectetaur adipiscing elit, sed do eiusmod tempor incididunt ut labore et dolore magna aliqua. Ut enim ad minim veniam, quis nostrud exercitation ullamco laboris nisi ut aliquip ex ea commodo consequat. Duis aute irure dolor in reprehenderit in voluptate velit esse cillum dolore eu fugiat nulla pariatur. Excepteur sint occaecat cupidatat non proident, sunt in culpa qui officia deserunt mollit anim id est laborum.

2-point Leading
Lorem ipsum dolor sit amet, consectetaur adipiscing elit, sed do eiusmod tempor incididunt ut labore et dolore magna aliqua. Ut enim ad minim veniam, quis nostrud exercitation ullamco laboris nisi ut aliquip ex ea commodo consequat. Duis aute irure dolor in reprehenderit in voluptate velit esse cillum dolore eu fugiat nulla pariatur. Excepteur sint occaecat cupidatat non proident, sunt in culpa qui officia deserunt mollit anim id est laborum.

FIGURE 8.26

Text Leading

FIGURE 8.27

Text Alignment

Left-Justified (or Ragged Right) Text
Lorem ipsum dolor sit amet, consectetuer adipiscing elit, sed diam nonummy nibh euismod tincidunt ut laoreet dolore congue nihil imperdiet doming id quod mazim placerat facer possim assum.

Right-Justified (or Ragged Left) Text
Lorem ipsum dolor sit amet, consectetuer adipiscing elit, sed diam nonummy nibh euismod tincidunt ut laoreet dolore congue nihil imperdiet doming id quod mazim placerat facer possim assum.

Full-Justified Text
Lorem ipsum dolor sit amet, consectetuer adipiscing elit, sed diam nonummy nibh euismod tincidunt ut laoreet dolore congue nihil imperdiet doming id quod mazim placerat facer possim assum.

Centered Text
Lorem ipsum dolor sit amet, consectetuer adipiscing elit, sed diam nonummy nibh euismod tincidunt ut laoreet dolore congue nihil imperdiet doming id quod m placerat facer possim assum.

whether the text is smoothed out at the margins. Edges are either justified or ragged. So text can be *left justified* (also called *ragged right*), *right justified* (also called *ragged left*), *centered,* or *full justified.* Full-justified text differs from centered text in that centered text generally has both ragged right and ragged left margins, while fully justified text has its right and left sides evenly lined up at the margins. Figure 8.27 shows how the different alignments look for the same text.

Why would you choose left-justified text over full-justified text? It's obvious why many people prefer full justification: the smooth margins are pleasing and neat on the page. And for hundreds of years, full justification was the mark of a printed (as opposed to typewritten or handwritten) document. When personal computers became available to individuals, understandably many chose to align their letters, papers, and other documents in such a way as to mimic a printed book. If you have decided on full justification, be aware that full justification works best with smaller type and narrower columns, since that combination provides less chance for distracting rivers of white space.

Some studies suggest that left-justified, ragged-right text is easier to read for many people, particularly those who have difficulty reading in the first place. Explanations vary, but the reason may be that the uneven line lengths prevent eye fatigue and help the reader find the correct next line as the eyes move down from one line to the next. Other studies find that either full justification or left-justification can be equally easy to read for experienced readers.

In addition to ease of reading, there may be other reasons for you to choose a ragged-right justification for your document. If you are using columns (such as in a newsletter), ragged-right column edges allow a greater separation between columns, making the page appear more attractive and less cluttered. With the full-featured word processors and layout programs available to most people, experimenting with different settings for spacing and alignment will help you arrive at the most usable and effective arrangement for your document.

USING COLOR

Color is perhaps the most predominant design element on a page or screen. The human eye has developed to discern subtle differences in color, and the perception of color can be pleasurable to the viewer. Color brings a message all its own to a text, and successful document designers take advantage of color's power to enhance the effectiveness of their designs. Use color well and you strengthen your message; use color poorly and you may detract from your document's impact or even send a negative message.

Color is an attribute that contributes to design in both subtle and dramatic ways. In certain media, such as film, color is the default. Ask most people what they notice about a picture, film, or graphic, and if it's not in color, they will say so. We are so used to seeing certain items in "living color," that if we see black and white, we feel as if our expectations have been thwarted. A director who makes a film in black and white is trying to make a point precisely by going against our expectations.

Because color is so important, work *with* it, not against it. Using color is like cooking with spices—the right ones in the right proportions work wonders to improve the flavor and memorability of the dish, but the wrong ones or the wrong amount turns a masterpiece into an unpalatable mess. See Figure 8.28a and b for examples of good and bad use of color.

FIGURE 8.28a

Using Color on the Page: A Magazine Ad with Overpowering Use of Clashing Colors

FIGURE 8.28b

Using Color on the Page: Two Ads Showing Tasteful, Effective Use of Color

Open up several magazines and see how different types of messages get different treatments. Advertisements are trying to attract your attention, so their written text and their color scheme together project a message designed to persuade you to buy the product, contribute to the cause, or change your behavior. Color can persuade very subtly. Colors have associations, even when we are not consciously aware of them. And bright colors have a different effect on people than do soothing, subdued colors.

Advertisers are well aware of the effect of color on persuasion, and they know that they can use color to help persuade you to buy or believe what they are selling. Articles and fictional pieces may use subdued colors to suggest reliability and truthfulness or garish colors to suggest excitement or suspense. When you look at a variety of color treatments, try to imagine what effect the designer was hoping to achieve. Once you have become tuned in to color, you can make it work for you to enhance and promote the message of the other elements on the page or screen. See Figure 8.29a and b for examples of the different effects of color.

FIGURE 8.29a

Color Moods: Two Ads Using a Restful, Subdued Color Palette

FIGURE 8.29b

Color Moods: Two Ads Using Bright, Exciting Colors

Designing with color is not simple, and to make things more difficult, colors convey subtle and not-so-subtle meanings of which we must be aware when we use them. If you put yellow into a scene with soldiers, you may give the subtle message of cowardice, since in our society yellow is a color we relate to cowardice. Yellow can also mean caution, so you can use it in messages that convey warnings. Purple suggests royalty; red suggests blood. Blue can be sad or peaceful. Green calls up the environment and nature, but it is also the color of envy and the color of American money. And some associations will change as your audience changes. Color associations are learned and almost entirely cultural.

You will not always want to use color in your printed documents. A term paper does not usually need it, for example. But many documents benefit from color if it is well managed. Treat color as a tool to help readers find and understand content, rather than as a camouflage for an otherwise poor design. And while color certainly can be decorative, for most applications decoration is not enough of a reason to incur the expense of printing in color.

For online use, color comes without cost, so you can afford to be more casual about including it. What you cannot afford to be is careless about its use. Color is a powerful tool. You should be able to justify each use you make of color on the basis of what you plan to accomplish with it.

Consider the following when using color.

- **Use color with restraint:** With color, less is more. And you have many alternatives to using full color, which is expensive for printed documents. Often merely adding a second color is enough to create a distinctive look. Using many colors is rarely necessary. Too many colors can add to design clutter, which can distract from your message. And be careful when you combine colors so that you do not put colors together that just don't seem to work next to each other. Use color to highlight a single important element, such as the company name or logo. If you are following a style manual that calls for color, follow that manual's requirements. See Figure 8.30 for an example of using color effectively.
- **Keep your text and your colors in harmony:** Be especially careful about setting text in color or against colored backgrounds. Color makes text harder, not easier, to read. In fact, even reversing black and white makes text difficult to read (white text on a dark background). See Figure 8.31 for an example of text and color.
- **Use typographic cues other than color:** Keep in mind readers who are color-blind or who are viewing your document on a monochromatic photocopy or screen. If you have graphics such as line graphs that depend on color to show different elements, make sure you make those elements different in other ways, too. In other words, make each colored line or colored area different in form (shape, shading, or thickness) as well. For example, lines can be solid, dashed, broken, or dotted. Areas can be shaded, striped, or cross-hatched.

(a)

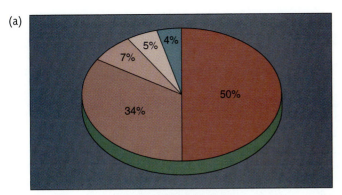

(b)

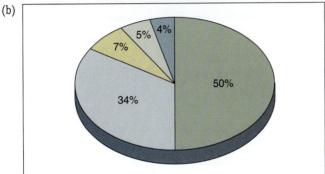

FIGURE 8.30

Using Color in Graphics

Notice how the choice of adjacent and background colors affects the attractiveness, readability, and usability of these pie charts. Which is easier to read—(a) or (b)?

Colored text is harder to read than black text on a white background.
Colored text is harder to read than black text on a white background.
Colored text is harder to read than black text on a white background.
Colored text is harder to read than black text on a white background.
Colored text is harder to read than black text on a white background.
Colored text is harder to read than black text on a white background.
Colored text is harder to read than black text on a white background.
Colored text is harder to read than black text on a white background.
Colored text is harder to read than black text on a white background.
Colored text is harder to read than black text on a white background.

FIGURE 8.31

Text and Color

Using Color Effectively

- Select a main color for your document and use complementary colors (red–green, blue–orange, yellow–violet) or adjacent colors (violet–blue–green, red–orange–yellow) as contrast.
- Use different shades of the same color to unify your page.

(continued)

- Keep in mind that very bright colors will attract the reader's attention. If you do not want to do that, avoid using them.
- Balance bright colors with text or other visually interesting material. Softer, lighter colors will not be able to compete for attention in the presence of bright, lively colors.
- Be aware that a few colors judiciously chosen and used in moderation can make a bigger impression than many bright colors all competing for the reader's eye.
- If you choose to use colored text, make sure it presents enough of a contrast with the background to be easily readable. Black is the easiest color text for most people to read on a white background. Yellow or white lettering on a deep blue background is also a good choice.

ADDITIONAL DESIGN PRINCIPLES FOR SCREEN AND WEB

The fact that there aren't universal standards for online design does not mean that anything goes. To the contrary: how you design and organize your Web site and its pages will in large measure determine whether it gets visited and revisited. Putting up a Web site is fairly easy. Putting up an effective Web site that accomplishes what you need to accomplish is not.

As for any other document creation, the first step must be planning. And for Web sites, top-down planning—that is, planning the navigation and major structural items first—is the way to proceed. Look first at the big picture: What is your purpose? Focus? Audience?

The answers to those questions will determine the direction your site plan—a map of the structural elements of your site and how they connect—will take. The navigation paths through your pages will depend on the logical connection of content between pages, and if you have not figured out where those connections belong, you will not be able to link the site properly.

You can probably guess that the design of your site will have to be different for different purposes and audiences. Your site will consist of Web pages linked to each other according to some arrangement. Start by sketching a schematic, such as those in Figure 8.32, representing the pages your visitors will see and how the pages are related.

Recall that in Chapter 4 you learned about various techniques for planning documents. Many of those techniques will work equally well when planning your Web site. And in Chapter 6 you learned about organizing and managing information. Those methods work here too. You may find that you can use some variation of outlines, trees, flowcharts, or storyboards to plan your site. Review those sections of Chapter 6 as you think about your Web site.

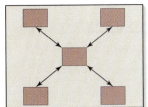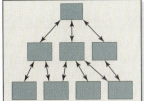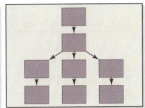

FIGURE 8.32
Site Plan Schematics

Elements in Common with Paper-Based Pages

Many of the elements of good design work both on paper and on screen. Review the guidelines for good design provided earlier in this chapter: simplicity, symmetry, consistency, readability, and usability. Each is just as important on the screen as it is on paper. In some ways, these principles are even more important when you design for a screen instead of the page, because the screen presents other challenges your readers don't face when they are confronted with printed pages.

Consistency in screen design is particularly important. The design elements should be consistent from page to page. Use *styles* to achieve consistency in your online page design. Styles are recurring characteristics that can provide your site with a pleasing rhythm. They help users see repeating features connecting similar elements. Typical style features are bold text, italic text, small capitals, paragraph alignment, color, and typefaces. Figure 8.33 shows examples of styled text.

When you use a word processor to create a print document, you use styles to give your headings, body text, headers, and footers a consistent look. These elements help unify your document and provide navigational aids to your readers. The online equivalent to the word processor's *style* is the *cascading style sheet (CSS)*. Use cascading style sheets to ensure that similar elements on your site are displayed the same way. Using a CSS unifies the look of your body text, headings, links, and other Web-page elements. Cascading style sheets are your instructions to the browsers as to how you want various types of elements displayed: which colors, sizes, fonts, and other characteristics the headings, links, and paragraphs will carry.

This is an example of **bold styled text.**
This is an example of italic styled text.
This is an example of underlined styled text.
This is an example of bold italic styled text.

FIGURE 8.33
Styled Text

> **The Advantages of Using a Cascading Style Sheet (CSS)**
>
> - CSS is vendor neutral, developed by the same consortium that oversees the Web (World Wide Web Consortium).
> - CSS is supported by most browsers.
> - CSS augments your options on your Web pages.
> - CSS allows readers and authors to define style sheets.
> - CSS uses standard desktop-publishing terminology.
> - CSS enables the use of organization-wide style sheets. When you want to make changes to the look of the site, you need only change the style sheet and not the whole site.
>
> Håkon Wium Lie and Bert Bos, *Cascading Style Sheets: Designing for the Web* (Reading: Addison Wesley Longman, 1997) vi.

> " "
> If you use a word processor, use styles; if you create Web pages, use cascading style sheets.

The fact that an entire site's "look and feel" can be controlled from one place is probably the best advantage of style sheets. If you use a word processor, use styles; if you create Web pages, use cascading style sheets. See Figure 8.34 for an example of a cascading style sheet.

Elements Unique to Screen and Web

Reading documents online, whether they are online articles, illustrations, help files, Web pages, or advertisements, requires more effort than reading the same material on paper. This difference occurs because the physical characteristics of screens differ greatly from those of paper. Even if you and your readers are experienced computer users, you and they have to deal with considerations that are quite different on the screen from on the page. And if your readers are not experienced in reading from screens, they will have even that much more difficulty using your documents. So you will have to plan for these differences in order to make your online documents as effective as possible. See Figure 8.35 for a comparison of print and online elements.

Designing Your Writing for Screen and Web

You have just seen that online design shares some attributes—simplicity, symmetry, consistency, readability, and usability—with print design. It should not surprise you to realize that online text similarly shares many characteristics with printed text. For example, you still must carefully select your words, write clear sentences, use topic sentences for your paragraphs, limit each paragraph to one main idea, and so on. Clarity and conciseness are just as important when you're writing the text for a Web page as when you're writing the text for any other kind of document. However, there are some essential differences, too. Review Chapter 7 on achieving an effective style.

FIGURE 8.34

Cascading Style Sheet

```
/*
BODY {
 font-family : Arial, Helvetica, sans-serif;
 font-size : 10pt;
 font-weight : normal;
}
TD {
 font-family : Arial, Helvetica, sans-serif;
 font-size : 10pt;
 font-weight : normal;
}
*/
H1 {
 color : Black;
 font-family : Arial, Helvetica, sans-serif;
 font-size : 16pt;
}
H2 {
 font-family : Arial, Helvetica, sans-serif;
 font-size : 10pt;
 font-weight : normal;
}
H3 {
 color : Black;
 font-family : Arial, Helvetica, sans-serif;
}
A:Link {
 color:#006600;
 text-decoration:none
}
A:Visited {
 color:#800080;
 text-decoration:none
}
A:Active {
 color:#FF0000;
 text-decoration:none
}
A:Hover {
 color:#330033;
 text-decoration:none
}
```

FIGURE 8.35

Print and Online Elements

	PRINT	ONLINE
Resolution	300 dpi or greater	72 dpi or 96 dpi
Orientation	Portrait (vertical) orientation	Landscape (horizontal) orientation
Lighting	Reflected from paper	Radiated from screen
Flicker	None	Governed by refresh rate of display
Color	Expensive to produce; CMYK system	Free; RGB system
Size	Fixed	Varies according to monitor
Appearance Predictability	Fixed: fonts, size, color, layout	Variable: fonts, size, color, layout

Conventional Publishing Versus Web Publishing

- Web publishing is restrictive. All that conventional publishing demands of its consumers is that they be sighted and literate; Web publishing remains inaccessible without the Internet and can be a lot poorer with limited bandwidth.

- Web publishing offers richer communication. Web publishing is free of many constraints that chain the print medium, namely space, high cost of color illustrations, sequential arrangement, and so on. But it also means that communicators need to be more versatile if they are to use Web publishing effectively and make use of such features as animation, audio, and video.

- Web publishing is flexible. With print, communicators can rest assured that their message, in terms of both content and presentation, will retain its form (its appearance); with the Web, this cannot be assured: different browsers, and different settings of the same browser, will display the same document differently. Only PDF (portable document format) can retain the graphical integrity of a document. More important, Web publishing makes it possible to tailor a document to its potential user, so much so that no two readers will read the same "document." Each, by following a different sequence of links, will be reading a different document.

- Web publishing is dynamic. Making corrections in a printed document is like trying to put the toothpaste back into its tube, whereas revising a Web document is almost as simple as replacing one file with another. More important, it is far easier to update a Web document (which also means that readers expect a Web document to be far more current, and the onus is on the communicator to meet that expectation).

Yateendra Joshi, director of information technology and services, New Delhi, India.

Your readers will have a range of backgrounds and computer skill levels, so you'll have to plan the prose style of your site accordingly. Work on adopting a prose style and tone that are easily accessible to the least sophisticated of your readers without offending or boring your more experienced readers. You'll also have to present text in highlighted keywords, headings and subheadings, bulleted lists, short paragraphs, and so on in such a way that your readers can easily scan the text. The wording of each and every link is also an important consideration. Make the link names short and descriptive; don't make the reader guess. The reader should know what to expect before clicking on each link.

Improving Your Web-Page Prose Style

Purpose

Consider your goals and what you hope to accomplish with your site. Is your site a student home page in which you share your favorite links with friends and visitors? Is it a company Web site to present your customers and investors with information about the company and its products and services? Is it an online sales outlet that promotes and sells products over the Web? Is it a promotional site to showcase your freelance or consulting business? Depending on your site's purpose, you will organize it and provide content that accomplishes what you want it to.

Focus

Consider the most likely audience for your Web site. People from all over the world may visit your site, but you probably have a more narrow audience in mind for what your particular site offers. You will have many of the same audience considerations as you would for your print documents, but for your Web audience you must also take into account the probable level of computer and Web experience of your potential audience and make style decisions accordingly.

Organization

Readers of online documents scan these pages looking for the information they need. They like summaries, a top-heavy (inverted pyramid) way of organizing the content, and graphics that complement the text. Give readers the most important information first. Begin with the conclusion. Then provide supporting and background information. See Figure 8.36 for an example of a Web page using an inverted pyramid style. Readers of Web pages are typically in a hurry, and few will read text word for word, from the top of the page to the bottom without scanning. Design elements can make Web pages much easier to scan: headings, large type, bold text, highlighted text, bulleted lists, graphics, captions, topic sentences, and tables of contents or main menus.

Meaningful Headings

Provide headings and subheadings that allow readers to find information quickly and easily. Avoid using clever wording in your headings. Tell readers exactly what they should expect to find under each heading.

Keywords

Choose important words that will need special emphasis, and highlight them with bold or colored text to help readers scan the text. However, keep in mind that hypertext is inherently highlighted. Because it is underlined and colored, the text draws readers' attention. Make sure you clearly distinguish between text you want to emphasize and text that links to somewhere else.

FIGURE 8.36
Web Page Using Inverted Pyramid Style

The more important information is at the top of the page so that it can be captured on a single screen.

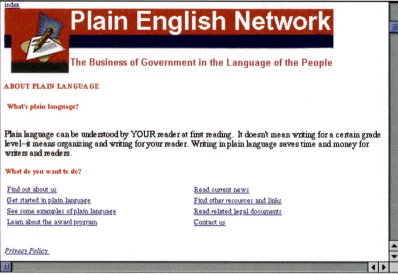

The interested reader can scroll down to get additional information at the bottom of the page.

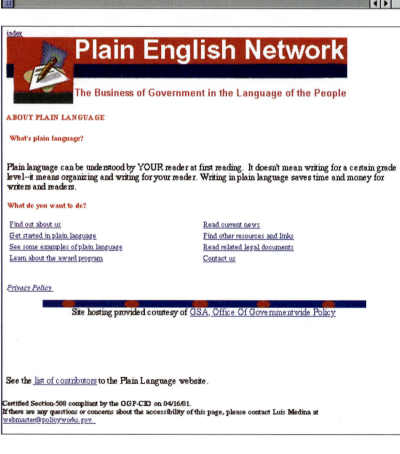

Chunked Information

Break information into small, digestible chunks. Limit each paragraph to one subject. In addition, screens vary in size from tiny (for hand-held personal digital assistants) to large (for a variety of page-layout and graphics uses). Long paragraphs that require the reader to scroll down to finish reading are less desirable than short paragraphs that can fit on the screen all at once. (See Figure 8.36.) Also, when you design your paragraphs for the screen, keep in mind that readers may have come to this screen from very different places. You will have to make sure that each chunk of text can stand alone without depending on information the readers may not have seen yet.

Bulleted Lists

Bulleted lists are easier to read on the screen than are long paragraphs. Lists help to organize information in a logical way and are a good format for presenting links. They are most effective on the screen when each list item is short. See the "Text Lists" section earlier in this chapter for more on this type of text presentation.

Informal Prose

The Web is an informal medium. Readers of most kinds of Web pages want an informal or conversational style. In general, simple and informal writing is preferred over complex and formal prose. Readers want to be able to understand the essential points quickly, particularly when they read online documents. A simple style means not only choosing simpler words over bigger words, but also shorter sentences and paragraphs over longer ones. Readers also seem to prefer more objective writing over promotional writing.

> **"** **"**
> Readers want to be able to understand the essential points quickly, particularly when they read online documents.

Humor

Web readers are also known for their appreciation of humor. Use humor to communicate with readers on a personal level and make your site more attractive. In general, readers of Web pages are receptive to a wide variety of humor on Web sites. They enjoy irreverent, cynical, satirical, sarcastic, or flippant pages, anything to help overcome the boredom of the page. Readers are receptive to humor even on corporate sites and pages. But keep in mind that humor is culturally dependent. Be careful that your humor doesn't have the unintended consequence of offending members of your audience.

Correct Mechanics and Grammar

Check for errors in mechanics and grammar before you upload your pages. Even though the Web is an informal medium, readers look for credibility. A site that looks well edited and well thought out will appear more credible than one that is sloppily thrown together without the author's paying attention to the basics of clear communication.

Credibility

Readers of Web pages typically are also concerned about the credibility of the information they obtain from Web sites. Readers are concerned about the motivations for the site and the qualifications and trustworthiness of the people who create the sites. The quality of a site's content can help users think it is a more credible site. Web writers can improve their credibility by offering their readers good writing with an objective tone and by keeping their site current and up to date.

Jargon

Remember that your audience will have varying knowledge of the Web and computer usage. To accommodate the largest audience possible, avoid jargon and other language that could exclude potential users. The Web is an international medium of information exchange. Jargon does not translate well from culture to culture.

Links

Don't use "click here" or "click me" to cue a navigational link. Always embed the link in the text for easier reading and so that printouts will make sense. Write links within a context that tells readers what information they will find if they follow the link. Don't highlight whole sentences with link text. It is distracting. Choose key words that indicate why a link is different from others. For the use of readers with disabilities or with older text browsers, provide Web addresses or e-mail addresses explicitly, not only as a link attached to a descriptive term.

International Audience

If you plan to take advantage of the Web to communicate with users from other countries, you must tailor your document to meet their needs. Avoid jargon, colloquialisms, and unexplained acronyms. Write simple sentences. Consider including a glossary, metric measurements, and dates that are formatted in the conventional style of users from your intended audience.

Be very careful about the graphics you choose to display. Suitability of images varies quite a bit from one culture to another. What may be commonplace in one culture—images of people or animals, for example—may be offensive in another. Color associations vary from country to country and culture to culture. Look at other Web sites that target the country or culture you want to reach and see what conventions—textual and visual—are observed.

Graphics and Text

The Web is a graphics-intensive medium, but it is also very much a text-based medium. Readers of Web pages expect an effective combination of words and text throughout a site. And these readers also typically believe that graphics that add nothing to the text are a distraction and a waste of time.

CHOOSING THE ETHICAL PATH

Because readers are often unsure of who has written the information at a site and how reliable the facts are, they search for sites that seem objective. Avoid exaggerated language and claims that may mislead your readers.

Writing for the Web

- Determine the purpose of your Web site so it will accomplish what you want it to accomplish.

- Narrow your focus so you can identify your audience and reach the users who will be interested in what you are offering.

- Write with an objective tone and keep your site current to increase your site's credibility.

- Make sure your pages are well organized and easy to scan. Use design elements including meaningful headings, large type, bold and highlighted keywords and text, bulleted lists, captions, and graphics.

- Avoid jargon, colloquialisms, and unexplained acronyms that could exclude potential users. Your prose can be informal and you can use humor. But correct mechanics and grammar still are critical.

- Embed links in the text for easier reading. Don't highlight entire sentences with link text; choose keywords to show why a link is different from others.

- Work for an effective combination of words and text throughout your site. Graphics that add nothing to the text are distracting and a waste of time.

Designing the Interface

Every place where a person and an object interact has some kind of interface. This applies to your furniture, your appliances, your telephone, your computer, and your Web site. Well-constructed furniture is comfortable, functional, and aesthetically pleasing. Well-engineered appliances are easy to use. Well-designed electronic equipment is logically organized. Similarly, the user interface is the part of your Web site that the visitor sees and interacts with, and like any other interface, it should be created with the user in mind.

When you create documents that are going to be printed, you have an expectation of how their various elements will be positioned. You read earlier in this chapter about readers' expectations for books, newsletters, and brochures. We see these kinds of documents all the time and usually do not question the standard ways they are designed and laid out. Another way of expressing this idea is to say that various documents are designed according to *convention*. Often we don't think about this matter explicitly because we are so used to seeing particular documents following their normal conventions.

In creating and publishing Web and other online documents, the situation is a bit different. For one thing, there is a great variety in arrangement of online documents, so conventions have not been developed and universally accepted in this medium. For another, talking about the design and layout of a Web document ignores the fact that Web documents have many purposes and audiences, so one conventional type of arrangement is unlikely to serve all documents. See Figure 8.37 for sample Web-site layouts.

FIGURE 8.37

Web-Site Layouts

Web sites with similar purposes and content can have very different layouts.

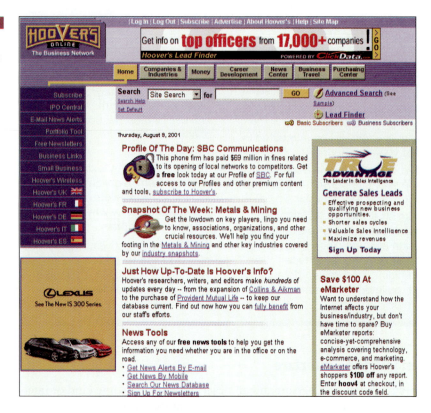

Recall that earlier in this chapter you learned about readers' expectations for books, newsletters, and brochures. These document types are organized in conventional ways to provide a familiar navigation for readers. In some ways, the same is true for Web pages, although there is much more variety for this type of "document." Conventions aren't written somewhere as a handy list of the things you should do on your Web site. But look around at other sites. Your visitors come to your site having seen those others. If your site is very different, make sure it's different for a good reason.

Users have certain expectations about what they will see and how they will move around. They expect that a Web site will have pages and links. The locations of certain elements on a page are, if not standardized, at least fairly predictable. When you design your site, think about whether you want to reinforce the expectations of your visitors and let them find your content where they expect it to be or whether you want to invent an original interface at the possible expense of difficulty and frustration for your audience.

Design your screen navigation (headings, navigation bars, hyperlinks, forward and back buttons, and help links) so that users become familiar with the layout and know where to look for what they need when they get to a new page.

A study conducted by Thomas S. Tullis and reported by Jakob Nielsen, the Web usability guru, showed that people could correctly identify the various elements on Web sites, even when all the text was nonsense words. They were able to do that because users are accustomed to seeing certain page elements appear in certain places in their browser window and can guess the function of text from its location. This result argues strongly that if you want your users to find information on your site easily, put it where they expect to find it.

See Figure 8.38 for typical Web-site elements.

The elements your readers expect to find on your Web pages include a title at the top of each page, with perhaps a subheading beneath it; your name and contact information at the bottom; a "date last revised" notice with the date of your last page revision; a graphic or list of links, usually on the left-hand side, with navigation buttons or hypertext links, used to access other parts of your site and to orient users as to where they are with respect to the whole site; and blue links for unvisited links and red or purple for visited links.

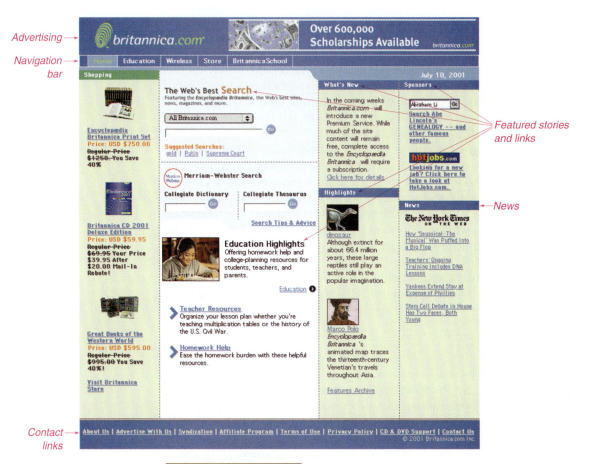

Advertising →

Navigation bar →

Featured stories and links →

News →

Contact links →

FIGURE 8.38

Web Site-Elements

Interactivity

Readers of paper documents have a limited number of ways to look at the text. They can turn pages, and they can glance down and up and back down again on each page. Readers of online documents can do similar things on the screen (go backward or forward one screen, scroll up and down on the same screen, and link to distant screens), but they have other possibilities that readers of printed documents do not have. So when you design documents for online use, you should be aware of the possibilities and take advantage of them when you can.

Multimedia

Multimedia means sound, video, movies, and animation. Designing for multimedia is complex and beyond the scope of this book. But if you are going to design Web pages, online help, or other kinds of online documents, you

---

DESIGNING WEB PAGES

The top four vertical inches of your home page are the most valuable real estate in your Web site and should be the most dense area in your site in both visual and functional complexity.

—Patrick J. Lynch,
Yale University's Center for Advanced Instructional Media

will sooner or later have to decide whether multimedia modules are appropriate for your needs. If you do decide that multimedia is just the thing you need for your online document, keep in mind its limitations.

Organizing Online Space

- Avoid frames. Frames are divisions of your page into separately scrollable areas. They make bookmarking pages difficult, if not impossible, and break up the already limited screen area into even smaller segments.
- Structure links to avoid having everything on one page. Show the overviews of several topics with links to further material for each one.
- Instead of bandwidth-hogging large graphics—graphics that take a long time to download—display small graphics or thumbnails that link to bigger graphics.

Give users the choice to view those larger graphics or not.
- Control the content display area to minimize scrolling. Very motivated users will scroll to see the bottom of your page; less motivated users will surf away. Users are more likely to see material that they don't have to scroll to access than material that is initially hidden from them.
- Put your most important information up near the top of the screen in an inverted pyramid order.
- Keep your pages uncluttered by putting less on the page.

Accessibility Matters

- Be aware that users with disabilities may not be able to see, hear, or understand your music or video files. Provide alternate access to your material: descriptive text instead of audio narration, captions with photos, and so on.
- Ask yourself if the content you are providing can be provided in a lower-tech way, without compromising quality and usability. Can the graphic be smaller? Can the video be presented instead as stills or a transcript? Can the audio be presented as captions or text?
- Consider site accessibility options for people who might need alternate types of presentations because of disabilities. Have you made it possible for visually impaired or hearing impaired visitors to use the information on your site? See Figure 8.39 on accessibility guidelines and Figure 8.40 on accessibility Web sites.

Multimedia files are large files. Downloading them takes a long time, especially for users with slow Internet connections. And playing or displaying multimedia files requires a reasonably fast processor. Older computers don't handle multimedia very well. Ask yourself if you really need multimedia in your documents, and if the answer is yes, think about how you can maximize its effect without overwhelming the user's computer system.

Scrolling

Because screen sizes vary, users may have to scroll down to read an entire screen's worth of information. Some users will not care to expend that effort, so try to have all your information visible at once. If you need to divide infor-

FIGURE 8.39

Accessibility Guidelines

Accessibility Guidelines of the HTML Writers Group (adapted)
<http://www.hwg.org/opcenter/policy/access.html>

1. Provide text equivalents for non-text elements.
2. Don't rely solely upon color.
3. Signal transitions from one language to another.
4. Make sure pages are usable with and without style sheets.
5. Update the text-equivalent of your information whenever you update the standard page elements.
6. Don't make the screen flicker.
7. Use plain, understandable English.
8. Use client-side imagemaps, not server-side, and provide lists of text links for imagemaps.
9. Use HTML 4.0 table markup on data tables.
10. Use NOFRAMES and TITLE tags within frame pages.
11. Don't rely solely upon scripts and applets.
12. As a last resort only, make an alternate, accessible page.

Web Accessibility Initiative (WAI)	http://www.w3.org/WAI/
WebABLE	http://www.webable.com/
Web Design Group Accessibility Page	http://www.htmlhelp.com/design/accessibility/
Federal IT Accessibility Initiative	http://www.section508.gov/
MIT Universal Design and Web Accessibility	http://web.mit.edu/ada/waccess.html
Designing More Usable Web Sites (Trace Research & Development Center, University of Wisconsin–Madison)	http://www.trace.wisc.edu/world/Web/index.html

FIGURE 8.40

Accessibility Web Sites

FIGURE 8.41

Window with Scroll Bar

Each item in the bulleted list is a link to information further down the page.

mation in such a way that not all the information is visible at one time, making your readers scroll to the bottom is a good idea. But if you want readers to see your message right away, put the important information near the top of the screen. Figure 8.41 shows a window with a scroll bar.

Linking

Another way to move readers to further information elsewhere in your online document is to have them jump to another page to see additional information. Hyperlinks make jumping from one page to another easy. By having users click on hyperlinks to move to another page, you ensure that they are paying attention, at least somewhat, to your document's content. And by offering them choices of where to jump, you can tailor their path through the material to better suit their needs.

On-Screen Color

The human eye can discern millions of colors, and many of them are easily available to you and your readers onscreen. What would be costly to produce in print is simple and cheap to accomplish online. So whereas you would have to be very careful about whether and how to use color in your print documents, you can be more relaxed and creative with your online documents. Nonetheless, you will find that the effective use of color is still something that comes with experience and practice.

Unlike color that is printed on paper, color on the screen displays differently on different monitors and systems. So your audience may not be seeing the same colors that you intend, depending on their computers and settings. Even viewing colors on the same monitor and system can yield a

FIGURE 8.42

Effects of Different Resolutions

Notice how the different resolutions affect the image.

different experience depending on how long the monitor has been on and whether the color settings for the monitor have been set in a uniform way. If getting the exact color is important to you, you may have to use paper instead of a computer to distribute your document.

Screen Resolution

Screen resolution refers to the number of picture elements (pixels) that can fit onto the screen. Resolution is described by two numbers, width (in pixels) and height (in pixels). Monitors also are rated by the distance between the dots that make up the images and text. This value, called *dot pitch*, normally is expressed as a decimal fraction, such as .28. The smaller the number, the sharper the image can be. The finer the resolution, the finer the detail that can be displayed and the crisper the appearance.

Design for the screen assuming your readers have low-resolution monitors, even though more and more monitors are reaching higher and higher resolutions. Set your monitor on a resolution of 640 by 480 or 800 by 600. Look at the results. Are they pleasing and do they convey your information well? Less-fine resolutions result in larger images on the screen, so make sure that you are not designing your screens to hold more information than your readers will actually be able to see. Information that cannot be correctly displayed on the screen will not convey your message effectively. See Figure 8.42 for examples of effects of different resolutions.

Fonts

Text is more difficult to read onscreen than it is on paper. That is because the resolution of a typical screen is much less fine than that of a typical printer. Because of this difference in resolution, choose fonts that do not need a high resolution to display clearly. In general, your text will be more legible on screen if you

- use a sans serif font, preferably one that is designed for screen use, such as Verdana
- keep the letters, words, and lines spaced well enough apart so that they don't run into each other
- use large enough letters so that smaller monitors and lower-resolution monitors can still display your text clearly

Another important issue to consider when planning fonts for screen use is whether your readers will have the same typefaces installed on their systems as you have on yours. If your text uses a particularly interesting typeface, you can be almost positive some of your readers will not be able to view the text properly. Instead of the typefaces you planned for, they will see other typefaces, which their systems or browsers or other software will substitute for the missing typefaces. Most often, the substituted typefaces will change the entire look of the piece and probably also change the line breaks and page breaks.

To avoid this problem, use commonly available typefaces—such as Times New Roman (a serif typeface) or Helvetica or Arial (sans serif typefaces)—and also specify acceptable substitutes in your Web-page coding. Your other alternative is to bundle in the typefaces with the document. Some software programs allow bundling; others do not. Check the manuals or online help files of your program or browser to see if bundling is a possibility. But to avoid the problem in the first place, plan to use conventional, rather than novel, typefaces.

Browser Capability

Some of your online documents may be designed for use on the World Wide Web or for display in a Web browser on an intranet. Browsers vary in how they display various elements, such as colors, fonts, paragraph spacing, animation, and graphics. In fact, some browsers display text only, and do not have the capability of displaying multimedia or graphics of any kind. Keep in mind when you are designing your online document that readers who are using text browsers need to be offered the chance to use your information too. Provide alternate, text-based routes through your document.

Even graphical browsers display text, graphics, and multimedia differently. At the very least, try to test your online documents for browser compatibility using Netscape Navigator and Microsoft Internet Explorer on a PC and a Mac. The latest versions of these browsers should be capable of handling almost any standard codes and files. But remember, too—many people who use these browsers do not have the latest versions. Readers who cannot read your message because you have used features not installed on their computers will be lost to you. If you want to reach as many people as possible, use standard features and avoid the ones that are recognized by one browser but not others.

> " " Readers who cannot read your message because you have used features not installed on their computers will be lost to you. If you want to reach as many people as possible, use standard features and avoid the ones that are recognized by one browser but not others.

Plug-Ins

Plug-ins are programs that can be added to browsers to enable them to perform a specific function (display or play a certain file type). If you depend on plug-ins to display your files, they should be plug-ins that are available to your readers, too. Often browsers will offer to install appropriate plug-ins when new file types are encountered. Be prepared to lose readers who do not want to install plug-ins to access your material.

Download Speeds

Files that are heavy in graphics, animations, and multimedia are files that are very large. And large files present a problem to users with slow Internet connections. Although state-of-the-art download speeds make downloading large files almost trivial, for a large number of computer users, perhaps the majority of your users, slower modems and connections are the rule. If your files are so large that users with slow modems have to wait minutes or longer for each file to download, your readers may decide that the wait is not worthwhile and may surf away to faster sites. Keep your graphics and other files small enough that they can be downloaded within reasonable times even by slow modems. And if you do have files that take a long time to download, be courteous and warn your readers that the files they are clicking to download are large.

FIRST AID FOR YOUR DOCUMENT DESIGN

When you design a document from scratch, you will of course try for the best and most effective design right from the beginning. But many times you will find that you are looking at documents designed by others or ones that have been returned to you for improvement. What do you do when you are faced with a document that needs help?

Triage is a term used in medicine to mean the identification of the most seriously ill patients in order to treat them before the less sick ones. You can perform triage on documents too. Improving the design of your documents or someone else's may seem a daunting task. But don't be overwhelmed or discouraged. Perform triage on your documents to fix the most severe problems right away. Fixing the easy-to-find problems will make a tremendous and immediate difference in the effectiveness and appeal of your documents. Once you have made these changes, you can then work on other, specific problems and fine-tune your design until it is as perfect as you would like it to be.

Document Triage

- Break long paragraphs into smaller units or chunks. Much technical writing is very dense, with an abundance of details that fill long paragraphs. Smaller paragraphs are easier to read and digest. Give your readers the chance to chew on smaller pieces of information so they can swallow and digest them easily.

- Provide headings that signal to your readers the topic of the next chunk or set of paragraphs. Make sure the headings are proportional in size to the font you are using, since headings that are too large or too small are jarring. Don't use periods or colons after headings. The fewer punctuation marks you use in headings, the better.

- Use plenty of white space. The difference between a hard-to-read document and one that readers find inviting is often simply the amount of white space between sections, in margins, and around illustrations.

From the workplace

Lise Hansen

Director of Information Architecture (Web-site designer)
Yamamoto Moss (Design Agency)
Minneapolis, Minnesota

Lise designs commercial Web sites. Her team researches a client's needs and proposes and develops customized sites that will meet those needs. To do her job well, Lise needs to figure out the best plan for the client's site and communicate her ideas to clients and co-workers. For that, she draws on a variety of skills: some she learned in school and others she developed on the job.

In my job, I work with clients and designers to create Web-site architectures, strategies, and prototypes, using case scenarios appropriate to the client's business objectives and the audience needs. I consult with our clients on Web strategy and content development and conduct usability testing for the sites we develop.

What I do now is called information architecture, but ten years from now, I think that the title "Information Architect" won't even mean the same thing, if it still exists. We structure information, but we also design and conduct end-user research, deal with marketing and brand, and try to translate business goals into Web strategy.

I arrived at information architecture indirectly. My undergraduate degree is in biology with a minor in technical writing. I initially wanted to work as a science writer. I figured out late that technical communication was a career that appealed to me. By that time, I was well on my way toward completing my biology degree, so I stuck with it and pursued the minor.

Our group creates the working documents for every site our agency creates. We create the site maps, copy documents, and site strategies that the team works from. The team includes account management, designers and developers, copywriters, and clients.

The information architects take the lead at the beginning of a project. We have the main responsibility for conducting research and developing site maps or reports, but we also gather contributions from designers and development staff (e.g., questions to ask during research, feedback on reports). Site maps and copy documents are always a collaborative effort with the client. Since our group helps identify the users, goals, and objectives of the site, we are very involved up front and continue to be consulted throughout the process. The input we have on development beyond the initial project varies from client to client.

The advantages of working as a team rather than individually are that everyone gets a chance to "buy in" to the direction being proposed and we get the advantage of different perspectives, which makes for much richer recommendations. The disadvantage is that getting everyone together takes time. Sometimes it feels as if we're always in a meeting. Additionally, working collaboratively costs the client money, so we

CHECKING WHAT YOU'VE LEARNED

Well-designed pages and screens do not happen by accident. Teach yourself to recognize and appreciate good design and you will be on your way to producing your own well-designed documents.

General Principles

- Have you planned your documents with the qualities of simplicity, symmetry, consistency, readability, and usability in mind?

are constantly having to sell the advantages of working closely this way.

In general, the collaborative process works pretty smoothly. We could benefit from having still more informal communication and developing mutual respect between team members who work in different areas. Ideally, other members of the team should be comfortable going to the designer with an idea.

As part of my job, I have to give presentations—some to clients and prospective clients, others to co-workers. I design my presentations according to the audience and purpose. My presentation style is to rely on some high-level talking points—I hate it when presenters just read from the slides. If it's a pitch, I'll pull together a lot of sample work we've done for clients in a similar industry.

Since I work for a design agency, visuals rule. If I can say something with visuals instead of text bullet points, I'll do it. In my type of work, presentations deal more with communicating concepts than with explaining particulars. Since information architecture can be intimidating, I use high-level diagrams to illustrate what we do. And if I'm in more of an instructional mode, I'll again use visuals to illustrate my points (e.g., screen shots of Web sites to illustrate navigational strategies).

What I've learned through my work is that to be a good writer, you must understand your audience and, more important, understand what action the audience is supposed to take based on the document. Then you write accordingly.

That advice will help you write better. But I've learned a few other things about how to be successful on the job:

- Join the professional association appropriate for your field.
- Volunteer—If you're not a joiner, start small and follow through on your commitment. Look for a volunteer opportunity that is very discrete and work your way into more advanced projects. This strategy works well if you don't like to (or don't think you are good at) "schmoozing." It gives you a chance to interact with people who are already established in the field. If you're still a student, volunteer to work on a project that will contribute to your portfolio.
- Take the initiative on projects while being wise about your company's culture and politics. In the same breath . . .
- Avoid the company politics. Try to be noncommittal if someone tries to bait you into weighing in on one side or the other.
- Create reasonable deadlines for yourself and keep to them. You'll get a bad reputation if you promise to get something delivered the next day but it doesn't show up until three days later.
- Propose solutions. If you've come up against a situation or problem that you could use your bosses' advice on, identify some possible solutions (and their pros and cons) before asking for their help. Presenting possible solutions makes it easier for your bosses to give you advice quickly and demonstrates that you have initiative and the ability to handle more complex projects.

- For each of these principles, could your treatment be improved?

Organizing Space

- Have you allowed enough white space or blank space to provide a pleasing and easy-to-follow text?
- If you are using grids, do all your elements line up properly with the gridlines?
- Do you have headers, footers, or both to provide consistency and navigational aids in your document?

Typography

- Have you chosen typefaces that work well together?
- Have you selected sizes and spacing that allow for the greatest legibility and readability of your text?
- Did you select a paragraph alignment style—generally left aligned–ragged right or full justified—that allows for the easiest access to your information?

Designing for Online Screens and Web Pages

- Have you planned the site structure, navigation, and page layout to maximize the effectiveness of your site?
- Can the reader easily move from one section of your site to another without getting lost?
- Have you provided common elements on each page: navigation bars, headers, update information?
- Have you chunked the information into small enough groupings so as to minimize scrolling?
- If scrolling is unavoidable, have you organized your information according to an inverted pyramid order (most important first)?
- If you use multimedia on your site, have you provided text alternatives for readers with accessibility needs or older browsers?
- Have you minimized the loading time of your pages by streaming multimedia files and providing thumbnails (smaller, low-resolution versions) of graphics files?

EXERCISES

REVIEW

1. Find three examples of an effective use of typefaces. What makes them effective? Bring them to class and be prepared to justify your selections.
2. Find two examples from a newsletter or magazine in which the designer has used grids to organize the placement of material on the page. One should feature a symmetrical arrangement of elements; the other an asymmetrical arrangement. Do they both work? Where are the grid lines? Sketch out the grid lines and bring them and the examples to class.
3. Design a poster advertising a forthcoming event. Decide where the gridlines will be and how you will balance the elements. Choose two typefaces that go well together and use them in the poster. Bring the poster to class and discuss how you chose the typefaces and why you believe they work well together.
4. Select a technical document from your discipline. Can the design be improved? How? Sketch

out an improved version of a page from the document. Why is your version better?

5. Find what you consider to be a well-designed page from a magazine, newspaper, book, brochure, or Web site. In several brief paragraphs, discuss how the elements of simplicity, symmetry, consistency, readability, and usability may or may not apply to the example you have found. Bring the paragraphs to class for class discussion.

 ### THE INTERNET

Look at the main pages of a dozen or more home pages or corporation Web sites. In a few paragraphs comment on the effective or ineffective use of color on one main page for one of the sites. Bring a printed copy (black and white will be fine) of the main page and your paragraphs to class for class discussion.

 ### ETHICS/PROFESSIONALISM

Look at the car ads in your local newspaper. In a few paragraphs comment on any questionable design practices (for example, large print, fine print, asterisks, and other notations) that may potentially mislead readers. Bring the ad and your paragraphs to class for class discussion.

 ### COLLABORATION

Working in small groups (no more than three students per group), provide a one-page design (on paper provided by your instructor) combining text, text art, and visuals (rough sketches will do for all three). This design should demonstrate as many of the major principles of design (simplicity, symmetry, consistency, readability, and usability) as you can incorporate (at least three). Collaboratively write a one-paragraph summary of how your design illustrates these principles. Be prepared to discuss your design and paragraph with the entire class.

 ### INTERNATIONAL COMMUNICATION

Find an advertisement in a travel magazine that advertises a resort or other place to visit in a country outside the United States. Discuss how the ad is designed to appeal specifically to American readers.

RESOURCES

Castro, Elizabeth. *HTML 4 For the World Wide Web: Visual Quickstart Guide.* 4th ed. Berkeley: Peachpit, 2000.

Hoft, Nancy L. *International Technical Communication: How to Export Information About Technology.* New York: Wiley, 1995.

Horton, William. *Designing and Writing Online Documentation: Hypermedia for Self-Supporting Products.* 2nd ed. New York: Wiley, 1994.

———. *Illustrating Computer Documentation: The Art of Presenting Information Graphically on Paper and Online.* New York: Wiley, 1991.

Lie, Håkon Wium, and Bert Bos. *Cascading Style Sheets: Designing for the Web.* 2nd ed. Edinburgh: Pearson Education, 1999.

Nielsen, Jakob. *Designing Web Usability: The Practice of Simplicity.* Indianapolis: New Riders, 2000.

Schriver, Karen A. *Dynamics in Document Design: Creating Texts for Readers.* New York: Wiley, 1997.

Weinman, Lynda. *Designing Web Graphics.3: How to Prepare Images and Media for the Web.* 3rd ed. Indianapolis: New Riders, 1999.

Yale Style Manual. Online. Available at <http://info.med.yale.edu/caim/manual/contents.html>. Accessed 7/17/00.

9

Illustrations

Appropriateness   295

Ethical Use of Illustrations   302

Tables   302

Graphs   305

Charts   311

Drawings, Diagrams, and Maps   314

Photos   317

Clip Art   319

Computer Illustrations   321

From the Workplace   322

IN THIS CHAPTER

You may think of the illustrations you use in your documents or presentations as secondary to other features. However, illustrations often are as important as any other element—your statement of purpose, your method of organization, the examples and other details in your prose, the style and tone of your communication, or the design. Illustrations are used primarily to demonstrate concepts, but they can also be used to help readers navigate through the text or clarify, simplify, emphasize, summarize, reinforce, attract, impress, show a relationship, and even save space. Illustrations can be used to show what something looks like or how it works, clarify information, distinguish among objects, and get quicker and more accurate responses from readers. Illustrations and text are not mutually exclusive. Ideally, they will be used to enhance each other's effectiveness and complement each other.

You will learn about:

- the appropriate uses of illustrations
- strategies for illustrating for print and for the screen and the Web
- strategies for properly labeling and displaying illustrations
- the ethical uses of illustrations
- strategies for creating illustrations: tables, graphs, charts, drawings, diagrams, maps, photos, clip art, and computer illustrations

> **VISUAL COMMUNICATION**
>
> Visual communication is critical to a successful documentation project. Whether viewed in hard copy, online, or on the Internet, graphic elements are a vital element to documentation in any medium. Different learning styles require the use of visual communication.
>
> —Marjorie Hermansen-Eldard, course developer, Orem, Utah

APPROPRIATENESS

Illustrations are just one of the major elements of effective document design, but handling them appropriately and effectively is important all by itself. Use illustrations to aid job performance, help to make documents internationally accessible, assist nonreaders, bring in wary readers, add credibility to work, and promote creative thinking and efficient reading.

Sometimes space in a report or other technical document is limited. Use illustrations in place of words for these situations if the concepts in the text use numbers, symbols, or measures; the ideas being presented are structural or pictorial; the readers are visually perceptive rather than word perceptive; the subject is too complex to explain in words; or your illustrative skills are stronger than your writing skills.

Illustrations serve three roles when combined with prose in a technical document:

- **Illustrations get the reader's attention and create interest.** They attract attention and generate interest by keeping the reader involved in the material, breaking up long passages, emphasizing specific data, making the reading enjoyable, and providing quick references.

- **Illustrations explain information.** They explain information by simplifying complex subjects, helping the reader to absorb many facts and figures, condensing detailed information, showing relationships between things, getting across concepts that words cannot convey, and comparing and contrasting diverse subjects.
- **Illustrations help the reader to retain the text material.** They help to retain information because illustrations can be remembered more easily than text and the reader may be able to retrieve words from memory that are associated with the pictures.

Illustrating for Print

People who must communicate technical information are challenged to make the information they portray as clear and concise as possible. Many times, to illustrate a point or make the text clearer, an illustration is inserted in a document. An illustration is a visual aid that helps the reader to access information faster.

Follow these basic guidelines when planning to use illustrations in a document. Consider first how people take in information and then how best to display the information you have. Motivate your readers by getting their attention and relating the material to them.

- Illustrations must be appropriately and effectively displayed to achieve the intended effect on your audience. All of us have seen textbooks, reports, manuals, and many other kinds of documents containing illustrations that seem out of place or that are placed far from where the discussion (if there is any discussion) of the illustrations occurs. It's not unusual to see a report, for example, in which all of the illustrations are placed at the end of the report or perhaps in an appendix. All essential illustrations should be placed in the report where they are discussed.
- Refer to illustrations before they are displayed. You may refer to an illustration or a table in several different ways. For example, "As Figure 1.1 illustrates. . . ." Or simply, "(See Figure 1.1.)" or "(Figure 1.1)." Sometimes informal illustrations (for example, cartoons or informal tables) are neither discussed nor referred to in the text. In general, all illustrations should be mentioned in the text. If you have an illustration that you don't mention, make sure it is necessary and adds something to the discussion.
- Number all figures consecutively as they appear in the document (Figure 1, Figure 2, and so on). Number all tables consecutively, too, separately from the figures (Table 1, Table 2, and so on).
- Illustrations should be properly labeled. Every illustration should be identified by type ("Figure" or "Table" or "Plate" [for art or sometimes

for photos]). Each should have a number, a title or caption, and, if necessary, a citation of its source. Use callouts (numbers and letters) to label and identify parts that are listed near the figure. Use a legend or key to identify symbols, variations, or the size scale. Do not directly label parts in an illustration if there is any possibility that it will be reused in another context. Callouts and a legend make the illustration more generic for reuse later, since it is far easier to make changes to callouts that are somewhat separated from the main part of a graphic than it is to make changes to labels that are an integral part of the visual itself. Use standard symbols and abbreviations for any text that is used. Be consistent with terminology in the text and on the illustration. See Figure 9.1 for a figure with callouts and Figure 9.2 for a table and caption.

■ Illustrations should not be too close to the surrounding text on the page. Allow for sufficient white space on all sides of the illustration, so that readers can easily read the text and so that the illustration does not make the page look crowded.

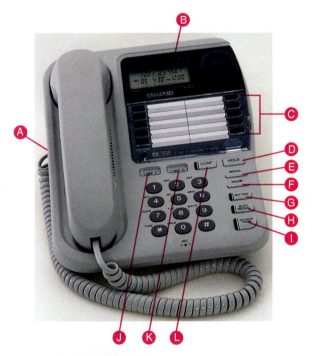

KEY

- A Headset jack
- B Display
- C Auto-dial buttons
- D Hold button
- E Redial button
- F Pause button
- G Muting button
- H Busy redial button
- I Speaker phone button
- J Line 1 button
- K Line 2 button
- L Conference call button

FIGURE 9.1

Figure with Callouts

The lettered callouts are explained in a key.

FIGURE 9.2
Table and Caption

**TABLE 1. THE TOP 10 LIST OF VENTURE CAPITAL
REGIONS FOR THE YEAR 2000**

Region	Funds raised in 1999	Funds raised in 2000	Change 1999–2000
1. Silicon Valley	$15.34 billion	$26.02 billion	69.6%
2. New England	$3.96 billion	$8.42 billion	112.6%
3. New York metro area	$2.67 billion	$5.97 billion	123.6%
4. Los Angeles/Orange County area	$2.71 billion	$3.91 billion	44.3%
5. Washington metro area	$1.84 billion	$3.12 billion	69.6%
6. Washington state	$1.40 billion	$2.03 billion	45.0%
7. Austin, Texas	$900 million	$1.65 billion	83.3%
8. Philadelphia metro area	$1.18 billion	$1.28 billion	8.5%
9. North Carolina/South Carolina	$795 million	$1.15 billion	44.7%
10. Connecticut	$515 million	$1.05 billion	103.9%

Source: *Infoworld*, 19 March 2001: 20.

- Place illustrations so that they fall within the top third, middle third, or bottom third of the page if possible, rather than randomly on the page. Use a balance of text and illustrations on any pages where illustrations occur. If an illustration occupies an entire page, make sure it is adequately sized to the page. It should not be too large or too small for the page. All captions, callouts, and legends should be clearly readable.
- Page-length illustrations printed in landscape format—wider than they are long—should be placed with the top of the document closer to the binding if the document is bound. (See Figure 9.3.)
- Foldout illustrations—extra-large pages that fold up to fit in with the rest of the pages—are acceptable in many kinds of documents but require special handling during printing and binding.
- All illustrations should have a professional appearance. Poor photocopies or copies printed with low-quality printers are not acceptable except in draft versions of documents.
- Don't glue, paste, or tape illustrations onto the pages of the final copy of a document. Doing so for photocopying purposes may be acceptable.
- Properly indicate the source of any illustration borrowed from or adapted from another source in the lower left-hand corner of the illustration. Make sure you have permission to adapt or borrow the source illustration, unless you have reason to believe your use qualifies as fair use under the copyright law. See Chapter 8 for more information on fair use.

FIGURE 9.3
Landscape-Oriented Art

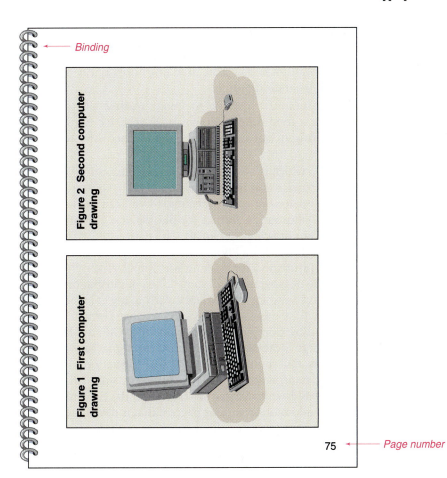

Binding

Figure 2 Second computer drawing

Figure 1 First computer drawing

75 — Page number

- Provide a list of tables and a list of figures as separate tables of contents. These lists can serve as additional reader aids.
- If any illustrations are not essential to the text of the document but you still want to include them, place them in an appendix for the document.

Illustrating for the Screen

Many of the basic principles of print illustrations apply to on-screen illustrations on CD-ROM and the Web. Because all on-screen illustrations generally must adhere to the same principles whether or not they are online, they are covered together in this section.

Much of the difficulty in planning on-screen illustrations stems from the wide variety of screen sizes and resolution. These differences mean that you must know exactly when and where to use an illustration. Try out your illustrations on a variety of monitors, platforms, and browsers if possible. Always remember to design screen layouts to be pleasing to the eye.

Follow these guidelines when using on-screen illustrations:

- Consider the medium that will be used to display an illustration. For example, if an illustration is also to be used in a book, is it necessary to include the same illustration online?

- Choose your illustrations according to image quality, size of image (large images take a long time to download), need for transparency, progressive rendering or streaming, and possible necessity to pay licensing fees.

- Select the format in which you want to present the illustration. Purchase and learn to use software that might assist you. Often, software is available in shareware versions or demo versions, so you can try before you buy. Use the JPEG illustration format for photos and GIF illustration format for solid color drawings or clip art. The name JPEG comes from the group that designed it, Joint Photographic Experts Group. It's a compression method (a method for making files smaller) specifically designed for handling photographs and some kinds of illustrations. JPEGs are the best format to use for photographs with many colors or subtle changes in color. GIF stands for Graphics Interchange Format. This format was developed by CompuServe for online use. GIFs are best used for images with large areas of solid color such as logos, cartoons, and simple illustrations. GIF should be used for any illustration in which a portion should be transparent against a background, since GIF illustrations can be rendered with transparent backgrounds. GIF animations are an easy way to add motion to your pages if that is desired. Provide a text-only option for readers who either won't or can't display illustrations as they browse.

- Decrease the size of your illustration files by saving them in a low-resolution format. Remember, computer monitors are low-resolution devices, so high-resolution graphics with 24-bit color are wasted in this medium. Worse, the size of the illustrations will make the loading time prohibitively long. Smaller files will look just as good in many cases and will download in a more reasonable length of time. File download time often makes the difference between a site that users like to visit and browse and one that is glanced at and abandoned. Design for screen sizes of 640 by 480 pixels, even though many monitors will do better than that. Most browsers default to 500 pixels wide. Headers should be less than 480 pixels wide so that viewers do not have to scroll. Issue size warnings for larger illustrations or sound and movie files.

- Choose small illustrations with few colors, since they are quicker to download than larger ones and those with more colors. Consider using interlaced illustrations (illustrations that originally appear in very low resolution and refresh at higher resolution) to download, since viewers are more willing to wait through a long download if they can see the picture becoming sharper and sharper than if they have to look at a blank screen slowly filling in from the top.

- Size your illustrations appropriately. The size of the illustration signals a certain degree of importance. Make the illustration appropriate to its context. If your illustration is too large to fit on the screen, eliminate unnecessary information, consider making the illustration smaller, break the illustration up into smaller parts, and only if absolutely necessary provide scroll bars.

- Illustrations should be close to their related text. Consider anchoring your illustration to the related text. *Anchoring* means that if the text moves, the illustration will move as well. If you have several illustrations, they can be clustered together or arranged in a vertical or horizontal arrangement. Your material can have different interpretations based on the position of the illustrations, so make sure you have placed the illustrations just where you mean them to be. Be aware that anchored illustrations—unlike floating illustrations—cannot be independently moved on the page. Once they are anchored, they stick with their associated text.

- The shape and orientation of an illustration can influence the attitude the reader will have toward it. For important illustrations, leave the shape and orientation basic so that users can recognize them easily. Textures and patterns can determine the sharpness of an illustration and make the illustration more recognizable. Size will affect the recognizability of illustrations as well.

- When applying text to your images, apply the text last and don't resize the image once the text is in place. Use anti-aliasing to make curves in text seem less jagged. *Anti-aliasing* is a technique that decreases the effect of low-resolution display on curved images such as letterforms. Instead of using stair-step jagged lines for diagonals and curves, anti-aliasing blurs those lines with the background pixels. The effect, rather than seeming more blurry, is to have the lines appear smoother. Ensure that the background and text contrast adequately by adjusting the color combinations, line weight, or stroke width.

- Adjust the contrast between the illustration and the background to make the illustration easier for the reader to interpret.

- Use color carefully. Color can enhance illustrations but may be difficult for some users who have monochromatic monitors or who are color-blind. Also variations in certain colors make illustrations difficult to distinguish. Mix color values (as few or as many as you have) to create more color options unless you are designing for the Web. Different Web browsers display colors differently; therefore, confine your Web page colors to the 216-color browser-safe palette.

- Allow viewers to zoom in on the illustration if possible. One way is to provide a low-resolution thumbnail that links to the full-sized illustration when the user clicks on the smaller image.

- Dynamics or movement of illustrations should be kept to a minimum. Marquee, blinking, or vibrating illustrations are distracting.

ETHICAL USE OF ILLUSTRATIONS

> " "
> There are many ways to present material deceptively, and it is your responsibility to ensure that your visuals are not only technically accurate but ethically presented as well.

You probably know the old saying: Figures lie and liars figure. The figures referred to in that remark are numbers, which can be manipulated in a variety of ways to support almost any conclusion. As true as that might be for numerical data, it is even more true for visual data. You might think that because something can be seen, it must be true. After all, if you see it, it must be there.

In fact, when it comes to representing information pictorially or graphically, how you present an item can completely change how it is interpreted. There are many ways to present material deceptively, and it is your responsibility to ensure that your visuals are not only technically accurate but ethically presented as well. Watch out in the sections that follow to see where there are opportunities for less-than-truthful illustrations, and make sure that you avoid these traps.

TABLES

Illustrations are generally divided into tables and figures. Tables show comparisons of numbers and other information by displaying them in rows and columns. Tables are convenient for displaying several factors at once. A reader can quickly and easily compare data in one column with data in another. Typical parts of a table include a table number, a table title, column headings, row headings, body, rules, source line, and footnotes. You can see each part labeled in Figure 9.4.

Tables are useful for presenting either simple information or technical data. Decide whether an informal table will provide sufficient clarity to the subject or whether a formal table will be necessary to illustrate complex information.

Informal Tables

Look at the informal table shown in Figure 9.5. Informal tables differ from formal tables in several ways.

Creating Informal Tables

- Keep informal tables brief and simple.
- Don't identify informal tables by table numbers.
- Omit titles for most informal tables.
- Omit the ruled frame around informal tables, and provide only the necessary minimum of internal ruled lines. Ruled frames are omitted so that informal tables are viewed as a continuation of text.
- Don't record informal tables in the lists of tables, illustrations, or figures, and don't list them separately in the table of contents.

Stub head →

Cut-in head →

Row head →

Cut-in head →

Number →

Title →

Straddle rule →

Column heads →

Table body →

Category	Employment Period					
	Nov 2000	Dec 2000	Jan 2001	Feb 2001	Mar 2001	Apr 2001
Labor Force Data						
Civilian labor force[1]						
Employment	2,900.2	2,922.6	2,932.2	2,931.4	2,932.5	2,924.2
Unemployment	99.7	102.3	115.7	132.2	127.0	128.7
Unemployment rate[2]	3.3%	3.4%	3.8%	4.3%	4.1%	4.2%
Nonfarm Wage and Salary Employment[3]						
Construction	126.7	126.3	127.2	128.1	127.9	126.0
Finance, insurance, and real estate	149.9	150.3	150.1	150.9	151.3	151.5
Government (federal, state, and local)	403.9	401.2	402.1	408.2	410.0	411.2
Manufacturing	615.3	614.0	612.6	608.7	605.6	603.2
Mining	2.6	2.6	2.7	2.7	2.7	2.4
Services	771.6	773.5	777.7	780.4	781.6	781.2
Trade (wholesale and retail)	637.7	639.3	638.8	639.4	639.0	638.2
Transportation and public utilities	134.9	135.5	133.7	133.7	134.3	135.0

Table 17
Employment in the State of Wisconsin
(November 2000–April 2001)

Source: Bureau of Labor Statistics. 5 June 2001 <http://stats.bls.gov/eag/eag.wi.htm >. ← Source note

[1] Number of persons, in thousands, seasonally adjusted.
[2] In percent, seasonally adjusted.
[3] Number of jobs, in thousands, seasonally adjusted.

Footnotes →

FIGURE 9.4

Parts of a Table

A table does not necessarily have to have every element.

Formal Tables

Formal tables are used more often than informal tables in reports. Also, they are presented as separate items rather than as ordinary paragraphs of text. Formal tables have framed borders, descriptive titles, and table numbers. As a result, formal tables are included in the list of illustrations or list of tables. See an example of a formal table in Figure 9.6. Tables are best used for displaying numbers and units of measurement that must be illustrated precisely. For example, there is an obvious difference between 2.0123 and 2.0150 when

FIGURE 9.5

Informal Table

Headings are sometimes omitted from informal tables.

Area of Study	Definition
Theoretical ecology	Use of math and computer models to explain scientific observations.
Field ecology	Collection of data from observation of different ecosystems.
Applied ecology	Focus on conservation, species extinction, and design of nature reserves.
Restoration ecology	Focus on rebuilding of habitats.

FIGURE 9.6

Formal Table

Table 5   Global Summary of the HIV/AIDS Epidemic, 1999

	Number of Persons			
	Adults	**Women**	**Children**[1]	**Total**
Newly infected with HIV in 1999	4,700,000	2,300,000	620,000	5,320,000
Living with HIV/AIDS	33,000,000	15,700,000	1,300,000	34,300,000
Died from AIDS in 1999	2,300,000	1,200,000	500,000	2,800,000
Died from AIDS since 1981[2]	15,000,000	7,700,000	3,800,000	18,800,000

Source: *Report on the Global HIV/AIDS Epidemic.* Joint United Nations Programme on HIV/AIDS. 5 June 2001 <http://www.unaids.org/epidemic_update/report/Epi_report_chap_glo_estim.htm> .

[1]Under the age of 15.
[2]Beginning of HIV/AIDS epidemic.

they are presented side by side in a table, but if they are shown as contrasting heights on a graph, the difference might not be so obvious, depending on the graph's scale.

Creating Formal Tables

- Provide a title for the table.
- Arrange information logically— least to greatest, greatest to least, or past to present.
- Frame the table, but avoid using so many rules that the table becomes cluttered and hard to read.
- Provide a heading for every column.
- Provide rows and columns in a readable width.
- Use parallel grammatical forms for words.
- Identify units used (meters, years, degrees Celsius, and so on).

(continued)

- Convert fractions to decimal fractions, and limit numbers to two decimal places, unless extra precision is required.
- Round off numbers if possible, especially when the added precision of exact figures is not necessary. Round numbers are easier for readers to remember and are easier to relate to other numbers.
- Avoid footnotes unless you must explain or define entries.
- Place the source of the table below the table.
- Place large tables perpendicular to regular text pages, that is, parallel to the binding of a print document, and align the top of the tables with the binding of the document.

GRAPHS

Graphs, sometimes called charts, are designed by plotting a set of points on a coordinate system. Coordinate systems vary, and this text will not teach you about choosing one type over another. You learn about these systems in your other classes. But you should be aware that a standard, two-dimensional Cartesian (x–y) coordinate system presents a conventional approach to displaying numerical data. And by convention, X is often used to represent the independent variable and Y the dependent variable.

One advantage of using graphs over tables is that measurements of trends, movements, distributions, and cycles can be presented more clearly and effectively with graphs. In using graphs to illustrate data, the essential meaning of large amounts of information can be visualized quickly. Also, graphs provide a more complete interpretation of data by offering a comprehensive view of a situation.

There are several basic types of graphs that can be used to illustrate statistical data. Some of the most typical kinds are bar graphs, line graphs, circle or pie graphs, and pictographs.

Bar Graphs

The simple bar graph is one of the most useful and widely used formal graphic aids. Use a bar graph to make comparisons between two or more coordinate items or comparisons based on linear values. The lengths of the bars are determined by the value of each category.

Bar graphs use bars to compare specific measurements. Bar graphs consist of horizontal or vertical bars of equal width that are scaled in length to represent some quantity. When bars are presented horizontally, the figure is referred to as a bar graph. When bars are presented vertically, the figure may also be identified as a column graph. See an example of a bar graph in Figure 9.7.

Bar graphs may be used to display a change in quantity over time, but they are intended to display static data or snapshots of data at various times. The

FIGURE 9.7

FIGURE 9.7

Bar Graph

Chart 1
Number of Children under Age 18

FIGURE 9.8

Bar Graph with Non-Zero Baseline

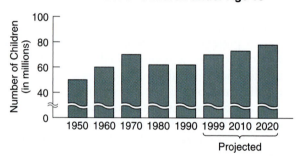

Chart 1
Number of Children under Age 18

FIGURE 9.9

Stacked Bar Graph

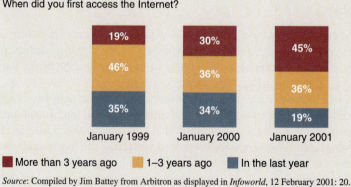

Figure 1. Fewer newbies are coming online this year

Nearly half of those currently accessing the Internet have been online for more than three years. In January, 19 percent of Internet users could be considered newbies, down from 35 percent in January 1999.

When did you first access the Internet?

■ More than 3 years ago   ■ 1–3 years ago   ■ In the last year

Source: Compiled by Jim Battey from Arbitron as displayed in *Infoworld*, 12 February 2001: 20.

FIGURE 9.10

Paired Bar Graphs

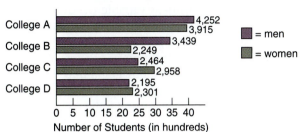

Chart 1
State University Full-Time Undergraduate
Enrollment 2001–2002

Source: State Education Report, pp. 75–80.

length of each bar represents a specific measurement. Because the reader uses the length of the bar to estimate differences between items, the value of the units at the beginning of each bar must be zero. If you have a compelling reason not to start at zero, then you must indicate on the bar graph that the information has been made to fit into the graph. Do this by indicating a break in the bars and labeling the *Y*-axis appropriately. Compare the bar graph with non-zero baseline in Figure 9.8 with the bar graph in Figure 9.7.

Stack information within bars if you want to show several components and how they make up a total. See Figure 9.9 for an example of a stacked bar graph. Group the bars when you want to show two or more sets of information occurring simultaneously. See Figure 9.10 for an example of a paired bar graph.

Creating Bar Graphs

- Make each bar the same width, and clearly label each one.
- Make the space between bars approximately one-half the bar width.
- Group bars according to categories when appropriate.
- Use a legend or a key, if appropriate, to distinguish different bars, and vary the pattern or color in multiple bar graphs.

- Try to make the vertical or *Y* scale at least 75 percent as long as the horizontal scale.
- Make the longest bar extend nearly to the end of its parallel axis.
- Stay with two-dimensional depictions for data in two dimensions. Adding a superfluous third dimension in the depiction can be misleading and unnecessary.

TIPS

Line Graphs

Line graphs are useful for showing how quantities change over time. Money, time, and temperature are common subjects for line graphs. The line graph can be used to plot the movement of two variables: an independent variable and its dependent variable. The independent variable is usually plotted horizontally. The dependent variable is plotted vertically. Often the independent variable denotes time and the dependent variable denotes a value changing over time. A point marks the recorded data and gives readers reference points for the graph as a whole. Since line graphs consist of connected points, their use implies that you are showing a continuous process. If instead you are describing necessarily discrete events, then a line graph may not be an appropriate choice.

Line graphs should have their axes clearly labeled, and if the scale is different for the X and Y axes, the axis labels should clearly state so. See Figure 9.11 for an example of a line graph.

Creating Line Graphs

- Place the independent variable on the X (horizontal) axis and the dependent variable on the Y (vertical) axis.
- Keep vertical and horizontal axes proportionate. Don't blow up the Y axis so that small differences look large.
- Make sure the slope or steepness of the line accurately portrays the trend indicated by the data.
- Place no more than three lines on each graph. If the lines fall very near each other, consider changing the scale of the graph to make the lines more distinguishable.
- Use colors and symbols (dots, dashes, x's) to distinguish lines. Color alone will not be useful if your graph is photocopied or is viewed by a color-blind person.
- Label each line or use a legend if necessary to avoid clutter.
- When showing positive and negative Y values, use the X axis to represent zero.

FIGURE 9.11

Line Graph

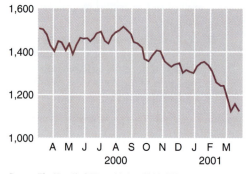

Source: *The New York Times* 10 Apr. 2001: W1.

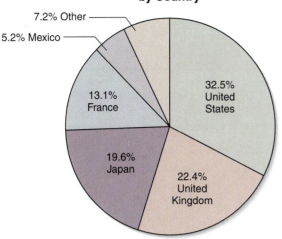

Chart 2
XYZ Fund Stock Allocations
by Country

7.2% Other

5.2% Mexico

13.1%
France

19.6%
Japan

32.5%
United
States

22.4%
United
Kingdom

FIGURE 9.12

Pie Graph

Pie Graphs

The pie graph or circle graph is another type of graph that can be used to present statistical information. This graphic aid allows easy and accurate interpretation of data. The primary advantage of the pie graph is that it clearly depicts proportions of a whole. This feature makes the pie graph a valuable tool for executives, for example, to use in financial reports. Another advantage of the pie graph is that data can be arranged in an orderly manner. A pie graph would not be a good choice to depict a large amount of data. See the pie graph in Figure 9.12.

Creating Pie Graphs

TIPS

- Use wedges to represent approximate, relative amounts of a whole. Some pieces of the graph can be exploded or separated from the whole. Separate at most one wedge when you are using the separation for emphasis.
- Place the largest segment of data at the twelve o'clock position. In clockwise order, arrange segments in decreasing size order.
- Percentage numbers and any description may be located inside the graph when space allows. But if your graph will be used in different cultural and linguistic contexts, descriptions should be outside the pie graph in a legend or in labeled callouts. It is far easier to replace callouts than to redraw visuals.

(continued)

● Combine very small wedges together into a larger category or under "other" if feasible. Keep in mind that very narrow wedges are difficult to see because each wedge is so small, so limit your pie graph to eight or fewer wedges.
● Do not use a pie graph if the purpose of the graph is to show precise amounts.

Pictographs

Creating Pictographs

● Keep the pictograph simple and clear.
● In drawing pictographs, make sure the design is displayed so that it easily can be seen in relation to the desired units.
● Choose symbols that closely represent your topic, value, or idea.
● Choose symbols that are readily understood and are simple and recognizable when reduced or enlarged.

● Space all symbols equally.
● When displaying different quantities, change the number of symbols, not the size or height. Changing the number of symbols provides a linear increase in the quantity shown. Changing the size of the symbols can provide an unintended quadratic (squared) increase.
● If possible, round off numbers to eliminate fractions.

A pictograph (or pictogram, visual table, or picture graph) is a graphic form that uses pictures to represent data. The advantage of using a pictograph to portray data is that it is an effective, interest-getting device that can

FIGURE 9.13

Pictograph

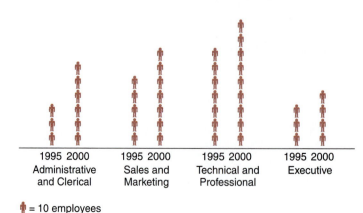

Chart 3 PQR Software Company

1995 2000 | 1995 2000 | 1995 2000 | 1995 2000
Administrative and Clerical | Sales and Marketing | Technical and Professional | Executive

👤 = 10 employees

be useful for a lay audience. The pictograph is essentially a pared-down graph that uses the objects displayed—stick figures, cows, or whatever else might be related in some way to the object being quantified—to represent the actual data. Unlike a bar graph, a pictograph uses no axes to show numeric value or scale, so any relevant information is shown through the number of the objects displayed. See the pictograph shown in Figure 9.13.

CHARTS

Charts show relationships instead of amounts. Flowcharts, organizational charts, and schedule charts are types of charts.

Flowcharts

A flowchart provides an overview of a process. A flowchart is an illustration that shows a sequence of stages displayed from beginning to end. The items in the chart should be connected according to the sequence in which the steps of the process occur. The main advantage of using a flowchart to illustrate information is that it displays an overview of the process, enabling the reader to comprehend the important steps of the process quickly and easily.

Several varieties of flowcharts can be used to signify the steps of a process: labeled blocks, pictorial representations, and standardized symbols. Elements in flowcharts should always be connected according to the order in which the steps occur. Flowcharts usually have left to right or top to bottom movement. Should the movement be otherwise, always use arrows to show the proper direction. See an example of a flowchart in Figure 9.14.

Creating Flowcharts

- Break down each step into the smallest unit appropriate for your purpose and scope. A broad overview will have a few very general steps. A detailed programming module may have many specific steps.
- Label or identify each step in the process by using either symbols, pictorial blocks, or captioned blocks. Use meaningful labels, keeping in mind your audience's needs and background.
- Include a key to identify symbols that may be unfamiliar to the reader.
- Provide ample white space on the page and avoid crowding the steps or placing arrows too close together.
- Use foldout pages if the flowchart is very large, rather than continuing it over several pages. If you must break it up over several pages, be sure the points of connection from page to page are well labeled.
- Verify each route through your flowchart by devising test data that will require following different paths through your chart.

FIGURE 9.14
Flowchart

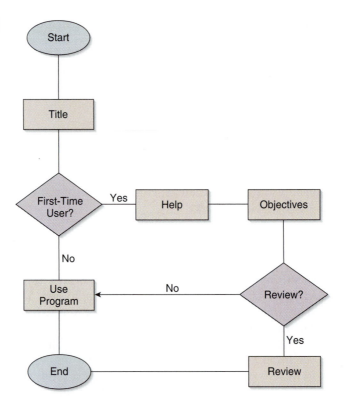

Organizational Charts

Organizational charts demonstrate the components of an organization and how they relate to each other. They emphasize the hierarchy of positions within a company or organization. These charts are effective for providing an overview of an organization to readers or to present the lines of authority within the organization. Figure 9.15 shows a typical organizational chart.

FIGURE 9.15
Organizational Chart

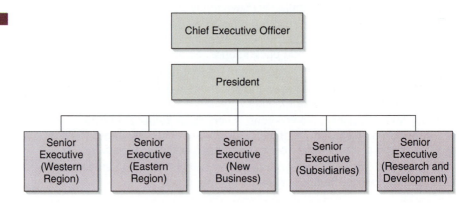

Creating Organizational Charts

- Specify each component of the chart in a single box.
- Ensure that boxes on the same horizontal level represent similar levels of authority.
- Clearly show how each position relates to those above and below as well as to the sides.
- Link the boxes appropriately to a central authority.
- Include in the box, if necessary, the names of personnel who fill each position.

Schedule or Gantt Charts

Schedule charts, also called Gantt charts, identify the major steps in a project and tell when they will be performed. A schedule chart enables readers to see what will be done, when each activity will start and end, and when activities will overlap. Schedule charts are often used in proposals to show the projected plan of work. They are also good for showing dependencies between various activities. You can also use them in progress reports to show what you have accomplished and what you still have to do. One of the principal considerations in creating a schedule chart is deciding how much detail to include. The scope of detail is determined by the purpose of the chart and the audience. Figure 9.16 shows a typical schedule chart.

Proposed Project Schedule September 10, 2____			October					November				December		
Task	Start	End	1	8	15	22	29	5	12	19	26	3	10	17
Define objectives														
Interview users	10/1	10/12	⊢—⊣											
Analyze system	10/8	10/19		⊢—⊣										
Research alternatives	10/10	10/19		⊢⊣										
Design solution														
Develop main design	10/18	11/9				⊢—⊣								
Code programs	10/24	11/22				⊢—⊣								
Draft manual	11/7	11/30						⊢—⊣						
Test system														
Meet with experts	11/19	11/30								⊢⊣				
Give to first users	11/28	11/30									⊢⊣			
Revise	12/3	12/7										⊢⊣		
Install	12/10	12/12											⊢⊣	
Train users	12/12	12/18											⊢—⊣	

FIGURE 9.16

Schedule (Gantt) Chart

Creating Schedule Charts

- When planning the schedule chart, decide on the appropriate time units for your chart: days, weeks, months, or longer.
- Show time along the horizontal axis.
- Label all activities clearly. The chart should be easy to read in its normal location (on a wall, in a report, under shop conditions, and so on).
- For each type of activity, designate a distinguishing color. For example, planning stages might be in blue, writing stages in green, review cycles in yellow, and evaluation or maintenance periods in red.

- Don't forget to allow for holidays, vacations, and schedule slippage from unanticipated causes.
- If some of the steps depend on activities of other divisions or organizations (such as a printing service bureau), place those steps on the chart on the basis of that entity's time constraints.
- Be prepared to modify the chart if deadlines are not being achieved. It is better to have a realistic schedule chart that functions as a helpful tool than one that is ideal but unusable.

DRAWINGS, DIAGRAMS, AND MAPS

Drawings, diagrams, and maps can be the most appropriate illustrations to use in many instances. All three have distinct advantages.

Drawings

Drawings are illustrations that are designed manually by professional artists or laypeople to portray a subject or object. Sometimes they are produced by mechanical means. Drawings have many advantages over photographs. They can convey ideas that are difficult to explain in prose. Also, they can include as much or as little information as needed, according to the purpose of the drawing.

Drawings can highlight details or relationships that photographs cannot convey. They can also display the main components of an object, eliminate clutter, enlarge important areas of a picture, cut away the outside view of equipment so that readers can see the insides, and offer an exploded view, in which the parts of the object are spread out so that the reader can see their relationship and how they fit when assembled.

Some commonly used drawings are artist's conceptions, block diagrams, cartoons, cutaway views, engineering drawings, exploded views, line drawings,

ON DRAWINGS

The drawings are useful for showing how the pieces fit together, and the text describes what the piece does. I try to keep each drawing to seven elements or less, and then each of those elements might be further broken down in another drawing.

—George Johnston,
software development engineer,
Redmond, Washington

Indicator lights

Power button

Keyboard

Touch pad

Touch pad buttons (2)

Options bay

Display release

Display

Main battery

Display latch (2)

Display close/
Suspend button

Microphone

Key lock

Optional modem jack

Air intake

Speaker

FIGURE 9.17

Drawing with Callouts

logic drawings, perspective drawings, and schematics (for example, for wiring circuits). (See Figure 9.17.)

Creating Drawings

- Select the amount of detail that will be most useful to your audience. Normally, use the minimum amount of detail that still conveys your point.

- Label clearly all parts, steps, or stages by horizontal, parallel labels and arrows.

- Select symbols that are familiar to your audience.

- Give dimensions, orientation, and point-of-view information about your object.

- If necessary, show how parts relate or are connected or attached to the whole and to each other.

- Use color, if possible, to highlight specific details where appropriate.

- Place drawings close to text that refers to them.

- Draw information to scale.

- Provide an inset schematic showing where the area in the drawing is located with respect to the larger object. If you are showing a blowup of a part of a larger unit, provide an outline sketch that shows its context in the bigger picture.

Diagrams

Diagrams are pictures of objects or events that use conventionally defined symbols to convey information. Diagrams may show, for example, the wiring of a room, the assembly of a computer, or the changes in a weather pattern. Diagrams combine literal elements (drawings of parts) and symbolic elements (arrows to show movement, direction, or associations; shading to show curvature). See Figure 9.18 for an example of a diagram.

FIGURE 9.18
Diagram with Callouts

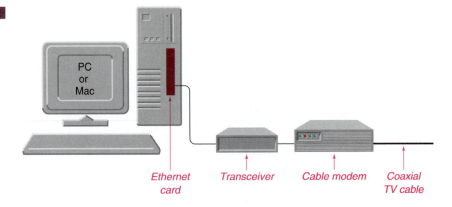

Ethernet card Transceiver Cable modem Coaxial TV cable

Creating Diagrams

- In an exploded diagram, show parts near their actual locations on or in the object depicted.
- Highlight the most important material and de-emphasize or delete unimportant material.
- Use the standard symbols of a discipline or profession where appropriate. Electronics, genetics, and linguistics, for example, all have their own standard symbols for representing various concepts.
- Clarify the meaning of any symbol through a caption if you think your audience may be unclear about a symbol.
- Provide context for the diagram by showing where it fits in the larger picture.

Maps

Maps are drawings that provide a physical layout. Like graphs, they can show quantitative information such as average temperatures for a region, voting patterns, and population distribution. Maps are used to portray geographic characteristics such as roads, mountains, or rivers. They are valuable for displaying geographic distributions such as housing and industrial centers. Also, simple maps are used to explain transit and highway systems. (See Figure 9.19.)

Creating Maps

- Clearly identify the map's boundaries, and eliminate unnecessary boundaries.

(continued)

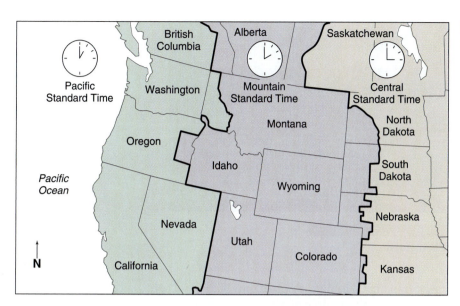

FIGURE 9.19

Map

- Leave out unnecessary information. For example, when displaying population, don't include rivers and roads. Omit features (rivers, elevations, county seats) that do not directly concern your topic.
- Use dots, lines, colors, symbols, or shading to indicate or emphasize features. Markings should be clear and distinct.
- If necessary, include a legend (map key), providing an explanation of dotted lines, colors, shading, or symbols.
- Indicate direction. Conventionally, maps show north, often by including an arrow and the letter N.
- Include a scale of miles or feet for proportions.
- Present proportions with as much accuracy as possible. If you are using a projection that has appreciable distortion, add a note to inform your readers of that fact.

PHOTOS

Photographs are preferred over drawings when a precise replica is needed. Photographs are useful to help technicians understand complex equipment. They are among the best ways to show results. Photographs can be visually appealing; however, a drawing of the same subject may provide more information. Consider using good-quality black-and-white photographs for reports when quick pictures are needed. Usually, photographs to be printed with text must be halftones (represented by a system of dots). Include photographs in your document by scanning a conventional photograph or using a photograph

FIGURE 9.20

Photograph

taken by a digital camera. Photographs with good contrast can be photocopied. Figure 9.20 is an example of a printed photograph.

Using and Handling Photographs

- Choose black-and-white or color depending on your budget and the requirements of your project. The annual report of a company probably needs color photographs. A progress report probably doesn't.

- Consider adding a familiar object to the photograph to help the audience gauge size and dimensions.

- Avoid too much detail in the photograph. (See Figure 9.21.)

- If you enlarge the photo, make sure the resolution of the original was fine enough to support the increase in size. If you shrink it, make sure you retain enough detail for the photograph to be recognizable and useful.

- If the photo reproduces poorly, consider choosing a drawing instead. A fuzzy photograph is worse than none at all.

- Crop your photo (cut away unneeded parts) to eliminate distractions and extraneous background.

- Use a photo-editing program to enhance contrast, retouch color, or add text or special effects.

- Correct optical artifacts (such as glare or red eyes).

- Consider adding callouts or small arrows to the photo to point to the main features.

- Consider adding a caption to help the readers understand what they are seeing.

- If the background is light, use a plain rule around the photo to frame it.

- Avoid using paper clips or staples on photographs.

- Avoid folding or creasing photographs.

- Avoid writing on either the front or back of photographs.

FIGURE 9.21

Cropping a Photo

The original photo at left shows too much detail; the photo on the right has been cropped to high-light the relevant information.

CLIP ART

Clip art consists of commercially produced drawings, symbols, and icons, licensed to be used in a wide variety of situations. Pictures in many cate-gories—office, people, home—are available for use in your documents to pro-vide instant visual interest. An immediate advantage of clip art is that most of it may be used without specific permission once you have purchased a license for the collection. You may insert, photocopy, or redraw and publish clip art without any attribution.

When you purchase a license to use a clip-art collection, you purchase the right to use it in your own work without paying further royalties or licensing fees. Some clip art carries restrictions about multiple uses within a given pro-ject, prohibitions against online or Web-page use, or limitations on resale. But, in general, you may use clip art freely in your work. Figure 9.22 shows typical examples of clip art.

Some libraries contain clip-art books, such as the *Dover Pictorial Archive* series. Up to ten illustrations may be reproduced from this source on any one project or in any single publication without permission or cost. In addition to clip art that can be photocopied and used, clip art traditionally is available as transfers (thin sheets with plastic symbols, letters, numbers, or pictures that

FIGURE 9.22
Clip Art

can be rubbed onto paper), and as templates (plastic sheets with cutouts of shapes such as furniture or computer terminals; math, logic, or electronic symbols; or numbers and letters).

Computer clip art and photo images are also widely available through numerous computer software programs and via the Internet. You can easily locate CD-ROMs that contain only clip art or find clip art packaged in with many different kinds of software. Microsoft Office, for example, provides a wide variety of clip art that easily can be inserted into documents. As you would expect, many graphics programs come with a clip-art library, and some include fairly extensive collections of photo images.

Sometimes the use of clip art libraries and photo-image libraries is restricted. Corel Draw, for example, provides many kinds of clip art and photo images but also restricts how you may use them. Restrictions involve a variety of issues: you may not redistribute or sell the images, link any images related to individuals to any products or services, or create obscene or offensive works using the images. You need to review carefully any restrictions specified by the company that licenses the clip art or the manufacturer of the graphics program you use.

In addition, you can find numerous clip-art sites on the Internet as well as many sites providing all kinds of photo images. You will have to be sure to distinguish between sites that are providing clip art that is clearly in the public domain and sites that provide clip art with certain restrictions. *Public domain* is a legal term referring to the status of a work or an invention whose copyright or patent has expired or that never had such protection. You must be especially careful in using graphics and photo images that you find on the World Wide Web and other Internet locations. Photo and graphic images are copyrighted and may be used only with the copyright owner's explicit permission. (See the "Copyright" section in Chapter 6 for a more detailed discussion of this important issue.)

In fact, the ease of copying graphics and photos has led to an overly casual concept of image ownership. Just because someone puts a picture or other graphic on a site does not mean that the image belongs to that person. It may be that the person using it has permission to do so. But that permission—if it exists—probably does not extend to members of the general public. If you use a graphic that turns out to have been taken from the actual owner's site, you can be held liable for copyright infringement. Even if you want to get permission to use an image you find on a Web site, it can take real detective work to find out who actually owns the copyright to it.

> " " You must be especially careful in using graphics and photo images that you find on the World Wide Web and other Internet locations. Photo and graphic images are copyrighted and may be used only with the copyright owner's explicit permission.

COMPUTER ILLUSTRATIONS

Computers have made it easier than ever before to create your own professional-looking illustrations in just a few minutes. With many computer programs, once you enter the essential information, you can switch almost instantly to viewing the data as a bar graph, a pie graph, or a variety of other illustrations. Then you can choose the illustration that you think best represents the data for your particular audience.

Computer programs may save you a lot of time and work in creating illustrations, but you will still need to learn the essentials of effective illustrations to get the most benefit from them. Because of the wide array of illustration tools available, it's possible even for design novices to create professional-looking designs and illustrations.

Computer programs for illustrating fall into two groups: vector programs and raster (pixel) programs. Raster programs are better for working on the graphics in areas or on individual pixels (picture elements). Neither is intrinsically better; the one that suits your purpose better is the better choice.

Vector Programs

Vector programs, such as Illustrator and FreeHand, help you create illustrations, logos, curved type, and other similar effects. Whatever you create in a vector program can be enlarged or shrunk without loss of smoothness. These programs give you the flexibility to create smooth lines at any resolution and are a good choice if you will have to change the scale of your graphics.

Vector programs use mathematical calculations to draw shapes. By layering these shapes, you get the appearance of an image. These programs are generally used for creating original artwork, logos, or special text effects that you can't create with a raster (pixel-based) program. (See Figure 9.23.)

Vector drawings, unlike their raster counterparts, can be scaled up or down in size without losing sharpness or introducing stair-step effects, called "jaggies." Once you create an image in this type of program, you can import it into a raster paint program to add more color or depth to the image. With vector programs, you do not save the image as a GIF or JPEG image; each program saves images in its own proprietary format. Use vector programs for a variety of drawing and illustrating needs and when you want to create certain specialized kinds of forms such as flowcharts.

slogan for the week

FIGURE 9.23

Vector Artwork

This artwork was created using a vector program, Microsoft's Draw add-on for Word. Other vector programs are Adobe Illustrator and Freehand.

Peter Ricciardi, Jr.
Freelance Photographer, Graphic Artist, Illustrator
Rockland, Massachusetts

Peter turned an employment setback into a career advantage when his company downsized him out of a job. His current success as a freelance commercial artist and photographer followed from his talents and also from his approach with new clients, tailoring his presentations to their interests and needs.

I trained to be a commercial artist, and I am now a freelance commercial photographer/artist. The art school I attended suggested that students work at a printing press to learn how art is reproduced in magazines and newspapers. I worked the press cameras and stripped film for offset press. Then I picked up photography courses to learn more about lighting and different film formats.

My first job out of art school was at a small advertising agency that needed a jack-of-all-trades—someone with art, photography, and printing experience. I got a lot of on-the-job training there to fill out my knowledge of both design and photography. I stayed with that company about 12 years. Since the job was always different, I never got bored doing the same thing every day.

I became self-employed when the ad agency I worked for downsized. I had two choices: work for someone else for 40 to 60 hours a week and not have control of what I was doing or be a freelancer and explore different types of assignments and push my creative horizons to see just what I could do.

I have been freelancing for about three years. Satisfied clients have been my best source for new business. They have been recommending me to their associates because they are comfortable with my demeanor and quality of work. I left on very good terms with my former employers and they also refer people to me from time to time. I send letters, do cold calls, and check the Sunday help wanted section. I also do freebies with a by-line for people and organizations, to gain more exposure for myself.

I usually present a portfolio with samples to a very small group or just one individual. I prepare "leave

Even though many of the photo-editing programs also enable you to create art and other graphics from scratch, there are programs that are specifically designed to do that and do it well. From a drawing and illustrating program, you should expect tools that enable you to draw complex shapes and fill them with a variety of patterns, fills, gradients, and textures. You can move shapes around, rotate and reflect them, distort them, group them, resize them, sharpen and unsharpen their edges, manipulate contrast, and apply a variety of text effects. Drawing programs can be used as page-layout programs, although they usually do not afford the same breadth of features as programs dedicated to that purpose.

Corel Draw is one of the most established drawing programs on the market and still one of the best. Adobe Illustrator provides numerous drawing and painting features along with sophisticated typographic controls. Microsoft Draw is an add-on program for Microsoft Office. The program functions as an integral part of Microsoft Word.

Visio Corporation provides four widely used specialty drawing programs with Visio Standard, Visio Professional, Visio Enterprise, and Visio Technical.

behinds" on a dye-sublimation printer. The dye-sub allows me to make custom or one-of-a-kind pieces that can be tailor-made for the person or organization. I have a Web site that functions as a portfolio/introduction letter.

I learned how to use computers on the job. Desktop publishing was just coming of age when I started working. Art then was prepared as paste-up mechanicals. I think nearly all art for printing is now prepared via computer. The computer lets me do the layout and the finished art nearly simultaneously. The ability to revise quickly has made the creative process more spontaneous than before.

Half my time is spent preparing letters to possible clients with graphics/photos of what I do and hi-how-are-you-doing letters with samples to clients I already have. When I write letters of introduction to new clients I can just ramble out whatever comes into my head and place what I think will be appropriate photos and graphics in them and then edit myself on the fly. Each letter can be custom-built for that client. I don't have to send out printed brochures that are just general in their approach. I believe that sending a well-put-together e-mail or letter can tell someone how "put together" I am. After all, presentation is half the job when one is in a visual career.

As a freelancer, I usually take care of my own documentation. When I am contracted to provide illustrations or photographs for someone else's work, I generally sit down with everyone concerned and take notes on what my client is trying to say and who he or she is going to be talking to. About half the time I'm on my own (which allows me to get different takes on a project); clients will often be pleased when I can present a new view on their subject. Other times I work with an art director or the client directly. The advantage here is that people get exactly what they think they want. Most of the time they're flexible to allow me to show a new angle on their subject matter. I think my clients are hoping I will come up with a fresh perspective on their product, service, or message and enhance the written word with a visual that'll clarify or call attention to what they are trying to say.

Insider Advice

My best advice to others just starting out would be to listen to people who have been at it for a while. Learn whatever anyone is willing to teach you. You just don't know what piece of knowledge will come in handy someday.

Visio Standard, for example, enables you to create many kinds of flowcharts, diagrams, organizational charts, project time lines, and maps. The three other programs offer other advanced features.

Raster Programs

Raster (or pixel, or paint) programs give you great control over every element of your graphic, but once you have created the graphics using these programs, they should stay the same size for best viewability.

Raster programs are ones with which you create or edit images made up of tiny rectangles of color called pixels (picture elements). Each screen pixel has only one color, which is described by its red, green, and blue (RGB) component values. Once all the colored pixels are side by side, they form an image. (See Figure 9.24.)

You will also see these images referred to as *bitmaps* or *bitmapped images*. All images on the Web (GIF, JPEG, and others) are bitmaps. Raster programs are useful when you want to edit scanned images or create your own images

FIGURE 9.24

Raster Artwork

This artwork was saved by a raster program; raster programs save images in GIF, JPEG, or other bitmap formats.

from scratch. They enable you to perform sophisticated transformations on the various colors and positions of items in a graphic image. The more powerful programs, such as Adobe Photoshop and Jasc Paint Shop Pro, have many useful options that mimic the effects of artists' tools. Photo editors and paint programs are examples of raster programs.

Graphics Utilities

Graphics utilities include screen capture programs as well as programs for organizing, managing, and viewing graphics.

In software documentation, screen captures are commonly used to show the various screens—main menus, dialog boxes, toolbars—of a software program. Using screen-capture software, you can easily show your readers exactly what they are going to see when they use a particular feature of the software you are describing. You can show toolbars, buttons, cursors, menu items, dialog boxes, error messages, and a variety of realistic examples in as much detail as you require. Some programs even enable you to show animations in your screen captures, so readers can better understand the processes you are describing. Figure 9.25 shows a typical screen capture.

Screen-capture programs have a variety of options, enabling you to select which portion of the screen you want to capture and the form in which you want to save the resulting image. HyperSnap-DX, for example, offers many fea-

FIGURE 9.25
Screen Capture

tures to edit your screen captures. SnagIt is a versatile screen-capture program that could also be listed along with the graphics-viewing and graphics-management programs, since it incorporates a thumbnail catalog browser and multimedia viewer.

Many kinds of commercial, shareware, and freeware graphics programs are available to help you organize, manage, and view the illustrations in your directories and files. Thumbs Plus and Hijaak Pro are well regarded, general-purpose image managers, for example. In addition to the programs listed here, many of the graphics programs listed in other categories will perform some of the same functions for you.

CHECKING WHAT YOU'VE LEARNED

- Have you selected the information that you want to display and decided whether the illustration will ask a question, provide an answer, or create an emotional response?
- Have you determined a specific objective including who your audience will be, what decisions its members will have to make, and how well they will be able to understand the illustration?
- Have you selected the type of presentation best suited to the data you are displaying: Lists of numbers in tables? Comparisons of similar items in bar graphs? The interaction of independent and dependent variables in line graphs? Percentages of a whole in pie graphs? Demographic data in pictographs? Processes and procedures in flowcharts? Systems of

mechanical and electrical components in diagrams? Geographical information in maps? Documentary evidence in photographs? Icons or general illustrative material in clip art?

- Have you conveyed information simply and directly?
- Have you labeled and annotated the illustrations to avoid ambiguity?
- Have you made the horizontal and vertical scales comparable? If not, have you explained why?
- Have you taken care when you displayed pictorial and graphical information to present it ethically and responsibly? Have you compared like items and avoided deceptive comparisons?
- Have you evaluated your illustrations and tested them with users to ensure that the message you want to deliver is being conveyed?
- Have you planned for change?

EXERCISES

 REVIEW

1. Evaluate the formal table (Figure 9.6) in this chapter, and decide whether it meets the criteria of an effective table according to the guidelines in the Tips list (page 304–305) for creating formal tables.

2. Using the guidelines for creating pie graphs discussed in the chapter, create a pie graph representing how you typically spend your time for 24 hours on a weekday (for example, sleeping, breakfast, classes, lunch, work, dinner, homework). Evaluate the effectiveness of using a pie graph for representing this information.

3. Find an example of clip art on your computer or on the Internet. Discuss the circumstances under which you think using this clip art might be appropriate for a technical document (for example, a memo, an e-mail message, a letter, a report, a proposal, instructions).

4. Review the discussion in this chapter on computer illustrations. Use one vector program and one raster program to create the same illustration. Compare some of the advantages and disadvantages of creating these two kinds of illustrations with these programs.

 THE INTERNET

Find a good example of an effective photograph used on the welcome page or home page of a Web site. Discuss what features make the photograph particularly effective for the Web site, and discuss why a photograph was a better choice than a drawing or some other kind of illustration.

 ETHICS/PROFESSIONALISM

Review the discussion concerning the ethical uses of illustrations. Find an example of an illustration (a figure or a table) where the information is distorted, inaccurate, or otherwise incorrect. Be prepared to discuss why you think the illustration was created this way.

 COLLABORATION

Bring a photograph of an object in your discipline (for example, a computer, an engineering compass, a microscope, a petri dish) to class for this group exercise. Working with two or three students, discuss ways you might crop the photo in a technical document to emphasize certain features or elements over others. Suggest ways your group members might crop their photos, too. Be prepared to discuss your conclusions.

 INTERNATIONAL COMMUNICATION

Discuss how different cultural values might influence your choice of the visuals you use in some documents or in a presentation when some members of your audience are from another country.

RESOURCES

Dayton, Linnea, and Jack Davis. *The Photoshop 5.0/5.5 Wow! Book.* Berkeley: Peachpit, 1999.

Harris, Robert. *Information Graphics: A Comprehensive Illustrated Reference.* Atlanta: Management Graphics, 1996.

Huff, Darrell. *How to Lie with Statistics.* Harmondsworth: Penguin, 1976.

Kosslyn, Stephen M. *Elements of Graph Design.* New York: Freeman, 1994.

Kostelnick, Charles, and David D. Roberts. *Designing Visual Language: Strategies for Professional Writing.* Boston: Allyn and Bacon, 1998.

Tufte, Edward R. *Envisioning Information.* Cheshire: Graphics, 1990.

———. *The Visual Display of Quantitative Information.* Cheshire: Graphics, 1993.

———. *Visual Explanations: Images and Quantities, Evidence and Narrative.* Cheshire: Graphics, 1997.

10

Editing, Revising, and Evaluating

Editing   329

Revising   339

Evaluating Drafts   350

From the Workplace   356

IN THIS CHAPTER

Writing a draft is just the first step when you are creating a document, either in print or online. Editing, revising, and evaluating are all aspects of the same process, a process that refines, smooths, and polishes a work until it is as good as it can be, whatever its constraints. Editing, revising, and evaluating are essential to ensure the quality of your documents. In fact, typically, you will be constantly writing, editing, revising, and having others review and evaluate your work. These activities go hand in hand, one following the other, and in recurring fashion. This chapter will help you go from first draft to polished final draft.

You will learn about:

- navigating around the types and levels of edit: when to use them and how they differ

- revising your document to improve its style

- evaluating drafts: submitting your draft for evaluation and reviewing drafts of others

- usability testing your documents: having others test the effectiveness of your text and visuals

EDITING

Editing is performed at many stages and by many people. You may, of course, edit your own work, and you should edit while you are writing and after you revise. More commonly, others will edit your work. If you are fortunate, a professional editor will examine every word, phrase, clause, sentence, paragraph, and larger segment. The review process occurs when others read your work and accept it, suggest modifications, or reject it.

As a college student, you may be involved in a peer review in which other students look over your work according to certain criteria provided by your professor. In industry, a review may involve many phases of review from peer to technical to legal. Finally, when the work has gone through its edits and reviews, it can be evaluated and tested to see whether the documents are appropriately written for their audience and whether they function as required.

In some ways, approaches to editing vary almost as much as editors. Editing is a task that probably no two people do the same way. (See Figure 10.1.) Some people edit their work page by page, simply looking at each word, sentence, paragraph, and larger section, making changes at both the micro level and the macro level at the same time. In short, they edit their work piecemeal and randomly. They don't have a system. Other people systematically use an approach called bottom-up editing. They begin editing at the sentence level

FIGURE 10.1

Editing Methods

PAGE-BY-PAGE EDITING	Work sequentially through the document making changes as each element is encountered.
BOTTOM-UP EDITING	Work a sentence at a time; then edit a paragraph at a time; then edit a section at a time.
TOP-DOWN EDITING	Work on the overall organization, design, and content; then move down to problems within each section; then work on individual paragraphs; then work on sentences and words.

and work their way to the larger elements of a document. Still other people prefer what is called top-down editing. They start with the larger features of the document—including content, organization, and design—and then work their way down to the sentence and word level of the document. People who use the top-down approach believe it saves time over the bottom-up approach. Using the top-down approach, editors will not have wasted time editing a subsection at the sentence level if they later decide to delete it. On the other hand, those who follow the bottom-up method find it distracting to read past word and sentence errors and awkwardness and believe that they can follow the motion of ideas through a text better when their view is not obstructed by lower-level errors.

Whatever system you use, the important thing is to have some kind of system. More important, it's necessary to understand that editing is a complicated process that comprises many types of oversight activities that can be performed on a document. It is almost meaningless to talk about performing an edit on a document without also specifying what kind of edit is meant. Van Buren and Buehler list nine types of edits—coordination, policy, integrity, screening, copy clarification, format, mechanical style, language, and substantive—which they group into five "levels" numbered one to five. (See Figure 10.2.) This breakdown of editing tasks is widely quoted and quite suitable for the rigidly defined editing process in a large company. Some of the elements in various types of edits concern fulfilling company requirements for placement of company logos and preventing derogatory or judgmental comments about private companies and governmental agencies. Others are more generally applicable.

In this chapter, the discussion about editing will be confined to the important phases of developmental editing, substantive editing, copyediting, and proofreading.

Developmental Editing

Editing is a deceptively short word for an extensive process that begins before you write your first word and ends when your work goes out in print. In between, you subject your projects to scrutiny at every level of organization and at every stage of preparation and production.

TYPE	LEVELS OF EDIT				
	1	2	3	4	5
Coordination	x	x	x	x	x
Policy	x	x	x	x	x
Integrity	x	x	x	x	
Screening	x	x	x	x	
Copy Clarification	x	x	x		
Format	x	x	x		
Mechanical Style	x	x			
Language	x	x			
Substantive	x				

FIGURE 10.2

Levels of Edit

SOURCE: Used with permission from *The Levels of Edit*, written by Robert Van Buren and Mary Fran Buehler, and published by the Society for Technical Communication, Arlington, Virginia.

The first step in that extensive process is the developmental edit. During developmental editing, you evaluate your design, the organization of your major areas, the genre of your deliverables, and many other aspects of your project. During developmental editing, you look at your documents, Web pages, online help files, graphics, and other output from the broad perspective of the user's needs and the producer's resources. Unlike the editing that you perform at the paragraph, sentence, or word level later on, developmental editing seeks to uncover fundamental weaknesses in organization, arrangement, or premise.

Developmental editing continues through the earlier stages of your project, during planning and early drafts. You are performing a developmental edit when you

- evaluate a project proposal
- develop and critique a project outline
- scrutinize models and flowcharts for appropriateness and logic
- redesign the visuals in your project
- test your concept of the project by interviewing users of your product to verify that your chosen genre is the most appropriate one for your purpose
- check your storyboards for appropriate continuity and technical feasibility
- evaluate your graphics for usefulness and clarity

Changes you make during developmental editing will save you time and money later, since you will catch problems before they have been elaborated on and while they can easily be undone.

> " " Unlike the editing that you perform at the paragraph, sentence, or word level later on, developmental editing seeks to uncover fundamental weaknesses in organization, arrangement, or premise.

The developmental editing stage is not the one in which you correct grammar, spelling, or punctuation. In fact, paying attention to those details during a developmental edit is a waste of time, since the very words you correct now may not even make it into the next draft once you have completed a developmental edit on the document.

Effective Developmental Editing

- Don't proofread. Don't copyedit. Developmental editing is a planning and evaluating tool, not a spelling checker.

- Put yourself in your reader's shoes. Will your document or Web site effectively convey its message? Could it be reorganized to do a better job?

- Ask yourself whether information is presented in a logical order. Does it build from general to specific, from specific to general, chronologically, in size order, in order of complexity, or in some other order?

- Check that similar items and subjects are treated similarly.

- Verify that the parts form a coherent whole.

- Make sure that the information is complete but not redundant.

- Consider whether the genre is appropriate for the content. Would the text be more effective converted to a visual? Paired with a visual? For an online project, would multimedia aids add to or subtract from the impact of the text?

- Use an appropriate level of theory. Is the text too theoretical? Should you have more concrete examples? Is it too concrete? Do you need to include more theoretical underpinning for your assertions?

- Take care of any legal issues that you must consider in presenting the content. Are copyright and trademark issues being respected? Are permissions needed?

Substantive Editing

In this phase of editing, the editor thoroughly checks the content and meaning of the technical document. The editor checks, for example, the purpose, scope, and accuracy of the information, and the organization, design and layout, style, and logic of the document. Substantive editing may occur with each successive draft of a document. While developmental editing will begin as the document is still being planned and substantive editing reviews the document after it has been drafted, both types of edits treat similar concerns. They both seek to ensure that the document is as effective as possible.

Effective Substantive Editing

- Check that material is presented in a logical order and that items are grouped logically.

- Verify that information is complete but not redundant.

- Establish that the information is presented appropriately for the audience, subject, purpose, and scope.

- Verify that the level of detail is appropriate for the audience, scope, and purpose.

- Work through the design of the document. Are the headings, headers, footers, and other design elements appropriate and helpful?

- Ensure that the tone is consistent and appropriate for the genre.

- Examine text to determine if visuals would be useful.

- If there are visuals, check that they are necessary, that they are clear and easy to understand, and that they display information appropriately and accurately.

Copyediting

Copyediting occurs after developmental and substantive editing. The copyeditor checks for punctuation and spelling errors, correctness, consistency, accuracy, and completeness. Many of these qualities are also evaluated during the revision process. (See the "Revising" section later in this chapter.) The difference is that at the copyediting stage, you are looking at the document with a narrower focus: one sentence and one paragraph at a time.

Effective Copyediting

- Evaluate the text for flow. Can the reader follow the argument from one sentence to the next? From one paragraph to the next? From one section to the next?

- Correct faulty grammar, spelling, punctuation, and capitalization.

- Verify cross-references to other sections of the work.

- Verify the consistent use of headings, terminology, spelling, and punctuation.

- Ensure that acronyms, initialisms, and abbreviations are explained when they are first mentioned unless they are in such common use that the reader can be expected to know them.

- Check for internal consistency throughout the document.

- Ensure that the information that is provided is correct and complete.

(continued)

FIGURE 10.3

Copyediting Symbols

Marks	Explanation	Example
ℯ ℯ	Delete	Use this mark to eliminate a a letter or a word word.
⌒	Close up	Use this mark to take out extra sp ace.
⌢⌣	Delete and close up	Sometimes you must eliminate a character and close up the space.
∧	Insert	Use the caret to insrt a letter, a word, or words.
∿	Transpose	This mark transposes lettres. You also can use it to transpose words.
◯	Spell out	Circling a number or an abbreviation—5 or U.S—means "spell it out."
≡	Capitalize	this mark changes a lowercase letter to a capital.
/	Make lowercase	This mark changes a Capital to a lowercase letter.
⊙	Make a period	Use this mark to add a period.
⌃,	Make a comma	Also use this mark to add a comma.
⹀	Add a hyphen	A well trained editor knows where to put hyphens.
¶	Start a paragraph	This mark indicates a new paragraph. It can be placed before any sentence.
⟋	Run in	This mark eliminates a paragraph. It runs the copy together.
⌄	Add an apostrophe	The apostrophe—its needed in contractions and elsewhere.
⌄⌄ ⌄⌄	Add quotation marks	Use quotes wisely.
——	Italicize	Use italics sparingly for emphasis.
∿	Make boldface	Use bold type for design elements.
· · ·	Stet (let it stand)	The dots say to ignore any editing marks and follow the original text.
⊗	Fix broken type.	Circle a broken type and put a mark in the margin ⊗
‖	Align type	This marks shows how to align the type.
ⓦⓕ	Fix wrong font	Sometimes the wrong typeface is used. Circle it and put "wf" in the margin. ⓦⓕ

- Check that text references match graphics, figures, and tables.
- Check that figures, tables, and illustrations are marked for insertion in the most appropriate location.
- Check the quality of graphics for accuracy and readability.
- Ensure that the text conforms to the chosen style guide and to house style.

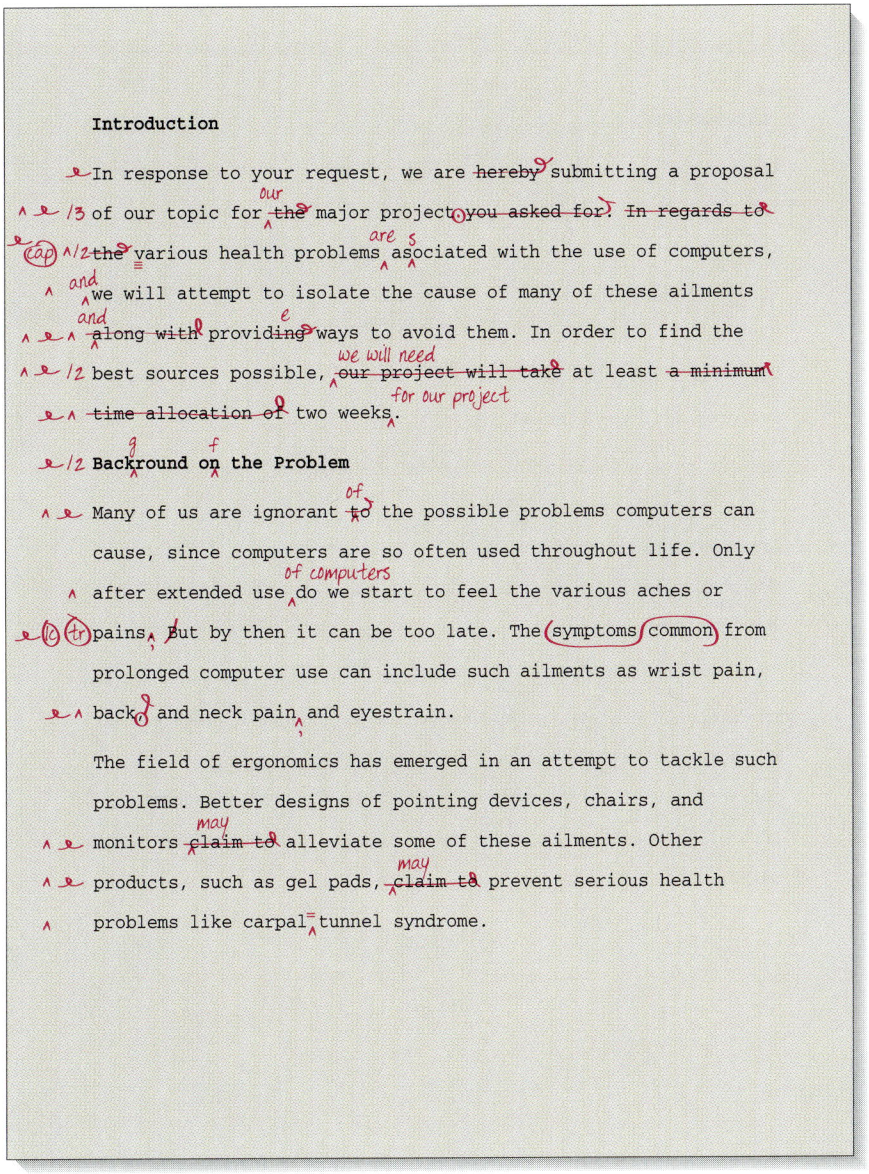

FIGURE 10.4a

Copyediting Example: The Marked-Up Copy

Introduction

In response to your request, we are ~~hereby~~ submitting a proposal ⅓ of our topic for ~~the~~ major project ~~you asked for. In regards to~~ *our* ~~the~~ various health problems ~~is~~ associated with the use of computers, *are s* we will attempt to isolate the cause of many of these ailments *and* ~~along with~~ providing ways to avoid them. In order to find the *e* best sources possible, ~~our project will take~~ at least ~~a minimum~~ *we will need* ~~time allocation of~~ two weeks. *for our project*

Background on the Problem

Many of us are ignorant ~~to~~ the possible problems computers can *of* cause, since computers are so often used throughout life. Only after extended use do we start to feel the various aches or *of computers* pains. But by then it can be too late. The ~~symptoms~~ ~~common~~ from prolonged computer use can include such ailments as wrist pain, back, and neck pain, and eyestrain.

The field of ergonomics has emerged in an attempt to tackle such problems. Better designs of pointing devices, chairs, and monitors ~~claim to~~ alleviate some of these ailments. Other *may* products, such as gel pads, ~~claim to~~ prevent serious health *may* problems like carpal tunnel syndrome.

Copyediting symbols are shown in Figure 10.3. Look at the two copyedited documents in Figure 10.4a and b. See where the editor has made changes to improve the order of the presentation, the tone of the work, and the mechanics of the sentences.

FIGURE 10.4b

**Copyediting Example:
The Corrected Text**

Introduction

In response to your request, we are submitting a proposal of our topic for our major project. Various health problems are associated with the use of computers, and we will attempt to isolate the cause of many of these ailments and provide ways to avoid them. In order to find the best sources possible, we will need at least two weeks for our project.

Background of the Problem

Many of us are ignorant of the possible problems computers can cause, since computers are so often used throughout life. Only after extended use of computers do we start to feel the various aches or pains, but by then it can be too late. The common symptoms from prolonged computer use can include such ailments as wrist pain, back and neck pain, and eyestrain.

The field of ergonomics has emerged in an attempt to tackle such problems. Better designs of pointing devices, chairs, and monitors may alleviate some of these ailments. Other products, such as gel pads, may prevent serious health problems like carpal-tunnel syndrome.

Proofreading

Proofreading occurs at the end of the publication process. It is sometimes confused with copyediting, but the two have distinct differences. Copyediting occurs earlier in the process; it helps you prepare the document for printing. Proofreading occurs after the document has been typeset and is the step that verifies that the text has been printed according to your requirements.

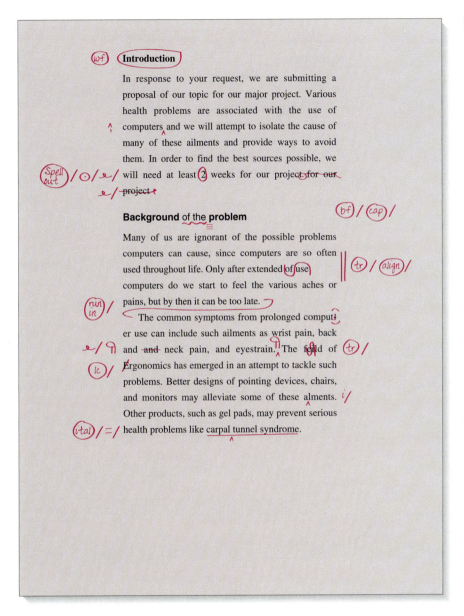

FIGURE 10.5a

**Proofreading Example:
The Marked-Up Type**

Copyediting marks and proofreading marks are similar. Proofreading marks are made chiefly in the margins of the printed copy; copyediting marks and comments are typically made both in the margins and within the lines of text in a manuscript. Many dictionaries and some style manuals list the standard proofreading marks. They can be found online as well, for example, at <http://www.eeicom.com/staffing/marks.html>. Figure 10.5a and b shows a proofreading example.

FIGURE 10.5b

**Proofreading Example:
The Corrected Document**

Introduction

In response to your request, we are submitting a proposal of our topic for our major project. Various health problems are associated with the use of computers, and we will attempt to isolate the cause of many of these ailments and provide ways to avoid them. In order to find the best sources possible, we will need at least two weeks for our project.

Background of the Problem

Many of us are ignorant of the possible problems computers can cause, since computers are so often used throughout life. Only after extended use of computers do we start to feel the various aches or pains, but by then it can be too late. The common symptoms from prolonged computer use can include such ailments as wrist pain, back and neck pain, and eyestrain.

The field of ergonomics has emerged in an attempt to tackle such problems. Better designs of pointing devices, chairs, and monitors may alleviate some of these ailments. Other products, such as gel pads, may prevent serious health problems like *carpal-tunnel syndrome*.

Effective Proofreading

- Check spelling, punctuation, and capitalization.
- Verify format consistency.

- Check line breaks and word breaks for correctness.

(continued)

- Eliminate repeated lines; replace missing lines.
- Review the placement of graphics for correctness.
- Ensure the consistent use of heading styles.
- Verify the alignment of text and figures.
- Review indentions, margins, and alignments.
- Verify page number accuracy.
- Check callouts for accuracy.
- Compare captions with text descriptions.
- Ensure that house style is followed throughout.

REVISING

Writing, editing, and revising are different activities in the writing process. Whether you are writing quickly or laboring over every word, effective writing still requires more refining and polishing. In revising, you reread what you have written and make an effort to improve the document in every way you possibly can.

Effective writing is achieved only by revising and then revising some more. You're not likely to make a technical document, whether it's a memo or a technical report, just exactly what it needs to be on your first, second, or even third try. The early drafts are rough drafts, and to achieve your final draft, you will have to do a great deal of polishing. After finishing a first draft, good writers will labor over every word choice, every phrase and clause, every sentence, every paragraph, and every section in the next draft and in the draft after that.

The first draft of any document may be detailed, but it's seldom adequately detailed. The style may be okay, but it's rarely completely suited to the audience. The grammar and spelling errors may be few, but there may still be errors. The design may appear to be fine, but it usually won't be as good as it can be. Illustrations may appear to be well suited to the text, but they often aren't. If you are fortunate enough to have someone else thoroughly edit your work, you will typically be surprised at the many areas for improvement. You'll have to continue revising until you finally create a document that is strong in all areas. Of course, even after you do all of this revising, your document may still not be perfect, but at least it will be far more effective than it would have been.

In some respects, revising occurs throughout the document process. As you plan your document, each time you make changes in your subject, purpose, or scope, you are revising. Each time you take a different approach to your subject after brainstorming, mind mapping, or freewriting, you are revising. Each time you make changes in your outline or other organizational plan, you are revising. And, of course, as you write every word, sentence, and paragraph and make even slight changes, you are revising. However, more formally

ON REVISING

Use of the computer has greatly improved the quality of my writing. I am a lazy writer, and an average typist. Re-keying documents on a typewriter was never my idea of recreation. But with the computer, revision is so easy that there is no excuse for not revising as many times as necessary to improve the document or message.

—Joel Hartman, chief information officer, Orlando, Florida

defined, revising is what you do after you have planned, researched, and written a first draft of your document. Now that you have a version of your ideas on paper or a computer screen, you'll need to go back through your document and make changes as necessary.

Revising is not the same as reviewing or evaluating. Revising occurs when you make stylistic, grammatical, or other kinds of changes in your document or someone else's document. Reviewing occurs when you submit your document to someone else to critique. Evaluating occurs when you or someone else tests the appropriateness or usability of what you have written or created.

Revising Your Work

- After you finish a draft, leave the draft alone for some time, preferably a day or two.

- For paper documents, revise on paper rather than onscreen, at least during early drafts.

- Examine each section to make sure you have followed your outline or storyboard.

- Check your level of detail. Ensure that it is consistent and appropriate for your audience, scope, and purpose.

- Review your material for completeness.

- Make sure that your paragraphs are organized logically and that the information is presented clearly.

- Review your material to eliminate redundancy.

- For on-screen material, make sure that each screen contains as much material as your readers can reasonably be expected to handle at one time and no more.

- Look over your illustrations to verify that they are placed appropriately. Consider adding nontext elements—figures or tables—to support your text.

When you are writing about technical subjects, you have to understand your subject well to express it clearly to your readers. If you don't understand the technical details, how will you explain them in your prose?

Accuracy and Precision

Accuracy—freedom from error—is important in many types of writing, but it is an absolute necessity in most kinds of technical writing. Accuracy has at least two senses or meanings in technical prose, one concerning the correctness of the information or content and one concerning precision or choosing the correct technical or familiar word. Properly, this second sense of narrowing the word choice to the word that targets just the meaning you want can be called *correctness* or *precision*. But since the two work so closely together, we'll consider both meanings in this section.

When you write technical prose, you provide your readers with information that they will depend on, and its accuracy ensures that they can understand, evaluate, and use the information you have conveyed. When you are writing about technical subjects, you have to understand your subject well to express it clearly to your readers. If you don't understand the technical details, how will you explain them in your prose?

Even if you are quite knowledgeable about your subject, you may find it useful to have your work reviewed for technical accuracy. For one thing, you may be so familiar with your subject that you omit information or steps that seem obvious to you but that would not be obvious to your readers. For another, even though you know you understand your topic, you want to make sure that you've correctly explained it from a technical standpoint. Whether your subject is highly technical, moderately technical, slightly technical, or not technical at all, accuracy is a basic requirement to create functional, effective documents.

Correctness or precision in the terms you use is also essential. Consider the following terms, for example: *DNA–chromosome* and *inapt–inept*. To a layperson there may not be much difference between each word in these word pairs. To a specialist, however, there are essential differences. For example, most people recognize DNA as the genetic material of living organisms, whereas a biologist would realize that DNA is a collection of nucleic acids that code for specific genes in chromosomes. Also, words such as *inapt* and *inept* sound similar but have different meanings: The former means "inappropriate," and the latter means "incompetent." It's essential that these terms and countless others be used correctly and not interchangeably. In Appendix A you will read more about commonly confused words.

> **ON CHECKING FOR ACCURACY**
>
> Most people don't seem to "get" the need for accuracy. In our work, all raw technical data should be reviewed and analyzed very, very carefully. Just because it came from an engineer, who is the expert on the hardware, does not mean the data is correct. So the process of verifying data thoroughly is much more involved than people think at first. Inaccurate data in our business can literally have tragic consequences.
>
> —Ray A. José, senior technical writer, New Britain, Connecticut

Appropriateness

The appropriateness of a document refers to a writer's degree of success in aptly choosing language that is especially suitable or compatible for a given subject, purpose, scope, and audience. When you choose a word, a phrase, or even a tone, your choice should be suitable for the situation. By using inapt language, you distract from your message and sabotage your document's effectiveness. When you choose words, their associations can make the difference between appropriate and inappropriate usage. Consider carefully the message your words carry beyond their dictionary denotation. Words bring connotations that help to determine their suitability in a given context. Every word you choose helps to shape your readers' perceptions of your subject matter. (See Figure 10.6.)

Consider, for example, the word *inspect*. The word means to examine carefully, especially for flaws. Synonyms are *investigate*, *probe*, or *scan*. Telling a client that you are going to *inspect* a product report has a different connotation from suggesting that you are going to *scan* the product report. *Inspect* is a more appropriate diction choice and suggests that you are going to examine the report very carefully, looking for flaws. *Scan* is a less intensive word and signifies that you are going to examine the report more superficially. Your word choices

> " "
>
> Every word you choose helps to shape your readers' perceptions of your subject matter.

FIGURE 10.6
Diction

MAKE AN EFFORT TO ACCOMPLISH AN END

attempt	stresses the initiation or beginning of the effort
try	stresses the effort or experimental nature
endeavor	involves exertion and difficulty
essay	involves difficulty and experimentation
strive	requires great exertion and persistent effort

MOVE OR ACT SLOWLY AND FALL BEHIND

delay	put off
procrastinate	suggests blameworthy delay
lag	implies a failure to maintain a speed set by others
loiter	delay while in progress of doing something
dawdle	aimless wasting of time while in progress
dally	delay through trifling or vacillation

SHOW IRRESOLUTION OR UNCERTAINTY

hesitate	pause before deciding or acting
waver	hesitation after seeming to decide
vacillate	prolonged hesitation
falter	wavering or stumbling

USE POWER OF CONCEPTION, JUDGMENT, INFERENCE

think	attain clear ideas or conclusions
cogitate	deep, intent thinking
reflect	unhurried consideration
reason	consecutive logical thinking
speculate	reasoning about the theoretical or problematical
deliberate	slow, careful reasoning to reach a conclusion

strongly influence the effectiveness of your prose and how your audience views your own seriousness, credibility, and persuasiveness.

Conciseness

"I made this letter longer than usual, because I lacked the time to make it short."

—Attributed to Blaise Pascal

When you write with conciseness, you capture your meaning in exactly the length and depth required, without stinting or overdoing. Your treatment is neither incomplete nor superfluous. It is actually more difficult to write fewer words that express your meaning than more words. Concise writing often requires lots of rewriting to eliminate unnecessary words from early drafts. But when you cut back to achieve conciseness, take care that you are not falling into the trap of writing cryptically. True conciseness consists of achieving a balance between lean prose and sufficient detail. Also see the "Telegraphic Writing" section later in this chapter.

Achieving Conciseness

- Reread and rewrite your material, always watching for superfluous words.
- Increase your vocabulary. By becoming familiar with the meanings of words, you will see that a single word can often substitute for a series of words. For example, *like* means *in the same way that*, *never* means *under no conditions*, *halve* means *cut in half*.
- Ask yourself whether each word in every sentence that you write is needed. Is each word essential? Does it contribute to or interfere with the meaning of your sentence? Does it add anything to your meaning that another, perhaps adjacent, word does not?

Unnecessary Words or Phrases

Unnecessary words and phrases or wasted words and phrases weaken your prose and add little or nothing to the meaning of a sentence. Unnecessary words include *totally, really, extremely, very, basically, completely,* and *essentially.* These are sometimes referred to as meaningless qualifiers. Unnecessary phrases include *as it were, it has been indicated that, at the present moment in time, it should be noted that, considering the fact that, despite the fact that, is composed of, on a regular basis, on the part of, regardless of whether, the reason is because,* and *while simultaneously.*

Often you may simply substitute a single word for a phrase:

Original:

Despite the fact that Hanson PLC has revenues of more than $12 billion, its corporate staff is exceedingly lean.

Revision:

Although Hanson PLC has revenues of more than $12 billion, its corporate staff is exceedingly lean.

Redundancies

Redundancy is one of the biggest problems all writers face. Often writers use more words than necessary to express an idea.

Original:

The reason for this price increase in this software program was probably due to the fact that the company's competitors also increased their prices.

Revision:

This software program costs more because competing programs also cost more.

Circumlocutions

A circumlocution is a long way of saying something—going around a topic with words. Some writers prefer circumlocutions because they sound formal, but circumlocutions create pompous and inflated language.

Examples:

In the modern world of today . . .
It is possible that there might be . . .
Submit suggestions that you may have in regard to the topic . . .

Prepositional Phrases

View critically all prepositional phrases, especially those longer than two words. We depend on these three- and four-word prepositional phrases because we are unfamiliar with the meanings of so many one-word prepositions. A prepositional phrase can often be reduced to a single word or deleted altogether.

Original:

Over the duration of the project, we expect there will be some disruption due to noise, dirt, and dust.

Revision:

During the project, we expect there will be some disruption due to noise, dirt, and dust.

Verb Phrases

Many verb phrases are redundant. In these phrases, two words (generally, a verb followed by a noun) do the work of one (the noun made into a verb).

Original:

Space probers are reluctantly *reaching the conclusion* that there is little likelihood that intelligent life is out there in the empty spaces beyond our solar system.

Revision:

Space probers are reluctantly *concluding* that there is little likelihood that intelligent life is out there in the empty spaces beyond our solar system.

Original:

Several economists predict that the expansion will *come to an end* in what is now its seventh year.

Revision:

Several economists predict that the expansion will *end* in what is now its seventh year.

Noun Phrases

These phrases often begin with *a* or *the* followed by a noun and end with *of*. They can easily be improved.

Original:

The maintenance of this flow is assured by their willingness to rubber-stamp the decisions of their benefactor.

Revision:

Maintaining this flow is assured by their willingness to rubber-stamp the decisions of their benefactor.

Original:

The installation and testing of a new product, *the conversion of* user files, and *the training of* users are not small matters.

Revision:

Installing and testing a new product, *converting* user files, and *training* users are not small matters.

Original:

Personal computers were meant to give people more flexibility *in the processing of information.*

Revision:

Personal computers were meant to give people more flexibility *in processing information.*

Expletive Constructions

An expletive is a syllable, word, or phrase inserted to fill a vacancy without adding to the sense. Some contexts require expletives: *It* is raining. But in many cases, you can substitute wording that will tighten the sentence and make it stronger.

Original with expletive "There was":

There was a short which burned out the circuit.

Revision:

A short burned out the circuit.

Original with expletive "It is":

It is absolutely essential to ground the device before charging it.

Revision:

You must ground the device before charging it.

Gobbledygook

When jargon, in the sense of pretentious and often unintelligible words, is part of long, convoluted sentences, gobbledygook occurs. Gobbledygook is inflated or pompous language at the sentence level.

Original:

Intercom utilization will be used to initiate substitute teacher involvement.

Revision:

The intercom will be used to help involve substitute teachers.

Telegraphic Writing

Telegraphic writing takes conciseness to an extreme. Some writers create a compressed style when they omit articles (*a, an, the*) and prepositions (*in, of, to*) from their writing. Technical prose that will be read by non-native speakers of English or that will be translated into other languages should never sacrifice clarity for conciseness by using telegraphic writing. For that matter, technical prose should not sacrifice clarity no matter what the reason and no matter who the audience.

Original:

Turn handle for faucet counterclockwise until handle can no longer be turned.

Revision:

Turn *the* handle for *the* faucet counterclockwise until *the* handle can no longer be turned.

Those "Unimportant" Little Words

Cary Grant's agent received a telegram attempting to find out Grant's age: "How old Cary Grant." Grant intercepted the message and replied: "Old Cary Grant fine. How you."

Concreteness

Concreteness refers to a quality of language that describes tangible things. Its opposite is abstractness. Concrete words refer to specific objects, persons, places, and acts, things that can be detected by the senses: *Apple Computer Corporation* is more concrete than *the computer industry*; *Gatorland* is more concrete than *zoological park*; *amylase* is more specific than *enzyme*; a *1999 Toyota*

REVISIONS ARE EASIER NOW

Now that I work mostly on a computer, everything happens faster. This is both good and bad. Delays on a project are costly. The bad part is there isn't as much time to think about things and faster processors are not a substitute for that. There is a lot more copy and paste work done now than when people had to do work manually. This is bad for original thought but great for revisions.

—George Johnston, software development engineer, Redmond, California

Corolla is more specific than *car;* and *using the Infoseek search engine to perform a Boolean search on frogs* is more specific than *using a search engine.*

Abstractness, in contrast, refers to general ideas, acts, conditions, relationships, qualities, or anything that cannot be perceived by the five senses, such as *courage, evil, goodness, truth, freedom,* and *justice.*

Concreteness and abstraction are rarely encountered as absolutes; they exist along a range. Choose words suitable for your audience. You will use both concrete and abstract words in your writing, but an overabundance of abstract words will mask your meaning and bore readers.

Use concrete details in conjunction with abstract words as well as examples to explain concepts. Many abstract words present readers with too many possibilities for interpretation. In technical prose, abstract words are often necessary, but there are times when a more concrete word is a better choice.

> You will use both concrete and abstract words in your writing, but an overabundance of abstract words will mask your meaning and bore readers.

Consistency

Consistency refers to your treatment of repeated elements in your document. You achieve consistency when you stay at the same level of formality throughout your document. You achieve consistency when you control your vocabulary and don't overuse synonyms. You achieve consistency when your punctuation and spelling of technical terms remains constant throughout your document.

You must be careful about spelling or punctuating certain words consistently. You need to decide, for example, whether you will refer to your audience members as *readers* or *reader(s)* or *users* or *user(s).* If you are referring to the document you are writing, will you use the term *book, guide, manual, instructions,* or *document?* Usually, you will want to make sure you are using terms consistently.

You may have been taught to vary your writing by using synonyms or rephrasings to avoid excessive repetition. Although this advice often holds for nontechnical prose, in technical writing you may have to forgo this nicety of expression in the interest of effectiveness. Readers assume that different technical terms refer to different items, and if you sometimes use *fixture* and other times use *light,* your audience may very well believe that you are talking about two different items even when you're not. So, in general, be consistent and use the same terms throughout the document.

Of course, you must make decisions about capitalization and usage as well. To achieve consistency, your company may have developed a style guide you must follow; if not, you can create your own to ensure consistency within your own documents. See Appendix A for help with these issues.

> Be consistent and use the same terms throughout the document.

Clarity

You want your readers to understand your prose without having to struggle over your meaning. One important way to achieve this effect is to strive for

ON REVISING FOR CLARITY

With some clarification of the objectives and purpose the product is much better. I find that the largest area of revising is clarity.

—Lisa Mezzatesta, director of learning and development, Atlanta, Georgia

clarity in your writing. Clarity, quite simply, is the state of being clear, so you can think of clarity as the absence of ambiguity. Writing clearly means using words in the right way and focusing on achieving a single meaning for your words, phrases, and sentences.

Far from being the exception in technical prose, ambiguity is all too often the rule. Unclear prose shows up in many technical documents, and ambiguity may occur at the word, phrase, clause, sentence, paragraph, or other segment level. If what you write can easily be misinterpreted by your readers, you have not been clear. If your readers misconstrue your message and interpret it in a different way from what you intended, you have not been clear. Sometimes, it is difficult to imagine how our words can be misconstrued, since to us they seem so unambiguous. Here is where an outside reviewer can be helpful in identifying possible sources of confusion in your writing.

Sincerity

Sincerity is not a feature you would expect to be concerned about for a technical document. After all, doesn't it go without saying that your user guide, for example, would present its instructions honestly? Why would technical writers intentionally try to deceive their readers? Although sincerity may not be a quality you strive for explicitly, it underlies all your writing. Yet even ethical writers grapple with these issues in technical prose.

To create a relationship with your readers, you will want to establish that you are a trustworthy source of information. If your readers don't believe in your sincerity, your text will not effectively convey its message. You may have valid reasons for withholding or distorting information, but sincerity is a powerful tool to achieve believability. Good writers establish a bond with their readers, and sincerity is an effective way to maintain that bond.

Write truthfully and honestly, and—unless using humor suits your purpose—treat your subject and your readers seriously. Choose words that help you to convey your tone, establish your credibility, and build trust with your audience. (See the "Establishing Your Credibility" section in Chapter 7.) Pay attention to those words, phrases, clauses, sentences, and larger segments that can undermine the relationship that you are carefully crafting with your reader. All these elements contribute to creating your own voice in your writing.

CHOOSING THE ETHICAL PATH

Sometimes insincerity is more a question of information misleadingly omitted than information falsified. For example, lapses in sincerity may occur when software bugs, often euphemistically lumped together with "undocumented features," go discreetly unmentioned in the reference manual or instruction sheet.

Negative Constructions

You have a double negative when you put two negatives within a sentence for emphasis. Sometimes double negatives are helpful to put a special emphasis on part of your sentence: "We were not ungrateful." But most of the time you should avoid double negatives in your writing because they create unnecessary ambiguities. Negative instructions can be confusing for readers.

Original:

The computer should not be shut off until Windows is no longer running.

Revision:

Shut off the computer after exiting from Windows.

Original:

Do not unplug the computer during an electrical storm if you don't want to risk being shocked.

Revision:

To avoid the risk of being shocked, do not unplug the computer during an electrical storm.

Another type of negative construction concerns using words to convey a negative meaning. Negative words and phrases are words or expressions that often create a defensive or hostile attitude in the audience. In a letter of complaint, for example, expressions such as *your fault, your mistake, your stupidity, your employee's blatant negligence,* or *your shoddy workmanship* may cause a hostile reaction.

Sentence Parallelism

If you are discussing two or more ideas that are basically equal in importance, you can convey this equality using parallel structure or putting ideas of parallel importance in parallel form.

Original:

Our problems with this client can be solved by notifying him of our plans in advance, if we meet with him at least once a week, and if we communicate more frequently by phone and e-mail.

Revision:

Our problems with this client can be solved by notifying him of our plans in advance, meeting with him at least once a week, and communicating more frequently by phone and e-mail.

Parallel Structure with Lists:

To install the printer board, first remove the case from the PC in the following manner:
1. Unplug the computer.
2. Remove the five screws from the back panel.
3. Lift the back of the metal cover.
4. Slide the metal cover back and off the computer.

Parallel Structures Beyond Paragraphs:

Our first objective must be to cut unprofitable operations . . .
Our second objective must be to consolidate management information . . .
Our third objective must be to eliminate cost overruns during production . . .

Faulty parallelism occurs when the sentence fails to make the verbs or nouns parallel to each other.

Original:

Taking all of the parts out of the boxes and check them with the parts list to make sure you received all of the parts required to set up your new computer properly.

Revision:

Take all of the parts out of the boxes and check them with the parts list to make sure you received all of the parts required to set up your new computer properly.

See Figure 10.7 for further examples on parallelism.

EVALUATING DRAFTS

You go through many steps between the time you are assigned a project and the time you finish it. Typically, you plan, research, organize, design, write, revise, and produce the document, either on paper or on screen. And each of these steps comprises many substeps. Sometimes you do all these things yourself; other times you are collaborating with a partner or a larger team. When you are working on your project with other people, you expect to integrate your work with theirs, and usually that means you will be reading each other's work to check for compatibility of style and content, flow of narrative, and comprehensiveness of treatment. (See Chapter 3 for detailed information on working collaboratively.)

Your drafts will undergo several types of evaluation. The first is your own two eyes. You write your document; then you edit it. Editing is a form of evaluation, where you look over what you have written and seek to improve it by correcting errors and smoothing the narrative. The next is the revision process, where you go back to your draft and make changes, such as you read about in the previous section. The last is the evaluation process, which consists of having your document reviewed and tested.

Review Cycles

Regardless of whether you work alone on your project or with others, an important stage in the writing cycle is the review cycle. When you are planning, you make a schedule. And one of the items you include in your schedule is one or more review cycles. A review cycle is the process of turning your document over to someone else—an editor, committee, supervisor, classmates, colleagues, your professor—for comments and suggestions and then

TWO PAIRS OF EYES

All of my work is done as a team effort and usually divided up into writing and editing. I see no drawbacks to that approach. In fact, I don't know how you could create good written work without at least two pairs of eyes looking at each project.

—Mark W. Sincell, Ph.D., freelance science editor and writer, Houston, Texas

FIGURE 10.7

Faulty Sentence Parallelism

Sample A

Original:

You can either *request "press grind"* available for selected coffee types, or when grinding at home, *the coffee should be coarse* (about 6 seconds with a blade grinder).

Revision:

You can either *request "press grind"* available for selected coffee types, or, when grinding at home, *grind the coffee* to a coarse consistency (about 6 seconds with a blade grinder).

Sample B

Original: Switch Calibration Test:

1. *Clamp* amp probe around one surface unit lead.
2. *Set* control to lowest heat setting (at WM) and allow switch to stabilize (3 cycles).
3. *Compute* percent-on time of switch by timing the ON and OFF times of the cycling switch. Percent-on time is found by dividing ON-time by total cycle time and multiplying by 100.
4. *Calibration limits:* 6 percent or less on-time at lowest operating point of switch

Revision: Switch Calibration Test:

1. *Clamp* amp probe around one surface unit lead.
2. *Set* control to lowest heat setting (at WM) and allow switch to stabilize (3 cycles).
3. *Compute* percent-on time of switch by timing the ON and OFF times of the cycling switch. Percent-on time is found by dividing ON-time by total cycle time and multiplying by 100.
4. *Verify* calibration limit of switch: 6 percent or less on-time at lowest operating point of switch

Sample C

Original: After Defrosting:

1. *Large items may be icy* in the center. Defrosting will complete during STANDING TIME.
2. *Let stand,* covered with plastic wrap, in the refrigerator for time shown in the chart below.
3. *See chart* below for standing time and rinsing directions.
4. *Items which have been layered should be rinsed* separately or have a longer standing time.

FIGURE 10.7

(continued)

Revision: After Defrosting:

1. *Allow large items,* which may be icy in the center, to complete defrosting during STANDING TIME.
2. *Let stand,* covered with plastic wrap, in the refrigerator for time shown in the chart below.
3. *See chart* below for standing time and rinsing directions.
4. *Rinse items* separately if they have been layered or have a longer standing time.

Sample D

Original: Using Your Thermal Carafe:

Rinse the inside of the carafe with hot water before brewing.
For best results, *brew* a full 8-cup capacity.
The *brew-thru lid must be in place* on the carafe before brewing.
Remove the carafe from the coffeemaker after brewing to seal in flavor and heat.
Keep the carafe lid closed when not pouring.

Revision: Using Your Thermal Carafe:

Rinse the inside of the carafe with hot water before brewing.
For best results, *brew* a full 8-cut capacity
Close the brew-thru lid, which must be in place on the carafe before brewing.
Remove the carafe from the coffeemaker after brewing to seal in flavor and heat.
Keep the carafe lid closed when not pouring.

Sample E

Original: Using Your Iron

1. *Fill* iron with water.
2. *Plug* cord into standard outlet.
3. *Move* Temperature Selector to desired setting.
4. *Release* steam button up.
5. *Water may drip* from steam vents if iron is not preheated at least 1–2 minutes.

Revision: Using Your Iron

1. *Fill* iron with water.
2. *Plug* cord into standard outlet.
3. *Move* Temperature Selector to desired setting.
4. *Release* steam button up.
5. *Preheat* iron at least 1–2 minutes to prevent water dripping from steam vents.

having that person or group return your document to you for further revision based on suggestions developed during the review.

You don't need to have someone review every e-mail or letter you send, but if the e-mail, letter, report, or other document is important, you need to have at least one other qualified person review your work. The qualified reviewer will spot shortcomings in your *logic*, your *organization*, your *design*, your *tone*, your *technical accuracy*, and so on. And as an added bonus, this person may spot problems with *mechanics:* the misspelled words and any other typographical errors that your word-processing program failed to pick up. Finally, the reviewer will alert you to problems with your *grammar*. In sum, if you want your communications to be as effective as possible, you can't rely on just your own judgment. You need the judgment and help of your peers, and, where appropriate, you need to test your documents to find out whether they are fulfilling their purpose as well as they should for their intended audience.

IN THE FAMILY

My favorite writing mentoring experience was helping my daughters with their writing assignments as they went through school. Even through graduate school, one of them would send me drafts of papers for review and editorial suggestions. Both daughters became proficient writers and good communicators.

—Joel Hartman, chief information officer, Orlando, Florida

Review For

- Logic
- Organization
- Design
- Tone
- Technical accuracy
- Mechanics: spelling, punctuation
- Grammar

Review is an important part of the document process, and when you plan your schedule, it is essential that you allow enough time for this phase of the work. See Figure 10.8 on review cycles. Keep in mind that your reviewers are busy people. Giving them your material to review immediately before you have to submit it for production puts an undue and unreasonable burden on them. Schedule enough time for them to give your document the careful attention it deserves and for you to implement their suggestions.

Sometimes you will need more than one review cycle to make your document suitable to its purpose. If you submit an article to a peer-reviewed journal, for example, the journal's reviewers may make many suggestions for substantive changes. Once you have implemented those changes, you will submit the revised manuscript to the journal for re-review. If the article still is found to need improvement, you will be asked to continue the revision process. This process can cycle several more times, and typically it does.

The main thing to remember is that whether you are working alone or in a group, your documents will benefit from review. Sometimes reviewing will be

FIGURE 10.8

Review Cycles

On this Gantt chart, the review cycles for the project are highlighted.

Proposed Project Schedule

✓	Task	Start	End	March				April					May	
				5	12	19	26	2	9	16	23	30	7	14
	Planning	3/5	3/16	▄										
	Research	3/12	3/23		▄									
	Writing	3/19	4/6			▄▄								
	Design review	4/9	4/13						▄					
	Accuracy review	4/9	4/13						▄					
	Technical review	4/9	4/13						▄					
	Revising	4/16	4/20							▄				
	Usability review	4/23	4/27								▄			
	Mechanical review	4/25	4/27								▄			
	Style review	4/25	4/27								▄			
	Revising	4/30	5/2									▄		
	Legal review	5/3	5/8										▄	
	Revising	5/9	5/11										▄	
	Production	5/14	5/18											▄

at your discretion; other times it will be required. Even if it's not required, having your document reviewed will result in a better document. See Figure 10.9 for types of review.

Style Review

There are many types of review. A style review covers many of the elements you learned about in Chapter 7 and many of the principles of good prose you have already read about in this chapter. But it also concerns checking a document to make sure it conforms to what is often described as *house style:* specific company requirements for capitalization, abbreviations, captions, use of numerals instead of spelled-out numbers, punctuation guidelines, required citation style, spacing around special elements, and so on.

Peer Review

In Chapter 3 you learned about peer review and its importance in college and in the workplace. Documents that have been reviewed by your classmates or colleagues have passed under the eyes of at least one other person who is familiar with your assignment or your subject. In some situations, peer review may be your only chance to have an assignment critiqued by someone else, and your documents will be better for the review.

EDITING AND REVISING

It is a good idea to have a separate set of eyes to edit documents if the staff supports this kind of division of labor. It is also a good idea if a separate person does the planning of what topics need to be edited and that same person does the review at the end to make sure nothing was overlooked.

—Laurie S. Benson, software development project manager, Altamonte Springs, Florida

FIGURE 10.9

Types of Review

Overall	Appropriateness for the audience Organization and accessibility of material Scope of content Appropriateness of tone, style, vocabulary Number and helpfulness of examples Avoidance of gaps or superfluities in treatment Similar treatment of similar elements
Legal Review	Liability Disclaimers Copyright/trademark infringement
Usability	Enough examples, clear examples Accurate visuals Avoidance of cultural biases Clear navigation Accurate and complete table of contents and index Easy-to-follow instructions Explanation of conventions Explanation of acronyms and abbreviations Definitions of new or difficult terms
Accuracy	Correspondence of objects or processes with descriptions Functionality of procedures Currency of screen shots Workability/usability of tutorials and instructions
Style (house)	Conformity to house style or a specified style manual (CBE, MLA, APA, IEEE, CMS) Consistent use of style Standard use of wording and terminology Absence of bias Control of tone Emphasis for important points
Mechanics	Spelling Punctuation Grammar Conventions: numbers, lists
Design	Usability Ease of navigation Use of visuals Use of features: headings emphasized, correct number of subheadings per heading, consistent subheadings Appropriateness of level of formality Consistency of level of formality with subject matter
Technical	Accuracy of content Detail level of visuals Clarity and conciseness of labels and captions

From the workplace

Yateendra Joshi

Director, Information Technology and Services
TERI (Tata Energy Research Institute)
New Delhi, India

Yateen is a careful observer of language and its uses. From the time he began working as a plant scientist through his present executive position directing a division of the respected Tata Energy Research Institute, Yateen's efforts to improve his and others' level of written communications, both for distribution within his organization and in its external publications, has very ably supported his role as technical communicator and disseminator of research information.

As director of the Information Technology and Services Division at the Tata Energy Research Institute in New Delhi, India, I hold the overall charge for all functions related to collecting, processing, refining, packaging, and disseminating technical information related to the Institute's mandate and serving a 350-strong staff of professional researchers. This position was a progression from my long-standing responsibilities as a technical communicator.

My education, both bachelor's and master's degrees, is in agricultural science, and I did work for 12 years in that field. My first job, after graduating with a bachelor's degree, was that of a farm supervisor. I was only partly trained for it. I knew the theory behind most of the farm operations, but I was ill-equipped to supervise or undertake those operations, and I lacked the business orientation necessary to run a farm as a commercial enterprise. In any event, I left

that job after about eight months to enroll in graduate school.

I joined the Indian Council of Agricultural Research as a staff scientist doing research on plant disease. While there, I was also assigned the duties of a technical information officer, and a part of that job was to edit and proofread technical documents. Along with my regular job, I enrolled in a correspondence course in book publishing.

It was then that I had a lucky break: I managed to attend an intensive 14-week course on editing and publishing scientific material, run jointly by the International Rice Research Institute in the Philippines and the International Development Research Centre and the University of Toronto Press in Canada. It was this course that made it possible for me to land a full-time job in science publishing: I joined TERI as publications officer toward the end of 1988.

Ten years ago, I knew next to nothing about PCs. Now, of course, computers are the backbone of any communication. E-mail discussion groups and the Web have enriched my professional life beyond measure. I use computers for writing almost to the exclusion of pen and paper (though I prefer to do most *editing* on hard copy).

Ironically, I find that PCs have considerably *added* to my overall workload: first because now I end up spending a lot more time on getting things just so (something that you do not venture to do if the only

In later chapters of this textbook, you will learn about writing different types of documents: résumés for obtaining a job or grant; letters, memos, and e-mail used for a variety of purposes; procedures, processes, and specifications; informal and formal reports; and instructions. All of these types of documents can benefit from peer review to improve their quality and effectiveness. Another way to think about the peer-review process is that it is a very basic form of usability testing. You submit your work to someone else to review, and that person evaluates it to see if it conveys the meaning it should

tool you have is a manual typewriter), which actually lowers productivity and boosts paper consumption. Second, probably much of the work would have been done by others in the past.

I supervise the writing of other members of my team. What I've noticed is that most people fail to recognize the need to tailor their writing to the intended reader. Most also overestimate the readers' knowledge of the subject and their motivation. As communicators, we should realize that we are competing for the readers' attention, that most are reluctant readers who would rather be doing something else, and that most nonfiction readers seldom read anything longer than a page from beginning to end in one go.

Meetings

In the course of my career so far, I've had to endure many, many meetings. Meetings often seem to me a device to avoid, or at best postpone, concrete thinking. Routine meetings rarely achieve something that cannot be achieved by means of reports. Meetings in large groups are suited only for imparting information, although many people do not realize this.

For meetings to be successful, the outcome needs to be defined in operational terms, as in "At the end of this meeting, we will have decided on a name for our proposed newsletter, its intended audience, budget, and a launch date." Alternatively, a meeting could be more or less unstructured and more in the nature of a brainstorming session, and this should be made clear in advance.

Insider Advice

Since I made a major career change by moving from research to technical communication, I have thought extensively about what a person can do to maximize the chances of job advancement. If I had to advise someone just entering the workforce in my field, I would say this:

- Technical expertise alone rarely helps you advance in your career although it is an essential foundation. Later, as you assume managerial responsibilities, you would find it increasingly difficult to keep pace with what is happening in your field. Often, you would be forced to make a choice between being an expert and being successful in material terms. Make that choice consciously and accept the trade-offs.
- Keep records. I wish I had kept such statistics as the number of manuscript pages I have edited so far, the number of letters I helped draft, the number of presentations that I was involved in, the total amount of money that was paid out with my authorization. One day, such statistics might be handy.
- Read selectively but read a great deal, especially when you have the time. You will unconsciously absorb good writing and it will be reflected in your writing—do not confine your reading only to newspapers, journals, and magazines.
- Be proactive, be visible, and be vocal. Technical communicators have a lot to contribute to a company's success but managers seldom realize that potential. It is up to you to make them realize it. Make sure that you are involved early on in all the projects or jobs for which your input will be sought later.

and functions as it is supposed to. Put another way, the reviewer ascertains if your document "works."

Reviewing Large Projects

Reviewing is an essential step in creating effective technical documents. Reviewing occurs when you submit your document to someone else to edit. (Some people use the term *checking* for when you examine your document yourself.) In some complex collaborative-writing college assignments and in major projects in a corporate setting, you will frequently encounter a much more established review procedure. In a collaborative college assignment your professor may require various kinds of extensive review of your collaborative document before you and your group members finally turn in the assignment. In a corporate setting you will often find that many different departments may have to be included in the review process because the company's reputation and profits may be at stake.

SCHEDULING REVIEWS

One challenging situation came up when I was working with a recent immigrant from China. His English was so poor that he could not review my documents—but he was too proud to admit this to his supervisor and went on promising that he would have it done "soon." In the end, nothing sufficed to get him to review the documents. He left the company, and I have no idea to this day if they are correct.

—Emily Cotlier, technical writer, Auckland, New Zealand

The review cycle may call for many phases of review including a documentation plan review, a peer review, a technical review, a customer-service review, a marketing review, an editing review, a management review, and a legal review. Of course, if a document requires many or all of these kinds of reviews, you and others in your company will need extensive project management skills to make sure the review cycle proceeds smoothly. For an excellent discussion of these advanced skills, see JoAnn T. Hackos, *Managing Your Documentation Projects*.

Usability Testing

Usability testing is common in many industries to determine the quality of a product or service. Usability testing is widely used in the computer industry, for example, for both software and hardware, and many companies have usability labs designed solely for this purpose. In software usability testing, a multi-step process is frequently used—a process that includes various pretest preparations, the actual testing, analysis of the test results, modifying of the software, and retesting of the product. All the steps are complex and can be time consuming. For information about usability testing of Web sites, see Chapter 8, and for information about usability testing for instructions, see the "Testing Your Instructions" section in Chapter 19.

A well-constructed usability test will use testers, facilitators, observers, and recorders to document every phase of the process. The testers, test subjects, or test users are the people who sit at the computer or other apparatus and perform the defined task. The facilitator plays the role of the host of the usability test. The observer's role is simply to watch the users as they perform the defined tasks and keep notes on where they have difficulty using the system. The recorder observes the test subjects as the tasks are being performed and records anything that must be measured. For example, if one of the tests concerns the time to perform each task, the recorder uses a timer and records the times required for each task. See Figure 10.10 on usability testing elements.

After the testing is performed and the results have been analyzed, further changes in the product, the documentation, or both, along with further testing, typically lead to a much improved product. Of course, a sophisticated

STEPS IN USABILITY TESTING	ACTIVITIES
1. Plan scope, issues, participants, location, budget.	■ What are you going to test? ■ What concerns do you have about the document or Web site that you want to test? ■ Which users should participate in the test? ■ Where will you conduct the test? In a fixed laboratory? In a conference room or other space with a portable lab? In a conference room or other space but without any recording equipment? Remotely? ■ What is your budget for testing?
2. Develop scenarios.	■ Select relevant tasks for users to try. ■ Prepare, try out, and refine scenarios for those tasks. ■ Make sure the scenarios are clearly written and not too much of a challenge for the allotted test time.
3. Recruit test participants.	■ Recruit users who accurately represent your current or potential users. ■ Consider using a firm that specializes in recruiting for usability tests. ■ If you do it yourself, build a database of users for future tests.
4. Conduct usability testing.	■ Have a trained facilitator interact with the user. ■ Have trained observers watch, listen, and take notes. ■ Make sure participants know that they are helping by trying out the document or Web site; the document is being tested, not them. ■ Get participants to think aloud as they work. ■ Let participants express their reactions. ■ Listen! Do not lead. Be sure to stay neutral in your words and body language. Be careful not to ask leading questions that may skew the participants' responses. ■ Take detailed, useful notes concentrating on observations of behavior rather than inferences.
5. Make good use of the test results.	■ Compile the data from all participants. ■ List the problems experienced by the participants. ■ Sort the problems by priority and frequency of the problem. ■ Develop solutions. Get expert advice if the solutions are not obvious. ■ Fix the problems. ■ Test the revised version to ensure you made the right design decisions.

FIGURE 10.10

Usability Testing Elements

software product will usually undergo many tests and versions before it is marketed; even after it is marketed many further improvements may be required before the product performs as to its specifications.

CHECKING WHAT YOU'VE LEARNED

After planning, researching, and writing a document, much work remains to be done to make it the best document it can be. Moving through the various types of editing, you will check your document for correctness, completeness, logical flow, tone, format, and other issues covered in this chapter.

Developmental and Substantive Editing

- Have you evaluated the document for overall logic and completeness?
- Is the document type appropriate for the intended audience, subject, purpose, scope, and context?
- Are there sufficient visuals?
- Are the visuals appropriate?

Revising

- Is the document concise, avoiding unnecessary words and phrases, long words where inappropriate, extraneous intensifiers, redundancy, circumlocutions, and overreliance on prepositional phrases, verb phrases, and noun phrases?
- Does the document avoid using expletive constructions and gobbledygook?
- While aiming for conciseness, does the document also avoid overly terse or telegraphic prose?
- Is the document free from ambiguous references?
- Are elements of all lists parallel with other elements in the same list?
- Have you ensured that your prose is clear, sincere, and unambiguous?

Evaluating Drafts

- Have you had the draft reviewed for style issues such as bias, tone, cultural sensitivity, appropriate diction, appropriate use of jargon, handling of abbreviations?

Reviewing

- Did you plan a review cycle into the schedule for your document?
- Was your document usability tested to ensure that typical users would be able to use the document easily for its intended purpose?

EXERCISES

 REVIEW

1. Rewrite the following sentences to make them more concise:
   A. You should check your computer for viruses on a regular basis.
   B. It should be noted that solving this problem will take more time than we first thought.
   C. While simultaneously pressing the Control key and the letter "I" on your keyboard, you can create italics.
   D. Our group must meet soon to discuss the project we are working on together if we want to keep from falling behind the other groups in class, groups that apparently have already met several times.
   E. It goes without saying that our team can be the best team in class.

2. Rephrase many of the sentences in the following paragraphs to make them more concise:

   Carpal Tunnel Syndrome (CTS), which is a Repetitive Stress Injury (RSI), is one of the leading causes of computer-related injuries caused by computers. Carpal Tunnel syndrome is caused by the effects of irritation and compression of the median nerve at the wrist. Constant flexing and compression of the wrist causes compression of the medial nerve, transforming into fibrosis (tough inflexible tissue). This can lead to constant pain in the wrist, numbness, and pins and needles, which may prevent full mobility in the hand.

   CTS has become largely notorious and well known because it can be highly debilitating and harmful. Advanced cases of CTS can leave permanent nerve damage, severely limiting hand and finger movement, and coordination. Symptoms of CTS include the symptoms of pain, numbness, and tingling in the hands, particularly in the first three fingers and thumb. The same symptoms can also appear in the forearms at the same time as the hands. Burning pain in the wrist during the time you are away from the computer and in the middle of the night are clear indications that you have signs of CTS.

   With CTS your muscles swell, growing larger, and this swelling in turn pinches the nerves in your hands and fingers, resulting in the numbness sensation where it's hard for you to feel anything in your hands and fingers. Fingers and hands begin to lose a regular supply of oxygen through the contraction of muscles. The contractions restrict blood flow through the capillaries, eventually cutting off all oxygen to the hand and fingers.

3. The following paragraphs contain gobbledygook. Rephrase and simplify the prose wherever possible:

   While motoring along paved, government sanctioned roadways, your vehicle begins to experience grave technical operational abnormal difficulties. When such an event occurs, several options are recommended.

   When the vehicle initially begins to manifest the abnormality, it is advised that you decrease, gradually, the amount of pressure you are applying to the pedal that controls the acceleration of the vehicle. Avoid applying either intense or sudden pressure to the pedal that controls the braking mechanism of the vehicle. Exercising extreme caution, maneuver your vehicle in a direction that leads off of the roadway surface.

   When on an interstate governmentally sanctioned roadway, attempt to maintain your vehicle's mobility and rate of travel at a level that you will be able to attain the next forward approaching off ramp. Be certain that the motorists to the rear of your vehicle can observe that you will be attempting to make changes in your vehicles orientation in relationship to their own vehicle.

   After you have ascertained that you have safely and completely exited from the roadway, determine a method for ensuring that your vehicle can be seen and identified by motorists in other vehicles. One method of doing this involves the utilization of your vehicle's emergency flashers or hazard lamps. If the grave technical difficulties being experienced by the vehicle you are motoring in occur at such a time when the solar orb is no longer visible, it would be advisable that you employ the "dome" light located within the interior of the vehicle. It is also advisable that you illuminate the area behind your vehicle, through the utilization of flares, warning flags, or reflective triangles.

4. Rephrase the following sentences to avoid errors in sentence parallelism:
   A. The supervisor recommended an increase in salaries and that other expenses be decreased.
   B. The group leader recommended that we get plenty of food, sleep, and exercising.
   C. Install the joystick by reading the installation directions, shutting off the computer, and begin with the first step in the instructions.
   D. This team was the most successful because of hard work, good people, and we were in the right place at the right time.
   E. My major responsibilities are to maintain the network, troubleshoot any problems, and supervising 18 employees.
5. Find an example of a memo, e-mail, or letter that contains problems in wordiness, gobbledygook, or any of the other problems discussed in this chapter. Revise the document and turn in both the original and your revision.

 THE INTERNET

Find an example of text on a Web page (for example, a home page, a company page, an organization page) that has at least one of these faults in

the prose: redundancies, problems in consistent use of terms, circumlocutions, unnecessary expletives, double negatives, or problems in sentence parallelism.

 ETHICS/PROFESSIONALISM

Review the discussion of gobbledygook in this chapter, and then find an example of gobbledygook in any printed or online document. For example, advertisements for computers and computer peripherals are one good source. Discuss whether you think the language was used intentionally to obscure and what you think the ethical consequences are of using language in this way.

 COLLABORATION

Working in small groups, review the discussion of appropriateness in this chapter and of the example word *inspect*. Brainstorm with members of your group to find another example of a word and its synonyms that can present problems in appropriateness to both writers and readers. Create an example where the use of one word is a more appropriate choice than the use of one of its synonyms. Be prepared to discuss your example with the class.

 INTERNATIONAL COMMUNICATION

Assume your instructor asks you to peer review the draft document of a student for whom English is a second language. Discuss the potential difficulties you might encounter in editing this student's document.

RESOURCES

The Chicago Manual of Style. 14th ed. Chicago: U of Chicago P, 1993.

Coggin, William O., and Lynnette R. Porter. *Editing for the Technical Professions.* New York: Macmillan, 1993.

Dragga, Sam, and Gwendolyn Gong. *Editing: The Design of Rhetoric.* Amityville: Baywood, 1989.

Dumas, J. S., and J. C. Redish. *A Practical Guide to Usability Testing.* Norwood: Ablex, 1993.

Dupré, Lyn. *BUGS in Writing: A Guide to Debugging Your Prose.* Rev. ed. Reading: Addison-Wesley, 1998.

Hackos, JoAnn T. *Managing Your Documentation Projects.* New York: Wiley, 1994.

Hackos, JoAnn T., and Janice C. Reddish. *User and Task Analysis for Interface Design.* New York: Wiley, 1998.

Hodges, John C., et al. *Harbrace College Handbook: With Revised 1998 MLA Style Updates.* 13th ed. New York: Harcourt Brace, 1998.

The Microsoft Manual of Style for Technical Publications. 2nd ed. Redmond: Microsoft, 1998.

Nielsen, J., and R. Mack. *Usability Inspection Methods.* New York: Wiley, 1994.

Rosen, Leonard J., and Laurence Behrens. *The Allyn & Bacon Handbook.* Boston: Allyn and Bacon, 2000.

Rubin, Jeffrey. *Handbook of Usability Testing: How to Plan, Design, and Conduct Effective Tests.* New York: Wiley, 1994.

Rude, Carolyn. *Technical Editing.* 2nd ed. Boston: Allyn and Bacon, 1998.

Tarutz, Judith. *Technical Editing.* Boston: Addison-Wesley, 1992.

Van Buren, Robert, and Mary Fran Buehler. *The Levels of Edit.* 2nd ed. Jet Propulsion Laboratory, 1980. Arlington, VA: Society for Technical Communication, n.d.

Weber, Jean Hollis. *Electronic Editing: Editing in the Computer Age.* New South Wales: Archer, 1999.

Wood, Larry E., ed. *User Interface Design: Bridging the Gap from User Requirements to Design.* Boca Raton: CRC, 1997.

Words into Type. 3rd ed. Englewood Cliffs: Prentice-Hall, 1974.

PART THREE

Job Search and Professional Development

Chapter 11
The Job Search   367

Chapter 12
Professional Growth   413

Chapter 13
Developing Presentation Skills   433

11

The Job Search

Where to Search   368

Job Correspondence   375

Résumés   388

Portfolios   400

Interviewing   402

From the Workplace   406

IN THIS CHAPTER

Searching for a job is a task virtually everyone faces at some time. For many people, it's a task that recurs every year or two. For some, it happens once in a lifetime. This chapter covers planning your job search and conducting it to a successful conclusion. Whether this is the first time you have had to apply for a job or the tenth, you may find yourself dreading the process. There is no need to feel that way. The job search can be rewarding and informative if it is approached correctly. If you view it as a learning experience in and of itself, one that will teach you about both yourself and your industry and lead to a rewarding employment situation, you will have benefited from the process and maximized your chances of finding what you're looking for.

You will learn about:

- job leads and where to find them
- application letters, thank-you letters, reference letters, update letters, accept and decline letters, and resignation letters, which are the crucial communication links between employer and prospective or departing employee
- résumés of various kinds: chronological and functional; print, online, and scannable
- portfolios: print and Web-based
- interviewing from both sides of the desk, both for information in preparation for applying for a job and the job interview itself

WHERE TO SEARCH

Successful job hunting requires a great deal of time and energy. One way to save time is to know where and how to find jobs. The following are the major sources to explore for good job opportunities.

School Career Counselors

If you are a student, the best place to begin your job search is on your own campus. But don't wait until you're ready to graduate to start thinking about your post-graduation plans. Begin early in your academic career. Having a good idea of what kind of work you want to do after school will help you to choose the courses you take and the programs you enroll in. You don't have to start with a well-defined idea of your career goals in order to make an appointment with a career counselor to investigate your options.

Visit or telephone the careers office before your appointment to find out what you will need to take with you to your meeting. You will probably have to have an up-to-date transcript to show the counselor. If you have prepared a résumé, take that along, too. In addition, write down whatever ideas you have

SEEKING HELP

The role of the career services office is to assist the job seeker in locating possible employers and to offer advisement on appropriate approaches and techniques for a successful job search.

—Career Resource Center, University of Central Florida

about possible career directions, being sure to include information about your willingness to relocate and your pertinent job skills and experience.

When you arrive at your appointment, the counselor will ask you many questions about your experience, talents, and interests. The counselor may ask you to undergo an aptitude evaluation, in the form of either a paper-and-pencil or computerized questionnaire. Answer as truthfully as possible. After all, the purpose of the questionnaire is to determine your interests and abilities. If you are not forthcoming about these matters, how can you expect the job prospects to fit your needs?

The counselor will review the information you have provided and offer suggestions for types of work that you may be suited for. If you arrive at the careers office with a good idea of what you are seeking, the counselor may make a few suggestions about your choice, but in either case the process will proceed the same way. Once your interests and abilities have been considered, the counselor will explain your options for finding employment. You may need further schooling to be eligible to work in your chosen field. Or you may need on-the-job or apprenticeship training. Your school may offer internships with local companies to give you a chance to try out the kind of work you want to do in an environment of training.

The jobs counselor will also have information about which companies in your field are looking for entry-level employees. If you already have some experience, you may qualify for a somewhat higher-level job. This information too will be available to you at the careers office. The counselor can give you an idea of what the salaries in your field are likely to be and what your prospects are for advancement.

After Your Careers Interview

- Follow up on the counselor's suggestions: refine your résumé, check ads (online, newspaper, journal, voice mail), and speak to your academic advisor to make sure your courses are going to prepare you for the type of work you want to do.
- Phone leads
- Attend job fairs on your campus or in other locations in your area

---

From the list provided by the counselor, you can telephone or write to companies to ask if they are accepting job applications. The human resources department of larger companies will direct you in the appropriate way to apply for their jobs. In smaller companies, you may speak with the owner, a manager, or an administrative assistant who will let you know what you should provide as part of the application procedure.

Often, representatives of larger companies visit college campuses in person on recruiting drives. The employment counselor at your school will know about these visits. And often, printed notices are posted on bulletin boards in the campus student center, the various classroom buildings, and the careers office itself. Make a habit of scanning these notices when you see them. They often provide good information about prospects you may not find out about anywhere else.

Job Fairs

In many colleges, job recruiters visit the campus to recruit new employees from the student body. Find out from your careers office when these visits are expected so you can plan to attend. When several companies send representatives on the same day, they are usually participating in a job fair. Job fairs are an excellent way to become acquainted with companies whose names may be unfamiliar to you. The nice thing about job fairs is that you don't have to know in advance which companies you want to speak with. You can go in the expectation that the companies that participate are eager to attract new employees, and you don't have to have made contact with the companies in advance for them to solicit your application.

Take along plenty of copies of your résumé when you attend the fairs, so that the recruiters have a good way of remembering you and finding you again later. Consider attaching a photo to your résumé to help the recruiter remember just which of the many students you are.

Trade Journals and Magazines

If you already have a pretty good idea of the field you will be seeking to work in, you should familiarize yourself with that field's organizations and the trade journals and magazines read by members of the profession. Become familiar with the journals and consult them frequently, since employers often will advertise job openings in a profession's key publications. For example, if you want to work in the field of mechanical engineering, you would check out the American Society of Mechanical Engineers' journal, *Mechanical Engineering*. For careers in the aerospace industry, you might consult the Society of Automotive Engineers' publication, *Aerospace Engineering*. If you want to be a plastics engineer, you could consult the Society of Plastics Engineers' *Plastics Engineering*. In the biomedical technology industry, the Association for the Advancement of Medical Instrumentation publishes the journal *Biomedical Instrumentation and Technology*.

If you want to work as an electronics engineer, you could check the publications of the IEEE Circuits and Systems Society, such as *Circuits and Devices*. For computer science, you could try the publications of the ACM, namely *Communications of the ACM*. And in chemistry, you could check the *Journal of the American Chemical Society*. If you are interested in working as a technical communicator, you would consult publications of by the Society for Technical Communication (STC). Its quarterly journal, *Technical Communication*, is mailed to the society's 24,000 members and contains a variety of job ads. The society also publishes *Intercom,* a monthly magazine that also has job ads. STC also has a variety of special interest groups that publish newsletters and often have their own discussion groups on the Internet.

Your instructors can tell you which professional journals are the primary ones in your field. Your college library will have copies of the major publications for many disciplines. And if you want to have your own copies, check to see if the organizations that publish the journals have student or introductory memberships. Very often, such memberships can get you valuable benefits at little cost while you're a student.

Newspapers

Many college students make the mistake of relying chiefly on their local newspaper or the local newspaper of the city where they hope to be employed. Typically, fewer than 20 percent of available job openings will be advertised in the paper. However, this fact does not mean that you should skip looking at ads in the paper altogether. Newspapers can be a valuable source for finding a possible job opening. And now that most newspapers publish at least a concise version—and often a full version—of their publication on the World Wide Web, you have a good chance to look over job ads for even distant locations from the comfort of your workstation at home or at school. Use these listings to find out what types of skills are in demand as you plan your coursework and prepare your portfolio. See Figure 11.1 for a sample newspaper job listing.

Employment Agencies

You might think that an employment agency is exactly the right place to start looking for a job. Actually, this path is not the first one to follow. Before

Engineer–Electrical Machine Controller resp. for design & troubleshooting electrical control boxes, mechanical analysis of industrial machinery & solving electrical service problems by phone. Deg. pref'd, exp. & strong comm. skills essential. Exc. bnft pkg w/401K. Resumes c/o HR, Peachtree Enterprises, 32 W. Main Street, Warminster, PA 18974, FAX 555-555-555. EOE.

FIGURE 11.1

Newspaper Job Listing

contacting an employment agency (or allowing yourself to be solicited by one), educate yourself about the possibilities in your job field. Speak to your friends and colleagues, your professors, and your school career counselor to find out what you should expect in terms of salary, benefits, job responsibilities, and—if you choose to go that route—agency fees. Be aware that there are different kinds of employment agencies. Many perfectly legitimate companies find and subcontract employees to other companies. The agency receives a percentage of salary—all paid by the employer—for the employee's services. In some professions in which highly skilled people are in demand, employers are more than happy to pay an employment agency to search for and place the right people. Many students in computer science, engineering, the sciences, and technical communication, for example, find jobs this way.

Other employment agencies are called career counseling or career marketing companies. You can easily find their ads in any major city newspaper. They charge you a fee to help you find a job (either an hourly rate, such as $50 to $100 an hour, or a flat charge for the service provided), and many also charge the employer if they place you in a particular job. Many of these companies are legitimate and do make a sincere effort to help you find a job; others are not.

Pitfalls of Job Agencies

Some job hunters have had bad experiences with career counseling companies that demanded excessive up-front fees and promised more than they could deliver.

- Be wary if you are asked to sign a contract requiring payment in advance.
- Avoid signing any contract with a company that offers help in exchange for 5 percent to 10 percent of your annual salary.
- Stay away from agencies that refuse to let you contact their other clients. You should be allowed to talk to other people who are using the company's services.
- Be skeptical of companies that promise access to unadvertised jobs. Many career marketing companies brag about their ability to tap into a supposedly hidden job market.
- Be careful if you are offered unlimited access to counselors. Any good career marketing company will give you an accurate assessment of the availability of its counselors, but it won't be unlimited.
- Reject agencies that insist that you are obligated to wait until they find a job for you. These agencies don't want you to find a job on your own or through another agency because then they would lose the commission.

There are many legitimate job-hunting resources. College students typically do not need to go to the expense of hiring a career counseling company. Searching for a job on your own may or may not take longer, but your own search will usually be far less expensive. Of course, if a legitimate contracting company wants to help you find a job at no cost to you, then take advantage of the extra help.

Networking

Networking—forming ties with colleagues outside of formal job contexts to exchange information or services—can be an extremely valuable source for finding out about job opportunities in your field. The longer you are in a profession, the easier it is to network. Your list of contacts will be extensive and will continue to grow. But if you are looking for your first full-time job, you may find networking a little intimidating or difficult. Networking is a process you do not need to feel apprehensive about. For a detailed discussion of networking, see Chapter 12.

For a start, you can get to know several of your professors. They often know many people in industry, and if the professors know that you are looking, they can be helpful in putting you in touch with people who might be hiring.

Earlier in the chapter you learned about the college careers office and about campus job fairs. Introducing yourself to the representatives from companies exhibiting at the job fair and speaking to a job counselor at the careers office are both forms of networking. At the very least, take some copies of your résumé with you when you expect to be among people who can pass along job leads, and take advantage of every opportunity to hand them out. Networking at a job fair requires preparation, but with some practice you can soon become an old hand at navigating the booths and the representatives.

Professional Meetings

Attending professional meetings is another excellent way to network. As an additional incentive to join, student memberships in professional organizations are often discounted, even though student members receive substantially the same benefits as regular members. Don't wait until you graduate to join the chapter of your professional organization. Become involved while you're still a student, and you will have a good basis for job searching later. The Society for Technical Communication, for example, has many student chapters; it also has professional chapters that encourage students to join. The professional members get to know the students, and the students become more involved in the profession before they graduate.

Many organizations encourage students to begin their professional affiliations while they are still in school by forming student chapters. Meetings often are held on campus. Professional organizations having student chapters include

KEEPING IN TOUCH

Get to know people around you and keep in contact with former co-workers and management staff as well as those you meet at professional meetings. Never burn your bridges. The information technology field is relatively small, and you never know who may have input on future promotions or opportunities.

—Diane J. Schneck, project leader, Kissimmee, Florida

the American Society of Mechanical Engineers (ASME), the Society of Women Engineers (SWE), the National Society of Black Engineers (NSBE), the Society of Hispanic Professional Engineers (SHPE), the American Institute of Chemical Engineers (AIChE), and the American Institute of Aeronautics and Astronautics (AIAA).

In addition to joining a society's key organizations, you can attend various local affiliated conferences and trade shows. For example, many students in technical communication attend not only the annual regional conference or national conference of the Society for Technical Communication, but also various meetings of other technical societies. Most major cities have a variety of professional societies of people who share common interests. And for the engineering professions, the IEEE has more than 300 local sections with more than 1,000 technical chapters. Ask your professor for information about professional organizations in your field.

Job Databases

Another helpful source of job information is a job database—essentially a list of job openings—available via telephone (as recorded job announcements), mail, or the Internet. Some computer databases are searchable on the Internet.

Job Databases on the Internet

<http://www.careerbuilder.com/> for nationwide job listings

<http://www.cweb.com> for CareerWeb Internet recruitment sites

<http://www.computerjobs.com> for computer jobs and career management resources

<http://www.careermag.com> for the *Career Magazine*

<http://www.headhunter.net/jobseeker/index.htm> for Headhunter.com

<http://ww1.joboptions.com/jo_main/> for online employment recruiting

<http://www.monster.com> for the Monster Board

<http://www.usajobs.opm.gov/> for government jobs and employment information

---

The amount of information that is available at these sites can be overwhelming and—like all Internet information—subject to frequent change. You will need to hone your job-searching skills so that you don't waste a lot of time looking at positions for which you are not qualified.

The Internet

In addition to attending the local and national conferences of a professional society, many people augment their knowledge of their disciplines through various mailing lists or discussion groups on the Internet. Here again, your instructors can help you find the ones that pertain to your field. There are numerous discussion groups on computer science, engineering, and the sciences. The Special Interest Group on Computer–Human Interaction (SIGCHI) (a part of the Association for Computing Machinery) has several. There are hundreds of engineering lists, such as the chemical engineering list, CHEME-L, and the civil engineering list for urban and regional planners, URBAN-L. In technical communication, many job openings are posted on the mailing list TECHWR-L. For those who are searching for a job teaching technical communication, job ads can often be found on the mailing lists for the Association of Teachers of Technical Writing (ATTW-L) and the Council for Programs in Technical and Scientific Communication (CPTSC-L).

The Internet is proving to be an invaluable resource for finding out about jobs. Just about every major company now has a Web site, and many such Web sites contain links related to job openings. In addition, various search engines and indexes are making it increasingly easy to track down job openings listed on Web sites or discussed in Usenet newsgroups.

You can also use the Internet to show off your own work and your credentials. More than a few students have been hired on the basis of their own personal Web pages and the portfolios of their work they have posted at their sites. The work you do while in school is not only good practice for work you will do after you are graduated, but can also provide prospective employers with a preview of your talents.

> **USING THE INTERNET**
>
> When I started working, electronic communications was not like it is today—getting a job was a matter of word of mouth. Now, I would tell anyone starting out to begin with the Internet. So many companies subscribe to job search sites and so many companies have their own Web sites that include employment pages.
>
> —Judith Honeywood, information designer consultant, Chicago, Illinois

JOB CORRESPONDENCE

Job correspondence includes more than just application letters and résumés. You will find that many kinds of letters can aid you during your job search. These letters share their formatting requirements with other types of business correspondence. Make sure that you know how to put together a business letter and that you are familiar with the conventions for content and placement of elements. (See Chapter 14.) In addition, since some job letters convey a request, others signal agreement, and still others express refusal, you should familiarize yourself with direct and indirect orders for letters (also covered in Chapter 14). Understanding tone is also essential for writing effective letters (see Chapter 7).

Some elements are common to most business letters; some elements are unique to the particular type of letter. The next sections will discuss the goals and fine points of certain job letters.

> **HELPING YOURSELF**
>
> Each person secures his or her own employment. The responsibility rests with the job seeker to persuade and prove to an employer that he or she is the most qualified candidate for a position.
>
> —Career Resource Center, University of Central Florida

The chief aim of an application letter is to help you get an interview.

Application Letter

You may be wondering why you need an application letter when all your pertinent information is already contained in your résumé. The reason is that your résumé is a one- or two-page summary of your achievements and background, while your application letter is the agent that introduces you to the prospective employer. The chief aim of an application letter (also called a job letter or cover letter) is to help you get an interview. Keeping this aim in mind will help you to focus on what to cover in your job letter. Unlike your résumé, which is a factual listing of your achievements, your job letter is intended to persuade the reader not only that you are a *qualified* applicant for the position, but also that you are the *best* applicant for the position. Use your application letter to highlight those parts of your background you want to emphasize. You may also use the application letter to introduce new information, data that you think will help the company view your application more favorably than everyone else's.

Some people have difficulty writing a persuasive cover letter, but that's chiefly due to a lack of extensive work experience. Once you are graduated and gain more work experience, writing the job letter often becomes easier. See Figure 11.2 for a sample job application letter.

Research the Company

Your application letters will be more effective if you can demonstrate in appropriate places in the letter some knowledge of the company, its reputation, its products, and its plans for future growth. You can gather this kind of information in many different ways. Call the company and ask to have an annual report sent to you. Use a search engine to find the company's Web site. Use standard sources in the library, such as the *Mergent* (formerly *Moody*) periodicals and *Standard and Poor's* publications, to find essential information on the company, its employees, and its products. Ask your professors and friends whether they know anything useful about the company.

Direct Your Letter to a Specific Person

Many job ads list only the title Human Resources Director or Personnel Director. Some provide only the address. Call the company to find out the name of the human resources director or personnel director. If you cannot obtain a name, consider obtaining the name of the supervisor or director of the division in the company where you hope to work and address your letter to this person. Your letter likely will be forwarded to Human Resources or Personnel if what you have written is of interest.

Write Your Application Letter

Follow all of the principles of good business letter correspondence.

- Include all of the major parts of a letter (heading, date line, inside address, salutation, body, complimentary close, and signature block).

FIGURE 11.2
Job Application Letter

1400 Green Badger Lane
Orlando, FL 32817

December 14, 2_____

Ms. Michelle Harris
Director of Personnel
Dynamic Healthcare Services
Orlando, FL 32816

Dear Ms. Harris:

I am applying for the opening you advertised in the *Orlando Sentinel* for an entry-level technical writer. As my enclosed résumé indicates, I am a senior at the University of Central Florida and will graduate in May with a Bachelor of Arts degree in English (concentration: technical writing) and a minor in Biology. As a writer with a strong interest in science, I believe I am well suited to work at Dynamic Healthcare Services.

Throughout my college career, I have held a variety of positions that have helped me to fund my college education. Most recently, I have worked for the Office of Sponsored Research and Graduate Studies as an Administrative Assistant. Through my various assignments at OSR, I have gained broad office experience that is essential to a technical writer at your company.

In addition to my part-time work, I have been a full-time student at UCF for the past two years and have achieved a 3.7 GPA in my major. To prepare myself for employment in the technical writing field, I have taken classes that teach advanced writing concepts such as Online Documentation, Techniques of Technical Documentation, Technical Report Writing, Graphics for Technical Writers, and Technical Writing Style. I am also pursuing a minor in Biology, which qualifies me further for the position because of my knowledge of biological principles. Since Dynamic Healthcare Services develops clinical information systems for use in laboratory, radiology, anatomic pathology, and anesthesiology applications, I am confident that my technical knowledge would benefit the company.

I have many computer skills, and I am able to learn new applications rapidly. I frequently use desktop publishing tools such as Word, Excel, and Adobe PageMaker. I am currently taking a course at UCF named Introduction to Computer Science in order to familiarize myself with general computing principles and applications, operating systems, and networks.

In closing, I want to stress that I have a strong desire to excel. I am very attentive to detail and maintain high standards of quality for my work. I am personable and diplomatic, and I enjoy collaborating with other writers. I realize that it is difficult for my résumé and application letter to convey the full breadth of my qualifications and skills. Would it be possible for me to meet with you to discuss what I have to contribute to your company? If so, please call me at (407) 555-7092 or e-mail me at npeters@pegasus.cc.ucf.edu.

Sincerely,

Nichola J. Peters

Nichola J. Peters

- Provide a minimum of one-inch margins on all sides.
- Use professional-quality stationery, avoiding unusually bright paper colors (such as green, yellow, pink).
- Use a high-resolution inkjet or laser printer.
- Remember to sign your name.

See Chapter 14 to learn about the standard parts of a business letter.

Create an Effective Opening

Identify how you learned about the position. For example, state whether someone told you about the job, you saw an ad in the paper (state which paper), you saw it mentioned on the Web, or you saw it listed in a trade magazine. Name-drop if possible. Perhaps a well-known member of your profession or an employee of the company told you about the opening. Mentioning the person's name will help to make your letter more noticeable than others.

State why you are writing by saying something such as, "I am applying for the opening you advertised in the *Atlanta Constitution* for a senior-level technical writer." Identify yourself, either in the opening paragraph of the letter or in the second paragraph. This strategy may be accomplished simply by writing, "I am a senior at the University of _____ and will graduate in May with a degree in _____."

Develop an Effective Middle

Mention your enclosed résumé. Often this strategy can be combined with that of identifying yourself. For example, you may write, "As my enclosed résumé indicates, I am a senior at the University of _____ and will graduate in May with a degree in _____."

Discuss your relevant work experience. If you have work experience that is pertinent to the position for which you are applying, emphasize the skills and achievements that are most applicable to the current opening. State confidently how you are qualified for the current opening because you have done similar work elsewhere. State how you believe you can make further contributions in these areas for this company.

If you have work experience that is less relevant to the particular opening, stress the values of the work experience you have. If you have experience based on unpaid work, such as work for a school course, describe that experience. Remember that all your full-time and part-time jobs have enhanced your skills in some way. If you have little or no work experience, devote more discussion to particular academic strengths.

After discussing your work experience, elaborate on your educational strengths, both major and minor, in the middle of the letter. This section may be part of the same paragraph discussing your work experience, or it may be a separate paragraph in the middle of your letter. For example, explain that your major in _____ required _____ semester hours of courses of the _____ semester hours required for a college degree. Discuss any coursework that is particularly germane to the job opening, any appropriate internships, any significant research work done for any of your professors, or any additional relevant coursework beyond the coursework for your major.

While emphasizing both your work and academic experience, mention the reasons for your interest in the company. For example, perhaps you have a special interest in one of the company's current or forthcoming products, or perhaps you know that the company has exceptional groups of employees and you would like to become part of one of the groups.

Use the "you attitude." The "you attitude" (or "you approach") means focusing on the reader and the reader's interests as much as possible. Emphasize how you believe you can make contributions to the company if you are given the opportunity. Your letter should reflect your knowledge of the company and its products wherever possible and also should convey an overall enthusiasm for the job opening throughout.

Provide an Effective Close

State that you are available for an interview at the reader's convenience. Don't restrict your availability to certain times or dates or until after final exams are over. If you are invited to an interview, you will make adjustments to your schedule accordingly.

Provide your phone number or several phone numbers (especially if you will be moving from one address to another during your job search) and your e-mail address, even though all necessary contact information should be on your résumé. Sometimes résumés are misplaced, and your cover letter may be all that is available for contacting you.

Provide a courteous ending. Emphasize, for example, your interest in working for the company. The ending "I look forward to hearing from you soon," is also acceptable if you cannot think of a more specific closing line.

Proofread Your Letter

Your letter should represent you in the best way possible. You can't afford to send out an application letter that has typos, spelling errors, punctuation errors, or errors in grammar. There are too many other applicants who will send out professional-quality letters.

Attach your résumé—with a paper clip is fine—and mail the letter and résumé in a properly addressed envelope or, if the employer requests it, send the letter and résumé as attachments to an e-mail.

Follow Up Your Letter

Follow up with a telephone call if you haven't heard from the company after two weeks. Ask whether your letter arrived and whether the intended recipient has had a chance to look it over. Request an interview if the person you are speaking to sounds receptive to that possibility.

Thank-You Letter

During the job application process you write thank-you letters as a follow-up to an interview. Thank your interviewer for having taken the time to

FIGURE 11.3

**Job Interview
Thank-You Letter**

2705 West Oak Lane
Worcester, MA 01603
August 20, 2_____

Mr. Phil Rouse, Manager
Software Documentation Department
Whitcomb Technical Solutions
4703 Haskell Rd.
Boston, MA 02122

Dear Mr. Rouse:

I am writing to thank you, Mr. Steve Jenkins, and Mr. Gray Appleton for the time you took out of your busy schedules to interview me this past Monday.

Once again I must say how impressed I am with your staff, your company products, and your company procedures. I am familiar with most of the companies in the Boston area, and your company is easily the most advanced for what it is doing with its software products and documentation.

During our interview, I forgot to tell you that I was under consideration for election to the President's Leadership Council. I just received a letter today notifying me that I have been selected as a member of this council. Every year this council chooses only a handful of students as members, and I am delighted that I have been fortunate enough to be chosen this year.

I am confident I can contribute a great deal to your company, and I hope I have the opportunity to prove myself.

I look forward to hearing from you.

Sincerely,

Sarah Chase

Sarah Chase

interview you. The proper time to send a thank-you letter is immediately after the interview.

See Figure 11.3 for an example of a job interview thank-you letter. In the opening, state simply that you are writing to thank the reader for the interview. If possible, try to mention the names of all of the people who were involved in your interview. You may address the letter to the principal interviewer and then, in the opening paragraph, extend your thanks to the others who took time to talk to you and to answer your questions. If you were impressed by the people, various projects, or company products, use the middle of the letter to say so. This kind of thank-you letter also provides the perfect opportunity to repeat how much you are interested in working for the company and to stress once again your strengths and qualifications for the position. You may want to emphasize these points in the closing of the letter in addition to providing a courteous ending.

Reference Letter

As a college student, you will often ask others to write a reference letter or a letter of recommendation for you. Perhaps you need such a letter for a job while you're in college or a full-time job when you're about to graduate. Or perhaps you need it as a required item for admission into a graduate program. Sometimes you will see these reference letters and perhaps receive a copy; other times you may never see the letter you ask someone else to write. When you ask others to write reference letters for you, be sure to ask people who you are confident will write strong letters for you. See Figure 11.4 for an example of a school letter of recommendation.

At certain times of the year, your professors may be inundated with requests for letters of recommendation. Since you are requesting a favor, try to lighten the burden by providing a stamped, pre-addressed envelope for the recommender to use, along with a brief list of the items you would like your professor to remember about you while the letter is being written. List the pertinent courses you have taken and the grades you received (if they were good). If you have been involved in service clubs or other organizations on campus, jot this information down for the professor, too. And if there is any other information you would like mentioned in the letter, let your professor know about it. Include a copy of your résumé with your request.

Update Letter

Like thank-you letters, update letters are helpful for maintaining your visibility to those with whom you interviewed or who are otherwise responsible for hiring someone for the position. An update letter may simply inform someone at the company that you have changed your address or phone number. Or it may stress some additional strengths that you forgot to mention during the interview. Or perhaps you were dissatisfied with the way you answered a particular question. The update letter provides an opportunity to give a better answer to the question or to answer a question you couldn't answer during the interview. Finally, an update letter may call attention to some achievements that have occurred since the interview. Perhaps you received an award or other distinction at your university, or perhaps you had a recent success with a project at your current job. Any of these situations would provide excuse enough to write an update letter. See Figure 11.5 for a sample update letter.

FIGURE 11.4

School Letter of Recommendation

May 11, 2____

To Whom It May Concern:

Carolyn B. is applying for admission into the master's program in Women's Studies at Northern State University and asked me to write a letter of recommendation. I am delighted to do so.

I have known Carolyn for ten years. She was a student in three of my technical communication classes while completing a minor in this field and a major in Organizational Communication. The three classes she took with me are ENC 4293 Technical Documentation I, ENC 4295 Technical Documentation III, and LIT 4433 Survey of Technical and Scientific Literature.

I have taught many outstanding students during my 20 years of full-time college teaching, and Carolyn is easily one of the best students I have ever taught. She excelled in all three of my classes. I was so confident in her writing, editing, and leadership abilities that I asked her to serve as class editor for the *Style Guide and Standards* manual created in the Technical Documentation I class. Carolyn's many skills assured that this manual was a quality product and one that was finished on time despite many difficulties.

Carolyn also repeatedly demonstrated her keen intelligence and communication skills in my discussion class, Survey of Technical and Scientific Literature. The course not only examines the varying prose styles of many classics, but also challenges many underlying assumptions concerning science and technology. Carolyn welcomed the class debates and contributed significantly to many lively discussions.

Because I have kept in touch with Carolyn since she graduated in 1991, I have become acquainted with her views on many issues. I can assure you that she definitely has a strong commitment to representing women and women's issues in all kinds of professional circles. And she certainly has the determination, intelligence, discipline, and communication skills necessary to succeed in even the most demanding graduate program. For all of these reasons, I highly recommend that you admit her into your program.

Sincerely,

Bob Smith

Bob Smith
Professor
Technical Communication

The Update Letter

- In the opening, state that you are writing to provide an update on whatever the topic is.
- In the middle of the letter, elaborate briefly on the topic.
- In the closing, thank the reader for taking the time to read your correspondence.

FIGURE 11.5
Update Letter

34 Sala Drive
Boston, MA 02107
August 21, 2____

Mrs. Stella Warner
Director of Human Resources
Whitcomb Technical Solutions
4703 Haskell Rd.
Boston, MA 02122

Dear Mrs. Warner:

As you know, I recently applied for an opening in the Software Documentation Division of your company. I am writing to let you know I have recently changed my address and home phone number.

My new address is 34 Sala Drive, Boston, MA 02107. My new home phone is 617-555-0270. I wanted you to have this information in case you had to get in touch with me before the scheduled interview.

Sincerely,

Troy Adkins

Troy Adkins

Accept/Decline Letter

In an acceptance letter you accept an interview offer, a job offer, an offer of a promotion, or some other offer for professional advancement. One of the most common purposes for an acceptance letter is to accept a job offer. Even if you accept the job offer over the phone, you still have to write a letter verifying your start date and starting salary. This letter sometimes precedes and some-times follows a letter from the company setting out some of the same points.

FIGURE 11.6

**Letter Accepting
a Job Offer**

34 Sala Drive
Boston, MA 02107
August 30, 2____

Mrs. Stella Warner
Director of Human Resources
Whitcomb Technical Solutions
4703 Haskell Rd.
Boston, MA 02122

Dear Mrs. Warner:

Thank you for your telephone call earlier today offering me the technical writer position in the
Software Documentation Department of your company. As I told you over the phone, I am
delighted to be offered this position, and, again, I gladly accept the offer.

To review the details, you mentioned that my starting date is Tuesday, September 4, and my
starting salary is $32,000 a year. Please take a few moments to verify these facts in a letter
to me.

I look forward to working at Whitcomb Technical Solutions.

Sincerely,

Troy Adkins

Troy Adkins

The acceptance letter is a way of ensuring that you will receive something
from the company in writing that verifies the terms of the job offer. It's very
important to have this information in writing, and you should make every effort to have a representative of the company provide you this information in
tangible form. See Figure 11.6 for an example of a job acceptance letter.

In the opening, thank the person you are writing to for the offer. State the date of the offer and that you are happy to accept the offer. In the middle of the letter, review any important details such as the start date, meeting place, and, if possible, the negotiated salary. In the closing, state that you are looking forward to beginning your job with the company.

Of course, you should not accept a job that isn't right for you (although you should not think that your first job will necessarily be a perfect, high-paying job). The purpose of a refusal letter is to decline a job offer or some other important job opportunity. As a college student who is about to graduate, you may feel fortunate to be offered any kind of job in your field. However, students in the scientific and technical professions frequently face choices among several job offers. Students often ask how they can politely decline one job offer and accept another or how they can decline one job offer even though they have no other offer. There are specific strategies that you can follow for properly declining a job offer if you feel it is not right for you.

In this kind of letter you should use an indirect instead of a direct pattern. (See Chapter 14 for more information about direct and indirect patterns in correspondence.) An indirect pattern means that you do not state your intention to decline the job in the opening paragraph. Instead, open the refusal letter by acknowledging any previous correspondence or other kind of communication (phone conversation, fax, e-mail, and so on) concerning the job offer. Then, in the middle of the letter, discuss any pluses in working for the company. You may then mention, for example, that you have another offer from a different company or that you have chosen to wait for other possible opportunities. In brief, politely and tactfully discuss any good reasons for declining the current opportunity, and then state that because of these reasons, you regretfully decline the job offer. In the closing, look to the future. Stress, for example, that you look forward to seeing the reader and other employees of the company at various trade shows or in other professional circumstances.

Be careful to remain pleasant and professional when you write a letter declining a job offer. It is not necessary to be blunt about your reasons for declining. The people you are writing to may be the same colleagues you will see at conferences, organization meetings, or across a classroom from you in graduate school. In fact, the job you decline today may be with the company you take a job with later in your career. Consider the people you met as you considered taking a job at this company to be possible leads for new jobs or other help to you in the future. See Figure 11.7 for an example of a letter declining a job offer.

Resignation Letter

People typically change jobs often during the course of a career, and many people have more than one career during a lifetime. It is almost inevitable that you will have to write a letter of resignation at least once.

CHOOSING THE ETHICAL PATH

You have an obligation not only to the company whose offer you are declining, but also to your peers and other graduates from your university who will follow in your footsteps. If you don't properly decline a job offer, you could end up making the company reluctant to interview any future candidates from your university.

FIGURE 11.7

**Letter Declining
a Job Offer**

34 Sala Drive
Boston, MA 02107
August 30, 2____

Mrs. Stella Warner
Director of Human Resources
Whitcomb Technical Solutions
4703 Haskell Rd.
Boston, MA 02122

Dear Mrs. Warner:

Thank you for your letter of August 27 informing me that I have been offered the position as technical writer in the Software Documentation Department of your company. I am very pleased that your company has chosen to extend this offer to me.

Unfortunately, I must regretfully decline this good opportunity. This morning I accepted the offer of a position with Orion Software. Both Whitcomb Technical Solutions and Orion have a great deal to offer any employee, but I feel that Orion Software is the better choice for me.

I want to thank you for taking so much time with me and, again, for offering me the opportunity to work at such a fine company.

Sincerely,

Troy Adkins

Troy Adkins

It's generally considered a professional obligation to give your employer at least two weeks' notice if you plan to quit a job, and the letter of resignation is your formal statement about this matter. Also, if the circumstances of your departure allow for it, you should have a face-to-face meeting with your supervisor to announce your plans before submitting the letter. However, bad feel-

FIGURE 11.8
Resignation Letter

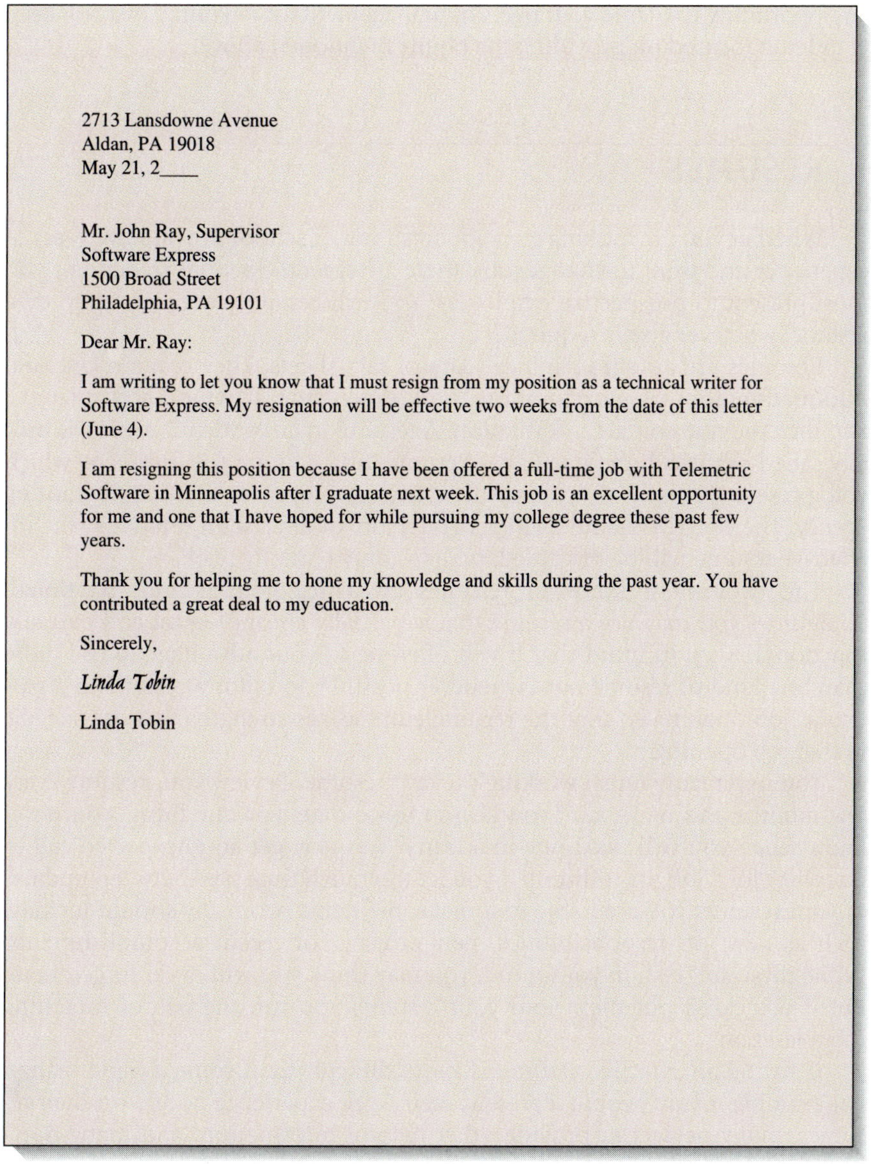

2713 Lansdowne Avenue
Aldan, PA 19018
May 21, 2____

Mr. John Ray, Supervisor
Software Express
1500 Broad Street
Philadelphia, PA 19101

Dear Mr. Ray:

I am writing to let you know that I must resign from my position as a technical writer for
Software Express. My resignation will be effective two weeks from the date of this letter
(June 4).

I am resigning this position because I have been offered a full-time job with Telemetric
Software in Minneapolis after I graduate next week. This job is an excellent opportunity
for me and one that I have hoped for while pursuing my college degree these past few
years.

Thank you for helping me to hone my knowledge and skills during the past year. You have
contributed a great deal to my education.

Sincerely,

Linda Tobin

Linda Tobin

ings on both sides may be involved; if so, a resignation letter suffices to replace any face-to-face meeting. (See Figure 11.8.)

A resignation letter states that you are resigning, offers reasons for your resignation, specifies your last of day of employment, and provides a courteous
close. Aim for a serious, professional tone throughout. Avoid using the letter as

an opportunity to blame your peers or management for anything. Instead, keep your letter focused on providing the points mentioned above.

RÉSUMÉS

Whether you are looking for a job fresh out of school or you have years of experience and want to change jobs, there are several essential credentials you must present to prospective employers. You will certainly need an up-to-date résumé, whatever else is required.

Résumés are autobiographical data or fact sheets. They contain essential information about your education, work experience, activities, and interests, and they provide contact information. A résumé in an academic setting is usually called a curriculum vitae (c.v.). Résumés and c.v.s are the means by which you present yourself to your prospective employer or a stipend-granting agency. The effective résumé will get you a job, or at least an interview; the ineffective résumé will be discarded, perhaps only partially read.

The two major kinds of résumés are chronological and functional. Sometimes you may use a résumé that is partially chronological and partially functional. Keep in mind that it will often be to your advantage to use more than one kind of résumé and, whenever possible, to tailor a résumé to a particular job opening so that the résumé emphasizes strengths that are specific to that job opening.

You never truly finish working on your résumé. Review your résumé every few months and make sure you keep it up-to-date. For one thing, you never know when you will need one in a hurry. You may get an unexpected call to interview for a job. In addition, if you let too much time pass between updates of your résumé, you are liable to forget some items you really should include, such as new job responsibilities, new projects, or recent accomplishments. While these are fresh in your mind, you may think you will never forget them. But if you don't put them into your résumé, you run the risk of forgetting them later on.

Creating an effective résumé is more difficult than some people realize. For example, many people represent their work experience poorly on their résumés, many neglect to provide other helpful information, and many don't devote enough attention to making their résumés easy to read. Creating an effective résumé requires numerous drafts before you achieve a balance of content and design.

General Requirements for Résumés

There are certain conventions you will follow when putting together your résumé. Using standard conventions does not mean that your résumé cannot be distinctive. In fact, you want your résumé to be noticed. But the notice, to get you the job, has to be a favorable notice. Include the information the prospective employer expects to find, generally in the format and places the employer expects to find it. That is the way to make sure that your qualifications are fully appreciated by the people reading your résumé. When you begin to create your résumé, you may find it useful to use your word processor's résumé template and then modify the result to suit your needs and preferences.

Contact Information

The first thing the reader will want to see is your contact information. That includes your name, address, telephone number, fax number (if you have one), and e-mail address. You can direct the reader's eyes to your name by displaying it in a larger type size than the rest of the elements in the résumé. Center or left-justify your name. Below your name, provide your address and the rest of the contact information. These items should be in a smaller type size than your name.

Job Objective

Next provide a job-objective statement so that your readers know what your immediate employment goal is. This statement could and should be tailored to the specific job you will be applying for. When you submit your résumé to several companies whose jobs bear different job descriptions, make sure that your résumé's job-objective statement reflects the particular job at that company. People who read résumés often say that they are bothered when someone doesn't provide a job objective. Don't make the human resources person guess what your employment goals are. State them up front. After all, if you don't know what job you are applying for, how should the prospective employer know?

Use a specific statement such as, "Seeking a position as a technical writer or editor in the aerospace industry" or "Seeking a position as a software engineer in the biomedical and pharmaceutical industry." Another way to word the job-objective statement is to go right to the job description itself: "Technical writer in the paper manufacturing industry," for example, or "Applications/database programmer in the banking industry." In that case, "Seeking a position as a" is implied.

Notice that these job objectives are specific about the type of position and the industry. When appropriate, you may also be specific about the department in which you would like to work.

Education

If your work experience is not extensive (three or four career-related jobs), discuss your education before you discuss your work experience. Omit high-school education from your résumé, unless you attended a special technical high school. If you have any special certificates or licenses, you could list them here. If you have an associate of arts degree or an associate of science degree, list it on your résumé and provide the name of the institution, the location, and the month and year you received the degree. Provide the same information for any four-year college degree. If you won't be graduating for a semester or two, simply use wording such as "Expected month/year." If you don't have a lot of work experience to emphasize, you may want to call attention to secondary academic strengths by listing, for example, a minor in addition to your major, specialized courses, an internship or co-op work experience (or discuss this under Work Experience instead), and grade-point average (if good: 3.0 or better).

Work Experience

For your work experience you should provide the job title, the company name and location, and the start and end date for each position. (Use "to present" to indicate the end date of your current job if you are working at the present time.) Make sure there are no gaps in the dates you list. If there are—representing times of unemployment, for example—account for them honestly. A gap in dates sends up a red flag to your readers. They will wonder what you were doing and why you didn't mention it.

Use action verbs to list in phrase form three or more specific job duties for each job, and emphasize the job duties that are related to the job for which you are currently applying. Also list any specific contributions or work-related achievements. It may also be helpful to indicate which jobs have been full-time and part-time. This part of the résumé becomes easier to write as you acquire more experience.

Résumé Action Verbs

achieved	adapted	administered	advised
arranged	constructed	controlled	coordinated
created	designed	determined	developed
directed	established	evaluated	formulated
guided	handled	implemented	instituted
maintained	managed	mentored	modeled
monitored	negotiated	organized	planned
programmed	provided	recommended	recruited
represented	resolved	selected	supervised
trained			

Of course, emphasize career-related jobs as much as possible or any job that specifically relates to the opening for which you are applying. If you are a college student and have had only part-time jobs that are unrelated to your career, it's still helpful to list these jobs and describe them at least briefly. For example, you may simply state, "Held a variety of part-time jobs including cook, waiter, and salesperson to help pay for 75 percent of my education."

Specialized Experience

If you are applying for a position in a technical field, you may also want to have a separate section titled "Computer Skills" or "Computer Experience." Here simply provide a listing of your chief software and platform experience. Extensive familiarity with e-mail is so common that it should not be listed on your résumé as a separate computer skill.

For a position in the science disciplines, list your research and laboratory experience, if relevant. And if you have coauthored any published papers, mention those too.

If you are majoring in a writing field such as technical communication or journalism, you may want to have a separate main section titled "Writing Experience" or "Writing Projects." Here you should list in reverse chronological order—most recent to oldest—the specific titles of your projects and publications. Place titles in italics (for manuals, brochures, and magazine titles) or in quotation marks (for article titles).

Achievements, Awards, Activities and Interests, and Professional Memberships

If appropriate, provide a section titled something like "Achievements," "Awards," or "Activities and Interests." List any academic honors and memberships in campus organizations. Describe any extracurricular and community activities, and mention any personal interests that will help your reader to have a better idea of who you are. If you belong to any professional societies, list them under "Professional Memberships." Listing such memberships shows a commitment to your discipline.

References

At the bottom of the résumé, state that references are available on request. If you have space, you may list three or four references directly on the résumé. Remember that it is a courtesy to ask before providing someone's name as a reference. List only those people who have agreed to provide references for you. Once you have obtained permission, provide each person's name, job title, company or organization, address, phone number, and e-mail address (if available). If you prefer, you may instead use a separate "List of References" on another page. Provide complete information about your references in one or two well-designed columns.

Availability

You may provide a date (month and year) for your résumé if you want, along with information such as "Willing to relocate" and "Available for employment immediately" or "Available for employment after [month]."

Designing Your Résumé

When you have finally listed all of the relevant information, then focus on the design of your résumé. The design choices that you make for this document are important, and you should consider design elements as carefully as you considered content and organizational elements. See Chapter 8 for extensive information on this topic.

Résumé Design

- Provide a minimum one-inch margin on all four sides. Too many résumés crowd the margins. You'll need to consider many factors—such as point sizes, spacing, punctuation, and styles—to help you place the essential information on one page.

- Use easily readable fonts. Some fonts are too difficult to read easily, and others are too boring (Courier, for example). For scannable résumés you may need to choose more "everyday" fonts rather than the more artistic or interesting ones.

- Stick to two or three fonts that look good together. Devote some attention to the font you will use for your name; consider a different font for the contact information and headings. Use an easy-to-read font for the body of your résumé. Avoid mixing more than three fonts on the page.

- Don't use print sizes that are too large or too small. Any type that

is smaller than 8 point will be too difficult to read, and point sizes larger than 24 point may be inappropriate. (See the "Typography" section in Chapter 8 for an explanation of point sizes.)

- Place major headings flush left, or center them on the page. Use a consistent font and point size for the headings. Leave enough space before and after the headings to make it easy for your reader to skim the résumé.

- Use styles (bold, italics) to call attention to job titles, company names, or other important information. Use these styles consistently for the same kinds of information, but don't overdo it. Having too many emphasized words dilutes the effect.

- Avoid clutter. Placing too many lines of text together makes the résumé more difficult to read and less visually appealing.

- Use consistent punctuation throughout the résumé.

After you have printed a draft of your complete and well-designed résumé, ask several people to critique it for readability, information completeness, and design effectiveness, and then make any necessary changes. When you finish your final draft and are sure that the résumé is free of errors, print multiple copies on high-quality paper. Use conservative paper colors—white, cream, or gray. Consider using matching stationery for your cover letters.

FIGURE 11.9

Chronological Résumé

Gerald Melendez

427 Vista Trail; Plymouth, MI 48170; (734) 555-2627; gmelendez@email.com

Objective	Seeking a position as a technical writer or editor.
Education	Bachelor of Arts degree in English. Michigan State University. May 1986.
Work Experience	
1992 to Present	Senior Technical Writer. *Institute for Simulation and Training.* Southfield, MI. Edit a variety of technical documents including grant proposals and reports.
1990–1992	Senior Technical Writer. *Credit Card Software, Inc.* Troy, MI. Documented credit card software for programmers and computer operators. Included flowcharts, program narratives, files and records, job steps, and control cards. Used Vollie on the IBM mainframe to scan COBOL source listings and copybooks.
1989–1990	Senior Technical Writer/Trainer. *Schoolcraft Community College.* Livonia, MI. Worked as a writer on a federal grant helping develop training materials for in-house employees for a local software company. Produced a task-oriented workbook to enhance and explain how the software worked and how customers used it.
1988–1989	Senior Technical Writer. *Software Design Group.* Southfield, MI. Worked as consultant organizing and revising database administrator's guide.
1986–1987	Senior Technical Writer. *Travelers/EBS, Inc.* Northville, MI. Documented insurance software to produce user guides, documented hardware, and administered new releases.
1984–1986	Technical Writer. *Dynamic Control Corporation.* Reford, MI. Documented software for hospital systems. Produced user guides, administrative guides, and reports manuals.
1983–1984	Technical Writer. *Assessment Designs, Inc.* Southfield, MI. Developed exercises for assessment centers, included writing scripts. Role played for assessment of candidates for promotion in major companies.
Computer Skills	Word, PowerPoint, RoboHelp, PageMaker, Excel, HTML.
Honors	Phi Beta Kappa and Cum Laude graduate in 1986.
References	Available on request.

Printed Résumés—Chronological Organization

In a chronological résumé, you provide traditional headings: education, work experience, writing experience, computer skills, personal data, and references—each arranged in reverse chronological order. For example, for work experience you provide your most recent job, then your next most recent job, and so on. In this kind of résumé, emphasize the dates and duties of each position. See Figure 11.9 for an example of a chronological résumé.

When preparing a chronological résumé:

- **Use conventional headings and place them in a standard order.** For example, use "Work Experience," "Employment History," or "Experience"; don't use headings such as "How I've Paid My Bills." Readers expect elements of a résumé to appear in a particular order: name, contact information, job objective (optional), education, work experience, personal data, and references.
- **Use reverse chronological order.** Use most-recent-to-past order for the information you provide in each section of the chronological résumé unless there is a good reason to bend this rule. For example, under "Education" list your four-year college degree before your community college degree. Under "Experience," list your most recent job first. However, you may list another job first if it is more relevant to the position for which you are applying.
- **Use phrases, rather than complete sentences.** Phrases make it easier for readers to skim your résumé. When putting the phrases together, make sure that they are consistent and parallel. Read them over to make sure that they sound right when they are put next to each other. If you have to use abbreviations, be sure they are not potentially unclear or confusing—for example, for specialized degrees or professional societies.
- **Provide accurate, thorough, and honest information.** Such detail includes dates for your degrees, training, certificates, jobs, achievements in college and in the workplace, awards, scholarships, professional memberships, and other distinctions (for example, Dean's List or honor-society memberships).
- **Limit your résumé to one page, if possible.** Don't provide too much information. If you must use two pages, the content of the information must justify the extra page. The exception to the two-page rule is for a curriculum vitae (c.v.). These can be quite lengthy to highlight the many papers the applicant has published and the number of committees on which the applicant has served. Unless you are preparing a c.v. for an academic position, limit yourself to one or two pages.
- **Don't provide too little information.** Too many people neglect to discuss important job skills, important secondary academic strengths, important achievements or awards, and other kinds of potentially relevant or helpful information.

CHOOSING THE ETHICAL PATH

Don't lie or distort information. Don't inflate a grade-point average if you choose to provide one on your résumé. Don't list degrees you haven't earned, skills you don't possess, memberships you can't claim, or achievements or awards to which you are not entitled.

Printed Résumés—Functional Organization

In a functional résumé (also known as a skills and accomplishments résumé) you use headings that draw attention to your key strengths—management skills, technical skills, selected professional achievements, and qualifications. See Figure 11.10 for an example of a functional résumé.

FIGURE 11.10
Functional Résumé

Seeta Narayan

1452 Terrace Drive; Baldwin, NY 11510; (516) 555-6104; Fax 555-2717

Dynamic professional with eight years of progressive experience in computer project planning and management, corporate training program development, documentation, and systems analysis and design. Innovative problem solver who takes initiative, works independently as appropriate, and also enjoys teamwork.

Areas of Expertise

Needs Definition; Training; Communication & Motivation; Program Development & Evaluation; Technical Writing & Editing; Translating Concept to Reality

Accomplishments

Management/Project Implementation

Managed major projects and information systems teams of 3 to 12 members including department managers; managed medical practices.

Planned, installed, and supported mainframe and personal computer systems; analyzed current business, needed outcomes, and costs/benefits; determined policy/procedure changes; designed and tested software; converted and monitored systems and their use. Maintained stable accounts receivable through conversion.

Provided consultant services and 24-hour customer support for 4 hospitals.

Initiated orientation program and manual, enhancing new employee value to organization.

Designed marketing materials which were used in proposals.

Training/Technical Writing/Editing

Developed training and inservice programs: trained classes and individuals; trained 100% staff with 97% success rate.

Wrote training reference manual; wrote organization-wide training proposal.

Coordinated training for 5-state region: designed annual survey of client and internal training needs; published annual training calendar; trained the trainers; designed client newsletter. Enhanced public relations between organization and clients.

Taught computer applications: healthcare-specific; Lotus 1-2-3 2.0; WordPerfect 5.1; Project Workbench; Stress and Time Management.

Electronic Résumés

Today, even if you have a well-designed traditional print résumé, you will find it useful to have several well-designed online résumés, too. Consider, for example, designing at least one online résumé for your home page on the Web (many companies look at home pages to find qualified applicants) and another kind of online résumé for various electronic scanning technologies.

FIGURE 11.10

Functional Résumé
(continued)

Community Resource Development

Initiated training, apprenticeship, and placement program for household workers: wrote successful grant proposal; secured generous in-kind contributions from professional, business, and academic sectors, with no refusals; advised curriculum design.

Program objectives were met: skills, pay, and fringe benefits were raised for graduates. Improved skills and increased business knowledge led to three minority-owned businesses. Well-publicized program instrumental in improving the working conditions of household workers throughout the community.

Professional Background

Long Island Institute of Photography, Rockville Centre, NY. 1991 to present.
Registrar & Computer Consultant.

Nassau Community College, Manhasset, NY. 1991 to present.
Adjunct Faculty, Community Education.

Mercy Hospital, Rockville Centre, NY. 1986 to 1990.
Project Leader, Information Services.

Hospital of the University of Pennsylvania, Philadelphia, PA. 1985.
Systems Analyst, Management Information Systems.

Outsourced Medical Systems, Philadelphia, PA. 1984 to 1985.
Regional Education Coordinator.

Education

Bachelor of Science degree in Public Administration, 1983
Hofstra University
Garden City, NY

References

Available on request.

Online Résumés

Your online résumé will probably be one you design for your home page. See Figure 11.11 (page 398) for an example of an online résumé. In this résumé, you don't have to use the standard order of a print résumé. Instead, you can organize the résumé alphabetically by topic or in any other logical order.

Functional Résumés: Sample Skills

Computer science:	development, coding, maintenance
Science:	research, experiments, reports, and papers
Technical communication:	writing, editing, illustrating, designing
	or
	print, multimedia, online/Web projects
	or
	brochures, manuals, newsletters

The reason you have this flexibility is that readers of your online résumé do not have to look at it sequentially. Since it is online, you will provide hypertext links from a list of contents at the top to the various sections such as Education, Work Experience, and Awards and Accomplishments. The various sections can appear on the same Web page or can be separated into separate pages. Consider including samples of your portfolio linked to the corresponding entry in Work Experience or School Projects.

When designing an online résumé, consider all the limitations inherent in viewing material on a screen instead of on a printed page. Make sure that your résumé is both readable and attractive to look at. View it on several different browsers operating on several different platforms. Review Chapter 8 for more suggestions on creating online documents.

Scannable Résumés

One of the technologies that employment agencies use, résumé management systems, scans electronic résumé databases for certain kinds of résumés according to specific criteria. These criteria vary, based on the needs of the company. When the search terms are entered by the operator, the program looks through the résumé database for those terms. If your résumé contains the looked-for term or terms, it will show up as a match for the search. Because this practice is now common, you need to know how to make at least one online résumé as computer and scanner friendly as you can to increase the chances that you will be identified as a good candidate. See Figure 11.12 for an example of a scannable résumé.

You don't abandon all the qualities of a good print résumé or a good online résumé designed for the Web when you create a scannable résumé. You just place more emphasis on some topics and take a different approach with others. The traditional job market still requires you to have and use multiple versions of print résumés, most of which are read in 30 seconds or less by prospective employers. Adding the online résumé to your job-seeking effort increases your chances of being hired, especially in instances in which certain companies are doing at least their initial screening electronically.

FIGURE 11.11
Online Résumé

John Doe

American Avenue #1 Any City, Any State 99999
E-mail: johndoe@xxxxx.xxx
Phone: (xxx) xxx-xxxx
My Homepage

Objective
Seeking full time, entry-level position in computer sales.

Education
University of America, Any City, State

- Bachelor's of Science in Liberal Arts, Expected graduation spring of 2000
- Minor in math

Any Community College

- Completed Associate of Arts, 1998

Leadership Experiences
Communications Chair, Any Fraternity, 1999

- Maintain the involvement of members by keeping them informed of all events

Fundraising Chair, Any Fraternity, 1998

- Responsible for maintaining contacts in the private sector for events
- Monitored members and kept records of events

Executive Committee of New Members, Any Fraternity, 1996–1998

- Ensuring the education and history of new members
- Responsible for coordinating events such as retreats
- Mentoring of new members

Work Experience
Specific Computer Corporation: Internship Sept. 1999–May 2000

- Support the front office staff with computer related problems

Second Restaurants: Corporate and store trainer, Jan. 1998–May 2000

- Responsible for the training of servers and managers
- Maintaining services standards and assistance to new managers

First Restaurants: Trained in all areas, July 1996–Jan. 1998

- Management of money and transactions of coworkers
- Ensuring quality in service and food

Extracurricular Activities
Contributions to the community include:

- Muscular Dystrophy Association: volunteer from 1993 to present
- Zora Neale Hurston Festival for the arts and humanities: volunteer 1999

Involved in several athletic and social activities, which include:

- Flag football, Basketball, Racquetball, Billiards, and Darts

Other Competencies

- Java, C, and HTML
- Computer proficient in MS Office '97 and Excel
- Bilingual in English and Spanish

References upon Request

Back to Top

FIGURE 11.12
Scannable Résumé

Miguel Gomez
4336 Maple Street
City, State 12345
E-mail: mgomez@xxxxx.com
Phone: (xxx) xxx-xxxx

Objective
    Software sales for business applications

Education
    Johnston State University, City, State
        Bachelor's of Arts in Communications, expected graduation 2002
    Martinsville Community College, City, State
        Associate of Arts, 2000

Leadership Experiences
    Communications Chair, Student Government Association, 1999–2000
        Maintained community involvement of club activities
    Fundraising Chair, Student Government Association, 1998–1999
        Distributed event information to the private sector for events
        Monitored members and kept records of events
    Executive Committee, Student Government Association, 1998–1999
        Oversaw the education and adjustment of new members
        Coordinated events such as retreats
        Mentored new members

Work Experience
    Computer Corporation: Computer Assistant, March 2000–present
        Managed business computer–related areas and customer service
    Tallow's Restaurant: Corporate and store trainer, January 1998–February 2000
        Trained servers and managers
    Italian Garden Restaurant: Trainee in all areas, July 1996–December 1998
        Ensured the quality of customer service and food

Extracurricular Activities
    Contributions to the community:
        Muscular Dystrophy Association: volunteer, 1993 to present
        Zora Neale Hurston Festival: volunteer, 1999
    Athletic and social activities:
        Flag football, Basketball, Racquetball, Billiards, Darts, and Tennis

Other Competencies
    Java, C, and HTML
    Computer proficient in MS Office, Excel, and Access
    Bilingual in English and Spanish

References upon Request

Word Choices for Scannable Résumés

- Use nouns as often as possible, since in scannable résumés, nouns dominate. Using nouns makes your résumé more easily searchable by a computer that is programmed to look for keywords.

(continued)

- Use keywords effectively. Keywords are the key for the scannable résumé. Use keywords for education, experience, interpersonal skills, technical skills, and tool skills that are most likely to be searched for in your discipline. The more keywords you use, the more likely that your résumé will be selected. Try to use the keywords and phrases that are most often used in your profession. Stated another way, maximize the use of your profession's jargon or buzzwords. Look at help-wanted ads in your field to see the buzzwords that appeal to employers.
- Keep abbreviations to a minimum.

Buzzwords

Business: account management, manager, sales, advertising

Computer Science: specific computer program names such as Pascal, C++, Visual Basic

Technical Communication: specific skills areas such as online help, Web-page design, graphic design, technical editing; tools skills such as RoboHELP, Adobe PageMaker, FrameMaker, Microsoft Word.

Designing a Scannable Résumé

- Place your name first with your contact information on a separate line.
- Keep the design simple. Scanners will have difficulty with graphics and tables, for example.
- Help the scanner to read the résumé. For example, left-justify the entire résumé. Avoid tabs, hard returns, italics, underlining, or bold. Avoid horizontal or vertical lines. Avoid parentheses, brackets, or other unusual punctuation marks.
- Stick to common fonts such as Helvetica, Times, Palatino, and Courier.
- Restrict the size of your font to the 10- to 14-point type range.
- Use a single-column format.
- Use page length to your advantage. Limiting your résumé to a page is less of a concern in designing résumés to be scanned.

PORTFOLIOS

Your portfolio is the tangible record of the projects and papers you have worked on. It is the permanent record of your accomplishments in school or on the job, and it can be your ticket to future employment. A piece of work needn't have been created entirely by you to be included in it, but do not incorporate someone else's work into your portfolio without giving credit to the other person.

An increasing trend among college students is to provide a version of their portfolio on the Web. Many students have personal Web pages, and in addition to providing information about themselves and their favorite links, they are providing online résumés and samples of their work linked to their home page. Samples may include papers, group work, design work, computer code, and so on.

Creating Your Portfolio

- Always ask for extra copies of documents you produce so that you can include them in your portfolio. Some writers actually put a statement in their contracts stipulating that they receive a certain number of copies of the documents they produce.

- Like your résumé, your portfolio should be updated periodically to keep it current.

- Logically organize your portfolio pieces, and include a table of contents. You may organize items to reflect different skills, such as writing, editing, illustrating, and designing documents, or to present different document types, such as brochures or newsletters, in different sections. If you have worked in several fields, you might choose to organize your pieces to reflect those fields.

- Be sure to use only originals or good-quality copies of the documents you include. Poor-quality photocopies will seriously detract from a professional image.

- Consider including a section on awards and honors.

- Use graphic elements—color, rules, bullets, and other icons—to tie together the pages of your portfolio. Background paper in a muted color may help to set off your documents and make your entire portfolio appear more unified.

- Annotate the pieces that you include in your portfolio. White cards or labels can be affixed to the bottom corners of pages to highlight relevant information, such as your role in a group project or an award won by a document you produced. Do not annotate the obvious; you should not need to tell your reader that a brochure is a brochure.

- Consider showing more than one view of documents such as brochures so that the reader can see your design skills.

- Make sure documents are firmly placed in sleeves so that they do not slip around and look messy and disorganized. Use rubber cement or a glue stick to set the documents securely in their places if they tend to shift around.

- Never leave your portfolio with a prospective employer. Consider creating a small packet of documents and other relevant materials, such as your résumé and references, that you can leave behind after an interview.

- If given the chance, use your portfolio to talk your way through an interview and demonstrate what you have accomplished.

INTERVIEWING

Interviewing skills are essential for researching information, regardless of what you need the information for. The interviewing skills covered here require many of the same approaches you take in researching information through other people. After all, you're still dealing with people, and whenever you're dealing with other people through interviewing or any other kind of communication, you have to use all the skills at your disposal to communicate successfully.

The job interview is just one type of interview, but it is probably the one that almost everyone encounters at some time during a working life. Most people are nervous about job interviews. They expect all of the questions to be tough, and they are worried that they will provide the wrong answers. It's perfectly normal to be nervous about a job interview. After all, you've worked hard in college, and now you're looking for a good job at a good salary in a good location. You want everything to go well. The keys to a smooth interview are relaxation and preparation. Of course, these two are related: thorough preparation helps you to relax.

The Informational Job Interview

One way to practice your interviewing skills and increase your knowledge about a career field or a specific company (including the people who work there) is to set up a series of informational interviews with knowledgeable corporate contacts. See also Chapter 5 on gathering information.

Researching for the Informational Job Interview

Use the informational interview as a tool for acquiring information that you would not find through other means. Before requesting informational interviews, you should do some self-assessment. Identify your skills, values, and interests. Also, obtain background facts and details on the company so that you can use the informational interview productively.

To prepare for a series of informational interviews, write a list of potential contacts. These individuals may be personal friends, relatives, and associates as well as alumni and others to whom you have been referred. Most people find that it is easier to approach those they know first. Once you have developed a comfortable style for requesting and handling the informational interview, you can begin to seek referrals from other sources.

Obtaining an Informational Interview

There are two ways to obtain an informational interview. The first is a written letter to unfamiliar contacts asking for assistance and mentioning how you received their names. Follow up the letter with a phone call to establish a date and time for a meeting. The second approach is more direct and is used with people you already know: either call or approach the individual in person to make your request.

Informational Interviews

- Plan what you are going to say and jot down notes to yourself.
- Once you reach the person on the telephone, state that you are not asking for a job (and make sure you mean it).
- Explain to the person that you are seeking certain kinds of information and ask whether this person would be able to find 20 or 30 minutes to meet with you to answer questions.
- When asking for an appointment, be thoroughly organized. Have your calendar ready so that you can quickly say whether or not the time suggested is possible for you. Do not expect this person to go out of the way to accommodate your schedule. You should be the one who is flexible.
- Offer to forward a copy of your résumé as a means of introducing yourself and your background.
- Ask for directions to the office. Make sure you know where you are going.
- Thank the person for being willing to spend time to meet with you. Restate the date and time for the meeting. Provide your phone number in case the person needs to contact you before the appointment.

Preparing Informational Interview Questions

After you have set up an informational interview, organize an agenda for the meeting. It is usually a good idea to ask general questions when you are seeking information about a company, function, division, or department. Specific questions are useful when speaking with a person about a job or responsibility that is of interest to you:

- **The job or career field.** Ask about major job responsibilities and skills required, what the individual likes and dislikes about the job, how many hours the person works each week, what kind of schedule is typical, the degree of flexibility in the schedule, the amount of travel required, the degree of interaction with co-workers and clients, fringe benefits, new projects that are under way or planned, types of decisions that are made, other positions that are possible in the field, and advice for beginning a job search.
- **The company.** Ask how the company differs from competitors, its type of management style, trends within the company, opportunities for

professional development, general company policies and expectations, and problems the company is facing.

- **The department.** Ask about the relationship of the department to the company, its current problems, current priorities, new programs, current staff and their backgrounds, and department goals.
- **Your background.** Ask about where the individual would see you fitting into this organization or one like it, who in the company would be most interested in your skills, what the individual thinks of your résumé, and whether you have the qualities and skills for positions in this type of department or organization.

Evaluating the Interview

As soon as possible after the interview is complete, evaluate the interview by answering the following questions: What impressions do you have of the position? Company? Department? How did your contact help you to clarify your career objectives? Finally, don't forget to send a thank-you note.

The Job Interview

There are three parts to the job interview process: preparing, participating, and following up. Each requires your careful attention.

Preparing for the Interview

Preparing for the interview involves knowing your own strengths and weaknesses, knowing about the company and the industry it is part of, anticipating the kinds of questions you are likely to be asked, having questions to ask, and allowing plenty of time for your arrival at the interview.

SUCCESS ON THE JOB

- Don't interview for the company or product. Instead, look for the kind of people you want to be working for and with.
- Make sure you will have mentor/buddy candidates.
- Be prepared to work hard. That alone will differentiate you from 75 percent of the people.

—Bob Shapiro, senior program manager, Burlington, Massachusetts

Top 10 Personal Qualities Employers Seek in Job Candidates

1. Communication Skills
2. Motivation/initiative
3. Teamwork skills
4. Leadership skills
5. Academic achievement/GPA
6. Interpersonal skills
7. Flexibility/adaptability
8. Technical skills
9. Honesty/integrity
10. Work ethic–Analytical/problem-solving skills (tie)

—*Job Outlook 2000,* National Association of Colleges and Employers

Interview Preparation

- **Assess yourself.** To help yourself relax at least a little, seriously assess your strengths and weaknesses. What are you best at? What qualities do others admire in you? Now is not the time to be modest. You need to know what makes you a good person before you can recognize the qualities that also make you a good prospective employee.

- **Research the company.** Never go to an interview knowing little or nothing about the company. Ideally, you'll already have reflected your knowledge in your application letter. Numerous resources can tell you about a company's prospects, its products, its employees, and its benefits packages. Good knowledge of a company will help you think of other questions as the interview proceeds.

- **Rehearse your answers to their most likely questions.** Make a list of questions you can expect to be asked and rehearse your answers. Be prepared to tell the interviewer about yourself: why you went to college, why you chose your discipline, what areas of your discipline interest you the most. Accentuate the positive.

- **Prepare your own questions.** Be prepared for the interviewer to ask you whether you have any questions, and make sure you do have some. For example, ask if a job description is available for your desired position, ask about product development and current products, and ask about benefits and work conditions.

- **Wait before asking about salary.** Should you ask about salary, and, if so, when? There is no easy answer to this question, but one effective strategy is to assume that the salary will be competitive, and, if you are truly interested in the position, do all that you can do to have the company offer the job to you. Once you have reached this point, discussion about salary can be meaningful.

- **Plan to arrive early.** Finally, consider traveling to the interview as part of planning for it. One of the worst mistakes you can make is to arrive late. Plan to arrive at the receptionist's desk at least 15 minutes before your scheduled interview. An early arrival allows time for you to relax and collect your thoughts and shows you are well organized and professional.

PREPARING FOR THE JOB INTERVIEW

I have served on several search committees, and it is now expected that by the time candidates are invited in for interviews, they will have used the Web (and other sources) to become knowledgeable about the institution. Candidates often arrive for their interviews with a good perspective of the university and more specific questions about the position.

—Joel Hartman, chief information officer, Orlando, Florida

You can get a good idea of typical salary ranges for the type of position you seek by looking at help-wanted ads in newspapers or online. Many professional organizations publish annual salary surveys of their membership, broken down by level of schooling, years of experience, and geographic region.

From the workplace

Helen Cygnarowicz

VP Operations: Software
MathXpert
Santa Clara, California

Helen has moved through an impressive variety of jobs and industries on her way to her current position with a firm that produces mathematics courseware. She mostly learned on the job and taught herself what she needed to know by asking the right people the right questions and by being receptive to new ideas and techniques. She combines her analytical skills with an active curiosity about how things work and how they can be improved, which are helpful traits in any job.

My degree is in speech communication with an emphasis in rhetoric, but my education had nothing directly to do with my work. It is incidental to my work, but it has been invaluable because it taught me to communicate and to persuade.

I have changed professions, industries, jobs, and career goals many times in my life. I started out as a building and planning department secretary for a residential community of upper-scale citizens where the art of persuasion was vital. They were not any more clever than people without money; they just thought they were. It was my job to help them maintain that illusion, while doing what the town needed.

I changed careers to records management and really got my start at technical writing in those years. I developed software applications for use in municipalities throughout the state of California, and I consequently needed to provide user guides for those applications. I also got my start at proposal writing, again using the art of persuasion to get contracts. I also did a lot of "speechifyin'" using the same techniques, because very frequently the city department did not really understand its own needs, and it was important to give them something they were lacking but did not realize they needed. I left that career and industry when the competition became cutthroat. It was truly a 24/7 job and I had children to raise.

I moved on to being an executive secretary at a hematology analyzer manufacturing company, where I continued with tech writing from the marketing perspective. I wrote catalog and brochure material. (I have no training in chemistry, just a profound interest, since the first college class I failed was chemistry.) I also did database management and, of course, all the secretarial compositions required by marketing and engineering. I got a good feel for the differences in the mind sets of the people in these departments and had no difficulty interacting with either department.

Participating in the Interview

To participate in an interview successfully, view it as a three-part process. Whether you or your interviewer is aware of it, most interviews have a beginning, a middle, and an end.

In many respects, your interview starts before it officially begins. Your clothing, your arrival at the company, your introduction of yourself to the receptionist, your demeanor as you wait, and your first handshake with the interviewer are all the beginning of your interview. Most of this part is nonverbal. Another part of the beginning occurs when you join the interviewer in his or her office or a conference room.

Body language is important here, too. Your posture, gait, eye contact, and composure tell the interviewer a great deal about you. Straight posture, an

I moved on to an engineering company and developed many inventory and sales forms for the company. I continued to improve my computer and software application skills by simply practicing anything I could get my hands on. From there I went to an object-oriented software language development company and worked as the tech writer devoted to the API. I first came across UNIX and FrameMaker at that time and also had to learn how to live with a Mac as well. I learned most of my file transfer and management skills there.

I subsequently got into contract technical writing. I spent 18 months on a "three-week project" for Hitachi Japan (but not in Japan, just with Japanese engineers locally). The culture shock was as great for the engineers as it was for me, as I am a very analytical person who needs to understand the hardware and software to some degree before I can write about it. I developed the specifications for every conceivable aspect of this huge clinical chemistry analyzer and its DOS help system. Then I helped the out-of-state developers produce the manual. I actually was the SME (subject matter expert) myself in that regard, because I knew every spec and what every part of that analyzer was intended to do overall, as well as independently.

After doing so much writing, I made a decision that I would change focus to a management career rather than solely a writing job. I worked toward that end by attending UCSC and getting a Certificate in Management of Technical Publications Departments, and ultimately I got the management position in tech pubs for which I was qualified.

When I was a contractor, the lines of communication were always open. I was given specs to read and could meet with the subject matter experts at any time. Otherwise, when SMEs got recalcitrant about providing information, I looked around to find someone who was not necessarily designated as one, but who was equally as knowledgeable. It was always a matter of my taking the lead and finding the answer one way or another. It usually worked, though, because I always tried to get the answer on my own. When I could not get it on my own, then I was a supplicant looking for an explanation about something that confused me, rather than just asking for an explanation cold.

Insider Advice

For a tech-writing career, my advice would be to write, write, write. Anything. Everything. About subjects that are strange or esoteric. About subjects dear to your heart. I would advise you not to bother if you simply are not curious about anything. I've always tried to approach the job as an opportunity to do well and gain the respect of others, not just collect a pay check. Enthusiasm for the work is a must.

To want to know is to want to see, is to want to do, is to want to use, is to want to tell somebody about it, is to learn more, is to be a tech writer.

even gait, direct eye contact, and calm composure: These signs tell the interviewer that you are steady and straightforward and that you are serious about getting the job. Slouching posture, needlessly fast or slow gait, little or no eye contact, and a nervous or jumpy composure: these signs can indicate that you may not be a direct or dependable person. You can't always control the signs of nervousness, but be aware of how you present yourself to others, and work on correcting or controlling those signals that present the wrong "you" to the interviewer. How you sit in your chair is another factor. Sit straight in your chair, feet placed flat on the floor. Don't cross your legs. Take care that you do not tap or wiggle your feet, which can be distracting and annoying to the interviewer. All these nonverbal signals are part of the beginning, and you need to be aware of them throughout the interview.

CHOOSING THE
ETHICAL PATH

You may like some candidates more than others, but maybe one of the candidates whom you find the least personable is actually the best candidate for the job. Also, be careful about other biases during the interview. For example, if you have biases concerning gender or ethnicity, you may fail to hire the best person for the job. You need to look past your own biases or preferences.

When the interviewer begins talking about the weather, the traffic, or anything else, the interview officially is under way. Now is the time to exchange pleasantries and to talk casually about anything the interviewer cares to talk about. Let the interviewer take the lead and follow his or her cues.

The middle and end parts of the interview are those that you have already prepared for and can anticipate. Remember the list of questions you expect to be asked as well as the questions you want to ask. Usually, when the interviewer asks you whether you have any questions, you are beginning the closing of the interview. Comments on how the job search will be handled at this point and when you can expect to hear from the company are part of the closing.

As you wrap up, don't forget all of the important body language—the eye contact, the firm handshake, the posture, the walk, and all the rest. Your body language tells the interviewer a lot about how interested you are in the job.

Do You Have Any Questions?

Toward the end of the job interview, you will be asked if you have any questions. Even though your questions will occur late in the interview, some employers will look very closely at your responses and judge you accordingly. The questions you ask are an important indicator to your interviewer as to your suitability for the position and your fit within the company culture. What you ask can reveal much about you.

If your questions focus mostly on vacations, holidays, and other time off from work, you give one impression. If they concentrate on opportunities within the company for training and advancement, they give another. If they dwell on particular projects you might work on or the composition of the project team, they give yet another. You have many ways to show your serious interest in the job, and the questions you choose can help your case or hinder your chances to get hired.

Following Up on the Interview

Now that you've survived the interview, your "ordeal" still isn't over. You need to follow up. You need to thank your interviewer, remain proactive, continue searching, and be persistent.

At the very least, promptly send a thank-you letter to the person or people who interviewed you. The strategies for writing this letter are provided earlier in this chapter. The thank-you letter shows your interviewer that you are professional and appreciative. And, of course, the letter helps to keep you visible during the decision-making process.

Many interviewees mistakenly take a passive role after the interview is over. The interviewer may have said something such as, "I'll call you in two weeks to let you know what we've decided." Many job candidates then wait two or three weeks hoping to hear from the interviewer. You can't be passive and expect a company to hire you. You need to be proactive. Send follow-up correspondence (or e-mail), and don't wait for the interviewer to call you. After a week or two, call the interviewer and say that you are just checking on the status of the job search. With most interviewers at most companies you won't jeopardize your chances of being hired; if you handle yourself professionally during the phone conversation, the interviewer will view you as acting professionally and as someone who is definitely interested in the job.

Conducting the Job Interview

Someday it will be your turn to hire others, and for this process you will need to know how to conduct a job interview. Conducting an effective job interview requires many additional skills. Unfortunately, many candidates are interviewed by interviewers who are not well prepared to interview.

Interviewing Job Candidates

- Familiarize yourself with the job correspondence (application letter, résumé, job application form, and other materials) of the candidates you are interviewing.

- Know what type of person you are looking for. You need to identify clearly the technical skills, the interpersonal skills, and the many intangibles that make a person an ideal candidate, and you need to measure each candidate according to these criteria.

- Give each interview a structure— a definite beginning, middle, and end. Know the general questions you want to use at the beginning of an interview. Typical questions might be, "Did you have any problems getting here?" or "Where were you coming from?" or "How long did it take to drive here?" or "How did you hear about this position?"

- Save the tougher questions concerning the candidate's preparation and suitability for the job for the middle of the interview. Typical questions might be, "Have you ever done work on projects similar to ours?" or "How would you describe your usual working pattern?" or "Why did you leave your previous job?"

- Bring closure to the interview and let the candidate know what to expect after the interview is over.

- Be realistic. Most of the candidates will not be ideal. Everyone has different strengths and weaknesses. You need to develop your intuitive sense or gut feeling about which strengths are the most important to enable this person to succeed.

- Hire the best person for the job, based on the needs of the department, division, or company.

CHECKING WHAT YOU'VE LEARNED

Job Leads

- Have you used your school's resources to their fullest: careers office? library? job fairs? your professors and other word-of-mouth sources?
- Did you start your planning early enough so that you have enough time to prepare yourself both academically and in the job search process?

Job Correspondence

- Do your letters present you in the most professional way?
- Do they follow the appropriate format for a business letter?
- Do they follow the appropriate format for an application letter, thank-you letter, reference letter, update letter, accept or decline letter, or resignation letter?
- Have you provided a well-expressed beginning, an appropriately detailed middle, a businesslike close?

Résumés and Portfolios

- Do you present your credentials in an appealing and logical order?
- Are your résumé and portfolio organized so that a prospective employer can find each element easily?
- Is the résumé detailed enough to give the prospective employer a good idea of your skills and expertise?

Interviews

- Have you researched the person and company you will be visiting?
- Have you practiced what you will say: how you will respond to questions and what questions you will ask when it is your turn?
- Have you followed up with a thank-you note and, if appropriate, other correspondence or phone calls?

EXERCISES

 REVIEW

1. Find out which journals or trade magazines advertise jobs in your field. Select an ad and compose a letter of application asking for an interview. Be prepared to discuss in class how you decided what to include and emphasize in the letter.

2. Prepare a functional résumé suitable for use when applying for a job in your field. If you are

applying for your first job, use experience you may have acquired by working on projects for courses you have taken. Have a classmate critique it for readability, information gaps, and design effectiveness, and then make any necessary changes.

3. Take the résumé you prepared in exercise 2 and convert it to a scannable résumé.

4. Select an job ad from your field and research the company that placed the ad. Draw up a list of questions you would want answered if you were interviewing for a job at the company.

5. Write an update letter that you might use after a job interview. Make up one new or changed fact that you want the prospective employer to know about in the letter. Make sure that you tie the information in to the interview.

 ### THE INTERNET

Access at least three of the job databases available on the Internet listed on page 374 of this chapter. Find and print a job advertisement that seems a good match for you. Bring the ad to class and be prepared to discuss why the ad is a good match for you.

 ### ETHICS/PROFESSIONALISM

Discuss in one paragraph some of the ways a student could be unethical or unprofessional in an application letter. And discuss in one paragraph some of the ways a student could be unethical or unprofessional in a résumé. Bring the two paragraphs to class for discussion, and be prepared to discuss the disadvantages of the unethical or unprofessional examples.

 ### COLLABORATION

For the following exercise, everyone must bring a good printed draft of a résumé to class. Working together in groups of three students, use the following role-playing approach to conduct a mock job interview:

1. Create one group with two students who represent the company conducting the interview.

2. Assign one student to be the person who will be interviewed.

3. The student who will be interviewed should give his or her résumé to the students conducting the interview.

4. Give the students five to ten minutes to review the résumé and to discuss with each other some questions to ask the "job seeker."

5. After the interviewing group is ready, these two students may use about ten minutes to conduct a brief interview of the third student.

6. After the interview is over, all three students should discuss constructively the strengths and weaknesses of the interview.

7. The group members should change roles until all three students have been interviewed by the others.

 ### INTERNATIONAL COMMUNICATION

Using any source you prefer, find a job opening specifically outside the United States. Make a list of the special additional qualities or skills required because the position is outside of the country. Bring the list to class for discussion.

RESOURCES

Atkinson, Toby D. *Merriam-Webster's Guide to International Business Communications.* New York: Macmillan, 1996.

Bolles, Richard Nelson. *What Color Is Your Parachute: A Practical Manual for Job-Hunters and Career-Changers.* Berkeley: Ten Speed, 2001.

De Vries, Mary E. *The Elements of Correspondence.* New York: Macmillan, 1996.

———. *Internationally Yours: Writing and Communicating Successfully in Today's Global Marketplace.* Boston: Houghton Mifflin, 1994.

Gonyea, James C., and Tom Jackson. *The On-Line Job Search Companion: A Complete Guide to Hundreds of Career Planning and Job Hunting Resources.* New York: McGraw-Hill, 1995.

Kramer, Marc. *Power Networking: Using the Contacts You Don't Even Know You Have to Succeed in the Job You Want.* Lincolnwood: NTC/Contemporary, 1997.

Merriam-Webster's Guide to Business Correspondence. 2nd ed. Springfield: Merriam-Webster, 1996.

Moore, David J. *Job Search for the Technical Professional.* New York: Wiley, 1991.

National Association of Colleges and Employers. *Job Choices in Science, Engineering, & Technology.* Bethlehem: NACE, 2000.

———. *Planning Job Choices.* 44th ed. Bethlehem: NACE, 2000.

12

Professional Growth

Career Development   414

Professional Organizations   415

Professional Journals   416

Online Forums   420

Conferences   421

Continuing Education   422

Professional Development through
  Establishing Contacts   424

From the Workplace   428

IN THIS CHAPTER

Professional development does not end when you are hired for the job. Finishing your course of study at school is only the beginning of your professional growth. You have many ways of improving your skills and enhancing your knowledge base.

You will learn about:

- professional organizations: the benefits of active participation in the organizations that promote the professional needs of those in your discipline
- professional journals: how to find the ones in your field and information about submitting articles for publication
- online forums: electronic ways to exchange information with your peers using mailing lists and newsgroups
- conferences: their importance in networking and staying current
- continuing education: various options for furthering your education after college
- establishing contacts: how you can meet people who may be your present or future colleagues
- interacting with your colleagues: at meetings, by working together collaboratively, and through mentoring

CAREER DEVELOPMENT

When you are a student and even after you are already employed, you naturally want to position yourself advantageously for job placement and professional development. Whether you work for yourself or for a large or small company, you want to be remunerated for the skills and knowledge you bring to the job. In the technical professions, that means you need to train up to the state of the art in your field. And once you have achieved this level of knowledge and expertise, you have to stay current by keeping up with new advances and trends. Finishing your course of study at school is only the beginning of your professional growth.

To make sure you are in a position to deliver that excellent work, start with a good foundation through your schoolwork and internship opportunities. Prepare yourself so that you will be seen as a desirable addition to the workplace. Remember that once you are in the job marketplace, several hundred other people may be competing for the same job opening or promotion, so do as much as you can to enhance your chances of being selected. Even when you have secured a position, you cannot afford to become complacent. You will have many opportunities to develop a variety of professional skills on the job, and you should take advantage of as many of them as possible.

Besides the at-work opportunities for developing your skills, there are a number of other ways you can promote your own advancement by maximizing what you can offer to your profession. Professional organizations, subscriptions, conferences, in-house seminars, meetings, networking, mentoring, collaborating, and negotiating are important areas that will help you get and keep the job you want and add to your job satisfaction.

PROFESSIONAL ORGANIZATIONS

Almost every discipline or profession has an organization that represents its interests, and many have at least one journal or trade magazine. (See Chapter 11 for additional information about professional organizations and journals.) Also, increasingly many disciplines have at least one mailing list or one discussion group on the Internet. Membership in a professional organization is so important that many companies will pay its employees' membership fees, which can amount to several hundred dollars a year or more. Even if you have to pay the dues yourself, membership in professional organizations can pay you back in many ways, both tangible and intangible.

One of the tangible benefits of membership in a professional organization is discounted entry to its professional meetings—regional, national, and international. These meetings can be expensive; registration fees in the hundreds of dollars are not unusual. Your membership in the organization will pay off here, since often members receive preferential registration rates. Additionally, many organizations have student memberships, which offer greatly reduced dues for the duration of your enrollment in college and even possibly for one or two years beyond college. Some organizations offer reduced membership rates for new members or members who are earning at lower income levels. These membership categories are intended to help newcomers to the field obtain the benefits of professional memberships without causing them undue financial hardship. If you are eligible for these discounts, by all means take advantage of them. The profession benefits from the influx of new members and their ideas; you benefit from the networking and information you receive as the result of learning from your more experienced peers.

Professional organizations often publish journals and newsletters. For example, in the field of information technology, the International Federation for Information Processing acts as an umbrella group for a variety of national organizations, many of which have their own publications. Most of these organizations publish newsletters or journals as well.

If you are entering the field of computer science and computer engineering, you may already know about the Computing Research Association, which supports basic computing research and affiliated professional societies. And the Association for Computing Machinery provides services for the members of its general organization as well as its 36 special interest groups.

In engineering, the largest professional organization is the Institute of Electrical and Electronics Engineers (IEEE). Engineers in several dozen areas are represented by its many technical groups. Each year, hundreds of meetings sponsored by one or another group are provided for members and interested nonmembers. But even if you can't attend its meetings, you can read the publications each of the technical groups provides in its own specialization. Membership in the general organization entitles you to join the affiliate organizations that cover the field of engineering that interests you.

Subscriptions to its publications are another tangible benefit of membership in a professional organization. For example, members of the Society for Technical Communication receive the quarterly journal, *Technical Communication;* the monthly magazine, *Intercom;* and the annual membership directory, in addition to other member benefits. People who teach technical communication and those who work in industry find these sources valuable for keeping current with research in the discipline.

You will learn about some of the intangible benefits of membership in professional organizations later in this chapter.

Professional Organizations Online

Association for Computing Machinery   <http://www.acm.org>

Computing Research Association   <http://cra.org/>

Institute of Electrical and Electronics Engineers <http://www.ieee.org>

International Federation for   <http://www.ifip.or.at/>
Information Processing

Society for Technical Communication   <http://www.stc.org/>

PROFESSIONAL JOURNALS

Finding Journals

Other journals or trade magazines may be essential to your discipline but unrelated to a particular professional society. You need to know what these journals and magazines are, and you should read them regularly. But how do you know which ones to look for? You have three excellent resources at your school. See Figure 12.1 for examples of professional journals.

The direct route to finding out which journals publish articles of interest in your field may be word of mouth. Ask your professors which journals they read for professional information. They may be able to point out journals that provide excellent material but that you may not have run across on your own.

A second method to find useful journals in your field is to see which journals publish articles you are interested in reading. Go to the library and look up articles in your discipline. Take note of which journals are publishing the

FIGURE 12.1

Professional Journals

articles. Most likely, the journals that publish articles in your area of interest will be the ones you will find yourself reading when you want to keep current in your field.

The third method is to ask a reference librarian. Librarians have a wealth of knowledge about how to find information, and if they don't know the answer, they know where to look for it. Of course you can't expect every librarian to be familiar with your particular field of knowledge. Librarians specialize in locating and managing information. The advice you get from the librarian may be in the form of instructions on how to find the information yourself.

Publishing Journal Articles

Journals can be an excellent way of keeping up with developments in your field. Professional journals are the research-oriented publications in a field; trade journals or trade magazines are less research oriented, but their content is nonetheless specific to a particular discipline. Once you have begun working in your area, consider what you can give back to the profession in the form of sharing what you have learned. Consider writing a short article for one of your professional journals or trade magazines. Writing and submitting an article is good practice for organizing and consolidating what you have learned. And

FIGURE 12.2

Guidelines for Authors

Instructions for Preparing Author-Produced Manuscripts for IGS Publications

These Instructions, dated June 2001, supersede any previous ones. Following these guidelines to the best of your ability will help to expedite the production process.

1.0 Input

1. The applications to be used for electronic transmission to the editor are listed below in the decreasing order of desirability:

   a. **Microsoft Word '97 or '98**   PC (version '97) or Macintosh (version '98)

   b. **Microsoft Word 6**   (document must be saved to MS Word version 6.0 for Windows or earlier, with all figures embedded)

   c. **Word Perfect 5 or 6**   Word Perfect 5 or 6 RTF

   d. **plain ASCII text**

2. Times Roman 12 point font should be used for the body of the text, with headings in Times Roman 12 point bold or bold italic.

3. Title for each contribution should be limited to 45 characters.

4. Text must be set to single-space.

5. To preserve graphics quality in the final printing phase, all articles *should* be accompanied by separate, stand-alone graphics files (or figures) in native format (MacDraw, Canvas, etc.), or PICT, TIFF, EPS, PS (postscript), JPEG or BMP files.

   See Section 2, *Illustrations, Tables, and Footnotes*, for further details.

1.1 Text Formatting

1. Body text will be formatted in a single column, 6 1/2 inches wide.

2. Top margin will be 1 inch, and bottom margin will be 1 inch.

3. Body text will be set justified. Bullet text will be set flush left/ragged right. Table text will be set flush left, flush right, or centered as required -- never justified.

4. Bylines and affiliations on the front page shall be limited to the primary author(s) only. Other contributors and their affiliations can be included as an appendix at the end of the article.

It may help to use the dimensions illustrated in Figure 1. If you encounter any difficulties, please contact Ken Gowey by phone/fax at (818) 354-4532, or via email at *kgowey@jpl.nasa.gov* .

your article may be helpful for someone else who is experiencing the same learning process you are going through. Additionally, submitting articles for publication is an excellent way to attract the notice of employers and prospective employers.

Perhaps one of your professors, fellow students, co-workers, or other colleagues can work with you on developing a publishable paper. You may have written an especially good paper for a course you were taking. Your professor or instructor can advise you on which topics may be of most interest to the journal editors and can give you tips on how to rework material to prepare it for submission to a journal.

If you do decide to submit an article to a professional journal or trade magazine, read carefully the guide to authors prepared by the editorial staff of

FIGURE 12.2

Guidelines for Authors
(continued)

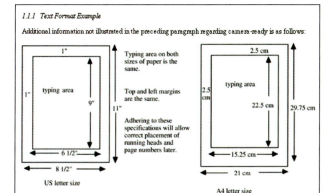

1.1.1 Text Format Example

Additional information not illustrated in the preceding paragraph regarding camera-ready is as follows:

Figure 1.

2.0 Illustrations, Tables, and Footnotes

Figure(s) may be embedded into the text document, *but should also* be submitted as self-standing, "native" art files in native format (MacDraw, Canvas, etc.), or PICT, TIFF, EPS, PS (postscript), JPEG or BMP files. Please do not submit GIF images or graphics captured from the World Wide Web, as resolution is generally poor.

These separate graphics files may be sent as a * .zip file (* .bin or * .hqx for Macs) and labeled accordingly.

In addition, to ensure that your article is reproduced exactly as intended, it is *recommended* that a hard copy of the finished article (with text and figure(s) integrated) be supplied by either postal mail or fax. (Please note: figures with fine detail are unusable when transmitted by fax. Also, any discrepancy in content between the electronic and hard-copy versions may create considerable delay in processing the contribution.)

Note: Authors who submit articles with graphics imbedded may elect not to submit separate graphics files, *however* exact replication of quality, in either the final printed copy, or replication for the World Wide Web, *cannot* be guaranteed.

2.1 Placement of Illustrations and Tables

1. Try to place figures and tables at the top of a page.

2. If a figure or table is less than 6 1/2 in. (162 mm), center it within the 6 1/2 in. (162 mm) image area. Do not turn a figure or table to landscape unless it is wider than 6.5 in. (162 mm). If a figure or table must be turned, the top should be at the left margin, the caption should run along the right margin.

3. Figure(s) must be legible after reduction (if necessary) to fit an image area no greater than 6 1/2 by 9 inches.

4. Figure captions must be in 12 point Roman, single spaced, and clearly tie the figure to the title or content of the text.

5. Do not attach actual photographs to the page. Submit them separately, properly identified on the back using a soft tip pen and indelible ink. You can indicate the placement of the photograph by pasting a xerographic copy to the page.

6. If electronic graphics files are not available, please remember to send the *original* photographs and line art. Xerographic copies of art, laser-printed photographs, or tear sheets (photographs from printed books or journals) produce poor quality results, and can not be used.

7. Avoid using compound art (photographs and line art combinations). If such an illustration is essential, submit a photograph of the entire figure.

2.2 Footnotes

A footnote must appear within the typing area. It should be separated from the text by one blank space, and should be indented 1 in. (2.54 cm), with a half line space between the footnote number and the footnote text.

---

that journal. Often the guide to authors is printed in each copy of the journal itself. The guide will tell you what types of submissions the journal accepts and in what format. If your topic is one that you believe will meet the journal's criteria, follow the guidelines and give it a try. See Figure 12.2 for an example of guidelines for journal authors.

Don't be surprised if you receive a response asking for further development on the paper. Professional journals are peer reviewed, which means knowledgeable people in the field check the paper to make sure it meets the standards of the profession, discipline, and journal. If your paper passes peer review, the editor will tell you when you can expect to see it in print. But don't expect to be paid for your article. Your reward will be in knowing that you have been given a forum to present your ideas to your peers. And of course, if you decide to pursue a career in academe, published papers are a must.

ONLINE FORUMS

The Internet has increasingly become one of the best ways to stay current in a discipline. Many disciplines have their own mailing lists or discussion groups—in effect newsletters that are mailed to you as e-mail—and newsgroups—essentially bulletin boards of messages "threaded" into topic streams. Online communication channels keep you informed about issues in your field.

PEER NETWORKS AND ONGOING LEARNING

I am a member of the Society for Technical Communication (STC), and I read their two journals (*Technical Communication* and *Intercom*). I also belong to the copyediting-I and techwr-I (technical writing) Internet discussion groups, which are a marvelous source of information and—in the context of training—an opportunity to help solve new problems that I don't face in my own job. Ongoing learning is probably the key to my success thus far; there's an awful lot more to learn than what they have time to teach you in school, and the profession is changing rapidly.

—Geoff Hart, publications coordinator, Québec, Canada

Finding Mailing Lists

- Get word-of-mouth recommendations. Ask your friends and colleagues for leads on valuable mailing lists in your field.
- Check in the main journals for your discipline. Often they will list pertinent mailing lists.
- Look at these sites for helpful information:

  Yahoo Groups <http://groups.yahoo.com/>

  Topica <http://www.topica.com/>

  tile.net <http://www.tile.net>

  Society for Technical Communication (check the SIG page) <http://www.stc.org/>

  IEEE societies and technical councils page <http://www.ieee.org/>

  TECHWR-L (Technical Writing Mailing List) <http://www.raycomm.com/techwhirl/>

As discussed in Chapter 11, there are probably thousands of online lists representing the interests of almost any field you can imagine. There are many such lists in engineering, such as the chemical engineering list, CHEME-L. In the field of technical communication, the mailing lists TECHWR-L, ATTW-L, and CPTSC-L are good ways to keep track of the concerns of others in this rapidly changing field. In addition to the broader concerns of the membership as a whole, more focused concerns can be handled within special interest groups (SIGs). For example, for those who have a special interest in contract work, there is the Consulting and Independent Contracting mailing list, CICSIG-L. People who want to share their problems with and concerns about contract work regularly post valuable information to this list. This special interest group also publishes a printed newsletter for its members.

Joining a mailing list can be as easy as sending an e-mail message to the listserver software that manages it or as complicated as applying to the moderator for permission to join. Each list owner has complete authority over how the list is managed and run. Usually, lists that service special interest groups require membership in that SIG before allowing you to join the list, but that is not always the case.

CONFERENCES

Most professions have societies or other organizations that provide those who work in the discipline with opportunities for networking with their peers, and much of that networking is accomplished at professional conferences. Attending conferences is not something just college professors and graduate students do. Attending conferences is one of many things professionals do to help stay current in their disciplines. Many professions have annual meetings, either as part of a larger conference or, if the organization is large enough, as a stand-alone annual conference. Larger conferences have many concurrent sessions in which experts discuss the latest trends and issues; smaller conferences may choose to present one session in each time slot so that all attendees can benefit.

Engineers in several dozen areas are represented by the Institute of Electrical and Electronics Engineers. Each year, IEEE groups sponsor hundreds of meetings for members and interested nonmembers. As posted on its Web site, "The IEEE hosts more than 300 conferences and meetings each year, covering a wide range of technical, professional, standards, education and career-related subjects." The Association for Computing Machinery (ACM) also sponsors many conferences on several continents. Its Web site <http://www.acm.org> is a good starting place to find conferences and learn about other member benefits in the computing field. The ACM's 36 special interest groups (SIGs) sponsor meetings and publish newsletters on a variety of computer-related topics.

Almost 3,000 technical communicators, professors, and students attend the Society for Technical Communication's annual conference in the springtime in a major U.S. or Canadian city. Each conference's proceedings are published, sampling papers from many of the presentations. STC also holds regional conferences, which are dedicated to specific areas of concern to technical communicators. Figure 12.3 shows a typical professional conference.

BUSINESS CARD NETWORKING

When I exchange business cards with someone at a seminar or meeting, I write on the back of the card something about how we met or something memorable. When I get in touch later I can refer to the card ("Hi! I'm not sure you remember me, but I was in your résumé writing seminar last fall with E. B. White. . . .").

—Diana Farrell, senior technical editor, Bala Cynwyd, Pennsylvania

FIGURE 12.3

Speakers Share Their Knowledge with Conference Attendees.

Many organizations in the sciences and other disciplines host professional meetings. To find out what is available in your particular area of interest, check your organization's Web site, or go to the library and review the professional journals in your field.

CONTINUING EDUCATION

To advance in your career, you need credentials. And to get credentials, you need training. Few employers in the technical fields will hire workers with no experience or training. There are several very good ways you can acquire credentials, and one of the most respected and accepted is to have a college degree or certificate in your field. Colleges and universities are typically the place where the latest knowledge and research in a field are to be obtained. It makes sense to start with your college education. When you declare a major, you are saying that you want to learn the specialized knowledge that practitioners in that field have mastered. Put another way, while you are in school, you are trying to come up to speed in your field.

Once you leave school, it is up to you to continue learning and growing professionally. After you leave the structured environment of a college or university and enter the workforce, further education is a choice, and that choice is not usually a progression along a predetermined path. Courses toward a certificate, a graduate research degree, a graduate teaching degree, or other credential will qualify you for advancement at work and often yield salary increases, too. That is why you should seek out educational opportunities and make time to pursue them. Learning is lifelong. And much of it takes place outside the classroom. Open yourself to the possibilities, because staying in one place often means falling behind.

> " "
> Learning is lifelong. And much of it takes place outside the classroom.

Seminars and Training on the Job

Many people cannot afford to take the time away from work to attend a conference out of town, and employers won't always pay for employees to attend outside seminars and meetings. For that reason among others, a common resource for professional development is the in-house seminar. These seminars may be as short as an hour or as long as a few months. Many large companies have their own staff members who provide seminars in professional development. Other companies hire outside experts to lead corporate seminars. At these seminars, employees can learn everything from using a computer tool to giving oral presentations to catching up with the latest findings in their discipline.

If you are offered the opportunity to attend a seminar or training course, do so even if you don't see an immediate application for the skills or information in your present position. You may want to apply for a different job someday—either at your present company or at another one—that will make use of exactly these new skills and knowledge. Figure 12.4 shows a typical seminar setting.

Degree and Certificate Programs

In many disciplines, the required educational credential is a bachelor's degree, master's degree, or doctoral degree. In others it is a certificate in a certain specialty area. Check into the requirements of your particular industry and profession. It may be that an associate degree or a bachelor's degree is just the first step on the road to professional certification. Once you leave school, you may also have to work on obtaining another credential in the form of a certificate or other diploma.

Your school library can give you a good idea of the possibilities in your field and geographic area. Perhaps you will have to move to a new location to

> ### TRADE SHOWS AND CONTINUING EDUCATION
>
> Networking is critical. Attendance at meetings such as trade shows and continuing education courses is indispensable in my opinion if you are a serious career practitioner. Be involved in community-related organizations, no matter what your other constraints might be.
>
> —Scott Mackler, principal cleanroom consultant, Fayetteville, New York

FIGURE 12.4

Seminars Provide an Oopportunity to Expand Your Knowledge.

obtain the further schooling you will need. Your professors will be a good source of information about educational possibilities in your field.

Individual Courses

Even if you are not enrolled in a degree or certificate program, you may still enroll in individual courses offered at local colleges and universities. Enrolling often involves no more than submitting a transcript of your previous educational history and paying a nominal application fee and a course fee. You are not required to matriculate (enroll as a degree-seeking student) in most schools in order to take courses. If you are not a regular student at the school, however, you may find that popular courses will be closed to you, since priority may be given to the school's own students.

If you decide to take individual courses, find out if the costs for the courses will be picked up by your employer. Many companies have a policy of paying for the further education of their employees, as long as the education can be deemed to benefit the company in some way. Taking a course in a subject related to your job may be reimbursed; taking a course in a totally unrelated field probably will not be reimbursed.

Correspondence Courses and Other Distance Learning

The traditional way to take a course is by enrolling and then attending classes. In most university and community college settings, that is what you will do. But increasingly, courses are taught either by correspondence (mail) or via the World Wide Web. Such courses form an area known as "distance education," since the students and the instructors may live in widely scattered areas and may seldom, if ever, meet in person.

Correspondence courses or other types of distance learning are good ways to obtain training in subjects that are not taught in a location geographically convenient to you. Suppose you are employed somewhere but want to take a course offered for an entire semester in another state. You could take a leave of absence from your job, but often this solution is not practical. If the course you want to take is also offered through correspondence or over the Web, you may be able to take the course without leaving your hometown. Lists of distance learning possibilities are available online and at the library. Often you will hear about opportunities by word of mouth—for example, from your professors while you are in college.

PROFESSIONAL DEVELOPMENT THROUGH ESTABLISHING CONTACTS

You grow in your job when you make the most of the professional opportunities available to you. An often overlooked opportunity is in the area of the interpersonal contacts you form on the job and through other work-related

SUCCESS ON THE JOB

- Be a sponge! Soak up as much information as you can. Make it clear that you want to learn and apply new things.
- Take big challenges and stay in touch with your progress on them.
- Don't be afraid to raise your hand and ask questions. Solving it yourself isn't always the best way.
- Pay attention to the responses you get, and try never to ask the same question twice.
- Acknowledge help. If you use something you got from others, tell them so as a part of keeping them informed and therefore keeping them prepped to help you should you need help again.
- Find a mentor who can coach you and a peer that you can partner with. Help each other.

—Bob Shapiro, senior program manager, Burlington, Massachusetts

channels. Such contacts are called networking, and they can take a variety of forms, among them chapter meetings, work collaborations, and mentoring.

Networking

Networking—forming ties with other people for friendships or professional relationships—is an essential professional development skill. Networking is reaching out and making others aware of who you are and what you would like to do or have. You network when you introduce yourself at meetings or conferences and exchange business cards with those you meet. You network when you reach out both to those you know and those you don't know through face-to-face conversations, phone calls, conference calls, video conferencing, e-mail, and so on. Some people have a talent for such networking; others find it difficult to do. If you are one of the latter, you need to relax and accept that networking is part of interacting with others. Networking is making professional ties so that you will have stronger professional relationships in your current job or so that you will have people to call on to help you if you should lose your current position. In sum, networking is a survival skill.

It is all very well to meet people and let them get to know you. It is entirely another thing to be able to call on them when you want their help. In order to do that, you have to have some way to keep track of the people whom you have met, so you can find their contact information later. A good way to do that is to compile a database of the people you meet (a database is simply a collection of information that is organized in some way).

A common way to keep track of those with whom you network is to keep a list of names, addresses, phone numbers, fax numbers, and e-mail addresses. Some people prefer to use a rotary card file, some an address book, some a conference attendee list with names highlighted, some a personal information manager or a database program on their computer, and some an electronic handheld organizer. There are computer programs to help you manage your networking file, and there are even Web sites that will provide an online address book you can use to store information. Database programs such as Access can do the same thing. The important point is to avoid having the names and contact information scribbled on all kinds of pieces of paper and the backs of business cards. Without an organized system, you will too often find it difficult to track down the one name you need.

Even before your professional career is established, begin to collect contacts for your database, and plan to add to the database regularly. You will find it an invaluable source for growing professionally within a company and for moving from job to job. Read about networking and the job search in Chapter 11.

Chapter Meetings

One place to meet people whom you may want to add to your contact list is at meetings. You have already learned a bit about professional meetings earlier in this chapter. Another kind of professional meeting—one that can be

NETWORKING AND THE JOB SEARCH

I have been a fanatic for networking ever since I realized that every job I have ever got was the direct product of networking.

—Mark W. Sincell, Ph.D., freelance science editor and writer, Houston, Texas

LEARNING THE ROPES

First job out of college I had two mentors. One was a technician (I was an engineer). He taught me all of the practical things that I hadn't studied in college. The other was an older man (at least he seemed like an old guy at the time, but he was probably only as old as I am now!) who was a consultant to the company I worked at. He knew I was hard working and could learn quickly, and since he worked at our company only a few days a week, he saw me as someone who could do work for him in between the days he was on site. He would always explain what he was doing and why, and would verbalize his thought processes as he worked something out. He counseled me on how to learn, on what to study, on the specific technologies we were working with, on how to "fit in" at this small, private company, and eventually on when it was time for me to move on. Both these mentors were incredibly helpful.

—Bob Shapiro, senior program manager, Burlington, Massachusetts

even more important than national conferences—is the chapter meeting. Many national and international organizations, such as the Institute for Electronic and Electrical Engineering and the Society for Technical Communication, have local area chapters that hold regular meetings. These meetings serve two purposes: they promote the agendas of the parent organization to advance professional standards and knowledge among practicing workers in the field, and they allow people who work in the same industry, profession, or field to meet, share information, and form ties based on common interests.

The advantage to participating in chapter meetings cannot be overemphasized. If you attend these meetings, you will not only learn what your peers are working on and interested in, but you will also meet the people who may be your next co-workers or even employers or employees. And as an added bonus, the educational programs offered by your local chapter will teach you some aspects of your field you may find interesting and even marketable eventually.

The flip side to what you learn from attending local meetings is what you yourself put into your local chapter. Participate in its programs as well as attend the meetings. You will find that you have information that others will find useful and interesting. And once you have attended a few meetings as an observer, you will see that the old-timers in the field are often very glad to give newcomers a hand up on their careers when they can. But none of this can happen if you don't join and attend meetings.

Collaborating

Collaborative work is a broad topic. As you learned in Chapter 3, few jobs today are performed in isolation. To get the job done, you will need to rely on others to perform a variety of roles, some formalized in protocols at your job, others more informal. Collaboration can aid in your professional development, because it lets you view at close hand the skills others bring to their part of the jobs you work on together. In fact, making the most of the collaborative process is a vital skill for almost any type of work. This knowledge will stand you in good stead if you can apply what you have learned about working with others to the many contexts of the work environment.

Mentoring

Mentoring has proved to be invaluable in a number of professions and activities. It is the process by which a seasoned, experienced person provides guidance to an inexperienced person outside of normal work channels. Mentoring can take many forms—from formal, assigned programs to informal, loosely structured ones.

In academe, full or associate professors often act as mentors for assistant professors. The mentor helps evaluate the assistant professor's teaching, research, committee service, and so on. By working closely with the assistant professor, the mentor is able to help the newcomer improve in teaching, become more productive in research, serve on the appropriate committees, and, in general, navigate the politics of a particular department or administration. Professors will also often mentor a promising student, particularly when it comes to participating in research or helping the student with recommendations to graduate school.

In the corporate world, mentoring is also essential for the success of any new employee. Often such mentoring is very unstructured. The new employee essentially finds out who holds the real power or who can be depended on for information or action. However, this common approach is not truly mentoring, and it requires far too much of the new employee's time. A true mentorship implies some kind of structured relationship. Certain mentors are assigned to specific people, and guidelines are followed. Two key characteristics define a formal mentoring relationship:

1. Pair a skilled (senior) professional with a novice.
2. Make sure the relationship is outside formal channels of supervision and evaluation.

Informal mentoring relationships are also possible and they are often quite successful. But to assure the benefits that mentoring can deliver, it's more certain if the relationship is planned for and made formal. Mentoring can occur even between colleagues who may not be working in the same location or even at the same company.

A novice who is lucky enough to find someone who is willing to act as a mentor will be able to bridge many of the difficulties newcomers face when entering a field.

Being Mentored

- Work to make the relationship a professional one.
- Remember that your mentor is a guide, a colleague, a friend. Your mentor is not your parent or your banker. The value of the relationship is in guiding you through the early stages of your employment and not in solving your personal, social, or financial problems.
- Remember that your mentor is more experienced than you are.
- Keep in mind that the goal is not to make you a clone of your mentor but to help you realize your own strengths.
- Schedule frequent meetings with your mentor but not so frequent that meeting with you represents an unfair burden on your mentor.
- Be honest, open, and receptive to benefit fully from the relationship.
- Make certain the mentor is aware of your concerns, fears, or worries.
- Keep in mind that suggestions and criticisms are meant to be helpful and to benefit you, so take them seriously and work toward improving your performance.
- When you disagree with your mentor, settle any disagreement amicably or at least amicably agree to disagree.

From the workplace

Marjorie Hermansen-Eldard

Course Developer
Legato Systems, Inc.
Orem, Utah

Marj found out through personal experience how professional memberships can make the difference between extended unemployment and immediate re-employment when you're laid off from your job. Her job search consisted of her choosing among several good offers that came her way as the result both of her good reputation in her field and the contacts she had made through her professional organization.

I am one of the fortunate few who are lucky enough to work in my field of study. Both my degrees are in English composition from Brigham Young University. I am a full-time technical writer and also a teacher of technical writing and composition at our local community college, Utah Valley State College. The school courses that helped prepare me for my first job—technical editor and desktop publisher—include an excellent document editing course and a basic technical writing course. I also learned a great deal on the job.

I have been both a full-time technical communicator and a teacher of technical communication. My classes are all computer aided—my students are taught the essential technical communication skills along with computer skills. My students take a real-world documentation project from concept to deliv-

ery. I have thoroughly enjoyed taking my "day job" into the classroom and teaching advanced students how technical writing happens in the real world.

It is of paramount importance to me that my students learn how to communicate in a team environment. As far as I'm concerned, there is no more critical skill in the technical communication field than being able to work, communicate, negotiate, and be productive in a team environment.

I find myself uniquely qualified, at this point, to discuss job searches, since I just finished a most successful one myself! Five months ago, I was laid off from the job at a software company due to financial difficulties within the firm. Within that week, I successfully interviewed at three different companies, and I accepted an outstanding offer to become a course developer—essentially a technical writer writing certification courses for top-level system administrative personnel.

From start to finish, here's the chain of events that led me to my great course development position (any teacher's dream job!):

The day I was laid off from the software company, I received a call from the senior course developer at Legato Systems. She asked if I'd be interested in inter-

At the beginning of your career it is more likely that you will be mentored than that you will be someone else's mentor. But you can learn the positive qualities of mentoring even when you are in school. Perhaps you have helped other students when they have needed information about how to navigate around the campus or figure their way through the paperwork required to complete their major. Perhaps you have participated in a study group with your fellow students and have helped the ones who seemed to need more assistance. Both situations are examples of mentoring behavior.

Once you are working, it is entirely likely that sooner or later either you will be asked to mentor another employee or you will suggest it yourself.

viewing for one of two course developer positions at Legato. I sent her my résumé and received an almost immediate invitation to interview at the Orem, Utah, office.

At the same time, I'd sent résumés to several other local companies and received several more calls to interview. All told, in that first week I had five interviews. I interviewed with an Internet service provider, a testing/certification company, a 3-D modeling company, an online job search company, and Legato Systems. (I actually had two interviews with them—one in person and one over the phone.)

Then, the second week, I received two e-mail messages asking if I'd be interested in doing contract work. One of the women was the manager of a writer's consortium. She had heard of me from some of her writers and said I'd come highly recommended. She had work I could start on that very day, if I wanted it. The same woman had been working with the testing/certification company I'd interviewed with. Without ever having met me, she called the hiring manager for that position and gave me a "glowing recommendation," based solely on what her writers had said about me.

My membership and involvement in the Society for Technical Communication (STC) had everything to do with the success of my job search. The majority of the positions I interviewed for were recommended to me by STC members. The individual interviews went smoothly as a result of knowledge and expertise I'd gained through professional development meetings, conference attendance, and the invaluable net-

working I'd done over nearly 12 years of membership in STC. When interviewers asked questions about tools, processes, and experiences I'd had in the technical communication field, I could speak to nearly every item, thanks to my STC experiences.

Networking is a critical aspect of my career. Just a little over two years ago, both my husband and I were laid off from our jobs. As two veteran technical communicators and senior STC members, we owe our "safe landing" in our jobs to our STC network.

I often receive calls, e-mails, even letters from people who say, "Are you still active in STC? Whom do I contact to list my needs for a technical writer?" I'm proud to be able to respond, "Yes, I'm an active STC member . . . here's the contact information for our Web coordinator. She can post your job needs."

Insider Advice

The best advice I could give a newcomer in a technical field is to get involved in your professional organization. Throughout my career, whether my company paid for it or not, I've always renewed my STC membership. Twice now, in the past three years, my STC network, my STC experience, as well as my professional development have netted me good jobs. The networking, the learning, the publications—all aspects of my membership in STC—are what have made me the competent, marketable technical communicator I am today.

Being someone's mentor is a great responsibility, and you will want to discharge it conscientiously.

Despite the best intentions of both parties, sometimes a mentorship may fail. The mentor and protégé may have been mismatched from the beginning. They may feel uneasy with one another or have unrealistic expectations. They may not have the strong trust a mentorship relationship must have. In these situations it's best to be candid about the problems and terminate the mentorship promptly. After all, the person being mentored is certainly not realizing a benefit from the relationship, and the time spent in the failed mentorship could be better spent paired with another mentor.

Mentoring

- Realize that high-quality mentoring requires a commitment of your time, energy, and expertise. Good mentoring is hard work.
- Establish mentoring guidelines and goals and make sure the person being mentored understands both.
- Promote the growth of the protégé through counseling and empathy, but also remain detached, avoid judgment, steer clear of personal problems, and set limits.
- Be a good communicator and a good teacher—well-organized, flexible, committed, and patient.
- Be honest, particularly in providing candid feedback.
- Always practice what you preach, since the person being mentored will often emulate your technique and style.
- Establish specific time allocations for assistance; meetings should occur regularly (at least once a month). Possible meeting venues are business lunches, coffee after work or after a professional association meeting, or a tour of the workplace. Telephone calls and e-mail are useful supplements to—but not replacements for—face-to-face sessions.
- At the end of the mentoring period, back away. Although the separation may be painful for the person being mentored, successful disengagement is important because it leads to a redefinition of roles and a new relationship as professional colleagues. Failure to disengage can lead to dependency and erode the success of the mentoring.

CHECKING WHAT YOU'VE LEARNED

Learning to do your job well doesn't end when you have trained for the position you were hired to fill. As a professional in a technical field, you have not only the challenges of your job to meet, but also the future challenges you will face throughout your working life.

Staying Current

- Have you joined the appropriate professional organizations that serve members of your discipline?
- Do you read professional journals or trade magazines to stay up to date?
- If you have experience or knowledge—either from work or school—that might be of interest to your peers, have you considered submitting an article for publication?

Professional Organizations

- Do you attend local chapter meetings of your professional organizations?

- If you attend meetings, do you exchange business cards and network with other members?
- Have you volunteered to work on committees as an opportunity to further the goals of your organization and to make yourself known to other people in your field?
- Have you attended professional conferences in your field? If you are not able to attend, do you read the published proceedings of those meetings to get an idea of what was covered in the sessions?

Continuing Education

- Do you plan to pursue further education in your field once you are graduated?
- Have you investigated opportunities for further training in your area?

Mentoring

- If you have been assigned a mentor, have you made every effort to benefit from the relationship?
- Have you made yourself available for mentor–protégé meetings?
- Have you been open and honest with your mentor?
- Have you been considerate of your mentor's time?
- Have you been receptive to your mentor's guidance?
- If you have mentored someone else, have you made yourself available, not only for scheduled meetings but for the occasional impromptu meeting?
- Have you been flexible and generous with your time?
- If the relationship did not work out, did you act in a professional manner and make an effort to part amicably?

EXERCISES

 REVIEW

1. Review the three major methods discussed in the chapter for finding the important journals in your field. Provide a list of the top five journals in your field, and be prepared to discuss how you found them.

2. Identify two major conferences in your field. Provide the dates and locations of the conferences for this year.

3. Discuss some ways you have already used networking to find contacts in your major or your field. Discuss the specific networking strategies you used and the advantages and disadvantages of these strategies.

4. Provide at least one paragraph discussing one experience you have had with in-house seminars, correspondence courses, or distance-learning courses. Discuss the advantages and disadvantages of the learning experience.

5. Create a list of the advantages of using the strategies discussed in the chapter for enhancing your professional development. Discuss the one strategy you found the most useful and why.

THE INTERNET

1. Using the Internet and some of the resources discussed in the chapter, find at least two mailing lists in your field. Provide the URLs for the lists and provide brief descriptions of what the lists offer subscribers.
2. Find the Web site of a major professional organization in your field. Write a paragraph describing how the site is organized and how effective you think the organization of the content is.

 COLLABORATION

Working in groups of three or four students, take turns discussing with the other members of the group the different kinds of strategies you have already used for professional development. Make a list of the common benefits you and the others agree on, and be prepared to share the list with the class.

 ETHICS/PROFESSIONALISM

Review both the guidelines for mentoring and being mentored. Then write at least a one-paragraph scenario or case study illustrating how a mentoring relationship can become unethical or at least unprofessional and present either the mentor or protégé with difficult choices. Be prepared to discuss your brief case study with the class.

 INTERNATIONAL COMMUNICATION

Assume you are assigned to work on a project with a co-worker who is from another country. Assume you have been asked to mentor the co-worker so that he or she will be an effective co-worker and one who understands clearly your company's corporate culture. Make a list of the challenges you think you will have to overcome to succeed.

RESOURCES

Bishop, Sue. *The Complete Guide to People Skills.* Oxford: Gower, 1997.

Kramer, Marc. *Power Networking: Using the Contacts You Don't Even Know You Have to Succeed in the Job You Want.* Lincolnwood: VGM Career Horizons, 1998.

Kratz, Dennis M. *Effective Listening Skills.* Toronto: Irwin, 1995.

Yager, Dexter. *Dynamic People Skills.* Wheaton: Tyndale House, 1997.

13

Developing Presentation Skills

Giving Oral Presentations   434

Kinds of Presentations   435

Preparation   436

Delivery   440

Presentation Tools   446

From the Workplace   458

IN THIS CHAPTER

Presentation skills are not incidental to your college studies and your career. They are an essential part of your competency in your discipline or profession. Preparing and delivering effective oral presentations are essential skills for students and technical professionals. You will often be called on to inform or persuade others in impromptu, outlined, or scripted presentations. Of course, as with many other communication skills, you must continue to practice your presentation skills if you are to improve. The more presentations you give, the better speaker you will become. Knowing how to present effectively will help you in your college classes and will enhance your professional career in numerous ways.

You will learn about:

- kinds of presentations: impromptu, outlined, and scripted; informative and persuasive
- preparation: how to plan, research, script, and rehearse the presentation
- delivery: the techniques for maximizing the effectiveness of your presentation
- presentation tools: how to select the ones you will need, how to prepare them, and how to use them

GIVING ORAL PRESENTATIONS

Few interpersonal skills are more important than the ability to give an effective oral presentation. In college you will often have to give individual or group reports depending on your major and your classes. And if you are a member of even just one campus organization or civic group, for example, you will probably have the opportunity to speak about your views concerning issues of interest to the group. In the workplace, you may be asked to speak at a brown-bag lunch, a staff or division meeting, a roundtable discussion, a panel discussion, a sales presentation, a press conference, or in some other context.

Many technical people have the skills and knowledge they need to succeed in their jobs, but sometimes they lack the ability for or interest in giving effective oral presentations. Some people do seem to have a talent for talking before groups of people, but most of us have to work at acquiring this important skill. Regardless of whether you enjoy speaking before groups or you dread it, you can learn about oral presentation skills the way you learn about anything else, and once you know what these skills are, you can practice and practice until they seem almost second nature to you.

KINDS OF PRESENTATIONS

Most presentations fall into one of three categories: impromptu, outlined, or scripted. These basically differ in the degree to which you have prepared for them and in their level of formality. Presentations also generally are informative or persuasive.

Impromptu, Outlined, or Scripted Presentations

Many of your presentations will be informal. You may be called on unexpectedly in a staff meeting just to summarize quickly a few points concerning your progress on a project. You'll have to respond with an ad hoc or impromptu presentation. You'll have to think quickly of what you want to say, and then you'll have to say it. Or you may have expected to give a brief presentation at the staff meeting and just jotted down a few notes to remind you of some of the key points you want to cover.

Other times you may be asked to prepare a formal presentation for upper management on the progress of a project you're working on. You'll have the time to prepare visuals and other aids for this more formal presentation. You'll probably organize your thoughts according to an outline, keeping in mind that the outline lists the main facts to help you stay on track.

Depending on your profession, you may also have the opportunity to present your ideas at a professional meeting or conference. Presentations at conferences also vary from the informal to the formal. One common kind of formal presentation is the scripted presentation. In a scripted presentation you write down word for word every sentence you will read to your audience or that you will memorize and recite for your audience. At many conferences an outlined presentation is preferred over a scripted presentation, and it would be a mistake to read your presentation at such conferences.

Whether your presentation is impromptu, outlined, or scripted, you need to know certain strategies to help you give the most effective presentation you can give.

Informative or Persuasive Presentations

Students and technical professionals are frequently called on to instruct or inform others. Presentations designed to provide information are called informative presentations. Typical informative presentations are lectures, product updates, conference presentations, procedural reviews, and some kinds of classroom presentations.

Students and technical professionals are also frequently called on to advocate one position or point of view over other positions or points of view. You will often have an occasion to speak where your major purpose is to change the mind of the audience, not merely inform. You might, for example, be called on to speak persuasively at a sales meeting, a community event, a proposal presentation, or a conference presentation.

PREPARATION

Many people have a fear of speaking in public. The best way to cope with nervousness is to prepare for and practice delivering your presentation. And even if you are a confident speaker, an effective presentation still requires preparation. The more you prepare for an outlined or scripted presentation, the more successful the presentation will be. And, of course, the more presentations you give, the better you will become at preparing for and delivering all kinds of presentations, even impromptu ones.

Planning

Plan your presentation. An effective presentation doesn't just happen. You have to spend a great deal of time thoroughly planning every part of a presentation. Ironically, the more you plan the more natural the presentation will often appear to be.

Knowing the Audience

Know your audience. Always keep in mind what the audience needs to know. This is true not only for writing to an audience effectively, but also for speaking to an audience effectively. What you want to talk about and what your audience needs to know are not always the same thing. By carefully determining who your audience is and what they need or want to know, you will avoid taking unnecessary digressions or covering unnecessary points. By knowing your audience, you can craft and shape your presentation to achieve your purpose.

But what does "knowing your audience" mean? See Chapter 2 on audience. You know your audience by considering what its members already know about your subject, what they need to know about your subject, what level of technical knowledge they possess, and what experience they may already have with your topic.

For some formal presentations, you may have to do a formal audience analysis to determine more carefully what your audience needs to know. A formal audience analysis considers various parameters that are relevant to the audience's relationship with your topic. For example, for an audience analysis, you might gather specific information on the levels of education (vocational school, university, graduate studies), years of experience, department (data processing, accounting), industry (e-commerce, financial software), and job position (entry level, middle management, executive).

KEEP IT SIMPLE

Keep the visuals simple and brief. I try always to remember the 7 +/− 2 rule: Lines should be 5 to 9 words long, paragraphs 5 to 9 lines long. Following this rule helps ensure transfer from short-term to long-term memory.

—Bob Shapiro, senior program manager, Burlington, Massachusetts

Researching

Research your presentation. You may be asked to speak about a topic that you know about entirely from personal experience, but more often than not you will be asked to speak on a topic that you will have to investigate further or that you have been investigating or working on for some time. See Chapter 5 for many strategies you can use to become more informed about your topic. Also, keep in mind and use the outlining techniques discussed in Chapter 6.

Organizing

Organize your presentation. Your presentation should have a distinct structure—an opening, a middle, and a closing. As the discussion below makes clear, there are certain strategies the audience expects you to use in the opening, middle, and closing of your presentation.

Using Appropriate Language

Plan to use language that is appropriate to your audience. Be appropriately informal or formal. Use clear, concise, accurate, and descriptive language. Keep your key points simple. In sum, talk to your listeners using language they will understand and appreciate. See Chapter 7 for a discussion of the many stylistic choices you must consider.

Beginning the Presentation

Prepare a good beginning. A good opening can boost your confidence in a way that will help you through the remainder of the presentation. Work hard from the beginning to establish your credibility. If necessary or appropriate, introduce yourself first. If you haven't already been introduced, give your name and perhaps a few relevant details about yourself. Your credibility as a speaker is established not only by your mastery of the content and your credentials for speaking on your topic, but also by your poise, confidence, gestures, eye contact, projection, and many other elements.

Prepare at least one specific strategy for getting your audience's attention:

- **Humor:** Humor can be an effective way to get your audience's attention quickly and to keep people listening. Of course, if you're not comfortable using humor, then don't. An ineffective joke, for example, may set a negative tone for the remainder of your presentation.
- **An anecdote:** Using an anecdote means telling the audience a story. An interesting story is one of the most effective ways to get your audience's attention at the very beginning.
- **A statistic:** Stating one or more well-chosen statistics not only helps you get your audience's attention but also may enhance your credibility.

ON HUMOR

Some audiences appreciate humor: I had great success with transparencies that visually depicted poorly constructed sentences ("I was trying to get a better radio station when the stop sign jumped out and surprised me."). Used judiciously, humor can lend punch to an otherwise dry presentation. But, should the audience be people who are trying to decide if you are the mortician to use, you may want to be more formal, not funny.

—Diana Farrell, senior technical editor, Bala Cynwyd, Pennsylvania

FIGURE 13.1

**Presentation Preview on a
PowerPoint Slide**

"Indexing 101"

- Introduction
- Analyzing the text
- Writing the index
- Editing the index
- Testing the index
- Resources

- **A quotation:** A well-chosen quotation can effectively set the tone for the entire presentation.
- **A dramatization:** Dramatizing an issue means personalizing it. For example, if you are talking to an audience about a decrease in sales, you might want to tell why one customer decided not to renew a contract.

Tell your audience the topic and purpose of your presentation. Don't take the purpose of your presentation for granted. You may know why you are talking to your audience, but your audience needs to be told in very clear terms why you are speaking. You may simply want to say something such as, "The major point I want to convey to you is. . . ." Give your audience a preview by telling them what you are going to cover in your talk. See Figure 13.1 for one way to prepare your audience for your talk.

Developing the Middle

The middle of the presentation poses special challenges. You have many possible ways of organizing the information presented in the middle of your presentation. Perhaps you will cover your topic chronologically, essentially offering a narrative of events; arrange your presentation topically, covering three or four key topics in the order of most-to-least important or least-to-most important; or provide an overview of a problem and then discuss one or more solutions.

Prepare a good middle, or body. Remember that for most class presentations you barely have time to cover five main points, and most often you have time to cover only two or three. Let the audience know when you have moved to the middle part of your presentation. Say something like, "For my first point. . . ." Use transitions to help your audience follow what you are saying.

Cover each main point in enough detail to suit your purpose. Support each main point adequately with facts, examples, expert testimony, and so on. If your chief purpose is to inform your audience, you want to make sure you cover each topic in enough depth so that your audience has a clear understanding of each point. If your chief purpose is to persuade your audience to accept or do something, then you need to make sure each point is covered in enough detail to help you make each point persuasively. See Chapter 2 on audience and persuasion.

Use appropriate link words to establish the relationship of each point to the previous one: *nevertheless, additionally, and yet, in contrast,* will act as navigation tools to point out the sequence of your remarks. While transitions are important in written works, they are especially important in oral presentations when your audience cannot go back and review the earlier sentences.

Ending the Presentation

Prepare a good ending. A conclusion is usually less than 10 percent of your presentation, but you should prepare it as carefully as you prepared both your introduction and the body of your presentation. Let your audience know that you have reached your conclusion. Say something like, "To wrap up" or "To conclude" or "Finally" or "In closing."

If appropriate, review your most important point or points. Use a quotation, a startling statistic, or a dramatization to help make the conclusion memorable. When you have completed your prepared remarks, tell your audience that you will be happy to answer questions and mention the availability of handouts, if any. Be sure to complete your talk promptly now that you have told your audience you are concluding.

Practicing

Prepare by practicing. Practice your presentation several times before you present it in public. Time your talk so that you can stay within the limits you are given. If possible, practice in front of a mirror and critique your gestures. Tape-record your talk and listen to your voice. Do you frequently use meaningless fillers in your speech? If you hear a lot of "ums" and "y'knows," work on eliminating such verbal tics, which distract from what you are saying.

Dressing Appropriately

Plan to present a well-groomed and professional appearance. If your professor requests that you dress appropriately for your classroom presentation, then you should wear a suit or other business attire. If your professor doesn't

ON PRACTICING

How to give good presentations? Practice, practice, practice. And not in your head. Say all the words out loud and preferably in front of an audience.

—Mark W. Sincell, Ph.D., freelance science editor and writer, Houston, Texas

GREAT PRESENTATIONS

Here are some tips on preparing great oral presentations:

- Decide in advance on the result you want and have all of your planning and presentation focused on obtaining that result.
- Know your agenda and communicate it clearly to your audience.
- Give participants input into the agenda.
- Set expectations early and often as to length, goals, and projected outcome—yours and the audience's.
- Review your presentation. Think carefully about the audience to be sure you aren't going to alienate someone, and to be sure your message/filter is appropriate.
- Provide handouts at the start so that people don't have to write detailed notes.
- Watch your audience carefully and figure out which things they are responding to and which ones they are shutting out. Depending on the purpose, either modify what you say to address their areas of interest as you determine them, or address head-on the items they are shutting out.

—Bob Shapiro, senior program manager, Burlington, Massachusetts

make your appearance an issue, you should still come to class dressed and groomed appropriately for your talk. Cut-off jeans, short skirts, or T-shirts aren't proper attire for presentations. And definitely, in a corporate setting, where your professional appearance is always an important factor, you must dress appropriately for staff, department, or division presentations. When you are speaking to the company's clients, your appearance takes on an added importance.

Setting the Stage

Become familiar with the room where you will speak in advance of your talk. If possible, visit the room beforehand and position yourself in the spot where you'll be standing or sitting later. Look out at your imaginary audience and try to imagine them, their interests, their concerns, and what they want to know.

Prepare the place for your talk:

- If you will be standing at a lectern, check that it is placed where you want it and that you have sufficient lighting to read your notes.
- If there is a microphone, adjust its height to accommodate your own and make sure you know how to turn it on and off.
- Listen to the room acoustics. You want your voice to carry easily to the last row without projecting into the hallway.
- If you need a screen, make sure that one is available and verify that it is ready for you. If you have brought a laptop computer to show a presentation, check that you can attach it appropriately to the display hardware in the room.
- Turn on your presentation equipment and make sure your images are placed and focused properly. Locate the light switches, and make sure you know who will be operating them for you if you need the lights out.
- If you will be reading notes, verify that they are where you expect them to be and that they are in the correct order. If you will read your notes in a darkened room, make sure you have adequate lighting.
- If you plan to use handouts, distribute them to the places where you want the audience to pick them up.

DELIVERY

Becoming a good speaker requires lots of time and practice. Perhaps it's true that some people aren't nervous when they give a talk or presentation. However, most of us have to work very hard at becoming good public speakers, and we have to work hard at overcoming our nervousness. Often, what you interpret as someone else's natural public-speaking ability is, in fact, the result of excellent preparation and careful practice. So even if you think you have little talent for speaking in public, you can learn the techniques that will take you through to a successful, effective presentation.

Lots of people have plenty of advice about various ways to deliver a presentation. You should read or listen to what others say and use the information that you think will help you to relax and to give a good presentation. It helps to watch other speakers and notice how they get their messages across to their audiences.

Relaxing

Remember to relax, now the time for your talk has arrived. You have been introduced, or you must introduce yourself. Before you begin speaking, take a few deep breaths and look at your audience. Remind yourself that these people want to hear what you have to say and that they want you to succeed.

> **GIVING A PRESENTATION**
>
> Giving a presentation is like being a deejay at a dance: if you can't maintain a continuously faster beat, jump to something new and start slow. Keeping the audience interested and involved is important, because it means they are thinking about the topics you're presenting.
>
> —Seth Maislin, freelance editor, indexer, information architect, Arlington, Massachusetts

First, before you begin speaking, find a quiet room where you can calm yourself and take some deep breaths. Imagine that you are standing before your audience, and look at this imaginary audience calmly. Tell yourself that you have much to offer this group and that they are looking forward to benefiting from your knowledge and experience. At many conferences, speaker rooms are set aside for the purpose of letting speakers collect their thoughts before giving their presentations.

Second, after you are introduced and before you begin speaking, take a few moments to look at your audience and take a few deep breaths. Take your time. You don't have to begin speaking immediately. Look at the audience confidently and remember to smile.

Third, focus on the fact that you will most likely be the expert about your topic. You have probably spent a great deal of time preparing for this moment. Try to enjoy this opportunity for sharing what you know with people who want your information. Remember that the audience wants to hear what you want to say. Your audience wants to know what you know.

Fourth, keep things in perspective. You may be nervous because you fear that you will make a fool of yourself or that you may make a mistake. Don't focus on yourself. Focus on your message. And don't be afraid of mistakes. If you make them, learn from them.

Finally, maintain a sense of humor. If it helps you, imagine your audience members sitting in their underwear or with dunce caps on. If you make a mistake and if it's appropriate to do so, laugh at yourself. Make the mistake work in your favor.

Controlling Nervousness

Control your nervousness. Remember that even the most experienced speakers are nervous before they give a presentation and that nervousness is a natural response to speaking in public. You can learn to control this nervousness in many ways.

Establishing Eye Contact

Look at your audience and remember to maintain eye contact during your presentation. Read your audience for signs. With practice you'll be able to tell whether your listeners are bored, interested, motivated, enthusiastic, and so on. (See Figure 13.2.)

Projecting

Project your voice appropriately for the size of the room; your voice will sound different, depending on the room acoustics and the size of the audience. Maintain your voice at a pleasant pitch. Pitch is the highness or lowness of your voice, its rise and fall as you speak, its intonation. Be sensitive to the sound you are producing and be prepared to modify it if you find that it is not appropriate for the room. Use sufficient volume to be heard easily, but not so much that you're shouting at your listeners. If you are using a microphone, verify that it is adjusted appropriately for your voice. Vary your speaking volume to attract your listeners' attention.

FIGURE 13.2

Speaker and Audience Interaction

Watch your audience for feedback on your presentation.

FIGURE 13.3

Gestures in Presentations
Your gestures reinforce your
message.

Using an Appropriate Pace

Maintain a steady pace or rhythm for your presentation. Don't speak too
quickly or too slowly. Cover your points at a pace that your audience can easily follow. Guard against speaking so steadily that your voice descends into a
drone. Your speaking pace should settle into a cadence that maintains audience interest with a balance and variety of rhythm.

Using Gestures

Use gestures appropriately. An experienced speaker will use all kinds of
gestures for emphasis; many will be so natural that the audience won't even be
aware that the speaker is using the gestures. Your hands, shoulders, eyes,
mouth, and eyebrows may be used to intensify all kinds of meanings. Of
course, your gestures may also be inappropriate to your point. Exaggerated or
erratic gestures may help undermine a point instead of intensifying it. You
need to learn how to make the gesture that is appropriate to the point and
how to time the gesture accordingly. Here is where your practice in front of the
mirror will pay off. (See Figure 13.3.)

Avoiding Distractions

Avoid distracting behavior, such as shaking your car keys in your pocket,
tapping the lectern with your pen or pointer, pushing your glasses up too frequently, coughing or clearing your throat too often, drinking from your glass
of water too often, shaking or tilting the podium, pacing the room too
quickly, or turning your back to the audience.

Using Auditory Clues or Signposts

Tell the audience what you are going to tell them, tell them when you move on to a new point, and tell them what you have told them. Give the audience a constant sense of the structure or organization of your talk. Let your audience know when you are moving on to your next important point. Give your audience frequent auditory and visual clues. Use words and phrases such as, "And now for my next main point" or "Now that I've summarized this issue, I want to move on to the next issue." Use your visuals to let your audience know where you are in your presentation, too.

Expecting the Unexpected

Be prepared for something to go wrong. Most often everything will go smoothly throughout your presentation, but something may surprise you, too. Perhaps the projector bulb will burn out in your overhead or slide projector. Perhaps you will drop your notes unexpectedly. Perhaps you will trip over a wire while you're pacing the room. Perhaps you will discover that your slides are in the wrong order even though you double-checked them just before your presentation. Perhaps you will find yourself unable to suppress a sneeze, cough, or hiccup. These and many other events have occurred to even the most experienced public speakers. Handle such events with grace and a sense of humor. Audiences are typically patient and will wait while a bulb is replaced, notes are reshuffled, and so on. If appropriate, apologize for the oversight and then continue. Don't dwell on what just happened. Get back into the rhythm of your presentation, and deliver the kind of presentation both you and your audience expect.

Using Presentation Tools Appropriately

Know how to use your presentation tools, but keep them from distracting your audience. Professionals use all kinds of tools during their presentations. These tools can become a distraction if the audience pays more attention to them than to you.

> " Used well, your tools can enhance your presentation tremendously. Used poorly, your tools can make your audience lose its focus on what you are saying.

For example, if you are using overhead transparencies, practice putting up one transparency after the other so that the process appears smooth and natural. If you are using a computer and a program such as PowerPoint or Presentations, avoid going from one slide to another too quickly. If you are using a pointer, use it sparingly and appropriately. Don't hide your audience's view of your visuals, keep your visuals simple, and make sure the information on them is clearly readable by someone in the back of the room. Avoid using too few or too many visuals: about one each minute is plenty. When in doubt, use fewer. Your audience wants to hear your presentation, not just read your slides. Used well, your tools can enhance your presentation tremendously. Used poorly, your tools can make your audience lose its focus on what you are saying.

Watching the Time

Don't speak longer than you are supposed to. Remember to manage your time effectively. You want the presentation to be just the appropriate length, rather than too short or too long. Many presentations are constrained by time limits. Presentations at conferences may be limited to fifteen minutes per panel speaker, for example. Or perhaps your supervisor simply asked you to speak to other employees in the division for thirty minutes. If your audience knows how long your presentation is supposed to be, make sure you stay within that time limit. Have a wristwatch or stopwatch in front of you where you can refer to it unobtrusively, or locate a wall clock you can glance at while you speak. Audiences aren't very forgiving of speakers who speak longer than they are supposed to.

Time your practice sessions and get a good idea of the length of your talk. Notice whether you tend to speak very quickly when you're nervous. If so— and that is a common situation—remind yourself to pace your presentation more slowly. Practice beforehand until the speed is just right. Ask someone else to critique your speed when you are practicing.

Using Handouts

If you use handouts, give them out before you begin your presentation or after you finish your presentation. Many audience members will appreciate having something to take notes on while you talk. Of course, some suggest that giving the audience handouts before you speak can be distracting because many in the audience will look through the materials you have provided while you are speaking. You'll have to determine if and when to give out handouts, depending on your purpose, audience, and other considerations.

Letting the Audience Know You're Wrapping Up

Let the audience know when you are going to begin your wrap-up. Look at your audience, take a deep breath, and say something like, "And now to wrap up" or "Let me conclude by saying" or "In closing, I would like to say . . ." You'll find that your audience appreciates hearing these words and will be even more attentive. This is a good time to remind your audience of your most important point or points. Remember, your closing is important and can be used effectively to inform, persuade, or motivate your audience.

Thanking the Audience

If appropriate, thank your audience for listening. If you have done well, your audience will let you know through applause or some other acknowledgment. Its members will thank you for your comments, and you should thank them for their participation. It's the professional thing for you to do.

PRESENTATION TOOLS

A wide variety of presentation tools are available to speakers. You need to decide which tool or tools are best suited to your particular topic and your audience. Of course, your choice of visual aids depends on the circumstances of your presentation, whether, for example, you are giving a formal presentation at a professional conference to a large audience in an auditorium or an informal presentation to a small group of peers in a makeshift meeting room.

In the formal situation, you should consider 35-mm slides or computerized projection. They present well and give your talk a polished, professional appearance. They cannot be created on the spur of the moment, though, so they would not be as appropriate for a less formal presentation. In the informal situation, overhead transparencies would be more appropriate. They can be created from computer files or from handwritten sketches. You can write on them during your presentation using a marking pen. Thus transparencies are suitable for a presentation that may be more interactive between you and your audience. Other circumstances may require other presentation tools including models, a chalkboard, posters, flip charts, or video. There are some important guidelines to keep in mind for each of these media. See Figure 13.4 to compare presentation tools.

Models

Models are physical representations of ideas or other kinds of objects. An engineering student, for example, may use a model of a bridge to illustrate various principles of design. A chemistry student may use models to demonstrate the structure of a molecule. Models can be effective for catching the attention of your audience, for dramatizing a particular point or concept, and for quickly making a complex point clear. See Figure 13.5 for an example of a model.

Chalkboards and Dry-Erase Boards

Despite all the other technology available to you, a simple chalkboard, chalk, and an eraser may often prove most useful. Most classrooms and many meeting rooms contain a chalkboard or a dry-erase white board with erasable markers. Either type of board can be used to demonstrate a variety of points quickly. However, if you spend too much time writing on a display board with your back to your audience, your audience's attention may wander. Unless you are a skilled presenter, you should take very little time during your presentation to put information on a board for your audience to read. Figure 13.6 shows a dry-erase board in use.

ON VISUALS

I always weave my visuals into my presentations so that I don't simply stand up and lecture. Visual communication helps the audience relate to what I'm presenting. Pictures, graphics, charts, and even music can solidify abstract concepts for listeners.

—Marjorie Hermansen-Eldard, course developer, Orem, Utah

TOOL	PURPOSE	ADVANTAGES	DISADVANTAGES
Models	■ concretize the abstract or simplify the complex	■ attention-catching ■ three-dimensional	■ difficult to see at a distance
Chalkboards and dry-erase boards	■ record information generated at the moment	■ readily accessible ■ demonstrate points quickly without prior preparation	■ time-consuming ■ can be difficult to read ■ force writer's back to face audience
Posters	■ display information prepared in advance	■ compact ■ easy to prepare	■ difficult to read at a distance
Flip charts	■ record information generated at the moment or present material prepared in advance	■ low cost ■ low noise ■ demonstrate points quickly with or without prior preparation ■ not dependent on prone-to-failure electronics	■ difficult to copy ■ difficult to read at a distance
Transparencies and overhead projectors	■ display prepared text and visuals	■ easy to see at a distance ■ easy to prepare	■ multimedia (animations, video, sound) not possible
35-mm slides	■ display prepared text, graphics, and photos	■ easy to see at a distance	■ expensive to prepare in quantity ■ require special equipment to display ■ multimedia (animations, video, sound) not possible ■ subject to equipment failure
Computers and presentation software	■ display text, graphics, and other multimedia in sequence ■ present audiovisual information in an unattended setting	■ easy to prepare ■ easy to incorporate multimedia	■ depend on equipment that is susceptible to failure or breakdown ■ require special equipment to project display
Video	■ present visual and auditory information and training	■ easy to play back ■ format familiar to audience ■ effective and efficient in conveying information	■ expensive to produce ■ require time and expertise to design and accomplish

FIGURE 13.4

Presentation Tools

FIGURE 13.5

Using a Model

Models make complex structures easier to understand.

Posters

To save time during your presentation, you can use a poster to provide the information you want your audience to see or to know. Of course, posters are more suitable for smaller audiences than larger ones, because they are difficult to read at a distance. Make sure that whatever you are presenting on your poster is large enough and clear enough to be viewed easily even from the back of the room.

In many of the sciences, poster sessions are common for showing others the results of your research on a particular project. Your aim should be to present visually the key concepts of your research. Use diagrams, arrows, photographs, and other visual indicators to show what you did rather than trying to explain your research using text alone. Your poster should address one central question. State the question on the poster, and instead of elaborating on various issues related to the question with text on the poster, clarify issues by discussing them with the people who stop to view the poster.

An effective poster in a poster session provides one major idea for viewers to take home and consider. Any conclusions should be summarized briefly and in

FIGURE 13.6
Dry-Erase Board

a straightforward style. If you must acknowledge any contributors or funding organizations, you may do so using smaller type than elsewhere on the poster. Ideally, any text on the poster should be large enough to be read easily at least six feet away. Group the text into sections and use headings. Your headings should be in a large type size—perhaps 36 point or larger—and the font for the headings should be different from the font for supporting text. Supporting text should be in 24-point type or larger. Keep in mind that posters in poster sessions are not publications. If any points need elaboration, bring handouts to the poster session. See Figure 13.7 for examples of posters.

Flip Charts

Like chalkboards, flip charts enable you to sketch your thoughts as you speak, although some speakers prepare a series of sheets on a flip chart in advance and then walk the audience through each sheet. Advantages of flip charts include their low cost, low noise, the possibility of creating visuals on the spot, and the fact that because they are low-tech systems, they are not dependent on electronics that may fail unexpectedly. Disadvantages include

FIGURE 13.7

Posters

their difficulty to copy and their "I just thought of this" connotation. See Figure 13.8 for an example of a flip chart.

Transparencies

Most college classrooms and company meeting rooms have overhead projectors for using transparencies. The projector and transparencies (also called viewgraphs or foils) are some of the most widely used communication tools. Like other media, this technology has both advantages and disadvantages. See Figure 13.9 for an example of a transparency and overhead projector and Figure 13.10 for advantages and disadvantages of transparencies.

Some common misuses are having too many transparencies (about ten per 40-minute presentation is adequate), presenting too many lines of print or too-small print, covering too much information (use a handout instead), producing unreadable graphs, showing cartoons with unreadable dialog or captions, and using unprofessionally reproduced photos and other visuals.

FIGURE 13.8

Flip Chart

Using Transparencies

- Make sure the projector is at the front of the room, with plenty of space on a nearby table for orderly placement of transparencies. This allows you to face your audience and encourages interaction.

- Keep the lighting dimmed.

- Do not read the lettering on transparencies to your audience. Instead, mention key points and elaborate with statistics or examples.

- Allow ample time for your audience to take notes, when appropriate.

- Be concise.

- Mention key points in words or phrases, with a maximum of six to eight words per line and seven lines per transparency.

- Use large lettering. Type should be at least 24 point for easy readability.

FIGURE 13.9

Transparency and Overhead Projector

FIGURE 13.10

Advantages and Disadvantages of Using Transparencies

ADVANTAGES	DISADVANTAGES
Allows clear visual explanation and reinforcement	Noisy projection
Pace and sequencing controlled by speaker	Acetate material subject to deterioration over time
Hard-copy prints easily made	Bright and true colors difficult to achieve
Attention getting	Color too expensive for large format
Easy technology to learn	Can't be rapidly sequenced
Can be created on the spot	Often overused (too many in one presentation)
Easy to change order	
Rehearsals possible without projection equipment	

35-mm Slides

Someone once said that the three most feared words in the English language are "Next slide, please." Yet slides are a common tool for oral presentations. With slides you can show many kinds of visual material—charts, graphs, bulleted lists, photographs, and a host of others. Although computers have taken over the role formerly held by the slide projector to some degree, there are times when only a slide show will do. Of course, you'll have to plan a slide presentation carefully. Not only do you have to ensure that your slides are set up in the correct order and ready to go, you also have to verify that the projector is working properly and that you know how to use it. See Figure 13.11 for an example of a projector and slide carousel.

Showing slides has some advantages: the ease of rearranging their sequence, the possibility of remote operation and long- or short-distance projection, the relatively low cost of producing color images in a photographic format, the visual realism that is possible with photographs, the inexpensive production of color visuals in quantity, and easy control over the pace of information. Other advantages include flexibility of positioning at the front of a

FIGURE 13.11

Projector and Slide Carousel

FIGURE 13.12

**Advantages and
Disadvantages of
Using Slides**

ADVANTAGES	DISADVANTAGES
Ease of rearranging their sequence	Long lead time for preparation
Possibility of remote operation and long- or short-distance projection	Diminished effectiveness in high ambient light
Relatively low cost of producing color images in a photographic format	Distraction of projector noise
Visual realism that is possible with photographs	Difficulty of obtaining hard-copy prints
Inexpensive production of color visuals in quantity	Dimness of lighting required
Easy control over the pace of information, flexibility of positioning at the front of a room or in a rear-screen projection	Inability to show continuous motion or processes
Ease of storage and transportation	Susceptibility of slides to getting out of order and causing confusion to your audience
Visibility to a whole room	
Ability of the speaker to point out critical items on a large screen	
Availability of special visual effects such as cutaway enlarged views or image distortion to enhance the impact	
Possibility of reviewing specific points easily by reversing slides	
Ease of quick rearrangement for revision	
Capability of being updated and adapted to different audiences or having the emphasis varied	

room or in a rear-screen projection, ease of storage and transportation, visibility to a whole room, the ability of the speaker to point out critical items on a large screen, the availability of special visual effects such as cutaway enlarged views or image distortion to enhance the impact, the possibility of reviewing specific points easily by reversing slides, the ease of quick rearrangement for revision, and the capability of being updated and adapted to different audiences or having the emphasis varied. (See Figure 13.12.)

Disadvantages include the long lead time for preparation, diminished effectiveness in high ambient light, the distraction of projector noise, the difficulty of obtaining hard-copy prints, the dimness of lighting required, the inability to show continuous motion or processes, and the susceptibility of slides to getting out of order and causing confusion to your audience.

For the most effective use, make sure visuals do not clutter the slide (avoid overuse of images); carefully integrate slide content with important handouts; make sure images can be seen by all audience members; plan ahead (when requesting a 35-mm projector, also ask for a remote controller and an extension cord if you'll need them). Place the projector a sufficient distance from the screen so that images are relatively large.

Computers and Presentation Software

Increasingly, computers, connected to multimedia projectors to project the computer image onto a large screen for the audience, are used for all kinds of oral presentations. For example, many presenters use portable projectors to project high-quality images from their laptop computers. And many presenters use full-featured presentation software programs to deliver their presentations. PowerPoint and Presentations have become favorites of speakers because of the many features these programs offer and their ease of use. They are equipped with preformatted presentation designs or templates and a variety of special effects, such as animations, sweeps, and fades. The slide templates make it easy for even novices to create a succession of text, illustrations, bulleted lists, and other slide formats, complete with graphics, clip art, and photographs. Music and other sound effects make the computer-presented slide show into a complete multimedia experience. The slide shows can proceed either automatically and unattended or at a pace controlled by the presenter. Just as with other audiovisual systems you might use during a presentation, you should check your slides from the back of the room to make sure they are legible. See Figure 13.13 for an example of an LCD projector, screen, and sample slide.

ON SLIDES

The better the slides, the better the presentation! I use visually interesting slides that differ from one another—this keeps the audience engaged.

—Rochelle Schwartz-Bloom, Ph.D., associate professor, Durham, North Carolina

FIGURE 13.13

LCD Projector, Screen, and Sample Slide

Making Your Transparencies and Slides More Legible

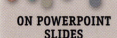

ON POWERPOINT SLIDES

I complained to a colleague that the slide size in PowerPoint was excruciatingly limiting. His response: just write less. Since then the quantity of information produced on my slides has declined, with no decline in quality. In fact, I'm sure that the quality of my presentations overall has improved because the audience listens better and I can be more spontaneous. As a result, my presentations are also more interactive.

—Seth Maislin, freelance editor, indexer, information architect; Arlington, Massachusetts

● Choose an appropriate color scheme. You can easily capture your audience's attention with an effective use of color, but be careful. Too many colors will be distracting. In general, use brightly colored text against a dark background. The darker background reduces glare. A dark blue background and yellow or white text are a good combination of colors.

● Choose an appropriate font. There are many fonts and it's important to choose those that will work best in a particular situation. For example, Arial Bold for headings and Times Roman for body text is an effective combination. Sans serif typefaces work well for slides. See the "Typography" section in Chapter 8.

● Choose an appropriate font size. The audience must be able to see the text on your slides. Of course, much depends on the size of the screen, the distance of the last row of seats from the screen, and so on. At a minimum, use 24-point type for the text on your screens. Headings and subheadings should be even larger.

● Don't use all capital letters. When you use all capital letters, you minimize the characteristic shapes of letters and their distinguishing marks. Capital letters are normally used to signal the beginning of a sentence and

proper nouns, so using all caps distracts from the message, since it runs counter to the audience's expectations.

● Choose an appropriate line spacing. If you provide generous spacing between lines, you make it easier to discern the letterforms and read the text.

● Choose an appropriate writing style. Don't provide too much text on any one slide. Provide bulleted lists of points wherever possible. Use phrases, not complete sentences. Use concrete, not abstract, language, and use specific words and phrases, not general ones. Use solid examples rather than generalities.

● Try to be conversational rather than too formal. You are making a presentation, not reading text out loud. Your audience members expect you to talk, not read, to them. Your slides or transparencies are chiefly lists of important points you want to cover. They are an overview, not a verbatim copy of your presentation.

● Make your slides legible. Limit the amount of text on each slide. Don't choose to use a smaller point size just to fit the text on the slide. Work on summarizing, condensing, and making the information more appealing to your audience instead of struggling with formatting issues.

Videos

Many people own or have access to camcorders. Families have hours of tapes of family get-togethers and other events. Video can also be just the right

FIGURE 13.14
Camcorder

tool to make a variety of points during an oral presentation. Videos are relatively cheap to produce, edit, and purchase, and videotape has a shelf life of five to nineteen years, depending on the frequency of use, and digital video's shelf life is even longer. It is available in a variety of formats, and it can easily be used to show motion, process, or interpersonal skills. (See Figure 13.14.)

Among video's advantages are that it allows points to be shown at various speeds and stopped or reversed, as necessary. Video magnifies processes, fine details, and operations, which can be helpful in demonstrations (through "zooming" by the video camera). Video allows the same information to be shown simultaneously to audiences in different locations. It provides the opportunity for immediate critique, analysis, or evaluation by replaying segments of the tape. Video allows individualized instruction by sequencing the content interactively with workbooks, guides, texts, or computers. Visual effects are an excellent way to enhance either the information or entertainment value of the presentation. Video allows material to be kept current through the editing or correcting of material. You can be sure of consistent quality in the presentation of the material. Video provides resource information on remote cultures and other countries and offers performances or interviews with noted individuals.

From the workplace

Joel L. Hartman

Vice President for Information Technologies and Resources
University of Central Florida
Orlando, Florida

Joel works in a university setting as chief informa-tion officer. His educational background prepared him well for this work, and he has been able to continue to develop his skills as he moved from a career in television to his current position in higher education.

In 1995 I came to the University of Central Florida (UCF), where I am chief information officer, with overall responsibility for campus information tech-nology and resource units. My original goal was to work in broadcast television production, so my under-graduate and graduate degrees are in journalism and communication. After several years of early experience in both commercial and educational television, how-ever, my job responsibilities continued to broaden, and within a few years I was no longer directly in-volved with television and was instead managing a va-riety of technology resources in a higher education setting. I fully expect to be doing this type of work un-til I retire. It is challenging and rewarding, and every day is different.

My typical workday consists primarily of two activi-ties: attending meetings and sending or receiving e-mail. One day recently I came into the office early to get started on the day's tasks, only to find that a network outage kept me from accessing any network resources. For a moment, I sat there looking at the PC screen won-dering what to do next. That event brought home to me the extent to which my work depends on network ac-cess. Over the past few years, the emphasis on PC usage in my job has changed from a tool to create documents to a tool for communication and collaboration.

Giving Presentations

I prepare my presentations by first outlining, and then creating bullet slides, finally adding graphics, an-imation, and sound as appropriate. I will often tinker with a presentation up until a few minutes before de-livering it.

Because of my near-total reliance on PowerPoint presentations, I usually take backups when delivering a talk to large or important groups. These may include a printed copy of the slides, a set of projection trans-parencies, or even a spare computer and projector. When possible, I try to bring my own PC and data projector, finding that using equipment I can trust leads to more consistency, quality, and reliability.

One lesson learned from delivering numerous presentations is that I tend to try to cram too much into a presentation, causing me to either run long or to have to hurry through some slides. The other is that I have to continually fight the form-over-sub-stance battle. I have found that on occasion I would have served my audience better had I concentrated more on the presentation's ideas, and less on produc-ing glitzy PowerPoint slides. I sometimes joke with my audience and tell them I am using a newly discovered presentation package: "WhatsthePoint." Sometimes my audience doesn't see the humor.

Working as a Team

I'm sort of the editor-in-chief for division reports and publications, only a few of which I actually cre-ate. Most of the articles and public presentations with which I am involved today are written by multi-ple authors. UCF is doing some very interesting things in distributed learning, and there are frequent opportunities to write or present on this topic. The co-authors are members of the team responsible for distributed learning at the institution, and all are ac-customed to producing multi-originator articles and presentations.

We usually begin as a group, reviewing the assign-ment, scope, focus, and individual writing assign-ments. On the assigned due date, each author's contri-bution is received and merged into a first composite draft. Following that, editing, revision, and prepara-tion for publication (or presentation) is a collabora-tive task. Usually, one or two members of the group volunteer to produce the PowerPoint presentation or to prepare and send the final draft.

In a sense, our author group mentors one another. We share suggestions, edit each other's work, and accept joint responsibility for the results. But these are more collaborative endeavors than mentoring.

Over the past 30-some years working in higher education, I have found that an ability to write and speak clearly have been critical success factors. Leadership requires the creation of a vision—a story about the organization's future. Communicating that vision to staff, institutional leaders, and others is an ongoing need.

Also, video is not novel to an audience that is familiar with television. (See Figure 13.15.)

Among the disadvantages are that illustrations and lettering are limited to a 3 to 4 ratio (television screen proportions). Audience size is limited unless multiple monitors, closed circuit or cable broadcasts, or video projection systems for large rooms are used. Video can be quite expensive if elaborate productions or a lot of equipment, materials, or personnel are involved.

To use video effectively, preface the material to be viewed by the audience with reference to presentation content and objectives. Prepare follow-up activ-

ADVANTAGES	DISADVANTAGES
Allows points to be shown at various speeds and stopped or reversed, as necessary	Limits illustrations and lettering to a 3 to 4 ratio (television screen proportions)
Magnifies processes, fine details, and operations, which can be helpful in demonstrations (through "zooming" by the video camera)	Limits audience size unless multiple monitors, closed circuit or cable broadcasts, or video projection systems for large rooms are used
Allows the same information to be shown simultaneously to audiences in different locations	
Provides the opportunity for immediate critique, analysis, or evaluation by replaying segments of the tape	
Allows individualized instruction by sequencing the content interactively with workbooks, guides, texts, or computers	Incurs great expense if elaborate productions or a lot of equipment, materials, or personnel is involved
Enhances either the information or entertainment value of the presentation using visual effects	
Allows material to be kept current through the editing or correcting of material	
Allows monitoring of consistent quality in the presentation of the material	
Provides resource information on remote cultures and other countries and offers performances or interviews with noted individuals	
Presents a familiar interface to an audience that is familiar with television	

FIGURE 13.15

Advantages and Disadvantages of Video in Presentations

ities to reinforce learning. Make sure video and audio quality are good. Make sure the videotape is not too long. (To allow adequate follow-up, it should not go over 30 minutes for a 50-minute time slot.) Make sure the entertainment value doesn't exceed the information value.

CHECKING WHAT YOU'VE LEARNED

Preparing

- Have you planned your presentation, taking into account your purpose and your audience's needs?
- Have you researched and organized your material and designed your talk so its organization is logical and easy to follow?
- Have you crafted an effective opening, establishing your credibility from the start?
- Have you presented your arguments in a logically structured middle?
- Have you summarized your main points in your conclusion?
- Have you practiced in front of a mirror to make sure your gestures and delivery are smooth and professional?
- Have you selected clothing appropriate to the setting?
- Have you checked that your items of equipment—microphone, lectern, projector—are positioned where you need them and will perform as desired?

Delivering

- Have you practiced to convert your good planning into a polished presentation?
- Have you established eye contact with members of your audience?
- Have you presented a calm and professional appearance?
- Have you projected your voice—and varied its tone and volume—for maximum effectiveness?
- Have you distributed handouts either before or after your presentation at a place where the audience can readily find them?
- Have you solicited audience participation and questions?
- Have you paced yourself to allow yourself to finish your entire talk?
- Did you thank your audience when you were finished?

Using the Tools

- Have you chosen the best tool or tools for your particular presentation and your audience?
- Have you learned how to use the tools effectively for presenting visuals?

EXERCISES

 REVIEW

1. Your instructor will call on you and other members of the class in turn to give a brief impromptu presentation. Discuss the topic for no more than two minutes. After you are finished speaking, make a list of those items you found difficult to do during your impromptu presentation.

2. Write a memo in which you discuss your major apprehensions and weaknesses concerning giving a presentation. In the closing of the memo, discuss how you think you can handle many if not all of these apprehensions and weaknesses after reading the chapter.

3. After reviewing the discussion of the advantages and disadvantages of the various presentation tools, make your own list of the tools you currently are most comfortable using and why you feel comfortable using them. Then make a list of the presentation tools you are least comfortable using and why you feel uncomfortable using them.

4. Recall a presentation you have listened to where the speaker was effective. Create a list of points concerning why the speaker was effective and be prepared to share your comments with the class.

5. The credibility of a speaker can be projected in many ways—knowledge of the subject, confidence, poise, projection, eye contact, and so on. Create a bulleted list of the strategies you would like to use to help improve your credibility as a speaker. Be prepared to share the list with the class.

 THE INTERNET

Using at least two different search engines, research the topic of giving an effective oral presentation. Make a list of what you consider the most useful tips after reading the sites you found.

 ETHICS/PROFESSIONALISM

1. Make a list of the ways a person can be unprofessional in giving an oral presentation. Then provide a list of tips on how to avoid being unprofessional.

2. Create a list of some unethical strategies a speaker can use during a presentation and discuss why these strategies might be considered unethical.

 COLLABORATION

Working with one or more students in the class, create a list of the challenges that a group would face in preparing for and presenting a group presentation. For example, some of the difficulties may be determining who will prepare which part of the topic, determining the order of the speakers, or determining how the presentation tools will be handled. Also create a list of strategies you and your group members could use to overcome these challenges.

 INTERNATIONAL COMMUNICATION

Write a paragraph discussing some of the difficulties you would expect students from other cultures to encounter when they give a presentation in an American college classroom.

RESOURCES

Bergin, Francis. *Successful Presentations.* New York: Prentice Hall, 1996.

Bishop, Sue. *The Complete Guide to People Skills.* Oxford: Gower, 1997.

Brown, William. *Interpersonal Skills for Leadership.* New York: Prentice Hall, 1998.

Gurak, Laura J. *Oral Presentations for Technical Communication.* Needham Heights: Allyn and Bacon, 2000.

Hager, Peter J., and H. J. Scheiber. *Designing and Delivering Scientific, Technical, and Managerial Presentations.* New York: Wiley, 1997.

Kratz, Dennis M. *Effective Listening Skills.* Toronto: Irwin, 1995.

Morrisey, George L. *Loud and Clear: How to Prepare and Deliver Effective Business and Technical Presentations.* Boston: Perseus, 1997.

Reimold, Cheryl, and Peter Reimold. *How to Prepare and Deliver Outstanding Presentations: A Practical Guide.* Piscataway: IEEE, 1999.

PART FOUR

Documents

Chapter 14
Correspondence   465

Chapter 15
Procedures, Processes, and
Specifications   510

Chapter 16
Proposals   545

Chapter 17
Informal Reports   583

Chapter 18
Formal Reports   622

Chapter 19
Instructions   682

14

Correspondence

Letters   466

Memos   493

E-mail   498

From the Workplace   504

IN THIS CHAPTER

The majority of your daily writing will be letters, memos, or e-mail in which you communicate directly with other people and try to provide what they want or need to know. Letters, memos, and e-mail are often no more than one page long, but don't let this brevity fool you. Writing an effective letter, memo, or e-mail requires many of the same steps that are involved in longer written communications. In many cases, you still will have to brainstorm or use some other technique to help you develop your ideas (see Chapter 4 for prewriting techniques), you still will want to establish your purpose and narrow the scope of your message, and you still may outline or organize to state the points in the order that will be the most effective for your reader. You also will find that careful control of tone and style makes the difference between an effective letter, memo, or e-mail that achieves your purpose and one that fails. (See Chapter 7 for information about achieving an effective style.)

You will learn about:

- the basic elements common to letters of various types
- letter formats: their differences and similarities, and when to select one format over another
- the usual organization of letters written for different purposes
- the features and uses of memos
- when and how to use e-mail as business correspondence

LETTERS

Letter writing is a vitally important skill in the business world. Letters are a basic person-to-person communication that takes place in a wide variety of settings and situations. Whether or not you ever have to write reports, proposals, or manuals on the job, you almost certainly will have to write letters. You have a limited opportunity to make your point and achieve your purpose in a letter, since letters tend to be much briefer than many other business communications. Therefore, more than for most other business communications, every word counts. Moreover, how you format your letter becomes part of the message, too.

You will have to write letters for a variety of professional, social, and personal occasions. The requirements for letters differ depending on the letter's purpose and audience. A letter of application has different requirements from those of a letter of complaint, and a personal letter to a close friend has different requirements from those of an invitation letter to acquaintances. Learn to use the correct formats, the appropriate strategies, and the widely accepted conventions, and your letters will accomplish what you want them to. Your professional letters say a great deal about you and, when you are an employee, about the company you work for. Letters that ignore accepted formats, use poor strategies for the kind of letter you are writing, or misuse conventions will fail to communicate the intended message. Therefore, understanding the basics of effective letter writing is essential both in school and on the job.

Parts of a Letter

Letters can have eight commonly used parts: a *heading*, a *date line*, an *inside address*, a *salutation*, a *body*, a *complimentary close*, a *signature*, and, when necessary, an *end notation* (or notations). However, other parts (including an *attention line*, a *subject line*, and an *identification line*) may sometimes be necessary. In professional correspondence you must use and provide these parts appropriately and correctly.

Heading

Headings (also called return addresses or outside addresses) differ, depending on whether they occur on company or organization stationery or on personal stationery. Official correspondence between an employee of a company and someone outside the company requires the use of letterhead stationery. Personal correspondence may be more appropriately carried out through electronic mail or on personal notepaper. See Figure 14.1 for a model of a typical letter.

A printed heading on business stationery—called letterhead—consists of the company or organization name, street address or post office box, city, state, zip code, phone number, fax number, and Internet addresses (e-mail and Web site). Many companies and organizations combine all these elements with a logo and other design elements at the top of the page, either flush left or centered. Some provide much of the same information at the bottom of the page and provide just the company or organization logo at the top of the page.

If you are writing a business letter on letterhead stationery, you do not repeat the information that is already printed. If you are writing a business letter and you are not using letterhead stationery, then your heading will consist of the company's address: street address or post office box, city, state, and zip code.

Date Line

The date line gives the date that the letter was written. If you are using company letterhead, skip at least two lines below the address and provide the date for the letter either flush left at the left margin or flush left at the center line. On personal stationery, you may provide the date as part of the heading or two or more lines below your address. Figure 14.2 shows a heading and date line.

The typical order for the date is month, day, and year: December 1, 2001. Spell out the month to avoid confusion. Using all numbers can be ambiguous. In the United States, by convention, dates are noted as month, day, and year—12/1/2001 means December 1, 2001. In many other countries, dates are noted as day, month, year—12/1/2001 means January 12, 2001. In the military the order is day, month, and year with no commas: 1 December 2001.

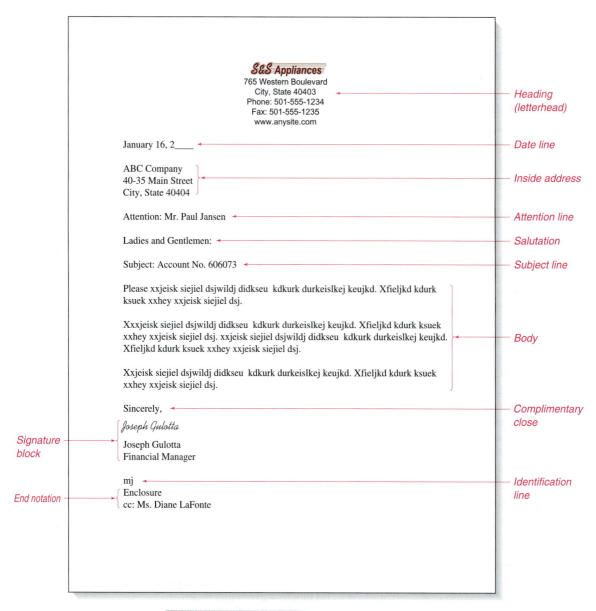

FIGURE 14.1

Business Letter

Not all letters need contain an attention line, a subject line, an identification line, or end notations.

Inside Address

The inside address is the address of the person, company, or organization to which you are sending your letter. Whenever possible, address your letter to a specific person rather than to the company or organization as a whole.

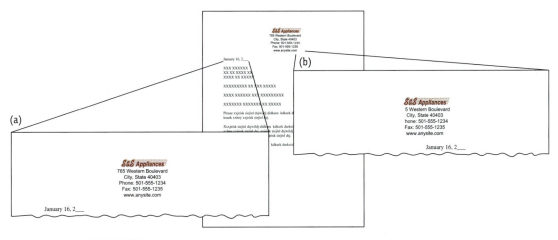

FIGURE 14.2

Heading and Date Line

The date line is two to six lines below the letterhead in (a) full-block and simplified formats and (b) semiblock and modified-block formats.

Mentioning the recipient's name in the inside address makes it more likely that your letter will not be delayed on its way to the appropriate reader. Typically, an inside address includes the name of the person you are writing to (including a courtesy title for the person and the person's job title), the company or organization name, the street address or post office box, the city, the state (either spelled out in full or abbreviated with the official postal service two-letter state code), and the zip code.

A courtesy title is the "Mr.," "Ms.," "Mrs.," "Miss," "Dr.," "Professor," "Reverend," or whatever is appropriate for the person to whom you are writing. If the person has a one-word job title, place this title on the same line; if the title is more than one word, place the job title on the line just below the person's name.

If you have questions about forms of address in the inside address and correct salutations for clerical and religious orders, college and university faculty and officials, consular officers, diplomats, foreign heads of state, government officials, military ranks, various professional titles, multiple addresses, and an assortment of special titles (for example, Doctor, Esquire, Honorable, Professor), consult a reference work such as *Merriam-Webster's Guide to Business Correspondence*, listed in the Resources at the end of the chapter. Figure 14.3 shows the placement of the inside address.

Attention Line

Attention lines are sometimes necessary in business correspondence if you want to address an organization in general and also bring your letter to the attention of a particular individual within the organization. If you address a letter to a company with an attention line for a particular person and that

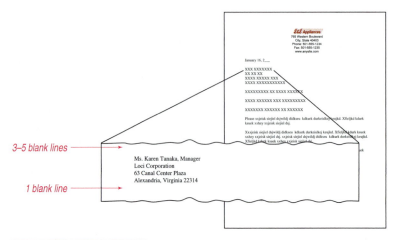

3–5 blank lines

1 blank line

Ms. Karen Tanaka, Manager
Loci Corporation
63 Canal Center Plaza
Alexandria, Virginia 22314

FIGURE 14.3

Inside Address

For shorter letters, allow more blank lines above the inside address; for longer letters, allow fewer blank lines.

person is unavailable to read your letter, then anyone representing the company may read it. If you address a letter to an individual and also provide an attention line to another person at the company, the letter will be forwarded to the person in the attention line if the addressee is unavailable.

Because a letter using an attention line is actually written to the company, the salutation following the attention line should be "Ladies and Gentlemen," "Gentlemen," or "Ladies" depending on who owns the company. (See the "Salutation" section that follows.) Place the attention line against the left margin in all letter formats, two lines below the inside address. The word *Attention* should be spelled out, and the first letter should be capitalized. Placing a colon after the word is optional.

Salutation

The salutation is your greeting to the person with whom you are corresponding. It should be placed against the left margin regardless of the letter format you are using, and it should be two line spaces below the inside address or the attention line. The salutation is followed by a colon except in personal letters, where a comma is commonly used. Typical salutations include the following:

Dear Mr. Doe:

Dear Mrs. Smith:

The courtesy title in the salutation must agree with the courtesy title that you use in the inside address. If you are writing to Mr. John Doe, for example, you should address him as "Dear Mr. Doe." If you know John Doe and have a good relationship with him, you may simply use "Dear John" for your salutation.

If you are writing to a company and do not know the name or gender of the specific person you are addressing, you have several choices. You can begin with "Dear Office Manager" or "Dear Personnel Supervisor," using the person's title as if it were a name.

If the owners of a company are both men and women, you may use "Ladies and Gentlemen" or "Dear Sir or Madam" for your salutation. If the letter is addressed to an all-female organization, the salutation "Ladies" is commonly used. If you have the name of an individual but you are uncertain of the gender, you might want to use the whole name, as "Dear Pat Smith."

"To Whom It May Concern" may be used if your letter is not addressed to any particular person or company. If at all possible, find a different salutation because this one is considered very impersonal. Letters of recommendation sometimes use this salutation because they are often sent to unknown addressees and are often distributed throughout a company or organization.

The guidelines concerning whether to use "Miss," "Ms.," or "Mrs." are complex. If you do not know the preferred title of address for the woman you are writing to, you should use "Dear Ms. Smith." If she has indicated a preference for "Miss" or "Mrs.," then you should use what she prefers.

In academic settings it is usually safest to write "Dear Dr. Smith" or "Dear Dr. Doe," even if you are not sure the person has a doctorate. Few people will be offended by being called "Doctor" inappropriately, but some who do hold doctorates will resent an omission of the title in correspondence. See Figure 14.4 for sample salutations.

FIGURE 14.4
Sample Salutations

TO ONE PERSON—TITLE PREFERENCE KNOWN

Dear Mr. Johnson:

Dear Ms. Rowland:

Dear Mrs. Shapiro:

Dear Miss Jefferson:

TO ONE PERSON—NAME UNKNOWN

Dear Editor in Chief:

Dear Accounts Manager:

TO AN ORGANIZATION—NAMES UNKNOWN

Dear Sir or Madam:

Dear Ladies and Gentlemen:

TO ONE PERSON—GENDER UNKNOWN

Dear Merle Sweeney:

TO A WOMAN—TITLE PREFERENCE UNKNOWN

Dear Ms. Haywood:

TO A COLLEGE INSTRUCTOR

Dear Dr. Chan:

(a)

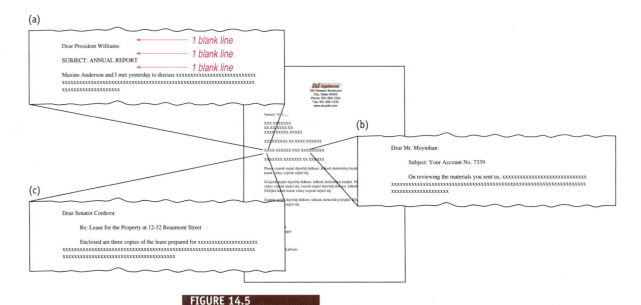

(b)

(c)

FIGURE 14.5

Subject Line

(a) The subject line is flush left in simplified and full-block formats. (b) The subject line may be indented in semiblock format, to match paragraph indents. (c) *Re:* usually replaces *Subject:* in legal documents.

Subject Line

A subject line is often used in professional correspondence to signal the content of the letter in a few key words. The subject line should be placed two line spaces below the salutation either against the left margin or indented, depending on the format of the letter you are using. For letters with indented paragraphs, indent the subject line. The word "Subject" should be followed by a colon. You may also provide a subject line and omit the word "Subject." Subject lines may be written in all capital letters. In some situations, notably in legal correspondence, "Re:" may be used instead of "Subject." See Figure 14.5 for sample subject lines.

Body

The body of a letter, also referred to as the message, consists of the text of the letter from the first sentence of the opening paragraph to the last sentence of the closing paragraph. If you want to write effective letters, remember that every letter has a definite structure and that even brief letters have an opening, a middle, and a closing.

Openings in letters vary according to purpose and audience. For many kinds of letters you need provide context for the letter and to state your purpose for writing in the opening. Providing context can mean acknowledging previous correspondence if you are responding to a letter or establishing a common ground when writing a letter of complaint. In one of the first few sentences, state why you are writing. Don't keep your reader guessing about why you wrote the letter. (See the "Patterns: Direct and Indirect" section later in this chapter for a description of a situation in which the purpose for writing is stated early but the conveying of bad news is delayed.)

One of the most common mistakes people make in writing letters is to bury their purpose somewhere in the middle of the letter. In general, letters are brief, and your reader needs to be told why you are writing. Put yourself in your reader's shoes and ask "Why am I reading this? Why was this letter sent to me? What does this writer want?" Most letters should answer these questions near the beginning—in the opening paragraph or two.

The middle of a letter may be only a sentence or two, or it may be several detailed paragraphs. This is the part of the letter in which you may use facts, statistics, examples, anecdotes, testimony, dates, names, reasons, and so on to support the purpose of your letter. In a brief letter on an ordinary or commonplace topic the middle won't be very involved. In a letter concerning a complicated or delicate issue the middle may be quite extensive. Whether the middle is brief or long, you must make sure it's appropriate to your purpose for writing.

How you end your letter also depends a great deal on your purpose for writing. The last few sentences of a letter typically enhance its professional tone. For example, you may write, "Please contact me if you have any questions" or "I am looking forward to discussing this matter with you soon." Use one of these or another closing that seems most natural to you and fits best with what you want to say.

Complimentary Close

Normally, your letter will end with a complimentary close and a signature block. The complimentary close is usually two lines below the last line of the last paragraph in the letter, aligned with the date at the top of the letter. If the date is flush left on the center line of the page, your complimentary close should be too.

The most common closes are the one-word closes "Sincerely" and "Cordially." Two-word and three-word complimentary closes such as "Sincerely yours" or "Very truly yours" are much less commonly used in correspondence today. Avoid original closes that are not appropriate in professional correspondence, such as "Later," "Signing off," or "Your humble servant."

International correspondence presents other problems where more formal closings, salutations, and so on, are common practice and in fact considered necessary in the well-written business letter. For example, as a rule, French business letters end with a formula, such as "Please accept, my dear sir or madam, the expression of my highest esteem." To omit this type of close in a formal French business letter would be considered poor form.

If you are unfamiliar with the cultural expectations of the person who will be receiving and reading your letter, consult a guide to international

> Don't keep your reader guessing about why you wrote the letter.

FIGURE 14.6

Complimentary Close and Signature Block

(a) The complimentary close and signature block are flush left at the left margin in full-block and simplified formats. (b) The complimentary close and signature block are flush left at the center of the page for semiblock and modified-block formats.

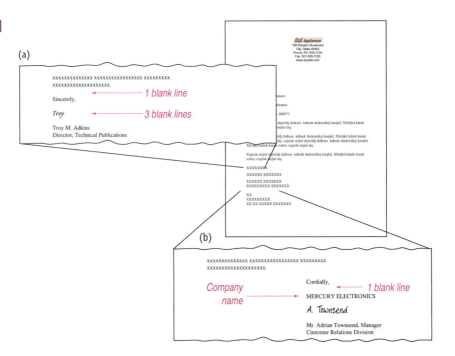

business communications or ask a knowledgeable colleague or friend to look over your letter before sending it. See Figure 14.6 for samples of the complimentary close.

Signature

The signature block, consisting of your signature and your typed name, follows at the bottom of the letter. Skip four lines between the complimentary close and the typed name. The signature block should be aligned with the date at the top of the letter. If the date is flush left on the left margin of the page, your complimentary close and signature block should be flush left on the left margin, too. If the date is flush left on the center line of the page, you will align your complimentary close and signature block on the center line. Your signature may be as flamboyant or illegible as you care to make it (that's why you also provide your typed name), but it's a good idea not to have a signature that's too large or too small. For business letters your signature should be written in blue or black ink, never in other colors and never in pencil.

In much business correspondence it's common practice to provide the company name as part of the signature block. The company name should be placed about two lines below the complimentary close. Then skip two lines and provide the letter writer's signature, printed name, and job title. See Figure 14.6 for samples of the signature block.

Identification Line

Sometimes assistants draft letters for their employers to sign, and often typists type letters written or dictated by others. The identification line informs the reader who wrote or dictated, who signed, and who transcribed or typed a business letter. If someone else drafted the letter for you to sign, that person's initials should be provided, aligned against the left margin two line spaces below the last line of the signature block. For example, if John Smith drafted the letter for Jane Doe's signature, the identification line would read JS:JD, with both sets of initials in capital letters.

If someone else typed the letter, the typist provides his or her initials after the writer's at the bottom of the letter. For example, if the writer's initials are ABC and the typist's initials are XYZ, the initials ABC:xyz (or the typist's initials alone) would appear at the end of the letter, aligned with the left margin of the page. Notice that the typist's initials are provided in lowercase letters. See Figure 14.7 for sample identification lines.

End Notations

End notations are often used in correspondence to indicate enclosures or to indicate the names of others who will receive copies of the letter. If you are providing enclosures, you can write "Enclosures" or "enc." (without the quotation marks) at the bottom of the letter, against the left margin, and

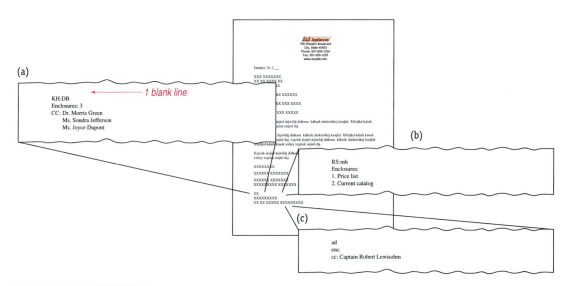

FIGURE 14.7

Identification Line and End Notations

(a) The letter was drafted by KH and signed by DB. (b) The letter was drafted and signed by RS and typed by MH. (c) The letter was typed by AD and drafted by whoever signed the letter.

even indicate the number of enclosures: "Enclosures: 2" or "enc. 2." The end notation "cc" (which formerly meant "carbon copy" but now can be taken to mean "courtesy copy") indicates who else is receiving a copy of the letter. See Figure 14.7 for sample end notations.

Letter Formats

The professional appearance of your letter is essential. Many readers won't bother to read a letter that looks unprofessional, so you need to devote attention to margins, line spacing, fonts, paragraph length, and so on. These elements differ, depending on the format you select. In addition, the alignment and indentions of various letter features can vary depending on the letter format you are using. Selecting a letter format may mean simply following your professor's or employer's preferred method. But often the choice will be up to you.

The differences between block, modified block, and semiblock reflect more on personal taste and the design of the preprinted letterhead (if any) than business requirements. Review each one and choose the one that suits you best and looks best with the placement of letterhead elements. The simplified style is often used when it has been adopted as "house" or company style. It provides a stripped-down approach to the business letter, one that can seem too sparse in some contexts. The personal style of letters is just what it sounds like. You usually would not use this style in business correspondence, but it would be perfectly suitable in personal correspondence when you want to send something more formal than an e-mail.

Consider the five common letter formats: block or full-block, modified block, semiblock, simplified, and personal.

Block or Full-Block

See Figure 14.8 for an example of a full-block letter.

Text alignment: All elements flush left on the left margin.

Spacing:

> **Date line:** Two to six line spaces below the last line of the heading or letterhead.
>
> **Inside address:** Placement varies depending on the length of the letter. A common spacing is four line spaces below the date line.
>
> **Salutation:** Two lines below the attention line (if an attention line is provided).
>
> **Body:** Two lines below an attention line or two to four lines below the last inside address line.

Paragraphs: Not indented; lines single spaced, with a double space between paragraphs.

FIGURE 14.8
Full-Block Letter

Orion Consulting
1254 Cactus Way
Phoenix, AZ 85014
(602) 555-7877

May 2, 2___

Mr. Mike Kendrall
Vice President of Operations
Loci Corporation
63 Canal Center Plaza
Suite 710
Alexandria, Virginia 22314

Dear Mr. Kendrall:

Thank you for your letter of April 27 providing me a copy of a Confidentiality Agreement with your company. As you requested, I kept a copy for my files, and I am enclosing a copy for you. I am also writing concerning some changes in possible starting dates for the seminars because of a change in my schedule.

First, because I have signed this agreement, I hope that you can now send me sample correspondence (memos and letters), sample reports, and any other relevant documents from those who will participate in the writing seminars. After I review these materials, I will have a better idea of what areas need to be addressed, and then I will promptly send you a proposal for the writing seminars. I hope this plan is okay with you.

Second, during our conference call on April 16, we discussed some possible dates in early June for starting these seminars. Because of recent changes in my schedule, the earliest I can conduct the first four-hour (9:00 a.m. to 1:00 p.m.) seminar is Friday, June 15, instead of Friday, June 1 or June 8.

During our conference call, I know there was some concern about the availability of participants for the latter part of June. I could offer the first seminar on June 15 (if this date is convenient), and if Friday, June 22, is not convenient for the second seminar, I will send you a proposal offering seminars for Friday, June 15, and several Fridays in September or October (for a total of three seminars). As I recall, we excluded conducting any seminars in July or August. Please let me know what Fridays are most convenient for you, and I will do my best to adjust my schedule accordingly.

Sincerely,

John Rodino

John Rodino

Modified Block

See Figure 14.9 for an example of a modified-block letter.

FIGURE 14.9

Modified-Block Letter

Orion Consulting
1254 Cactus Way
Phoenix, AZ 85014
(602) 555-7877

May 2, 2___

Mr. Mike Kendrall
Vice President of Operations
Loci Corporation
63 Canal Center Plaza
Suite 710
Alexandria, Virginia 22314

Dear Mr. Kendrall:

Thank you for your letter of April 27 providing me a copy of a Confidentiality Agreement with your company. As you requested, I kept a copy for my files, and I am enclosing a copy for you. I am also writing concerning some changes in possible starting dates for the seminars because of a change in my schedule.

First, because I have signed this agreement, I hope that you can now send me sample correspondence (memos and letters), sample reports, and any other relevant documents from those who will participate in the writing seminars. After I review these materials, I will have a better idea of what areas need to be addressed, and then I will promptly send you a proposal for the writing seminars. I hope this plan is okay with you.

Second, during our conference call on April 16, we discussed some possible dates in early June for starting these seminars. Because of recent changes in my schedule, the earliest I can conduct the first four-hour (9:00 a.m. to 1:00 p.m.) seminar is Friday, June 15, instead of Friday, June 1 or June 8.

During our conference call, I know there was some concern about the availability of participants for the latter part of June. I could offer the first seminar on June 15 (if this date is convenient), and if Friday, June 22, is not convenient for the second seminar, I will send you a proposal offering seminars for Friday, June 15, and several Fridays in September or October (for a total of three seminars). As I recall, we excluded conducting any seminars in July or August. Please let me know what Fridays are most convenient for you, and I will do my best to adjust my schedule accordingly.

Sincerely,

John Rodino

John Rodino

Text alignment: Some elements flush left at left margin (inside address, salutation, body, identification line, and enclosure notation); some elements flush left at center line (date line, complimentary close, and signature block).

Spacing: Same as full-block style.

Paragraphs: Not indented; lines single spaced, with a double space between paragraphs.

Semiblock

See Figure 14.10 for an example of a semiblock letter.

FIGURE 14.10

Semiblock Letter

Orion Consulting
1254 Cactus Way
Phoenix, AZ 85014
(602) 555-7877

May 2, 2___

Mr. Mike Kendrall
Vice President of Operations
Loci Corporation
63 Canal Center Plaza
Suite 710
Alexandria, Virginia 22314

Dear Mr. Kendrall:

    Thank you for your letter of April 27 providing me a copy of a Confidentiality Agreement with your company. As you requested, I kept a copy for my files, and I am enclosing a copy for you. I am also writing concerning some changes in possible starting dates for the seminars because of a change in my schedule.

    First, because I have signed this agreement, I hope that you can now send me sample correspondence (memos and letters), sample reports, and any other relevant documents from those who will participate in the writing seminars. After I review these materials, I will have a better idea of what areas need to be addressed, and then I will promptly send you a proposal for the writing seminars. I hope this plan is okay with you.

    Second, during our conference call on April 16, we discussed some possible dates in early June for starting these seminars. Because of recent changes in my schedule, the earliest I can conduct the first four-hour (9:00 a.m. to 1:00 p.m.) seminar is Friday, June 15, instead of Friday, June 1 or June 8.

    During our conference call, I know there was some concern about the availability of participants for the latter part of June. I could offer the first seminar on June 15 (if this date is convenient), and if Friday, June 22, is not convenient for the second seminar, I will send you a proposal offering seminars for Friday, June 15, and several Fridays in September or October (for a total of three seminars). As I recall, we excluded conducting any seminars in July or August. Please let me know what Fridays are most convenient for you, and I will do my best to adjust my schedule accordingly.

Sincerely,

John Rodino

John Rodino

Text alignment: Flush left at left margin (inside address, salutation, body, identification initials, and enclosure notation); some elements slightly to the right of dead center or flush right (date line, complimentary close, and typed name).

Spacing: Same as full-block style.

Paragraphs: First line indented five spaces; lines single spaced, with a double space between paragraphs.

Simplified

See Figure 14.11 for an example of a simplified letter.

Text alignment: All elements flush left on the left margin.

Spacing:

> **Date line:** Two to six line spaces below the last line of the heading or letterhead.

> **Inside address:** Placement varies depending on the length of the letter. A common spacing is four line spaces below the date line.

> **Subject line:** Replaces salutation; placed two lines below the attention line (if an attention line is provided); typed in all caps.

> **Body:** Two lines below subject line or two to four lines below the last inside address line.

> **Complimentary close:** Omitted in this format.

> **Typed name (and business title, if necessary):** Placed at least five lines below the last line of the body; typed in all caps.

Paragraphs: Not indented; lines single spaced, with a double space between paragraphs.

Personal

See Figure 14.12 for an example of a personal letter. Personal correspondence is much more informal in format and tone than professional correspondence. Personal letters are usually written on plain stationery, without a letterhead, and the recipient may be addressed by first name, depending on the relationship between the sender and the receiver.

Text alignment: Some elements flush left at left margin (salutation, body); some elements flush left at center line or slightly to the right of center line (address of sender, date line, complimentary close, signature).

Spacing:

> **Address of sender (return address):** At the top; normally two lines (street address and city, state, zip code).

> **Date line:** Immediately below inside address (or sometimes two lines below city, state, zip code).

> **Salutation:** Two to six lines below the date line.

FIGURE 14.11
Simplified Letter

> **Orion Consulting**
> *1254 Cactus Way*
> *Phoenix, AZ 85014*
> *(602) 555-7877*
>
> May 2, 2___
>
> Mr. Mike Kendrall
> Vice President of Operations
> Loci Corporation
> 63 Canal Center Plaza
> Suite 710
> Alexandria, Virginia 22314
>
> STARTING DATES
>
> Thank you for your letter of April 27 providing me a copy of a Confidentiality Agreement with your company. As you requested, I kept a copy for my files, and I am enclosing a copy for you. I am also writing concerning some changes in possible starting dates for the seminars because of a change in my schedule.
>
> First, because I have signed this agreement, I hope that you can now send me sample correspondence (memos and letters), sample reports, and any other relevant documents from those who will participate in the writing seminars. After I review these materials, I will have a better idea of what areas need to be addressed, and then I will promptly send you a proposal for the writing seminars. I hope this plan is okay with you.
>
> Second, during our conference call on April 16, we discussed some possible dates in early June for starting these seminars. Because of recent changes in my schedule, the earliest I can conduct the first four-hour (9:00 a.m. to 1:00 p.m.) seminar is Friday, June 15, instead of Friday, June 1 or June 8.
>
> During our conference call, I know there was some concern about the availability of participants for the latter part of June. I could offer the first seminar on June 15 (if this date is convenient), and if Friday, June 22, is not convenient for the second seminar, I will send you a proposal offering seminars for Friday, June 15, and several Fridays in September or October (for a total of three seminars). As I recall, we excluded conducting any seminars in July or August. Please let me know what Fridays are most convenient for you, and I will do my best to adjust my schedule accordingly.
>
> *John Rodino*
> JOHN RODINO

Body: Two lines below the salutation.

Paragraphs: Not indented; lines single spaced, with a double space between paragraphs.

In a personal letter, using only a first name in the salutation (followed by a comma) is fine, and providing a personal complimentary close is common, too.

FIGURE 14.12

Personal Letter

The return address and date line can be aligned flush left at the center line or, if preferred, centered to create a simple personal letterhead.

229 Peachtree Hills Avenue
Atlanta, GA 30355
December 20, 2____

Dear Phil,

Thanks again for your phone call. As always, I enjoyed talking to you and catching up on news. I'm enclosing a map to our place. If you have any problem with the directions, give me a call. We look forward to your visit.

Yours,

Dave

Formatting Letters

- Use at least a one-inch margin on all sides. For a one-page letter, position the text slightly higher than the middle of the page. (See Figure 14.13.)
- Single-space your letter using extra space between paragraphs.
- Use a conservative-looking typeface that does not distract the reader from your message.
- Use only one typeface. If your letter is very long and you have provided descriptive headings for various sections, those headings may be in a second typeface that complements the body text.
- Use italics, bold, and underline only to provide emphasis for a word, phrase, or short passage. If every sentence contains styled text, it loses its effectiveness.
- Use point sizes in the average range—10 to 12 point is usual.

Your word processing software has a setting for font size.

- Keep your paragraphs short. Try to keep your paragraph length under ten lines.
- Use good quality stationery in conservative colors (white, cream, or gray) for business correspondence.
- Use color sparingly if at all in correspondence.
- If you are using letterhead stationery, a second and subsequent pages should be on matching nonletterhead paper. At the top of the second and subsequent pages provide the name of the person you are writing to (including courtesy title), the page number, and the date. Figure 14.14 shows a sample second page.

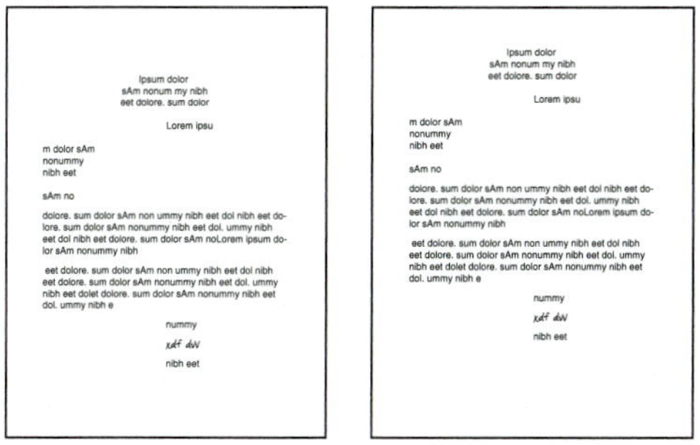

(a) (b)

FIGURE 14.13
Positioning Short Letters

(a) A one-page, vertically centered letter looks crowded at the bottom. (b) A one-page letter positioned slightly *above* the center of the page looks attractive and well-spaced.

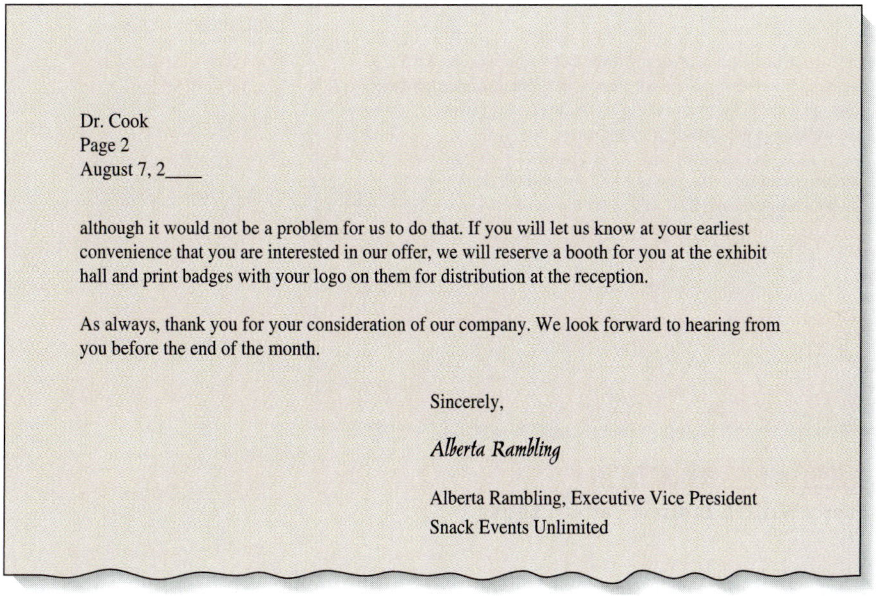

Dr. Cook
Page 2
August 7, 2____

although it would not be a problem for us to do that. If you will let us know at your earliest convenience that you are interested in our offer, we will reserve a booth for you at the exhibit hall and print badges with your logo on them for distribution at the reception.

As always, thank you for your consideration of our company. We look forward to hearing from you before the end of the month.

Sincerely,

Alberta Rambling

Alberta Rambling, Executive Vice President
Snack Events Unlimited

FIGURE 14.14
Second-Page Header for a Letter

Patterns: Direct and Indirect

In correspondence—letters, memos, and e-mail—the terms *direct* and *indirect* refer to the order in which you present good or bad news or delicate information. These patterns are also sometimes referred to as the "yes/no" order. If you are offering good news, then present it in the opening of the letter (the direct pattern). If you are providing bad news, then place it toward the end of the middle or in the closing of the letter (the indirect pattern).

The indirect pattern is a challenging way to organize the information of a letter. In addition to stating the purpose of your letter in the opening (as you should try to do in all your correspondence), you are preparing the reader for

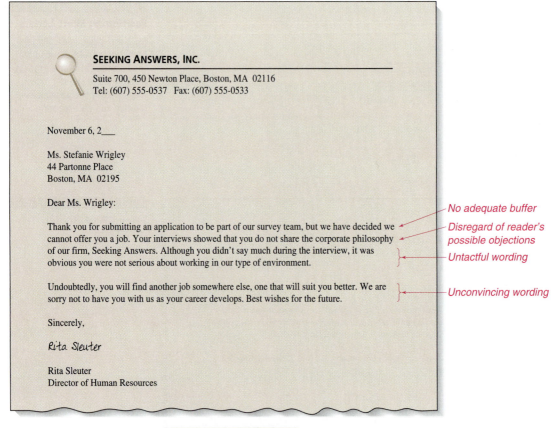

SEEKING ANSWERS, INC.

Suite 700, 450 Newton Place, Boston, MA 02116
Tel: (607) 555-0537 Fax: (607) 555-0533

November 6, 2___

Ms. Stefanie Wrigley
44 Partonne Place
Boston, MA 02195

Dear Ms. Wrigley:

Thank you for submitting an application to be part of our survey team, but we have decided we   — *No adequate buffer*
cannot offer you a job. Your interviews showed that you do not share the corporate philosophy   — *Disregard of reader's*
of our firm, Seeking Answers. Although you didn't say much during the interview, it was   *possible objections*
obvious you were not serious about working in our type of environment.   — *Untactful wording*

Undoubtedly, you will find another job somewhere else, one that will suit you better. We are   — *Unconvincing wording*
sorry not to have you with us as your career develops. Best wishes for the future.

Sincerely,

Rita Sleuter

Rita Sleuter
Director of Human Resources

FIGURE 14.15

Poorly Written Indirect Pattern Letter

the bad news that you will state later in the letter. This type of delay is often necessary and will make your letter more effective than if you simply state the bad or blunt or delicate news without preparing the reader for it.

An indirect pattern is demanding because it constantly challenges you to see your subject and purpose from the reader's point of view. When using an indirect pattern, carefully consider the following questions:

- Have you provided an adequate buffer in the opening of your letter?
- Have you considered possible concerns or objections the reader may have or make concerning the bad or delicate news?
- Have you stated the bad or delicate news as tactfully as possible in the best place in the letter?
- Is your wording convincing?

Knowing how and when to use an indirect pattern will help you in many kinds of correspondence situations. See, for example, Figure 14.15, a poorly

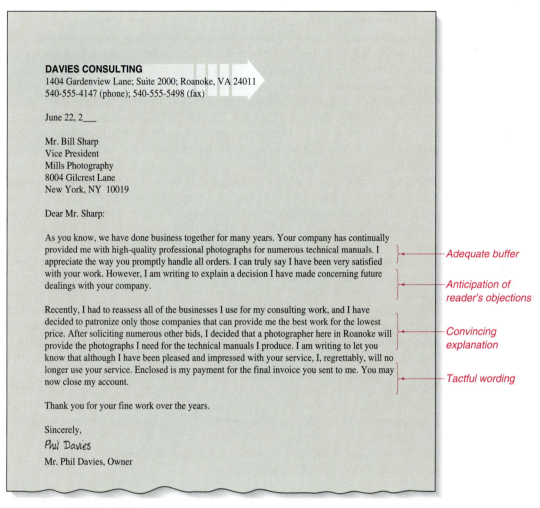

DAVIES CONSULTING
1404 Gardenview Lane; Suite 2000; Roanoke, VA 24011
540-555-4147 (phone); 540-555-5498 (fax)

June 22, 2___

Mr. Bill Sharp
Vice President
Mills Photography
8004 Gilcrest Lane
New York, NY 10019

Dear Mr. Sharp:

As you know, we have done business together for many years. Your company has continually provided me with high-quality professional photographs for numerous technical manuals. I appreciate the way you promptly handle all orders. I can truly say I have been very satisfied with your work. However, I am writing to explain a decision I have made concerning future dealings with your company.

— *Adequate buffer*

— *Anticipation of reader's objections*

Recently, I had to reassess all of the businesses I use for my consulting work, and I have decided to patronize only those companies that can provide me the best work for the lowest price. After soliciting numerous other bids, I decided that a photographer here in Roanoke will provide the photographs I need for the technical manuals I produce. I am writing to let you know that although I have been pleased and impressed with your service, I, regrettably, will no longer use your service. Enclosed is my payment for the final invoice you sent to me. You may now close my account.

— *Convincing explanation*

— *Tactful wording*

Thank you for your fine work over the years.

Sincerely,

Phil Davies

Mr. Phil Davies, Owner

FIGURE 14.16

Well-Written Indirect Pattern Letter

written indirect pattern letter, and Figure 14.16, a well-written indirect pattern letter.

Types of Letters

All letters do not have the same purpose, so all letters do not have the same organization. Think about why you are writing your letter before you begin and keep that in mind as you review the section you have just read on direct and indirect order. The following sections discuss complaint, adjustment, refusal, inquiry, and transmittal letters. For information on writing a job-application letter, see Chapter 11.

Complaint Letters

Unfortunately, at some time—and probably not just once—you will find you have to write a letter complaining about a product, service, or incident. Perhaps the product you purchased was overpriced or is faulty; perhaps you received substandard service; or perhaps a store clerk treated you rudely. Often the only way to get satisfactory action is to write a complaint letter. You may be angry about the product, service, or incident, but you'll have to learn how to set some of that anger aside if you want your letter to achieve positive results. You can write an angry letter simply to vent your emotions, but don't expect to receive satisfaction if you mail it. Sometimes you can achieve a satisfactory result by writing the letter and putting it aside. Come back to it in a few days. You may find that you overreacted or that you can express your displeasure more effectively now that you've had some time to cool down. See Figure 14.17 for an example of an overemotional complaint letter.

The purpose of a letter of complaint is to obtain some kind of action concerning the product you purchased, the service you received, or the incident in which you were ill treated. Your purpose may be to obtain a refund, an exchange, or a better product for the same price as the defective product that you purchased; to have the service provided again for no cost or to have better service provided the next time; or to obtain an apology for the way you were treated or to have someone reprimanded for the way he or she treated you. These are among the many possible reasons for writing a letter of complaint. But it isn't enough just to write out your complaint and hope for the best. You'll need to control carefully the organization, content, style, and tone of your letter to achieve your letter's purpose. See Figure 14.18 for an example of an effective complaint letter.

Well-written complaint letters are composed carefully, with attention given to all three parts of the letter's body:

1. In the opening of the complaint letter, establish a common ground with your correspondent. Identify your relationship with the recipient or company. Tell your reader why you have purchased products or had services provided by the company or organization before. Your goal here is to establish a courteous tone and to build rapport with the reader. In the last sentence or two of the opening, make your purpose for writing clear by simply stating you are writing because of a recent problem or incident that you hope can be resolved.

2. In the middle of the letter, discuss the particulars of your complaint. Be specific about product names, serial numbers, invoices, dates, and anything else that might help to identify the transaction and persuade your reader to your point of view. Avoid negative phrases such as "your mistake" or "your fault." Avoid insults. Maintain a courteous tone throughout, and you'll more likely achieve the results you seek. Toward the end of the middle of your letter, state your specific request for action. Request the refund, exchange, apology, better service, or

FIGURE 14.17

**Over-the-Top
Complaint Letter**

SHOCKTACKLE BIKE AND KITE SHOP
2727 Lakeview Avenue, Sea Side Groves, VA 23205
277-555-2468 (phone); 277-555-2469 (fax)

July 16, 2___

"Here In Town" Directory
150A Tabler Street
Sea Side Groves, VA 23205

To the Editors of the "Here In Town" Directory:

I can only believe that it is your intention to RUIN the highly regarded standing of the ShockTackle Bike and Kite Shop with a listing in your directory in which you take it upon yourself to RENAME OUR SHOP the "ShockTICKLE Bike and Kite Shop."

WHO gave you permission to rename the ShockTackle Bike and Kite Shop? For 28 years—as you know very well—we have been the ShockTackle Bike and Kite Shop. Mr. Shocktackle's name is an integral part of our name. With the name change and the omission of our telephone number, it is obvious that you would NEVER want to be so informative as to allow people the opportunity to actually SHOP at the very store you write about: That might actually be helpful. Now you have taken it upon yourself—through yet another of your unbelievable acts of hubris—to rename our store.

The "Here In Town" Directory has no idea what kind of effort it takes to bring the world's great recreational equipment to Sea Side Groves. And you make that more evident all the time. For those of us who actually place the orders, stock the shelves, and conduct well-timed sales—in spite of an article's placement ON THE DAY OF THE SALE and WITHOUT A PHONE NUMBER—the ultimate insult is to have the local directory rename one's store without permission. THAT IS NOT FOR YOU TO DO—no matter how powerful you may think you are. When you write about us again—IF you write about us again—let me remind you that we are the SHOCKTACKLE BIKE AND KITE SHOP. Please do us the courtesy of remembering that in the future. And our store telephone number is 277-555-2468, since you seem to have forgotten that as well.

Angrily yours,
Arnold Esterling
Arnold Esterling, Manager

whatever else you want to receive. If necessary and appropriate, offer a compromise.

3. In the closing of the letter, look to the future, for example stating that you would like to continue as a loyal customer, and provide a courteous ending, such as, "Thank you for your careful attention to this matter. I am looking forward to hearing from you soon."

Adjustment Letters

Adjustment letters are responses to letters of complaint from customers or clients. In these letters you are offering some kind of adjustment or compromise

FIGURE 14.18

**Well-Written
Complaint Letter**

1201 Winterwood Boulevard
Oakland, CA 94601
June 25, 2____

Ms. Phyllis A. Dow
Bay Professional Consultants
934 N. Orange Avenue
San Francisco, CA 94103

Dear Ms. Dow:

Over the past few years, you have provided valuable advice to my wife and me concerning our
son, Jeff. We appreciate the attention and time you have devoted to our situation. It isn't often
that we encounter such professionalism. However, I am writing concerning a billing issue that I
hope can be resolved soon.

Recently, we experienced a misunderstanding with your billing office. After our last
appointment with you, we stopped by the front desk, where we learned we had a balance due in
the amount of $55.00. The staff member did not know what the charge was for and said she
would find out on the next day. Because we were in a hurry to pick up our son, I asked my wife
to pay the amount, feeling we could sort out the details later.

The next day we found out that the $55.00 is a charge for our supposedly missing an
appointment on May 25 at 2:00 p.m. This news was a big surprise to my wife and me. I
checked my detailed phone log and verified that I had called your office on the morning of May
23 to cancel the appointment and reschedule it for a later date. In addition to the entry in my
log, I specifically recall the telephone conversation.

In sum, my wife and I ask that you and your office staff void the $55.00 charge. It would be
unfair to charge us $55.00 when we canceled our May 25 appointment more than 48 hours in
advance. I am particularly conscientious about keeping all appointments I make, and if I cannot
keep an appointment, I always cancel well before the appointment.

If you would like to discuss this matter with me, please call me at 555-2627.

Considering the amount of time my wife and I have spent with you, this particular incident is
relatively minor. We hope it will be resolved amicably, and we look forward to future meetings
with you.

Thank you.

Sincerely,
Bob Smith
Bob Smith

in response to what was requested in the letter of complaint. Adjustment letters
provide good opportunities to strengthen relations between the organization or
company and the customer. They can be difficult to write because you may not
be able to agree to provide exactly what your reader is requesting, but you will
still want to maintain or build goodwill. See Figure 14.19 for a sample adjustment letter.

FIGURE 14.19
Adjustment Letter

Bay Professional Consultants

934 N. Orange Avenue; Suite 200; San Francisco, CA 94103; 415-555-4142 (phone); 415-555-3467 (fax)

June 29, 2___

Mr. Bob Smith
1201 Winterwood Boulevard
Oakland, CA 94601

Dear Mr. Smith:

Thank you for your letter of June 25. I am happy to have you and your family as our clients, and I am grateful for the details you provided about the recent problem.

As I understand the situation, you have been charged $55.00 for possibly missing an appointment. I have checked with all of my staff members and have reviewed various files, particularly the telephone log. We log all of our phone calls here at Bay Professional Consultants. However, I will admit to you that it is possible that my staff sometimes forgets to log some phone calls. Your thorough explanation of how you view the events is satisfactory to me. I have instructed my staff manager to void the $55.00 invoice.

My staff and I look forward to working with you and your family in the future.

Sincerely,
Phyllis A. Dow
Ms. Phyllis A. Dow

Well-written adjustment letters make effective use of their three main sections:

1. In the opening of the letter, acknowledge that you received the reader's letter and state the date of the letter you are responding to. Thank the reader for taking the time to write to the company, and tell the reader how much his or her business means to the company. In these ways and others you are establishing a courteous and professional tone. If you are granting exactly what the writer of the complaint letter requested, then state in the opening paragraph that you are enclosing a refund, offering a discount for the next visit, or providing whatever adjustment you are able to offer. If your response is positive, then use the direct or "good news" approach for your reader.

2. In the middle of the letter, summarize your understanding of the situation as it was described by your reader. This summary shows that you have read the letter closely and that you are paying careful attention to the reader's point of view. After you finish summarizing the reader's view, offer the company's position on the particular complaint. State whether or not it is company policy to offer an exchange or refund or whatever. If you are free to offer the reader what was requested, then you may state at this point in the letter that you are offering what was requested (if you haven't already done so in the opening). If you must offer a compromise, then state what the compromise is. Maintain a respectful, professional tone throughout. You aren't representing yourself; you are representing the company, and your goal should be to maintain goodwill as much as possible.

3. In the closing of the letter, mention that you are looking forward to a continuing relationship with your reader, and provide a courteous ending.

Refusal Letters

You can think of a refusal letter as an adjustment letter that says "no." In a refusal letter you are declining to offer the writer what was requested in a letter of complaint to your company or organization. This kind of letter will be more effective if you prepare your reader for your refusal. See Figure 14.20 for a sample refusal letter.

1. In the opening of the letter acknowledge that you received the letter sent to you ("Thank you for your letter of June 29 . . .") in order to establish a common ground. This common ground provides a buffer for the bad news that you will provide a little later in the letter. It also helps you establish a professional tone and maintain a "you attitude" in your letter. Maintaining a "you attitude" (also called a "you" approach) means focusing on the reader and the reader's interests as much as possible. Use the word "you" frequently instead of "I," "we," and "our." And for the "you attitude" to be successful, your efforts to appeal to the reader must be honest and sincere rather than contrived.

2. In the middle of your letter, focus on the reasons you must decline the request. Then, after you state the reasons, politely state that you regretfully must decline the request. Offer convincing reasons, and be fair to the reader.

3. In the closing of the letter, look to the future. Remember that you still want your reader to be a customer. Provide a courteous close.

Inquiry Letters

Often you have to make a formal request to a person, a company, or an agency to obtain information. Letters of inquiry are necessary when you need

FIGURE 14.20
Refusal Letter

Bay Professional Consultants

934 N. Orange Avenue; Suite 200; San Francisco, CA 94103; 415-555-4142 (phone); 415-555-3467 (fax)

June 29, 2___

Mr. Bob Smith
1201 Winterwood Boulevard
Oakland, CA 94601

Dear Mr. Smith:

Thank you for your letter of June 25. I am happy to have you and your family as our clients, and I am grateful for the details you provided about this recent problem.

As I understand the situation, you believe you called on May 23 to cancel a scheduled May 25 appointment, and you believe you have been mistakenly charged for not canceling an appointment. For many years my staff has logged all of the calls that come to the office. In fact, last year I put an automated system into place, so that all of the calls are logged electronically. My staff and I have reviewed these logs carefully, but, unfortunately, we can find no record of a call by you on May 23. I have had the automated phone system checked and have been assured everything is working properly with this system. Is it possible that you canceled some other appointment with a different office on that day?

Regrettably, I cannot authorize my staff to void the $55.00 invoice for the missed appointment. I hope you will understand our position.

We appreciate your continued patronage and look forward to working with you in the future.

Sincerely,
Phyllis A. Dow
Ms. Phyllis A. Dow

to find information about a person, a product, or a service, for example, and you haven't been able to find the information from some other source. Knowing how to write this kind of letter can be helpful in many research situations. If no action on the part of the person or company has prompted your letter, then it is considered an *unsolicited letter of inquiry.* If you are responding to a product ad suggesting that you write for more information, then your letter is a *solicited letter of inquiry.* See Figure 14.21 for guidelines concerning solicited and unsolicited inquiry letters.

Solicited and unsolicited letters require similar and yet slightly different strategies. Figure 14.22 shows a sample unsolicited inquiry. Either type requires the following:

FIGURE 14.21

**Guidelines for
Inquiry Letters**

SOLICITED LETTER OF INQUIRY	UNSOLICITED LETTER OF INQUIRY
■ State letter is in response to ad or other solicitation. ■ Mention source or location of request. ■ Explain what information is needed.	■ Identify yourself. ■ State why you are writing. ■ Apologize for any inconvenience. ■ Enclose a self-addressed, stamped envelope if you need a written reply.

1. In the opening of a solicited or unsolicited letter, state who you are and why you are writing. If you are writing a solicited letter, state how you heard about the opportunity to request information (through a print, television, newspaper, or magazine ad, for example). If you are writing an unsolicited letter, take a more careful approach in the opening, explaining briefly who you are and why you need the information. Use a serious tone and a formal style throughout either letter. Consider offering your reader some kind of compensation for the time it will take to fulfill your request, whether by providing a copy of your research results or by paying for any expenses in addition to postage.

2. In the middle of either letter, state what kind of information you need. Be direct and clear about the information you need, and provide a deadline so that the person you're requesting information from will know when to respond. If you need to ask a list of questions, enclose the list on a separate sheet and simply use the letter to introduce yourself, state why you need the questions answered, and provide a deadline. Make it easy for the person to respond to your questions, for example, by providing plenty of space below each question so that he or she can simply return your list to you.

3. Provide a courteous close. In a solicited letter, simply thank the correspondent for sending the information. In an unsolicited letter don't thank the recipient in advance for sending the information, but apologize for any inconvenience your request may cause. Include a self-addressed stamped envelope to make it easier for the person to whom you are writing to respond.

Transmittal Letters

A transmittal letter is a cover letter that is attached to, but is not part of, a proposal, report, manual, or some other document you are sending to someone. Transmittal letters are essential for providing a record of how, when, and to whom documents are distributed in an organization or company. Your transmittal letter identifies what is enclosed, provides an overview of the contents (optional), identifies to whom the material is being sent, and provides a courteous close. See Figure 14.23 for a sample transmittal letter. You will learn more about transmittal or cover letters in Chapter 18.

FIGURE 14.22
Unsolicited Inquiry Letter

1404 Victory Garden Lane
New York, NY 10019
October 11, 2___

Mr. Bruce Chen
Vice President of Operations
Orange Sky Software Company
Suite 3000
1803 Dumont Circle
Anaheim, CA 92801

Dear Mr. Chen:

I am a graduate student majoring in technical communication. I am working on a research project concerning different online help programs, and I am writing to ask you some questions concerning your online help program. If you can take 20 minutes of your time to answer the attached list of questions and return your answers to me in the enclosed envelope, I will gladly share the results of my comparative study with you when it's finished.

To save you time, I have provided a space of several inches below each question. If you don't mind, just jot down your answers in the indicated space. Also, if it's not too inconvenient, I will need to receive your response by November 1.

I can assure you that your answers to these questions will be quite helpful for my study. I look forward to hearing from you.

Sincerely,

Jack Baxter

Jack Baxter

MEMOS

Even though corporate e-mail has considerably reduced the paper flow at many companies and organizations, many people still write and send memos on all kinds of topics. You will spend a considerable amount of time on the job reading and responding to memos. Unlike letters, which are chiefly intended to be read by people outside of the company, memos are a

FIGURE 14.23
Transmittal Letter

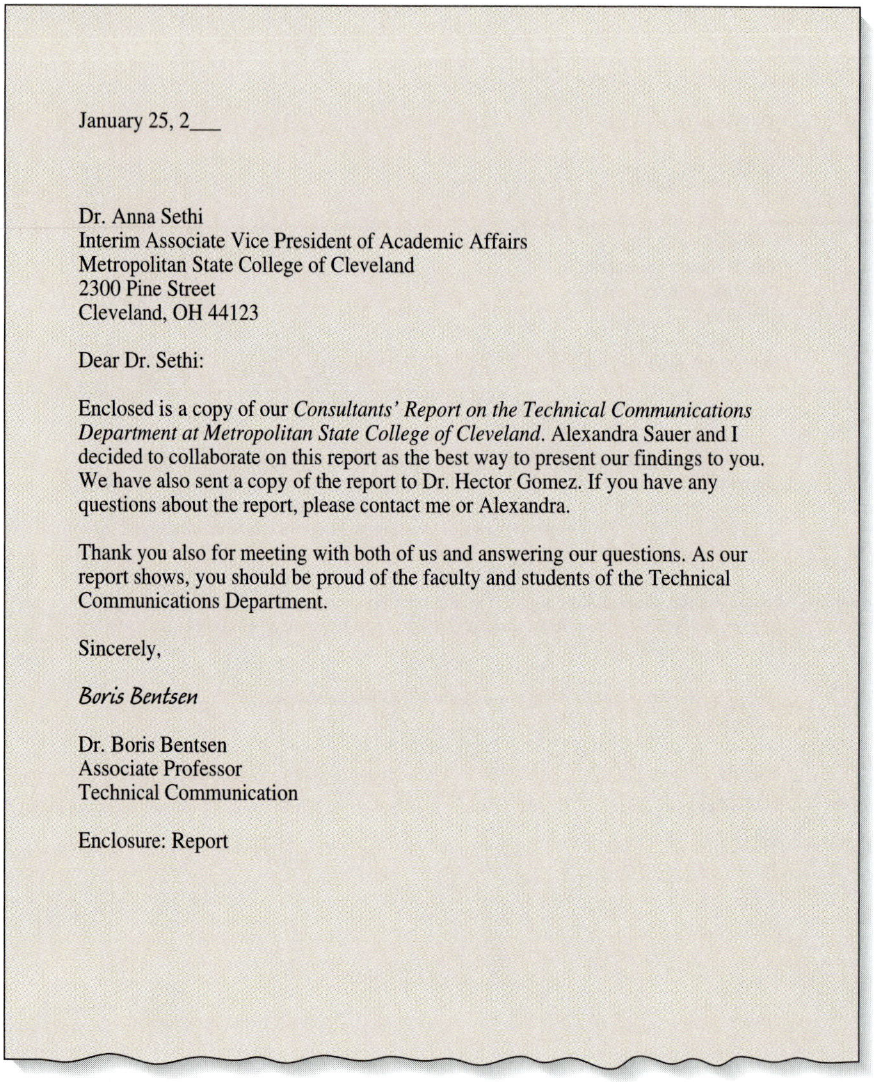

January 25, 2___

Dr. Anna Sethi
Interim Associate Vice President of Academic Affairs
Metropolitan State College of Cleveland
2300 Pine Street
Cleveland, OH 44123

Dear Dr. Sethi:

Enclosed is a copy of our *Consultants' Report on the Technical Communications Department at Metropolitan State College of Cleveland.* Alexandra Sauer and I decided to collaborate on this report as the best way to present our findings to you. We have also sent a copy of the report to Dr. Hector Gomez. If you have any questions about the report, please contact me or Alexandra.

Thank you also for meeting with both of us and answering our questions. As our report shows, you should be proud of the faculty and students of the Technical Communications Department.

Sincerely,

Boris Bentsen

Dr. Boris Bentsen
Associate Professor
Technical Communication

Enclosure: Report

form of internal correspondence for employees. The format of memos varies considerably from the format of letters. Formats of memos may also vary from individual to individual within a company or organization. In addition to the regular contexts in which you will find memos, the memo format also is a useful one to use when you need to create a fax cover sheet.

Formats

Look at Figure 14.24 and refer to it as you read the next two sections.

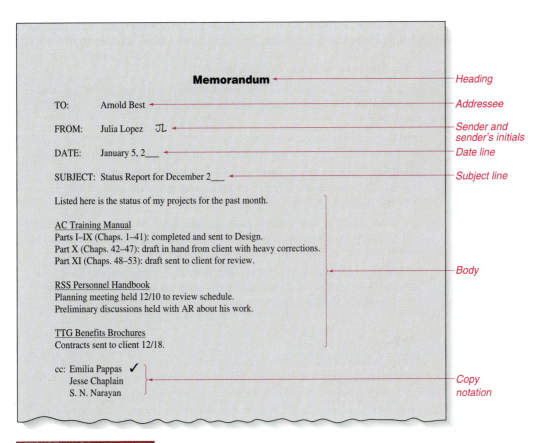

Memorandum ———————————— *Heading*

TO: Arnold Best ←——————————————— *Addressee*

FROM: Julia Lopez   JL ←——————————— *Sender and
                                        sender's initials*

DATE: January 5, 2___ ←————————————— *Date line*

SUBJECT: Status Report for December 2___ ←———— *Subject line*

Listed here is the status of my projects for the past month.

AC Training Manual
Parts I–IX (Chaps. 1–41): completed and sent to Design.
Part X (Chaps. 42–47): draft in hand from client with heavy corrections.
Part XI (Chaps. 48–53): draft sent to client for review.

RSS Personnel Handbook   *Body*
Planning meeting held 12/10 to review schedule.
Preliminary discussions held with AR about his work.

TTG Benefits Brochures
Contracts sent to client 12/18.

cc: Emilia Pappas ✓
    Jesse Chaplain ←——————————————— *Copy
    S. N. Narayan   notation*

FIGURE 14.24

Memo

Heading

The heading for a memo often contains the word "Memo" or "Memorandum" at the top of the memo, either aligned flush left or centered. A fax cover sheet will have "Facsimile" or "Fax Cover Sheet" in place of "Memo" or "Memorandum." Many people omit the word "Memo," believing that the other heading information makes it clear that the form is a memo. Notice that you don't provide the kind of heading information you provide in a letter (although many companies and organizations have preformatted memos that contain the company name, address, and other information). Many word processing programs can provide you with various designs for your memos.

Heading elements appear aligned on the left margin:

Addressee: The addressee line, labeled "To:" stands in place of an inside address. Provide the addressee's full name and, if appropriate or necessary, the person's complete title and address, as you would in the inside address of a letter.

Multiple addressees: If several recipients are listed in the addressee line, each person's copy should have some indication by the name showing to whom that copy is addressed. The indication can be as simple as a check mark placed next to the name or colored highlighting over it.

Sender: The sender line of a memo takes the place of a signature line used in a letter. After the word "From:" provide your full name and your job title if necessary.

Initials: Traditionally, you handwrite your initials to the right of your name instead of providing a signature block and signature at the bottom of the memo.

Date line: The date line consists of the word "Date" followed by a colon. The date for a memo is written in the same way it is written for a letter: December 1, 2001.

Attention line: For some memos you may also use an attention line. An attention line may be used in a memo for the same reason it is used in a letter: to ensure that the letter will be read even if the addressee is unavailable.

Subject line: The subject line is one of the most important lines in a memo. You should provide in a few key words the contents of the memo. The subject line is typically the last line to appear before the body of the memo.

Body

The body of a memo is the opening, middle, and closing paragraphs. How you open, develop the middle, and close depends on your purpose for writing. However, even a brief memo has a definite structure. Some memos also use a signature line, an identification line, enclosure notation, mail notation, and copy notation.

Signature line: Most memos do not use a signature line, but sometimes a company style allows a space for signing memos. If you have written your initials after your name on the "From:" line at the top, it is not necessary to initial or sign the body of the memo.

Identification line: An identification line in a memo may provide the same information it provides in a letter: identification of who wrote, dictated, signed, sent, transcribed, or typed the memo.

Enclosure and copy notations: Enclosure notations and copy notations in memos provide the same information they provide in letters.

Writing Memos

- Keep your memo as brief as possible. There is no prescribed length for a memo—some memos may be many pages long depending on the subject, purpose, scope, audience, and other factors; more often they are much shorter.

- Use a prose style and tone that are appropriate for your subject, audience, and purpose. For example, if your memo is going to

(continued)

FIGURE 14.25

Second-Page Memo Header

Dr. Haddock
Page 2
May 15, 2___

xx xx xxxxxxx xxxxxxx xxxxxx xxxxx xxxxx xxxxxx xxxx xx xxxxxxxxx xxx xxxx xxxx
xxx xxxxxx xxxxxxx xx xxx xxx xxx xxx xx xxxxxxx xxxxxxxxxxx. xx xx xxxxxxx
xxxxxxx xxxxxx xxxxx xxxxx xxxxxx xxxx xx xxxxxxxxx xxx xxxx xxxx xxx xxxxxx
xxxxxxx xx xxx xxx xxx xxx xx xxxxxxx xxxxxxxxxxx.

xx xx xxxxxxx xxxxxxx xxxxxx xxxxx xxxxx xxxxxx xxxx xx xxxxxxxxx xxx xxxx xxxx
xxx xxxxxx xxxxxxx xx xxx xxx xxx xxx xx xxxxxx

FIGURE 14.25

Second-Page Memo Header

your professor or your boss, make sure it reflects the formality of that situation.

- State your purpose in the opening brief paragraph. Don't waste your reader's time. Get to the purpose quickly.

- Use a forecasting statement, if appropriate, to tell your reader what you will cover in the memo. For example, write, "This memo addresses the key issues discussed in our last meeting, provides some new alternatives, and recommends our next course of action."

- Keep the paragraphs brief. Paragraphs should not exceed ten typed lines.

- In a longer memo, use headings and subheadings if necessary to help your reader recognize the organization of your memo.

- If the memo has a second or third page, indicate the recipient at the top of those pages in a continuation page header, as you would do in a letter. If you are sure the pages will remain stapled together, you may omit the header. See Figure 14.25 for an example of a second-page header.

Styling Memos

- Don't use many different typefaces or styles (italics, underlining, bold). Stick to one typeface for the body. If your memo has sections that have descriptive headings ("Background," "Resources," etc.), those headings may be in a different—but coordinating—typeface to set them apart from the following paragraphs.

- Avoid using point sizes for your typefaces that are smaller than 8 points or larger than 14 points.

- Avoid novelty or hard-to-read typefaces.

E-MAIL

Electronic mail (also known as e-mail, email, or Email) has been available for several decades but has become enormously popular within only the past five years or so. E-mail enables users to send and receive messages electronically. Messages are sent and received in seconds or minutes—much more quickly than is possible by surface mail ("snail mail"). See Figure 14.26 for a sample e-mail.

Advantages of E-mail

E-mail has many advantages over other kinds of correspondence. E-mail is easy to learn and easy to use and it is convenient. You can just as easily send a message to one person or the same message to thousands. And unlike the telephone, which can and often does interrupt at inconvenient times, e-mail messages can be read at the convenience of the reader.

E-mail is inexpensive. As a student, you may have an Internet account through your school. You may also have an account through a national or regional commercial provider, such as America Online, Prodigy, CompuServe, Microsoft Network, AT&T, or BellSouth, or you may have an account through a local Internet provider. Or perhaps you use one of the free Internet service providers for dial-up access to the Internet or just free e-mail. Even if you pay for Internet access, you probably don't consider the cost too expensive. And most companies offer flat-rate monthly plans, which limit your costs considerably.

E-mail is efficient. It's possible to handle numerous messages in very little time. With just a few keystrokes, you can also manage your correspondence by placing messages in electronic mailboxes and by updating your e-mail address book. E-mail also is quick. Most e-mail is delivered within a few minutes or less. Rarely will e-mail require more than a day to arrive.

E-mail can be useful for recording progress on projects (since messages can serve as a log of communications), for getting identical information to a large group of people, and for automatically receiving information that may be of interest to you. Additionally, e-mail is good for the environment. In many places, e-mail has replaced the massive use of paper to handle the day-to-day need to communicate via memo within a company or organization or from one company to another.

Disadvantages of E-mail

E-mail has some important disadvantages that should be considered carefully for every e-mail message you send. For example, e-mail is so convenient that you may neglect to use print correspondence (a letter, memorandum, or handwritten note) when print correspondence may be more appropriate. If you are sending someone information that must be filed in company archives,

THE DOWNSIDE OF E-MAIL

A worrying trend is that the more you use e-mail, the less inclined it makes you to use other forms of communication, especially letters ("snail mail"), which means that, without realizing it, you cut off all those whom you cannot reach electronically.

—Yateendra Joshi, director of information technology and services, New Delhi, India

FIGURE 14.26
E-mail Message

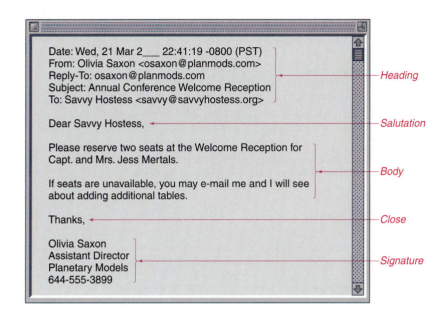

Date: Wed, 21 Mar 2___ 22:41:19 -0800 (PST)
From: Olivia Saxon <osaxon@planmods.com>
Reply-To: osaxon@planmods.com
Subject: Annual Conference Welcome Reception
To: Savvy Hostess <savvy@savvyhostess.org>   ← *Heading*

Dear Savvy Hostess,   ← *Salutation*

Please reserve two seats at the Welcome Reception for
Capt. and Mrs. Jess Mertals.
                                                             ← *Body*
If seats are unavailable, you may e-mail me and I will see
about adding additional tables.

Thanks,   ← *Close*

Olivia Saxon
Assistant Director   ← *Signature*
Planetary Models
644-555-3899

e-mail would not be the preferred medium. And for legal protection, e-mail notifications and interchanges are much weaker than paper correspondence.

Tone in e-mail is difficult to convey. It's easy for a reader to misinterpret a humorous or sarcastic message, for example. To help you convey the appropriate tone, you should become familiar with and use smileys or emoticons, such as those discussed later in this chapter. Be careful not to use these information tools in formal e-mails, for example in e-mails to your boss or your clients. The examples in Figure 14.27 show casual e-mail messages that could easily be misinterpreted.

E-mail can be easily lost. Sometimes a service provider's main computer will go down, not only making it impossible for you to send e-mail until repairs are done, but also sometimes losing e-mail that has been sent to you. Once e-mail is lost, it usually is lost forever. Worse, you will probably not know that your message was not delivered or that you were supposed to receive a message that never arrived.

If you don't check your e-mail frequently, your unread messages may create a backlog on your service provider's system. Many e-mail providers set a limit on how much space messages may take up before new messages are refused. Once that limit is reached, new messages will be turned away. Also, the person to whom you send an e-mail message may not check e-mail very often, so your message could go unread for a very long time.

Some providers charge a fee for each message you receive. If you are on several high-volume mailing lists, your costs could quickly get out of hand. Also, service providers with many subscribers may have insufficient resources to let all those who want to use their accounts be online at the same time. If

FIGURE 14.27

Vague or Misleading E-mail Messages

How many different ways could a recipient interpret these e-mail messages?

Dear Alex,

Your presentation was completely unlike any I had ever seen before, and I don't expect to see another like it again.
You are really something.

Jack

Javier: You ought to take the day off. You look as if you could use it. We'll let you know when to come back.

Steve

Hi Megan,

Thank you for your response to my e-mail last month. Now that I know where you stand on the lab layout, I'm sure we'll have plenty to talk about next month.

Thanks a bunch for the suggestions. How did you come up with them?

Sarah

you absolutely must have access to your e-mail account, you may have to change to a provider that can accommodate the traffic.

Not everyone has an e-mail address, and it can sometimes be very difficult to find an e-mail address for someone if you don't already have it. Often you can look up e-mail addresses in an online database such as <people.yahoo.com> or <www.555-1212.com>, but if you select the wrong person's address, your e-mail will not reach its intended target. The best way to find out someone's e-mail address is to ask that person.

> "
> The best way to find out someone's e-mail address is to ask that person.

Unfortunately, sometimes your message will go astray. Mistype one letter or number in the recipient's e-mail address, and that person will not receive it. If the mistyping results in a valid address, someone else will receive your message. If your message is not delivered at all, you may or may not receive notification of nondelivery.

If your computer is invaded by a computer virus or has some other kind of problem, you risk permanently losing all your unanswered or saved e-mail and your address book. To prevent this loss, keep a copy of your e-mail addresses on a backup diskette.

E-mail is not private. Internet service providers, university servers, and corporate intranets routinely back up their drives, so messages you want to delete may still have a permanent home somewhere in a backup file.

Sending E-mail and Attachments

How you send your e-mail, send attachments, or read the e-mail you receive varies from one e-mail program to another. Become familiar with the essential features of the e-mail program you prefer. Regardless of which one you use, there are a few conventions or guidelines you should follow.

Verify that you have specified the proper e-mail address for the person to whom you are sending your message. Many e-mail programs allow you to insert a person's e-mail address automatically, but you still need to manage your e-mail address book and keep your addresses current. Check that your own name and e-mail address also appear in your e-mail headers. Most e-mail programs insert this information automatically.

Provide a clear subject in the subject line of your e-mail message. If you are responding to someone else's message, most e-mail programs insert the original subject into the subject line of your e-mail message. You are free to change the subject line if circumstances warrant the change. If you are composing a new message, be certain to provide a subject in the subject line. E-mail programs will not insert one for you, although many will query you if you forget to provide one.

Consider whether you are sending formal or informal e-mail. If you are sending formal e-mail, use a salutation ("Dear Ms. Carter"), use a more formal style and tone, and provide a more formal signature. If you know your correspondent, you may simply write "Dear Stephanie" or "Hello" or provide no salutation at all.

Make your e-mail easily readable. Try to limit the width of each line to approximately 55 characters, so that your reader can skim your message easily. Keep the prose style relatively simple, and avoid overly long paragraphs.

Be cautious when using colors, fonts, styles, and other design features in some e-mail programs. Increasingly, e-mail programs enable you to use different colors for your text, different typefaces and sizes, styles such as italics and bold, and even different colors for your background. However, your readers will see none of these features if they do not have an e-mail program that can detect the features. Even if they do, be careful not to mix too many elements.

If your e-mail program doesn't have the color and design features, you may put words between asterisks (*) to indicate emphasis or use underscore characters (_) before and after a word or phrase you would like underlined. Some e-mail programs, such as Eudora, handle replies containing styled text differently from text without colors, styles, and the like. It can be quite annoying to reply to a styled e-mail when the program insists on providing an unusual treatment for the cited text. Therefore, use styles in e-mail sparingly if at all. Some e-mail programs provide an option to strip off styling from text before sending an e-mail.

Use a "signature" for your e-mail when appropriate. See Figure 14.28 for a sample signature. An e-mail signature is a few lines of identifying information that you can have your e-mail program automatically add to the end of

FIGURE 14.28

E-mail Signature

E-mail signature files can be customized for different uses.

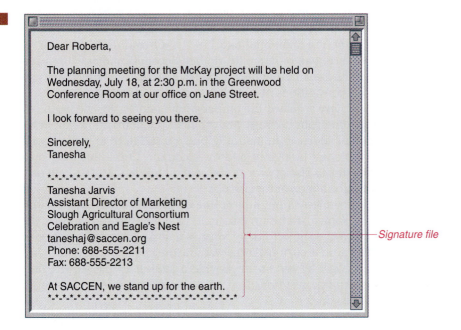

each message you send. It may include your name, job title if appropriate, address if you want to provide one, phone numbers, and so on. Or a signature may simply be a favorite quotation. Many e-mail programs automatically insert a signature into the bottom of your e-mail message, and many e-mail programs offer you the option of having many kinds of signatures. You should use a formal signature for formal e-mail correspondence and a personal signature for informal correspondence to friends and family. You also have the option of providing no signature, and for much e-mail this may be appropriate as well.

Proofread your message carefully before sending it. If your e-mail program has a spelling checker, use it.

Respond to messages appropriately. If you are replying to a long e-mail message, include just the relevant part or parts instead of the entire message. There is no need to include the entire original message. This point is especially important when your e-mail message will be seen by many people who are following your topic on an Internet mailing list or Usenet newsgroup. Usually, you should provide the original e-mail message at the top and then your response below it, which provides your readers with a context for your message. They will immediately see what original message you are responding to. Most e-mail programs automatically preface the original message with something such as, "On 10/12/01 [often including the time] you wrote:" or simply "Jane Doe wrote:" This is followed by the original message and then your response. Your response will be followed by your e-mail "signature," if any.

Keep your response short whenever possible. An e-mail message is comparable to a memorandum, and while it's true that a memorandum can be several pages long or longer, most memos are brief and to the point. Follow this practice and keep your e-mail message brief and to the point as well.

Plan ahead when providing attachments. Many e-mail programs make it possible to attach text, graphics, Web pages, audio, and video files. Some do not. Make sure you know whether your correspondent can receive attachments. For example, if you wanted to attach a photograph to an e-mail you are sending to your parents or friends, they must also be using an e-mail program that allows them to view the attachments you send.

Be considerate when sending attachments. Consider the size of the attachment. Files smaller than 100 kilobytes are generally acceptable. You may want to warn your correspondent with a separate e-mail message if you are sending any attachment that is longer. A 2-megabyte high-resolution graphic, for example, could take a long time to download and could cause the recipient's Internet mailbox to overflow, preventing further e-mail from being delivered.

Be vigilant when sending attachments. While many so-called computer viruses (such as the Good Times virus) are bogus, others are very real and can be transmitted in e-mail attachments. Before you attach a document to your e-mail message, make sure you have checked it for viruses. The people you're sending it to may not have a virus checker installed on their computers. Additionally, be wary when opening attachments sent to you by others. Malicious code can find its way onto your computer by masquerading as messages and attachments supposedly sent by people you know.

Netiquette

In addition to following basic e-mail conventions, you should observe proper e-mail etiquette, often referred to as *netiquette*. Guidelines for proper behavior concerning you and the e-mail you send include the following:

Be aware that what you send in an e-mail message may become public knowledge. Generally, you should assume that your worst enemy is reading everything you post—or at least could if he or she wanted to. Many employers do read their employees' e-mail and have a legal right to do so. So never assume that your e-mail is a private correspondence between you and your reader. All e-mail is saved routinely when service providers back up data on their servers or on the computers that handle your e-mail. These backup copies are not available to you for deletion.

Don't send abusive messages. The practice of sending such messages, called flaming, is unfortunately a common practice in many Internet newsgroups and mailing lists. There are even newsgroups devoted to flaming. Basically, you should not write in an e-mail message anything that you would not say to your correspondent in person. Be considerate of your reader's feelings and how your reader may interpret and react to your e-mail message. Also, be careful about

From the workplace

Bob Shapiro
Senior Program Manager
Lightbridge, Inc.
Burlington, Massachusetts

In his early schooling, Bob worked particularly hard on developing his communication skills. Over the past 25 years, he has held seven different jobs in four different professions, in industries as diverse as publishing, telecommunications, multi-media training, and the military. He was able to make the transition from job to job and industry to industry by making use of those same communication skills whose importance he had recognized so many years before.

My degree is in electronic engineering from Brown University. Brown was a school where the emphasis was on thought processes and learning, not necessarily on specific knowledge. As a result, it was easy for me to make the various slides I have made from one career emphasis to another.

Currently, I am a senior program manager for Lightbridge, Inc., a company that creates client acquisition and fraud prevention software for the mobile telecom industry. As program manager, I supervise a team of software engineers, writers, graphic artists, quality-assurance engineers, and tech writers.

Even from childhood, I knew that I wanted to do something technical. I also knew that I was weak in the areas that engineers are stereotypically weak: oral and written communication and interpersonal skills. So starting in high school I worked on those areas and have now turned them into strengths. In both high school and college I took speaking and writing courses as electives. I arranged to write and speak on technical topics so that I would be able to practice communicating to technical and nontechnical audiences about technical subjects.

I was a good electronic engineer, but I had better skills at managing people and projects, so I made the switch from engineering to program management. There seemed to be more opportunity for advancement and more money on the management track. I also wanted to be more involved in the overall project/ program, and moving to management seemed the best way to do that.

using an angry tone. If you absolutely must write an angry e-mail message, consider waiting a day before you send it. If you send the message immediately, you may well regret doing so.

Use sarcasm cautiously, and not at all in business correspondence. Sarcasm is a special tone that must be handled carefully in any medium. Much of what we communicate in face-to-face conversation is actually conveyed through tone of voice, facial expressions, and body language. The written word allows for none of these. If you are determined to be sarcastic in your e-mail, make sure you provide enough context and perhaps even use an appropriate emoticon or abbreviation to help your reader appreciate, or at least recognize, your sarcasm. Look over your e-mail before sending it, in case your wording could be mistakenly interpreted by someone else as being sarcastic.

Be aware that some people see e-mail as an informal and conversational medium while others see many e-mail communications as formal. Ideas that you may think are to be taken lightly or casually may be taken seriously by others.

Written communication is a huge portion of my job. I do most of my work using computers: communicating with others, writing documents, editing online documents, using spreadsheets, reviewing online help, testing programs, surfing the 'Net to look for competitive information, researching new technologies, finding training courses, and so on. Other than the 'Net surfing, most of this is work I did previously on paper.

I still plan my work the same way I always did on paper though: when writing I still create an outline, then a rough draft. I do make more edits and try for a more polished final result compared with when I worked on paper and with secretaries. When I am the typist, I tend to be more picky, being more comfortable expecting high standards from myself than asking someone else to type a fourteenth draft.

Working as a Team

Where I work, all documents are collaborative in terms of review and approval; most are individual in terms of creation and ownership. Typically one individual takes ownership of creating each document, spec, or other aspect of a project. That individual is then responsible for doing the work, seeking whatever help is needed in doing it, reviewing the document with the appropriate team members, and editing the document to reflect that input and any other decisions made at the review meeting. Sometimes for consistency across a project, a single individual has ownership of a whole suite of documents. Other people may help out in working on the details of some of the documents, but that one individual "owns" all of them.

The initial assignments are based on the skills and experience required for the job. You have some trade-offs when you have documents created collaboratively. Successful collaboration is consensus driven, which means that it is going to take longer. On the plus side, if you had only one person creating the whole suite of documents, others couldn't work in parallel and you wouldn't necessarily get buy-in from the team members who weren't involved. It's a complicated equation: You have to remember that doubling team size does not double output or halve completion time.

One thing I would like to see change: I think the flow of information between developers, designers, and documenters could certainly be improved. For example, the developers and designers could involve the documenters in writing error messages and specifying on-screen text. That extra involvement would serve to make the writers feel part of the team, give them ownership, and not incidentally improve the quality of the screen text.

Use upper- and lowercase letters as in any other correspondence. The same conventions that are used by writers of printed messages apply to e-mail. Some people use all caps in e-mail because they have a preference for doing so, and they are totally unaware that others will view their messages as shouting at the reader. All caps are also more difficult to read than mixed case. And just as you wouldn't use all capital letters, don't use all lowercase; doing so makes it difficult to tell when sentences end or begin. Capitalize the beginnings of sentences and the personal pronoun *I*. Just because you are creating an electronic document, don't imagine that your readers will see it with electronic eyes. Since plain-text e-mail does not allow for stylized text such as italics or boldface type, use all capitals if you need to emphasize one or two words.

Limit your signature file (the few lines following the body of your e-mail) to several brief lines, if any. Many newsgroups and mailing lists have rules about the length of signatures. Your readers shouldn't have to wade through fifteen lines of information about you or your favorite joke just to get to the end of your message.

> " "
> Just because you are creating an electronic document, don't imagine that your readers will see it with electronic eyes.

FIGURE 14.29

Emoticons (Smileys)

:-)	Smiley	:-0	Uh oh!
:)	Smiley without nose	;-(	Crying smiley
(-:	Left-handed smiley	|-)	Sleeping smiley
;)	Winking Smiley	:-o	Surprised smiley
8-)	Smiley with glasses	:-0	Very surprised smiley
8-)>	Smiley with glasses and beard	:-P	Disgusted smiley
< :-)	Smiley with dunce's cap	:-D	Very pleased smiley
:-|	Serious smiley	:-X	Keeping lips sealed
:-I	Indifferent smiley	:-Q	What?
:-/	Skeptical	:-}	Ditto
:-7	Wry	:-@	Screaming
:->	Sarcastic	: 0	Yelling
: (	Sad smiley		

FIGURE 14.30

E-mail Abbreviations

AFAIK	as far as I know	LOL	laughing out loud
BRB	be right back	OBTW	oh, by the way
BTW	by the way	ROTFL	rolling on the floor laughing
CUL	see you later	ROTFLMHO	rolling on the floor laughing my head off
FYA	for your amusement		
FYI	for your information	RTFM	read the "fine" manual
HTH	hope this helps	TIA	thanks in advance
IIRC	if I remember correctly	TNX	thanks
IMHO	in my humble opinion	YMMV	your mileage may vary
IMNSHO	in my not-so-humble opinion		

Emoticons and Abbreviations

People on the Internet have become quite adept at inserting emotion and self-expression into computer messages by using typographic characters and other tricks of the keyboard. While their use in business e-mail and other formal correspondence should be limited or even absent, in less formal settings, they can be helpful in setting the proper tone to an exchange. Figure 14.29 shows examples of emoticons. Also, many common expressions are abbreviated in e-mail to save time. Figure 14.30 shows a few common e-mail abbreviations.

CHECKING WHAT YOU'VE LEARNED

Correspondence in the age of electronics has become more, rather than less, prevalent. Knowing how to select the appropriate form of correspondence and how to craft the most effective communication is more important than ever.

Correspondence

- Have you followed the standard format for the type of correspondence you are writing: letter, memo, or e-mail?
- Do your letters, memos, and e-mails project the image of a competent, knowledgeable, professional person?

Letters

- Have you included a heading if you are not using letterhead stationery?
- Are the parts of your letter placed appropriately and aligned in keeping with the format preferred at your job or selected by you: full-block, modified block, semiblock, or simplified?
- If you are writing a personal letter, have you followed the format for this type of letter?
- Have you stated early in the letter your purpose in writing?
- If you are relating good news, do you mention that fact early in the letter?
- If you are writing a refusal letter, have you used an indirect pattern to defer the bad news to the late middle of your letter?
- Have you maintained a professional and courteous tone throughout the letter, regardless of your purpose in writing?
- Does the closing of the letter make reference to the expectation that you will continue to have a cordial professional relationship with the recipient?

Memos

- Does your subject line clearly express the main topic of your memo?
- Have you used headings to signal the content of various sections of the memo?
- Have you used one or perhaps two typefaces to give the memo a unified and attractive appearance?

E-mail

- Have you suited the tone of your e-mail to its purpose: informal for casual correspondence and formal for more serious business correspondence?

- Have you followed the rules of netiquette in your online correspondence?
- Have you used generally accepted typographic conventions—mixed upper- and lowercase, correct spelling, simple, easy-to-read typefaces—to allow the recipient to read the message easily?
- Have you used plain, unstyled text (no bold or italics or colored text) as a courtesy to readers with e-mail programs that do not display styled text?
- Have you limited the length of your signature lines at the end of your message?
- Have you reread your e-mail before sending it to check for possible wordings that could be misunderstood by the recipient?
- If the situation and context warrant it, have you used emoticons to make your tone apparent?

EXERCISES

 REVIEW

1. Review the discussion of a complaint letter in the chapter. Then choose a topic concerning a complaint you have about a product, service, or incident, and write a complaint letter to obtain action on a request. Create your own personalized letterhead for this assignment containing your address in the heading. Provide a separate date line. Use one of the formats (block or full-block, modified-block, semiblock, or simplified) discussed in the chapter and meet all of the requirements of a good business letter.

2. Assume you are the employee of the company or organization who receives the complaint letter described in Exercise 1 above. Write a refusal letter in response to the complaint letter. Meet all of the requirements of a refusal letter, and provide at least one good reason (appropriately placed in the letter) for refusing the action requested in the complaint letter.

3. Assume you are the employee of the company or organization who receives the complaint letter described in Exercise 1 above. Write an adjustment letter in response to the complaint letter. Meet all of the requirements of an adjustment letter, and provide at least one good reason for granting what is requested in the complaint letter or provide at least one good compromise concerning the request.

4. Write an unsolicited letter of inquiry to a company or organization of your choice concerning a person, a product, or a service. Meet all of the requirements of a good business letter and of an unsolicited letter of inquiry.

5. Assume that all of the members of your class are employees of the same company. Write a memo to another class member concerning a topic of your choice. Make sure the memo meets all of the requirements of a good memo.

6. Rewrite the complaint letter in Figure 14.17, so that it meets all of the requirements of an effective complaint letter.

 THE INTERNET

1. Review the discussion of e-mail and sending attachments via e-mail. E-mail your instructor a brief message concerning a short (one or two pages) attached file. Then send both the message and the attached file to the e-mail address provided by your instructor.

2. Find an example of an e-mail message written by a friend or someone else that contains what you consider to be an effective use of emoticons to help establish the tone of the message. Bring

a printed copy of the message to class, and be prepared to discuss the message with the class.

ETHICS/PROFESSIONALISM

Review the discussion of netiquette in this chapter. Create your own tip list of things you can do via e-mail that would be considered unprofessional and perhaps unethical. In other words, create a list of tips on how to be unprofessional and perhaps unethical in your e-mail communications. Be prepared to share your tip list with the class.

COLLABORATION

Working in groups of three or more students, compare your complaint, refusal, and adjustment letters written in response to the review exercises 1, 2, and 3 above. Each student in the group should make a list of decisions that were made to make the refusal and adjustment letters different from each other. Be prepared to discuss your list with the class.

INTERNATIONAL COMMUNICATION

Review the discussion of direct and indirect patterns for correspondence discussed in the chapter. Keeping in mind that many cultures prefer an indirect pattern (for example, Japan and many countries in the Middle East), make a list of the additional challenges presented in writing correspondence to someone who is a member of another culture. Be prepared to discuss your list with the class.

RESOURCES

Atkinson, Toby D. *Merriam-Webster's Guide to International Business Communications.* New York: Macmillan, 1996.

De Vries, Mary E. *The Elements of Correspondence.* New York: Macmillan, 1996.

———. *Internationally Yours: Writing and Communicating Successfully in Today's Global Marketplace.* Boston: Houghton Mifflin, 1994.

Merriam-Webster's Guide to Business Correspondence. 2nd ed. Springfield: Merriam-Webster, 1996.

Murdick, William. *The Portable Business Writer.* Boston: Houghton Mifflin, 1999.

Poe, Ann. *McGraw-Hill Handbook of More Business Letters.* New York: McGraw-Hill, 1998.

Poe, Roy W. *McGraw-Hill Handbook of Business Letters.* 3rd ed. New York: McGraw-Hill, 1994.

15

Procedures, Processes, and Specifications

Definitions   511

Technical Descriptions   513

Processes   517

Policies and Procedures   519

Specifications   526

From the Workplace   534

IN THIS CHAPTER

The documents you will learn about in this chapter—definitions, technical descriptions, processes, policies and procedures, and specifications—are the workhorses of the technical communication genres. They don't enjoy the prominence of proposals, reports, and instructions (which you will learn about in other chapters), and they often are not as weighty as the other genres, but they are central to what communication in the technical professions is about. In a real sense, without these documents, the larger documents would be lacking a vital infrastructure.

You will learn about:

- definitions: how to identify and explain the meaning of technical terms in order to reach a common ground for understanding with your readers

- technical descriptions: how to provide text and visual explanations for how things are constructed

- processes: how to show how things work

- policies and procedures: how to direct employees and a variety of types of applicants toward compliance with the goals and methods of the organization

- specifications: how to set out requirements for products and services

DEFINITIONS

If it's necessary to provide a definition as part of a technical description, or for some other document, you should be aware that there are informal and formal definitions and various strategies for creating both of these kinds of definitions. Extended definitions also may be required in longer documents. (See Figure 15.1.)

Informal Definitions

An informal definition simply provides other words that have meanings similar to that of the term you are trying to define. For example, to define *search engine,* you might write "a tool used to locate information and resources on the Web." Informal definitions can be provided in a variety of ways.

Parenthetical definitions: Too many protons in a nucleus lead it to emit a positron (*positively charged electron*).

Phrase definitions: We are going to study ions, *which are atoms or molecules that do not have the normal number of electrons,* as part of our unit on radiation.

Sentence definitions: *The effective dose of radiation is the sum of the equivalent doses of the various types of irradiated tissue, each properly weighted for its sensitivity to radiation.*

FIGURE 15.1
Types of Definitions

TYPES OF DEFINITIONS	WHEN USED	EXAMPLES
Informal	In text in which you don't want to break up the narrative and can define the term simply in a few words or a sentence: in reports, process descriptions, policies and procedures.	Gamma and x-ray radiation consists of packets of energy known as photons.
Formal	In more formal text situations where it is natural to stop the narrative flow to explain your terms: as part of a report, in a glossary section of a proposal or report, in instructions.	absolute coordinate: a number (usually an integer) that describes a specific position on a nucleic acid or protein sequence.
Extended	In text where you are explaining background information in some detail and the readers require a clear understanding of the meaning of terms and expressions used in the document: in reports, scientific papers, proposals.	plörk: Play-work. Plörk is what scientists do. It is the enthusiastic, energetic application of oneself to the task at hand as a child excitedly plays; it is the intense arduous, meticulous work of an artist working on her lifelong masterpiece; it is joyful work. [A truly extended definition would not fit into a table like this one.]

Some definitions explicitly limit their use to the current context only:

Computer: A "computer" is defined for Current Population Surveys as a personal or home workstation having a typewriter-like keyboard connected to a laptop computer, minicomputer, or mainframe computer.

Rural: All areas not classified by the Census Bureau as urban are defined as rural and generally include places of fewer than 2,500 persons.

Computer and *rural* can certainly be defined in other ways, but the U.S. Census Bureau states explicitly what it means by the terms for its Current Population Survey.

Formal Definitions

A formal definition offers a more structured approach to a term. In a formal definition you may provide a formal sentence definition in which you identify the term, the class, and how the term is different from other members in the class. (See Figure 15.2.) For example, you may write, "An animated GIF is a multi-image digitized graphic where images appear to create motion." The term is *GIF,* the class is *multi-image digitized graphic,* and the distinguishing feature is *where images appear to create motion.*

TERM	CLASS	DISTINGUISHING FEATURES
animated GIF	multi-image digitized graphic	images appear to create motion
trestle ladder	self-supporting portable ladder	nonadjustable in length, consisting of two sections hinged at the top to form equal angles with the base
mutation	nucleic-acid sequence change	affects biological function

FIGURE 15.2
Formal Definitions

Here is another example: "A *trestle ladder* is a self-supporting portable ladder, nonadjustable in length, consisting of two sections hinged at the top to form equal angles with the base." The term is *trestle ladder,* the class is *self-supporting portable ladder,* and the distinguishing feature is *nonadjustable in length, consisting of two sections hinged at the top to form equal angles with the base.*" A collection of definitions in a report, proposal, technical description, or other document is called a glossary.

Extended Definitions

Alternatively, you may provide an extended definition. See Figure 15.3 for an example. An extended definition typically provides several paragraphs that offer first a sentence definition and then a detailed discussion of the term. In the detailed discussion of the term you may provide graphics, examples, comparisons, analogies, negation (defining the term by discussing what it is not), function (what it does), and etymology (origins of the term) to define the term further. Extended definitions are often placed into longer documents—proposals or formal reports—that will be read by people not in the discourse community of the writer. (See Chapter 2 for information on discourse communities.)

TECHNICAL DESCRIPTIONS

Technical descriptions provide information about a product to readers who may use it, buy it, or assemble it. Technical descriptions may be brief or they may be quite lengthy and detailed, depending on the complexity of the product or mechanism being described.

A description of a relatively simple mechanism typically includes a description of the overall appearance; a description of its component parts, how each one functions, and other details readers might need to know; and visuals depicting the mechanism: schematic drawings, photographs, exploded drawings, flowcharts, site elevations, and so on.

A description of a complex mechanism is, of course, longer than that of a simple mechanism. And as with other types of documents it will have a

FIGURE 15.3

**Extended Definition—
Ionizing Radiation**

SOURCE: U.S. Department of Energy, Office
of Human Radiation Experiments.

What are the basic types of ionizing radiation?

There are many types of ionizing radiation, but the most familiar are *alpha*, *beta*, and *gamma/x-ray* radiation. *Neutrons*, when expelled from atomic nuclei and traveling as a form of radiation, can also be a significant health concern.

Alpha particles are clusters of two neutrons and two protons each. They are identical to the nuclei of atoms of helium, the second lightest and second most common element in the universe, after hydrogen. Compared with other forms of radiation, though, these are very heavy particles—about 7,300 times the mass of an electron. As they travel along, these large and heavy particles frequently interact with the electrons of atoms, rapidly losing their energy. They cannot even penetrate a piece of paper or the layer of dead cells at the surface of our skin. But if released within the body from a radioactive atom inside or near a cell, alpha particles can do great damage as they ionize atoms, disrupting living cells. Radium and plutonium are two examples of alpha emitters.

Beta particles are electrons traveling at very high energies. If alpha particles can be thought of as large and slow bowling balls, beta particles can be visualized as golf balls on the driving range. They travel farther than alpha particles and, depending on their energy, may do as much damage. For example, beta particles in fallout can cause severe burns to the skin, known as beta burns. Radioisotopes that emit beta particles are present in fission products produced in nuclear reactors and nuclear explosions. Some beta-emitting radioisotopes, such as iodine 131, are administered internally to patients to diagnose and treat disease.

Gamma and *x-ray* radiation consists of packets of energy known as *photons*. Photons have no mass or charge, and they travel in straight lines. The visible light seen by our eyes is also made up of photons, but at lower energies. The energy of a gamma ray is typically greater than 100 kiloelectron volts (keV–"k" is the abbreviation for *kilo*, a prefix that multiplies a basic unit by 1,000) per photon, more than 200,000 times the energy of visible light (0.5 eV). If alpha particles are visualized as bowling balls and beta particles as golf balls, photons of gamma and x-radiation are like weightless bullets moving at the speed of light. Photons are classified according to their origin. Gamma rays originate from events within an atomic nucleus; their energy and rate of production depend on the radioactive decay process of the radionuclide that is their source. X rays are photons that usually originate from energy transitions of the electrons of an atom. These can be artificially generated by bombarding appropriate atoms with high-energy electrons, as in the classic x-ray tube. Because x rays are produced artificially by a stream of electrons, their rate of output and energy can be controlled by adjusting the energy and amount of the electrons themselves.

beginning or introductory section, a middle or body, and a conclusion. The introductory section may have such items as a definition, function, and background of the item; purpose; an overall description; principles of operation; and a list of major parts.

The body would contain a detailed description of each major component, including definition, shape, dimensions, material, subparts (if any), function,

FIGURE 15.3

Extended Definition
(continued)

Both x rays and gamma rays can penetrate deeply into the human body. How deeply they penetrate depends on their energy; higher energy results in deeper penetration into the body. A 1 MeV ("M" is the abbreviation for *mega*, a prefix that multiplies a basic unit by 1,000,000) gamma ray, with an energy 2,000,000 times that of visible light, can pass completely through the body, creating tens of thousands of ions as it does.

A final form of radiation of concern is *neutron* radiation. Neutrons, along with protons, are one of the components of the atomic nucleus. Like protons, they have a large mass; unlike protons, they have no electric charge, allowing them to slip more easily between atoms. Like a Stealth fighter, high-energy neutrons can travel farther into the body, past the protective outer layer of the skin, before delivering their energy and causing ionization.

Several other types of high-energy particles are also ionizing radiation. Cosmic radiation that penetrates the Earth's atmosphere from space consists mainly of protons, alpha particles, and heavier atomic nuclei. Positrons, mesons, pions, and other exotic particles can also be ionizing radiation.

and relationship to other parts. The conclusion of a complex description might contain a summary (for quite complex mechanisms), a discussion of the interrelation of parts, and a walk-through of one complete operating cycle.

One of many challenges is deciding on the best order or sequence for describing the mechanism: spatially, functionally, chronologically, or a combination method. The choice will depend on the audience's needs. Although it is

FIGURE 15.4

**Technical Description—
Calorimeter-Cycler for
Evaluating High-Power
Battery Modules**

SOURCE: U.S. Center for Transportation
Technologies and Systems.

Description of Test Equipment

The combination of the large, custom-made calorimeter and the high-power battery cycler is a one-of-a-kind piece of special purpose test equipment for battery calorimetry. Here, we provide a description and the capabilities of each component.

Calorimeter Description

The calorimeter is of the heat conduction type and is based, in part, on a commercially available isothermal calorimeter (CSC Model 4400 Isothermal Microcalorimeter). Heat-conduction calorimeters sense heat flux between the sample and a heat sink. The heat sink is the enclosure containing the sample and is fabricated with aluminum surrounded by an isothermal bath. If the sample is hotter or colder than the heat sink, heat flows between the heat sink and the sample. In actual practice, the thermal conductivity of the path between the sample and the heat sink is matched to the expected heat flow so that the temperature difference between the sample (the battery, in this case) and the heat sink is minimized. The temperature of the heat sink is kept constant and the entire calorimeter shielded from its surroundings by a constant-temperature bath. The temperature control of the heat sink, together with proper matching of the thermal conductivity of the path between the sample (or measurement cavity) and the heat sink, renders a passive isothermal measurement condition.

The large, custom-made battery calorimeter is pictured in Figure 2 and a block diagram of the calorimeter with a listing of critical components is shown in Figure 3. The measuring unit of the calorimeter includes a 39 cm long, 21 cm wide, and 20 cm high aluminum enclosure connected to a large aluminum heat sink via heat

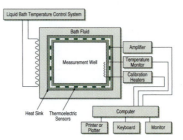

Figure 3. Block Diagram of the Heat Conduction Battery Calorimeter

flow sensors (semiconductor thermoelectric devices) that are located between the heat sink and the sample cavity. The bath temperature operating between –30°C to +60°C is controlled with a stability of 0.001°C. For calibration purposes, the measuring unit also incorporates electrical heaters, allowing for heat input at rates of 1 to 80 W. The measuring unit is designed so large-gauge leads, which must be connected to the sample battery for charging and discharging experiments, achieve thermal equilibrium. The large-gauge leads generate a negligible amount of heat even at very large currents. Further, they are attached to the isothermal aluminum enclosure, resulting in an insignificant impact on the accuracy of heat generation data obtained for battery modules. The battery temperature (internal or surface) in the calorimeter is measured with an accurate platinum RTD.

The measurement cavity can be either dry or filled with a dielectric, inert heat-transfer fluid. The air in the dry chamber can be stirred with small fans and the liquid-filled chamber is stirred with constant-speed stirrers to speed heat transfer from samples to the measurement chamber walls. The small amount of heat added for mixing is taken into account in calculations. The time response of the calorimeter is not affected by stirring within the measurement cavity. However, the time required to reach a steady-state response for a battery at constant power will be shortened significantly by stirring due to improved heat transfer between the sample and the calorimeter. Even under the best circumstances, the time constant for a typical large battery module will be much longer than the response time for the calorimeter.

Figure 2. Large Cavity Battery Calorimeter

tempting to describe an object or process according to the writer's own understanding, viewing the same object from the user's perspective will often result in a far different decision about organizing the document. See Figure 15.4 for an example of a technical description.

PROCESSES

Process descriptions focus on how things are done or how they work. They may focus on processes concerning products made by people—for example, how televisions, computers, radios, car engines, or cellular phones work. They may also cover, for example, natural processes such as how volcanoes erupt, how tornadoes are formed, or how photosynthesis works. Process descriptions are often an integral part of many other kinds of technical documents, including instructions.

Processes differ from instructions, although they have features in common. Processes describe how something happens, often in a step-by-step, sequential manner. Instructions tell the reader how to perform a procedure. In the first instance—processes—the writing is descriptive. That means that the writer describes a sequence of events. In the case of instructions, the writing is prescriptive. That means that the writer tells the reader how the sequence of events is supposed to happen in order for the instructions to be completed correctly. In instructions, the reader is a participant in the process and must be able to accomplish what the writer requires. See Figure 15.5 for a comparison of procedures, processes, and instructions.

As you can see from Figure 15.6, a process description does not instruct the reader on how to accomplish something. Rather it explains the way some-

TYPE OF DOCUMENT	CHARACTERISTICS
Policies and Procedures	Imply or state philosophy, ethos, or standards; broad in scope, but sometimes detailed and step-by-step.
Processes	How something happens; writing is descriptive; often sequential and step-by-step.
Instructions	How to perform an activity; writing is prescriptive; reader is a participant; reader must be able to accomplish what the writer requires; often detailed and step-by-step.

FIGURE 15.5

Characteristics of Policies and Procedures, Processes, and Instructions

After the female mosquito obtains a blood meal (male mosquitoes do not bite), she lays her eggs directly on the surface of stagnant water, in a depression, or on the edge of a container where rainwater may collect and flood the eggs. The eggs hatch and a mosquito larva or "wriggler" emerges. The larva lives in the water, feeds and develops into the third stage of the life cycle called a pupa or "tumbler." The pupa also lives in the water, but no longer feeds. Finally, the mosquito emerges from the pupal case and the water as a fully developed adult, ready to bite.

FIGURE 15.6

Process Description— Four-Stage Life Cycle of Mosquitoes

SOURCE: U.S. Environmental Protection Agency, Office of Pesticide Programs.

FIGURE 15.7

**Process Description—
Uranium 238 Decay**

SOURCE: U.S. Department of Energy, Office
of Human Radiation Experiments.

1. Uranium 238 emits an alpha
2. Thorium 234 emits a beta
3. Protactinium 234 emits a beta
4. Uranium 234 emits an alpha
5. Thorium 230 emits an alpha
6. Radium 226 emits an alpha
7. Radon 222 emits an alpha
8. Polonium 218 emits an alpha
9. Lead 214 emits a beta
10. Bismuth 214 emits a beta
11. Polonium 214 emits an alpha
12. Lead 210 emits a beta
13. Bismuth 210 emits a beta
14. Polonium 210 emits an alpha
15. Lead 206, which is stable

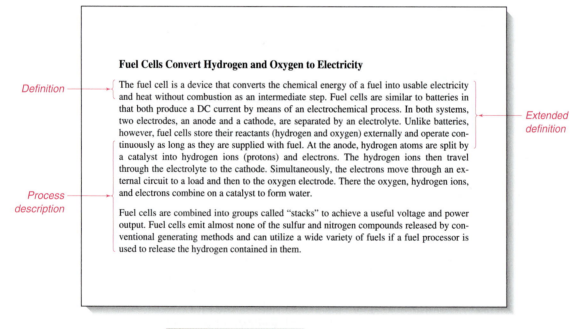

Fuel Cells Convert Hydrogen and Oxygen to Electricity

Definition

The fuel cell is a device that converts the chemical energy of a fuel into usable electricity and heat without combustion as an intermediate step. Fuel cells are similar to batteries in that both produce a DC current by means of an electrochemical process. In both systems, two electrodes, an anode and a cathode, are separated by an electrolyte. Unlike batteries, however, fuel cells store their reactants (hydrogen and oxygen) externally and operate continuously as long as they are supplied with fuel. At the anode, hydrogen atoms are split by a catalyst into hydrogen ions (protons) and electrons. The hydrogen ions then travel through the electrolyte to the cathode. Simultaneously, the electrons move through an external circuit to a load and then to the oxygen electrode. There the oxygen, hydrogen ions, and electrons combine on a catalyst to form water.

Extended definition

Process description

Fuel cells are combined into groups called "stacks" to achieve a useful voltage and power output. Fuel cells emit almost none of the sulfur and nitrogen compounds released by conventional generating methods and can utilize a wide variety of fuels if a fuel processor is used to release the hydrogen contained in them.

FIGURE 15.8

Process Description—Fuel Cell Process

SOURCE: U.S. Department of Energy, Office of Transportation Technologies.

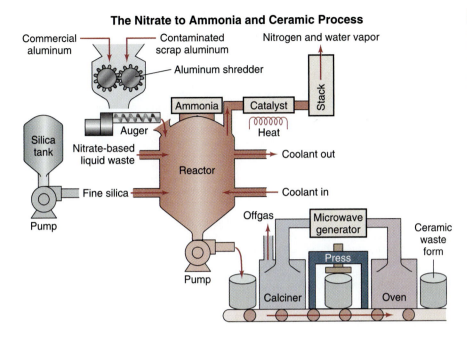

The Nitrate to Ammonia and Ceramic Process

FIGURE 15.9

Process Description—Nitrate to Ammonia and Ceramic Process

SOURCE: Pacific Northwest National Laboratory.

thing happens. The mosquito example shows a process description in narrative form. Some process descriptions lend themselves more readily to a list form. Figure 15.7 shows another process description. Process descriptions can be quite lengthy. See Figure 15.8, Figure 15.9, Figure 15.10, and Figure 15.11.

POLICIES AND PROCEDURES

Policies and procedures, also called directives, provide information for your readers on how things are done in an organization. They are the standardized ways of doing things in many organizations—for example, taking inventory, organizing incoming mail, stamping a time card, applying for a sabbatical, or taking vacation time. Often you will see policies and procedures linked together—as here—almost as if they were the same thing. They are often paired because they both concern a company or organization's philosophy of operation. But the difference is important. *Policies* are the standards an organization wants to enforce. *Procedures* are the methods for accomplishing those standards.

Rules and regulations are another kind of policy document. Many organizations cover all kinds of policies and procedures thoroughly in policies and

FIGURE 15.10

**Process Description—
Arkenol's Process**

SOURCE: U.S. Department of Energy, Office
of Transportation Technologies.

The heart of the process is the decrystallization followed by dilute acid hydrolysis. The original Peoria process, and a modified version proposed by Purdue, carry out dilute acid pretreatment to separate the hemicellulose before decrystallization. The biomass would then be dried to concentrate the acid absorbed in the biomass prior to addition of concentrated sulfuric acid. Purdue proposed recycling sulfuric acid by taking the dilute acid/water stream from the hydrolysis reactor and using it in the hemicellulose pretreatment step.

In Arkenol's process, decrystallization is carried out by adding 70%–77% sulfuric acid to biomass that has been dried to 10% moisture. Acid is added at a ratio of 1.25:1 (acid:cellulose+hemicellulose), and temperature is controlled at less than 50°C. Adding water to

dilute the acid to 20%–30% and heating at 100°C for an hour results in the release of sugars. The gel from this reactor is pressed to remove an acid/sugar product stream. Residual solids are subjected to a second hydrolysis step. The use of a chromatographic column to achieve a high yield and separation of acid and sugar is a crucial improvement in the process that was first introduced by TVA and researchers at the University of Southern Mississippi. The fermentation converts both the xylose and the glucose to ethanol at theoretical yields of 85% and 92%, respectively. A triple effect evaporator is required to reconcentrate the acid. Arkenol claims that sugar recovery in the acid/sugar separation column is at least 98%, and acid lost in the sugar stream is not more than 3%.

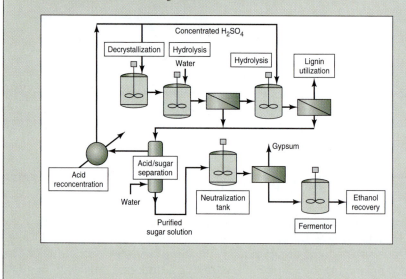

procedures manuals or employee handbooks. But policies and procedures do not always have to be very elaborate. Even a brief e-mail directive about employee time off during the holiday season qualifies as a policy.

Standard operating procedures (SOPs) are widely used in some industries to help workers complete a job safely, to ensure that production operations

FIGURE 15.11

**Process Description—
Hydrolysis of Wood**

SOURCE: U.S. Department of Energy, Office
of Transportation Technologies.

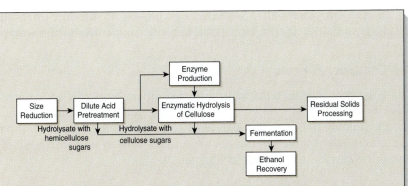

Figure 1: The enzyme process configured as separate hydrolysis and fermentation

The first application of enzymes for hydrolysis of wood in an ethanol process was obvious—simply replace the acid hydrolysis step with an enzyme hydrolysis step. This configuration, now often referred to as separate hydrolysis and fermentation (SHF), is shown in Figure 1. Pretreatment of the biomass is required to make the cellulose more accessible to the enzymes. Many pretreatment options have been considered, including both thermal and chemical steps.

The most important process improvement made for the enzymatic hydrolysis of biomass was the introduction of simultaneous saccharification and fermentation (SSF), as patented by Gulf Oil Company and the University of Arkansas. This new process scheme reduced the number of reactors involved by eliminating the separate hydrolysis reactor and, more importantly, avoiding the problem of product inhibition associated with enzymes. In the presence of glucose, ß-glucosidase stops hydrolyzing cellobiose. The build up of cellobiose, in turn, shuts down cellulose degradation. In the SSF process scheme, cellulase enzyme and fermenting microbes are combined. As sugars are produced by the enzymes, the fermentative organisms convert them to ethanol. The SSF process has, more recently, been improved to include the cofermentation of multiple sugar substrates. This new variant of SSF, known as SSCF for Simultaneous Saccharification and CoFermentation, is shown schematically in Figure 2.

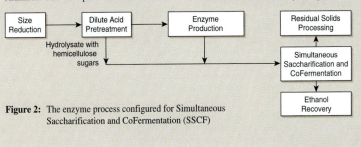

Figure 2: The enzyme process configured for Simultaneous Saccharification and CoFermentation (SSCF)

are handled consistently, to prevent failures in manufacturing that cause harm to people, and to ensure that official procedures are properly followed to comply with company or government regulations. An SOP may also function as a training document for teaching users about a process, serve as a checklist for co-workers or auditors, provide a historical record, or help in the investigation of an accident. Essentially, SOPs help employees to produce high-quality products so that their companies can be more competitive in the workplace.

Company Policies

If you are charged with writing your company's policies and procedures documents, your first step will be to plan what you will do and how you will go about doing it. Figure 15.12 shows a company policy document. If part of the procedures you are writing about concerns how to do something, follow the guidelines for instructions in Chapter 19.

FIGURE 15.12

Company Policy Document

SOURCE: Ernest Orlando Lawrence, Berkeley National Laboratory, *Regulations and Procedures Manual*.

B. WORK PERIODS

1. Workday

The standard workday for full-time employees is 8 hours per day, 8 a.m. to 5 p.m. Exceptions are necessary in certain operating situations such as:

Laboratory protection.

Accelerator and computer operations.

Scientific experiments in which experimental needs determine coverage requirements.

Additional exceptions may be allowed as defined in RPM §2.23(D) (Flextime).

2. Work Week

Normally, a work week consists of the five consecutive workdays, Monday through Friday, within a calendar week. A calendar week is defined as Saturday midnight to the next following Saturday midnight. Exceptions are allowable under the same circumstances noted in Paragraph (B)(1), above.

C. WORK SCHEDULE

Employees should be aware that, under University policy, no portion of time due the Laboratory may be devoted to private purposes and no outside employment may interfere with the performance of Laboratory duties. These requirements apply regardless of the percentage of time worked. Abuses may be grounds for disciplinary or corrective action. See PRM §2.20(A) (Outside Business Activities).

Use of Laboratory telephones for brief calls within the local commuting area is permitted, however, when required by changes in work plans, emergencies, or coordination of work activities with family members or others who can be reached only during working hours. If an employee finds it necessary to use a Laboratory telephone for a call outside the local commuting area, the employee must reimburse the Laboratory for the call or charge the call to his or her home telephone number or personal calling card. See RPM §9.02(A)(2) (Communications and Networking Systems).

1. Full Time: A schedule involving complete work weeks or work months.

2. Part Time: A schedule involving a specified percentage of each work week or work month.

3. Indeterminate Time: An unspecified number of hours per work period.

D. OVERTIME

Overtime in most cases is time worked over 8 hours per day or 40 hours per week. For some classifications, however, other provisions determine overtime; the specific provision and applicable pay basis for each classification are shown in Appendix A to Contract 98.

Company Policies—Planning

- Consider whom the document is for. Does it apply to the whole company? Employees in just one department?
- Determine the purpose and scope of the policies. Will they cover one type of activity or many? Do they address benefits and schedules? Workplace safety? Customer relations?
- Gather together the information you need to include. Are there previous documents of this kind in use at your company? Have there been directives—memos, letters, or other correspondence—dealing with specific issues and policies? Have some directives superseded others? Make sure your document is completely up to date.
- Try to consider all possibilities on a given issue, and make sure your document covers them. Don't leave loopholes: they will only lead to trouble. Try to anticipate what your readers might need to know and make sure to include that information.

Company policies should never be created in isolation. Many people are "shareholders" in the policies, and they should be consulted.

Company Policies—Reviewing

- Make sure your document is reviewed by the people who will be using it, as well as your supervisors, to make sure it is complete, accurate, specific, easy to understand, and usable. An important element of any document is its readability and usability.
- If your company requires it, submit your document for legal review. Procedures and policies have legal ramifications, and your document is an official representation of your company's way of conducting business.

How you format and produce your company policies depends on a number of considerations.

Company Policies—Formatting and Producing

- When you have all the information, decide how to format it. If your company has a style guide or follows a standardized document format, follow that. Use a published style guide, such as the *Chicago Manual of Style,* for topics not covered in your company's style guide or if your company does not have its own guide.

(continued)

- If you include warnings, cautions, alerts, and safety information, make sure that they are easy to find and that they are emphasized appropriately.
- Plan for page elements, such as headers and footers, heading styles, spacing, margins, and typefaces. (See Chapter 8 for more information on these topics.) Use front matter—cover page and table of contents—and back matter—glossary, appendixes, and index—for longer documents, if appropriate.
- Since policies can and do change over time, provide a way to incorporate new information without having to rewrite or republish the document. You might produce the document with a loose-leaf binding to allow for updates, or keep a list of changes or even an updated copy of the policies on the company's intranet or Web site.

Other Procedures

Another type of procedure you may be writing does not concern employee policies or standard operating procedures. These are procedures a company uses to inform its employees, job applicants, grant applicants, service providers, or supply providers about the company's expectations or requirements in a variety of specific situations. For example, you followed your school's procedures when you applied for admission. The procedures probably were available in the school's catalog, in other admissions material, on a Web site, and on the application form itself. Figure 15.13 is an example of a document that explains how to prepare proposals.

Procedures and policies can be similar to instructions, but they differ in several ways. The term *procedures* can also mean directions on how to perform an action. More often, those kinds of procedures are called *instructions.* You will learn about instructions in Chapter 19.

Instructions are often detailed and step-by-step. Procedures may be detailed and step-by-step, but they are not necessarily so. Procedures can be broader in scope and often include—either explicitly or implicitly—the philosophy, character, or standards the company wants its readers to follow.

Consider Exhibit 15.1 on pages 539–544, an example of procedure and policy guidelines provided for ethical and legal research using human pluripotent stem cells. Because research on human stem cells is a controversial topic raising many concerns on the part of the public, the National Institutes of Health (NIH) issued guidelines on procedures to be followed by applicants for NIH funding for research in the field. Before the guidelines were issued, draft copies were published for public comment. Based on the concerns raised by the public, members of Congress, lobbyists, special-interest groups, religious organizations, and patient advocacy groups, the NIH revised the document somewhat before its official release.

Just as with any other documents, the body of policies and procedures is organized into logical groupings, in this case:

Getting Started

Envision what improvements your project will make, and then ask yourself what activities and course(s) must be developed, what instruments will be needed, or what coalitions must be formed to make the desired improvements. Focusing first on the goals and objectives helps ensure that the activities are designed to reach those goals.

After the goals and associated activities are well defined, **consider what resources (e.g., people, time, equipment, technical support) will be necessary** as part of the request to NSF. A better proposal is likely to result if the goals and activities are clear before resources are considered.

Mention what work has been done in preparation for the project, and describe specific attempts that have been made to try the proposed improvement on a small scale. Evidence of preliminary work demonstrates planning and commitment to the project and often indicates the project's potential for success.

When the proposal requests significant funds for equipment, it is helpful to **consider alternatives** and **explain why the instruments chosen are particularly suitable for the project** and why others, especially less expensive ones, are less suitable.

Get advice from people who have been successful in the proposal process. (See the Getting Advice Section listed in Step 3 and consider these activities early in the process.)

Gathering Background Information

When writing a proposal, **look for previously awarded NSF projects** or work supported in other ways that are similar. The relationship of the proposed project to work of others should be described. In addition, the proposal must give appropriate attention to the existing relevant knowledge base, including awareness of current literature. Results of previous projects may have been presented at professional meetings or published in journals, and NSF regularly publishes abstracts of its recently awarded grants.

FIGURE 15.13

Procedures—Advice to Proposal Writers

SOURCE: National Science Foundation, Directorate for Education and Human Resources.

I. Scope of Guidelines
II. Guidelines for Research Using Human Pluripotent Stem Cells That Is Eligible for NIH Funding
III. Areas of Research Involving Human Pluripotent Stem Cells That Are Ineligible for NIH Funding
IV. Oversight

As the guidelines in Exhibit 15.1 show, the document's purpose is to inform scientists of the conditions that they must meet in order to qualify for research funding from the NIH. The scope section comprises two paragraphs, one that tells what the document addresses and the other that specifies whom the document applies to.

The first paragraph in the scope section of the NIH guidelines tells what the guidelines will cover. This paragraph is a definition paragraph, including the definition of human pluripotent stem cells: "cells that are self-replicating, are derived from human embryos or human fetal tissue, and are known to develop into cells and tissues of the three primary germ layers. Although human pluripotent stem cells may be derived from embryos or fetal tissue, such stem cells are not themselves embryos."

The next paragraph states that the policies apply to: "(1) awardees who want to use existing funds; (2) awardees requesting an administrative or competing supplement; and (3) applicants or intramural researchers submitting applications or proposals."

Section II sets out the requirements for compliance for applicants for funding. A list of documents that must accompany each application is stated: an assurance that the cells used in the research follow the conditions set forth in the guidelines, a sample informed consent form, an abstract of the protocol used, documentation of Institutional Review Board approval of the derivation protocol, and several other requirements.

Section III lists seven categories of research that are ineligible for funding under the guidelines. Section IV puts forth the review process for funding requests, the annual reporting process that will account for the approved funds, and the group of people who will assist in future recommendations and revisions to the guidelines.

SPECIFICATIONS

Specifications refer both to the design and function requirements for technologies of all kinds—for everything from space shuttles to household appliances—and to the requirements for services. All the technology around you is built, either well or poorly, according to specifications of one kind or another. Obviously, if the specifications are not carefully considered—and sometimes even if they are—the technology won't be well designed, or it will be designed with flaws—even minor ones—that could have major consequences. So writing precise, accurate, and clear specifications becomes not only a desired accomplishment but a necessary one, requiring a great deal of skill.

Some specifications consist of a collection of items to be included in the final product, along with detailed descriptions of each item. Examples of this would be the specifications for a construction project or the specifications for equipping a laboratory. Other specifications set out in detail how an objective is to be accomplished or how the component parts of a system are to function. This type of specification is what you see when you look at a device, such as a photocopier or facsimile machine, and you see a list of the dimensions, power consumption, operating temperatures, and features.

The specifications normally form a complete statement either of what you are requiring from someone else or of what you will provide to someone else. For example, if you want to build a house, you discuss your requirements with an architect. The architect then provides a design that includes a list specifying what type of each element you require and how many (for example, 14 double-glazed, 2-foot-by-3-foot single-casement windows with 15 percent bronze tint). You would then invite several general contractors to bid on the job. The specifications list would form the central list of materials for your house, and any quote would have to incorporate those materials. The materials list is an example of the first kind of specifications, the one that describes the collection of items to be included in the final product.

The second kind of specifications—functional specifications—describe the requirements for what something or someone must do. Specifications express the requirements of the person, company, government, or agency in a particular context. A required item must be provided in order to satisfy the specification.

Sometimes you will want to specify that an action or attribute is desired but not required. For example, if you are responding to a job ad and you do not have all the requisite attributes mentioned in the ad, you might apply anyway, just in case the attribute you lack is desired but not required: experience with a certain type of hardware or software or sales experience, for instance. Be very careful when writing specifications that you require compliance for the items that are mandatory and that the wording you choose—your diction—makes that clear.

> Specifications normally form a complete statement either of what you are requiring from someone else or of what you will provide to someone else.

Precision and Accuracy

The key to successful specifications is precision and accuracy of language. Precision and accuracy are not the same things, although they often appear together. (See Chapter 7 on achieving an effective style.) When you use precise language, you narrow the object, system, or process you are describing until the words you are using uniquely define just the exact object, system, or process you mean them to. Accuracy refers to the truth of what you describe. When you use accurate language, you provide a true listing of an object's attributes or its functioning.

Precise and accurate language is always important when writing about technical subjects, but in specification writing, it is crucial. How you write your specifications depends—as with so much other writing—on your audience and purpose. If you are required to write specifications, you probably will have guidelines to work from and possibly other specifications written for similar purposes. Use such resources as models, and modify them to suit your needs.

Depending on your purpose, your specifications may include sections on the appearance of the parts of the system; how each part will function; listings and descriptions of the materials that will be used to construct the system; accompanying diagrams, photographs, or parts lists; and detailed performance requirements of the described system or the protocols and standards to which it conforms.

Note: As a legal matter, if the specifications you write are for something you are offering to supply, make sure you are capable of supplying it and that you will deliver what you are offering. If you can't deliver, don't make the offer or you will find yourself facing penalties for nonperformance.

Writing Effective Specifications

- Write achievable specifications. Make sure individual and combined requirements are mutually achievable.
- Write verifiable specifications. Write in such a way that you can determine whether the requirements have been met.
- Write specifications, not explanations. Remember: Specifications specify.
- Provide performance specifications rather than design specifications. Tell people what to do, not how to do it.
- Cite standardization documents; that is, established standards promoted by government or industry sources.
- Use consistent and accurate terminology and be careful with your words. Differentiate between *shall* and *will*; use *or* correctly, and avoid using *any*. Such attention ensures your specifications will say what you intend them to say.

Writing Specifications

Write achievable specifications. Complex technical specifications usually comprise a large number of individual requirements, which often affect the accomplishment of each other. When taken one at a time, each requirement may be easily met, but when combined—three, four, five, or twenty or more together—they may form a set that is mutually unachievable. Making sure that the specifications do not become overwhelming is the responsibility of the person who drafts the specifications.

Write verifiable specifications. Always specify things in such a way that you can verify whether the requirements have been met. Verification methods include inspection, measurement, testing, and demonstrations. Definite pass-or-fail criteria, with no element of judgment or opinion involved, must be assigned to every verification method. Otherwise, disputes are likely to arise over the acceptability of the product.

Write specifications, not explanations. Readers of your specifications should be able to rely on such statements as *true* and *correct* and be able to act on them in preparing bids without any further investigation to verify the specifications. If you believe that you must make explanations, be sure to check them carefully to make sure that they are true in all cases, regardless of what approach the bidders may take toward satisfying your requirements. Remember, specifications specify. They do not explain.

Provide performance specifications rather than design specifications. Put simply, the difference is between telling people what to do and telling them how to do it. Performance specifications are stated only in terms of the result required; design specifications stipulate what materials and methods are to be used in producing goods or rendering services. Most specifications that you encounter in practice are an unwitting combination of the two types. All it takes to categorize a specification as a design specification is one design requirement. In general, writers of mixed specifications are held responsible when a contractor adheres to the design requirements and claims that doing so prevented satisfaction of the performance requirements.

Cite standardization documents such as those put out by government or industry agencies. When you cite a published specification or standard, be sure that you have read the document and understand it fully. Be sure you include in your own specifications all the information required by the text of the document you are citing. Avoid creating unnecessary work for your readers by citing documents in their entirety. Instead, tell your readers specifically which paragraphs of the cited document apply. If only a few sentences of the cited document really apply to your specifications, then eliminate the citation by spelling out the requirements as part of your own specifications.

Be consistent. Specifications must be rigorously consistent throughout. This means that every mention of each topic covered must be in logical conformance with everything else that is said about all the related topics. Editing a document for this degree of consistency requires a sharp memory and a great deal of concentration, especially when the document is a long one.

Use terminology consistently. Even if your specifications sound odd when read aloud, you should use exactly the same terms every time you refer to the same item. Also, be very careful of pronouns, since readers sometimes choose a different antecedent for them from the one you intended.

Carefully differentiate between *shall* and *will*. *Shall*, when used in specifications, imposes a binding requirement on the offering entity. On the other hand, the word *will* usually is used only when the specifier wants to make some kind of promise to the offerors. Careless errors in the *shall*s and *will*s often lead to very unpleasant surprises when work is being done under contract.

Be sure that whenever you use *or* you do not really mean *and*. Also be sure that you have not granted someone permission to make a choice of doing either one task or another when you intend for them to do both. Inspect the text of your specifications for occurrences of the word *or*, and check each one carefully to make sure that its logic is correct. Using commas in sequences will help avoid ambiguity.

Avoid using *any*. *Any* is an ambiguous word. Often it can be simply deleted from specifications without altering the meaning of the text; in other cases, the words *each* and *every* may be useful in rewriting the requirement for better clarity.

Presenting Specifications

Specifications can be as complicated as plans for satellite guidance systems or as simple as rules for letterhead stationery. Look at Figure 15.14 for an

FIGURE 15.14

**Specifications—
Department of Defense
(DoD) Letterheads**

SOURCE: U.S. Department of Defense.

Department of Defense

INSTRUCTION

NUMBER 5330.2

February 13, 1984

ASD(C)

SUBJECT: Specifications for DoD Letterheads

References: (a) DoD Instruction 5330.2, subject as above,
November 27, 1979 (hereby canceled)

(b) Federal Property Management Regulations (FPMR), GSA, August
26, 1983, to Subpart 101-11.6, Records, Equipment, and Supplies;
Stationery Standards

1. REISSUANCE AND PURPOSE

This Instruction reissues reference (a) to update policy,
procedures, and responsibilities concerning specifications for
official letterhead stationery used within the Department of
Defense and to provide for the use of computer and word
processor equipment in the preparation of correspondence.

2. APPLICABILITY

This Instruction applies to the Office of the Secretary of
Defense, the Military Departments, the Organization of the Joint
Chiefs of Staff, and the Defense Agencies (hereafter referred to
collectively as "DoD Components").

3. POLICY

DoD preprinted letterhead stationery shall be uniform and shall
contain only those elements described in this Instruction.

4. PROCEDURES

4.1 Preprinted official letterhead stationery:

4.1.1 Shall be used for all correspondence prepared for the
signature of the Secretary and Deputy Secretary of Defense, and
the Executive Secretary of the Department of Defense.

4.1.2. Shall be used for all correspondence to addressees
outside the Department of Defense.

4.1.3. Shall be 8-1/2 by 11 inches.

example of specifications. You will see it is broken into sections detailing the purpose of the specifications, to whom they apply, the details of the requirements and possible exceptions to those requirements, and when the specified rules go into effect.

The first section, Reissuance and Purpose, tells the reader what the specifications address and how they apply. The purpose of the specifications is to "update policy, procedures, and responsibilities concerning specifications for

FIGURE 15.14

Specifications *(continued)*

4.1.4. Shall bear the seal of the Department of Defense, which shall be 1 inch in diameter and 1/2 inch from the upper left and top edges of the stationery.

4.1.5. Shall carry no other decorative or distinguishing insignia, printed or otherwise.

4.1.6. Shall show the name of the principal activity to which this Instruction applies (such as Department of the Army, or Defense Logistics Agency, or Defense Communications Agency) centered horizontally, 5/8 inch from the top of the sheet, and printed in 12-point, heavy plate Gothic small capital letters, or equivalent.

4.1.7. Shall show the name of the department, agency, office, bureau, administrative or technical service, or principal command centered immediately under the name of the principal activity to which this Instruction applies printed in 6-point, heavy plate Gothic large capital letters, or equivalent.

4.1.8. Shall carry the address and ZIP code number centered horizontally beneath the name of the department, agency, office, bureau, or administrative or technical service, or principal command printed in 6-point, heavy plate Gothic large capital letters, or equivalent. The bottom of the printing shall be 1-1/16 inches from the top of the trimmed sheet.

4.1.9. Shall be printed in black or blue ink.

4.1.10. May incorporate the following options:

4.1.10.1. The phrase "In reply refer to," printed in 5-point, light plate Gothic large capital letters, or equivalent.

4.1.10.2. Corner markings to indicate the address area for window envelopes.

4.1.10.3. Fold Markings.

4.1.10.4. A 1/2-point guideline, 3/4 inch long, placed 1-1/2 inches from the bottom and 1/8 inch from the left side.

4.1.10.5. Appropriate slogans, approved by the head of the DoD Component concerned, or designee, and printed in the bottom margin approximately 1/2 inch from the bottom edge of the sheet.

4.1.11. Shall be printed on paper, the quality of which conforms with the provisions of the FPMR (reference (b)).

official letterhead stationery used within the Department of Defense, and to provide for the use of computer and word processor equipment in the preparation of correspondence." The section tells readers why the specifications were written.

Applicability—to whom or in what cases the specifications apply—is stated: "This Instruction applies to the Office of the Secretary of Defense, the Military Departments, the Organization of the Joint Chiefs of Staff, and the Defense

FIGURE 15.14

Specifications *(continued)*

4.2. Computer- or word processor-generated letterhead stationery may be used for correspondence wholly within the Department of Defense provided:

4.2.1. Such correspondence is not prepared for the signature of the Secretary or Deputy Secretary of Defense, or Executive Secretary of the Department of Defense.

4.2.2. No element of the letterhead is larger than that authorized for preprinted stationery.

4.2.3. No seal, emblem, decorative device, distinguishing insignia, slogans, or mottos are used.

4.2.4. Stationery size conforms to that required for preprinted letterheads.

4.2.5. Such correspondence conforms with paragraph 4.1.6., above.

5. RESPONSIBILITIES

Heads of DoD Components, or designees, shall comply with the provisions of this Instruction.

6. EFFECTIVE DATE AND IMPLEMENTATION

This Instruction is effective immediately. Forward one copy of implementing documents to the Assistant Secretary of Defense (Comptroller) within 120 days.

Agencies (hereafter referred to collectively as 'DoD Components')." This section tells readers whether the document concerns them directly or not.

The next section, Policy, states the objective of the specifications: "DoD preprinted letterhead stationery shall be uniform and shall contain only those elements described in this Instruction." The Department of Defense wants documents coming out of its various offices to have a uniform appearance.

FIGURE 15.15

**Specifications—
Occupational Health and
Safety Administration
(OSHA) Head Protection
Standards**

SOURCE: U.S. Department of Labor,
Occupational Safety and Health
Administration.

Sec. 1910.135 Head Protection.

(a) General requirements.

(1) The employer shall ensure that each affected employee wears a protective helmet when working in areas where there is a potential for injury to the head from falling objects.

(2) The employer shall ensure that a protective helmet designed to reduce electrical shock hazard is worn by each such affected employee when near exposed electrical conductors which could contact the head.

(b) Criteria for protective helmets.

(1) Protective helmets purchased after July 5, 1994 shall comply with ANSI Z89.1-1986, "American National Standard for Personnel Protection—Protective Headwear for Industrial Workers-Requirements," which is incorporated by reference as specified in Sec. 1910.6, or shall be demonstrated to be equally effective.

(2) Protective helmets purchased before July 5, 1994 shall comply with the ANSI standard "American National Standard Safety Requirements for Industrial Head Protection," ANSI Z89.1-1969, which is incorporated by reference as specified in Sec. 1910.6, or shall be demonstrated by the employer to be equally effective.

The information that follows, listed under Procedures, gives the specifications themselves. It delimits when official letterhead stationery is to be used, who is to use it, the size of the paper, the size and placement of the department seal, what the stationery is *not* to include ("other decorative or distinguishing insignia, printed or otherwise"), how and where the agency name is to be printed, ink color, and a list of optional features (reply information, fold markings, slogans, paper quality).

Responsibilities is the section that details who must conform to these specifications, and the last section, Effective Date and Implementation, tells when the specifications are to be implemented.

Another example of specifications is shown in Figure 15.15, which presents standards on protective equipment from the Occupational Safety and Health Administration. As you see, the specifications are divided into two sections. The first, General Requirements, sets out the conditions under which the specifications will apply: when the employee works in an area with either falling-object or electrical hazards. The second section, Criteria for Protective Helmets, stipulates the American National Standards Institute (ANSI) standard that applies to the helmets, depending on when they were purchased—before or after July 5, 1994. You will notice that the specifications incorporate requirements by reference (ANSI Z89.1-1969, for example), rather than repeating all the particulars contained in the ANSI standards themselves.

Note: Be very careful writing specifications. If you leave something out, you could find yourself with legal liabilities you hadn't bargained for or financial

From the workplace

Scott Mackler

Principal Consultant
Cleanroom Consulting, LLC
Fayetteville, New York

Scott developed a successful consulting business in the field of cleanroom engineering (the creation and maintenance of contamination-free facilities, processes, and spaces). He keeps his competitive edge by using the Internet to his best advantage to reach potential clients.

My bachelor's degree from Rensselaer Polytechnic Institute is in mechanical engineering, and my master's from the University of Houston is in business. The undergraduate engineering curriculum mainly consisted of "read a book, take a test" and only a few labs (at that time; hopefully it has now changed). The program was probably geared more toward turning out grad students than practicing engineers. Actually, even my high school experiences working on automobiles turned out to be more useful than my undergraduate engineering degree, at least for my first job right out of college.

After working for others, I realized that it was not hard work, but rather the misalignment of philoso-

phies and ethics, that caused stress. Therefore I decided to resign and start my own business. I founded Cleanroom Consulting, LLC, in 1999 to provide cleanroom design and applications engineering, contamination control consultation, new cleanroom product introductions, and industrial sales and marketing. The MBA courses were far more useful toward this endeavor, although the technical undergraduate degree was certainly a plus. My contact base from my last place of employment began to seek me out, and so I was quite fortunate in that the work pretty much came to me. After about six months, I landed a large retainer contract that "put me on the map."

I am uncertain as to what I will do in the future, and when I will formally retire, but I am okay with that uncertainty. Well, to be perfectly truthful, I *would* like to be a wealthy philanthropist, but those jobs are really scarce.

I do a fair amount of writing, and while there's quite a range of deliverables, e-mail is certainly the "killer ap" and the preferred way of managing all cor-

penalties you can't afford. In the above example, for instance, helmets purchased exactly on July 5, 1994, would not have to comply with either of the two ANSI standards.

CHECKING WHAT YOU'VE LEARNED

Definitions

- Have you written definitions appropriate for your audience and its background?
- Are your definitions clear, complete, and unambiguous?
- Do your parenthetical definitions, sentence definitions, and extended definitions provide enough information in the context so that the reader can follow the remainder of the documents?

respondence. It's an on-going daily activity, without exception! I do still take notes by hand on construction sites, at trade shows, or in meetings, since that seems easiest, fastest, and least obtrusive. Except for sketches, all of my written communication is either e-mail or MS Word attachments to e-mail.

E-mail is the primary reason for my computer use. I also prepare many Word docs, about half as many Excel spreadsheets, also occasional brochures, but I strongly encourage all brochures today to be Web-based, either directly as a page or downloadable as an Adobe file. In fact, I myself have *no* printed brochure for my practice; I simply direct all non–Internet-based inquiries to my Web site for further information. This has actually led to some unanticipated work creating Web pages for others!

As an independent consultant, I think that the next logical step for me is a Web site that incorporates project-by-project archival nodes where each of my clients can log on and review all correspondence and deliverables generated to date on that particular assignment.

I create many of my own Web graphics, either scanned in or captured off the Web. The first tool I bought when I started my practice was a digital camera; that turned out to be a terrific investment. I have used it on practically every project. When I need more sophisticated graphics, I have a network of pre-screened independent subcontractors that I use on a project-by-project sourcing basis. I produce my own documents on my office system, simply a color inkjet printer (but using really high-quality paper). I have been considering upgrading to a color laser printer. For outsourced client documents, I use ad agencies and print shops.

What I've noticed is that people who don't seem to be able to communicate well in writing are the ones who cause the most problems whenever you are dealing with projects involving multiple people, locations, and complex systems. The mistakes I see most often are unclear sentence structure, ill-formed thoughts, and total misuse of the English language. Most people seem to never actually *read* what they have written! People who cannot communicate usually end up causing the project to incur losses, and these people must either be taught the importance of clear communication and how to provide same, or they must be replaced.

But I must say that I would rather have something, even if it's wrong, than have to rely on oral communications for business and business-related transactions. After all, "if it ain't written, it don't exist."

- Are your definitions written in a consistent format with *term, class,* and *distinguishing features* easy to locate?
- If you have many definitions, have you put them in a glossary?

Technical Descriptions

- For text descriptions, have you provided descriptions in an appropriate order: chronological, spatial, functional, or a combination of these?
- For a description of a mechanism, have you provided a description of the whole, the parts, each part's function, and other appropriate details?
- Where visuals would be helpful, have you provided them?
- For a complex mechanism, have you defined the terms you will use and labeled the parts in all visuals?
- For each subpart of a larger mechanism, have you described its shape, dimensions, materials, function, and relationship to other parts?

- Have you summarized the description?
- Have you described a walk-through of a complete operating cycle for machinery and processes?

Processes

- Have you defined unknown or unfamiliar terms?
- Have you broken down the activity you are describing into distinct steps?
- Have you provided illustrations where they would be helpful?
- If you provided illustrations, are they labeled with captions and call-outs and perhaps a legend to help readers better understand what they are seeing?
- Have you identified—and if necessary, defined—every part of the process that will appear in your description?
- Have you checked the process description for chronological accuracy? Is the sequence of events accurate?
- Have you used a level of technicality appropriate for your audience, purpose, scope, and context?

Policies and Procedures

- Have you identified the audience for your policies and procedures: researchers, office workers, telephone clerks, machine operators, maintenance staff, technical support staff?
- Are the policies written clearly and unambiguously?
- Are the policies internally consistent with no contradictory rules or regulations?
- Have you submitted the policies or procedures for review to the human resources department? To the legal department?

Specifications

- Have you made your specifications complete, without omitting any elements you require?
- Have you avoided including unnecessary or contradictory requirements?
- Have you clearly differentiated between *shall*—items or actions that are required—and *will*—items or actions that are optional?
- Have you used precise and accurate language?
- Have you used consistent terminology?
- Have you reviewed your specifications to make sure there are no ambiguous words, references, antecedents, or other potential loopholes?
- Have you written achievable, verifiable specifications?
- Have you included performance criteria rather than design criteria?

- Have you incorporated standards, regulations, or other available requirements by referring to them rather than by including them within your document?
- Have you had your specifications reviewed to make sure you understand the legal ramifications of the wording for each item?

EXERCISES

 ### REVIEW

1. Consider the following definition of JPEG taken from a popular book intended for readers who want to know more about various kinds of graphics files—how to distinguish them from each other, how to create them, and how to use them effectively. As you might expect, defining one term often requires using other terms that may or may not be familiar to your audience. Keeping in mind an audience of people who are relatively inexperienced with graphics files, make a list of the effective ways, if any, definitions of terms are handled here, and make a list of the ineffective ways, if any, definitions of terms are handled here.

What Is JPEG?

Technically speaking, JPEG is not a file format at all, it's a compression method that is used in file formats such as TIFF and JFIF. But most people refer to JFIF (JPEG File Interchange Format) as JPEG and give it the filename extension .jpg or .jpeg. When I refer to the JPEG file format in this book, I actually mean the JFIF format.

Note: Occasionally, you'll see the JPEG files with the extension .jif or .jfif.

JPEG (pronounced "jay-peg") gets its name from the committee that designed it, the Joint Photographic Experts Group. The key phrase here is photographic experts—this group was formed especially to design a better means of storing photographic and other photorealistic images. True color (24-bit color) was almost a given, so they concentrated on developing a good compression methodology.

Note: JPEG uses 24-bit color for RGB images. You can also save standard grayscale images (8 bits per pixel), extended grayscale images (12 bits per pixel), and CMYK images for four-color printers (32-bit color).

The advantage of JPEG over GIF and most other methods is this—it provides true color while compressing image files more than the lossless compression methods. The disadvantage is, of course, that it must use a lossy compression method to do that, so some image data is lost, but not as much as when you reduce a photorealistic image to 25 colors. The task of the JPEG committee was to decide which data were the most expendable.

Judi N. Fernandez, *GIFs, JPEGs & BMPs: Handling Internet Graphics* (New York: MIS, 1997), 18.

2. Review the discussion of technical definitions and descriptions in this chapter. Write a one-sentence definition of a pencil and then provide a one- or two-paragraph description. Assume that the pencil is a new standard number 2 (the type of lead used) pencil that has just been sharpened. And assume that your audience needs an exact definition and description to share with a client.

3. Review the example of a technical description titled Calorimeter-Cycler for Evaluating High-Power Battery Modules in Figure 15.4. Make a list of the strengths of this technical description.

4. Review the sample process descriptions provided in this chapter. Make a list of the features they share and a list of any features that are distinct for a particular process description. Are there any weaknesses in any of the process descriptions? If so, make a list of the weaknesses.

5. Find a brief example of policies or procedures from your workplace or from another source. Keeping in mind the discussion in the chapter that policies and procedures are different, write a paragraph discussing how your sample document concerns policies (rather than procedures) or procedures (rather than policies).

 THE INTERNET

Find a process description by using various search engines on the Internet. For example, search for information on how cell phones work, how a two-cycle engine works, or how a DVD player works. Evaluate the effectiveness of the process description according to the criteria discussed for process descriptions in the chapter. Provide a list of the strengths, if any, and weaknesses, if any, of the process description.

 ETHICS/PROFESSIONALISM

After reviewing the discussion of specifications in the chapter, write a two- or three-paragraph scenario involving a company failing to build something according to the required specifications and discuss the ethical issues involved. For example, imagine a company signed a contract to build a warehouse according to the specifications provided, but also imagine that some of the specifications are worded ambiguously and that the company building the warehouse has decided to take advantage of some of the ambiguities.

 COLLABORATION

Working in groups of three or more students, share the ethical scenario you created in the ethics/professionalism exercise above with other members of your group. Make a list of some common concerns and conclusions, and be prepared to share these with the class.

 INTERNATIONAL COMMUNICATION

Many companies have employees from other cultures. Make a list of issues a supervisor may want to take into account concerning the company's culturally diverse audience before composing and distributing policies or procedures. Be prepared to share your list with the class.

RESOURCES

Blake, Gary, and Robert W. Bly. *The Elements of Technical Writing.* New York: Macmillan, 1993.

Finkelstein, Leo. *Pocket Book of Technical Writing for Engineers and Scientists.* Boston: McGraw-Hill, 2000.

Pearsall, Thomas E. *The Elements of Technical Writing.* 2nd ed. New York: Allyn and Bacon, 2001.

Pfeiffer, William S. *Pocket Guide to Technical Writing.* Upper Saddle River: Prentice Hall, 1998.

Schultz, Heidi. *The Elements of Electronic Communication.* Boston: Allyn and Bacon, 2000.

Exhibit 15.1

539

National Institutes of Health Guidelines for Research Using Human Pluripotent Stem Cells

I. Scope of Guidelines

These *Guidelines* apply to the expenditure of National Institutes of Health (NIH) funds for research using human pluripotent stem cells derived from human embryos (technically known as human embryonic stem cells) or human fetal tissue (technically known as human embryonic germ cells). For purposes of these *Guidelines*, "human pluripotent stem cells" are cells that are self-replicating, are derived from human embryos or human fetal tissue, and are known to develop into cells and tissues of the three primary germ layers. Although human pluripotent stem cells may be derived from embryos or fetal tissue, such stem cells are not themselves embryos. NIH research funded under these *Guidelines* will involve human pluripotent stem cells derived 1) from human fetal tissue; or 2) from human embryos that are the result of *in vitro* fertilization, are in excess of clinical need, and have not reached the stage at which the mesoderm is formed. ← *Definition*

In accordance with 42 Code of Federal Regulations (CFR) § 52.4, these *Guidelines* prescribe the documentation and assurances that must accompany requests for NIH funding for research using human pluripotent stem cells from: 1) awardees who want to use existing funds; 2) awardees requesting an administrative or competing supplement; and 3) applicants or intramural researchers submitting applications or proposals. NIH funds may be used to derive human pluripotent stem cells from fetal tissue. NIH funds may not be used to derive human pluripotent stem cells from human embryos. These *Guidelines* also designate certain areas of human pluripotent stem cell research as ineligible for NIH funding.

Requirements for compliance → **II. Guidelines for Research Using Human Pluripotent Stem Cells that is Eligible for NIH Funding**

   A. Utilization of Human Pluripotent Stem Cells Derived from Human Embryos

   1. *Submission to NIH*

   Intramural or extramural investigators who are intending to use existing funds are requesting an administrative supplement, or are applying for new NIH funding for research using human pluripotent stem cells derived from human embryos must submit to NIH the following:

      a. An assurance signed by the responsible institutional official that the pluripotent stem cells were derived from human embryos in accordance with the conditions set forth in Section II.A.2 of these *Guidelines* and that the institution will maintain documentation in support of the assurance;

      b. A sample informed consent document (with patient identifier information removed) and a description of the informed consent process that meet the criteria for informed consent set forth in Section II.A.2.e of these *Guidelines*;

EXHIBIT 15.1

Procedures and Policies—National Institutes of Health Guidelines for Research Using Human Pluripotent Stem Cells

SOURCE: <http://www.nih.gov/news/stemcell/stemcellguidelines.htm>.

EXHIBIT 15.1

Procedures and Policies
(continued)

c. An abstract of the scientific protocol used to derive human pluripotent stem cells from an embryo;

d. Documentation of Institutional Review Board (IRB) approval of the derivation protocol;

e. An assurance that the stem cells to be used in the research were or will be obtained through a donation or through a payment that does not exceed the reasonable costs associated with the transportation, processing, preservation, quality control and storage of the stem cells;

f. The title of the research proposal or specific subproject that proposes the use of human pluripotent stem cells;

g. An assurance that the proposed research using human pluripotent stem cells is not a class of research that is ineligible for NIH funding as set forth in Section III of these *Guidelines*; and

h. The Principal Investigator's written consent to the disclosure of all material submitted under Paragraph A.1 of this Section, as necessary to carry out the public review and other oversight procedures set forth in Section IV of these *Guidelines*.

2. *Conditions for the Utilization of Human Pluripotent Stem Cells Derived from Human Embryos*

Studies utilizing pluripotent stem cells derived from human embryos may be conducted using NIH funds only if the cells were derived (without Federal funds) from human embryos that were created for the purposes of fertility treatment and were in excess of the clinical need of the individuals seeking such treatment.

a. To ensure that the donation of human embryos in excess of the clinical need is voluntary, no inducements, monetary or otherwise, should have been offered for the donation of human embryos for research purposes. Fertility clinics and/or their affiliated laboratories should have implemented specific written policies and practices to ensure that no such inducements are made available.

b. There should have been a clear separation between the decision to create embryos for fertility treatment and the decision to donate human embryos in excess of clinical need for research purposes to derive pluripotent stem cells. Decisions related to the creation of embryos for fertility treatment should have been made free from the influence of researchers or investigators proposing to derive or utilize human pluripotent stem cells in research. To this end, the attending physician responsible for the fertility treatment and the researcher or investigator deriving and/or proposing to utilize human pluripotent stem cells should not have been one and the same person.

Exhibit 15.1

541

EXHIBIT 15.1

Procedures and Policies
(continued)

c. To ensure that human embryos donated for research were in excess of the clinical need of the individuals seeking fertility treatment and to allow potential donors time between the creation of the embryos for fertility treatment and the decision to donate for research purposes, only frozen human embryos should have been used to derive human pluripotent stem cells. In addition, individuals undergoing fertility treatment should have been approached about consent for donation of human embryos to derive pluripotent stem cells only at the time of deciding the disposition of embryos in excess of the clinical need.

d. Donation of human embryos should have been made without any restriction or direction regarding the individual(s) who may be the recipients of transplantation of the cells derived from the human pluripotent stem cells.

e. Informed Consent

Informed consent should have been obtained from individuals who have sought fertility treatment and who elect to donate human embryos in excess of clinical need for human pluripotent stem cell research purposes. The informed consent process should have included discussion of the following information with potential donors, pertinent to making the decision whether or not to donate their embryos for research purposes.

Informed consent should have included:

(i) A statement that the embryos will be used to derive human pluripotent stem cells for research that may include human transplantation research;

(ii) A statement that the donation is made without any restriction or direction regarding the individual(s) who may be the recipient(s) of transplantation of the cells derived from the embryos;

(iii) A statement as to whether or not information that could identify the donors of the embryos, directly or through identifiers linked to the donors, will be removed prior to the derivation or the use of human pluripotent stem cells;

(iv) A statement that derived cells and/or cell lines may be kept for many years;

(v) Disclosure of the possibility that the results of research on the human pluripotent stem cells may have commercial potential, and a statement that the donor will not receive financial or any other benefits from any such future commercial development;

(vi) A statement that the research is not intended to provide direct medical benefit to the donor; and

(vii) A statement that embryos donated will not be transferred to a woman's uterus and will not survive the human pluripotent stem cell derivation process.

f. Derivation protocols should have been approved by an IRB established in accord with 45 CFR §46.107 and §46.108 or FDA regulations at 21 CFR §56.107 and §56.108.

EXHIBIT 15.1

Procedures and Policies
(continued)

B. Utilization of Human Pluripotent Stem Cells Derived from Human Fetal Tissue

1. *Submission to NIH*

Intramural or extramural investigators who are intending to use existing funds, are requesting an administrative supplement, or are applying for new NIH funding for research using human pluripotent stem cells derived from fetal tissue must submit to NIH the following:

a. An assurance signed by the responsible institutional official that the pluripotent stem cells were derived from human fetal tissue in accordance with the conditions set forth in Section II.A.2 of these *Guidelines* and that the institution will maintain documentation in support of the assurance;

b. A sample informed consent document (with patient identifier information removed) and a description of the informed consent process that meet the criteria for informed consent set forth in Section II.B.2.b of these *Guidelines*;

c. An abstract of the scientific protocol used to derive human pluripotent stem cells from fetal tissue;

d. Documentation of IRB approval of the derivation protocol;

e. An assurance that the stem cells to be used in the research were or will be obtained through a donation or through a payment that does not exceed the reasonable costs associated with the transportation, processing, preservation, quality control and storage of the stem cells;

f. The title of the research proposal or specific subproject that proposes the use of human pluripotent stem cells;

g. An assurance that the proposed research using human pluripotent stem cells is not a class of research that is ineligible for NIH funding as set forth in Section III of these *Guidelines*; and

h. The Principal Investigator's written consent to the disclosure of all material submitted under Paragraph B.1 of this Section, as necessary to carry out the public review and other oversight procedures set forth in Section IV of these *Guidelines*.

2. *Conditions for the Utilization of Human Pluripotent Stem Cells Derived from Fetal Tissue.*

a. Unlike pluripotent stem cells derived from human embryos, DHHS funds may be used to support research to derive pluripotent stem cells from fetal tissue, as well as for research utilizing such cells. Such research is governed by Federal statutory restrictions regarding fetal tissue research at 42 U.S.C. 289g-2(a) and the Federal regulations at 45 CFR § 46.210. In addition, because cells derived from fetal tissue at the early stages of investigation may, at a later date, be used in human fetal tissue transplantation research, it

Exhibit 15.1

543

is the policy of NIH to require that all NIH-funded research involving the derivation or utilization of pluripotent stem cells from human fetal tissue also comply with the fetal tissue transplantation research statute at 42 U.S.C. 289g-1.

b. Informed Consent

As a policy matter, NIH-funded research deriving or utilizing human pluripotent stem cells from fetal tissue should comply with the informed consent law applicable to fetal tissue transplantation research (42 U.S.C. 289g-1) and the following conditions. The informed consent process should have included discussion of the following information with potential donors, pertinent to making the decision whether to donate fetal tissue for research purposes.

Informed consent should have included:

(i) A statement that fetal tissue will be used to derive human pluripotent stem cells for research that may include human transplantation research;

(ii) A statement that the donation is made without any restriction or direction regarding the individual(s) who may be the recipient(s) of transplantation of the cells derived from the fetal tissue;

(iii) A statement as to whether or not information that could identify the donors of the fetal tissue, directly or through identifiers linked to the donors, will be removed prior to the derivation or the use of human pluripotent stem cells;

(iv) A statement that derived cells and/or cell lines may be kept for many years;

(v) Disclosure of the possibility that the results of research on the human pluripotent stem cells may have commercial potential, and a statement that the donor will not receive financial or any other benefits from any such future commercial development; and

(vi) A statement that the research is not intended to provide direct medical benefit to the donor.

c. Derivation protocols should have been approved by an IRB established in accord with 45 CFR §46.107 and §46.108 or FDA regulations at 21 CFR §56.107 and §56.108.

III. Areas of Research Involving Human Pluripotent Stem Cells That Are Ineligible for NIH Funding

Research ineligible for funding

Areas of research ineligible for NIH funding include:

A. The derivation of pluripotent stem cells from human embryos;

B. Research in which human pluripotent stem cells are utilized to create or contribute to a human embryo;

EXHIBIT 15.1

Procedures and Policies *(continued)*

C. Research utilizing pluripotent stem cells that were derived from human embryos created for research purposes, rather than for fertility treatment;

D. Research in which human pluripotent stem cells are derived using somatic cell nuclear transfer, i.e., the transfer of a human somatic cell nucleus into a human or animal egg;

E. Research utilizing human pluripotent stem cells that were derived using somatic cell nuclear transfer, i.e., the transfer of a human somatic cell nucleus into a human or animal egg;

F. Research in which human pluripotent stem cells are combined with an animal embryo; and

G. Research in which human pluripotent stem cells are used in combination with somatic cell nuclear transfer for the purposes of reproductive cloning of a human.

Review and reporting processes ⟶ **IV. Oversight**

A. The NIH Human Pluripotent Stem Cell Review Group (HPSCRG) will review documentation of compliance with the *Guidelines* for funding requests that propose the use of human pluripotent stem cells. This working group will hold public meetings when a funding request proposes the use of a line of human pluripotent stem cells that has not been previously reviewed and approved by the HPSCRG.

B. In the case of new or competing continuation (renewal) or competing supplement applications, all applications shall be reviewed by HPSCRG and for scientific merit by a Scientific Review Group. In the case of requests to use existing funds or applications for an administrative supplement or in the case of intramural proposals, Institute or Center staff should forward material to the HPSCRG for review and determination of compliance with the *Guidelines* prior to allowing the research to proceed.

C. The NIH will compile a yearly report that will include the number of applications and proposals reviewed and the titles of all awarded applications, supplements or administrative approvals for the use of existing funds, and intramural projects.

D. Members of the HPSCRG will also serve as a resource for recommendations to the NIH with regard to any revisions to the *NIH Guidelines for Research Using Human Pluripotent Stem Cells* and any need for human pluripotent stem cell policy conferences.

EXHIBIT 15.1

Procedures and Policies *(continued)*

16

Proposals

The Proposal-Writing Process   546

Kinds of Proposals   548

The Request for Proposal (RFP)   549

Elements of a Proposal   551

The Successful Proposal   565

From the Workplace   572

IN THIS CHAPTER

A proposal is a persuasive offer or bid to do something. As a college student you may have to write a few proposals, and as an employee you probably will have to write many.

You will learn about:

- the difference between solicited and unsolicited proposals
- the process of writing proposals: planning, research, writing, reviewing, producing, submitting, revising, and resubmitting
- the request for proposals (RFP) and the importance of adhering to its requirements
- the standard elements of a proposal
- how proposals are evaluated and reviewed
- how to maximize your chances of submitting a successful proposal

THE PROPOSAL-WRITING PROCESS

> "Writing a proposal is partly a matter of following directions and partly a matter of creating an original document.

Writing a proposal is partly a matter of following directions and partly a matter of creating an original document. Just as with any other document type, successful proposal writing requires following certain steps: planning, research, writing, editing, revising, and producing. Skipping any of the steps handicaps your proposal. Time is usually a consideration when you prepare any document, so be sure to give yourself enough time for each of the steps to ensure that you will be able to produce the best proposal possible for your situation.

Planning

The planning step begins when you identify a need and decide to propose a solution. In the next section you will learn about solicited and unsolicited proposals. In either situation you make a decision to submit a proposal. At that point you will start to gather the information you will need, considering the same points as for any other document:

- Who is your audience? What information does your audience need in order to understand fully what you are proposing? Who will approve or reject the plan you are proposing?
- What is your subject? What is the need you are addressing?
- What is your purpose? What do you want to accomplish by your proposal and its proposed course of action?
- What is the scope of your situation? Are you covering your subject in enough detail to give your audience a good understanding of the problem and your solution? What aspect of the problem or need will you satisfy?

Researching

Before writing your proposal, you gather information on the problem and its background so you can write a better proposal and also show the readers of your proposal that you are knowledgeable about the situation and how others have dealt with it previously.

Writing

When you write your proposal, you will follow the items in the formal request for a proposal issued by the funding agency or—for an unsolicited proposal—the guidelines presented in this chapter. The form and length of a proposal depend on its purpose and on several other factors.

- Is your proposal a response to your professor's requirement to develop a project for your class?
- Is your proposal an offer to do something that you have decided would be useful to your employer or a company for which you want to work?
- Is your proposal a response to a request for a proposal from an outside company, a government agency, or a grant-funding foundation or other entity?

Editing and Revising

Your proposal goes through editing and revision to make it as good as it can be. Sometimes the company or agency to which you are submitting the proposal will ask for changes or clarifications, and in that case you will revise the proposal and resubmit it. In some circumstances, that option is not possible and is, in fact, prohibited. For certain agencies, you may not amend your proposal once it is submitted. Therefore you should always try to make your proposal as complete and persuasive as you can.

In other cases, you may have your proposal rejected but decide to resubmit a revised version at a later time. It is not unusual for a proposal to be rejected several times until finally it is improved enough to be accepted and funded. Naturally, not every proposal will be funded, but a rejection does not mean you can't try again later with an improved version.

> " Always try to make your proposal as complete and persuasive as you can. "

Producing the Proposal

Once you have completed writing and revising the proposal, you will submit it in the form requested. A short proposal can be in memo format. Longer proposals may be submitted in loose-leaf binders or bound into volumes. In the case of solicited proposals, be very sure you submit your proposal before the deadline.

In short, preparing a proposal is like preparing any other kind of document: you have to follow a process to do it effectively.

> " Be very sure you submit your proposal before the deadline. "

KINDS OF PROPOSALS

You will write a proposal in one of two situations. If you are offering a proposal based on someone else's request—your professor, your employer, a company or government agency—you are offering a *solicited* proposal. Solicited proposals acknowledge the need articulated in a Request for Proposals and must convince their readers that the solution proposed is the best one to solve the problem. In the questions cited earlier in the "Writing" section, the first and last items refer to solicited proposals. Your professor, the outside company, the government agency, and the grant-funding entity all have identified a need that your proposal will offer to satisfy. For example, if a specific agency in the federal government needs computers, it will provide the specifications for them to various suppliers. Usually, the supplier with the lowest bid obtains the contract. A Request for Proposals may list numerous required specifications, or it may allow suppliers to propose their own, according to certain guidelines.

> Solicited proposals acknowledge the need articulated in a Request for Proposals and must convince their readers that the solution proposed is the best one to solve the problem.

If you are offering a proposal based on something you would like to do for which you see a need, you are offering an *unsolicited* proposal. The offer to do something that you have decided would be useful to your employer or another company represents an unsolicited proposal. You are offering your services to your employer or another company to accomplish some goal or solve some problem. Unsolicited proposals must convince their readers that a need or a problem exists. The recipient of your proposal may not be aware of the problem you want to solve or may not have thought to ask you to attend to it.

When you submit a proposal—either solicited or unsolicited—you are trying to convince your readers that what you are proposing is something they need and also that it is something that you are in the best position to accomplish. You may be requesting funding, you may be requesting time off from other responsibilities, or you may be requesting approval to turn your attention to a specific matter to fulfill a class assignment.

> Unsolicited proposals must convince their readers that a need or a problem exists.

Proposals can vary in length and scope and can take several forms:

- A letter, for example, may be used to ask your professor to accept your topic choice for a technical report or a project due later in your writing course.
- A memo, for example, may be used to convince your supervisor at work to provide new equipment for your office.
- A loose-leaf–bound book, for example, may be used to request a grant from a foundation.
- A multi-volume text, for example, may be used to seek a contract from a large company or the government.

In addition to differentiating proposals according to whether they are solicited or unsolicited and by length and scope, proposals can be distinguished by their audiences. Some proposals are internal: they are submitted within a company or organization. Internal proposals may be either solicited or un-

TYPE OF PROPOSAL	INTERNAL	EXTERNAL
UNSOLICITED	Propose a project at work, asking for permission to research the purchase of new equipment	Offer to develop an index for a company's Web site
SOLICITED	Propose the development of a new program to train new employees	Apply for a contract to provide computer-maintenance services

FIGURE 16.1

Types of Proposals

solicited. Other proposals are external: they are submitted to outside or independent companies or organizations. A typical external proposal is written by a consultant who is trying to obtain a contract with a company or organization. External proposals—like internal proposals—may be solicited or unsolicited. See Figure 16.1.

THE REQUEST FOR PROPOSAL (RFP)

The Request for Proposal (sometimes called a Request for Quotes) is a document setting forth the information required in the solicited proposal. In it, the agency or organization soliciting your proposal or bid tells you why it is requesting the information, what the proposal should include, who may submit a proposal, when and where the proposal is to be submitted, how the proposal will be evaluated, and other information you need to know in order to prepare a successful proposal. See Exhibit 16.1 (pages 578–582) for an example of a Request for Proposal.

RFPs can be very long and detailed or they can comprise simply a brief paragraph inviting proposals on a particular topic. They can be distributed by publication in periodicals, listing on an organization's Web site, distribution in targeted mailings, or posting on a company bulletin board. Sometimes a summary of the highlights of the RFP refers the reader to contact information where more detailed information can be obtained.

RFPs come in different formats, depending on the needs of the granting agency or institution and often on the amount of money to be distributed. Many RFPs will have some or all of these sections and others:

- Overview or Introduction: a statement that the agency is seeking proposals for certain goods or services to be provided
- Background: the history or situational information that may be useful to put the agency's needs in context
- Scope of proposal: what the agency wants to accomplish; what the successful proposal will offer to do or provide
- Technical Specifications: the requirements the proposal must fulfill for technical equipment or performance

- Qualifications: the training, experience, staffing, and equipment levels required of applicants
- Proposal Content: a listing with explanations of the specific types of information the proposal must provide
- Proposal Format: how the proposal is to be submitted, such as production requirements (type of printing, binding) and number of copies
- Checklists: reminder information to allow proposers to ensure that their proposals meet all the requirements set forth in the RFP
- Submission Information: how and where proposals are to be submitted; whether proposals, once submitted, can be revised and resubmitted
- Evaluation Criteria: the factors that will be used to enable the agency to select the winning proposal
- Timeline: when the proposal is due; when the decision will be made; when the decision will be announced

The RFP is your guide when you write a solicited proposal. The surest way to guarantee that your proposal *won't* be accepted is to ignore even one of the requirements in the RFP. Consider Exhibit 16.1 on pages 578–582, which shows grant guidelines. The document is an RFP setting out the criteria for applying for STC funding for special programs, with the RFP divided into sections.

The "About the Grants" section informs prospective applicants of the existence of the grants and describes how much (the maximum funding available), when (the maximum duration of the supported projects), who (eligibility requirements for applicants), and what (the type of project that qualifies as a "special opportunity"). In this important first section, prospective applicants can determine whether the grant will suit their needs and whether their project will suit the granting organization's goals for funding. At this pre-application stage of learning the requirements for the grant, time spent evaluating your project's suitability for funding by the organization will prevent wasting your time applying for something you don't have a chance of receiving.

The next section, "Deadlines and Review Schedules," gives the reader another type of *when* information: the application and review schedule. Here, too, careful reading will save you possibly wasted effort. If you can't submit the application before the stated deadline, don't submit the application. Very seldom will a fund-granting agency extend a deadline, and then only in very unusual circumstances. Plan on submitting your proposal on time or not at all.

The "Required Sections for Grant Proposals" section is the heart of the RFP. This section spells out the precise content of your proposal. For each subtopic in this RFP section, your proposal has a corresponding section. The STC-required sections are a cover page, table of contents, abstract, problem statement/rationale, survey of current practice (literature review), expectations/applications (goals), benefits to technical communicators, objectives/methods, facilities, deliverables and progress reports, milestone schedule, cost breakdown, qualifications, and bibliography.

SECTION	UNSOLICITED PROPOSALS	SOLICITED PROPOSALS
Background	Persuade the reader that there is a problem.	Persuade the reader that you understand the problem and can solve it.
Description of what is proposed	Persuade the reader that your solution will solve the problem.	Specify that you will provide what was asked for in the RFP.
Methods	Your plan for implementing your solution.	Your plan for implementing your solution.

FIGURE 16.2

Purpose of Sections in Solicited and Unsolicited Proposals

Note: When you read the rest of the chapter, you will notice that some of the proposal sections in "Elements of a Proposal" match exactly the ones in the STC guidelines. Others are equivalent but worded differently. Use the information in "Elements of a Proposal" to help you decide how to fulfill the requirements of the RFP you are responding to. When there are differences between what is stated in this textbook and what the RFP states, you should follow the requirements in the RFP. This chapter is a guide to successful proposal writing; it is one of the resources to call on as a supplement to the RFP.

If you are submitting an unsolicited proposal, you will not have an RFP to follow. In that case, the sections that follow in this chapter will provide good general guidelines. See Figure 16.2 for similarities and differences between sections of solicited and unsolicited proposals.

ELEMENTS OF A PROPOSAL

Proposals vary a great deal in the elements that are covered. For many proposals, what must be covered is specified. For other kinds of proposals, you must cover what your readers need to know, which varies according to the particular situation. Your subject, purpose, scope, audience, and context determine what you include in your proposal. If you are a consultant who is trying to obtain a client's business, you will take a different approach in your proposal from the approach of a person who is suggesting a course of action to a supervisor. If you are a college student writing a proposal concerning a class assignment, you may be required to take an approach different from approaches mentioned for the workplace.

Some proposals simply have an introduction, a body section, and various attachments. Other proposals, particularly those in response to government or corporate RFPs, are long, elaborate, and formal. For those proposals, you may need to provide a letter of transmittal (see Chapter 18 on formal reports), a binding, cover, table of contents (including a table of figures and a table of illustrations), abstract, the body of the proposal (see below), and appendixes. When an elaborate proposal is required, you will probably be working on the

> " Your subject, purpose, scope, audience, and context determine what you include in your proposal. "

proposal as part of a team. The important thing to remember is that you are responding to a request; therefore, you have to tailor your response to the information requested in the RFP or by your professor or other requestor.

Proposal Elements

Proposals can be solicited or unsolicited and can vary in their scope and length. Some proposals may include only an introduction, a body section, and attachments. Others may be long, formal, and elaborate. A proposal can include

- a letter of transmittal
- a binding
- a cover
- a table of contents (including a table of figures and a table of illustrations)
- an abstract
- background on the problem or need
- a description of what is proposed
- a methods section or specific plan
- a schedule
- a description of the qualifications of those who will carry out the plan
- a budget
- a conclusion
- appendixes
- attachments

An informal, unsolicited, internal proposal can be as short as one sentence ("I am offering my services to clean up the storage room to make more room for office supplies") or a memo. A solicited, external proposal can be hundreds of pages long. A proposal longer than three paragraphs probably has several sections, often set off by headings. Longer proposals will certainly have many, if not all, of these elements. Consider the sample proposal in Figure 16.3, which provides many of the sections discussed below.

Abstract

The abstract (also called, simply, the summary) is the section where you summarize the problem or need and your proposed solution. See Chapter 18 for a discussion of the differences between an abstract and an executive summary. A shorter proposal may not need an abstract; a longer proposal probably will. And even though the abstract is usually the last major section of the proposal to be written, it is the one that appears first.

MEMORANDUM

TO: Dr. Fellowes

FROM: Nancy Williams and Kay Collins

DATE: March 20, 2002

SUBJECT: Proposal to Write a Recommendation Report on a PC Maintenance Program

Introduction

We request permission to write a recommendation report to present a PC maintenance program to Integrated Marketing Company. This organization has a network of 50 personal computers, with no current maintenance program in place. We have had preliminary discussions with Katherine Roberts, Director of Administration, and she has expressed an interest in receiving a formal report discussing a program aimed specifically at Integrated's needs.

Background

During our initial meeting, Ms. Roberts discussed the rapid growth her company has undergone and the fact that total personnel has increased from 10 employees to 50 employees in the past six months. Ms. Roberts acknowledges that during this growth period, the company's focus has been in the development of new marketing materials, hiring additional employees, servicing existing clientele, and developing a program designed to expand their client base. Unfortunately, Integrated has spent little time and effort in maintaining their computer equipment on which they depend so highly in their growing marketing business. The company has spent considerable money on the purchase of new computer equipment for their expansion and is interested in protecting that investment.

During the past several months, Integrated has had several problems with their local area network (LAN). First, frequent power failures at their business location have shut down their entire computerized operations for several hours at a time, resulting in a crucial loss in productivity. Secondly, since the addition of new personnel on the network, the LAN is running much more slowly, and there has been a noticeable reduction in access time.

Another critical area of concern is that Integrated does not have a system for backing up files. If a computer virus were to infect their network, there is the potential for all of their files and documents to be destroyed. Further, the company's hardware has been subjected to high temperatures when the air conditioning was turned off each weekend during this past summer and previous summers as well. While this procedure has certainly reduced

---

You may be given specifications for the length of the abstract. If you aren't, then plan for a sentence or two summarizing each of the proposal's sections. Except for the very longest proposals, most abstracts can be as short as one paragraph and at most two paragraphs. Let the material be your guide. Be brief, but not cryptic. Make sure that your sentences flow logically from one to the next.

FIGURE 16.3

(continued)

Dr. Fellowes   2   March 20, 2002

Integrated's power bill, it has unnecessarily exposed the electrical and mechanical components to unsafe temperatures and has placed their equipment at risk of malfunction.

Finally, the hardware hasn't received any type of cleaning, and no preventive measures have been taken to keep dirt and dust from entering the various equipment vents and fans. The keyboards, monitors, printers, and other pieces of equipment in many of the workstations we saw during our visit were in need of cleaning.

Description of Project

Our proposal is to provide Integrated Marketing Company with a recommendation report for the purpose of presenting an overall PC maintenance program. Our approach to this report is to address many subject areas and provide a plan that is not only well-rounded, but also easy to implement and cost-effective.

To address the issue of file loss prevention, an educational summary of computer viruses will be presented, along with recommended safeguards to ensure proper document protection against viruses and other mishaps. These areas include the recommended purchase of a utility package, a power supply back-up, and a file back-up system. As files can inadvertently be deleted even with these systems in place, software that is able to recover deleted files will also be presented.

In order to improve the speed of the LAN, procedures for freeing up disk space and disk defragmentation software will be discussed. We will also explore and recommend the purchase of software updates on a regular basis for installation on the network.

Another topic of discussion in our proposed recommendation report is proper care, cleaning, and maintenance of the PC peripherals. This section will provide helpful tips to maximize the life of the peripherals and keep the equipment running efficiently. We will also suggest the purchase of supplies to be used for housekeeping.

Finally, we will recommend that one or more of Integrated's employees be fully trained on implementing and continuing this maintenance program. We will both provide this training at their offices in one eight-hour training session upon Ms. Roberts' approval of our proposed program.

Please refer to the attached outline for a list of the various topics to be included in our report.

Specific Plan

In order to prepare our report, we will need to carefully follow a formal process to ensure all areas of our proposed PC maintenance program have been thoroughly and effectively covered. This process has already begun with our initial meeting with Ms. Roberts.

FIGURE 16.3

(continued)

Dr. Fellowes   3   March 20, 2002

During that conference, we received sufficient background on the equipment history and current status, as well as various problems Integrated has experienced. Additionally, we were given a list of the quantities and types of peripherals they currently have, and we will use this information for providing some specific recommendations and purchase suggestions.

Based on our meeting with Ms. Roberts, we have come up with major topics that address Integrated's needs and problem areas, and these subjects will all be included in the report. We will research equipment purchase alternatives and then discuss the cost and pros and cons of each option so that Ms. Roberts will have several selection choices. This research will be conducted through the Internet and various libraries, and we will rely on our own personal knowledge as well. These research methods will allow us to confidently provide a thorough discussion within each subject area.

Plan Schedule

Our approach for preparing the report body will be to split the subject areas between ourselves and then have individual responsibility to conduct all of the research for those areas, as well as write the accompanying sections of the report. The report attachments will also be split equally and prepared individually. Additionally, we will regularly review each other's work so that we can keep our draft as updated as possible on an ongoing basis. One face-to-face meeting is planned when the draft is near completion, and other, regular communication is also planned. This will help us stay on track with our schedule and provide an opportunity to exchange additional thoughts and ideas. A complete plan schedule is attached for your review.

Qualifications

We are both Computer Science majors and have had some coursework with discussions about PC maintenance. Additionally, we have both worked for companies that have had various levels of PC maintenance programs in place and have therefore been exposed to many of the areas that we will be discussing in our report. Please refer to the attached résumés for full details of our qualifications.

Conclusion

We are both excited about the opportunity to work on this project. Ms. Roberts' initial enthusiasm for our thoughts and ideas was encouraging, and she remains quite open to considering a formal PC maintenance program for Integrated Marketing Company. We both feel well qualified to create a formal program for this organization and believe we can provide helpful information for Ms. Roberts as her company begins to address current needs and plans for the future as well. We hope you will give us your approval to work on this project and look forward to your response.

FIGURE 16.4

Proposal Abstract

The Orlando Chapter of the Society for Technical Communication sponsors an annual high school technical writing competition every fall. Next fall will be the chapter's 5th competition. Over the past four years, chapter members have made every effort to obtain invitations into various high school classes to promote both technical communication and the contest but with limited success. Members of the Education Committee believe that a more high-tech approach using a laptop computer, an LCD projector, and multimedia presentations on technical communication and the writing competition will be a much more effective way to inform teachers and students about technical communication and to motivate students to submit their work.

These two presentations will nicely supplement the information on the contest available on the chapter's Web site (http://www.stc-southeast.org/orlando/education/highsch/hghsch.html) and available in the literature mailed to area high schools every September. These two presentations will be developed as nonproprietary programs and as pilot programs. They will be tested thoroughly this fall and early next year before being distributed to other chapters in the state for use in the fall of 2001. Other STC chapters in the state should then be able to sponsor their own writing competitions more effectively if they choose to do so.

A grant amount of $9,952.20 is requested to fund this project.

Remember that the purpose of the abstract is to give an overview of the rest of the document, so that readers who do not have time to read the entire proposal will have a good idea of what you are proposing and why. Consequently, the abstract is not the place to put in the details that you use to support your persuasive arguments in the body of the proposal. If your readers need that information, they can go to the other sections of the proposal and read them there.

The Society for Technical Communication's guidelines for research-grant proposals include this description of an abstract section:

Proposal Abstract Specifications

On a separate page, include an abstract that summarizes the need for the research, the objectives and methods, and the funding amount requested. Include a brief statement of the type of results you expect (such as a book or a paper reporting on the study) and how the project will benefit the profession. In particular, indicate the expected benefits to all of STC, particularly practitioners.

—Used with permission from the Society for Technical Communication, Arlington, Virginia.

Figure 16.4 shows a proposal abstract; consider how it fits the requirements stated in the STC specifications.

Introduction

The introduction of a proposal is like the opening fanfare of a musical composition or the curtain's opening at the beginning of a play. In those settings, the audience is made aware that a performance is beginning and is given a chance to hear or see the players. Likewise, in the introduction to a proposal you are presenting yourself and introducing the subject of the document to follow.

In your introduction you should state that you are providing a proposal. Your introduction may be no more than an acknowledgment that the reader has invited the proposal and that you are responding to that invitation. Provide some context, for example, stating that you have had previous contact with the reader or that you are responding to an RFP from the reader or the reader's company.

A good introduction for a proposal should not overwhelm the reader with details. At this point you should provide only a general overview of what you want to do and of what the proposal contains. You want to generate interest in your idea, motivate the reader to read further, and help the reader to understand what will be covered. You can think of it as the "What's in it for me?" section, since that is how the reviewer will be looking at it.

Example: This proposal requests permission to research and design a new language-media center for the Department of Foreign Languages and Literatures.

Example: The Keynote Speakers Bureau seeks funding to prepare a series of lectures suitable for use by executives of the XYZ Company when they deliver speeches to prospective investors.

Example: We are requesting permission to research, analyze, and compile information regarding the health problems related to operating computers. The resulting report can be used to educate computer operators about workplace risks and advise them about ways to avoid them.

Background on the Problem or Need

The background section most often follows the introduction or is sometimes part of the introduction. This section offers a thorough review of the problem your proposal is addressing. Here you provide the appropriate context to show that there is a need for your proposed service, product, or solution, and how your proposal relates to that need. If, as in many cases, your audience is familiar with the background issues, you may omit this section or make it very brief. However, it is a good idea to include this section, if only to show your audience that you understand the problem. Discuss your understanding of the requirements in detail, and provide a thorough analysis of the requirements. If your readers need to be persuaded that there is a problem, this is the section where you must persuade them. If not, this is the section where you show you understand the problem that the reader is already aware of.

In longer proposals, this section includes a literature review. (See Appendix D for help on writing literature reviews.) The purpose of including a literature review is to show the proposal recipient that you are aware of past work that has been done to address the problem or need you are identifying. After all, if the problem has already been solved by someone else, why should the company pay for you to solve it again? So in this section, you want to show how others have approached the problem and why there is still a need for a solution, perhaps because previous solutions applied to a different context. Reviewing the literature will also increase your credibility with your readers. They will see that you are knowledgeable about not only the particular subject you are addressing but also its possible relationship to other projects.

Description of What Is Proposed

In this section you cover the specifics of what you plan to do or what you have to offer. In addition to providing a detailed description of the proposed service, product, or solution, you discuss the specific advantages of your service, product, or solution. If your proposal is unsolicited, this section helps to persuade your audience that the need you have argued for in the background section of your proposal has its satisfaction in your described solution. So in addition to selling the need for your solution, you must persuade your audience that your proposed course of action will be effective.

Another part of your message in this section is a clear identification of what you hope to accomplish if your project is approved. You can think of this part of your proposal as a goals and objectives section. You have told your readers about the problem and its background. Now you want to say what you would like the result of your efforts to be. You will describe goals—the broad end-products of your project—and objectives—specific accomplishments that will lead to the fulfillment of those goals.

What Is the Difference between Goals and Objectives?

Goals are the larger, perhaps long-term, ends toward which you work.

Objectives are the more immediate steps you accomplish on the way to achieving your goals. Objectives are more tangible and narrowly focused than goals.

Be as specific as you can when you recount your objectives. In order to have your proposal approved, your objectives must be concrete and achievable. Verifying the achievement of your objectives is one way the company or agency can make sure you are following the plan you are proposing. On the other hand, proposing vague objectives waves a red flag in front of the proposal evaluator that your proposal is not worthy of support. If you cannot articulate your objectives, you cannot expect the granting agency to figure out what you are trying to accomplish either. The following are examples of proposal objectives.

Goal: Improve elementary-school students' math skills.

Vague objective: Teach fourth-graders how to do long division.

Concrete objective: Bring the long-division scores of 100 percent of the target fourth-graders up to grade level or higher, as measured by the FCAT standardized exam.

Goal: Avoid buying software that duplicates functions we can already perform.

Vague objective: Organize the software library.

Concrete objective: Discard superseded and unusable software, and catalog the actively used software by function and hardware requirements.

A vague objective is an unattainable objective, since by its nature it is unspecific. A concrete objective is a potentially attainable objective because it targets a tangible and specific result.

Methods Section or Specific Plan Statement

In the methods or specific plan section you provide detail about implementing your approach. You may cover many topics here, including, for example, how the project will be organized, who will manage it, and what the specific plans and procedures are. Put another way, in this section you explain how you (or you and your team) will run the project, conduct the research, and organize the tasks necessary to complete it successfully. Specify your approach to satisfying the objectives you have spelled out in the preceding section. At this time, you want to persuade your audience that you are able to manage the project. For some kinds of proposals—usually those requesting funding for scientific research—this section discusses in detail the method (how you will accomplish the objectives you have described in the previous section) and resources (facilities, equipment, and other resources) necessary for your approach. In a grant proposal, this part is sometimes called the methodology section.

Methods Section

● Review both the methods and objectives to make sure they work together.
● Target each method to one or more of your objectives. State why you are proposing these methods, using as justification the objectives you have put forth previously.

(continued)

- Draw the reader's attention specifically to how each method relates to an objective.
- Verify that all the objectives, not just some of them, are accomplished by your methods.
- Revise the methods, the objectives, or both until they dovetail.

Schedule for Carrying Out the Plan

A thoroughly detailed schedule is one helpful element for persuading your audience that you can deliver your service, product, or solution on time. In the schedule or timetable you should discuss in detail how you plan to achieve each phase of the work proposed and attach a schedule showing how various deadlines will be met. Sometimes a brief schedule is included as part of a memo or letter simply by discussing the major tasks and expected dates of completion. Sometimes a more thorough schedule is created, for example, in the form of a Gantt chart. (See Chapter 9 for more on Gantt charts.) The more complex the proposal, the more complex your schedule will be. For very detailed proposals you will need to indicate your proposed work on every phase of the project. (See Chapter 4 for a discussion of estimating schedules.)

Your schedule must be realistic: you must also budget time for the unexpected. People go on vacations or get sick. Equipment breaks down. Offices and labs close for holidays. If you fail to take such all-too-possible events into consideration, you leave yourself open to schedule slippage and possible noncompletion penalties.

Qualifications of Plan Participants

In the qualifications section you need to discuss your specific credentials if you are writing your own proposal for an assignment or project. If your proposal is part of a team effort, discuss the staff and the specific credentials of all involved. If appropriate, you may also have to provide an overview on your organization or company. For this part you will often provide a prose discussion of the credentials and qualifications of the team members, and you will often include curricula vitae (in academe) or résumés (in the corporate world) as an appendix to the proposal. Where appropriate, identify those who are specifically responsible for management of the project if more than a few people are involved. In a very detailed proposal you will also discuss the management structure of the group.

Budget

Many proposals require no budget, other than the time and effort of the participants. If you are writing a proposal for your professor concerning an assignment, you may not have any budget considerations to cover. However, sometimes in college assignments and often in company proposals there are production, research, or equipment costs. For grant proposals requesting funding for research projects, this is an extremely important section. In the budget section you list and explain the costs related to the project. Your explanation must persuade your audience that what you propose is necessary. You will have to justify every item and verify each and every cost.

You will probably find you have to work and rework the figures to make everything come out within the limits you can reasonably expect to receive. As you recalculate the various figures, you may find it helpful to link your spreadsheet (if you are using one) into the proposal document so you can keep the numbers updated whenever you make changes. If you are proposing an expenditure to your company, you may need to discuss how it will be funded. The budget is literally the bottom line, and decisions to go ahead with a project are often heavily influenced by the information in this section.

Budget sections often have two parts—the item-by-item list of expenditures and an explanatory narrative. The narrative is particularly useful if some of your budget items require elaboration. If the amount of information you need to provide is short, you can provide this elaboration in the form of notes at the bottom of the list of figures. But for a large project with many items, the figures requiring elaboration may be numerous and may best be explained in paragraph form.

For a very large project, the expenditures section of the budget will itself be divided into sections. For example, expenses are often separated into direct and indirect costs. Direct costs are the amounts you are requesting to cover salaries, equipment, supplies, travel expenses, and other tangible and specific expenses. Indirect costs represent the overhead or administrative costs of running a project. You can think of these costs as the money it would cost to rent the space in which you work and the equipment you already own that you will be devoting to the project. Sometimes you will be given a maximum percentage, for example 8 percent, that you may bill for overhead. Other times you must come up with these numbers yourself. (See Figure 16.5.)

OBTAINING FUNDING

Researchers need to be able to communicate with funding sources, be they government agencies or industry clients. Effective communication is key to financial survival in research.

—Ron Crotogino, Ph.D., principal scientist, Québec, Canada

Conclusion

For some proposals, no formal conclusion is necessary. The last item may simply be your budget or various attachments, such as a schedule or résumés for those involved. However, many proposals benefit from having a conclusion that discusses, for example, testimonials about past successes on other, possibly related, projects. A conclusion can also be helpful for once more appealing to your audience for approval of the project and the requested funding. Also, your conclusion may reaffirm the overall confident tone of your proposal. Whether your proposal ends with a formal conclusion or not, review the proposal to ensure that it closes appropriately, giving the reader a sense that it is a complete entity.

FIGURE 16.5

Proposal Budget Section

SOURCE: California Department of Health
Services.

Appendix M—Budget

A. PERSONNEL

1. *Position Title*

   $3,000 paid monthly $\times$ 100% $\times$ 12 pay periods $36,000

   Responsibilities include overall planning, supervision, development training, report writing, fiscal and general coordination of project. Approves budget, invoices, ensures timely progress on grant obligations, and other duties as required. Responsible for Objectives 1, 2, 3, 4 and 5.

2. *Position Title*

   $2,000 paid monthly $\times$ 100% $\times$ 12 pay periods $24,000

   Develops and implements education program on teenage pregnancy prevention. Responsible for Objectives 2 and 3.

3. *Position Title*

   $2,000 paid monthly $\times$ 50% $\times$ 12 pay periods $12,000

   Conducts intake of program participants, provides referrals, transports participants to needed services. Responsible for Objective 4.

B. FRINGE BENEFITS: At approximately 20% of Total Salaries $14,400

C. TOTAL PERSONNEL COSTS $86,400

D. OPERATING EXPENSES

1. *General Expenses:* $7,044

   a. Office Supplies

      Pens, pencils, paper, etc., approximately $100 per month $\times$ 12 months = $1,200.

   b. Communications

      Includes installation and monthly costs related to the telephone system and FAX services, estimated at approximately $352 per month $\times$ 12 months = $4,224.

75

Appendix

The appendix section is where you place supporting materials that do not belong in the body of the proposal. Here is where you can put information about your company or organization, sample documents you have referred to in the main part of your proposal, statistical data you relied on to form your

FIGURE 16.5

(continued)

c. Postage

Includes expenses for postage costs for general correspondence, estimated at approximately $35 per month $\times$ 12 months = $420.

d. Duplicating

Includes expenses for internal, routine duplicating costs for correspondence, estimated at approximately $100 per month $\times$ 12 months = $1,200.

2. *Space Rent/Lease:* $3,000

(250 sq. ft. $\times$ $1.00 per sq. ft. $\times$ 12 mos.) = $3,000.

3. *Equipment Rentals:* $1,200

Two (2) IBM compatible computers at $100 per month x 12 months = $1,200

4. *Independent Financial Audit* $2,500

     TOTAL OPERATING EXPENSES $13,744

E. EQUIPMENT PURCHASES $1,200

The agency needs to purchase the following equipment to be used in producing program reports, educational handouts, and other materials.

Quantity	Description	Approx. Unit Price	Total
2	Laser Printer	$600	$1,200

F. TRAVEL AND PER DIEM (at State DPA Rates) $2,500

Program Staff

Includes travel and per diem expenses in accordance with current State DPA rates (local travel reimbursed at 31 cents per mile). Approximately 400–425 miles per month $\times$ 31¢ per mile $\times$ 12 months = $1,500

Travel to State CCG Conference and Regional Meetings for 2 staff = $1,000

G. SUBCONTRACTS/CONSULTANTS

1. *Consultant Services* $2,800

A consultant agreement with Dr. XYZ to conduct focus groups and modify curriculum (Objective 3). $350 per day $\times$ 8 days = $2,800

76

objectives, or letters from your university or company supporting your participation in the project you are proposing. If the résumés of the people who will be working on the project were not included in the qualifications section, include them here, too.

FIGURE 16.5

(continued)

2. *Contract* $20,000

A subcontract with XYZ Mentoring Agency to provide mentoring services to program participants (detailed budget attached). (Objective 5)

TOTAL SUBCONTRACTS/CONSULTANTS $22,800

H. OTHER COSTS

1. *Training* $1,000

a. Agency Staff Development: Includes registration costs and fees for meetings and conferences to be attended by program staff. Specific events undetermined at this time. Estimated budget amount is $1,000.

2. *Educational Materials* $2,000

Curriculum, books, videos, and other materials for educational programs relating to teenage pregnancy prevention.

3. *Transportation* $2,688

Includes all costs to transport program participants to agency for participation in educational programs. $100 of bus tokens per month × 12 months = $1,200; 400 miles per month × 31¢ per mile × 12 months = $1,488.

4. *Subcontract Administration* $1,000

5% of $20,000 subcontract to cover administration support.

TOTAL OTHER COSTS $6,688

I. INDIRECT COSTS: Maximum 10% of Total Personnel: $8,640

J. TOTAL PROJECT COSTS $141,972

Proposal Writing

- Think imaginatively and creatively when it comes to proposals, and don't be afraid to submit a proposal if you have a good idea. Many people have good ideas but are reluctant to write a proposal that will enable them to implement their idea.

- Make sure your proposal adds value or is worthwhile. Many ideas for proposals are bad ideas and should not be submitted at all. Don't just submit a proposal for the sake of submitting one. Make sure that you and perhaps some peers you have consulted think your idea is a good one.

- Make sure your proposal idea is adequately focused. Many proposal ideas are too broad or too vague. It requires considerable effort to narrow a proposal idea adequately.

- Always keep your audience in mind. Many proposals are submitted by peers to other peers, but

(continued)

more often, proposals are submitted to a combined audience. (See Chapter 2 for a discussion of various audiences.) Your proposal should be able to reach all your readers, even those who may not be familiar with your subject.

- If your proposal is a collaborative effort, make sure everyone has the opportunity to contribute equally. (See Chapter 3 for tips on working collaboratively.)

- Suit your proposal to the format. Some proposals are brief memos, some are letters, some are e-mail messages, and some are perhaps even several volumes long. Regardless of the format, your proposal should have an introduction, a body (with some or all of the standard sections), and a conclusion.

- Review the literature on your subject if you are responding to an RFP that requires this section. Many proposals require that you have reviewed the literature extensively before the proposal will be convincing. Your proposal should reflect that you

are thoroughly familiar with the literature.

- If the proposal requests funds, carefully scrutinize the costs and account for any variables (delays, materials costs, salaries or stipends, support staff, photocopying and other services, office space, equipment, and so on). You don't want to request too little funding to carry out the tasks you are proposing to accomplish.

- Carefully scrutinize your schedule. Make sure you give yourself and, if applicable, your co-applicants plenty of time to do the proposed work. Be especially careful to account for delays due to holidays, illness, vacation time, equipment failure, and so on.

- Make certain your proposal is persuasive before you submit it. Is your case made for the need to solve the problem or for the request? Are you convincing about how and when the work will be done? Do you effectively represent the qualifications of those involved? Are your expenses justified?

THE SUCCESSFUL PROPOSAL

When you write your proposal, you naturally try to make it as persuasive and complete as you can. But many proposals, even those that follow all the guidelines and suggestions mentioned in this chapter, do not get approved.

Following the Evaluation Criteria

Reviewers follow guidelines when they evaluate proposals in which various aspects of the proposal are given weighted scores. The scores are then added up and the proposal is given a "grade." The competing proposals then are ranked in order of their scores and the proposal with the highest score is approved, assuming the score is above a threshold figure. A proposal that

FIGURE 16.6

Request for Proposal with Evaluation Criteria

SOURCE: National Institutes of Health.

Malaria: Clinical Research and Trial Prevention Sites in Endemic Areas

You are invited to submit a proposal in accordance with the requirements of this RFP for "Malaria: Clinical Research and Trial Preparation Sites in Endemic Areas." The Government anticipates that three (3) to five (5) contracts will be awarded for a period of five (5) years as a result of this RFP.

The Business and Technical proposals must be separate portions in the proposal package.

The Business Proposal must be signed by an authorized official of your organization and must contain a detailed breakdown of costs by year for each cost category/element; the basis for all costs must be explained, and the supporting documentation must be submitted with the proposal.

The Statement of Work is composed of two parts, the second of which, Part B, would expand the contract to perform safety, immunogenicity and efficacy testing of drugs or vaccines. The government will decide whether and when to go forward with Part B. All offerors must address both parts A and B in their proposal.

It is recommended that any proposed annual increase in costs for inflation be limited to no more than 3% of total costs per year, which is also the maximum currently allowed by NIH for research projects.

The original and nineteen (19) copies of your technical proposal and the original and five (5) copies of your business proposal must be received by the Contracting Officer no later than January 23, 2____, at 4:00 p.m. local time.

WORK STATEMENT — PART A

Independently and not as an agent of the Government, the Contractor shall furnish all the necessary services, qualified personnel, material, equipment, and facilities not otherwise provided by the Government as needed to perform the work described below.

WORK STATEMENT — PART B

Independently and not as an agent of the Government, the Contractor shall furnish all the necessary services, qualified personnel, material, equipment, and facilities not otherwise provided by the Government as needed to perform the work described below.

The business proposal should present TOTAL COSTS including: 1) FIXED COSTS to include effort in trial design, meeting costs, data analysis costs, technical and financial reporting costs; 2) VARIABLE COSTS to include costs related to the actual conduct of the clinical trial. These costs should include related effort, patient treatment costs, materials and supplies, and assays.

> " "
> Maximize your chances of submitting a successful proposal by knowing what qualities the organization is looking for and making sure you are proposing what the sponsor wants.

meets all the requirements in full gets a score of 100; lesser proposals receive lower scores. In this way, reviewers can objectively evaluate the merits of the respective proposals. See Figure 16.6 for a typical breakdown of proposal evaluation criteria, and Figure 16.7 for an example of a proposal.

A variety of reasons account for failure to win proposal approval. The two main ones are that your proposal was in competition with other, better proposals and that your proposal failed one or more of the approval criteria set up by the proposal recipient. And while you cannot do anything that will prevent others from submitting competing proposals, you can maximize

FIGURE 16.6

(continued)

Proposal Evaluation Criteria

Proposals submitted in response to this RFP will be evaluated based on the following factors, which are listed and weighted in order of their relative importance. Proposals will be judged solely on the written material provided by the offeror. Part A and Part B will be evaluated separately. In order to be eligible for a contract award, both Part A and Part B must be determined to be acceptable. Following evaluation of both Part A and Part B, a final score for each proposal will be calculated by weighting as follows: 75% Part A and 25% Part B.

Technical Evaluation Criteria–Part A

1. Technical Approach (80 Points)

The technical adequacy and feasibility of the proposed plans for establishment of multidisciplinary field sites for clinical and field-based research on malaria, including:

a) Documented adequacy and feasibility of the proposed methods for epidemiologic studies, development and validation of case definitions and diagnostics, training, and collection of reagents (40 Points)

b) Documented adequacy and suitability of the field sites (20 Points)

c) Documented adequacy and suitability of the methods and approaches proposed for the integrated research component on malaria pathogenesis and immunity (20 Points)

2. Personnel and Experience (20 Points)

Documented adequacy and relevance of the expertise, experience, education, and availability of the personnel.

TOTAL 100 Points

Technical Evaluation Criteria–Part B

1. Technical Approach (80 Points)

The technical adequacy and feasibility of the proposed plans for conducting safety, immunogenicity and efficacy trials of vaccines or drugs against malaria, including:

a) Documented technical adequacy and feasibility of the methods and approaches proposed and appropriateness of the overall plan for management of this clinical research effort (50 Points)

b) Adequacy, suitability and availability of the necessary populations, including demonstrated ability to recruit, retain and follow-up patients (30 Points)

2. Personnel and Experience (20 Points)

Documented adequacy and relevance of the expertise, experience, education, and availability of the personnel

TOTAL 100 Points

Attachment D

The **narrative** description of the Technical Plan **must not exceed 100 pages**. The front side of the page equals one page (front and back of a page equals two pages). Type density and size must be 10 to 12 points. If constant spacing is used, there should be no more than 15 cpi, whereas proportional spacing should provide an average of no more than 15 cpi. There must be no more than six lines of text within a vertical inch.

your chances of submitting a successful proposal by knowing what qualities the organization is looking for and making sure you are proposing what the sponsor wants. Granting agencies help you to tailor your proposal to their needs by publishing guidelines and evaluation criteria for your reference, as shown in Exhibit 16.1, discussed earlier in this chapter. Refer to the evaluation criteria, if any, as you plan and write your proposal.

FIGURE 16.7

**Proposal for a
Background Report**

MEMORANDUM

TO: Dr. Sam Tobias
FROM: Ginger Puryear and Laura Martinez
DATE: March 29, 2____
RE: Proposal for a Background Report on Health Problems Related to
          Computer Operators

Introduction

We are requesting permission to research, analyze, and compile information regarding the Health Problems Related to Computer Operators. This background report will help educate computer operators regarding the health risks associated with computer use and the precautions they can use to diminish the effects. This information is designed for supervisors, managers, and business owners who use computers on a regular basis to be informed of the health problems related to computer operators.

Background on the Health Risks Related to Computer Operators

Within the last decade, the computer has become a staple in our society. Human adaptation to such rapid development in computer technology has lagged. As a result, many debilitating injuries linked to excessive computer use are surfacing.

There are new terms, such as *Computer Induced Repetitive Stress Injury* and *Work-Related Musculoskeletal Disorder*, which are affiliated with computer use. Furthermore, there has been a great increase in other injuries associated with computers. Eyestrain, Carpal Tunnel Syndrome, headaches, back/neck strain, and stress are being reported in record numbers. Even more serious injuries such as radiation exposure are feared.

These injuries are often the cause of lost money for employees and their employers. Because of work-related injuries, employees are missing work and losing pay. As a result, the companies they work for are losing money in both paid wages to sick employees and Worker's Compensation.

Project Description

We propose to provide a background report covering the many health hazards that face computer users, looking into the symptoms, causes, treatment, and prevention of major computer-related injuries. Our report will cover eyestrain, carpal-tunnel syndrome, headaches, back/neck strain, and stress. In addition, our report will cover health risks of a more serious nature. The possibility of hazardous magnetic fields as well as electromagnetic radiation will be investigated.

FIGURE 16.7

(continued)

Dr. Tobias
Page 2
March 29, 2____

Through our extensive research using the Internet, magazine articles, and library books, we hope to educate others in the area of computer-related injuries. Our report will enable our readers to take precautions to avoid further injuries or to prevent them altogether.

A formal outline, which details the contents of our report, is attached.

Specific Plan for Providing Background on the Health Risks Related to Computer Operators

For this report, we will research the scientific and popular literature for information concerning computer-related injuries. We will cover specific information and background for each of these computer-related injuries. By jointly developing a list of sources and then assigning half to each person to research, we will be able to do an in-depth study within our assigned time frame. We will use our outline to organize the information we discover. Writing and editing will be shared tasks, and we will review each other's work to provide a seamless, inclusive report.

Schedule

We can research, analyze, and compile the information on Health Risks Related to Computer Operators in four weeks beginning April 3, 2____.

Attached is a schedule for the completion of our report.

Qualifications

We have had extensive experience with computers in home, school, and work. We have encountered the same problems we listed in the proposed report. Both of us have experienced Carpal Tunnel Syndrome, eyestrain, neck/back strain, and other related problems while using the computer on a daily basis.

In addition to personal experience, we have conducted extensive research on the subject at hand. With our combined knowledge of the subject through research and personal experience, we are qualified to write a background report on this subject. Attached are our résumés for you to view.

Conclusion

The health risks associated with computer use are very real, and people should be well informed of these risks. We are very determined and dedicated to writing this report and having it available for the average person to review, understand, and learn from.

FIGURE 16.7

(continued)

Dr. Tobias
Page 3
March 29, 2____

**Outline on Background Report on
Health Problems Related to Computer Operators**

I.   Introduction
      A. Background of Health Problems Related to Computer Operators
      B. Purpose of Report
      C. Importance of the Research

II.   Eyestrain
      A. Symptoms
      B. Causes
      C. Treatment
      D. Prevention

III. Carpal Tunnel Syndrome
      A. Symptoms
      B. Causes
      C. Treatment
      D. Prevention

IV.   Headaches (Severe)
      A. Symptoms
      B. Causes
      C. Treatment
      D. Prevention

V.   Back and Neck Strain
      A. Symptoms
      B. Causes
      C. Treatment
      D. Prevention

VI.   Stress
      A. Symptoms
      B. Causes
      C. Treatment
      D. Prevention

FIGURE 16.7

(continued)

Dr. Tobias
Page 4
March 29, 2____

VII. Hazardous Magnetic Fields and Electromagnetic Radiation
    A. Causes
    B. Potential Risks
VII. Conclusion
    A. Restate general facts about health problems related to computer operators

Schedule for Background Report on
Health Problems Related to Computer Operators

Task	Time to Complete	Estimated Start Date to Estimated Completion Date
Research	2 Weeks	April 3, 2____ to April 17, 2____
Compile Research	1 Week	April 3, 2____ to April 10, 2____
Compile Charts/ Visual Aids	1 Week	April 3, 2____ to April 10, 2____
Draft Report	2 Weeks	April 10, 2____ to April 24, 2____
Proofread/ Revise Report	1 Week	April 24, 2____ to May 1, 2____
Completion of Report		May 3, 2____

From the workplace

Harlan Hammack

Training and Change-Management Consultant
Clarkston Group
Atlanta, Georgia

As a change-management consultant, Harlan realizes more than most people the value of promoting a sense of teamwork in the workplace. His communications take the form of both face-to-face contact at client sites and electronic interactions with more distant clients. Skills that work well in person may not be effective at a distance and vice versa, but understanding the different requirements increases the likelihood of successful interaction.

My degree is in English with an emphasis on narrative writing. I have worked as a technical writer and now work as an instructional designer/developer. The courses I took were very beneficial, most importantly the courses on technical writing. We were given various assignments and asked to write for different audiences. The approach to each assignment was different, which gave us the opportunity to experience many different facets of writing.

As for my first job out of school, my situation was a bit different from most. I spent ten years at Lockheed Aeronautical Systems Company (now Lockheed-Martin) before pursuing my degree. When I graduated, I moved to Atlanta, Georgia, and started working as a contract technical writer. The assignments were usually short-term, but I gained a lot of valuable skills and experience.

I've changed jobs quite often since graduating. I was a contract technical writer, then moved into consulting. I've worked as a technical writer in the telecommunications industry and in the health-care industry. Currently, I am a project manager for a consulting firm. My focus is on training and performance improvement. I got my first job through a temporary agency. From there, every job came from networking or word-of-mouth referrals. My current position as a senior training and change-management consultant came through networking.

Building a Team

At the beginning of any project, we try to incorporate some kind of team-building exercise to get all the consultants and client personnel comfortable with each other. One of the biggest hurdles we face is that some clients are afraid that the consultants will come in and eliminate jobs. Once we let everyone know that we are there to assist and support them, they usually drop the resistance. If everyone would take time to acknowledge, address, and eliminate the fears and misunderstandings, everything would run much more smoothly. That goes for every area of life.

I think that if more time were spent at the beginning of a project on team-building exercises, there would be less chance of communication breakdowns later. Too often, teams are thrust together without getting to know the team members, their work styles, their sense of humor, etc. If the team members were comfortable with each other, their working relationships would be much better.

Currently, I play both the roles of developer and of manager. I create multimedia on some projects while I delegate the development to team members on other projects. I'm working with developers in our India office to create multimedia-based training. I do the instructional design and creative treatment (including storyboards) and send the final drafts to India for development. We have conference calls and Web conferences when necessary, which really help the development process.

All of the documents we use to communicate back and forth are important to the process and the finished project. Since e-mail is a quick communication tool (and, with the time difference between here and India, e-mail is a lot more civil), we communicate electronically more often than not. Without communication, we couldn't successfully complete a project remotely.

One problem with new writers is that they fail to identify the audience and the purpose of the document being created. The old saying "form follows function" is just as true for writing as it is in engineering. If you've successfully identified the audience, how and when they will use the material, and the objective or goal of the document, the formats will more or less define themselves. Without this crucial first step, any document created will be relegated to a shelf as it will serve no purpose to the end user.

Networking is a large part of my job as a consultant. It's also the way I've landed my last few jobs. You never know whom you will meet or what connections the person may have. I belong to several professional organizations, but I've found that I have many more networking opportunities through friends, casual conversations on airplanes, etc.

Insider Advice

Some of the keys to successful consulting are flexibility, the ability to draw from past experience, to be a "quick study," and to be creative or innovative. My advice to someone new to the field would be to stay current on new technology, trends, and innovations, continue learning and expanding your skills, and network at every opportunity. The broader your experience and skill base, the more marketable you are. Never quit learning.

Appearance Counts

Well-organized, well-expressed content is the most important factor in getting your proposal approved. But do not underestimate the role appearance plays. Many organizations evaluate dozens or hundreds of proposals every year, and many of those proposals are worthy of funding. Yet not every worthy proposal gets approved. The qualities that distinguish the successful proposal from the unsuccessful proposal can ultimately come down to appearance, if both are equally worthy.

Swing the odds in your favor: select heading styles, typefaces, and page designs that feature your proposal in the best light. And here's a trick you can try: As Miner and Miner point out, "A familiar proposal is a friendly proposal." What they mean is that you can tailor your proposal to resemble the corporate style of the sponsoring agency's own documents. Your document, having a similar look to documents put out by the company itself, may signal a quality of reliability to the minds of your reviewers.

Pitfalls to Avoid

If you have selected a worthy project and it is one that could feasibly be supported by the person, company, or agency you are addressing, then you have made a good beginning. But it's just a beginning. Your proposal also must be presented well and avoid the pitfalls that lead to a rejection notice.

Don Thackrey, of the University of Michigan, reviewed an older survey of 605 unsuccessful proposals and found that proposals will stand or fall based not only on the merit of the project and the strength of the proposal, but also on the availability of funding and geographical and political considerations. Further, Thackrey identified several reasons why proposals fail, including:

- The problem is not sufficiently important to merit funding.
- The proposed methods do not apply to the stated objectives, the methods are described in such a way that they cannot be evaluated, or the approach is weak or not well thought out.
- The proposer is not sufficiently experienced or trained, doesn't have sufficient familiarity with recent relevant literature, or doesn't have an adequate background in the field.
- The requirements for equipment or personnel are unrealistic.

Many of the reasons stated above will not apply to proposals you prepare. But it is still a good idea to review the reasons proposals fail before you submit a proposal, to make sure you are not overlooking a possibly correctible fault in your proposal.

CHECKING WHAT YOU'VE LEARNED

General Issues

- Have you written your proposal with the needs of the requesting agency—rather than your own—in mind? Your proposal is a persuasive offer. It will not be persuasive if it fulfills your needs but not the company's. If you had questions about what was required, did you ask the requesting agency or office to clarify the points you didn't understand?
- For a solicited proposal, have you provided all the parts required in the RFP or other request form? Does your terminology match the requesting terminology? Have you followed the formatting (margins, fonts, headings, caption styles) specified in the RFP?
- Who is the audience for your proposal? Is this audience a one-person audience? What is this person's job title? Is this proposal appropriately written for the audience's knowledge about the subject and type of job position—managerial, technical?

Content Issues

- Have you organized your proposal according to the guidelines presented in the chapter: abstract, introduction, background, description, plan, schedule, qualifications, budget, conclusion, appendix?
- Does the proposal provide an introduction? Does the introduction contain at least a general overview of what you are proposing? If you are proposing to write a report, does this section include a discussion of who the intended audience is for the report? Who is the audience? Is this audience a good audience for the proposed report?

- Does the proposal provide a discussion of the background of the problem or need? Does this section provide a general discussion of the problem or topic you propose to address?
- Does the proposal provide a description of what is proposed? Does this section discuss, for example, the specific details of the problem you are proposing to solve or report on and the advantages of your approach to the problem or topic? Does this section include a reference to an attached outline, if you are proposing to write a report? Is the rationale for the organization of topics discussed in this part of the proposal? Is this section persuasive about why what you are proposing is needed?
- Does the proposal provide a specific plan for providing what is proposed? Have you explained in detail how you will manage and carry out the tasks necessary to achieve your goals? Are the research methods (personal knowledge, library research, Internet research, surveys) discussed? Have you discussed the management of the project and the rationale for your management plans?
- Does the proposal provide a discussion of a schedule for carrying out the plan? Does this section discuss how what you propose will be completed in the time frame spelled out in your schedule? Does this section include a reference to an attached schedule?
- Does the proposal provide a discussion of the qualifications of those who will carry out the plan? Are the general qualifications of everyone in the group discussed here? Does this section refer to attached résumés for every member of the group?
- Does the proposal provide a discussion of a budget if appropriate? Does the budget account for all the expenses you will incur in fulfilling what you are proposing? Have you accounted for all the items including salaries, supplies, overhead, travel?
- Does the proposal provide a conclusion? Is the conclusion adequately persuasive? Can it be improved to be more persuasive?
- Does the proposal have all the required attachments? An outline of your proposed report (for a report proposal)? A schedule? A résumé for each member of the group? Do you have any ideas for improving the outline or the schedule?

Design Issues

- For a solicited proposal, have you followed the required design details, either from the RFP or some other publication or notice?
- Have you used headings to help readers navigate through the various sections of your proposal? Have you used headers and footers as navigation aids?
- Have you used typefaces that are easy to read? Have you chosen one typeface for body text and perhaps a complementary typeface for headings?
- Have you allowed plenty of white space using margins, spacing between lines and paragraphs, and space around any illustrations?

Illustration Issues

- Have you provided tables, illustrations, or other visuals to support your proposal?
- If you provided photographs, have you cropped them to show just the information you require along with enough of the surroundings to provide context?
- Are your tables and other figures captioned properly and consistently?
- Did you place each illustration close to the text that refers to it? Do you refer to all tables and figures in the text?

Style Issues

- Have you reviewed your proposal to ensure that the level of formality and diction are appropriate for the audience? Have you written your proposal using language typical of your audience's discourse community?
- Have you avoided using inappropriate jargon?
- Have you strengthened your prose by using active voice and action verbs, especially when describing what you are proposing to do?
- Have you carefully controlled the tone of your prose?
- Have you avoided expressing bias in your prose?
- Have you used accurate and precise language?

Credibility and Consistency Issues

- Have you been realistic and honest about what you will provide? Promising what you are unable to deliver is unethical. If you are unsure, what steps will you take to make sure that you will make good on your promises?
- If you have included an outline of topics you will be providing or reporting on, is the outline a topic outline (topics and subtopics, not a sentence outline)? Are the topics and subtopics parallel (all nouns or noun phrases or verbs and verb phrases, but not a combination of nouns, noun phrases, verbs, and verb phrases)? Are the topics too general? Is the outline complete?
- Can you think of ways to improve the proposal? Are there errors in style (word choice, sentences, paragraphs), grammar (comma splices, subject–verb agreement, pronoun case), or mechanics (numbers, abbreviations, spelling, capitalization, punctuation)?
- Have you submitted drafts to other people in your organization who can critique them for correctness, accuracy, style, and content?
- Have you edited the final draft for consistency, especially if the proposal was written by several people?
- Have you proofread the proposal? Have you had at least one other person proofread it? Proposals with typographical or spelling errors are proposals that fail to be accepted.

EXERCISES

 REVIEW

1. Review the discussion of the elements of an abstract for a proposal. Then review the abstract in Figure 16.4. Discuss how effectively you think the abstract meets the requirements of a good abstract for a proposal.
2. Review the discussion of the elements of an introduction for a proposal. Then review the introduction of the proposal in Figure 16.3. Discuss how effectively you think the introduction meets the requirements of a good introduction for a proposal.
3. Review the discussion of the remaining elements of a proposal in the chapter. Review the remaining elements in the proposal in Figure 16.3. Discuss how effectively you think the remaining elements meet the requirements for a good proposal.
4. Review the proposal in Figure 16.7. Create a list detailing the strengths and weaknesses of this sample proposal.
5. Compare the two proposals in Figure 16.3 and Figure 16.7. Write a paragraph discussing which proposal you think is more persuasive and why. Be prepared to discuss your views with the class.

 THE INTERNET

Using a Web browser, go to the Web site for the National Science Foundation at <www.nsf.gov>.

Using the Search NSF Web feature, type in "proposal samples" to find a list of sample proposals submitted to the National Science Foundation. Review one sample proposal and discuss whether it provides all the major elements of a proposal as they are discussed in the chapter. Make a list of any additional elements that are provided.

 ETHICS/PROFESSIONALISM

After reviewing the elements of a proposal as they are discussed in the chapter, make a list of some of the ways you think information may be distorted in some sections of a proposal. Write a paragraph discussing how the distortions may or may not be unethical or at the very least unprofessional.

 COLLABORATION

Working in groups of three or four students, discuss the strategies you would use to improve the student sample proposal in Figure 16.3.

 INTERNATIONAL COMMUNICATION

Many companies must submit proposals to companies from other cultures to conduct business. Make a list of what you think might be some special challenges a company might have to overcome in writing, designing, and illustrating a proposal to be submitted to an audience from another culture.

RESOURCES

Miner, Jeremy T., and Lynn E. Miner. "A Guide to Proposal Planning and Writing." Online. Available at <http://www.oryxpress.com/miner.htm>. Accessed 12 July 2000.

Society for Technical Communication. "Guidelines for STC Research Grants." Online. Available at <http://www.stc.org/PDF_Files/51-97.pdf>. Accessed 16 July 2000.

Thackrey, Don. "Proposal Writer's Guide." Online. Available at <http://www.research.umich.edu/research/proposals/proposal_dev/pwg/pwgcomplete.html>. Accessed 16 February 2001.

EXHIBIT 16.1

**Request for Proposal—
STC Special Opportunities
Grant Guidelines**

SOURCE: Used with permission from the
Society for Technical Communication,
Arlington, Virginia.

Guidelines for STC Special Opportunities Grants

About the Grants

Introduction

Upon approval by the Society for Technical Communication's board of directors, one-time money grants may be awarded for special opportunities that support the purposes of the Society.

Allocation of Funds

The maximum allocation for a grant is $10,000.00 (US). Recipients submit receipts for expenses incurred during the special opportunity and are then reimbursed out of the grant fund. Up to 75 percent of the grant is available for reimbursement throughout the project, with 25 percent held back until the final report is received.

Timeframe

The typical grant is for one year. Grantees are expected to prepare a paper worthy of publication in *Technical Communication* or *Intercom* by the end of that period. Normally, all funding must be disbursed within eighteen months of the award date. Exceptions to this policy, such as no-cost extensions for a specific amount of time, will be considered individually.

Subsequent Applications by Grant Recipients

All grants are for one-time projects. Awarding of a grant does not constitute a guarantee of subsequent grants for projects related to the original grant. Grant recipients may apply for subsequent grants by submitting new proposals for evaluation during subsequent funding periods.

Who May Submit Proposals

Proposals may be submitted by student members, regular members (except voting members of the STC board of directors), and nonmembers of the Society.

What Constitutes "Special Opportunities"

To qualify for STC grant funding, a special opportunity must be a controlled activity that can develop and communicate new information to the STC membership. Therefore, the development of proprietary curricula or proprietary information, while important and valuable, would not qualify for an STC special opportunities grant. However, developing new curricula, a pilot program, or innovative teaching methods that could be shared could qualify for an STC special opportunities grant.

Deadlines and Review Schedules

Submitting Proposals to the Special Opportunities Grants Committee

The STC special opportunities grants committee reviews proposals twice a year, using a referee process, to determine whether to recommend them to the STC board of directors for approval. Deadlines for submission are February 15 and

15-1

Exhibit 16.1

579

EXHIBIT 16.1

(continued)

October 15. For proposals submitted by February 15, applicants can expect to hear in June whether a proposal was accepted. For proposals submitted by October 15, applicants can expect to hear in February.

Process

Select an opportunity that meets the purposes of the Society, preferably one that supports an objetive within the current STC Strategic Plan. The Society's mission, purpose, objectives, and goals are included in the appendix to these guidelines.

Prepare a proposal to justify the grant request. Send ten copies of your proposal to the following address:

> Special Opportunities Grants Committee
> Society for Technical Communication
> 901 N. Stuart Street, Suite 904
> Arlington, VA 22203-1854

Required Sections for Grant Proposals

The following sections are generally required in all proposals. If a particular section does not apply to your proposal, include the section heading and explain why it does not apply.

Cover Page

Include the title of the project and the name, mailing address, e-mail address, phone number, and signature of the project's principal requester.

Table of Contents

List the headings and page numbers of the proposal's major sections.

Abstract

On a separate page, include an abstract that summarizes the need for the project, the objectives and methods, and the funding amount you requested. Include a brief statement of the type of results you expect, such as model curricula, or a paper reporting on the project, and how the project will benefit the profession. In particular, indicate the expected benefits to practitioners or to the field of technical communication in general.

Problem Statement/Rationale

In two or three paragraphs, provide an explicit statement of your special opportunity objective. Explain why this objective needs focus and how this focus will benefit the practice of technical communication. It is common to identify a gap in practice or in the state of current knowledge about technical communication. Explain how your project speaks to the gap you have identified.

Survey of Current Practice

Your proposal should include a survey of current practice that establishes the relevancy and need for your proposed project, and presents a basis for the focus and methodology you will employ. This section should synthesize in a coherent narrative the state of the field relevant to the problem your proposal addresses, as

EXHIBIT 16.1
(continued)

presented in the Problem Statement section. Any citations discussed in this section should be listed in a biography at the end of the proposal.

This section should

1. establish the context and significance of the project

2. identify existing work that can be extended or applied to your proposed project

3. identify any gaps in the current state of knowledge or practice

4. support the importance and relevance of the focus and method that you plan to use in your project

5. create a basis for the expectations and applications of your project

Expectations/Applications

Based on your analysis of the problem and your review of the field, characterize the expectations you have for the project. State your goals and assumptions and what you anticipate your project will yield. Detail how you will modify or extend those assumptions by carrying out this work.

Benefits to Technical Communicators

Explain who will benefit from the results of your project. Explain how the project will expand knowledge about technical communication or provide a benefit to practitioners of technical communication.

Objectives/Methods

Describe and justify the objectives and methods for each phase of the project. Be clear about the objectives of the project, their scope, and their significance to the future practice of technical communication. Make sure that the methods selected and the anticipated results of your project will support your objectives.

Any workable method is welcome; however, you must make the case that the method fits the issues and will bring useful results. You must explain the methods to be used.

Facilities

List schools, libraries, laboratories, other organizations, sites, participants, consultants, and databases that you can use to accomplish the goals of the project. State any interdisciplinary support you have in implementing your work.

If you plan to use the facilities of your employer, your proposal must state that you have permission to use these facilities for an STC special opportunity project. If you are a student and plan to use the facilities of your college or university, you must have permission from your educational institution. A signed statement from your department chair or employer indicating that you may use the facilities for your project will suffice. Any additional contribution from these sources is also welcome and indicates that your organization will support your STC efforts; see the cost breakdown section.

Deliverables and Progress Reports

In your proposal, explain what you will deliver to the Society as a result of the project. Be specific. Include a list of deliverables and a schedule for the delivery of each. Progress reports should be provided at least three times a year during the

Exhibit 16.1

581

EXHIBIT 16.1

(continued)

project, in time for the board of directors meetings. The special opportunities grants committee manager will need these reports in August, December, and April. Your progress reports must be clearly written in English so that board members will understand what the project is about, what has happened so far, and what you expect to happen in the next third of the year.

STC expects that your project will result in a paper that would be appropriate to publish in the STC journal, *Technical Communication* or in *Intercom*. Papers for the STC journal must be written in language that practitioners understand, because 96 percent of the STC membership are practitioners.

Recipients are also free to write up their results for other audiences and to publish in other journals or by other means, but their first obligation is to write a paper for the STC audience. If the resulting product is a book, the recipients must first offer it to the STC Press, although neither the journal nor STC Press is obligated to accept the product.

Milestone Schedule

Provide a schedule with dates for key milestones and deliverables. Ideally, projects should be scheduled to commence within one month of funding approval from the Society.

Cost Breakdown

Explain in detail what you expect to spend for equipment, materials, and personnel (including costs for your own time) and when you expect to spend it. List all sources of support (such as financial aid, in-kind contributions such as mailing and telephone privileges, and donated printing service and computer time) as well as how much you need from the Society. Although your project budget may include a line item for overhead (usually for university-conducted projects), overhead may not exceed eight percent of the total budget.

Any expense that the recipient can show is required for conducting a project outlined in an approved proposal may be reimbursed up to the maximum $10,000.00 (US) grant amount. Among the expenses that the Society will consider for reimbursement are travel, release time, office expenses (such as telephone and mailings), and honoraria for participants.

Explain in detail what you expect to spend for personnel (including costs for your own time), materials, and equipment. If the grant proposal includes funding for any equipment that will not be used up during the grant period, you must justify why it is more cost-effective to buy such equipment than to gain use of it some other way, such as through equipment rental or buying services. Because STC wants this grant funding to be spent entirely on the STC special opportunity project, purchases for equipment that will not be consumed or obsolete by the end of the grant period will be disallowed unless you clearly demonstrate the lower cost of this approach.

Qualifications

Describe the education (including degrees, years granted, and institutions), job experience, and previous projects of the principal requester and all co-requesters for the project. Also include information about your level of activity within STC, such as any positions you have held, what you have done for the Society, any earlier work published in Society journals or newsletters, and so forth.

EXHIBIT 16.1
(continued)

Bibliography (optional)

When appropriate, a bibliography should list complete citations (APA format preferred) for all references in the proposal.

Criteria for Evaluating Proposals

The committee members use the following criteria to evaluate all proposals:

Background

1. Has the applicant clearly researched the context of this project and its potential contribution to the practice of technical communication?
2. Has the applicant demonstrated how this particular project could address this need?

Strength of Design

1. Are the methodologies appropriate for the topic?
2. Is the plan reasonable? Can it succeed?
3. Will the project further the goals of the Society?
4. Will the project benefit the profession?

Proposal

1. Is the proposal statement clear, concise, and well presented?
2. Can a reviewer determine the organization of the project and its major components from the proposal?

Budget

Does the budget seem reasonable? Is there any additional support (such as in-kind matching)?

Personal Considerations

1. Does the proposer have a history of activity as an STC member?
2. Does the proposer have the qualifications necessary to successfully complete the project?

15-5

17

Informal Reports

Types of Reports   584

Informal and Formal Reports   586

Common Types of Informal Reports   586

Choosing the Most Appropriate Format   598

Strategies for Preparing Informal
    Reports   599

From the Workplace   604

" "

You will read, write, and respond to more informal reports than any other kind of document.

IN THIS CHAPTER

Reports—documents about something that was done or something that needs to be done—are some of the most common documents written for organizations or companies in most disciplines or professions. Both in college and in the workplace, you will read, write, and respond to both informal and formal reports (see Chapter 18 on formal reports), but you will read, write, and respond to more informal reports than any other kind of document.

You will learn about:

- informal and formal reports
- common types of informal reports, including progress reports, periodic reports, trip reports, laboratory reports, meeting minutes, and forms
- choosing the most appropriate format
- strategies for preparing informal reports

TYPES OF REPORTS

If you look through the reports of a typical organization, you'll find reports of all kinds from annual reports to trip reports. The various types of reports are listed and described in Figure 17.1.

As a college student, you may be asked to provide information about a new trend, for example, in a background report. More than any other kind of report, the background report resembles a term paper, and as a college student you will probably write a dozen or more of these during your college career. Or you may be asked to document and interpret the results of a carefully controlled experiment in a laboratory report, analyze a problem and recommend a solution in a recommendation report, or gather original data and analyze its significance in an empirical research report.

If you are a company employee, you may be asked to give a progress report on your work on a project, submit a trip report listing your activities and expenses for a recent company trip, issue a policy report on a change in company policies, or submit a feasibility report concerning whether one course of action is preferable to another.

Trying to determine the kind of report that is most appropriate for a particular audience and purpose can be confusing. Sometimes the assignment in a college class or the conventions at a company make it very clear what kind of report you must write. At other times, you may find yourself free to choose. Either situation can still make report writing difficult and challenging.

Keep these important points in mind:

First, there is no single general kind of report. There can be as many different kinds of reports as there are problems within an organization or company. The bottom line in the workplace is that the report must deliver what it

TYPE	PURPOSE
Annual report	Provides a summary and evaluation of the activities and finances of an organization or a company for a 12-month period.
Environmental impact study	Assesses the potential impact on the environment of a course of action.
Feasibility report	Determines the best course of action concerning, for example, a product, purchase, service, or market.
Laboratory report	Describes the testing and research that are performed in a laboratory.
Maintenance report	Provides information showing the maintenance records for equipment.
Meeting minutes	Provides notes concerning major issues that were discussed and decisions that were made during a meeting.
Periodic report	Provides updates on work at regular intervals—daily, weekly, monthly, quarterly.
Progress report	Provides updates on work completed and work remaining on a particular assignment, task, product, or process.
Recommendation report	Suggests a particular course of action or several alternative courses of action.
Research report (also called empirical research report)	Relays information about tests, surveys, or experiments.
Trip report	Provides a detailed summary of the important events and other details concerning a business visit to another destination.
White paper	States a position on an issue or a problem.

FIGURE 17.1

Types of Reports

promises to deliver. Fulfilling the requirements of a report genre is less important than creating the right kind of document for the particular occasion.

Second, any report can be provided in memo, letter, e-mail, or a more formal book format. The form of a report is determined by many factors that will be discussed in more detail below.

Third, there is no consensus in academe or industry about what to call the different kinds of reports. For example, a progress report in one company may be referred to as a status report by another company or a periodic activity report by a third. Every company uses reports of many kinds to serve its needs and is less concerned about categorizing different kinds of reports. Even introductory technical communication courses don't classify reports in the same way. Some of the courses use textbooks that classify reports as informal and formal; others that classify reports as either informational or analytical; and still others that classify reports as informational, analytical, and recommendation reports. See Chapter 18 on formal reports for a discussion of these categories.

> " The bottom line in the workplace is that the report must deliver what it promises to deliver.

Fourth, the content and organization of similar kinds of reports can vary considerably from company to company. However, the differences are often minor. Even though one company may cover some additional or different content or organize a particular report differently, the structure of a report genre still requires that some common elements be covered. The body of most empirical research reports, for example, consists of an introduction, results, conclusion, and recommendations. See the "Common Elements in Formal Reports" section in Chapter 18 for a discussion of sections commonly found in most formal reports.

Fifth, the design of reports can vary considerably within just one department at a company, especially if no department-wide or company-wide style guide and standards manual is used. (See "Setting and Following Standards" in Chapter 4.) Even the design of one writer's report can be quite different from that of another writer in the same department.

INFORMAL AND FORMAL REPORTS

Many reports are informal; these often are written as memos, forms, e-mail, or letters. Many informal reports are essential for helping everyone at a company to complete a variety of tasks. Typically, informal reports are much shorter than formal reports, seldom exceeding five pages in length. They may simply be routine communications on everyday issues—for example, a memo approving the transfer of funds from one department to another or an e-mail message announcing the details of a recent company purchase. Sometimes a report is simply a form that must be filled out and filed.

If the topic requires in-depth discussion or is written for submission to another company, government agency, fund-granting organization, or the company's shareholders, a formal report is provided instead of a memo, letter, e-mail, or form. Formal reports are more commonly done in book format and include many of the elements discussed in Chapter 18.

COMMON TYPES OF INFORMAL REPORTS

Any of the kinds of reports discussed in the beginning of the chapter may be written as informal reports. Proposals are one good example. Some proposals are long, but many are brief and best suited to a memo, letter, or e-mail format. See Chapter 16 for a more detailed discussion of the different kinds of proposals. In the same way, any of the reports discussed below may be written as formal reports. However, more often they appear as informal reports.

Progress Reports

Progress reports provide your readers with updates on work completed and work remaining on a particular assignment, task, product, or process. A progress report also discusses any problems that have to be overcome and provides an overall assessment of the progress to date. In school you may write a progress report on the status of your paper or class project. In industry you may provide a progress report on a product, schedule, or budget.

Progress reports may be organized in several different ways. The most common way to organize a progress report is according to time: work completed and work remaining. You may also organize the progress report according to the tasks performed, describing, in order, each task that is necessary to complete the project and what has been accomplished on each major task.

Whatever method of organizing you choose, you begin a progress report by providing a brief introduction discussing the background for the project you're working on, including a discussion of the subject, purpose, and scope. Not everyone reading your progress report may know the reasons for or history of the project. You need to provide a brief paragraph providing the context for the project.

Organize the middle of the progress report according to the way that seems most logical to you—if you have the choice—or according to the conventions your instructor or your company requires, if any. If you are organizing the report according to time, first discuss work completed and any problems encountered during the particular reporting period. Then, in the next section in the middle of the progress report, provide an overview of the work that remains. If you are organizing the report according to tasks, then simply list each task (perhaps using a numbered or bulleted list) and describe your progress on each task.

For the final section of your progress report, provide a conclusion summarizing any key points, if necessary assessing your overall progress and forecasting or predicting the progress you expect to make until the next reporting period. There's usually no need to summarize key points in a brief progress report, but a summary is necessary in a longer progress report. As for assessing your overall progress, the major reason you're writing the progress report is not only to inform your reader of your progress on individual tasks, but also to give your reader an assessment or evaluation of your progress. Simply stated, you are writing to tell your reader how well you're doing concerning your assignment or project. The conclusion is an effective section for providing an overall assessment, but sometimes you can provide an assessment concerning your progress on each particular task if you choose to organize your progress report this way. Figure 17.2 shows a progress report using a work completed and work remaining format.

Periodic Activity Reports

A periodic activity report is a report submitted at regular intervals to provide information on the activities or status of an organization. One example is the monthly bank statements or credit union statements that bank customers or credit union members receive in the mail. Annual reports are another example. These reports provide an update to the stockholders and prospective

FIGURE 17.2

Progress Report

Memorandum

To: Dr. Phillip Lathrop
From: Robert Hagen
Date: April 3, 2____
Subject: Progress Report for *Tae Kwon Do Student Manual*

Introduction

The title of my project is *Tae Kwon Do Student Manual*. The project is a print manual for students of Centerville Tae Kwon Do. The purpose of the manual is to provide students and their parents with a useful source of information about Centerville Tae Kwon Do. The student manual will cover all the material that students of Centerville Tae Kwon Do are required to learn from white belt to first-degree black belt. The primary audience for the manual is students of Centerville Tae Kwon Do, both at the beginner and advanced levels. The secondary audience is the instructor and parents of the Centerville Tae Kwon Do students.

Work Completed

When I conceived of the idea to write a Tae Kwon Do student manual, I had to define the need, audience, purpose, and scope. After defining those elements of the project, I began to conduct research.

On March 8 I drove to Centerville and met with Masters Tony Lopez and Victor Martinez. They gave me direction as to what would be valuable in a student manual. Master Lopez, for instance, recommended that I include a glossary of Korean terms. Master Martinez provided me with the documentation that he gives to beginner students, which helped with the writing of the student manual.

While in Centerville, I also met with Ron Avery, a personal friend who agreed to design the cover of the student manual. Ron and I discussed the tone that the cover should create and specifics about the central image and typography. We decided to use a central image of two figures kicking simultaneously encircled by a glowing globe. We also decided that the words "Tae Kwon Do" would run across the top of the globe, and the words "Student Manual" would run along the bottom of the globe.

When I arrived back in Iowa City, I drafted a detailed outline for the student manual. I also completed a written proposal and a proposed timetable for the completion of the project. I then began to write the first draft of the student manual. The writing of the first draft went

---

stockholders of a company concerning the performance of the company for the year. Figure 17.3 shows an example of an annual report title page.

Trip Reports

Trip reports or travel reports concern the activities and expenses of a company employee while traveling on company business. Often these are forms,

FIGURE 17.2

(continued)

Dr. Lathrop   2   April 3, 2____

smoothly, and it is fully complete. I did not run into any complications. In fact, I saved several hours by using the Master Document feature in Microsoft Word. This was the first time that I used the Master Document feature, and I feel that it made the writing process dramatically easier. The first draft is complete.

Work Remaining

The following is a list of tasks that remain to be done to complete the student manual:

- Make revisions based on first set of peer edits and comments from you
- Meet again with Masters Lopez and Martinez and have them verify the technical accuracy of the student manual
- Meet with Ron Avery and have him add "Student Manual" to the cover
- Create a table of contents
- Conduct a usability test with three Centerville Tae Kwon Do students, two parents of Centerville Tae Kwon Do students, and one Centerville Tae Kwon Do instructor
- Complete Progress Report Two and hand in second draft
- Make further revisions based on second set of peer edits and comments from you
- Complete and hand in the final draft of the student manual

Conclusion

Overall, I am making good progress on the student manual. As I have stated earlier, the first draft is complete. By the next reporting period, I plan to have a revised draft completed. This draft will reflect the revisions suggested by you and my peers, as well as the results from a usability test, which I plan to conduct by the next reporting period. I also plan to have a revised draft of the cover from Ron Avery. I do not anticipate any complications.

but they can also be memos, letters, or e-mail. Most companies require such reports before you will be reimbursed for your expenses. If you are fortunate to travel with a company credit card, you still typically must list all your expenses in a trip report and provide details about all business-related activities. See Figure 17.4 for an example of a trip report.

In the trip report introduction provide a brief background discussion. Give an overview of the destination and dates for the trip, the purpose of the

FIGURE 17.3

Annual Report Title Page

SOURCE: <www.reportgallery.com>.

UNITED STATES
SECURITIES AND EXCHANGE COMMISSION
Washington, D.C. 20549

Form 10-K

ANNUAL REPORT PURSUANT TO SECTION 13 OR 15(d) OF THE
SECURITIES EXCHANGE ACT OF 1934

For the Fiscal Year Ended January 28, 2000

Commission File Number: 0-17017

Dell Computer Corporation
(Exact name of registrant as specified in its charter)

Delaware	**74-2487834**
(State or other jurisdiction of	(I.R.S. Employer
incorporation or organization)	Identification No.)

One Dell Way, Round Rock, Texas 78682-2244
(Address, including Zip Code, of registrant's principal executive offices)

(512) 338-4400
(Registrant's telephone number, including area code)

Securities Registered Pursuant to Section 12(g) of the Act:

Common Stock, par value $.01 per share
Preferred Stock Purchase Rights

Indicate by check mark whether the registrant (1) has filed all reports required to be filed by Section 13 or 15(d) of the Securities Exchange Act of 1934 during the preceding 12 months (or for such shorter period that the registrant was required to file such reports), and (2) has been subject to such filing requirements for the past 90 days.   Yes ☒   No ☐

Indicate by check mark if disclosure of delinquent filers pursuant to Item 405 of Regulation S-K is not contained herein, and will not be contained, to the best of registrant's knowledge, in definitive proxy or information statements incorporated by reference in Part III of this Form 10-K or any amendment to this Form 10-K. ☐

Aggregate market value of common stock held by non-affiliates of the
     registrant as of March 24, 2000 . . . . **$124,995,093,710**
Number of shares of common stock outstanding as of March 24, 2000 . . . .   **2,586,748,307**

DOCUMENTS INCORPORATED BY REFERENCE

The information required by Part III of this Report, to the extent not set forth herein, is incorporated by reference from the Registrant's definitive proxy statement relating to the annual meeting of stockholders to be held in July 2000, which definitive proxy statement will be filed with the Securities and Exchange Commission within 120 days after the end of the fiscal year to which this Report relates.

---

trip, and a brief overview of the results of the trip. In the middle of the report discuss any significant accomplishments, grouped, for example, by task; discuss any conclusions you have to offer about these accomplishments; provide any recommendations if you have any to offer; and provide a brief overview of the expenses for the trip. In the conclusion, assess the value or usefulness of the trip. If any follow-up activities are required, discuss these as well.

FIGURE 17.4

**Trip Report in
Memo Format**

Memorandum

Date: May 16, 2____
To: Al Smith, Manager
From: Fernando Rodriguez   *FR*
Subject: Trip to Jackson Manufacturing, Austin, Texas
                    May 14 to May 15, 2____

Introduction
This trip report concerns my May 14–May 15 visit to Jackson Manufacturing in Austin to
discuss a possible contract with the company to manufacture covers for our new line of
computers. As you know, we have not yet signed a contract with a company to
manufacture the covers for our new computer line. I was asked to meet with Sam Jackson,
the owner of the company, and to review in detail the company's proposal. After an
impressive tour of the company's facilities and after lengthy discussions with Mr. Jackson
and his associates, I now have a clear understanding of the company's proposal and the
company's ability to deliver a quality product to us by our deadline.

Accomplishments
I arrived at the company at 9:00 A.M. on Monday, May 14, and met with Mr. Jackson and
two of his associates from 9:00 A.M. until noon. We spent most of the morning touring the
company's extensive facilities. After lunch, various company representatives gave
presentations on how the company could easily meet our technical specifications for the
covers we will need. When I asked if they could provide 10,000 covers by August 18, they
assured me they could, and they showed me how they planned to meet this deadline.

I returned to the company the next morning (May 15) at 9:00 A.M. to review all the details
of the company's proposal and to address a few issues. I expressed my concern that the
company would have to hire, temporarily, an additional ten employees and hire them soon.
I was assured that finding ten additional employees on short notice would not be a
problem. I also expressed some concerns about the quality of the materials that would be
used, but I was provided additional test data showing how durable the materials are.

I recommend that we call our staff together to review the proposal one more time and then
sign a contract with Jackson Manufacturing no later than this Friday.

Assessment
Overall this was an extremely useful and productive trip. I was able to see first-hand the
concern for quality that Mr. Jackson and his employees have, and I was persuaded by their
commitment to provide our company the quantity of covers we will need within our three-
month deadline.

Lab Reports

Laboratory reports describe the testing and research that are performed in
a laboratory. They seldom evaluate or interpret the information or data. They
essentially just document work that is in progress in the lab. Information in
these reports is often helpful for the methodology section of research reports.

FIGURE 17.5

Test Section of a Lab Report

Roberts   2

Subjects, Materials, and Methods

A 50 ml round bottom flask equipped with Claisen head septum and drying tube was used in the preparation of the Grignard Reagent. A syringe was used for dispensing the ether and bromobenzene solution into the flask; .300 grams of shiny magnesium turnings were placed into the round bottom flask. A drying tube was prepared with anhydrous calcium chloride.

Next, 40.0 ml of anhydrous diethylether was placed into a dry 50 ml Erlenmeyer flask and corked. Ether was removed as needed from this flask during the course of the experiment.

Next, 1.40 ml of bromobenzene was placed into a pre-weighed test tube. Then 8.00 ml of anhydrous ether was transferred to the vial.

After the bromobenzene was dissolved, 1.60 ml of this solution was drawn into the syringe and the vial was capped. The syringe was inserted through the rubber septum and the bromobenzene solution was added to the flask.

This apparatus was placed above a hot plate, turned to the lowest setting, and stirred gently. After the mixture was stirred and heated slowly for about 10 minutes, bubbles started to evolve, and the originally colorless mixture started to turn yellow and then brown. The reaction took more than 30 minutes to complete. After this time, some magnesium still remained on the bottom of the flask. A stirring rod was then used to break up and crunch the remaining magnesium, to which more anhydrous ether was added. The reaction started bubbling. The rest of the bromobenzene solution was then added slowly over 15 minutes.

While the phenylmagnesium bromide solution remained heating, a solution of 2.18 grams of benzophenone in 4 ml of anhydrous ether was made in a 4-inch test tube. The test tube was capped until the reflux period was over. Once the Grignard reagent was cooled to room temperature, some of the benzophenone solution was added rapidly to the stirred Grignard reagent. The remainder of the benzophenone solution was then added. The mixture was then cooled to room temperature. The solution turned red and then gradually solidified, eventually

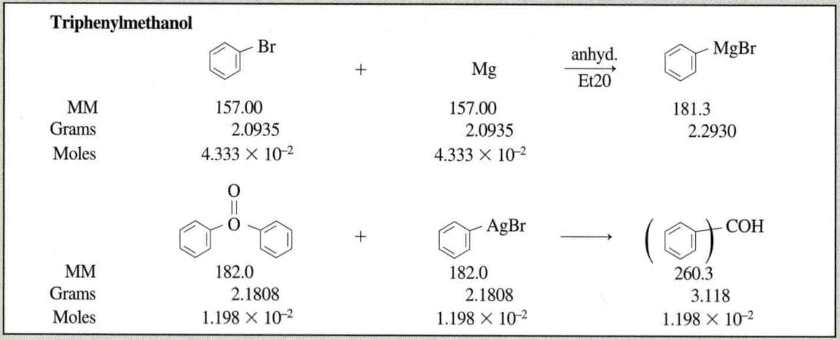

Triphenylmethanol

	Br		Mg	anhyd. Et20	MgBr
MM	157.00	+	157.00	→	181.3
Grams	2.0935		2.0935		2.2930
Moles	4.333×10^{-2}		4.333×10^{-2}		

	O=O		AgBr		COH
MM	182.0	+	182.0	→	260.3
Grams	2.1808		2.1808		3.118
Moles	1.198×10^{-2}		1.198×10^{-2}		1.198×10^{-2}

Often lab reports are submitted on a standard or in-house form. For college students, a laboratory report is sometimes referred to as a project report. A professor may give you specific requirements for how you are to proceed, asking you to demonstrate a theory or hypothesis, for example. You'll have to document how you followed the procedure, how you used the lab equipment, what results you found, and how you interpreted the results. See Figure 17.5 for an example of a lab report.

FIGURE 17.5

(continued)

Roberts   3

turning white as the adduct was formed. The syringe and septum were removed when stirring was no longer effective, and the mixture was stirred with a spatula. The tube containing the benzophenone solution was rinsed with about 2 ml of anhydrous ether and added to the mixture. The reaction flask was removed and capped. The contents were occasionally stirred. The flask was recapped and allowed to stand for 1 week.

Next, 12 ml of 6 M hydrochloric acid was added to neutralize the reaction mixture. A spatula was used to break up the solid while the hydrochloric acid was added. Some ether was lost to evaporation, so enough additional ether was added to maintain at least 10 ml volume in the upper organic phase. Two distinct layers were eventually obtained. The upper ether layer contained triphenylmethanol. The lower aqueous hydrochloric acid layer contained the inorganic compounds. At this point some solid remained, so additional hydrochloric acid was added to dissolve the remaining solid.

The entire contents of the reaction flask were transferred to the separatory funnel. The contents were 2 distinct clear yellow layers. The top layer was darker than the bottom layer.

A small amount of ether was used to rinse the reaction flask and was added to the separatory funnel. More ether was added to dissolve the remaining solid and shaken until everything dissolved. Eventually, 2 distinct layers appeared. The aqueous layer was removed from the separatory funnel and drained into a beaker. The top ether layer was poured into an Erlenmeyer flask. The aqueous layer was poured back into the separatory funnel and reextracted with 10 ml of ether. The lower aqueous layer was removed and discarded, and the remaining ether phase was combined with the first ether extract. The ether solution was dried with granular anhydrous sodium sulfate.

The dried ether solution was decanted into a small Erlenmeyer flask, and the drying agent was rinsed with more diethyl ether. The solvent was evaporated in a hood in a hot water bath at 50° Celsius using a dry air steam. After removal of the solvent, an oily yellow solid-like mixture remained.

The byproduct biphenyl was removed by adding 6 ml of petroleum ether. The mixture was heated slightly and stirred, and then cooled to room temperature. The biphenylmethanol was collected by vacuum filtration on a Hirsch funnel and rinsed with small portions of petroleum ether. It appeared dark yellow with very small cubic crystals. The solid was air dried and weighed at 1.7357 grams. The percent yield of the crude product was 76%.

The total product was crystallized from hot isopropyl alcohol in an Erlenmeyer flask using a hot plate. The hot solvent was slowly added just until the product dissolved. The flask was allowed to cool slowly, and when cooled, it was placed in an ice bath to complete the crystallization. The solid was given the I.D # -2-8-4, collected in a Hirsch funnel, and washed with cold isopropyl alcohol. The crystals formed were light-yellow, a little larger than before, and cubic. This product was allowed to air dry. The product was then weighed at 1.039 grams, and the percent yield was calculated at 33%.

A laboratory report typically begins with an introduction, which briefly discusses the subject, purpose, and scope of the procedure. The introduction may include or be followed by a background section discussing any applicable theory or research. Next is a methods section discussing the procedure you followed and the apparatus you used. This section is followed by a findings section discussing your interpretation of the data and your conclusions based on the interpretations. If necessary or appropriate, a lab report may also contain a recommendations section. (See the "Scientific Papers" section in Chapter 18 for a discussion of a related topic.)

Meeting Minutes

Minutes are the notes concerning major issues that were discussed and decisions that were made during a meeting. They are the official record of a meeting, and many companies, organizations, and clubs require that minutes be taken at meetings. Since minutes are the official record of the proceedings and are often incorporated into the permanent records of the company, accuracy and completeness are essential. In addition, minutes can be helpful for informing all members about what occurred at a meeting. You never know when you may be asked to take the minutes at a meeting, so it is important to know how to take complete and accurate notes. See Figure 17.6 for an example of meeting minutes.

Writing Minutes

- Make sure that the meeting has a printed agenda.
- Organize the minutes according to the topics and subtopics provided on the agenda.
- Record the date and the starting time of the meeting.
- Provide the names of all of those attending the meeting, if appropriate or if requested.
- Listen carefully to what is said, and make sure you understand what is being discussed and what decisions are being made.
- Take careful and thorough notes.
- Interrupt the discussion, if necessary, to make sure you are recording various motions and decisions correctly.
- Become familiar with *Robert's Rules of Order.* As the person recording the minutes, you won't usually be the chair of the meeting, but it helps to be familiar with the rules of procedure so that you can more easily understand what

is being discussed and why it is being discussed that way.

- Be consistent and specific when referring to people. For example, include the name of any person who makes a motion. Give the exact name of the person and use people's names consistently throughout the minutes.
- Be sure to record all motions word for word. Other matters and discussions may be summarized or paraphrased. Record the disposition for each motion. If the motion is voted on, record the result of the voting (passed, defeated). If the motion is tabled for later discussion, record that, too.
- Record the ending time of the meeting.
- Make sure your notes are complete and accurate. If possible, have someone else who attended the meeting review your minutes while both you and that person have a fresh memory of the meeting.

(continued)

- Sign your name to the minutes document.
- Provide copies to all members of the group (including those who were not able to attend) as soon

as it is convenient to do so after the meeting. Keep a copy on file for future reference and as a record of the meeting.

FIGURE 17.6

Informal Meeting Minutes

Minutes of March 26, 2____, Staff Meeting

In attendance: John Davis, Joyce Henderson, Phil Johnson, Cecilia Rodriguez, Jake Rubin, Marsha Schmidt, Fernando Torres, Jason Williams

Absent: Amy Lee

The meeting was called to order at 9:00 A.M.

1. General Announcements
   A. Awards
      Joyce Henderson and Cecilia Rodriguez were recognized as employees-of-the-month. John Davis was recognized by the mayor for contributions to the city's youth league.
   B. New Employees
      Fernando Torres was introduced as a new employee.
   C. Policy changes
      Jake Rubin announced that quarterly bonuses are now subject to review by a team of managers instead of just one manager.

2. Team Reports
   A. Team 1
      Team 1 reported that it was on schedule with the three computer products.
   B. Team 2
      Team 2 reported that it was still debugging the code in the software and would need three more weeks to complete work.
   C. Team 3
      Team 3 reported that six new U.S. clients have signed contracts for the new software release.
   D. Team 4
      Team 4 reported that five international clients will soon sign contracts.

3. Old Business
   A. Contract with Oilco Company
      The contract with Oilco Company is still under discussion.
   B. Contract with Netco Company
      The contract with Netco Company was signed last Friday.

4. New Business
   A. New Product Line
      Next January Teams 1 and 2 will be assigned to develop a new product line.
   B. New Competitor
      WinTech has moved into the same market and is expected to offer stiff competition.

The meeting was adjourned at 10:00 A.M.

Minutes submitted by Marsha Schmidt.

Marsha Schmidt

FIGURE 17.7

Form Report

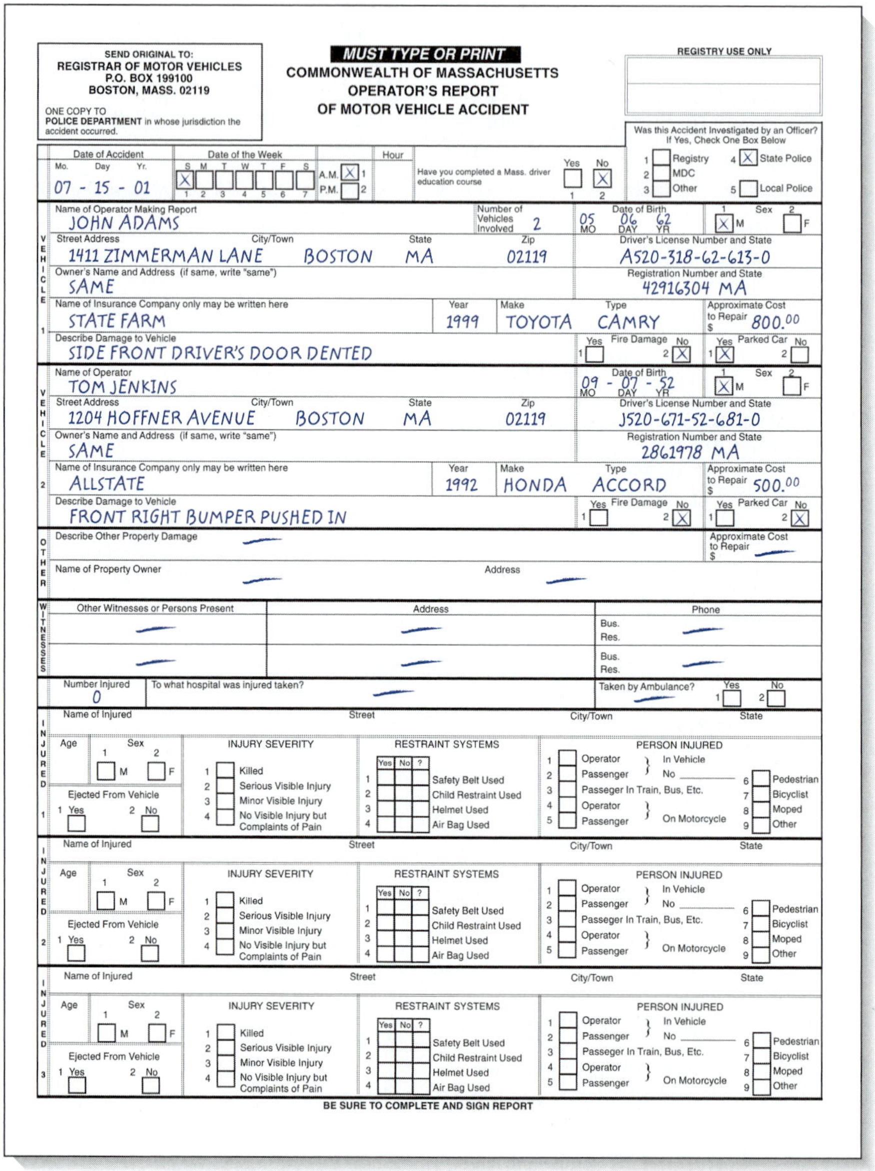

Forms

Many purposes in written communication are achieved simply through forms alone. As a college student, you are typically asked to complete forms when you apply for admission to a college, when you apply for residency in a college dorm, when you register for classes, and when you apply for a part-time job. Your professors may require you to provide information about yourself on a class form, or you may have to record the results of a laboratory experiment

FIGURE 17.7

(continued)

NOTE: Mark all items which apply. The diagram and description of what happened (below) need not be completed if separate 8½ x 11 size sheet with same detailed information is attached. Please sign report in space provided below.

LOCATION

City or Town Where Accident Occurred: BOSTON   Nearest Mile Marker   Number of Lanes   At Rotary Yes 1 No 2   If Accident Occurred on Ramp Fill in Below:

Street Name or Route Number: HOFFNER AVENUE   at intersection with: BLAKE STREET

1 On ramp to route number ___ N S E W going

Which direction was each vehicle traveling?   Or ---- If not at intersection, fill in below:

Vehicle No. 1 N S E W   Vehicle No. 2 N S E W [X]   _____ feet   N S E W Of nearest intersection, bridge, mile marker, railroad

2 On ramp from route number ___ N S E W going

Other Landmarks _____

TYPE — Accident Involved Collision With:

1 Pedestrian   4 Railroad Train   7 Overturned in road   B Truck
2 Motor Vehicle in Traffic   5 Ran off roadway hit fixed object ___ feet from road   8 Ran off roadway -- non-collision   C Moped
3 [X] Motor Vehicle Parked   6 Bicycle   9 Fixed object on shoulder, sidewalk or island   D Other
A School Bus

If Collision involved two or more vehicles mark one of the following:
1 Rear End 2 [X] Angle 3 Head On

COLLISION CONDITIONS

What were vehicles doing prior to accident? Mark appropriate box — Vehicle 1 | 2

	1	2	
1			Making right turn
2		X	Making left turn
3			Making U Turn
4			Going straight ahead
5			Passing on right
6			Passing on left
7			Stop sign
8			Skidding
9			Slowing or stopping
A			Crossing median strip
B			Driverless moving vehicle
C			Backing
D			Starting in traffic
E			Starting from parked position
F	X		Parked
G			Stalled or disabled
H			Stalled or disabled with flasher on
J			In process of parking
K			Entering or exiting from alley or driveway
L			Making right turn on red
M			Entering median
N			Crossed median
O			Other

Where was pedestrian located at time of accident? Mark appropriate box:
1 At intersection; 2 Within 300 feet of intersection; 3 More than 300 feet from intersection; 4 Walking in street with traffic; 5 Walking in street against traffic; 6 Standing in street; 7 Getting on/off vehicle; 8 Working on vehicle; 9 Working in street; A Playing in street; B Not in street; C Other

ROAD SURFACE: 1 Dry; 2 Wet; 3 [X] Snowy; 4 Icy; 5 Other

ROAD CONDITIONS: 1 [X] No Defects; 2 Holes, ruts, bumps; 3 Foreign matter on surface; 4 Defective shoulder; 5 Road under construction; 6 Other

COLLISION CONDITIONS: 1 Hit median barrier; 2 Hit guard rail; 3 Hit curbing; 4 Hit abutment; 5 Hit signpost; 6 Hit utility or light pole; 7 Hit tree; 8 Embankment; 9 Ditch; A Rock ledge; B Stone wall; C Bridge rail; D Other

LIGHT CONDITIONS: 1 Daylight; 2 Dawn or dusk; 3 [X] Darkness - road lighted; 4 Darkness - road unlighted

WEATHER CONDITIONS: 1 Clear; 2 Foggy; 3 Cloudy; 4 Rain; 5 [X] Snow; 6 Sleet

CONDITIONS — TRAFFIC CONTROLS:
1 Stop sign; 2 Yield sign; 3 Warning sign; 4 Signal light; 5 Officer or flagman; 6 Railroad crossing gate; 7 Railroad automatic signal; 8 Control device not working; 9 No control present; A No turn on red

DIAGRAM

INDICATE ON THIS DIAGRAM WHAT HAPPENED. Use one of these outlines to sketch the scene of your accident, writing in street or highway names or numbers.

1. Number each vehicle and show direction of travel by arrow:
2. Use solid line to show path before accident, dotted line after accident
3. Show pedestrian by:
4. Show railroad by:
5. Show distance and direction in landmarks; identify landmarks by name or number
6. Indicate north by arrow, as:

INDICATE NORTH BY ARROW

Describe What Happened: (Refer to Vehicles by Number)

VEHICLE 2 SKIDDED ON ROAD AND RIGHT FRONT BUMPER HIT DRIVER'S SIDE DOOR ON VEHICLE 1

My speed immediately prior to the accident was approximately _____ m.p.h.

Signature of operator making report _____   Date _____

on a form. In the workplace, forms include job application forms, job benefits forms, personnel evaluation forms, and travel forms, to mention only a few examples. And, increasingly, both college students and people in the workplace are called upon to complete all kinds of Web forms. Web forms are forms you access on a company or organization Web site. You may complete a Web form to order a product, to enter a contest, to request information, or to complete a survey, for example. See Figure 17.7 for an example of a form report.

CHOOSING THE MOST APPROPRIATE FORMAT

As you have already learned, most informal reports appear in the form of memos, letters, and e-mail messages. Often determining which of these formats to use is an easy decision, and at other times the decision can be more difficult.

When to Use Memo, Letter, or E-mail Format for Reports

- Memo reports are for internal use within a company or organization. They are generally more informal in format and style than formal reports. See the "Memos" section in Chapter 14.

- Letter reports are usually documents for audiences outside the organization or company; like memo reports, they are typically brief—four or five pages at most. Letter reports should follow the principles of effective letters discussed in Chapter 14.

- Increasingly, both memos and letters are attached to e-mail messages. The e-mail message serves as a cover message for the attached report. When the intended readers receive the e-mail message and attached file or files, they simply open the attached documents. However, the rapidly increasing sophistication of many e-mail programs also makes it easy to include an entire informal report within the e-mail message itself.

- Keep in mind that e-mail isn't private. If you want a message to remain personal or confidential, it's best to use a memo or letter format.

- The formatting you apply to your message may not be viewable by others. If the appearance of your report depends on lining up columns of numbers or other elements, emphasizing headings or text using styles (bold, italics, underlining), or displaying other visual features, you may prefer to use paper-based methods to send out your report.

- Informal reports on sensitive or delicate issues are often best written in memo or letter format. Memos and letters require more time to prepare and distribute than e-mail. The importance of the subject determines if a memo or letter is warranted over an e-mail message. A more important subject often justifies the extra effort.

- Consider the practices (or conventions) of your company or organization. Often news is distributed by e-mail, changes in policies by memo, and complaints or suggestions by letter. Personnel evaluations typically are written in memo or form format. Many communications such as hiring, firing, promotions, and demotions are best done face-to-face instead of in writing.

- Think of e-mail as primarily effective for messages about subjects of less importance, the

(continued)

day-to-day activities of the company or organization.	may be permissible to notify an employee of a promotion via e-mail, but would it be ethical to notify an employee via e-mail that he or she has been fired?
● Ethical considerations may also help determine which format is best for you. In some cases it	

STRATEGIES FOR PREPARING INFORMAL REPORTS

While it's true that informal reports are typically much shorter than formal reports, they still require careful preparation to be effective. You must employ a variety of strategies to prepare an informal report: focusing, gathering information, interpreting information, organizing, designing and illustrating, writing and revising the first draft, and using an appropriate prose style.

Focusing

As discussed in Chapter 4, focusing your topic means understanding your audience, identifying and narrowing your subject, determining your purpose, and limiting your scope. Properly focusing in an informal report often presents as many difficulties and challenges as focusing in many other kinds of technical documents.

Before you begin writing your informal report (whether it's in memo, letter, or e-mail format), you'll have to understand your audience's background and determine what your audience needs to know. A proper audience analysis (see Chapter 2) helps you to narrow your subject and determine your purpose for writing. Only by understanding whom you are writing for can you understand what you want them to know, do, or accept, and ascertain the best way to achieve one or more of these purposes. A proper consideration of audience also helps you to limit the scope of your report.

Because memos, letters, and e-mail messages are typically brief, state your purpose clearly in the opening, preferably in the first sentence. Of course, there are reasons for a more indirect approach (see the "Patterns: Direct and Indirect" section in Chapter 14), but in most cases you should state your purpose clearly and at the beginning.

Gathering Information

An informal report typically does not require the in-depth research of a longer, more formal report, but you still need to gather information to provide good content in this kind of report. For most informal reports, you may rely on only a few of the research strategies discussed in Chapter 5. If the information you need is known by others, you can interview them, have them fill out a survey form or questionnaire, or participate in an informal focus group. If appropriate, you can experiment to find out what you need to know. You may try the library or the Internet for written information.

The type of report and its subject matter will govern where you go for the information you need. If the report is about how employees are complying with a company directive, for example, you can observe the employees, ask them if they are able to comply, ask them for suggestions, and verify compliance objectively by noticing the results of their compliance. If you are reporting on the type of computers the company should purchase, you can visit stores, browse Web sites, ask others for recommendations, speak to manufacturers' representatives, review printed and online reviews, and try the equipment at other companies or in other departments. If you are providing a trip report for reimbursement of your expenses, you will gather all your receipts, ticket stubs, meal checks, and other supporting material in order to have a complete list in your report.

Interpreting the Information

Once you have gathered the information you need, spend some time interpreting it to understand what it means and to see if it supports your purpose for writing. Depending on the kind of informal report you are providing, interpreting the information may take only a few minutes or it may require many hours. A brief memo report on a policy change may require little time to analyze, whereas a laboratory report can involve many hours of sorting through the data to determine what should or should not be discussed.

Organizing

As with every technical document, give careful consideration to how you want to organize the key points in the introduction, middle, and closing of the informal report. Give special emphasis to audience considerations and cover the information in the order most effective for your particular purpose for this particular audience. The order of an informal report can be a major psychological factor in determining the success of the report. See, for example, the discussion of direct and indirect patterns in Chapter 14.

Regardless of the type of informal report you are writing, the introduction typically discusses the subject, purpose, scope, and any essential or relevant background. Sometimes a background section will follow the introduction if the report topic is complex enough or if the report is more than a few pages long. The middle of an informal report contains the major sections of the report, adhering, of course, to the demands of the particular kind of informal report. The sections may be organized using any one of many possible methods of organizing: from most important point to least important, least important

> " "
> The order of an informal report can be a major psychological factor in determining the success of the report.

to most important, chronologically, topically, and so on. (See the "Outlines" section in Chapter 6 for some organizing strategies.)

The closing of an informal report is an effective place for specifying what you will do or what you want your readers to do. For some informal reports, this will be an action statement. You may want to provide a numbered or bulleted list to help highlight the important actions. Depending on the kind of informal report you are writing, you may also want to provide an overall assessment, a summary of key points covered in the report, recommendations, or simply a courteous closing concerning future business dealings. See Exhibit 17.1 on pages 610–621 for an example of recommendation report. (For a discussion of recommendation reports, see Chapter 18.)

Designing and Illustrating

A report provided in the format of a memo, letter, or e-mail can be designed in many ways. Unless your professor prescribes a specific format or your employer requires you to follow a style guide, you may create any number of designs for an effective informal report. Even an informal memo still requires certain common elements, as do the letter and e-mail forms. See Chapter 14 for a discussion of these elements.

Informal reports can benefit from many of the same design elements you might use in instructions, a manual, or a more formal report. For example, in a memo report you may want to use headings to enhance the readability of the report. You may want to use "Introduction" as a heading, the major headings of the body in the body or middle of the report, and "Conclusions" and "Recommendations" in the closing of the report. In any informal report you may also use white space, typography, bulleted and numbered lists, line spacing, and other design elements to great advantage. The increasing sophistication of e-mail programs now makes it possible for writers to use all kinds of styles (bold, underlining, italics) as well as different typefaces, font sizes, and colors in their messages. See Figure 17.8 for an example of an e-mail report using styles.

Additionally, illustrations can play a major role in many informal reports. Illustrations require as much planning as any other part of the report. Determine what kinds of figures and tables will most effectively support the points you make in the paragraphs of your report. Keep in mind that a well-constructed bar chart or pie graph or a nicely done table can be one of the informative or persuasive parts of your report. See Chapter 9 for a discussion of how to create a variety of illustrations and place them effectively within your report.

Writing and Revising the First Draft

Every technical document requires at least several drafts before it becomes a polished report. Informal reports, however brief, can require much rewriting before you finally have the exact wording you need. See Chapter 10 for a more

FIGURE 17.8

E-mail Report

SOURCE: U.S. Department of Health and Human Services. Food and Drug Administration. Office of Device Evaluation.

X-Sender: tester@device.xx.com
X-Mailer: QUALCOMM Windows Eudora Version 5.0.2
Date: Thu, 13 Dec 2001 11:39:56 –0500
To: All Manufacturers
From: Testing Center <tester@device.xx.com>
Subject: Acute Upper Airway Obstruction Devices

- -

Background
This document describes a means by which acute upper airway obstruction devices may comply with the requirement of class II special controls. Manufacturers of **Acute Upper Airway Obstruction Devices** that follow the recommendations listed in this report before introducing their device into commercial distribution in the United States will be able to market their device. Manufacturers must maintain in their device master records and be able to demonstrate that their specific device complies with either the recommendations of this guidance or some alternate means that provides equivalent assurance of safety and effectiveness. If the manufacturer cannot comply with either of the above, they will not be exempt from the requirements of premarket notification and will need to submit a premarket notification submission and receive clearance prior to marketing.

Scope
FDA identifies an acute upper airway obstruction device as a raised rounded pad that is intended for use in relief of choking in acute upper airway obstruction in victims who weigh approximately 80 pounds or more. This generic type of device is an anesthesiology device classified under 21 CFR 868.5115, product code MZT. It is for over-the-counter use and, in the event of choking on a foreign body, can be applied to the abdomen and pushed upward to generate expulsion pressure to remove the obstruction.

Risks to Health
FDA has identified two risks to health associated with this type of device. These risks involve

1. incorrect use resulting in damage to the internal organs of the thorax and/or the abdomen, and

2. faulty device design that generates and applies too much pressure to the abdomen resulting in patient injury.

Special Controls Guidance
FDA believes the following controls, when combined with the general controls of the act, will provide reasonable assurance of the safety and effectiveness of this type device: Labeling that includes instructions for reporting complications resulting from the use of the device directly to the manufacturer, as well as any applicable medical device reporting requirements (21 CFR 803).

1. Labeling for the lay user that includes adequate instructions for use including (i) a clear identification of the minimum victim size threshold (weight), as well as any device-specific limitations identified through application of design controls, and (ii) instructions for use of the Heimlich maneuver.

2. Design controls that satisfactorily evaluate
  • the potential for excessive generation and application of pressure to the abdomen that can result in damage to the internal organs. The generated

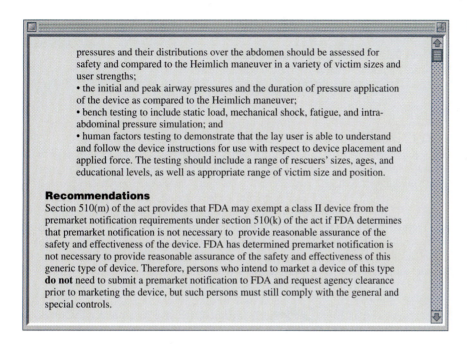

FIGURE 17.8

(continued)

detailed discussion of writing and revising. One common fault of many reports is that writers often expect readers to accept their conclusions without providing the convincing and adequately detailed evidence showing why the conclusions are warranted. A great deal of writing and revising is necessary to convince readers that your conclusions are valid. And, depending on the kind of report you are writing, some effective persuasion techniques may be necessary, too. (See Chapter 2 on audience and persuasion.)

Using an Appropriate Prose Style

Determining whether to use an informal or formal style in informal reports depends on your audience, subject, purpose, scope, and other rhetorical contexts. The prose style for informal reports may vary from very informal to formal, but the style is typically more informal in memos, letters, and e-mail. A formal style also can be appropriate in all kinds of memos, letters, and e-mail messages and is actually preferred in many situations. In general, a formal style has a serious tone, avoids second-person pronouns, avoids contractions, uses longer sentences and longer paragraphs, uses less familiar words, and uses abstract words. See Chapter 7 for a discussion of these and many other strategies for achieving a formal or informal prose style. Also see Figure 17.9 for an example of a memo illustrating an informal prose style.

From the workplace

Ron Crotogino, Ph.D.
Principal Scientist and Director of Marketing
Pulp and Paper Research Institute of Canada
Pointe-Claire, Québec, Canada

Ron is a scientist and administrator who has learned that clear communications are critically important for obtaining funding and reporting on research. He also has learned that scientists in general are tolerant of poor writing, and they shouldn't be.

My education was in chemical engineering. I went on to earn a Ph.D. as I wanted to work in research. Since graduating, I have been involved in research as a researcher, an adjunct professor, and a research manager.

I am required to do a lot of writing in my job, including reports, proposals, letters, memos, e-mail, instructions, newsletters, press releases, advertising copy, and translations. I wrote procedures manuals several years ago but do not yearn to repeat that experience.

The English courses I took at university were completely unsuitable—to some extent counterproductive—for learning to write about technical material. The focus was on creative writing rather than clear, concise, and unambiguous reporting. Technical writing does not have to be dry and boring. One can develop a good style in technical writing—just as one can in creative writing—without losing the conciseness and accuracy required in a good report or technical paper. These I learned by having my work mercilessly critiqued and edited by superiors and colleagues.

Most of my work is now carried out using a computer. (Before I had the computer I would type my drafts, as I am afflicted with illegible handwriting.) Most of my correspondence, internally and with clients and other outside contacts, is done by e-mail.

The way I write has not been affected substantially by the use of the computer, but the subsequent editing has. Word processors have made it much easier to edit and produce a clean first draft. My typed drafts were often embellished with a lot of sticky tape. The computer's cut-and-paste feature has eliminated the scissors and tape jobs. Occasionally, I would also write a first draft by hand, scribble notes all over it and then dictate it, as these manuscripts were totally illegible to anyone but me.

Until recently, I have had to edit a lot of reports written by my subordinates. The most frequent problem was gauging the audience. This is particularly difficult for researchers, who like to write for a small group of peers, not for the funding agency or client that paid for the work. Another related problem is clarity in explaining complex concepts. Good scientific or technical writing is a very challenging form of creative writing. Complex physical phenomena have to be described in terms of imagery that connects new findings with common experiences. I have been fortunate to have had mentors who excelled in this art.

For a while I worked at McGill University as a lecturer and thesis supervisor. I taught technical writing to engineers for six years. The courses I taught were barely sufficient to raise the students' consciousness about the need to acquire good writing skills. I did manage to get across some basic concepts about how to structure good technical writing. Many professors tolerated atrocious writing from the students, provided the answers presented were correct. This made it somewhat more difficult to get across the need for good writing.

The most difficult part of writing is to understand the audience. Academics most often err on the side of profundity at the cost of clarity, and many of their students emulate this style. A good scientific paper should be readable by nonspecialists.

The development of written and oral communication skills is a key to success in research, once the researcher has something worthwhile to communicate. Most researchers need to develop these communication skills. Seeking a critique of one's writing from others and editing their writing are the most effective ways to improve this skill. Colleagues will critique most of the reports and papers I write. Few things give subordinates or former students greater pleasure than to critique the writing of their boss or former professor.

FIGURE 17.9

Memo Written in an Informal Prose Style

Memorandum

To: Jack Jason
From: Ken Smith *KS*
Date: March 13, 2____
Subject: Print Room Improvements

I've noticed several wasteful activities while working in the print room, and I have solutions to save the company money.

First, there is a large amount of paper that is wasted during the printing of daily reports. The reason for such a waste is the header and footer pages attached to each individual report. There are two pages at the beginning and two pages at the end. This means a single-page report results in 5 printed pages—4 of which are thrown away. I understand that these pages were originally attached so that the reports could be easily separated and identified, but they are not necessary now. The print operators are familiar with every report and can easily identify each without needing cover sheets. Taking away these cover sheets would save the company supplies. Consider the 30 reports that the second shift prints. Using no cover pages would result in 120 saved sheets a night. That's over 1.5 boxes a week for one shift alone!

Next, screen prints from the Daily Sales floor are printed on the 08E. These pages are given a lower priority than other reports and are thus printed hours after they were actually created. When they are finally delivered to the appropriate person, the screen prints are usually out of date and unusable. A way to alleviate this problem is to send the screen prints to a less expensive printer, such as a bubble jet printer, that can be placed on the Daily Sales floor. This printer can be dedicated solely to screen prints. This way the screen prints would be timely, and the bigger printers can stay focused on the higher priority and time-consuming jobs.

Finally, printer ribbons are being wasted. Current policy requires the print operator to change the ribbons on printers PRT020700 and PRT020701 before printing AP checks. By doing so, the operator throws away ribbons that usually have very little use. These ribbons are being wasted since they could still print another 500 pages.

I propose we do not print the AP checks at a set time each night. Instead, AP checks should be printed after the ribbons need to be changed on the printers. This way the checks would be printed with a fresh ribbon, and the old ribbons would be completely used. This method will not create any problems with delivery of the checks since the checks are normally placed in the AP box, where they are picked up 8 hours later.

These improvements will help cut down waste in the print room and will help save the company money in supplies.

Achieving an Informal Prose Style

- Choose the familiar word over the unfamiliar word.
- Use unpretentious language.
- Aim for a plain style instead of a complex style. See the "Plain Style" section in Chapter 7.
- Keep your sentences short (but avoid a choppy sentence style).
- Use sentence variety.
- Use first- and second-person pronouns.
- Use contractions, such as *didn't* (for *did not*) and *couldn't* (for *could not*), unless their use would be jarring in the particular context.

- Keep the paragraphs short, usually six or fewer sentences and definitely fewer than ten.
- Use the "you-attitude" as much as possible. Focus on the reader and the reader's interests. Use the word *you* frequently, instead of *I, we,* and *our.*
- Establish your own voice. Don't try to sound like a textbook, encyclopedia, or journal article. Write conversationally, but check what you have written to make sure the level of formality or informality is appropriate for the context.

CHECKING WHAT YOU'VE LEARNED

Introduction

- Have you stated the subject and purpose of your report clearly for your intended audience?
- Have you stated your purpose as soon as possible in your report?
- If appropriate, have you provided the scope of your report?
- Have you provided a brief discussion of background if appropriate?

Body

- Is the body of the report effectively organized for the particular audience or audiences?
- Have you considered the best psychological order for your major points, depending on whether your audience is expecting to receive your communication, is receptive, or is resistant to your ideas?

Conclusion and Recommendations

- Are the conclusions based on only what is discussed earlier in the report?
- Have you adequately prepared your audience for the conclusions?
- If any recommendations are provided, are they stated as specific actions?
- Have you stated your recommendations so that your audience can easily understand what they are?

Design and Illustrations

■ Have you chosen the most appropriate format (memo, letter, e-mail) for the particular report?
■ Are illustrations provided wherever necessary or appropriate?
■ Are design elements (for margins, headings, typography) used consistently and appropriately throughout?

Prose Style and Mechanics

■ Is the prose style clear, appropriate, and informal or formal as necessary?
■ Is the report free of errors in grammar, punctuation, spelling, abbreviations, numbers, and capitalization?

EXERCISES

 ### REVIEW

1. Revise the prose style of the memo in Figure 17.10 to make the style more informal.
2. Read the progress report in Figure 17.11 and reorganize the report to make it more effective.
3. Review the recommendation report in Exhibit 17.1. Make a list discussing the advantages, if any, of providing this report in the form of a memo.
4. Review the conclusion and recommendations of the recommendation report in Exhibit 17.1. Discuss how the content of the two sections is different and how clear the difference is to you.
5. Review the prose style in the recommendation report in Exhibit 17.1. Discuss whether the style is formal or informal and why. Also discuss whether the prose style is appropriate for the audience. Identify any elements in the prose that you think would make the prose style even more appropriate.

 ### THE INTERNET

It's no overstatement to suggest that the Internet is changing the way people communicate in profound ways. E-mail, e-mail attachments (text, graphics, audio, and video files), interactive Web sites, discussion groups, and electronic newsletters are just some of the ways we use this medium to communicate. Write a paragraph discussing your views on how we may increasingly use this medium for more formal communications as well as informal communications.

 ### ETHICS/PROFESSIONALISM

Suppose you are an employee at a major corporation and that after working for the company for six months you receive an e-mail message from your supervisor informing you that your job has been terminated and that you have until the end of the day to pack up your possessions and leave. What are the ethical and professional issues that must be considered in a scenario such as this one in which an important message was transmitted through an informal medium?

 ### COLLABORATION

Working with at least two other people in groups in the class, make a list of the ways you can effectively use tools (word processing, e-mail, e-mail attachments, desktop publishing programs, file transfer programs, the telephone, fax machines) to collaborate effectively on an informal report. Be prepared to discuss your findings with the rest of the class.

FIGURE 17.10

**Memo Written in a
Formal Prose Style**

Memorandum

TO: Department Managers
FROM: Phil Jason
           Vice President of Operations
DATE: January 3, 2_____
SUBJECT: New Communications Program

Because of some recent problems with several company contracts with clients, the company is launching a comprehensive program to improve its written communications, including memoranda, letters to customers and vendors, reports, various manuals (for example, training, policies and procedures, user, and reference), and forms. The objectives of this program are to reduce communication misunderstandings, reduce communication costs, standardize communication practices and forms, and develop a company style guide and standards manual. I am writing to request specific contributions from each of you.

Manuel Rodriguez, Manager of Documentation, asked me to write to all department managers to request the following information to help meet these goals:

• your opinion on establishing standard procedures for all company documents for both internal and external communications

• photocopies or copies on disk of all memoranda and letters sent from your department for the past five business days

• a list of all company manuals both you and your employees use in their routine work

• your suggestions concerning how we can cut costs and increase the effectiveness of company communications

The success of this initiative depends on your cooperation and the cooperation of the employees you supervise. Please provide the above requested information no later than February 3.

Thank you.

INTERNATIONAL COMMUNICATION

You often may find yourself having to write an informal report for an audience that has at least some members of another culture, or perhaps all some members of the audience are from another culture. Make a list of the challenges you foresee in writing an informal report, with all of the features discussed in the chapter, for one or both of these audiences.

FIGURE 17.11

**Poorly Written
Progress Report**

To: Professor Tobias
From: David Johnson
Date: February 15, 2____
Subject: Progress Report

Introduction

Herein I update progress on the work that my team and I are working on in collaboration with ABC, Inc. ABC is working with several utilities companies in the country to improve efficiency and service. ABC has a project summary for each of the companies it has contracted with. The company wants us to organize the summaries using the template we will create and to compile all the new project descriptions (PDs) into a single notebook.

The audience for these project descriptions will be ABC employees. John Adams, the project manager, will assist with some of the project descriptions as an ABC employee and will be the final authority on their acceptability.

Work Completed

Since receiving the assignment, the team has done the following:

- Visited with ABC and John Adams
- Written and submitted a proposal
- Divided into subgroups
- Received project summaries
- Created a template for the project descriptions

Work Remaining

Two main phases of the work remain, the bulk of which is rewriting the project summaries. Once we paste them into the new template, we will refer to them as project descriptions. ABC handed us 20 folders, consisting of a total of 286 project descriptions. We will need time to work on these. We will work on these in our subgroups.

I need to familiarize myself with the template and the specific kind of work I will participate in.

The final phase of the project is to compile the 286 project descriptions into a single notebook. I would like to visit with Anne Lee in person one more time before finishing this phase.

Conclusion

At this point, we still need to work out glitches in the template. We asked for a two-day extension on our proposal. And I sense that some confusion about the project still lingers with the team. Otherwise, we're on task. Delays have not been unreasonable, and the team seems anxious to complete work on the project descriptions.

RESOURCES

Blake, Gary, and Robert W. Bly. *The Elements of Technical Writing.* New York: Macmillan, 1993.

Finkelstein, Leo. *Pocket Book of Technical Writing for Engineers and Scientists.* Boston: McGraw-Hill, 2000.

Pearsall, Thomas E. *The Elements of Technical Writing.* 2nd ed. Boston: Allyn and Bacon, 2001.

Pfeiffer, William S. *Pocket Guide to Technical Writing.* Upper Saddle River: Prentice Hall, 1998.

Schultz, Heidi. *The Elements of Electronic Communication.* Boston: Allyn and Bacon, 2000.

EXHIBIT 17.1

Memo Report

Memorandum

To: Ms. Katherine Roberts
            Director of Administration
            Integrated Marketing Company
From: Nancy Williams and Kay Collins
Date: April 24, 2____
Subject: A PC Maintenance Program

INTRODUCTION

Background

Integrated Marketing Company (IMC) has undergone rapid growth in business in recent months. The number of employees has increased from 10 to 50, an increase of 400 percent. During this growth period, the company's focus has been on developing new marketing materials, hiring additional employees, servicing existing clientele, and developing a program designed to expand their client base. You acknowledged that little time and effort have been placed in maintaining the company's computer equipment, and, in fact, no maintenance program is currently in place for the network of 50 personal computers. However, considerable money has been spent on the purchase of new equipment for this business expansion, and IMC has shown a strong commitment to protecting that investment.

Various problems relating to IMC's computer equipment have been identified:

- Power failures have shut down the network for several hours at a time.
- The network is running much more slowly with the increase of new personnel.
- No file back-up system is in place.
- Hardware has not received regular cleaning or maintenance.

Project Overview

The goal of our PC maintenance program is to provide a plan that is both prescriptive and flexible. We will present the major considerations and components of an effective maintenance program, not only addressing the problems identified during preliminary discussions, but also including other areas to provide a well-rounded, comprehensive program. Where applicable, we will present several alternatives, allowing you to tailor the program based on projected needs and budget constraints. Of course, no maintenance program will be successful if it is implemented but not continued; therefore, our intent is to create a program that is fairly quick to learn, with steps that are easy to follow and which take a minimal amount of time.

Exhibit 17.1

611

EXHIBIT 17.1

(continued)

Ms. Katherine Roberts   2   April 24, 2____

Importance of a Formal PC Maintenance Program

Without a formal PC maintenance program, a computer system might not operate optimally. Further, it might be unstable, mysteriously crashing at a most inopportune moment, or it might cease to operate at all. Without routine care and cleaning, computer peripherals can experience a shortened life span and work less efficiently. Inadequate housekeeping will lead to disk defragmentation, sluggish systems, and minimal free disk space. Finally, lack of data backups opens the door for disaster to strike when a virus infects a system, a hard drive crashes, power is lost, or files are inadvertently or maliciously destroyed. With today's business and industry in a constant state of change, a company must get the best performance from its computer equipment in order to remain competitive and maintain its edge in the marketplace. Investing today in a good maintenance program will most certainly prove to be productive in the long run in the sense that it will inevitably save time and money.

INVESTIGATIVE PROCEDURES

Audit of Present Software Maintenance Program

No regular software maintenance program is currently in place. Among the 50 personal computers, various versions of software programs are in use. Additionally, we observed that some of the computers have different collections of software loaded on the hard drives, and this situation has resulted in the need for periodic computer sharing between employees to allow access to the required software programs. We noted that these differences originated before the local area network (LAN) was installed and that they have not yet been addressed. Finally, some of the software accessed through the network has not been upgraded for some time.

Audit of Present Hardware Maintenance Program

No regular hardware maintenance program is currently in place. Because the majority of the 50 personal computers were purchased within the past six months, most of the machines have been running well. Hardware maintenance, therefore, has not been much of a priority. We observed during our visit, however, that various pieces of equipment in many of the workstations were in need of cleaning. Also, the hardware has been subjected to high temperatures during the summer months when the air conditioning was regularly turned off each weekend.

EXHIBIT 17.1
(continued)

Ms. Katherine Roberts   3   April 24, 2____

AREAS OF CONCERN

File Loss Prevention

Viruses

One particular area of concern is the lack of protection the computerized network currently has against computer viruses and the devastating effects they can have should one invade the network. Computer security experts estimate that more than 40,000 different viruses exist, although only a relatively small number of these viruses are responsible for most infections. Computer viruses can make their way into a PC by many different means, such as through hard or floppy disks, across networks, and over the Internet. Once on a PC, they can play music or create and display messages. More seriously, however, they can delete files and randomly change data. In order to comprehend fully the potential severity of a virus infection, it is important to first have a clear background and understanding of computer viruses.

The most basic definition of a computer virus is, simply, a computer program written by someone intending to do harm to computer programs and data. Typically, upon entering a PC or network environment, a computer virus will reside in memory and attach itself to another computer program. Once this newly infected program is run, the attached virus is activated and attaches itself to other programs. Just like biological viruses, these computer virus types need hosts to infect, and they survive by duplicating. Still other viruses are created for the sole purpose of damaging data by corrupting programs, deleting files, and even by reformatting an entire hard drive.

Computer viruses can only infect files and corrupt or destroy data. They cannot damage hardware in any way. Often a computer does not respond as expected to keyboard commands or display data appropriately on the computer monitor. This does not mean any hardware is damaged, however. Rather, it is the result of the computer virus in action, and it is the virus that is now in control of the PC.

Computer viruses are classified by the types of items they infect. Three common classifications include 1) program viruses; 2) boot viruses; and 3) macro viruses.

Program viruses—These types of computer viruses infect executable files, such as word processing software, spreadsheet software, and operating system programs.

Boot viruses—Viruses that attach to programs used to start up a computer are referred to as boot, or system sector viruses. This type of virus can infect a disk drive once it becomes attached.

Macro viruses—Macro viruses infect data in files that have macros defined within them. These virus types are typically found in word processing and spreadsheet applications.

Exhibit 17.1 **613**

EXHIBIT 17.1

(continued)

Ms. Katherine Roberts   4   April 24, 2____

The computer virus life cycle consists of three stages: infection, detection, and recovery. When it has entered a program or file, a virus is in the infection stage. Once it has been discovered and hopefully identified and isolated on the system, it is in the detection stage. A virus is often detected when the system behaves strangely or files or programs are not working properly or are even missing. Finally, the recovery stage occurs when the virus is destroyed and eliminated from the system.

Safeguards

Various anti-virus packages are available on the market, all aimed at protecting a PC from computer viruses. Programs like Norton AntiVirus from Symantec or McAfee VirusScan by McAfee Software alert the computer operator to potentially infected files as they routinely inspect your computer, and they will eliminate viruses they find. Both software companies sell complete suite packages, well worth the nominal price as they are capable of doing many other PC maintenance jobs presented later in this report. An analysis of Norton SystemWorks 2000 and McAfee Office 2000 is shown in Table 1.

<table>
<tr><td colspan="2" align="center">**Table 1.**
Utility Software Analysis</td></tr>
<tr><td>**Norton SystemWorks 2000**
Unit Cost: $42.95
Total Cost: $2,190.45</td><td>*Features*
Norton AntiVirus—Protects against computer viruses.
Norton Utilities—Provides crash protection and increases Windows performance.
Norton CrashGuard—Protects against system crashes and freezes.
Norton CleanSweep—Removes unneeded files and programs safely and completely.
Norton.com—Provides most current software patches, virus definitions, and hardware drivers to keep systems up-to-date.
Bonus Pack—Includes file compression, Web, fax, encryption, and Year 2000 utilities.</td></tr>
<tr><td>**McAfee Office 2000**
Unit Cost: $44.85
Total Cost: $2,287.35</td><td>*Features*
VirusScan—Protects against computer viruses.
First Aid 2000—Automatically fixes Windows problems.
Nuts & Bolts 98—Fixes up, tunes up, and speeds up the computer system.
Y2K Survival Kit—Fixes hardware and software Y2K problems.
Oil Change—Automatically updates computer software.
UnInstaller—Removes unneeded and unwanted files and programs.
McAfee Virtual Office—Provides Web site building pages and templates.</td></tr>
<tr><td colspan="2">(Source: Created by authors.)</td></tr>
</table>

EXHIBIT 17.1

(continued)

Ms. Katherine Roberts   5   April 24, 2____

Once anti-virus software has been installed, immediate protection will be provided automatically. The software will perform various tasks, including checking system files and boot records for viruses at start-up, checking programs for viruses at the time they are run, scanning the computer for viruses at regular intervals, monitoring the computer for suspicious activity that may indicate a residing virus, and checking floppy disks for boot viruses when they are used. Additionally, files, folders, and drives can be scanned for viruses manually, and periodic scans can be set to run at scheduled dates and times. These features may be customized to meet your particular needs and infection risk level.

More than 300 new viruses are created each month. Therefore, when purchasing anti-virus protection software, it is important to select a package which will quickly and conveniently provide monthly updates for continued protection against existing and newly defined viruses. More information about Norton, McAfee, and other anti-virus software may be obtained by visiting www.trusecure.com, a computer security firm that tests and certifies anti-virus products.

Of the many elements that play a role in running our business, power is one of the most critical. Implementing a fail-safe power management solution is not trivial; rather, it is a necessary and vital component to an organization's operations. It has been noted that frequent power failures at IMC's offices have shut down computerized operations for as long as several hours at a time. Consequently, data has been lost, and there has been a critical loss in productivity.

To address this problem, we recommend a proactive approach with the purchase of a UPS (uninterruptible power supply) system for IMC's computer network. A UPS runs continuous power directly from the line into a battery and subsequently to a PC. The primary purpose of a UPS is to provide sufficient time to save work in progress and allow the system to be shut down gracefully. If desired, however, a UPS can be attached to a system to allow it to continue operating for longer periods.

Additionally, the UPS acts as a surge suppressor in that any power surges affect the battery-charging mechanism and not the computer. Because the mean annual number of days with thunderstorms in the Southeast is 100, surge protection in our geographic area is most definitely a necessity.

American Power Conversion is a recognized leader in the manufacture of power protection products. We have therefore limited our analysis to models within this brand. APC's Smart-UPS line is a network-grade model that would be installed on the server only. This product line comes with PowerChute *plus* software that will safely store data and automatically shut down the network operating system before the battery is fully discharged. When purchasing a UPS, the primary consideration is how long you wish to have the computer network operate on battery back-up. Table 2 below outlines several such options for the IMC server.

Exhibit 17.1

615

EXHIBIT 17.1
(continued)

Ms. Katherine Roberts   6   April 24, 2____

Table 2.		
Network UPS Analysis		
ITEM	*BATTERY TIME*	*COST*
Smart-UPS 420	37 min.	$229.00
Smart-UPS 620	1 hr. 8 min.	$283.00
Smart-UPS 1000	2 hrs. 16 min.	$475.00
Smart-UPS 1400	3 hrs. 42 min.	$617.00
(Source: Created by authors.)		

In order to protect the 50 personal computers, additional UPS equipment would be required. Table 3 lists several options we selected with your particular PC specifications in mind.

Table 3.			
PC UPS Analysis			
MODEL	*FEATURES*	*UNIT COST*	*TOTAL COST*
Back-UPS 650	Instant emergency battery back-up for brief power outages; high performance surge suppression	$279	$13,950
Back-UPS Office 400	Instant emergency battery back-up for brief power outages; high performance surge suppression for both AC lines and datalines	$350	$17,500
Back-UPS Pro 650	Instant emergency battery back-up for extended power outages; high performance surge suppression for AC and network lines and also datalines	$379	$18,950
(Source: Created by authors.)			

Hard drive failures are the main reason for investing in a backup system. The more a computer is used, the more likely a crash will occur eventually, destroying your data in the process. For adequate protection, data must be backed up regularly and reliably. It is typically recommended that complete hard drive backups be done biweekly. The four major steps to a secure and dependable backup system are 1) getting a backup system; 2) testing the system on a monthly basis; 3) setting up a regular backup schedule; and 4) storing the data offsite.

EXHIBIT 17.1

(continued)

Ms. Katherine Roberts   7   April 24, 2____

There are various methods of backing up data. Our comparisons explore tape and removable media drives. The tape drive is one of the oldest forms of backup systems. It consists of a drive that is installed inside or connected to the computer by a cable. The drive reads and writes data onto a tape cassette. Table 4 below lists several external tape drive options.

Table 4.
Tape Drive Analysis

MODEL	COST	DATA TRANSFER RATE	TAPE CAPACITY	TAPE COST
Sony SuperStation 10GB	$139.00	50 megabytes/min.	10 gigabytes	$39.99/ea.
HP Colorado 14GB	$349.00	80 megabytes/min.	14 gigabytes	$35.99/ea.
SureStore T20 20GB	$529.00	120 megabytes/min.	20 gigabytes	$44.00/ea.

(Source: Created by authors.)

A removable media drive is similar to the hard drive that is built into the computer. Because it is external, it is quite easy to install. Additionally, the relatively low cost, high capacity, and ease of use make this type of backup system an attractive option. Whereas a tape drive copies data onto tape cassettes, a removable media drive reads and writes the data onto disks. In Table 5 we have compared several popular types for your consideration.

Table 5.
Removable Media Analysis

MODEL	COST	DISK CAPACITY	DISK COST
Iomega Zip 100	$99.95	100 megabytes	$10.00/ea.
Iomega Zip 250	$199.95	250 megabytes	$16.50/ea.
Iomega Jaz 2GB	$349.00	2 gigabytes	$124.95/ea.
Castlewood Orb	$199.95	2.2 gigabytes	$150.00/ea.

(Source: Created by authors.)

Even with our recommended safeguards in place, mishaps can occur. As we mentioned above, a comprehensive utility package is a necessary and worthwhile investment for proper system and data protection. In the event files are lost due to such problems as a computer virus infection, system crash, or application problem, the lost data and files can be recovered by utility software. Both Norton SystemWorks 2000 and McAfee Office 2000 presented above include this valuable feature with their software package.

Exhibit 17.1

617

EXHIBIT 17.1

(continued)

Ms. Katherine Roberts   8   April 24, 2____

Network Disk Management

Disk management is an important factor in optimizing IMC's network efficiency. Having adequate disk space, defragmenting the server hard drive, and using memory caching techniques can make a significant difference in your network productivity. Moreover, simply knowing the location of programs and properly organizing them on IMC's server will help reduce the possibility of duplicated data files, incompatibilities due to multiple versions, and data loss.

Disk Space

One technique to optimize network performance is to adequately free up the server's disk space. At least 20 percent of your server hard drive space should be kept free to maximize network access speed and overall performance. One common technique used to facilitate this task is to look at the date each data file was last modified. This strategy will quickly separate those files that have not had recent activity. Each file can then be reviewed to see if it can be deleted or permanently moved off the server to another form of storage. Additionally, both the Norton and McAfee utility packages presented above can assist you in performing this maintenance item with their built-in features. They both come with step-by-step instructions for this process and will even recommend files for deletion.

Memory Caching

Memory caching is a technique in which frequently used segments of main memory are stored in a faster bank of memory, referred to as a cache, that is local to the central processing unit, or CPU. In most cases, cache memory increases the performance of the processor dramatically. We recommend you test IMC's applications in order to fine-tune your required memory allocation for the disk cache. Either of the utility packages described above in Table 1 provides memory-caching features built into the software.

Disk Defragmentation

Defragment your disk biweekly. Defragmentation refers to the pulling together of scattered fragments of files to regain space lost through the daily creation, manipulation, and removal of files. When a small file is created, it uses a full disk sector of between 2–32 kilobytes to store the file. If full disk sectors are unavailable, the system will transparently break the file into smaller segments that will fit within the available space. After a period of time, the disk will become fragmented and inefficient. To defragment the server, you can use System Tools available through Windows. Additionally, the Norton and McAfee utility packages both contain this tool and provide several extra features, such as analyzing the hard drive and recommending a specific type of defragmentation procedure given the disk's current status.

EXHIBIT 17.1

(continued)

Ms. Katherine Roberts   9   April 24, 2____

Software Requirements

Annual Needs Audit

As manufacturers are constantly upgrading programs, new versions of software are frequently available on the market. It is therefore important that all software on the computerized systems be reviewed on an annual basis to ensure they do not become antiquated and will still be compatible with other, new software programs you may purchase. Further, this review can provide a good check to determine whether the current software will be adequate for anticipated business needs and demands in the upcoming year.

Software Upgrades and Standardization

In order to maximize productivity of IMC's software, periodic updates should be made to the current configuration following an annual audit. One particularly critical update will be that of IMC's anti-virus software once it is installed. Updates that provide protection against the latest known viruses should be downloaded from your software provider at least on a monthly basis. This can either be done through update tools built into the program itself or by downloading the new virus definitions from your provider's Web site.

We also recommend that all of your personal computers be standardized with the same software. This lack of consistency resulted in several employees having to share computers to have adequate access to required programs. While standardization is not a major issue, it would increase employee efficiency and make future upgrades less confusing.

Hardware Care and Maintenance

Importance and Benefits of Maintenance

Without routine care, personal computers can deteriorate rapidly and tend to be more prone to malfunction. Accumulations of dust, smoke, and grease on peripheral components can lead to all kinds of problems, from poor performance to even a complete system crash (Steers 404). The problems may linger on for some time and effect intermittent errors, or they may occur suddenly, as with a loss of IMC's entire system. Proper care and maintenance of computerized systems play a key role in maximizing the life of computer peripherals, keeping your PCs and network running efficiently, minimizing downtime, and containing repair and replacement costs. Experts recommend a thorough cleaning every six months in addition to a general surface cleaning every one to three months (Lindsey 3).

Exhibit 17.1

619

EXHIBIT 17.1

(continued)

Ms. Katherine Roberts   10   April 24, 2____

Cleaning and General Care

Dust is everywhere and originates from many sources. It can enter and clog vents in computer peripherals, be drawn into floppy drives, and stick to circuit boards and other electronic components. Over time, this coating becomes an unwanted thermal insulator to PC circuitry. Dust may also contain conductive elements that can cause partial short circuits in a system in addition to accelerating corrosion of electrical contacts, causing improper connections (Steers 404).

Some basic tools needed to periodically clean the PCs include lint-free wipes, swabs, and brushes. Basic cleaning kits are available at local office supply stores for as little as $10 to $30. Soap and water on a lint-free cloth works well on cleaning plastics, but an alcohol-based antistatic cleaner is needed for cleaning the electronics. Another necessity is a can of compressed air, which is very useful in removing dust and particles from hard-to-reach areas, such as the spaces between keyboard keys. We also recommend the purchase of one data vacuum cleaner, at $70, for personal computers and printers. The cleaning itself will take perhaps an hour or two, and the training program we are offering will provide in-depth instruction for this important maintenance step.

It is important that IMC's computerized equipment operate within safe temperature ranges. Electronic components have a temperature range within which they are designed and built to work, typically between 60 and 85 degrees Fahrenheit (Minasi 132). Because a personal computer is warmer inside than outside, changes in room temperature can become multiplied inside, leading to thermal shock. Thermal shock occurs when components have been subjected to rapid and large changes in temperature, and it can cripple your computer by causing repetitive expansion and contraction damage (Minasi 133). Keeping offices at a comfortable temperature at all times will keep equipment in proper working condition.

It is also important to keep liquids away from computer equipment. A common problem is drink or food spills by employees. To avoid this hazard, eating and drinking at computer workstations should be discouraged.

Finally, as each of your computer peripherals has its own user guide, we would also recommend two additional maintenance steps. First, the user guide, complete with model and serial numbers, can assist you in developing a list of all equipment you currently own and operate. This list should be regularly maintained for use as a quick reference when conducting annual audits, exploring future purchases, and comparing equipment compatibility, for example. Secondly, we recommend referring to each user guide and adding to IMC's formal program any additional maintenance items that may be specific to the equipment.

EXHIBIT 17.1

(continued)

Ms. Katherine Roberts   11   April 24, 2____

CONCLUSIONS AND RECOMMENDATIONS

Based on our initial audit of the computerized systems, we previously concluded a formal PC maintenance program would prove beneficial to IMC. We stand by that early recommendation and have put the above, specialized program together in a way that will best suit IMC's immediate and future needs. Be assured that all components of our maintenance program have received the thorough and comprehensive analysis necessary for you to make sound business decisions regarding equipment and its usage. We present to you below our specific product recommendations as an additional aid in your decision process.

Purchase Recommendations

Software

We recommend purchasing Norton SystemWorks 2000 over the comparable McAfee product. The Norton software is slightly less expensive, yet it has the same features as the McAfee program and includes the bonus pack.

To eliminate the need for the ongoing computer sharing by three of your employees, we additionally recommend the purchase of one copy of ACT! 2000 5.0 and two copies of Lotus SmartSuite Millennium Edition 9.5 priced at $189.95/each and $399.95/each, respectively.

Hardware

We recommend several hardware purchases at this time. First, to supply surge protection and power supply backup, we suggest the Back-UPS Pro 650 model for all personal computers. While this is the most expensive of the UPS options we presented, it provides the most protection and appears to be the best value. It will protect all computer, data, and network lines and provide backup power. The Smart-UPS 620 is our choice for the server because it provides an adequate length of power backup for a moderate price.

For data back-ups, we recommend the purchase of a removable media drive and further suggest the Castlewood Orb model over the other options listed. Purchasing a drive with a high data capacity is the most cost-effective approach, and the cassette drives provide the quickest backups. Of the cassette drives, the Castlewood model has the highest data capacity, yet it is considerably less expensive than the Iomega brand.

Miscellaneous Supplies

We recommend the purchase of five computer equipment cleaning kits and suggest the Starter Kit by ComputerBath priced at $12 per kit. Also suggested is the purchase of one Metro data vacuum priced at $70.

Exhibit 17.1

621

EXHIBIT 17.1

(continued)

Ms. Katherine Roberts   12   April 24, 2____

Training

We suggest that at least one designated employee be responsible for implementing and managing the PC maintenance program. Additionally, this technical staff member would be available to solve a wide variety of PC hardware and software problems, troubleshoot, and assist employees with user questions. In order for this staff member to be able to carry out these responsibilities, we recommend that formal training be provided. We are willing and available to provide this training at your offices in one eight-hour session.

Our training plan consists of a comprehensive approach to all areas outlined in our recommended PC maintenance program. Once training is complete, IMC employees will be fully knowledgeable and able to confidently carry out all aspects of the program. Additionally, we will assist with the installation of all equipment and software purchases related to acceptance of our program recommendations. We will provide a one-day training session and a complete PC maintenance program manual specifically designed for the company.

REFERENCES

Lindsey, Elizabeth. "Keying In on Computer Problems." *Business Insurance* 13 Sept. 1999: 3–4.
Minasi, Marak. *The Complete PC Upgrade and Maintenance Guide*. Alameda, CA: Sybex, 1994.
Steers, Kirk. "Keep That PC Clean!" *PC World* Dec. 1997: 404–405.

18

Formal Reports

Informational and Analytical
  Reports   623

Strategies for Preparing a Formal
  Report   636

Common Elements in Formal Reports   641

From the Workplace   652

IN THIS CHAPTER

As you learned in Chapter 17, any report may be presented as either an informal report or a formal report. And any report may be presented in memo, letter, e-mail, or book format. If the audience, subject, purpose, scope, and other contexts or constraints suggest or require a more formal approach, then your report should be created as a formal report and should include many of the elements discussed in the "Common Elements in Formal Reports" section later in this chapter.

You will learn about:

- informational and analytical reports
- strategies for preparing formal reports
- common elements in formal reports

INFORMATIONAL AND ANALYTICAL REPORTS

Because there are so many kinds of reports and so many purposes for reports, distinguishing one kind of report from another can be confusing. And trying to determine clearly what kind of report you should write for a particular audience and purpose can be difficult. This section provides some simple distinctions to guide you in your report writing. Also, keep in mind that many formal reports both in college and in the workplace are often written by teams. This kind of collaboration is often required because of the complexity of the project, the urgency of the deadline, and the necessity to draw upon different kinds of expertise, to mention only a few reasons. See Chapter 3 for a more detailed discussion of strategies for collaborating.

Most reports fall into one of two categories: informational reports and analytical reports. Informational reports chiefly give readers an understanding of a problem, an approach, a method, an issue, a product, a company, a trend, a technology, or some other topic. See Figure 18.1 for the key features of informational reports. Informational reports are contextual rather than evaluative. That is, they report but don't evaluate information. They provide essential background or other kinds of details to inform or to introduce but do not typically analyze or dissect a problem, issue, trend, or other aspect.

Analytical reports chiefly evaluate some issue, problem, condition, situation, trend, or other topic. See Figure 18.2 for the key features of analytical reports. To analyze something means to break it down into its component parts to see how the parts relate to each other. Analytical reports try to understand underlying relationships, causes and effects, and potential solutions of a particular topic. They are more than just informational, since their aim is to provide more than simply an understanding. Analytical reports may or may not lead to recommendations, but this is one of their most important uses. They help decision makers understand complex information so they can determine a proper response or course of action.

Analytical reports offering recommendations are sometimes referred to as recommendation reports. Because these reports offer recommendations, they are sometimes—but not always—distinguished from informational and analytical reports. In general, analytical reports concern themselves with questions such as why did this happen, is this a good idea, how does this plan compare to that plan, and so on.

In fact, some reports are both informational and analytical: progress reports, personnel reports, and trip reports, for example. A progress report informs readers about the current state of a project—the work completed and the work remaining—and it often discusses and analyzes any problems encountered or anticipated in the project. See the "Progress Reports" section in Chapter 17.

Background Reports

Background reports (also called general reports) are the most common type of informational technical report. They provide information to individuals or companies who need it. They are written to provide information only—

FIGURE 18.1

Key Features of Informational Reports

Informational reports chiefly give readers an understanding of a problem, an approach, a method, an issue, a product, a company, a trend, a technology, or some other topic.

Informational reports are contextual rather than evaluative. That is, they report but don't evaluate information.

Informational reports provide essential background or other kinds of details to inform or to introduce but do not typically analyze or dissect a problem, issue, trend, or other aspect.

FIGURE 18.2

Key Features of Analytical Reports

Analytical reports chiefly evaluate some issue, problem, condition, situation, trend, or other topic.

Analytical reports try to understand underlying relationships, causes and effects, and potential solutions of a particular topic. They are more than just informational, since their aim is to provide more than simply an understanding.

Analytical reports may or may not lead to recommendations, but this is one of their most important uses. They help decision makers understand complex information so they can determine a proper response or course of action.

for example, an update on trends in the marketplace or the history of some event or product. Since the chief concern is not with how readers will use the information, background reports seldom offer any recommendations. Background reports typically don't provide enough information on which the readers may act.

Consider, for example, the background report in Exhibit 18.1 (pages 659–681). The purpose of the report, stated in the second paragraph of the introduction, is to provide an overview of virus vulnerabilities to an information technology manager of a small company: "This report will provide a clear definition of the major vulnerabilities IT managers will encounter in providing computer-based business systems to customers. Vital data files, employee workstations, and network servers may be at risk if vulnerabilities are not addressed. The damage represented by a genuine vulnerability can translate into expensive recovery procedures."

Feasibility Reports

Feasibility studies are written to determine the best course of action concerning, for example, a product, purchase, service, or market. A feasibility report lets readers know whether it is practical or possible to pursue one or more courses of action. Basically, the report answers the question, "Is it a good idea?" or "Is this something our company should pursue?" Sometimes feasibility studies recommend that no course of action be taken. Typical feasibility studies include market analyses concerning opening a new business in a particular area, purchasing one product rather than a competing product, committing funding to one area of research instead of another, and so on. Often feasibility studies compare alternatives, analyzing the pros and cons and suggesting the most feasible alternative.

Feasibility reports require comparing at least two alternatives based upon various criteria. Consider, for example, a feasibility report concerning whether the purchasing department of a mid-sized company should purchase Apple laptop computers or Dell laptop computers for employees who frequently travel for the company. A rough outline for such a study might look something like the outline below:

Introduction
This section states the purpose of the report.

Problem
The section discusses the problem that purchasing one kind of laptop or another will address. For example, employees who frequently travel for a company need computer access for communication, for data analysis and other tasks, and for convenience.

Scope
This section states what alternatives are under consideration.

REPORT WRITING

I write reports for basically two purposes. One is to provide information to the university administration as part of the accountability and resource allocation process. These reports are important because they create a positive image of the program, and being thought of as good is just as important as being good. Decisions are made by a combination of perception and fact. Therefore, effective communications are important. The other purpose is to keep people who give us money well informed on how we have put it to good use. These funds include donations and research contracts. We depend on this outside funding for much of our success.

—Gregory D. Reed, Ph.D., university professor and department chair of civil and environmental engineering, Knoxville, Tennessee

Body

This section discusses the alternatives and the criteria used. The criteria are typically standards by which the alternatives are evaluated. In this case, the products are compared using standard criteria for laptop computers:

Purchasing an Apple Laptop Computer
  Features
  Ease of Use
  Available Software
  Hardware Reliability
  Service Options
  Cost
  Savings
Purchasing a Dell Laptop Computer
  Features
  Ease of Use
  Available Software
  Hardware Reliability
  Service Options
  Cost
  Savings

Conclusion

This section covers the key findings discussed in the body.

Recommendation

This section recommends a course of action for the company to take. For example, a recommendation may be to purchase the Apple laptop, purchase the Dell, or purchase neither. Keep in mind that a recommendation to take no action is sometimes the best recommendation.

Recommendation Reports

Whereas many analytical reports do not offer a specific course of action to take, recommendation reports always suggest a particular course of action or several alternative courses of action. Typically, in a recommendation report you analyze a problem, determine the possible solutions to the problem, and then recommend the best solution or solutions. Some example recommendations include funding or not funding a research program, developing a new product, acquiring a company or building site, or buying a piece of equipment. See Exhibit 17.1 for an example of a recommendation report. As with the other reports discussed in this chapter, recommendation reports can range in length from a page (for an informal recommendation report) to a single volume of several hundred pages to many volumes containing thousands of pages (such as the five-volume Warren Commission report on the assassination of President John F. Kennedy).

FIGURE 18.3

Exxon Valdez **Oil Spill**

In 1989, an accident in Alaska involving the oil tanker caused a massive spill that severely damaged local wildlife, such as this cormorant.

Consider, for example, the recommendation report titled *Spill: The Wreck of the* Exxon Valdez, the final report of the Alaska Oil Spill Commission concerning the disastrous oil spill of 1989. (See Figure 18.3.) The 223-page report provides 59 recommendations discussed in the 42-page section titled "Findings and Recommendations." The chief purpose of the report was for the Alaska Oil Spill Commission to offer recommendations to Steve Cowper, the governor of Alaska, and the Alaska legislature. In preparing their recommendations, the commissioners decided, "The report must be a call to public attention and legislative action. It should provide an overall, unbiased account of the disaster as it illustrated failures in planning and regulation. It should shape future debate; persuade the electorate to demand improvements; convince legislators of the need for bold action; and create the energy to propel debate into the future."

The major sections of the report are as follows:

Introduction

The Spill: Maritime Disaster Becomes a Crisis

History: Oil in Alaska

Preparedness: Alaska's Oil Spill Contingency Plans

Response: Chaos in the Coastal Communities

History: Oil Spill Prevention and Response

Technology: Cleaning Up Crude

After the Spill: Oceans at Risk

Findings and Recommendations
    Comprehensive Prevention Policy
    Responsibilities of Industry
    State Regulation and Oversight
    Federal Regulation and Oversight
    Government Response and Posture
    Implementing the Response
    Research and Development

Analysis of Commission Process

Conclusion

Bibliography

Appendixes

Empirical Research Reports

Research reports—also called empirical research reports—relay information about tests, surveys, or experiments of some kind. (See also "Scientific Papers" on page 633.) Research reports analyze information or data and follow a rigid structure of introduction, methods, results, and discussion. Often they rely on data provided in a laboratory report or information from a questionnaire or survey. Many scientific publications are basically research reports. They analyze a problem in the context of the existing research on the topic, propose a solution, subject the proposed solution to various tests, and then discuss whether or not the solution, tested through experimentation, is viable.

Research reports are the most common reports written by engineers, scientists, and other technical professionals. Professionals at many government agencies, for example, the General Accounting Office (GAO), the National Transportation Safety Board (NTSB), and NASA, devote much of their careers to writing research reports. They write the reports to help others within their agencies to make decisions or to extend human knowledge in a specific area. See Figure 18.4 for an example of some of the sections usually included in empirical reports—cover, title page, abstract, and table of contents.

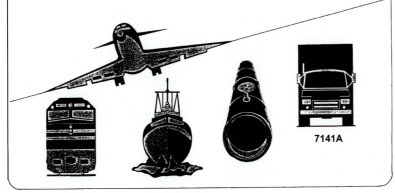

FIGURE 18.4

Empirical Report—Cover, Title Page, Abstract, and Table of Contents

PB99-917005
NTSB/HZM-99/01

NATIONAL TRANSPORTATION SAFETY BOARD

WASHINGTON, D.C. 20594

HAZARDOUS MATERIALS ACCIDENT REPORT

**FIRE AND EXPLOSION OF
HIGHWAY CARGO TANKS, STOCK ISLAND
KEY WEST, FLORIDA
JUNE 29, 1998**

7141A

FIGURE 18.4
(continued)

Hazardous Materials Accident Report

**Fire and Explosion of
Highway Cargo Tanks, Stock Island
Key West, Florida
June 29, 1998**

NTSB/HZM-99/01
PB99-917005
Notation 7141A
Adopted September 10, 1999

National Transportation Safety Board
490 L'Enfant Plaza, S.W.
Washington, D.C. 20594

FIGURE 18.4

(continued)

National Transportation Safety Board. 1999. *Fire and Explosion of Highway Cargo Tanks, Stock Island, Key West, Florida, June 29, 1998.* Hazardous Materials Accident Report NTSB/HZM-99/01. Washington, DC.

Abstract: About 5:14 a.m., eastern daylight time, on June 29, 1998, at Stock Island, Key West, Florida, a Dion Oil Company (Dion) driver was on top of a straight-truck cargo tank checking the contents of its compartments and preparing to transfer cargo from a semitrailer cargo tank when explosive vapors ignited within the straight-truck cargo tank. The ignition caused an explosion that threw the driver from the top of the truck. The fire and a series of at least three explosions injured the driver and destroyed the straight truck, a tractor, the front of the semitrailer, and a second nearby straight-truck cargo tank. Damage was estimated at more than $185,000.

The safety issues discussed in this report are the adequacy of Dion's product-transfer procedures and training, the adequacy of the Federal Highway Administration's oversight of motor carriers' procedures and training for loading and unloading hazardous materials, and the adequacy of Florida's oversight of the fire safety of storage tanks.

As a result of its investigation, the National Transportation Safety Board issued recommendations to the Federal Highway Administration, Dion, the Florida State Fire Marshal, the Florida Department of Transportation, the Florida Department of Agriculture, the Florida Department of Environmental Protection, the National Fire Prevention Association, the National Association of State Fire Marshals, and the International Association of Fire Chiefs.

The National Transportation Safety Board is an independent Federal agency dedicated to promoting aviation, railroad, highway, marine, pipeline, and hazardous materials safety. Established in 1967, the agency is mandated by Congress through the Independent Safety Board Act of 1974 to investigate transportation accidents, study transportation safety issues, and evaluate the safety effectiveness of government agencies involved in transportation. The Safety Board makes public its actions and decisions through accident reports, safety studies, special investigation reports, safety recommendations, and statistical reviews.

Recent publications are available in their entirety at **http://www.ntsb.gov/.** Other information about available publications may also be obtained from the Web site or by contacting:

National Transportation Safety Board
Public Inquiries Section, RE-51
490 L'Enfant Plaza, East, S.W.
Washington, D.C. 20594

Safety Board publications may be purchased, by individual copy or by subscription, from the National Technical Information Service. To purchase this publication, order report number **PB99-917005** from:

National Technical Information Service
5285 Port Royal Road
Springfield, Virginia 22161
(800) 553-6847 or (703) 605-6000

FIGURE 18.4

(continued)

iii   **Hazardous Materials Accident Report**

Contents

Executive Summary v

Factual Information 1
    Accident Narrative 1
    Emergency Response 1
    Vehicle Information 3
    Damage 4
    Driver Information 6
    Carrier Information 7
    Hazardous Materials 9
    Sources of Ignition 9
    Federal Regulations 11
    State Regulations 12
    Federal/State Oversight 13
    Statistics 16

Analysis 17
    Propagation of Fire 17
    Ignition Source 18
    Cargo Tank Loading and Unloading 19
    Oversight of Intrastate Motor Carriers 20
    Oversight of Cargo Tanks Used to Store Flammable Liquids 21

Conclusions 23
    Findings 23
    Probable Cause 23

Recommendations 24

Appendix 27
    Investigation and Hearing 27

Abbreviations 28

Typical report titles for research reports from the GAO include

Operation Desert Storm: Evaluation of the Air Campaign. GAO/NSIAD-97-134.

Patriot Missile Defense: Software Problem Led to System Failure at Dhahran, Saudi Arabia. GAO/IMTEC-92-26.

Foreign Missile Threats: Analytic Soundness of Certain National Intelligence Estimates. GAO/NSIAD-96-225.

Typical reports from NTSB on highway safety include

Safety Report Regarding Action to Reduce Fatalities, Injuries, and Crashes Involving the Hard Core Drinking Driver. NTSB Report Number: SR—00-01, adopted on 07/11/2000.

Deterrence of Drunk Driving: The Role of Sobriety Checkpoints and Administrative License Revocations. NTSB Report Number: SS—84-01, adopted on 04/03/1984. NTIS Report Number: PB84-917001.

Safety Aspects of Recreational Vehicles. NTSB Report Number: HSS-72-02, adopted on 06/14/1972. NTIS Report Number: PB-211651.

Typical reports for NASA include

What Does the First Manned Mars Mission Cost? Technical and Economic Issues of a Manned Mars Mission. Document ID: 19970027264 N (97N26294).

Mars Surveyor Program 2001 Mission Overview. Document ID: 20000012696 File.

Report at a Glance: Report of the Presidential Commission on the Space Shuttle Challenger Accident. Document ID: 19930010847 N (93N20036).

Scientific Papers

If you are a researcher, writing and publishing your results are important parts of your job. After all, research results are meaningless if no one knows about them. The scientific paper is the standard vehicle for reporting on experimental work. Other scientists read scientific papers to learn what is happening in their field and to obtain information on procedures so they can attempt to replicate or refute the results. A typical scientific paper has eight sections: title, abstract, introduction, materials and methods, results, discussion, acknowledgments, and references.

Title

Often your scientific paper will begin with a title page, consisting of the title of your paper; your name and the names of any other authors, in an agreed-upon order; and the name of your school or company affiliation. Sometimes the title, authors, and affiliations will be at the top of the first page of your paper, followed immediately by the abstract and other sections. At other times, the title, authors, and affiliations will be on their own title page.

Select a title for your paper that succinctly but accurately describes what the paper is about. Include keywords in the title that will help other researchers find your title when they do a bibliographic library search. Make the title specific enough so that the reader has no doubt about your topic but not so long that the meaning is left behind in excessive verbiage. Try to limit your title to ten or fewer words.

FIGURE 18.5

Scientific Paper Abstract

Pomplun Marc, Lorenz Sichelschmidt, Karin Wagner, Thomas Clermont, Gert Rickheit, and Helge Ritter. "Comparative Visual Search: A Difference That Makes a Difference." *Cognitive Science* 25.1 (January–February 2001): 3–36

[Copyright © 2001 Elsevier Science Inc. All rights reserved.]

In this article we present a new experimental paradigm: comparative visual search. Each half of a display contains simple geometrical objects of three different colors and forms. The two display-halves are identical except for one object mismatched in either color or form. The subject's task is to find this mismatch. We illustrate the potential of this paradigm for investigating the underlying complex processes of perception and cognition by means of an eye-tracking study. Three possible search strategies are outlined, discussed, and reexamined on the basis of experimental results. Each strategy is characterized by the way it partitions the field of objects into "chunks." These strategies are: (i) Stimulus-wise scanning with minimization of total scan path length (a "traveling salesman" strategy), (ii) scanning of the objects in fixed-size areas (a "searchlight" strategy), and (iii) scanning of object sets based on variably sized clusters defined by object density and heterogeneity (a "clustering" strategy). To elucidate the processes underlying comparative visual search, we introduce besides object density a new entropy-based measure for object heterogeneity. The effects of local density and entropy on several basic and derived eye-movement variables clearly rule out the traveling salesman strategy, but are most compatible with the clustering strategy.

Abstract

An abstract is a brief version of your work, condensed to 100 to 200 words. See Chapter 16 concerning how abstracts differ from executive summaries. Readers look at abstracts to discover if the paper contains the type of information that merits further reading or to discover what your findings were so they don't have to read the whole paper. Make sure any findings are included in the abstract, along with enough information for readers to decide if they want to read further. Include in your abstract why you did the research, what you found out, and how you interpret what you have found. After reading your abstract, readers should have a good idea of your paper's overall significance. See Figure 18.5 for an example of a scientific paper abstract.

Introduction

In the introduction, you tell readers what your paper is about. This section introduces the reader to the need for the research you have done and gives background information so the reader can evaluate the importance of the work. The introduction section answers the questions, "Why was this work necessary?" "What was already known about this subject?" "What did the researchers hope to accomplish by this work?" Scientific research often follows the steps of the scientific method. (See Chapter 5.) In the Introduction section of your scientific paper, you present your hypothesis and review the literature about your topic. (See "Literature Reviews" in Appendix D.)

Materials and Methods

In Materials and Methods, you describe what actions you took to prove or disprove your hypothesis. You tell your readers how you performed your research. To do that—and to make it possible for others to duplicate your work in their labs—you must be very specific. If you performed a test or measurement in a particular way, describe it or—if it is a standard test or measurement—name it and tell the reader where it was previously written up. If you modified someone else's method, give that person credit and describe what it was that you did.

Results

Summarize your findings in this section, but do not interpret them. Describe and relate your results specifically in text and accompanying tables and graphs where appropriate. The purpose of this section is to let readers "look over your shoulder" as you obtain your results.

If some of the information illustrates changes over time, a line graph may be an appropriate way to report it. Other types of information might lend themselves to other graphical displays, such as bar graphs or pie charts. (See Chapter 9 for more information on graphical reporting of information.) Pictorial and graphical material are collectively known as *figures.* Often, you will have numerical results that are better displayed in a table. Tables are presented in clearly labeled rows and columns. Tables and figures are each numbered sequentially but separately. Refer to all tables and figures in the text, as in "Mean time to onset of decay decreased with the age of the specimen (Figure 7)."

Discussion

In the discussion section, interpret the results you presented in the previous section and propose your explanation for their significance. Explain to your readers what your results mean and how they either confirm or refute the hypothesis you were testing. Summarize what you have accomplished and identify, if appropriate, avenues for further research.

Acknowledgments

Often in the sciences, research is dependent on the assistance of organizations or people who may not necessarily appear on the title page of your paper. In this section, you have the opportunity to acknowledge help—time, finances, expertise of others—you received as you did your research and prepared your paper. Here is where you thank financial aid–granting agencies, lab assistants, art and photography professionals or volunteers, statistical analysts, and others whose support enabled you to complete your work.

References

As part of your background research for your work, you relied on the work of others. You discussed and evaluated these other sources in your literature review in the Introduction section. Now you must give the exact citation information for those books, articles, and other sources. Use the citation style required by your professor, your lab, your department, your company, or your discipline.

Often, scientific papers conform to the citation style of the Council of Science Editors (formerly the Council of Biology Editors) or the American Psychological Association. (See Appendix C for more information on the specifics of some of these styles.) Most often, you will be told which citation style you must follow. If you are submitting your paper for publication in a professional journal, check the journal's advice to authors or similar section for information on its required style.

STRATEGIES FOR PREPARING A FORMAL REPORT

You need to know more than the essential differences among the various kinds of reports to write an effective technical report. A technical report typically requires carefully analyzing your audience and purpose, identifying the major question or questions explored in the report, conducting the necessary research, interpreting the results of your research, (when appropriate) stating your recommendations, organizing your report, determining the design and illustrations, and writing and revising various drafts.

Focusing the Report

> Focusing means analyzing and understanding your audience, narrowing your subject, determining your purpose, and properly limiting the scope of your document.

As discussed in Chapter 4, focusing is an essential part of working on any technical document whether it's a brief memo or a long formal report. Focusing means analyzing and understanding your audience, narrowing your subject, determining your purpose, and properly limiting the scope of your document.

Before you can narrow your subject properly, state your purpose clearly, or limit the scope of your document appropriately, you have to have a thorough understanding of your audience—what it needs or wants to know, its level of expertise concerning your topic, its preferences for the kind of report you're writing, and so on. See the "Audience" section in Chapter 2 for a discussion of various techniques for analyzing your audience.

To narrow your subject in a technical report, you must typically determine what key question or questions you are attempting to answer in the report. You may have an interest or a broad topic, but you still have a lot of work to do before you have a properly defined topic. Typically, this will be an ongoing process throughout the report-writing activity. You may begin with one or more good questions, but it may not be until late in the project that you come up with more significant questions.

In *The Craft of Research*, Wayne Booth, Gregory Colomb, and Joseph Williams discuss a three-fold process involving explaining what you are writing about (your topic), what you don't know about it (your question), and why you want to know about it (your rationale).

First, name your topic. Start with a sentence such as "I am learning about/working on/studying _____." Then fill in the blank with a few noun phrases: "I am studying repair processes for cooling systems." Second, add to this sentence an indirect question that states something about your topic you don't know or understand completely: "I am studying X because I want to find out who/what/when/where/whether/why/how _____." So for the example above: "I am studying repair processes for cooling systems, because I am trying to find out how expert repairers analyze failures." Now you have a reason for pursuing your topic. Third, motivate the question. In other words, "add an element that explains why you are asking your question and what you intend to get out of its answer" (43). State the rationale for the question and the project: "in order to understand how/why/what _____." So for the repair processes topic above: "in order to understand how to design a computerized system that could diagnose and prevent failures." This three-fold process typically leads not only to a well-focused subject and purpose of interest to you, but also one of interest to others.

The completed focus is the following sentence: "I am studying repair processes for cooling systems, because I am trying to find out how expert repairers analyze failures in order to understand how to design a computerized system that could diagnose and prevent failures." Of course, it's difficult to formulate such a well-focused subject and purpose early in a project. Often you may not be able to focus a report this effectively until much later in the report preparation process.

Identifying your key question or questions helps you to determine the specific purpose of your report. For example, in Exhibit 18.1's background report, the author states, "This report will provide a clear definition of the major vulnerabilities IT managers will encounter in providing computer-based business systems to customers."

Finally, to complete your work on focusing your report, you have to determine the scope. Even once you have narrowed your topic after considering your audience and determining your purpose, your report won't be properly focused unless you also determine the scope. For example, in Exhibit 18.1's background report, the author limits the focus of the report "to business application deployment on a Microsoft NT Network with an NT Exchange Mail system supporting a user base of approximately two thousand workstations."

Gathering Information

Any kind of report you write requires you to gather information. For some brief informal reports, simply collecting your thoughts before you compose the two- or three-page memo will do. In other cases, you'll have to do more extensive research using a variety of the strategies discussed in Chapter 5.

In formal empirical research reports, you'll have to gather the data for the report systematically and very carefully. Keep careful records of any data you collect during all the phases of data collection, and begin writing opinions about the data early in the process so that you can help yourself interpret the data more carefully later on. Even at this early stage, give some thought to how the data you are gathering will be presented in the report, and even make some notes concerning this issue. Doing so will help you determine later if you will need additional data in any part of the report.

Interpreting the Information

Now that you have gathered much if not all of the information for your report, the next important step is to interpret the information you have gathered. Again, this can be relatively simple for a brief informal report; it can be relatively simple for a more formal background report or feasibility report, too. The information you have collected may point clearly to one course of action over another in a feasibility study. However, it can prove to be much more difficult to analyze and sort data for a formal empirical research report.

You begin analyzing data when you begin collecting data. However, much of your analysis of the data takes place after you have gathered most of the information you will use. Work on some tentative conclusions at this point based on the data you have collected. Determining the conclusions now will help you determine what to include in the report and how to analyze it. Begin by writing down all the important results in random order, then group any overlapping results, and then list the results in order of most important to least important. Now sort through the data that best show the conclusions you have reached. It's even possible that some contradictory results may appear.

At this point, it's also important to determine how some of the data might best be turned into illustrations—either figures or tables for the report. The illustrations will be an important part of your report because they are often the most effective ways to help you support your conclusions. Make some notes on the rough illustrations concerning what they are supposed to show, how the data were gathered, and any other relevant factors. You'll be able to use this information later when you begin writing the report.

CHOOSING THE ETHICAL PATH

Be sure to discuss contradictions instead of ignoring them or—worse—trying to hide them.

FIGURE 18.6

**Planning Outline
for a Report**

Background Report on Health Problems Related to Computer Operators

Introduction

Health Problems

    Eyestrain

        Symptoms and Causes

        Treatment and Prevention

    Carpal Tunnel Syndrome

        Symptoms and Causes

        Treatment and Prevention

    Headaches

        Symptoms and Causes

        Treatment and Prevention

    Back and Neck Strain

        Symptoms and Causes

        Treatment and Prevention

    Chronic Stress

        Symptoms and Causes

        Treatment and Prevention

    Hazardous Magnetic Fields and Electromagnetic Radiation

        Sources

        Potential Risks

Conclusion

Organizing the Report

After you have gathered your information, analyzed it, and sorted it where necessary or appropriate, the next step is to outline your report. See Figure 18.6 for an example of a planning outline. Now your focus should be on how the results should be presented. The early outline you prepared before you began gathering information can be helpful here. Revise and expand it to emphasize the conclusions you have drawn. Review Chapter 6 for strategies on developing outlines.

The outline should contain concise and descriptive headings for every significant section of the report. Make the outline as detailed as possible. You should even include headings you may not use later in the report. This phase helps you organize your thoughts. Later some headings may be combined and some may be replaced with better wordings or more descriptive headings. Your final outline should contain all the exact headings and subheadings that will appear in the report. (The table of contents in Figure 18.4 is the result of good work on various outlines early in the report-writing process.) Remember that every major heading should have at least two subheadings or, in some cases, no subheadings. A topic cannot be subdivided into fewer than two parts.

After you have completed the final outline, you can use any number of methods for providing the content for each heading. You may write down all the points you want to cover under a particular heading in a random order. You may want to use index cards or sheets of paper containing paragraphs or the outline feature in your word processing program. Use whatever outlining approach works best for you.

> Use whatever outlining approach works best for you.

Designing and Illustrating the Report

As discussed earlier, while you are gathering your information you should give careful thought to the illustrations—both figures and tables—that you will use in the report. Illustrating your report shouldn't be an afterthought or something that's done after the report is complete. Your illustrations can be some of the most effective elements in your report.

All the illustrations in your report should be properly labeled, displayed, and discussed in the report. See Chapter 9 for information on properly labeling and displaying illustrations. If you use tables, make them as simple as possible. Readers will often ignore overly detailed or complex tables. All the tables in the report should be numbered in the order in which they appear in the report.

When you are ready to create your final draft, give careful consideration to all the design elements that will make your report the most effective. Of course, the earlier in the report-writing process that you think about design issues, the easier it will be to design the final version later.

Writing and Revising Various Drafts

Expect to write at least several drafts before you have an acceptable final version. As soon as you complete the final outline, begin writing the first draft. Write this draft as rapidly as possible. Focus more on what you want to say rather than how to say it most effectively. Don't worry at this point about going over what you have written. Instead, just continue writing until you are finished with the draft. After you have finished the draft, look over the report for whether you have discussed all of the ideas you wanted to discuss, whether there are any irrelevant ideas, or whether the organization could be more logical, requiring some changes in the outline.

In the next draft, focus more on improving the writing style. In other words, focus more on how you say what you want to say. Focus on your readers here and why they are reading your report. Focus on all the elements of style. (See Chapter 7 on achieving an effective style.) Also, consider setting aside the draft for a day or two, so that when you return to the writing you have a fresh start or point of view for the material.

As you revise, focus on various aspects of the report to help you make further improvements. (See Chapter 10 for a discussion of revising.) You may want to focus first on the content: Are the conclusions of the report valid? Are they adequately supported by the discussion in the body of the report? Have you provided enough background information where appropriate? Then focus on subject, purpose, and organization. Is the purpose clearly stated? Are the major sections of the body arranged in the most effective order? Then review for errors in mechanics—spelling, capitalization, punctuation, numbers, abbreviations, and grammar (see Appendix A and Appendix B). Also, review for weaknesses in style.

COMMON ELEMENTS IN FORMAL REPORTS

Most formal reports typically contain the following:

- **Front matter:** The front matter includes a letter of transmittal, cover, title page, abstract, executive summary, table of contents, and list of illustrations. The front matter helps readers to find the information they need, helps readers to decide whether they want to read the report, and gives readers the essential purpose, scope, and conclusions (and recommendations, if any) of the report.
- **Body:** The introduction, methods section, results section, conclusion, and sometimes the recommendation section make up the body of a formal report. The body is a discussion of the data—facts, figures, expert testimony, and other relevant factual information. This information must be adequately detailed.
- **Back matter:** The back matter of a report can include a glossary, a list of symbols (if any), any appendixes, reference lists, and an index. These important sections provide explanatory material, raw data, information on outside sources, and navigation tools to help the reader evaluate the worth of the material in the report.

Letter of Transmittal

A letter of transmittal is a letter that explains the purpose and content of the report. It accompanies most formal reports or proposals and usually precedes the title page. Sometimes it is bound in with the report; sometimes it is simply placed on top of the report. A letter of transmittal enables you to acknowledge those who helped with the report, highlight parts of the report that are of special interest, discuss any drawbacks of the study or any problems, and offer any personal observations. For an example of a letter of transmittal, see Figure 14.23 in Chapter 14.

Cover

A cover may be either hard or soft; its chief purpose is to protect the contents of the report. Covers should be used only for long documents. On the cover you may provide the document title, the writer's name, the date of submission, and the name or logo of the company or organization. Often all the items are centered about four or five inches from the top of the page. Alternatively, the cover may contain no information. For an example of a report cover, see Figure 18.4.

Title Page

A title page provides the title, author(s), intended recipients (including the organization for whom the report is intended), and date the report was submitted. Sometimes it contains a report number or identification code, applicable contract numbers if the report was done under contract, and proprietary and security notices. Make your title as descriptive as possible. If required, indicate whether the report is an analysis, a feasibility study, or whatever. The title page does not contain a page number, but it is counted in the pagination as page i. For an example of a title page, see Exhibit 18.1.

Abstract

An abstract is a condensed version of a longer piece of writing that highlights the major points covered, concisely describes the content and scope of the writing, and reviews the contents in abbreviated form. Abstracts are commonly descriptive or informative.

Descriptive abstracts tell readers what information the report, article, or paper contains. See Figure 18.7 for an example of a formal report descriptive abstract. This kind of abstract includes the purpose, methods, and scope of the report, article, or paper, but it does not provide results, conclusions, or recommendations. Descriptive abstracts introduce the subject to readers, who must then read the report, article, or paper to find out the author's results, conclusions, or recommendations. These abstracts are very short, usually less than 100 words.

Informative abstracts communicate specific information from the report, article, or paper. They include the purpose, methods, and scope of the report, article, or paper, and they provide the report, article, or paper's results, conclusions, and recommendations. Informative abstracts allow readers to decide

FIGURE 18.7

Formal Report Descriptive Abstract

TITLE AND SUBTITLE:
Design, Fabrication, and Testing of an Auxiliary Cooling System for Jet Engines

AUTHOR(S):
Kevin Leamy, Jim Griffiths, Paul Andersen, Fidel Joco, and Mark Laski

REPORT DATE:
January 2001

FUNDING NUMBERS:
WU-529-40-14-00 NAS3-27395

PERFORMING ORGANIZATION NAME(S) AND ADDRESS(ES):
GE Aircraft Engines One Neumann Way Cincinnati, Ohio 54215-6301

PERFOMING ORGANIZATION REPORT NUMBER:
E-12402

SPONSORING/MONITORING AGENCY NAME(S) AND ADDRESS(ES):
National Aeronautics and Space Administration Washington, DC 20546-0001

REPORT TYPE AND DATES COVERED:
Final Contractor Report

SPONSORING/MONITORING AGENCY REPORT NUMBER:
NASA CR-2001-210353 R2000AE114

ABSTRACT:
This report summarizes the technical effort of the Active Cooling for Enhanced Performance (ACEP) program sponsored by NASA (NAS3-27395). It covers the design, fabrication, and integrated systems testing of a jet engine auxiliary cooling system, or turbocooler, that significantly extends the use of conventional jet fuel as a heat sink. The turbocooler is designed to provide subcooled cooling air to the engine exhaust nozzle system or engine hot section. The turbocooler consists of three primary components: (1) a high-temperature air cycle machine driven by engine compressor discharge air, (2) a fuel/air heat exchanger that transfers energy from the hot air to the fuel and uses a coating to mitigate fuel deposits, and (3) a high-temperature fuel injection system. The details of the turbocooler component designs and results of the integrated systems testing are documented. Industry Version-Data and information deemed subject to Limited Rights restrictions are omitted from this document.

whether they want to read the report, article, or paper. Informative abstracts are short—usually no longer than 250 words. See Figure 18.4 for an example of an informative abstract in a formal report.

The practice of using keywords in an abstract is crucial because of today's electronic information retrieval systems. Titles and abstracts are often filed electronically, and keywords are put in electronic storage. When people search for information, they enter keywords related to the subject, and the computer lists the titles of articles, papers, and reports containing those keywords. Consequently, an abstract must contain keywords that accurately reflect what is essential in an article, paper, or report so that someone else can retrieve information from it.

Writing an Abstract

- Reread the article, paper, or report with the goal of abstracting in mind.
- Look specifically for these main parts of the article, paper, or report: purpose, methods, scope, results, conclusions, and recommendation.
- Use the headings, outline heads, and table of contents as a guide to writing your abstract.
- If you're writing an abstract about another person's article, paper, or report, the introduction and the summary are good places to begin. These areas generally cover what the article emphasizes.
- After you've finished rereading the article, paper, or report, write a rough draft without looking back at what you're abstracting.
- Don't merely copy key sentences from the article, paper, or report; you'll put in too much or too little information.
- Don't rely on the way material was phrased in the article, paper, or report; summarize information in a new way.

- Provide one or more well-developed paragraphs, and make sure that the paragraphs are unified, coherent, concise, and able to stand alone.
- Provide an opening, a middle, and a closing in the abstract. In the opening of the abstract of an article, paper, or report you discuss the purpose. In the middle you discuss the results and conclusions. In the closing you discuss the recommendations.
- Follow the order of the topics of the article, paper, or report.
- Provide logical connections or transitions between the information included. Your abstract should not add any new information but should simply summarize. Your abstract should be accessible to a wide audience through its handling of language, specifically technical language.
- Use passive verbs where appropriate to downplay the author and emphasize the information.

Executive Summary

An executive summary reviews the essential points of a report. (See the executive summary in Exhibit 18.1.) Executive summaries are useful for people who have neither the time nor the inclination to read a lengthy document but who want to scan the primary points quickly and then decide whether they need to read the entire version. These documents are called executive sum-

Writing an Executive Summary

- Read the entire original before writing a word. Get the complete picture. If you were the author of the report, review the material to refresh your memory of the overall picture.

- Reread and underline significant points (usually in the topic sentence of each paragraph).

- Rewrite the significant points in your own words.

- Don't sacrifice meaning for brevity. A summary should be short enough to be economical and long enough to be clear and comprehensive. A short, confusing summary will take more of a busy executive's time than a somewhat longer but clear one.

- Capture the essential meaning of the original document. A good summary always includes the original's significant points; primary findings; important names, numbers, and measurements; and major conclusions and recommendations. The essential message is the minimum that the reader needs to understand the shortened version of the whole.

- Write at the lowest level of technicality, translating specialized terms and complex data into plain English, because your summary will not include the support-ing information for technical statements. If the executive summary is part of a report, more people may read the summary than the entire report. When in doubt, simplify.

- Structure your summary to fit your audience's requirements. Some summaries follow the organization of the report, dealing briefly with the information in each chapter (or section) in order. Others highlight the findings, conclusions, and recommendations by summarizing them first, before going on to discuss procedures or methodologies.

- Avoid introducing new data into the summary. Represent the original faithfully. An executive summary is not a book report. Avoid opinions such as, "This report was very interesting" or "The author seems to think that . . ." You don't need to try to put the work into a particular perspective.

- Write your summary so that it can stand alone. It should be a self-contained message. Your readers should read the original only if they want to get a fleshed-out view of the subject. They should not have to read it to make sense of what you say in your summary.

- Edit your draft, cutting unnecessary words and phrases.

maries because they are often geared to the usual reading style of busy managers. Managers typically do not want or need an in-depth discussion of the many details of one project or another.

Executive summaries differ from abstracts. Abstracts concisely summarize the major points of an article or report and seldom are more than 200 words. A descriptive abstract discusses the subject, purpose, scope, and methodology of an article or a report, and often does so in 100 words or less. An informative abstract covers these topics and also provides any conclusions and recommendations. Like the informative abstract, an executive summary summarizes the subject, purpose, scope, methods, conclusions, and recommendations. However, an executive summary summarizes the entire report for executives who often must make decisions based on the conclusions or recommendations of the report. Executive summaries are usually 10 percent of the length of the report.

Table of Contents

A table of contents is a list of the headings along with the page numbers where the headings can be found in the report. It is an essential reader aid for longer formal reports. A table of contents helps readers to find what they want and understand quickly the overall organization and approach of the report. Generally, providing up to third-level headings in the table of contents suffices. Start by listing the abstract or summary, the list of illustrations, the introduction, various body sections, the conclusion, the glossary (if provided), appendixes, and references. Only headings that appear in the report may be included in the table of contents, but not all levels of headings go into the table of contents. For an example of a table of contents in a report, see Exhibit 18.1.

List of Illustrations

A list of illustrations is essentially a table of contents for the tables and figures in the document. It is a listing of all formal illustrations used in the report. You may provide the list of illustrations on the same page as the table of contents, unless the report has more than five figures or tables. In that case, place the list of illustrations on a separate page. The list of illustrations is called a list of figures if the report contains only figures and a list of tables if the report contains only tables. If you have both figures and tables, title the page "List of Illustrations." Then list the figures in numerical order first, followed by the tables in numerical order. For an example of a list of illustrations in a report, see Exhibit 18.1.

Introduction

The introduction of a report is a discussion of the subject, purpose, organization, and scope. Most introductions for most reports are several paragraphs long and seldom longer than a page; however, a longer introduction of two or three pages may be required if more background information needs to be provided.

You should employ a number of strategies in the introduction:

- Concisely identify what you are writing about or the subject.

- Identify your primary aim. Basically, tell your readers why the report was written, why they should read the report, and what benefits it will have for them. Identify how your report is organized and your approach.
- Tell your readers what the major sections of the report are and the order in which they will be covered. Think of this discussion as forecasting for the audience what will follow in the report.
- Tell your readers the scope and limitations of the report. Identify anything that makes this particular report unique in its focus on its subject.

For an example of a report introduction, see Exhibit 18.1.

Methods

A methods section, if it's appropriate for the kind of report you're writing, tells your readers what you did. This section discusses how your study or project or test was set up and why. The methods section is a common and major section of a research report. For this kind of report, a methods section may contain experiment descriptions (perhaps using the heading "Apparatus and Procedure" instead of "Methods"). If you do provide test procedures, describe them in enough detail so that your readers can see the value of the results and, if necessary, repeat the experiment. The amount of detail depends on the complexity of the procedure. See Figure 18.8 for an example of a formal report methods section.

Results or Discussion

The results in a report are the key data that you found or created. However, some key data may also be included in the appendix of a report. The results section, also referred to as the discussion section in some reports, tells your readers about your observations. This section comes between the introduction and conclusion (and the recommendation section, if appropriate)

FIGURE 18.8

Formal Report Methods Section

Methodology. New plants were identified through personal business contacts and through contacts in state development offices; manufacturing plants in the United States that had been in operation at least one year but less than ten years were considered for inclusion. Recruitment of new plants was done by phone. The plants included in this study represent a diverse group of new plants and are described in Table 1. Products include food and beverages, consumer products, heavy manufacturing, pharmaceutical and automotive-related; distribution centers were also included. Many of these plants represent Fortune 500 companies. Plants range in size from 61 to 1150 employees. Labor costs as a percentage of total costs range from 6 to 50%. Locations vary across the United States, with 11 plants in the Northeast, 10 in the Midwest, 9 in the Southeast, 2 in the West and 1 plant in the Northwest. Date of plant openings range from 1988 through 1998. All but 2 of the plants currently operate in non-union status.

and consists of the major sections and subsections of the report. Make sure you present the results in a well-organized and objective manner. The discussion and analysis of the results should help show that the conclusions are valid or warranted. Make sure each conclusion is clearly explained. Keep in mind that your readers are not as familiar with the material as you are, so avoid taking too much for granted, providing overly complicated discussions, or providing discussion that is too long. Your first priority should be on presenting the data as clearly and simply as possible. For an example of a results section, see Exhibit 18.1.

Conclusion

The conclusion is a concise interpretation of the facts that are covered in the body of the report. A good conclusion covers only what the data in the body of the report will support. There should be no conclusions in the report that are not derived from or built on the data covered in the body. Essentially, in this section you tell readers what you have told them earlier in the report.

Keep in mind that many people read the concluding section of a report first. The section must stand on its own and be independent of the body of the report. A good conclusion avoids equations, tables, figures, references, appendixes, undefined symbols, and the introduction of new material. For an example of a report conclusion section, see Exhibit 18.1.

> " "
> There should be no conclusions in the report that are not derived from or built on the data covered in the body.

Recommendations

Recommendations are the particular actions the reader should take on the basis of the conclusions of the report. Reports do not necessarily include recommendations. Most informational reports and many analytical reports offer no recommendations or specific courses of action for the readers to follow. See Figure 18.9 (pages 649–651) for an example of a formal report recommendations section.

Glossary and List of Symbols

A glossary is an alphabetical listing of key terms in the report, providing definitions in the form of phrases or complete sentences. If you provide the definitions in the form of phrases, then all of the definitions should be listed as phrases. If you provide the definitions in the form of complete sentences, then all of the definitions should be listed as complete sentences. (Review the "Definitions" section in Chapter 15.)

Glossaries are essential if you are writing for both technical and nontechnical readers, since words and expressions can have different meanings in general use and technical use. You should include and define all terms that you think will be unfamiliar to a general reader, being careful to coordinate

FIGURE 18.9

**Formal Report
Recommendations Section**

24   **Hazardous Materials Accident Report**

Recommendations

As a result of this accident, the National Transportation Safety Board makes the following safety recommendations:

to the Federal Highway Administration:

Add elements to training programs for Federal and State inspectors that include instruction on determining whether motor carriers have adequate written procedures for driver training in loading and unloading cargo tanks. (H-99-30)

Evaluate the adequacy of cargo-tank loading and unloading procedures of and driver training for hazardous-materials motor carriers and require changes as appropriate. (H-99-31)

Issue an "On Guard" bulletin to emphasize the danger of splash filling materials into cargo compartments and of switch loading materials having flash points at or above 100° F (National Fire Protection Association Class II and III liquids) into compartments that last contained materials having flash points below 100°F (National Fire Protection Association Class I liquid). (H-99-32)

to Dion Oil Company:

Establish written procedures for safely loading and unloading cargo tanks. (H-99-33)

Give drivers function-specific training on the written procedures developed in conjunction with Safety Recommendation H-99-33. The training should explain the danger of discharging static electricity when flammable liquids are poured into open cargo-tank compartments that contain explosive vapors, the danger of transferring flammable liquids between cargo tanks that are not bonded, and the danger of explosive vapors produced by switch loading gasoline and diesel fuels. (H-99-34)

to the Florida State Fire Marshal:

Make all local jurisdictions in Florida aware of the circumstances of the fire and explosions that occurred on Stock Island, Florida, on June 29, 1998. In addition, ensure that each local jurisdiction has a program to identify and inspect cargo tanks used as storage tanks for flammable liquids to be sure the tanks meet all the fire safety standards applicable to storage tanks. (H-99-35)

the definition with the context the reader will encounter in the report itself. Glossary definitions for the same term can be quite different for different reports, depending on how the term is used in each report. Once you have decided on a format for your definitions, make sure that each entry conforms to that format. For an example of a glossary, see Exhibit 18.1.

FIGURE 18.9

(continued)

| Recommendations | 25 | Hazardous Materials Accident Report |

Coordinate the help that the Florida Departments of Transportation, of Agriculture, and of Environmental Protection give local jurisdictions in identifying cargo tanks used as storage tanks for the transfer of flammable liquids to be sure that the tanks meet all fire safety standards applicable to storage tanks. (H-99-36)

to the Florida Department of Transportation:

Assist the Florida State Fire Marshal in helping local jurisdictions identify cargo tanks being used as storage tanks so that the tanks can be inspected to ensure that they meet all fire safety standards applicable to storage tanks. (H-99-37)

to the Florida Department of Agriculture:

Assist the Florida State Fire Marshal in helping local jurisdictions identify cargo tanks being used as storage tanks so that the tanks can be inspected to ensure that they meet all fire safety standards applicable to storage tanks. (H-99-38)

to the Florida Department of Environmental Protection:

Assist the Florida State Fire Marshal in helping local jurisdictions identify cargo tanks being used as storage tanks so that the tanks can be inspected to ensure that they meet all fire safety standards applicable to storage tanks. (H-99-39)

to the National Fire Prevention Association:

Make your members aware of the circumstances of the fire and explosions that occurred on Stock Island, Florida, on June 29, 1998, and urge them to develop a program to identify and inspect cargo tanks used as storage tanks for the transfer of flammable liquids to be sure that the tanks meet all fire safety standards applicable to storage tanks. (H-99-40)

to the National Association of State Fire Marshals:

Make your members aware of the circumstances of the fire and explosions that occurred on Stock Island, Florida, on June 29, 1998, and urge them to develop a program to identify and inspect cargo tanks used as storage tanks for the transfer of flammable liquids to be sure that the tanks meet all fire safety standards applicable to storage tanks. (H-99-41)

For some reports, a list of symbols and abbreviations may also be necessary. Depending on the document standards for the company, the list of symbols may be placed after a glossary or, more often, may be placed in an appendix. (See "Appendixes" below.) Such a list provides a complete catalog of the symbols and other abbreviations that are used in a report. Standard symbols for

FIGURE 18.9
(continued)

Recommendations 26 Hazardous Materials Accident Report

to the International Association of Fire Chiefs:

> Make your members aware of the circumstances of the fire and explosions that occurred on Stock Island, Florida, on June 29, 1998, and urge them to develop a program to identify and inspect cargo tanks used as storage tanks for the transfer of flammable liquids to be sure that the tanks meet all fire safety standards applicable to storage tanks. (H-99-42)

BY THE NATIONAL TRANSPORTATION SAFETY BOARD

JAMES E. HALL
Chairman

ROBERT T. FRANCIS II
Vice Chairman

JOHN A. HAMMERSCHMIDT
Member

JOHN J. GOGLIA
Member

GEORGE W. BLACK, JR.
Member

September 10, 1999

FIGURE 18.10
Formal Report List of Abbreviations

ALR	Administrative License Revocation
BAC	Blood Alcohol Concentration
BAIID	Breath Alcohol Ignition Interlock Device
DDMP	Drunk Driver Monitoring Program (State of Maryland)
DOT	U.S. Department of Transportation
DUI	Driving Under the Influence (of Alcohol)
DWI	Driving While Impaired (by Alcohol)
DWS	Driving While (License) Suspended
DWU	Driving While Unlicensed
FARS	Fatality Analysis Reporting System
FY	Fiscal Year
IID	Ignition Interlock Device
ISP	Intensive Supervision Probation
ISTEA	Intermodal Surface Transportation Efficiency Act of 1991

From the workplace

Steve Steinman

President, Steinman Associates, Management Consulting Organization (biotechnology, pharmaceutical, and biologics industries), Alexandria, Virginia

Steve's consulting company routinely writes documents that can span tens of thousands of pages. The successful ones enable large pharmaceutical companies to develop and test new drugs, some of which may lead to more effective treatments for a variety of diseases. A well-constructed application can set into motion medical advances of incalculable value. With the stakes so high, strong communication skills are a must.

I am the president and founder of a small consulting organization that operates in the fields of drug development and regulatory affairs. My college and graduate courses (bachelor's degree in zoology and graduate studies in the basic medical sciences) were necessary but not sufficient to support the work that I am currently carrying out. I needed a substantial measure of on-the-job training.

I have previously held positions in Quality Assurance, Quality Control, and Government Regulatory Affairs for large and small corporate entities dealing with high-tech medical devices, low-tech medical devices, radioactive diagnostic drugs, and biological products. I initially elected to leave the corporation that I served for ten years in order to advance myself professionally and financially and to work on more challenging projects.

Subsequent to my second job in the drug/device arena, I took eighteen months to travel around California with a successful candidate for statewide constitutional office. In that job, I was forced to do a substantial amount of writing, because the campaign lacked the resources to hire someone else to do it.

My current occupation as a management consultant—and a manager of consultants—principally involves written communication. Among the tasks that we are most frequently assigned is the drafting of applications to the Food and Drug Administration to convince that agency to authorize the conduct of a clinical trial of a new drug (an Investigational New Drug [IND] application) or the drafting of applications to market a new drug (New Drug Application [NDA]). These documents may run from five hundred pages at one extreme to tens of thousands of pages at

> You may think of an appendix as a reference section for the report. In this section you give the reader the opportunity to review and evaluate information you have used in forming your conclusions and recommendations.

most quantities have long been available in the sciences. The standard symbols have been adopted by various international organizations, and you should use them whenever possible. Creating or inventing your own symbols may confuse the reader. See Figure 18.10 (on page 651) for an example of a formal report list of abbreviations.

Appendixes

Appendixes include additional material that is useful but not essential to understanding the body of the report. In fact, sometimes appendixes are written by an author other than the author or authors for the report. You may think of an appendix as a reference section for the report. In this section you

the other extreme. The writing tasks encompass a logical presentation of experimentation and clinical trial data, including text, statistical analysis, displays, and argumentation. The basic science and clinical research underpinning a New Drug Application may easily require as many as 7 to 10 years to carry out.

Appearing at meetings with government regulators on behalf of client companies is another major function of our organization, and it is frequently possible to influence the quality and outcome of these meetings through thorough preparation and use of good communications techniques and skills.

Interacting with clients over drug-development strategy is a third major function of our office. The direction of client companies in policy and strategy takes the form of standard memoranda. For those clients with whom we work on a regular—even day-to-day—basis, e-mail may also be used. I personally generate upwards of 50 memoranda in a week.

I usually carry a laptop computer with me when I am on business travel, thus facilitating my ability to carry on any project currently in progress. I use e-mail with some clients and not others, depending upon my responsibility to the client. My principal use of the Internet is for rapid searches of the research and business literature. In my company we make regular use of spreadsheets, databases, and project management software.

Some of the documents that this office prepares for clients incorporate graphics; outputs dealing with statistical considerations are generated by our statistician who has significant proficiency in this arena. The remaining tasks fall between the project consultants and professional editors, depending on who has the relevant skills.

In general I do not approach writing tasks very differently whether using a legal tablet or a Mac. Here at Steinman Associates, we all generate our own correspondence and moderate-sized documents via computer. In the case of certain applications, there is no real choice: quite obviously, statistical analyses and database applications *require* the use of a powerful computer. Large documents, such as the NDAs and INDs I mentioned before, are published by a professional editor having the requisite software skills.

In my experience most writers lack the ability to gauge or evaluate the information that is actually required by the recipient and then present it logically and succinctly. We are making a substantial effort, both in our company and with the regulatory affairs staffs of our client companies, to raise the level of technical writing. Toward this end, I recently persuaded several client companies to use communication skills as a factor in employee reviews.

give the reader the opportunity to review and evaluate information you have used in forming your conclusions and recommendations. Readers who want to examine your raw data will find them in this section. Many reports have appendixes, and many do not. Typical items to include in an appendix are complex formulas, additional illustrations, questionnaires, symbol lists, and lab results. Detailed descriptions of techniques, procedures, or equipment not essential to the main purpose of the report may also be included.

Each appendix in a report should have a title. Multiple appendixes are usually identified as Appendix A, B, C, etc. The appendixes should be referred to in the appropriate places in the main body of the report. Illustrations included for the first time in an appendix continue the numbering used for illustrations in the main body of the report.

References

References are a listing of sources you consulted, provided in the documentation style that is preferred by the discourse community for whom you are writing. For an example of a references section (called "Works Cited"), see Exhibit 18.1. Also consult Appendix C for information about documentation styles.

Index

An index is a guide to the contents of a work. It differs from a table of contents in its level of detail and arrangement. While a table of contents normally lists major sections in the work arranged by page number, an index will list specific topics covered in the work, arranged according to some logical scheme—usually alphabetical or chronological. Readers check indexes when they want to find information that they have seen in a work but cannot locate, when they want an overview of the coverage on a particular topic, or when they need help locating material that might not be listed in a table of contents.

Creating an Index

- Be aware of any specific requirements that your instructor or your employer has imposed. If there is a style sheet, follow its guidelines.

- Decide whether you will be providing a page number index, a chronological index, or something else.

- Edit your index. Once you have finished creating your entries, they will have to be edited, just as you would edit any other work you create. Eliminate duplicate or redundant entries, and make sure your entries are useful, are arranged logically, and correctly point to the appropriate location in the text.

- Ask yourself whether each entry is necessary, phrased usefully, and located where the reader will look for it. If a concept can be referred to in more than one way, make sure you have cross-references from the alternative forms to one indexed term.

- Avoid circular entries, that is, entries that point to each other without actually sending the reader to a location in the text.

- Verify that your locators are correct. Select entries at random and check that their page numbers or other locators are accurate. If possible, sort your entries according to page number to check the correctness of locators more easily.

- If possible, have someone else check your index for usability.

CHECKING WHAT YOU'VE LEARNED

Front Matter

- Is a letter of transmittal provided first? Is it addressed to one specific individual, and is a job title provided for this person? Does the letter have a correct business letter format? If not, how can it be improved? Does the letter provide the necessary information for a letter of transmittal?
- Is a cover for the report provided? If so, does it provide the necessary information—title of the report, the author or authors' names, the date the report was submitted?
- Is a title page provided? Does it provide the necessary information—title of the report, intended audience, name of the author or authors, the date the report was submitted, copyright notice (optional)?
- Is an executive summary provided? Does it meet the requirements of a good executive summary?
- Is a table of contents (TOC) provided? Does the TOC begin by listing the executive summary? Is the list of illustrations listed in the TOC? Are the introduction, the major headings (up to three levels of the body of the report), the conclusion, recommendations, appendixes (optional for some reports), glossary, references, and index (optional for some reports) listed?
- Is a list of illustrations provided? For reports containing five illustrations or fewer, is the list of illustrations on the same page as the table of contents?

Introduction

- Does the introduction begin on a new page? Does it discuss the subject, purpose, organization, and scope (specific limits, focus, concerns, depth of detail) of the report?
- Is the purpose of the report clearly stated?
- Could a forecasting sentence or paragraph be provided in the introduction to help the reader understand what will be covered?

Body

- Does the first major heading of the body of the report begin on a separate page?
- Is the appropriate number of first-level major headings provided in the body of the report? Are the headings presented in an effective order?
- If a topic has subheadings, are there at least two for that topic?
- Are the paragraphs within the body of the report adequately detailed?

- If sources are paraphrased or quoted verbatim, are they documented properly?
- Are the within-the-text citations handled correctly for MLA, APA, CSE, Turabian, IEEE, or other documentation style? (See Appendix C.)

Conclusion and Recommendations

- Is a conclusion provided after the last paragraph of the body of the report? Does the conclusion adequately summarize the key points covered in the body of the report? Does the conclusion avoid discussing any data not covered in the body of the report?
- Is a recommendations section (unnecessary for a background report; required for a recommendation report or a feasibility report) provided? Are the recommendations specific actions for the audience of the report to consider? Can the recommendations be improved in any way?

Back Matter

- Are any appendixes (optional for some reports) provided? Appendixes typically include extra information or supplemental information such as price sheets, extra illustrations, and data not essential to the body of the report. If separate appendixes are provided, does each one have a title?
- Is a glossary provided? Does it define the key technical terms provided in the report? Are the definitions provided as all phrases or complete sentences? Either (but not a combination) is fine.
- Is a page titled "Works Cited" or "References" provided? Are the references in the correct format, accurately documented, alphabetically arranged, and complete?
- Is an index provided? If so, does it meet the requirements of a good index for a report? Are important concepts listed under terms where readers will look for them?

Design and Illustrations

- Does the report have an overall effective design? Are several different complementary typefaces used—one for the headings and another for the body text?
- Are the various heading levels (first, second, third) clearly distinct from each other and applied consistently throughout the report?
- Are the pages of the report numbered correctly—small Roman numerals beginning with the title page (the page is counted in the numbering but no number appears on the page) and Arabic numerals beginning with the introduction?
- Are illustrations—figures and tables or just figures or just tables—provided in the body of the report? Are these illustrations appropriately

displayed, labeled, and documented? Are the figures and tables numbered in the proper order?

Organization

- Are the major sections and subsections of the report presented in the most effective order?
- Are there any psychological advantages to presenting the content in a different order?

Style and Mechanics

- Are there any errors or weaknesses in style?
- Are there any weaknesses in mechanics (grammar, punctuation, spelling, capitalization, numbers)? Are all acronyms, initialisms, and abbreviations identified or defined?

EXERCISES

 REVIEW

1. Review the sample student background report in Exhibit 18.1. Write one or two paragraphs discussing the kinds of changes you would have to make in the report to make it a suitable feasibility report or a recommendation report.
2. Review the discussion of strategies for preparing a technical report. Write a paragraph discussing the strategies that you think will be the most difficult for you as you prepare to work on a technical report for this class.
3. Review the sample descriptive abstract in Figure 18.7 and sample informative abstract in Figure 18.4. Make a list of any elements the two abstracts have in common. Provide a separate list of some key differences between the two abstracts.
4. Review the elements of an effective introduction for a formal report. Review the introduction in Exhibit 18.1. Identify the effective elements in the introduction to the report.
5. Review the elements of an effective conclusion for a formal report. Review the conclusion in Exhibit 18.1. Identify the effective elements in

the conclusion to the report. Also discuss whether there is any information in the conclusion that does not belong in the conclusion to the report.

 THE INTERNET

Access some of the electronic databases available to you through your university library and find some sites for technical reports. Sites mentioned earlier in this chapter include the General Accounting Office, the National Transportation Safety Board, and NASA. Find a site relevant to your major and provide a list of five or more technical reports available at this site.

 ETHICS/PROFESSIONALISM

Review the sample background report in Exhibit 18.1. Create a list of the strategies used in the design, organization, content, and prose style of the report that you believe make it a professional (or conscientiously written) report. Be prepared to discuss your list with the class.

COLLABORATION

Working with two or more students in the class, use various brainstorming and mind mapping techniques (review these in Chapter 4 if necessary) to create a list of topics you and your group members might explore for a technical report. Also discuss what kind of reports (background report, feasibility report, recommendation report, research report) would be most suitable for the topics you discuss.

 INTERNATIONAL COMMUNICATION

Review the discussion of executive summaries in the chapter. Discuss how you might have to use different strategies for an executive summary if some or all of your audience for your formal report is from another culture. Discuss, for example, whether some key elements of an executive summary may have to be covered in a different order and why.

RESOURCES

Allen, Jo. *Writing in the Workplace.* Boston: Allyn and Bacon, 1998.

Booth, Wayne C., Gregory G. Colomb, and Joseph M. Williams. *The Craft of Research.* Chicago: U of Chicago P, 1995.

Pearsall, Thomas E. *The Elements of Technical Writing.* 2nd ed. Boston: Allyn and Bacon, 2001.

Exhibit 18.1

659

EXHIBIT 18.1
**Background Report—
Computer Virus
Vulnerabilities for
Networked/Computer-
Based Business Systems**

The *title page* gives the title, the author,
the person and organization for whom
the report was written, and the date.

Background Report on Computer Virus Vulnerabilities for Networked/Computer-Based Business Systems

Written by
Russell Jarvis

Prepared for
Mr. John Jackson
Information Technology Manager
Space Gateway Support Company
(SGS)

Submitted June 19, 2000

EXHIBIT 18.1

(continued)

An *executive summary* gives the highlights
of the report without the details and is geared
to the needs of the manager.

Executive Summary

Introduction:

The vulnerability of computer-based business systems can be examined from two perspectives:
- Preventing virus damage with antiviral software
- Limiting virus damage with network security

Apply these two perspectives to the business system environment:
- The Microsoft NT Network
- The Microsoft NT Exchange Mail System
- The Work Habits of the User

The Vulnerabilities of the Microsoft NT Network:

The key concept in NT security is "damage control." Start by restricting all users to every network resource and then apply NT security permissions allowing only users who have valid needs to access files, directories, or servers.

Professionally deployed and configured antiviral software is required. It should be of enterprise caliber. The viral pattern updates should be applied to workstation, servers, and Exchange servers in a timely manner. The preferred method is an automated process via the Internet on a daily (minimum) basis.

Business applications should be deployed with the business application on one server and the application database on a separate server. Users should only have access to the business application server. The business application (not users) should be the only entity with access to the application database. This isolates the data from areas where users have security permissions.

The Vulnerabilities of the Microsoft NT Exchange Mail System:

Exchange is the most susceptible element in the business system environment. Worms (self-propagating viruses) can send malicious code attachments from infected workstations to hundreds of recipients using the addresses contained in the local PAB (Personal Address Book) file.

ii

Exhibit 18.1

661

EXHIBIT 18.1

(continued)

The standard mechanism used by most vendors of enterprise level antiviral software for Exchange can only scan "incoming messages." This mechanism will not prevent an infected Exchange client from sending out hundreds of e-mails with infected attachments each time the machine is booted and validated to the NT domain.

The Vulnerabilities of the User's Work Habits

User education is very important. Educate the user concerning virus-like activities and the common methods of delivery. The user is the strongest or weakest link in the chain of events that must happen to develop a low-risk environment for computer-based business systems.

Users should be informed of their responsibility to safeguard vital business data and should be reminded of their responsibility on a regular basis. Warnings should be sent via e-mail when virus threats are imminent.

iii

EXHIBIT 18.1

(continued)

A good *table of contents* reflects
a well-organized report.

Table of Contents

Executive Summary ii
List of Illustrations v
Introduction 1
Definition of "Vulnerability" 3
    Danger of Corrupting Data Files.. 3
    Danger of Making Servers Inoperable.. 3
    Danger of Making Workstations Inoperable... 3
The Vulnerability of the Microsoft NT Network... 4
    Danger to the Client Workstations... 4
    Danger to the Network Servers.. 5
    Danger to Business Applications.. 9
        Logistics and Financial Databases... 9
    Antiviral Software... 9
        What Antiviral Software Will Do 10
        What Antiviral Software Will Not Do.. 10
Vulnerability of the Microsoft Exchange Mail System 11
    E-mail Administration... 11
    Antiviral Software 12
        What it will do 12
        What it will not do 12
Vulnerabilities of Users' Work Habits 12
    User Awareness 13
    MS Exchange Personal Folders 16
    File Housekeeping 16
    Antiviral Software 16
        What it will do 16
        What it will not do 16
Conclusion 17
Glossary 18
Works Cited 19

iv

Exhibit 18.1

663

EXHIBIT 18.1

(continued)

A *list of illustrations* is especially important
in a report with many figures or tables.

List of Illustrations

Figure 1: Server Vulnerability from an Infected Workstation 7
Figure 2: Security Model for Limiting Virus Damage 8
Figure 3: Communication Around the World via E-mail 10
Figure 4: Virus Information for Norton Antivirus Users 12
Figure 5: Virus Information for TrendMicro OfficeScan Users 13
Figure 6: TrendMicro's Virus Information Center 14

v

EXHIBIT 18.1

(continued)

The report's *introduction* explains the purpose of the report and describes any significant limitations or conditions governing the report.

Introduction

Discovery of vulnerabilities to computer-based business systems from malicious computer virus attacks is vital to the success of Space Gateway Support Company. The devastating effects of the new generation of computer viruses have proven that successful companies cannot ignore this threat. The informed Information Technology (IT) Manager will be aware of the dangers posed by these new "super" viruses and take steps to minimize these vulnerabilities.

This report will provide a clear definition of the major vulnerabilities IT managers will encounter in providing computer-based business systems to customers. Vital data files, employee workstations, and network servers may be at risk if vulnerabilities are not addressed. The damage represented by a genuine vulnerability can translate into expensive recovery procedures.

The scope of the report will be limited to business application deployment on a Microsoft NT Network with an NT Exchange Mail system supporting a user base of approximately two thousand workstations. It should be noted that web servers, which are fast becoming a major part of many private networks, will not be included because of the special complexities involved in "browser" interpreted code and permission configurations. The use of firewalls will not be covered because their usefulness as a tool for protecting business systems is so significant, it merits a report of its own.

A natural tendency will be to protect vital networked services with antiviral software only. Of course this will be necessary to achieve an adequate protection against a virus attack. However, it is imperative to understand that the vendor providing the antiviral software must have a "pattern" or "definition" of the virus readily available to the protected systems to actually identify the malicious code and neutralize it. This means that the actual vulnerability of any computer-based business system must be analyzed assuming the attacking virus is so new that no definition of the virus is available to enable the antiviral software to detect it as a threat. Total dependence upon antiviral software is dangerous.

This report will explain the vulnerability to virus attack of the Microsoft NT Network. The Microsoft NT Network must be correctly implemented and maintained to contain virus inflicted damage to a single file, directory, drive, workstation, server, or network. Security permissions must be used and updated. Network security must be a vital part of network administration.

Exhibit 18.1

665

EXHIBIT 18.1

(continued)

The Microsoft Exchange mail system is the single most used vehicle for delivering computer viruses. An experienced professional must properly administer it. Correctly deployed antiviral software designed specifically for Exchange is critical for reducing the company's exposure to vulnerability. The danger due to virus attack is not only real to Space Gateway Support Company, but to everyone with whom the company communicates via email.

Finally, this report will provide information concerning the computer work habits of the typical user. Elevating the user's awareness of viruses and using caution in file maintenance can determine whether a virus will be introduced into the network environment and how much damage it can do when a viral infection does occur.

EXHIBIT 18.1

(continued)

In this report, pages 3–16 constitute
the *results*, or *discussion*, section.

Definition of "Vulnerability"

According to *Merriam-Webster's Collegiate Dictionary*, Tenth Edition, one definition of
vulnerability is "open to attack." This is the type of vulnerability we are talking about. To
understand more about computer vulnerability and why you should know about it, we need to
first explain it. First of all, you need to know how virus vulnerability can affect your business.
There are three important ways a virus can affect your business. The first way a business is
vulnerable is through the corruption of its data files. A second way is letting servers become
inoperable. A third way a business becomes vulnerable is through workstations becoming
inoperable. Knowing about virus vulnerability is important for a business's survival.

Danger of Corrupting Data Files

In your business, computers are an essential component. Therefore, the vulnerability of data
files getting corrupted by a virus is very dangerous for you, your business, and your clients.
One important reason you need to know and understand vulnerability is that viruses can delete
all your files on your hard drive. This can include the operating system that turns on and off
your computer. Without the use of your computer, you have no business. Since most businesses
store all their files on a computer, losing the information can be devastating.

Danger of Making Servers Inoperable

Being vulnerable to viruses can also put your servers at risk. If a virus attacks your computer,
then the server may become inoperable. With a server inoperable, your can't e-mail anyone,
which includes the other employees or clients. If your e-mail has been infected, that also means
that you may have infected someone else's computer. Another thing that a virus may affect is
Microsoft Word. Without the ability to use MS Word, you cannot type a report, proposal,
memo or business letter. If Word or your e-mail goes down, communication may become
difficult. If you are unable to communicate, how can you get any work done? When this
happens, communication between everyone stops and it can hurt the business.

Danger of Making Workstations Inoperable

With a workstation inside a business, having it be vulnerable to viruses can be very dangerous.
If a virus gets inside one computer on the workstation, most likely the rest of the computers on
the workstation will become affected. This can also affect the production of the business.
Without any work getting done there is no business, which also means no money for the

3

Exhibit 18.1

667

EXHIBIT 18.1

(continued)

business and you. As we all know, we need money to have a business. Everyone will also lose all the files on the computer that are not saved on a disk. This can put the business behind or out of service, and we all know we do not want that.

The Vulnerabilites of the Microsoft NT Network

The Microsoft NT Network can be a very secure environment for business applications and data files. When properly deployed, it can limit the damage incurred from a malicious virus attack. Security measures can be applied to the user and the user's workstation.

Security can be applied to servers, limiting access to files, directories, and what can be done to them. These security measures are not in force after initial installation of the operating system by *default* (Howard 64). Whenever data is made available on a *network share*, the default for the security applied to that data is to allow all users to have full control of the directory and its contents. A network administrator must manually apply stricter security to the network share and its contents. The key concept is "damage control." If a virus outbreak occurs, how far can it go? Think of this method as a firebreak to prevent spreading damage.

If a virus is not found in the antiviral software's pattern or definition file, it will be undetected. If the code is executed, it will successfully perform all the procedures it can within the scope of the user's NT permissions. This would put the files and file folders on servers at risk as well as the local workstation.

Danger to the Client Workstations

The most obvious danger to a user's workstation is the introduction of a virus to that workstation and then the execution of the virus on that workstation. Files can be copied or moved to a local workstation through a floppy (removable) disk drive. Files can be copied or moved to workstation from a server or other workstation via a network connection.

However, the virus does not have to reside on the workstation to infect it. A virus can reside safely on a server while the user executes it. The workstation becomes the target of the virus attack and the virus remains on the server undetected.

The virus may be designed to perform any legal action permitted by the operating system. Deleting files and changing the contents of files are considered legal operations of the operating system.

Since all viruses are programs (or code), the virus must be started like any other program. This means that a user would normally start the malicious program under the pretense the program is a productive tool. However, some malicious code is hidden to the user and the user does not realize that a given mundane procedure is actually launching or interpreting code. The classic example of this is the MS Word macro virus.

4

EXHIBIT 18.1

(continued)

In short, a Word *template* is used to create a Word document. The average user is unaware that a template can contain Visual Basic code that is interpreted (executed) every time the document is opened. The execution of the code is transparent to the user. Malicious code can hide within a Word document, which is not normally associated with an executable file such as a virus. This was the method used by the famous "Melissa" virus. Antiviral software is being modified to deal with the specifics of such a virus (*TrendMicro Announces New Content Security Solution for Microsoft Exchange 2000* Web Site).

Windows95 or 98 does not have the robust security that the NT Workstation employs. The Windows95 and 98 operating systems are more vulnerable by virtue of the fact that every user has permission granted by the operating system to perform almost any action to the local machine (*Introducing Microsoft Windows95* 50).

The virus employs the permissions of the user to perform all its functions. If a virus is only designed to destroy files, the NT Workstation security can limit the scope of access a user has, thus restricting the scope of damage a virus can do. By default, the system is unrestricted. Security permissions must be applied and tested.

Danger to the Network Servers

The most obvious danger to a network server is an infected workstation with a valid network connection by a user who has security permissions to perform legal operating system actions. Servers are at great risk from worms that make their targets network drives instead of only the local hard disk. Applying the normal NT security to network shares can limit this vulnerability (Thompkins 63). See Figures 1 and 2.

Every user who validates to an *NT Domain* has a USERID, which can be restricted in its ability to connect to a server. By default, servers are not restricted (*Microsoft Windows NT Server Installation Guide* 92). When data is made available via a network share, the folder and its contents are made available to everyone with full control of the folder and its contents. Security must be applied manually or else the network shares are vulnerable to attack from an infected workstation.

Viruses exploit the permissions of the USERID currently logged on to the infected workstation. They can propagate themselves by using permissions granted through the Exchange mail system to send the virus to other Exchange clients. Worms can search for network connections, probing everywhere they have permission to go.

Worms can cause extreme damage to servers that are not infected with the virus itself. Though the virus inflicts the damage, much of the damage is preventable if proper permissions are in place. It is possible for one infected workstation to literally destroy every vital data file on every server if the USERID logged on the infected workstation has the permissions of a network administrator.

5

Exhibit 18.1

669

EXHIBIT 18.1

(continued)

Figures should be placed in the report right where they are discussed. Supplementary figures and tables may be placed in an appendix.

Unnecessary access to servers increases the exposure of clean systems to damage caused by only one infected workstation.

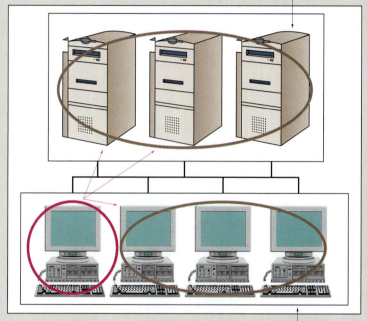

Figure 1: Server Vulnerability from an Infected Workstation
Source: Created in MS PowerPoint by the author

Workstations are also exposed to danger if their resources are shared on the network.

6

EXHIBIT 18.1

(continued)

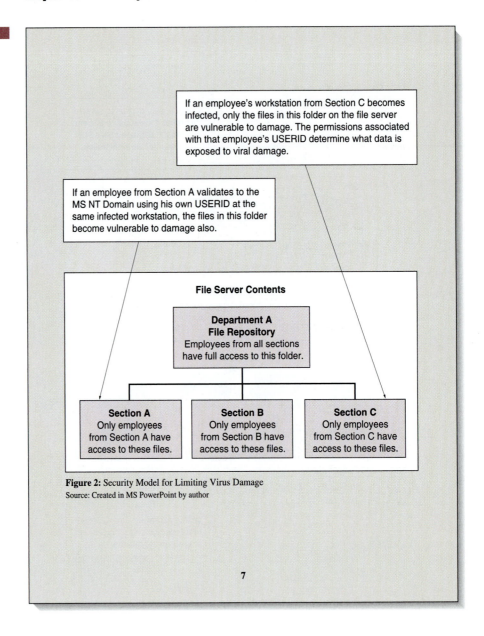

If an employee's workstation from Section C becomes infected, only the files in this folder on the file server are vulnerable to damage. The permissions associated with that employee's USERID determine what data is exposed to viral damage.

If an employee from Section A validates to the MS NT Domain using his own USERID at the same infected workstation, the files in this folder become vulnerable to damage also.

File Server Contents

**Department A
File Repository**
Employees from all sections have full access to this folder.

Section A
Only employees from Section A have access to these files.

Section B
Only employees from Section B have access to these files.

Section C
Only employees from Section C have access to these files.

Figure 2: Security Model for Limiting Virus Damage
Source: Created in MS PowerPoint by author

7

Exhibit 18.1

671

EXHIBIT 18.1

(continued)

The styling of *headings* should clearly
distinguish their relative weights.

Danger to Business Applications

Only employees actually performing tasks in a networked business application should have
access to that application. Security permissions should be applied as tightly as possible to lower
the exposure of the application to as few people as possible. Should a virus attack take place
and a virus is distributed to hundreds of employees, the exposure of vital business data to actual
vulnerability is reduced greatly. Vulnerability is realized only if workstations of the few
employees who have security permissions to business data becomes infected.

Logistics and Financial Databases

Proper deployment of major databases supporting logistics and finance is critical to lower
vulnerability to damage from virus attacks. The data should never reside on the same server as
the application. The database administrator is the only *person* who should have access to the
database server.

A special USERID that can only be used by the application should be used to access the
database. This means normal users can access the application, but not the database. Only the
application can access the database. The application server may be destroyed by an infected
workstation, but the workstation never has direct access to the data files.

Since proper backups are assumed to be in place, damaged data can be restored. However, even
a few hours of work multiplied by an entire finance department can escalate to an expensive
loss.

Antiviral Software

Only antiviral software developed for an enterprise level should be considered for protecting
network deployed business applications. This means a fully integrated suite of applications that
work together to protect workstations, file/application servers, and Exchange servers. They
must be specifically written to work with these Microsoft applications (*Antivirus Scanner
Implementation Considerations* Web Site). They should be professionally installed and
configured. Improper configuration can be as bad as having no software at all.

8

EXHIBIT 18.1
(continued)

What Antiviral Software Will Do

Antiviral software can prevent malicious code from being copied to (or from) a server or a workstation. This assumes that the virus has been identified by the antiviral software vendor, who has supplied the current viral pattern update to their customers to enable the software to detect the virus. *The timely delivery and deployment of these pattern files is critical to the success of viral detection* (*Norton Antivirus Solution Implementation Guide* 5-23).

For the workstation, most antiviral software packages will allow a user to schedule an automatic scan of any drive available to the user. This assumes the machine will be on during the scheduled time. When a file is attached to an e-mail message, the software considers it as a movement of that file and can be configured to scan the file. This prevents viruses from being sent from a protected workstation.

Files received at a workstation via e-mail attachment will be scanned when the file is opened (*Norton Antivirus User's Guide* 2-7). That is because the file attachment is copied to a temporary directory on the local machine during the opening process. Therefore, detectable viruses can be stopped by a protected workstation.

Most antiviral software for servers provides protection for file movement only. Files copied (or moved) to or from a server will be scanned. Most servers are designed to provide service twenty-four hours a day. Most antiviral software can be configured to scan the server automatically during slow business hours.

What Antiviral Software Will Not Do

Antiviral software will not protect a server or a workstation from the legal operations of an infected computer. It is not a virus-like activity to delete files or change the contents of files. Therefore an infected computer may execute the malicious code of a virus and do extensive damage to a workstation or server even though they are protected by antiviral software with a current viral pattern file.

Antiviral software will not stop a virus it does not recognize as a virus. The authors of computer viruses know that they will probably have one good chance to destroy their targets. Once the antiviral software vendor has identified the virus, the "inoculation" is made available to their customers. Failure to keep the pattern files current may have devastating consequences even if the virus has been in the wild for some time.

9

Exhibit 18.1

673

EXHIBIT 18.1

(continued)

Vulnerability of the Microsoft Exchange Mail System

If your business is going to be open for an attack by a virus, this is the first place to look. Most virus attacks are delivered through e-mail. Microsoft Exchange lets you communicate with other employees, clients and the world. See Figure 3. This may be great for the business but it is also a point of vulnerability. Microsoft Exchange only deals with communication, not protecting users from virus invasion. Working with Microsoft Exchange is like living in a large city where people come and go from all over the world. Any one of them could be infected with a contagious or possible fatal disease, such as a virus. It is nearly impossible to screen everyone coming in or going out because it would slow down the process of quick communications. This is the same for the Microsoft Exchange Mail System.

Figure 3: Communication Around the World via E-mail
Source: Microsoft Clip Gallery

E-mail Administration

The administrator of Exchange can allow your users to do the following: *send information to and receive information from users in other sites, organizations and systems; store and organize all types of information; share information by using public folders to participate in discussions, post information on a bulletin board, track customer accounts from a shared database, or access product information from a reference library; schedule appointments and group meetings; and track tasks* (*Microsoft Exchange Server 5.5 Documentation* Web Site).

10

EXHIBIT 18.1

(continued)

This is a great advantage to a business because it offers speed and volume to communicate with employees, clients and the world. Even though this is a great advantage, it is also extremely dangerous to a business, since it leaves the business vulnerable to virus attacks. Also with the administration, it may be able to protect the user's privacy but not from virus attacks.

Antiviral Software

The chosen type of antiviral software must be compatible with Microsoft Exchange. Experienced antiviral technicians should deploy the software. This way there will be no problem of anything going wrong and the software not working.

What it will do

The chosen antiviral software will check e-mail for known viral patterns. It can identify and isolate suspicious-looking code in an e-mail or attachments. The software has the ability to eliminate the virus from infected e-mails and files. It can provide continuous protection by scanning for known viruses automatically or at the direction of the software user.

What it will not do

The software cannot recognize new or unknown virus patterns. It will not restrict the transmission of viruses by legal and legitimate computer users. The software cannot do anything for already infected computers.

Vulnerability of Users' Work Habits

The vulnerability of users' work habits is another important issue to be aware of. The users are the ones who actually download the viruses on to computers. Users need to be aware of the types of viruses and how they may be received. Two types that are very common are worms and Trojan horses. *The computer worm is a program that is designed to copy itself from one computer to another, leveraging some network medium: e-mail, TCP/IP, etc.* (Symantec AV Center Web Site). *A Trojan horse is a program that performs some unexpected or unauthorized, usually malicious, actions, such as displaying messages, erasing files or formatting a disk* (TrendMicro Antivirus Glossary Web Site). If users do not know how to keep their computers from being vulnerable, they may receive a virus.

11

Exhibit 18.1

675

EXHIBIT 18.1

(continued)

User Awareness

Users need to know about how viruses may enter the computer system. One way viruses may enter the system is by users opening e-mail or downloading attachments from an unknown person. They also need to know how to use their antiviral software once installed on their computer. Knowing how to be aware is one of the first steps in decreasing the vulnerability to virus attacks. Another way is keeping up with virus updates. One example is looking on the Internet for daily updates about viruses and the solutions on how to get rid of them. There is an example below showing this (Figure 4). Users also need to be aware of letting others use their computer because they may not have the same work habits as themselves.

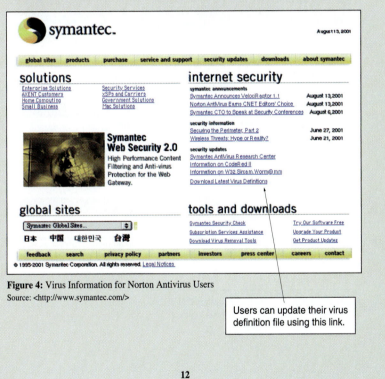

Figure 4: Virus Information for Norton Antivirus Users
Source: <http://www.symantec.com/>

Users can update their virus definition file using this link.

EXHIBIT 18.1

(continued)

MicroTrend's OfficeScan is a sample of the desktop portion of an enterprise level antivirus product. The update pattern file is distributed from a central point from an administrator without the user's interaction. See Figure 5.

> Users may check their Web site to verify that they are using the most current pattern file.

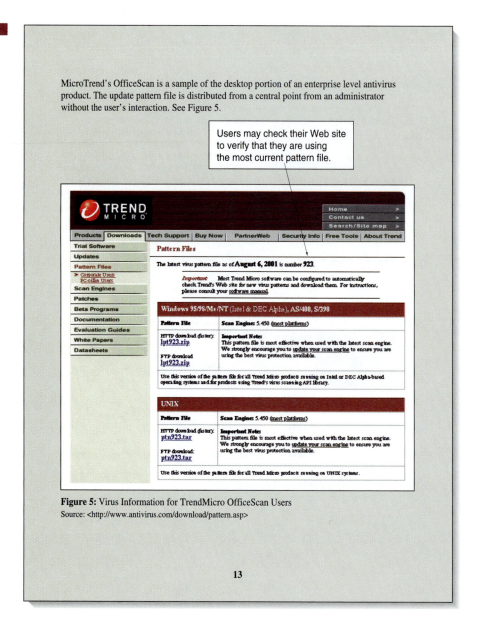

Figure 5: Virus Information for TrendMicro OfficeScan Users
Source: <http://www.antivirus.com/download/pattern.asp>

13

Exhibit 18.1   **677**

EXHIBIT 18.1

(continued)

TrendMicro (as well as most major vendors) provides a virus encyclopedia for users to explore and educate themselves on current viruses. See Figure 6.

These links provide the names of the most active viruses in the "wild." More detailed information is provided when the user drills down via the link.

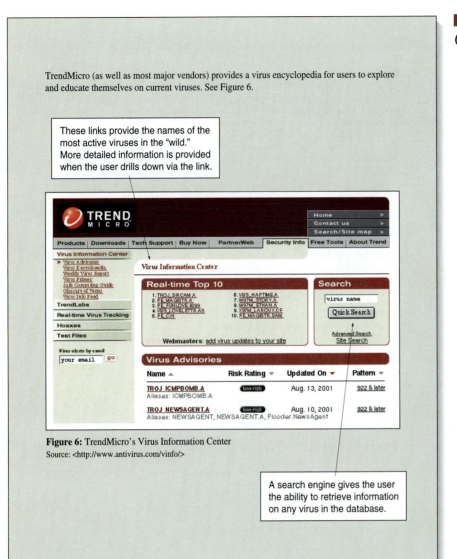

Figure 6: TrendMicro's Virus Information Center
Source: <http://www.antivirus.com/vinfo/>

A search engine gives the user the ability to retrieve information on any virus in the database.

14

EXHIBIT 18.1

(continued)

MS Exchange Personal Folders

Your MS Exchange personal folders are where most viruses can be hidden. Putting e-mails or downloaded attachments into your personal folders are a great way for viruses to get into your computer system. Letting viruses into your personal folders can also let the viruses into other people's computer systems. This may happen by using your address book in your personal folder. If the viruses do get into your address book, They may be sent to everyone in your address book. This can include other employees, clients and other businesses around the world. Being aware of what users allow into their personal folder is one way to prevent virus attacks.

File Housekeeping

With file housekeeping, the user needs to be in the habit of backing up files and keeping them separate from the hard drive. The user needs to keep them in a safe but easily accessible place. Users need to regularly upgrade the antiviral software so that it can keep their files clean of viruses. Users need to remember to protect themselves against new and old viruses. To help maintain a healthy hard drive, they need to scan all e-mails, attachments, floppy disks, and CD-ROMs.

Antiviral Software

The antiviral software needs to be reputable and user friendly. It can be deployed by antiviral technicians but needs to be run by an average user. The software must be written and compatible for the users to use with their computer network.

What it will do

The software will only protect against known viruses. It can scan your e-mail, attachments, disks and files for known viruses. If you suspect a virus, you can contact the antiviral software provider for help on identifying and eliminating the suspected infection.

What it will not do

The antiviral software cannot protect the user against unknown viruses or legal access by other infected computers in the user's network.

15

Exhibit 18.1

679

EXHIBIT 18.1

(continued)

The *conclusion* condenses and focuses the critical information in the report. It differs from the executive summary in not summarizing the report on a section-by-section basis. In some reports, the conclusion is followed by a *recommendations* section.

Conclusion

Microsoft NT Security must be employed effectively. The key concept is "damage control." Start by restricting all users to every network resource and then applying NT security permissions only to users who have a valid need to access the file, directory, or server.

Business Application Deployment must be done properly. They should be deployed with the application on one server and the database on another server. Users should only have access to the application server. A USERID employed by the application alone should have access to the data server.

Antiviral Software for Servers and Workstations must be deployed and configured professionally. It should be of enterprise level caliber. The viral pattern updates should be applied to workstation, servers, and Exchange servers in a timely manner. The preferred method is automated update via the Internet on a daily basis.

The Microsoft Exchange Mail System has become the delivery vehicle of choice for inflicting damage from malicious code. It is the most susceptible element vulnerable for exploitation. Self-propagating viruses (worms) can send malicious code attachments from infected workstations to hundreds of Exchange clients.

Antiviral Software for Exchange must be written specifically for Exchange. It must be able to scan incoming attachments for malicious code. Its configuration is critical to meet the special needs of the company or the product may prove ineffective.

Users must be made aware of vulnerabilities that do exist. They should be informed of their responsibility to safeguard vital business data and should be reminded of their responsibility on a regular basis. Warnings should be issued via e-mail when virus threats are imminent.

Educate the user concerning virus-like activities and the common methods of delivery. The user is the strongest or weakest link in the change of events that must happen to reduce vulnerability to virus attacks.

EXHIBIT 18.1
(continued)

A *glossary* lists, in alphabetical order, words and names used in the report that might be unfamiliar to the reader. A glossary may be followed by a *list of symbols and abbreviations* used in the report. *Appendixes* also follow the glossary.

Glossary

Default (or Default Settings)	Configuration settings provided automatically from an initial installation
Logged On	To validate to an NT Domain with a valid user account
Network Share	A directory available to network users
NT	New Technology
NT Domain	For Windows NT Server, a collection of computers that share a common domain database and security policy
Permission	A rule associated with an object (usually a directory, file, or printer) to regulate which users can have access to the object and in what manner
Shared Resources	Resources such as directories, printers, and ClipBook pages that are available to network users
User Account	Consists of all the information that defines a user to Windows NT
USERID	A unique name identifying a user account to Windows NT
Worm	A self-propagating computer virus

17

Exhibit 18.1

681

EXHIBIT 18.1

(continued)

The *works cited* page gives the citations for all the references made in the report. Citations should be complete enough for readers to verify the information by themselves. An *index* may be included in a very long report. It follows the works cited page and is the last item in the report.

Works Cited

<http://msdn.microsoft.com/workshop/security/antivirus/overview/overview.asp>. *Antivirus Scanner Implementation Considerations.*

<http://www.antivirus.com/corporate/media/2000/pro060a00.htm>. *TrendMicro Announces New Content Security Solution for Microsoft Exchange 2000.*

<http://www.antivirus.com/vinfo/virusencyclo/glossarg.asp>. *Glossary of Virus Terms.*

<http://www.microsoft.com/Exchange/en/55/help/documents/server/xcp01001.htm>. *Microsoft Exchange Server 5.5 Documentation.*

<http://www.symantec.com/avcenter/virus.backgrounder.html>. *Antivirus Research Center—Virus Descriptions.*

Howard, Paul, Janet Sheperdigian, and Lori Oviatt. *Support Fundamentals for Microsoft Windows NT.* Redmond: Microsoft, 1995.

Microsoft Corporation. *Introducing Microsoft Windows 95.* Redmond: Microsoft, 1995.

Microsoft Corporation. *Microsoft Windows NT Server Installation Guide.* Redmond: Microsoft, 1994.

Symantec Corporation. *Norton Antivirus Solution Implementation Guide.* Cupertino: Symantec, 1998.

Symantec Corporation. *Norton Antivirus User's Guide.* Cupertino: Symantec, 1998.

Tompkins, Cindy, Jeff Madden, Susan Greenberg, and Marilyn McGill. *Supporting Microsoft Windows NT Server.* Redmond: Microsoft, 1995.

19

Instructions

Instructions as Technical Prose   683

Elements of Instructions   684

Strategies for Preparing Instructions   689

Testing Your Instructions   698

From the Workplace   698

IN THIS CHAPTER

Instructions inform readers how to assemble, make, create, or otherwise manipulate something. You will find instructions everywhere you look—at college, in the workplace, at home, and even at recreation areas—and they are commonplace in all kinds of media, including film, audio, print, television, online tutorials, kiosks, Web sites, and e-mail. Knowing how to write effective instructions is a major asset for any student or employee.

You will learn about:

- the elements of instructions: writing introductions; discussing theory for certain kinds of instructions; providing lists of materials, tools, or equipment; and creating steps, troubleshooting sections, and warnings
- strategies for preparing instructions, from focusing your topic to producing the instructions
- testing your instructions

> " " Knowing how to write effective instructions is a major asset for any student or employee.

INSTRUCTIONS AS TECHNICAL PROSE

Instructions are among the most common types of document in technical prose. Instructions are different from process descriptions or policies and procedures. Process descriptions tell you how something works. You might read a process description, for instance, on how your VCR works or on how a cellular phone works. Policies concern the standards established by a company or organization, for example those concerning how to train new employees. Procedures concern the ways the policies or standards will be accomplished. In the case of training new employees, procedures would cover the steps necessary to train the employees according to company policy. See Chapter 15 on procedures, processes, and specifications.

As a college student, you've no doubt repeatedly followed instructions to obtain money from an ATM, log onto a computer in a computer lab, or place a parking sticker on the rear bumper or rear window of your car. These and many other simple instructions are a regular part of campus life. As an entry-level employee, you no doubt have received instructions on everything from how to use the photocopier to how to use the network printer.

Instructions are also commonplace outside of college campuses and the workplace. Most taxpayers are familiar with the federal government's instructions for filling out a tax return. Homeowners typically have dozens of appliance manuals filed away for occasional reference concerning appliance maintenance and use; hobbyists constantly are using instructions to further their skills in their particular crafts or activities; and computer enthusiasts continually are consulting printed or online instructions for troubleshooting or for learning new computer skills.

FIGURE 19.1

A Simple Instruction

A note is placed next to a classroom light switch.

PLEASE SHUT
OFF THE LIGHTS
WHEN YOU LEAVE

**JUST-IN-TIME
SOLUTIONS**

I appreciate intuitive software. However, in a pinch a
well-written manual or
online help system can be
worth its weight in gold. I
rely on those sources for the
occasional just-in-time
solution. If I acquire a new
piece of software that I will
need to use frequently or for
important tasks, I will try to
attend a few classes to
master the basics. Following
that, the manual becomes a
reference document.

—Joel Hartman, university chief
information officer, Orlando, Florida

The content and length of instructions vary, of course, depending on the complexity of the subject as well as the purpose, scope, audience, and context. In some cases a sentence or two will be all that is required. For example, a note placed in a classroom that states "Please shut off the lights when you leave" is an instruction. See Figure 19.1.

For complex topics, instructions may occupy several or more volumes. Manuals of many kinds contain instructions and are used at every university, company, and organization. Many are written by professional technical communicators; others are written by subject matter experts, programmers, or engineers. Typical manuals containing instructions or consisting entirely of instructions are software user manuals, assembly manuals, owner's manuals, tutorials, training manuals, safety manuals, installation manuals, and operator manuals. (See Figure 19.2.) These manuals cover a wide range of steps necessary for completing many complex tasks. However, keep in mind that many of the types of action you take in creating short lists of instructions can be generalized to larger lists, too.

Many technical manuals have purposes other than to provide instructions. Various technical manuals such as reference manuals, procedural manuals, and sales manuals often provide readers with information other than instructions and are invaluable resources for many companies and organizations.

ELEMENTS OF INSTRUCTIONS

The most common elements of instructions are an introduction; a theory section; a list of materials, tools, or equipment needed; a discussion of the steps that must be followed to complete the instructions; a section on troubleshooting; and, depending on the topic, warnings. Some instructions may also contain a glossary. Some instructions will need only a few of the elements; others will need all of them. Refer to Exhibit 19.1 (pages 703–715) as you read the next few sections describing the elements typically found in instructions.

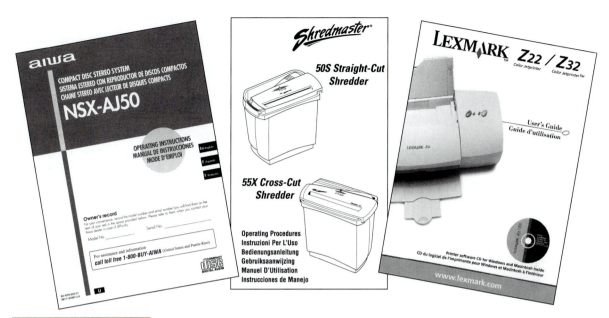

FIGURE 19.2

Longer Sets of Instructions

Manuals such as these give lengthy, and often complex, sets of instructions.

The Introduction

Instructions don't always require an introduction. The title of your instructions often will suffice to tell your readers what your document is about. However, sometimes you will want to provide a paragraph or more providing context or background information, identifying the audience for which the instructions are intended, stating the purpose of your instructions (if it isn't obvious), and identifying the scope or depth of detail. It's also helpful to tell your reader what won't be covered in your instructions.

Sometimes you may also want to set your readers at ease by reviewing the kinds of knowledge and background that are necessary to use the item you are describing, motivate your readers to carry out the tasks in the order provided, tell them how to use the instructions effectively, or comment on the organization of the instructions. If possible, provide an overview of what the instructions cover. (See the introduction in Exhibit 19.1.)

Theory

Sometimes your readers require a discussion of how certain equipment works or perhaps a brief discussion of some other underlying principles concerning the instruction topic. In these instances you may need to provide a theory section. Often your readers will have a better understanding of how to assemble something or how to carry out other kinds of instructions if they have an understanding of the underlying processes that are involved. For example, if you are writing instructions for how to clean a VCR, it would be helpful to discuss briefly how and why the heads of the VCR come into contact with the tape and require regular cleaning.

The theory section of your instructions is like a process description. (See Chapter 15 on procedures, processes, and specifications.) It provides your readers with necessary background or context so that the remainder of the instructions make more sense. If your instructions require someone to repair or to use equipment, you will need to explain how the equipment works and identify the essential parts. A diagram or photograph, with accompanying labels or callouts, can visually depict the various component parts.

List of Materials, Tools, and Equipment

A list of materials or tools and equipment needed is one of the most common elements of many instructions. The list may simply be a one- or two-column listing, or the list may be part of a diagram illustrating all of the materials, tools, or equipment needed (see the "Drawings, Diagrams, and Maps" section in Chapter 9). Be as specific as possible so that your readers will have everything they need to carry out the instructions. (See "What Will You Need to Get Started?" in Exhibit 19.1.) For some instructions, you may also need to tell your audience where they can obtain some of the materials, tools, or equipment. In some cases, certain materials, tools, or equipment may be rare or hard to find.

Steps Involved

The actual steps of the process are another common part of instructions. The steps are the directions for assembling, creating, or using something. For relatively simple instructions, a concise series of steps often suffices. For more complex instructions, you may have to perform a task analysis to determine the actual number of steps involved. See the "Gathering and Interpreting Information" section later in the chapter for a discussion of a task analysis.

Once you have done a detailed task analysis, several strategies are available to help make your instructions useful. The strategies include clearly identifying each step with a number, bullet, icon, or other symbol; giving your readers enough information to do what is required of them; and adequately covering alternative steps readers may perform when necessary.

Keep the steps brief and simple. Each should typically be one or two sentences long. Provide more steps if you find that one part of the instructions is too involved or long. However, you should follow the seven-steps rule of thumb. Keep to seven steps or fewer or, if necessary, break the steps into sublists or separate lists. See the numbered instructions in Exhibit 19.1. Your task analysis should help you to keep your steps manageable. Anticipate in any earlier step what readers may need to know to perform later steps. Many of us have been victimized by instructions that either omit essential steps or put steps in the wrong order. See the "Organizing" section later in the chapter for a discussion of various ways to organize the steps of your instructions.

If you have written many kinds of simple and complex instructions, it's hard not to notice the relationship between design and ease of use. The more effectively and carefully something has been designed, the easier it is for people to use it. This is true of practically everything from ATMs to software programs. (Think, for example, how easy it is to use a browser such as Netscape or Internet Explorer.) If you find yourself writing instructions concerning how to use something that has been poorly designed, your task of providing clear and easy-to-use instructions will be all the more difficult. Still, your goal should be to aim for simplicity. Make your instructions as easy to use as possible. Few people will complain that your instructions were too easy to understand and follow.

> Make your instructions as easy to use as possible. Few people will complain that your instructions were too easy to understand and follow.

Troubleshooting

Many instructions require a troubleshooting section. In this section you tell your readers how to check or retry various tasks if their first efforts are unsuccessful. A thorough troubleshooting section can be one of the most important parts of a set of instructions.

Troubleshooting sections may be organized in different ways. Sometimes they are simply titled "Troubleshooting," and sometimes they are titled "Frequently Asked Questions (FAQs)," although typically FAQs include all sorts of information, not just solutions to problems. Information in FAQs is often provided in a table, chart, or list of bulleted questions followed by answers. Troubleshooting information is usually not numbered, unless you are providing a series of steps for a specific task to help address a problem. In the instructions on woodworking in Exhibit 19.1, the author provides a simple list of three problems and possible solutions. Sometimes a troubleshooting section can be many pages.

Warnings

Provide warnings in your instructions to notify users of the possibility of undesired consequences. Warnings may be an essential part of your instructions, used to help ensure that instructions can be successfully carried out, or they may alert users to ways to prevent damage to equipment or injury or death to themselves or others. Many kinds of instructions are written without any warnings. If no risk of ruining the results, harming the equipment, or injuring users or others is involved, then no warnings are necessary. However, if damage or injury is a possibility, use warnings in your instructions. Figure 19.3 shows examples of the various kinds of warnings.

Warnings are typically classified into three major kinds, depending on their severity: caution, warning, and danger.

FIGURE 19.3

Caution, Warning, and
Danger Signs

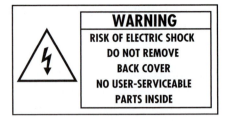

1. *Caution* makes readers aware that they may damage or ruin a project if they do not follow the steps exactly as they are listed. See page 10 of Exhibit 19.1 for an example of a caution notice.
2. *Warning* tells readers that they may damage equipment or tools if they do not follow the instructions exactly. See page 6 of Exhibit 19.1 for an example of a warning.
3. *Danger* warns readers of potential injury or death to themselves or others. See pages 4, 7, and 8 of Exhibit 19.1 for examples of danger notices.

It's important to place safety warnings where they will do the most good. Make sure you place them in the instructions where the reader will see and read them *before* carrying out the potentially risky step or steps. In Exhibit 19.1's woodworking instructions, the author provides one caution concerning careful use of a horsehair brush to keep surfaces clean of debris and foreign objects, and several danger warnings chiefly concerning power tools, combustibles, and chemicals.

Other Elements

Often instructions will contain other sections, for example, a glossary of terms or perhaps a list of additional resources. See, for example, the table containing a glossary of terms in Exhibit 19.1. Of course, for many brief instructions it's best to use straightforward language and to define any terms you use as you use them.

If, however, your instructions contain quite a few technical terms, a glossary will be helpful, even if the audience is familiar with many of the terms you are using. Also, sometimes readers want more information on the topic of the instructions. They appreciate additional resources on the same subject if it's appropriate to include them. Finally, for some complex instructions, appendixes that contain additional supplemental illustrations, for example, may be necessary.

STRATEGIES FOR PREPARING INSTRUCTIONS

Whether you write instructions in college or in the workplace, many of the challenges are the same. You must focus the subject, gather and interpret information, organize, design and illustrate, write and revise, achieve an appropriate prose style, and produce the instructions in an appropriate format for the audience and purpose.

Focusing

As discussed in Chapter 4, focusing is a matter of understanding your audience, narrowing your subject, stating your purpose clearly, and limiting your scope. It's especially important to do all of these well if your instructions are to be effective.

You can't begin to write instructions unless you know the background, level of expertise, interest level, motivations for reading, and other factors concerning your audience. You have many important questions to answer: Are your readers performing the instructions for the first time? Are they technically inclined or complete novices when it comes to using any of the required tools or equipment? Did they request the instructions? Will they enjoy an informal, conversational prose style? Will the readers appreciate your using humor in the instructions?

Completing the remaining steps for focusing—narrowing your subject, stating your purpose clearly, and limiting your scope—depends on answers to these questions and others concerning how and why your audience will be using the instructions.

Gathering and Interpreting Information

You may gather information for instructions in the same way you do for almost any other technical document—from personal knowledge, from interviews, from library and Internet research, from surveys and questionnaires, from focus groups, from experimentation. See Chapter 5 for a more detailed discussion of these and other strategies. Many instructions are written by writers who are thoroughly familiar with the subject from the start, and many instructions are written by writers who must become thoroughly familiar with the subject.

Of course, interpreting information for instructions means in part achieving a thorough understanding of everything involved in making, assembling, or creating the subject of your instructions. And interpreting information for instructions means figuring out how to explain in simple terms everything

FIGURE 19.4
Sample Task Analysis

Task Analysis

Obtaining the Recommended Tools and Equipment

　　Obtain the Recommended Tools.
　　Obtain the Recommended Equipment.

Choosing Suitable Softwood

　　Examining the surface
　　　　Reject boards with excessive scratches, gouges, planer grooves, etc.
　　　　Evaluate the coloring and the grain.
　　　　Match the coloring and grain for the entire lot.
　　Determining if the board is warped
　　　　Check the board from all angles.
　　　　Don't worry about slight curvatures.
　　Determining the density of the wood
　　　　Make sure the density is about the same for all of the wood.
　　　　Reject any pine that is excessively dense.

Cutting and Shaping Softwood

　　Cutting and ripping
　　　　Make crosscuts with a power miter saw or a radial arm saw.
　　　　For the power miter saw, pull the handle down slowly, keeping control of the speed of the travel.
　　　　For the radial arm saw, force the saw to travel across the board at a slow, uniform speed.
　　　　Use the table saw to cut boards lengthwise (ripping).
　　Shaping with routers
　　　　To shape board edges, use a router table with a router mounted underneath.
　　　　Make sure the height is adjusted appropriately for the proper shape.
　　　　Feed the board against the rotation of router bit, keeping a firm grip on the board.
　　　　Keep your fingers clear of the bit.
　　　　Don't feed the board into the router bit at the very end of the board.
　　　　As you feed the board into the router bit, only apply the amount of pressure needed to keep the roller bearing against the wood.

Preparing the Surface

　　If your project is designed to have a rustic look, just leave the knots as they are. If you're going for a more finished look, you'll have to dress them up with wood filler.

your readers will need to know in order to do whatever you're asking them to do. Creating easy-to-use instructions is a challenging exercise in making the unfamiliar familiar. Your skills at interpreting complex information both for yourself and for others will be tested in ways that few other kinds of technical documents test you.

An essential part of gathering and interpreting information for instructions is a task analysis. (See Figure 19.4.) In a task analysis you identify all of

FIGURE 19.4

(continued)

Filling Cracks and Knots
  Use wood filler to fill cracks and openings in knots.
  Use a 180-grit sanding disk with an orbital sander to remove the excess wood filler
  after it is completely dried.
Sanding
  Use a 180-grit sanding disk with an orbital sander to remove planer grooves, scratches,
  and dents.
  Use a 220-grit sanding disk with an orbital sander for the final surface preparation.

Finishing

Staining
  Using disposable staining gloves, apply the appropriate stain with a cotton wiping cloth
  to your pine project.
  Wipe the stain off completely, paying close attention to remove any fingerprints.
  Allow the stain to dry completely.
Waxing
  Allow the wax to warm to approximately 80 degrees.
  Apply with a clean cotton cloth keeping your strokes in the direction of the grain of
  wood.
  Work the wax into the wood until streaks cannot be seen.
  Allow the wax to dry completely.
  Hand buff the wax with a clean cotton cloth until the surface is not dull.

Wrapping Up
  Apply a polyurethane finish or wax finish.
  Apply multiple coats.

Troubleshooting

the steps your readers must perform to carry out your instructions. Then you
take each major step or task and break it down into smaller steps until all
parts are covered. The major task may already be a relatively simple one, in
which case your task analysis would not involve many substeps. Complex instructions will require a much more thorough task analysis. You must identify
all the major tasks that are involved in the complex set of instructions; then
you must break each major task down into smaller tasks. Each of the smaller

FIGURE 19.5

Instructions—Fixed Order of Steps

The steps for installing the computer drive must be performed in the order in which they are given. Numbering the steps reminds the reader of the correct order.

SOURCE: From *Dell Dimension XPS M166s and XPS M200s Systems Reference Guide.* Dell Computer Corporation, 1996. 5–2.

Before Installing Your Drive

Before you install a new drive, there are several preparatory steps you must complete:

1. **Remove the computer cover according to the instructions in "Removing the Computer Cover" in Chapter 3.**

2. **Remove the front bezel and the front-panel insert covering the drive bay you plan to use.**

   Empty drive bays contain a front-panel insert to protect the inside of the computer from foreign particles.

   NOTE: Whenever you remove drive, be sure to replace the front-panel insert in the empty bay.

   See "Removing and Replacing the Bezel" and "Removing and Replacing Front-Panel Inserts," found later in this section, for more information.

3. **If you are installing a drive in the drive cage, remove the drive cage from the chassis.**

   See "Removing and Replacing the Drive Cage," found later in this section.

4. **Configure the drive.**

   See "Configuring Your Drive," found later in this section.

5. **Determine the type of cables you will need to connect to your drive during the installation procedure.**

   See "Connecting Your Drive," found later in this section.

tasks may need further refinement until all the actions have been broken down into their component steps.

Organizing

There are many ways to organize instructions, and much depends on the complexity of the instructions you are creating. As mentioned earlier, you typically begin instructions with an introduction, a theory section if appropriate, and a list of materials and tools or equipment. The real challenge begins when you consider the various ways you can order the steps involved in the instructions. You have three basic orders to choose from—a fixed order, a variable order, and an alternative order.

A fixed order of steps means that the steps must be performed in the order in which they are discussed. (Figure 19.5 shows a set of instructions where the order of the steps is fixed.) A numbered list indicating the precise sequence is the best choice for this situation. See the "Text Lists" section in Chapter 8 for reference.

A variable order of steps means that the steps may be performed in different sequences. A bulleted list is often helpful for indicating this kind of order. Figure 19.6 shows a set of instructions where the order of the steps is variable.

Sometimes an alternative order of steps is useful. For example, if one kind of condition exists, the reader may follow one order; if a different condition

FIGURE 19.6

Instructions—Variable Order of Steps

The steps "Delete Unnecessary Files," "Run ScanDisk," and "Defragment Your Hard Drive" can be performed in any order. Also the bulleted steps under "Delete Unnecessary Files" can be performed in any order.

To keep your computer running at optimum performance, you need to perform these maintenance tasks at least once a month.

- Delete Unnecessary Files

    Your computer probably has numerous files that are not being used and will never be used again. If your hard drive space becomes limited, performance will suffer.

    - **Delete Internet Files**—While exploring the Internet, you will keep copies on your computer of much of the content you view. This automatic feature provided by your browser allows you to navigate from page to page more quickly. The files accumulate on your hard drive and take up precious disk space. Open Windows Explorer by selecting **Start/Programs/Windows Explorer**. Open the directory labeled "Windows" and scroll down to the directory named "Temporary Internet Files." Select all the files and press "delete" on the keyboard, sending them to the Recycle Bin.

    - **Delete Temporary Program Files**—If you download programs from the Internet, you normally download one file that expands into several files once run. After this is done, the file becomes worthless (unless you want to install the program again later) and takes up disk space. You must keep track of what directory you download files to. Create a directory called "Download Temp" and store them there. Locate your downloaded programs and send them to the Recycle Bin (see Internet Files).

    - **Delete Programs You Do Not Use**—Often you will install a program or a game, run it a couple of times, and then forget it and never use it again. If you still need to free hard drive space, uninstall programs you no longer use. To uninstall a program, select **Start/Settings/Control Panel** and then double click the icon labeled "Add/Remove Programs." Select any programs you do not use and press "Add/Remove." This should uninstall the program from your computer. If you are uncertain if you use a program, **do not uninstall it**.

    - **Empty the Recycle Bin**—You are probably already familiar with the Recycle Bin. Once you delete most files, they are kept in the Recycle Bin and still occupy hard drive space and resources. Open the Recycle Bin by double clicking the icon on the desktop (the desktop is your computer's main screen). Make sure that there are no files you need in the Recycle Bin and then select **File/Empty Recycle Bin**.

- Run ScanDisk

Open the **System Tools** menu and select **Scan Disk**. Your hard disk will have errors on it if normal program operation does not occur (such as a power outage, a system crash, or not properly shutting down your computer). Choose to scan each of your hard drives. Select

FIGURE 19.6

(continued)

"Thorough" as the type of test and check the box next to "Automatically fix errors." Press the start button to begin the scan. It will take a few minutes so you may check on it later.

NOTE: Make sure you close any running programs before running ScanDisk.

• Defragment Your Hard Drive

Open the **System Tools** menu and select **Disk Defragmenter**. Normal use of your computer will c cause your hard drive to become fragmented. When you use your computer, Windows will move files around to make them easier to access. Eventually, performance will suffer. You should "defrag" your hard drive regularly. Choose to scan each of your hard drives. Select "Thorough" as the type of test and check the box next to "Automatically fix errors." Press the start button to begin the scan. It will take a few minutes so you may check on it later.

exists, the reader should follow a different order. Figure 19.7 shows a set of instructions with alternative sets of steps.

Finally, a series of substeps is often necessary for complex instructions. Sometimes you have to take one major step and break it down into smaller substeps, particularly if the number of steps in a particular sequence exceeds seven or so. Indicate substeps either by indenting further or by creating a substep sequence of a, b, c, and so on. For example, in Exhibit 19.1, the author groups the steps into categories: "Choosing Suitable Softwood," "Cutting and Shaping Softwoods," "Preparing the Surface," "Finishing," and "Wrapping Up."

FIGURE 19.7

Instructions—Alternative Order of Steps

Alternative steps give different ways of accomplishing the same operation.

SOURCE: *Dell Dimension XPS M166s and XPS M200s Systems Reference Guide.* Dell Computer Corporation, 1996. 2-1.

Entering the System Setup Program

Enter the system setup program as follows:

1. Turn on (or reboot) your system.

2. When prompted, press <Del> *immediately* **to enter the system setup program.**

If you wait too long and the operating system begins to load into memory, *let the system complete the load operation.* Then shut down the system and repeat steps 1 and 2.

An alternate way of entering the system setup program when the system is already running is to reboot using the <Ctrl><Alt><Del> key combination, holding down the <Del> key until the system setup program screen appears.

NOTE: To ensure an orderly system shutdown, consult the documentation that accompanied your operating system.

You can also enter the system setup program by responding to certain error messages.

Designing and Illustrating

Use visual aids wherever possible in instructions. Visual aids include a combination of well-chosen design elements as well as effective illustrations. Together, these elements of design and illustration help readers grasp a concept, a step, or a context much more quickly.

Designing and Illustrating Instructions

- Provide only illustrations that are essential to the instructions. Determining which illustrations are essential depends on your audience, subject, purpose, scope, and context. For novice readers, providing illustrations of the necessary materials, tools, or equipment can be very helpful.

- If possible, provide an illustration for each major step.

- Provide a drawing or photograph of the final assembled product to give readers a good idea of what they are trying to achieve.

- As you write a draft of your instructions, think visually. Continually ask yourself if an illustration would help further clarify the point you are making in the prose. If so, make every effort to provide an illustration.

- Take care that you do not provide too many illustrations or you may find yourself facing an overwhelming task. Creating illustrations can be quite time-consuming and expensive, depending on the kinds of illustrations you are considering.

- Give your reader as many methods for locating information as possible. For example, in addition to a table of contents and an index, include section contents pages, tabs, different colors or icons to highlight each section, headers and footers, a glossary, a sectional page numbering system, and numerous heads and subheads.

- Consider carefully the kind of illustration that will be most helpful to your readers. For example, select a table, a list, a drawing, or a photograph, depending on which will best demonstrate the particular concept, step, or point. See Chapter 9 for a more detailed discussion of the appropriateness of various kinds of illustrations.

- Whenever possible, place illustrations on the same page or on the facing page near the text to which they relate. Your readers will appreciate being able to read about a particular step and at the same time see an illustration showing part of the step or the result of performing the step.

- Carefully integrate illustrations into your instructions and edit them for consistency in their use, placement, numbering, and labeling.

- Be sure that all illustrations are sized large enough to be read easily.

- Use at most two or three complementary typefaces, and use them to differentiate body text from headings.

(continued)

● Use different type styles (for example, bold, italic, condensed, outline) judiciously, and clearly signal to the reader that each type represents a particular kind of information. For example, italics may be used to present only captions or words that are defined in a glossary.

Writing and Revising

Some people may think that writing the steps of instructions is the most difficult part. After all, you may have many ways to organize that discussion, and it can be difficult to choose the best order. It can be even more difficult to be clear and concise in your discussion of every step. However, all the sections of instructions present their own challenges, and all can be difficult to write well. Review "Elements of Instructions" from earlier in the chapter for the many possible strategies you can employ in just the introduction, and you'll realize that writing even just the introduction can be time-consuming.

Using these elements as a guide, perhaps the best approach is to write a quick draft covering all of the essential points you want to cover in the various sections of your instructions. (See Figure 19.8.) While writing the rough draft, focus on writing down the key points (you can expand on them later) and covering the steps in the order that you have determined, at least for now, is the best one. As you write, note where an illustration may be necessary or

FIGURE 19.8

The Process of Creating a Quick Draft

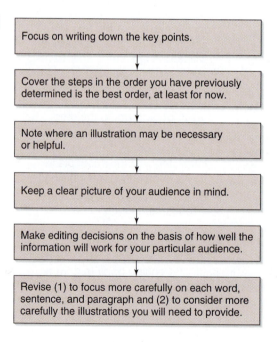

Focus on writing down the key points.

Cover the steps in the order you have previously determined is the best order, at least for now.

Note where an illustration may be necessary or helpful.

Keep a clear picture of your audience in mind.

Make editing decisions on the basis of how well the information will work for your particular audience.

Revise (1) to focus more carefully on each word, sentence, and paragraph and (2) to consider more carefully the illustrations you will need to provide.

helpful. Always keep a clear picture of your audience in mind, and make editing decisions on the basis of how well the information will work for your particular audience. For example, you may choose to delete a complex description—even one that is well done—because it is beyond the scope of your audience's needs and interests. When you revise, you can focus more carefully on each word, sentence, and paragraph, and you can more carefully consider the illustrations you will need to provide.

Using an Appropriate Prose Style

The formality of your prose depends on your audience, subject, and purpose. Many technical instructions are formal, but many are not. Keep the prose style informal in instructions whenever possible. For instructions aimed at homeowners, novice hobbyists, and other kinds of first-time users, an informal style can help the readers to relax and feel less intimidated. See the "Using an Appropriate Prose Style" section in Chapter 17 for a detailed discussion of the many strategies you can use to make your prose style effective in your instructions. A few other issues to consider concerning the style of your instructions are the imperative mood, a telegraphic style, tone, consistency, and terminology. See Chapter 7 and Chapter 10 for more information on these style issues.

Prose Style in Instructions

- Use the imperative mood (the command form of the verb) in the steps of the instructions. Each step should have no more than one imperative. Many of the steps will consist of brief sentences that tell your readers what to do: *To check for viruses on a disk in the A: drive, first place the disk in the drive. Second, open your antivirus program. Third, find the A: drive icon on the dialog screen.*

- Avoid a telegraphic prose style. The need for brevity in instructions sometimes leads writers to omit articles (*a, an, the*), conjunctions (*and, but, or*), and prepositions (*to, of*), creating a style that reads like a telegram: *Boot up computer. Turn on monitor. Click on "Start."* This style can easily become annoying and distracting.

- Provide a reader-friendly tone. A friendly tone, like an informal style, can help your readers to relax and feel less intimidated.

- Strive for consistency in your prose style. For example, do not refer sometimes to a "manual" and other times to a "guide" when you are talking about the same document. Choose one term and stick with it.

- Define terms within the context of a sentence or paragraph if possible. Also consider including a glossary of key terms in your front or back matter.

From the workplace

Rob Williams

Software Development Manager
Siemens ICN
Lake Mary, Florida

Rob has a few clearly defined goals for the progress of his career: get a job, get a better job, continue to improve his career progress, and retire at a relatively early age. So far he seems to be on track with that plan. In his present job, he manages a team that develops and documents software. Communicating with each other and with their customers is an important feature of the team's work.

I have a bachelor of science degree in computer science. My first job was as an entry-level programmer for Harris Corporation. I took customer requirements and made software modifications to an existing minicomputer to implement the functionality.

I obtained that first job through the school placement service. Every job after that one I obtained utilizing the services of a job recruiter ("headhunter") who was compensated by the company that hired me. In my industry, it's easier to advance or obtain desired experience by switching companies ("job hopping") than by staying in the same company.

I expect to continue do what I'm doing now until I reach retirement, which should still be at what I consider a young age (50 years). If I am successful in being financially "set" at that age, I intend to indulge myself—spending more time with my kids (Little League baseball coach?), doing once-in-a-lifetime activities (climb Mount Everest?), and perhaps tackling an entirely new field within my industry, such as 3D graphics.

I supervise a team of 11 engineers. I have supervised teams as small as 6 and as large as 29. My company has very technically advanced capabilities, including state-of-the-art "group development" software, state-of-the-art PCs, high-speed LAN connections, Internet connections, and video conferencing. One disadvantage, though, is that we have two large development staffs at diverse locations, one in Lake Mary, Florida, and the other in Boca Raton, Florida.

Producing the Instructions

When making production decisions, always consider how your readers will be using your instructions. For example, a binding that allows the instructions to be folded over would be best for instructions that readers may want to use while performing tasks. Laminated pages may be best for brief instructions that may be used frequently in an environment where the pages may easily become soiled. Tabs might be helpful if your instructions are complex and contain many sections.

TESTING YOUR INSTRUCTIONS

One of the most valuable things you can do is to test your instructions on the intended audience. If the intended audience isn't available, then test your instructions on other members of your class or other employees in your office. (See Chapter 10 for a more detailed discussion of the testing process.)

Make certain your instructions are complete. Don't omit an essential tool, part, step, illustration, warning, or helpful troubleshooting explanation. If

The most effective way for engineers to work would be to be co-located on the same site and for the smallest team possible to take full responsibility for the implementation of a given feature. The practicalities of a large company such as the one for which I work do not always allow this, but it's the ideal way to manage a project.

Technical writers are formally part of the development team for each feature. They are free to contribute to the design, and they are included in feature team meeting notices and document reviews, but in actual practice their role is primarily one of receiving information. Most of their input into the feature development is in the form of ensuring the customer perception of the product (that is, the user interface) is consistent.

The members of the software development community are responsible for producing their own documents. The company provides a strong base of training in this regard, including video tapes, electronically accessible work instructions, computer-based training (CBT), and, of course, on-the-job training through peers.

Many people don't realize that it's easy, in a written communication where the reader cannot provide feedback or acknowledgment, to confuse the reader by omitting information or being ambiguous. It's also easy for the reader take the wrong tone of the message. For example, an innocent query can be interpreted as an accusation.

Insider Advice

Get industry-relevant experience and be prepared to change jobs a few times. You must be willing to relocate. Look to see what types of expertise pull in the highest salaries, then go get that expertise.

The tried-and-true method of career advancement in my industry is to: First, get a job; second, get a better job; third, get an even better job; repeat as necessary. The crucial ingredient is to acquire industry-relevant expertise within a job so that other companies will value your skills. Engineers are in very short supply, and engineers with industry-relevant expertise can "write their own ticket"—perhaps a ticket like "do non-physical work from 8 to 5 in an air-conditioned environment for way too much money in low cost-of-living Florida next to Disney World."

possible, have someone unfamiliar with your instructions follow them. Note where steps seem unclear or confusing and revise the directions accordingly.

CHECKING WHAT YOU'VE LEARNED

The Introduction

Does the introduction tell readers the things they want to know or would find useful to know about the following topics? (Note: Some of the last few items may not be included in every introduction.)

- Subject of the instructions?
- Purpose of the instructions?
- Scope of the instructions?
- Intended audience for the instructions?
- Organization of the instructions?
- Ways to use the instructions effectively?
- Conventions (for example, indicators for notes, directory and file names, computer program names)?

- Persuasion (motivation for the readers to read the instructions)?
- Safety (may or may not appear in the introduction)?

Theory

- Is a theory section provided? If so, does it provide a good and clear overview of the important underlying principles involved to help the reader understand the instructions?
- If a theory section isn't provided, should one be? And, if so, what should it discuss?

List of Materials, Tools, or Equipment

- If the instructions concern the operation or repair of complex equipment, have the readers been told anything they would find useful to know about the location and function of the equipment's key parts?
- Have the readers been told about any materials and equipment they should gather before starting the procedure? Is the list complete?

Steps Involved

- Are the steps easy to understand and follow?
- Are the steps provided in the best order?
- Are notes or tips provided? If not, could some be provided?

Troubleshooting

- Have readers been told how to overcome any problems they are likely to encounter?
- Are troubleshooting tips provided throughout or toward the end of the instructions?

Warnings

- Are any safety warnings needed to protect the readers from harm? Are they provided, and, if so, are they effective?
- Are different kinds of warnings—caution, warning, danger—provided, and, if so, are they used properly?

Other Elements

- Is a glossary provided, and, if so, does it define all the necessary terms clearly?
- If a glossary isn't provided, would a glossary be helpful?

Design and Illustrations

- Are the pages effectively designed (good margins, fonts, line spacing, spacing between elements on the page, and so on.)? If not, what can you do to improve the design?
- Do the instructions use at least one level of heading throughout?
- Would headers, footers, or rules help the design?
- If notes or tips are provided, would they be more effective in text boxes?
- Is at least one effective illustration included?
- Are all illustrations appropriately placed, displayed, and labeled?
- Are any illustrations too large, too small, or difficult to read?
- Should you add additional illustrations or improve upon any of the existing illustrations?

Style and Mechanics

- Are all technical terms clearly defined?
- Are plain words used over fancy ones?
- Are the sentences appropriately simplified?
- Are the sentence length and structure varied?
- Are the paragraphs appropriately short, so that they can be read and easily understood?
- Overall, is the prose completely clear to a novice audience?
- Do the instructions avoid errors in grammar, abbreviations, numbers, punctuation, spelling, and capitalization?

EXERCISES

 REVIEW

1. Review the sample student instructions in Exhibit 19.1. Create a list of the ways the introduction in the instructions effectively fulfills the requirements of a good introduction.
2. Review the design choices and the illustrations used in Exhibit 19.1. Make a list of the effectiveness of the design choices and of the illustrations. If you think there are any weaknesses, make a list of these, too.
3. After reviewing Exhibit 19.1, create a list of what you consider to be the major strengths of the in-

structions. Justify each of your choices with a brief sentence or two.
4. Find a set of printed instructions in your house, apartment, garage, or car glove compartment. Bring the instructions to class and be prepared to discuss the strengths and weaknesses of the instructions with the class.
5. Review the instructions intended for homeowners in Exhibit 19.2 (pages 716–719) on installing a ceiling fan. Discuss the weaknesses of the instructions based on what you have read in the chapter. Make a list of the improvements you would make to these instructions.

THE INTERNET

The Internet is a great resource for instructions of many kinds. Search for a set of instructions on the Internet (for example, how to use a cell phone, how to shop for a used or new car, how to install a surround-sound theater system in your home). Make a list of the strengths and weaknesses of the instructions based on the elements covered in this chapter. Be prepared to discuss your list with the rest of the class.

 ETHICS/PROFESSIONALISM

Many instructions provide excellent warning labels (caution, warning, or danger) in the most appropriate places in the instructions. Provide a brief paragraph or create a list of the ethical issues you perceive when a company deliberately creates instructions in which essential warnings are either omitted or placed ineffectively in instructions.

 COLLABORATION

Working in groups of two or more students, create a simple set of instructions (a simple list of numbered steps will do) for one of the following: inserting a graphic into a Word document, creating a simple macro in Word, using the comments feature in Word, or using the track changes feature in Word. After your group is satisfied with the sequence of the steps, exchange your group's brief sample instructions with those from another group. While the other group is using Word on a PC to test your instructions, your group should take notes on anything members of the group testing your instructions comment on. Use the comments to improve your group's instructions. Then your group should test the instructions of the other group. Be prepared to discuss with the class anything your simple usability test revealed.

 INTERNATIONAL COMMUNICATION

Translating instructions can present special challenges whether the instructions concern installing new software or hardware on your computer or concern how to use, clean, and maintain a new appliance for your kitchen or a tool or a machine stored in your garage. Many instruction booklets for household appliances, watches, and so on come with instructions in English, Spanish, and French, for example. Find an example of instructions in one document in which the instructions are provided in two or more languages. Make a list of any design differences for the different translations, if there are any, and discuss why you think the designs are different.

RESOURCES

Pearsall, Thomas E. *The Elements of Technical Writing.* 2nd ed. Boston: Allyn and Bacon, 2001.

Pfeiffer, William S. *Pocket Guide to Technical Writing.* Upper Saddle River: Prentice Hall, 1998.

Exhibit 19.1

703

EXHIBIT 19.1

**Sample Instructions—
How to Use Softwood in
Woodworking**

SOURCE: Russell N. Jarvis. Printed by
permission of author.

How to Use Softwood
in Woodworking

by Russell N. Jarvis

EXHIBIT 19.1

(continued)

Introduction

Why Use Softwood in Crafts?

Softwood is quickly becoming the wood of choice for most novice woodworkers. It is easy to use and inexpensive. If you have ever worked with wood before, you know just how expensive hardwoods such as oak and maple have become. The necessity of conserving our natural resources and protecting our environment requires all of us to become more creative. So if you're interested in saving a few hardwood trees (and a few dollars!), here are some useful tips on how to use softer woods such as pine to create very attractive works of art.

The scope of these instructions will not differentiate among the many types of softwoods available to the woodworker. Instead, it is assumed that the reader will use the most available type of softwood, pine. Since there are many different types of pine, it will also be assumed that you will only have the worst type of pine available at your local lumberyard, yellow and sappy pine.

The novice woodworker will find this information especially useful since mistakes can not only cost money; they can be very dangerous. Easy-to-follow instructions for using softwoods are provided in four sections:

1. **Choosing Suitable Softwood**
2. **Cutting and Shaping Softwood**
3. **Preparing the Surface**
4. **Finishing**

Each section is self-contained and can be used without reading the previous sections. The material is presented in a logical order to coincide with the steps required to complete an actual wood project. The instructions, however, are designed to be generic in nature and applicable to any type of project you are undertaking whether it be a small shelf or a home entertainment center.

Exhibit 19.1 | **705**

EXHIBIT 19.1

(continued)

Figure 1. Sample pine shelf

What Will You Need to Get Started?

If you are starting from scratch as a woodworker, the following list of tools is recommended. This list is by no means all-inclusive, and your particular project will determine whether they are even required. If you are like most beginning crafters, this list will look more like a wish list for Christmas.

Recommended Tools

Tools

Formica tabletop	Radial arm saw
Router with shaping bits	Table saw
Eye protection	Band saw
Orbital sander	Scrolling saw
Horsehair brush	Drill press
Measuring tape	Air compressor
Carpenter square	Pneumatic brad nailer
Power miter saw	

Figure 2. Sample tools

3

EXHIBIT 19.1

(continued)

I strongly recommend the first item on this list, a Formica tabletop. It may be the most critical item for working with softwoods. Softwoods are especially susceptible to marring and scratching. A very smooth tabletop is best suited to prevent damage during sanding and shaping. These tabletops are easy to clean and maintain. If you get too much glue or dings on the tabletop, just rub it down with mineral spirits, let it dry, and sand it smooth!

> **Danger:** *Use every power tool in accordance with its user's manual to prevent personal injury.*

Recommended Materials

Supplies

Sandpaper (180, 220, 400 grit)
Tacky cloth
Stain
Wood finishing wax
Mineral spirits
Cotton wipe cloth
Disposable staining gloves
Soft lead pencils
Various size brads for nailer
Wood glue
Wood filler

Figure 3. Sample materials

You may need to add to this list depending on your project. You may find that you will not need many things suggested here, but I highly recommend that you invest a small amount of money into protecting your personal health and buy disposable staining gloves. Constant exposure to chemicals can produce toxic buildup in your body.

> **Danger:** *Use all combustibles and chemicals in accordance with the directions on their labels.*

4

Exhibit 19.1

707

EXHIBIT 19.1

(continued)

Getting Started . . .

Choosing Suitable Softwood

Selecting a good piece of wood is very important. There is no doubt that a gifted seamstress can make a "silk purse out of a sow's ear." But an experienced seamstress would be the first to tell you that it is easier to make a silk purse out of a piece of silk. So make it easy on yourself and take the time to select the best wood from the available stock.

Examine the Surface	*Tricks of the Trade*
1. Reject boards with excessive scratches, gouges, planer grooves, etc.	*If a scratch is deeper than the width of a normal paper clip wire, reject it. Though pine is easily sanded, it would not be cost effective to repair such a board.*
2. Evaluate the coloring and grain. Try to match the coloring and grain for the entire lot for a complete project.	*Usually a shipment of lumber is fairly uniform in grain, color, and density. However, shipments become mixed in the lumberyard. Take the time to select enough uniform wood for an entire project at one time.*
3. Reject boards with excessive number of knots, especially along the edges.	*Pine is susceptible to fracturing at knots when shaped by a router.*

Is the Board Warped?	*Tricks of the Trade*
1. Check the board from all angles. Remember that every board has six sides!	

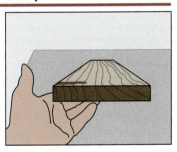

Figure 4. *Sample pine board*

5

EXHIBIT 19.1

(continued)

2. Slight curvatures in long boards may be acceptable if you plan to cut the board into smaller pieces.

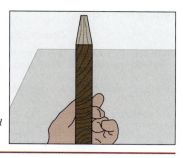

Figure 5. *Sample pine board*

Does the Pine Have Uniform Density?	*Tricks of the Trade*
1. Make sure the density is about the same for all the pine required for a complete project.	*This promotes uniform stain absorption.*
2. Reject any pine that is excessively dense.	*This indicates that a high quantity of sap is present in the wood.*

Cutting and Shaping Softwoods

Keeping blades and router bits clean and sharp is critical in making pine look good. Pine can have a relatively high sap content in comparison to hardwoods. Sap buildup on cutting edges can blunt the sharpest carbon-tipped edge and cause excessive drag on your power tools.

A cotton cloth saturated with mineral spirits will do the job nicely. Use extreme caution when cleaning power tool cutting edges.   Clean, sharp cutting edges will give you smooth cuts without burn marks.

> **Warning:** *Clean and inspect power tools frequently to keep them working properly.*

6

Exhibit 19.1

709

EXHIBIT 19.1

(continued)

> **Danger:** *Always unplug power tools*
> *before cleaning their cutting edges.*

Cutting and Ripping	*Tricks of the Trade*

1. Crosscuts (cutting against the grain) are best made with a power miter saw or a radial arm saw. This will guarantee a perfect 90-degree cut.

Figure 6. *Miter saw*

2. For the power miter saw, pull the handle down slowly, keeping control of the speed of travel.

When a circular blade encounters a section of wood denser than usual, the blade will grab the wood, pulling it into the direction of the rotating blade. This can bind the saw and produce a ragged cut.

3. For the radial arm saw, force the saw to travel across the board at a slow, uniform speed.

The radial arm saw is even more susceptible to grabbing the wood than the miter saw. Be prepared for sudden jerks.

4. Cutting boards lengthwise (ripping) is best done on a table saw. Always keep the wood flush against the guide and watch for dense areas such as knots.

"Kickback" can occur using any power saw. The table saw is notorious for grabbing a board suddenly and kicking it back at you during ripping.

7

EXHIBIT 19.1

(continued)

> **Danger:** *The following set of instructions deals with shaping softwood boards with a router. The cutting edge of a router bit is invisible when rotating. Keep your fingers clear of the cutting edge. Do not grip the board in a way in which your hand would enter the path of the router bit should you slip.*

Shaping with Routers	*Tricks of the Trade*

1. To shape board edges, use a router table with a router mounted underneath as shown in Figure 7.

    Always feed the wood in the direction of router bit rotation. Don't apply excessive pressure to keep the board against the bit.

2. Make sure height is adjusted appropriately for the proper shape.

    Unplug the router while making height adjustments. Check to make sure the bit is not loose. Make sure the bearing moves freely. If needed, clean with mineral spirits.

3. Feed the board against the rotation of router bit keeping a firm grip on the board. Keep your fingers clear of the bit.

This router bit has sap buildup. It could leave burn marks.

Figure 7. Router bit and table

3. Don't feed the board into the router bit at the very end of the board. Pine is susceptible to splintering when this is done.

Feed the board slowly into the router bit starting here. Move the wood carefully to the right until you reach the end. Then continue feeding the board to the left as indicated by the arrow.

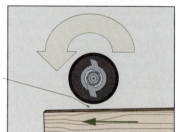

Figure 8. Router bit and table

Exhibit 19.1

711

EXHIBIT 19.1

(continued)

4. As you feed the board into the router bit, apply only the amount of pressure needed to keep the roller bearing against the wood.

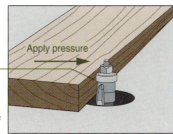

Apply pressure

This roller bearing will leave a groove on the edge of the wood if too much pressure is applied.

Figure 9. Router bit and table

Preparing the Surface

Pine will often have a variety of knots on a visible surface of a project. If you must have a clear surface without knots, be prepared to pay top dollar for your wood.

If your project is designed to have a rustic look, just leave the knots as they are. If you're going for a more finished look, you'll have to dress them up with wood filler.

Filling Cracks and Knots	*Tricks of the Trade*
1. Use wood filler to fill cracks and openings in knots.	*If the crack is wider than 1/8th inch, use two applications. Apply the filler exactly where it is needed only. Spreading filler to surrounding areas will cause uneven stain absorption.*
2. Use a 180-grit sanding disk with an orbital sander to remove the excess wood filler after it is completely dried.	*Follow the specific directions supplied by the manufacturer of the wood filler and always allow the proper amount of time to dry.*

EXHIBIT 19.1

(continued)

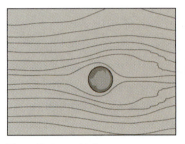

Figure 10. Acceptable knot

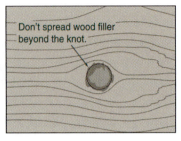

Figure 11. Application of filler

Sanding	*Tricks of the Trade*
1. Use a 180-grit sanding disk with an orbital sander to remove planer grooves, scratches, and dents.	*Check your sanding disks often, especially when working with dense pine. The disk can become caked with sap, and the friction heat can make the sap glaze on the surface, causing uneven stain absorption.*
2. Use a 220-grit sanding disk with an orbital sander for the final surface preparation. (A 400-grit sandpaper can be used for a third sanding if desired.)	*The surface will appear smooth after using the 180–grit sandpaper, but the wood fibers will absorb too much stain and the finish will feel rough to the touch.*

Caution: *Use a horsehair brush to keep all surfaces clean of debris and foreign objects. The Formica tabletop should be completely clean and smooth. Each board should be brushed off thoroughly before and after sanding.*

10

Exhibit 19.1

713

EXHIBIT 19.1

(continued)

Figure 12. Sanding with an orbital sander

Finishing

Staining	Tricks of the Trade
1. Using disposable staining gloves, apply the appropriate stain with a cotton wiping cloth to your pine project.	*This should be done in a well-ventilated place.*
2. Wipe the stain off completely, paying close attention to remove any fingerprints.	*Have a place prepared to place the project where it can remain clean and dust free.*
3. Allow the stain to dry completely. Consult the directions for the stain for drying times.	*Be patient.*

Waxing	Tricks of the Trade
1. Allow the wax to warm to approximately 80 degrees.	*Set the can of wax out in the sun for about an hour. It will go on smoothly and evenly when warm.*

11

EXHIBIT 19.1

(continued)

2. Apply with a clean cotton cloth, keeping your strokes in the direction of the grain of the wood.

Watch for uneven streaks of wax. This wax will harden when it dries. You will not be able to buff out a stubborn streak of wax.

3. Work the wax into the wood until streaks cannot be seen.

Be diligent.

4 Allow the wax to dry completely. Consult the directions for the wax for drying times.

Be careful handling the waxed surfaces. You can leave fingerprints in the wax and you will have a difficult time buffing them out.

5. Hand buff the wax with a clean cotton cloth until the surface is not dull.

Rub the surface as hard as you can without causing damage by breaking fragile parts.

Wrapping Up

You may wish to apply a polyurethane finish to your project, but I highly recommend you try the wax. A professional-looking job with polyurethane requires multiple coats with a high-quality sprayer. After you see and feel a hand-rubbed finish, you will be impressed.

Figure 12. Sample triangular corner shelves

12

Exhibit 19.1

715

EXHIBIT 19.1

(continued)

Troubleshooting

Problem: "There are too many knots in this pine."
Solution: You bought the wrong piece of wood.

Problem: "I did all this work, and my kid put a big scratch in it."
Solution: Rub a little stain on it. Rub it out completely. Wax it. Buff it. Tell your friends the antique look is no extra charge.

Problem: "I paid thousands of dollars buying everything in the recommended tools list, and I didn't use half of them."
Solution: I will buy them at a deeply discounted price.

Definition of Terms

Air compressor	A power tool designed to supply air pressure to pneumatic tools.
Band saw	A power tool with a blade in the shape of band looped around two large wheels, used in cutting intricate designs
Brads	Nails
Carpenter square	A tool used to determine square corners
Disposable staining gloves	Inexpensive rubber gloves resistant to petroleum products
Drill press	A power tool designed to drive precision holes
Eye protection	Goggles
Formica tabletop	A table with a hard plastic-like surface
Horsehair brush	A fine brush used for cleaning
Mineral spirits	A petroleum-based product used in cleaning oil-based paints
Orbital sander	A power tool for sanding
Pneumatic brad nailer	A pneumatic tool used to shoot small nails
Power miter saw	A power tool designed to crosscut at designated angles
Radial arm saw	A power tool designed to roll the saw along an extended arm for ` crosscuts
Ripping	Cutting a board lengthwise
Router	A power tool for shaping wood
Sandpaper (180, 220, 400-grit)	Sand paper with different degrees of coarseness
Sap	A gooey tarlike substance in wood
Scrolling saw	A power tool with a small, straight, vertical blade used in cutting intricate designs
Table saw	A power tool with a stationary circular blade, which can be adjusted in height
Tacky cloth	A special cleaning cloth designed to pick up dust
Wood filler	A plastic substance that dries with the characteristics of wood
Wood finishing wax	A wood finishing product

13

EXHIBIT 19.2

**How to Install a Ceiling
Fan in Your Home**

How to Install a Ceiling Fan

These instructions will explain how to properly install an overhead, ceiling fan. The instructions cover step-by-step how to prepare, assemble, wire, and mount your fan securely.

Properly installing the ceiling fan involves the following major steps: gathering necessary hardware and tools, preparing the ceiling, hanging the fan, wiring the fan, and attaching the fan blades. Proper operation and care for your new ceiling fan is also covered.

Read all instructions thoroughly. Failure to follow all instructions may result in damage to equipment and risk of injury.

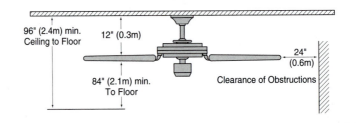

Included Hardware

1. Fan Motor Assembly (1)
2. Canopy (1)
3. Fan Blades (5)
4. Fan Blade Brackets (5)
5. Light Kit (1, optional)
6. Ceiling Mounting Plate (1)
    a. Bracket Attachment Hardware (10 screws, 10 lock washers)
    b. Blade Attachment Hardware (10 screws, 10 washers)
    c. Mounting Hardware (2 washers, 1 bolt, 1 nut, 1 pin, 4 screws)
    d. Electrical Hardware (5 wire nuts, 2 pull chains, 2 lock washers, 2 bolts, 2 screws)

Exhibit 19.2

717

EXHIBIT 19.2

(continued)

Required Tools

1. Phillips Head Screwdriver
2. Flat Head Screwdriver
3. Adjustable Wrench
4. Step Ladder
5. Wire Strippers

Before continuing, turn off all power to the electrical outlet being worked on to reduce the risk of electrical shock or fire.

1) Prepare the Ceiling

1. Remove existing fixture from outlet box.
2. Disconnect existing wiring.
3. Cut off exposed wire at end of wires in outlet box.
4. Strip wires in outlet box exposing 1" of bare wire.

2) Hang the Fan

1. Pass exposed wires in outlet box down through opening in ceiling mounting plate.
2. Screw ceiling mounting plate to outlet box using provided hardware. Ensure plate is flat against outlet box.
3. Lift fan motor assembly to mounting plate and hang fan temporarily by hole in canopy with hook protruding from the mounting plate.

3) Make Electrical Connections

Live wires can cause severe electrical shock. Ensure power to the electrical box is off.

1. Connect ground wire (green) on fan to ground wire (green or bare) in electrical box. Secure with wire nut.
2. Connect white wire on fan to white wire in electrical box. Secure with wire nut.
3. Connect black and blue wires on fan to black wire in electrical box. Secure with wire nut.
4. If using optional light kit:
   a. Attach white wires together. Secure with wire nut.
   b. Attach black wire on light kit to blue wire in fan. Secure with wire nut.
   c. Tuck wires into housing on fan, being careful not to kink the wires, and secure light kit with provided screws.
5. Tuck wires into electrical box behind mounting plate being careful not to kink the wires.

Ensure all wire connections are secure and no bare wire is exposed excluding the ground wire.

EXHIBIT 19.2

(continued)

4) Finish the Installation

1. Thread two screws from mounting hard into ceiling mounting plate.
2. Remove fan from hook.
3. Slide the fan mounting ball into mounting plate, aligning slot in ball with hook in plate.
4. Align locking slot on canopy with screw in mounting plate.
5. Push canopy upward, turning counter-clockwise to lock the canopy in place.
6. Tighten two canopy screws.
7. Thread in remaining two canopy screws.
8. Ensure all screws are secure.

5) Attach the Fan Blades

1. Attach fan blade brackets to fan blades using supplied screws and washers.
2. Attach fan blades to fan motor using supplied screws and washers.

6) Operating the Fan

Before operating fan, remove rubber stops from bottom of fan motor.

1. Turn power on to electrical outlet.
2. Attach pull chains.
3. Control fan speeds as follows:
   a. High: 1 pull
   b. Medium: 2 pulls
   c. Low: 3 pulls
   d. Off: 4 pulls
4. Control direction of airflow with switch on fan motor as follows:
   a. Forward (switch down): use in warm weather to provide downward airflow, cooling the room
   b. Reverse (switch up): use in cool weather to provide upward airflow, moving warm air off the ceiling and into the center of the room.

7) Care of Fan

1. The high speed of your fan can cause screws to come loose. Check that screws in canopy and fan blades are secure at least once a month.
2. Your fan will collect high amounts of dust. Dust the fan at least once per month to keep it looking new.

Exhibit 19.2

719

EXHIBIT 19.2

(continued)

8) Troubleshooting

Q. My fan will not start.
A. Check that power to electrical outlet has been turned back on after installation.
Make sure any light switches that may control the outlet are turned to the on position.

Q. My fan wobbles.
A. Check that the fan blades are mounted level. Use balancing kit if necessary.

Q. My fan is noisy.
A. Allow at least 24 hours for your fan to "break-in."
Make sure all screws are secure.
Make sure wire nuts are not rattling around inside electrical box or inside fan
beneath light kit.
Make sure pull chains are not rattling against fan body.

Appendixes

Appendix A
Mechanics of Good Prose   722

Appendix B
Grammar Issues   737

Appendix C
Documentation Styles   745

Appendix D
Other Documents   756

Mechanics of Good Prose

SPELLING

Many people are poor spellers. Even many good writers are poor spellers. While it's true that full-featured word-processing programs have spelling checkers, even a first-rate spelling checker won't catch certain kinds of spelling errors. It certainly won't catch words that are confused with similar words (*here, hear; their, there; your, you're*). There are no easy shortcuts to improving your ability to spell correctly. Reading constantly and widely can certainly help. Sounding out words can help, too. And caring about correct spelling is a factor as well. Make a list of words that you commonly misspell. (You'll find that many people misspell many of the same words.) Also, be aware that many words may be spelled in more than one way (for example, *employee, employe; judgement, judgment; online, on-line; disk, disc*). In these cases you should use the preferred spelling or the more common spelling. Your professor may require you to follow a specific style guide on these and other issues.

CAPITALIZATION

Capitalize the first word of a sentence. Use a capital letter for titles before the names of officials. Capitalize a title, rank, and so on, followed by a proper name or an epithet used with—or in place of—a proper name.

Dr. Sinclair passed the gavel to President Phil Smith, who will now address us.

Capitalize proper nouns and adjectives formed from proper nouns. Don't capitalize generic nouns unless they are part of a proper name.

Do you know what committee she is on?
She is serving on the Promotion and Tenure Committee.

Capitalize every word except conjunctions, articles, and short prepositions in the names of organizations, businesses, institutions, agencies, and geographical places. Do not capitalize derived nouns, adjectives, or verbs that have taken on specialized meaning ("balkanization," "americanized") unless they are parts of titles. In general, do not capitalize prepositions of fewer than four letters or the articles *a* and *an* unless they are the first word of a title. The article *the* is capitalized only under special circumstances. Capitalize *north, south, east,* and *west* only when they are locations or are part of a proper name. Don't capitalize them if they are directions.

Your appointment is at the United Telecom office at 4 p.m.
From her office, she can see the Statue of Liberty.
They filed a lawsuit against the Jarvis Tool and Die Company.
Drive east to get to the office. They work in the East.

Capitalize titles of published works (except articles, coordinating conjunctions, and prepositions).

Have you read the book *Illustrating Computer Documentation?*

The professional journal is called *Intercom*.

We follow the *Publication Manual of the American Psychological Association*.

Capitalize names of important historical events, holidays, months, and days of the week, but not the seasons of the year.

Valentine's Day   Tuesday   February 14
the Fourth of July   autumn

Nonsentence elements, such as table entries, captions, or footnotes, are often capitalized as a matter of style. The first word of these elements is capitalized: run-in headings; table subtitles, headnotes, box heads, and entries consisting of words, phrases, or sentences; footnotes to either the text or a table; and figure captions. Figure and table titles may be capitalized headline style or sentence style.

Figure 1. Three-view sketch of the research aircraft. Dimensions are in inches.

Figure 1. Computing Scheme for Algorithm.

Figure 1. Technology majors in U.S. colleges.

Capitalize references to specific departments but not general references.

English Department members are involved in computer technology.

Each department is invited to submit a proposal.

Capitalize subjects such as art, geography, and accounting only if they are part of a specific department or specific course title.

She is a journalism major and plans to enroll in "Introduction to Journalism" this fall.

The Journalism Department will hold a faculty meeting on Wednesday.

PUNCTUATION

Punctuation is the use of standard marks, such as commas and periods, to separate sentences, change tone, or indicate pauses. The purpose of punctuation is to increase clarity and readability of text. Use punctuation consistently; that is, punctuate similar situations in the same way.

Period

The principal use of a period (.) is to indicate the end of a sentence. It is also used in abbreviations, after numbers in a numbered list, and in Internet addresses to separate elements of domain names.

Question Mark

The question mark (?) is used at the end of a question sentence. It can be used to separate smaller question elements within a sentence.

Was it at the library? the laboratory? the operating room?

Exclamation Point

The exclamation point (!) is used to indicate surprise, irony, or strong emotion.

Never close your file without first saving it!

Comma

The comma (,) is a mark of separation and enclosure that indicates a grouping of words in a sentence. A comma is used to add emphasis or to indicate a pause. A comma helps your audience to read the text with ease. Use a comma to set off an introductory clause, phrase, or word.

After running the setup program, look at the Readme file.

A series is composed of three or more words, phrases, or clauses of equal grammatical rank. Use a comma to separate items in a series, including before the conjunction (*and, or*).

You will learn to use the menus, toolbar, and keyboard macros.

The old computer was slow, dirty, small, and unusable. (adjectives)

The software package contained five disks, two compact disks, one user guide, and a manual. (nouns)

She started the computer, inserted the disk, and ran the program. (phrases)

Larry installed the floppy drive, Mort wired the wall, and I bought the software. (independent clauses)

Use a comma in dates, before abbreviations after names, and in addresses.

Monday, February 11, 1991   Sam Scientist, M.D.   New York, NY

When dates occur in text, use commas to separate the day from the year and the year from the rest of the sentence. If the day is not specified, commas are omitted.

We signed the contract on February 28, 2002, in the corporate headquarters.

We signed the contract in February 2002 in the library.

Use a pair of commas to enclose parenthetical interrupters.

A mouse, while not a necessity, is certainly a convenience.

Commas are used to separate parts of a sentence to make the sentence clear and direct. Use a comma before *and, but, for, or, nor,* and *yet* when they join the clauses of a compound sentence.

The printer light blinked, but the document didn't print.

I knew the problem was fixed, for the document printed.

Do not use commas to separate a subject from its verb or a verb from its complement.

INCORRECT:	The researcher, removed the specimen from the cooler.
CORRECT:	The researcher removed the specimen from the cooler.
INCORRECT:	The committee and guests attended, the award ceremonies.
CORRECT:	The committee and guests attended the award ceremonies.

Use a comma between coordinate adjectives preceding a noun. A comma separating two adjectives indicates that the two adjectives are equal in their modifying force.

He bought a fast, powerful computer.

Semicolon

A semicolon (;) marks a major break in a sentence and indicates a pause. The semicolon shows that two statements within one sentence are related. A semicolon is also used to separate major sentence elements of equal grammatical weight. It signals a greater break in thought than a comma. Use a semicolon to separate independent clauses when there is no connective word.

The programmer completed the revisions; the system rebooted successfully.

Use a semicolon to separate items in a series when the items contain internal punctuation.

We visited Portland, Oregon; Seattle, Washington; and Vancouver, British Columbia.

Colon

A colon (:) indicates that what follows is an example, explanation, or extended quotation.

Use colons in bibliographies before page numbers of journal articles if the citation style you are following calls for it. (See Appendix C for details on citation styles.) Use colons in an informal table or unnumbered figure.

Table 1.1: Sample spreadsheet

Figure: Start-up screen

Use colons in a memorandum after identification words.

TO:

FROM:

DATE:

SUBJECT:

Use colons after the salutation in a business letter.

Dear Dr. Berger:

Use colons as a separator.

Hours and minutes: 14:50

Use colons in a ratio.

The ratio of computers to personnel is 1:4.

Use colons to introduce a quotation.

In my computer class, my professor says about the Internet: "The Internet is an indispensable tool for the completion of this course."

Use colons at the end of a sentences that introduce lists. The first letter after the colon may be either a capital or lowercase letter. The usage must be consistent throughout the document. Do not use a colon between a verb and its complement or object.

INCORRECT:	Each person must bring: a blank floppy disk, a mouse pad, and a lab manual.
CORRECT:	Each person must bring a blank floppy disk, a mouse pad, and a lab manual.
CORRECT:	Students must bring their own equipment and supplies to class: a blank floppy disk, a mouse pad, and a lab manual.
INCORRECT:	The winners were: Pat, Lydia, and Jack.
CORRECT:	The winners were Pat, Lydia, and Jack.
CORRECT:	There were three winners: Pat, Lydia, and Jack.

Do not use a colon between a preposition and its object, or after *such as*.

INCORRECT:	Many people do not take advantage of computer capabilities, such as: software, e-mail, games, and desktop publishing.
CORRECT:	Many people do not take advantage of computer capabilities, such as software, e-mail, games, and desktop publishing.

Dash

There are two kinds of dashes, and they differ in both length and function. The em dash (—), so called because it is the approximate width of a capital M, is used to show an abrupt change of thought in a sentence. It must be used sparingly and never as a substitute for other punctuation marks.

Properly loaded paper—notice the word *properly*—will not jam in the printer.

The en dash (–), which is approximately the width of a capital N, is used to indicate a range, such as of pages, dates, or times: *Lab hours are 11 a.m.–7 p.m.* It can also be used to separate the two numbers in a sports score: *The Yankees won, 7–2.* Use an en dash to join equal partners in an adjective pair, such as, *He never involved himself in PC–Mac debates.* In addition, en dashes are used in place of hyphens when an element of the hyphenated expression consists of more than one word, for example, *The company developed Year 2000–compliant software.*

Hyphen

A hyphen (-) is used to connect words to make a compound word. The hyphenated word is read as a single unit, as in *an up-to-date system.* Be consistent throughout the document with compound words that are hyphenated. Use a hyphen for compound numbers from twenty-one to ninety-nine, if the style is to spell out those numbers. Use a hyphen between the number and the unit of measure when they modify a noun.

110-pound weight

Use a hyphen to join words used as a single adjective before a noun.

full-time job
well-written manual

Omit the hyphen when a compound adjective occurs after the noun it modifies.

Her job was full time.
The manual is well written.

Slash

Slashes (/) are short diagonal lines sometimes used between two words to show that either word applies in the sentence, such as *and/or.* Avoid this usage in technical prose. Slashes are also used in dates and fractions. Slashes indicate the word *per.* For example, *feet/second* means "feet per second."

Apostrophe

The apostrophe (') has three uses: to form the possessive case of nouns and indefinite pronouns; to indicate contractions; and sometimes to form the plurals of numbers, letters, and symbols.

Apostrophes are used to stand for the omitted material in contractions.

doesn't	does not
can't	cannot
o'clock	of the clock

Learn to distinguish between the following pairs of contractions and possessives:

it's (it is)	its
there's (there is)	theirs
they're (they are)	their
who's (who is)	whose
you're (you are)	your

Apostrophes indicate contractions and sometimes possessives. Contractions are shortened forms of two words. For example, the contraction for the words *do not* is *don't*. Do not use contractions in formal writing. When writing less formal documents, such as letters of complaint or praise, you may use contractions to give your writing a conversational tone. Form the possessive of a noun that does not end in *s* by adding an apostrophe and an *s*.

Programmer's code

Form the possessive of a noun that ends in *s* by adding an apostrophe after the *s*.

Congress' recess

Use an apostrophe at the end of the word to form the possessive of a plural noun that already ends in *s*. Plurals that do not end in *s* form their possessives by adding *'s*.

All of the programmers' codes are easy to use.

Paint the men's locker-room door.

Use apostrophes to form the plurals of letters, but do not use them in plurals of abbreviations or numbers.

p's and q's

VDTs

4680s series

Exception: Sometimes you have to mix plural forms to avoid a more awkward formation.

do's and don'ts

Quotation Marks and Ellipses

Quotation marks (" ") are used to enclose quoted material and words that are used in some special way. Quotation marks always come in pairs. The marks show the beginning and the end of a speech, whether it is part of a sentence, one sentence, or several sentences. If a speech is interrupted by material showing who said it, quotation marks set off the quoted material from the explanatory material. Indirect quotations are not set off by quotation marks. Use quotation marks to enclose the exact words of a quoted speech.

"I am sure," agreed Jan, "that your answer is correct."

Peggy answered, "I worked hard on this. I checked all my data."

Peggy answered that she had worked hard and checked all her data.

Note: The last example is an indirect quotation. Words that are not directly quoted do not need quotation marks.

Use quotation marks to set off subdivisions of books, names of songs, and titles of units of less than book length, such as short stories, short poems, essays, and articles.

The second chapter of the manual is titled "Installing a Hard Drive."

The first article I read when researching recommendations for computer memory was "Questions about RAM" in the consumer magazine.

Use quotation marks to set off slang words used in serious writing.

If the computer has an undetected virus, the entire system can "crash."

Do not use double punctuation when ending a sentence with a quote.

INCORRECT:	John asked, "Where are the extra floppy disks kept?".
CORRECT:	John asked, "Where are the extra floppy disks kept?"

Follow these rules for placing quotation marks in relation to other punctuation marks:

Place commas and periods inside quotes.

"Come in," said John, "and have a seat."

"Jenny," he said, "let's have lunch."

Place semicolons and colons outside quotes.

Mr. Lowe said, "I heartily endorse this brand"; unfortunately, the customer thought he said "hardly" instead of "heartily."

In the summary of the article, Judy referred to "programs"; however, I remembered only one.

Place question marks and exclamation points inside if they belong to the quoted part, outside if they do not belong to the quoted part.

"Heavens!" he exclaimed. "Is this the best you can do?"

Can you believe he said "no"?

Use single quotation marks (' ') to enclose a speech within a speech or a quoted word within a speech.

Jim said, "The tech support guys told me, 'Give it a kick!'"

Ellipses (. . .) are used to mark an omission from a quoted passage and to mark a reflective pause or hesitation. Use the three-dot ellipsis to mark an omission from a quoted passage.

In the article about the use of color, Harriet Burke writes, "When designing GIF images . . . avoid using subtle gradations of color."

Use ellipses to mark a reflective pause or hesitation.

Computers, like other technological devices, can be . . . temperamental.

Use the four-dot ellipsis to indicate material omitted at the end of a sentence.

The hard drive just stopped working. . . .

Parentheses and Brackets

Parentheses ( ) are used to enclose explanatory or supplementary information and to indicate that the enclosed words are of lesser importance. When parentheses are used at the end of a sentence, put the period after the closing parenthesis. When the entire sentence occurs within parentheses, though, punctuate the sentence as usual, within the parentheses. Use parentheses to reference other text.

Before inserting a diskette into the A drive, verify that it is not write-protected (see Figure 3.1).

Use parentheses to enclose enumerated points.

To reboot the system, (1) remove any diskette from the A drive; (2) press and hold the ALT and CTRL keys; (3) press the DEL key; (4) release all keys.

Brackets [ ] are used to set off interpolations in quoted material and to replace parentheses within parentheses.

The reporter wrote: "No one could have predicted that it [the computer] would have had such an impact."

Not every expert agrees. (See Colin Wheildon [*Type & Layout*].)

In some discourse communities, such as mathematics, brackets are placed outside the parenthetical expression, with inner groupings indicated by parentheses.

$$[(a - b)x + (c - d)y]$$

MARKS OF EMPHASIS—BOLD, UNDERLINE, AND ITALIC

Modifying your text with bold, underline, and italic effects draws attention to the marked words. While marks of emphasis have a place in technical writing—where they are sometimes called text styles—their overuse detracts from their effectiveness. If you use them, use them for a good reason and use them consistently. Bold text should be used very sparingly for emphasis, but it can be useful in headings.

Underlined text is the handwritten and typewritten equivalent of italics. If you can use italics instead of underlined text, do so. Italics are used to differentiate regular text—set in roman, or regular, style—from unusual text. Italics are used for titles of books, operas, periodicals, plays, and films; names of genus, species, and varieties; for emphasis; to refer to less commonly used foreign words; and for names of boats, trains, airplanes, and spacecraft. Words used as words, rather than for their meaning, are italicized, as in "*Supersede* is often misspelled." Unfamiliar words are often set in italics the first time they appear in text. The variables in mathematical expressions are set in italics:

$$ax - 4y = 20$$

BULLETS

Bullets (•) are used before each item in a list of equally important items. Bullets are often used in lists when rank or sequence is not relevant or important. Try not to use bullets for a list of fewer than three items. Bulleted items should be constructed of parallel items. For example, if some list elements are noun phrases, they all should be noun phrases. If some are complete sentences, all should be complete sentences.

Capitalize and punctuate items in a bulleted list consistently. If each item is a complete sentence or a group of complete sentences, capitalize and punctuate accordingly. If each element is a word or phrase, either capitalize or not, depending on the style you are following. Do not use sentence punctuation for nonsentences unless you need to do so for consistency with other lists or to solve other formatting problems.

ABBREVIATIONS, ACRONYMS, AND INITIALISMS

Abbreviations are used to save space. They can be shortened words, contractions, acronyms, or initialisms. Some abbreviations are so well known that many people use them without thinking about what the letters actually stand for. This practice leads to redundancy in abbreviations at times. For example, if you say that you are looking for an ATM machine, in effect you are talking about an "automatic teller machine" machine. And when you finally locate this device, don't expect to be asked for your "PIN number," since that would be your "personal identification number" number.

While contractions and many other abbreviations are quite well known and need no explanation, others, particularly some acronyms and initialisms, are not so familiar. Define such abbreviations the first time they appear and any other time you think your readers need the reminder. For a document that is not read sequentially, that is, cover to cover in page order, define abbreviations every time they appear in a new paragraph unless the paragraphs are short and appear near each other.

Many common abbreviations are in everyday use. Abbreviate the words *avenue, boulevard, street, drive,* and *road* in numbered addresses but not when they are used without numbers.

You'll find the San Elijo Campus on Manchester Avenue.

Write to the San Elijo Campus at 3333 Manchester Ave., Cardiff-by-the-Sea.

When a month is used with a specific date, the following abbreviations may be used: *Jan., Feb., Aug., Sept., Oct., Nov., Dec.* Do not abbreviate *March, April, May, June,* and *July* in text. Spell out month names used without a date or with a year alone. In tabular material, use these three-letter forms without a period: *Jan, Feb, Mar, Apr, May, Jun, Jul, Aug, Sep, Oct, Nov, Dec.*

A sale is slated for Feb. 12, 2002.

February 2002 was our biggest month ever.

Acronyms and initialisms are abbreviations formed from the first letter or letters of the words in a multiword phrase. They are a special type of abbreviation, since they are not words that have been shortened but are rather a combination of several words. Acronyms are pronounced as words; initialisms are pronounced as letters. For example, *LAN* is an acronym formed from *Local Area Network*, while *FTP* is an initialism standing for *File Transfer Protocol*. Some acronyms have become accepted as actual nouns, and they are written in lowercase letters, as, for example, *sysop* (systems operator). But, in general, both acronyms and initialisms are written in all capital letters, without punctuation.

Two exceptions to this rule are geographic names, which are often (although not always) punctuated (such as *U.S.A.*) and academic degrees, such as *Ph.D.* or *B.A.* (By convention, the *h* in *Ph.D.* is written lowercase.)

In the computer industry, common usage has not definitely settled on whether certain abbreviations are acronyms (and therefore pronounced as words) or initialisms (and therefore spelled out). This topic is endlessly debated in various online forums. Whether *FAQ* (Frequently Asked Questions) is pronounced "fack" or "eff-ay-cue" may not seem to matter very much. But if you are a writer, it is exactly in these situations that you will find yourself challenged to be inventive in order to avoid problems. If *FAQ* is an acronym, then you would write about it as "a FAQ." If it is an initialism, then you would write "an FAQ." Sometimes you will have to spell out an abbreviation to avoid just such a problem: "a Frequently Asked Questions list."

NUMBERS

Write out (as a word) all numbers below ten, except units of measure, age, time, dates, page numbers, percentages, money, and proportions.

nine floppy disks

zero quality defects

Write any number greater than nine in numerals, unless you are following a style guide that recommends another system. (Some guides recommend writing out numbers under 100 or numbers that can be expressed in two words.)

20 times better

6,000 members

45,000 computer users

When two or more numbers are presented in the same section of writing, write them as numerals.

The upgrade system contains 32 megabytes of RAM, 3 disk drives, and 1 scanner.

If none of the numbers is greater than nine, write them all out as words.

The upgrade system contains three disk drives, one scanner, and two speakers.

Spell out one of two numbers—usually the shorter or the one that is not attached to a unit of measurement—that appear consecutively in a phrase.

7 four-color photos

two 3-inch disks

three 5-person teams

forty-five 4,500-component radar systems

Do not begin a sentence with numerals; instead spell them out.

Two thousand test subjects participated.

A quarter of a million dollars went into the preparation of the system.

Write large numbers in the form that is most familiar to your audience and easiest to understand.

The company lost 2.3 million dollars.

Limit repeating a spelled-out number as a numeral to legal documents.

Either party may terminate the agreement within three (3) months.

Measurements

Keep all units of measure consistent. Use the correct units for the system of measurement you have chosen. Write basic units of measure in word form, derived units of measure as symbols.

8 hours

5 seconds

9 feet

24 ft/s

45 m/s

Place a hyphen between a number and unit of measure when together they modify a noun (used as an adjective).

2-year-old system

15,000-volt charge

8-ounce disk

12-inch-high monitor

Fractions and Decimals

Use the singular when fractions and decimals of 1 or less are used as adjectives.

¼ pound

0.6 centimeter

0.22 cubic foot

0.3 kilometer

Write decimal fractions as numerals, not words.

0.68	*not* zero point six eight
2.312	*not* two point three one two
0.4	*not* zero point four

Treat decimal representations consistently, especially when presenting them in columns, rows, or groups. Precede decimal fractions of value less than one with a leading zero before the decimal point.

0.28	*not* .28
0.8000	*not* .8000

Exception: Numbers that can never be greater than 1, such as probabilities, do not take the leading zero.

$p < .05$

Do not inflate the degree of accuracy by writing decimals with too many digits. If you divide 2.34 by 5.55, your calculator displays 0.4216216, which should be written as

0.42

Writing a number as a decimal implies precision to the last decimal place: *the nearest 0.25 cup* implies more precision than *the nearest quarter cup*.

If a number is merely an approximation, then say so.

about half a glass of milk

approximately one-third less area

Percentages

Use numerals for percentages in the text unless doing so makes the text less clear.

On average, 18 percent of the devices failed in the first year.

Addresses

Spell out numbered streets from one to ten.

West Third Street

Write all building numbers, except for the building number one, as figures.

3804 East Broadway Street
One West Eighth Street

Time

Use *a.m.* and *p.m.* rather than *AM* and *PM*. Avoid superfluous letters and numbers.

The show starts at 5 p.m. (*not* 5:00 p.m.).
The program lasts from 7 to 9 p.m. (*not* 7 p.m. to 9 p.m.).

Dates

Do not refer to dates entirely in numbers, unless you know that your audience follows the same conventional order as you do. The date 2/11/02 means *February 11, 2002,* to Americans, but *November 2, 2002,* to Europeans. Express days of the month as cardinal numbers, not ordinals.

The show runs until Dec. 6 (*not* Dec. 6th).

Appendix B

Grammar Issues

PARTS OF SPEECH

Noun

A noun is the name of a person, place, thing, or abstraction. Examples: *PC, pointer, placement*. Nouns function as the subject of a sentence, as the complement of a verb, as an appositive, and as a term of direct address.

Pronoun

A pronoun substitutes for a noun. Pronouns can be personal (*you, me, ours, mine*), interrogative (*who, what, which, whom*), indefinite (*one, some, each, all*), relative (*who, whose, which, that*), demonstrative (*this, that, these, those*), reciprocal (*one another, each other*), reflexive (*himself, myself*), or intensive (*myself, herself*). The same pronoun can function differently, depending on the context.

Verb

Verbs perform an action or describe a state of being. Action verbs express a physical action (She *pressed* the enter key; He *shut* down the computer). Other verbs express a mental action (He *thought* he *understood* the computer operating system). Verbs can appear in many forms. They change tense to indicate time (*walk, walked*); voice to move from actor to acted upon (*sing, is sung*); mood to show action, command, or wish (*he is staying; halt!; so be it*). Verbs, unlike most other parts of speech, can carry a sentence by themselves.

Adjective

An adjective describes or modifies a noun or pronoun. Adjectives may modify nouns or pronouns in one of several ways. An adjective may tell what kind (a *large* laptop; a *fast* computer processor); may point out which one (*this* technical manual; *that* document plan); or may tell how many (*several* volumes; *nine* computers).

Adverb

An adverb modifies a verb, adjective, other adverb, or sentence. An adverb most commonly modifies a verb. Modifying a verb, an adverb tells how (he worked *quickly*), when (he called *immediately*), where (the team worked *there*), or to what extent (the team worked *hard*). Adverbs may also modify an adjective (she is *extremely* knowledgeable). Adverbs may modify another adverb (the program worked *very* slowly) or an entire sentence (*luckily,* the glue held).

Preposition

A preposition describes the relation of a noun or verb to another word. Prepositions form phrases along with their noun or pronoun objects and modifiers. The company *across* the street went out of business; Our meeting is *after* lunch; Everyone *in* the workroom escaped injury.

Conjunction

A conjunction joins words, phrases, and clauses. Conjunctions can be co-ordinate conjunctions, which join words, phrases, or clauses of equal importance (*and, but, or, nor, for, so, yet*); conjunctive adverbs, which join independent clauses (*accordingly, afterward, also, besides, consequently, furthermore, hence, however, later, moreover, otherwise, still, then, therefore*); or subordinate conjunctions (*until, since, if, because, after, before, although, that, as if, so that, though, unless, while, when, where*).

Interjection

An interjection is a word or phrase that expresses emotion or surprise (*Wow! Hey! No way!*). Interjections have no grammatical relationship to other words in a sentence.

COMMONLY CONFUSED WORDS

Your readers are distracted when you misuse words that are similar. If you say *infer* and you mean *imply,* your message is distorted. If you want *continuously* but substitute *continually,* your readers will wonder whether your other points are equally incorrect. There are many more words that people often confuse. Make sure that you know the exact meanings of the words you use. See Figure B.1 for a table of commonly confused words.

FIGURE B.1
Commonly Confused Words

Affect/effect. *Affect* is a transitive verb meaning to influence or to pretend; *effect* as a verb means to bring about; *effect* as a noun means result.

Adverse/averse. *Adverse* means harmful or inclement; *averse* means disinclined or unwilling.

Anxious/eager. *Anxious* expresses apprehension or fear; *eager* expresses enthusiasm or impatience.

(continued)

FIGURE B.1

(continued)

Appraise/apprise. *Appraise* means estimate the value of; *apprise* means inform.

Assure/insure/ensure. All three can mean to make sure, but *assure* means to give positive guarantee, *insure* means to take out insurance, and *ensure* means to make certain.

Average/mean/median. *Average* and *mean* are the same. Each is the sum of the items divided by the number of items. The *median* is the number that falls in the middle of the items: Half of the numbers are higher than the median and half are lower than the median.

Between/among. *Between* is used for relationships concerning two entities; *among* is used for relationships concerning three or more entities. However, if one item is being considered in relationship to each of the others individually in turn or if a succession is meant, then *between* is used even though there are more than two items. (*The traffic light cycled between green, amber, and red.*)

Bring/take. *Bring* is to cause to move toward the speaker or the subject; *take* is to cause to move away from the speaker or the subject.

Can/may. *Can* expresses ability; *may* gives permission.

Compliment/complement. A *compliment* expresses praise; a *complement* completes something.

Comprise/constitute. The whole *comprises* (includes) the parts; the parts *constitute* (make up) the whole.

Continuously/continually. *Continuously* is all the time; *continually* is over and over again.

Imply/Infer. A speaker or writer may *imply* more than he or she says; the hearer *infers* what the speaker intends.

Its/it's. *Its* is the possessive of the nonpersonal pronoun *it*. *It's* is the contraction meaning *it is*.

Lay/lie. *Lay* is usually transitive and takes a receiver of its action; its principal parts are *lay, laid,* and *laid*. *Lie* is intransitive in its usual meanings and does not take an object; its principal parts are *lie, lay,* and *lain*.

Less/fewer. *Less* refers to quantity; *fewer* refers to number.

Shall/will. *Shall* is the verbal auxiliary indicating the simple future for first person (I, we) and determination or a command for second and third person (you, he, she, it, they). *Will* is the reverse, indicating the simple future for second and third person and determination for first person.

That/which. *That* is restrictive and tells "which one." *Which* is a nonrestrictive and describes what something is like. *We installed the software that was developed by Microsoft.* (There are other software packages, but we chose this particular one.) *We installed the software, which was developed by Microsoft.* (This is the software we installed, and it was developed by Microsoft.)

Who/whom. *Who* functions as the subject of a verb; *whom* functions as the object of a verb. *Who is going there? Whom do you see?*

PROBLEMATIC GRAMMAR ISSUES

We have all been taught grammar since grade school, but several issues seem to provide problems for many people. To be effective, your writing should be as free from error as possible. If you haven't mastered the use of your language and its grammar, those in your audience will question the accuracy of the information you are trying to convey. Correct grammar and usage are the prerequisites to believable prose.

Fragments

Fragments are incomplete sentences. Sometimes professional writers use fragments for a deliberate effect, but often inexperienced writers create fragments when they think they are writing complete sentences.

INCORRECT: Waiting for the computer to boot up.

CORRECT: Wait for the computer to boot up.

INCORRECT: After recording the test results.

CORRECT: After recording the test results, we calculated the distributions.

Run-on Sentences

Run-on sentences are unnecessarily long or wordy sentences:

INCORRECT: After connecting all of the necessary wires to the CPU, printer, speakers, and scanner, we turned on the computer to see if it would work properly only to discover that something was not properly connected because the printer was not working at all and we knew the problem was not a software problem.

CORRECT: After connecting all of the necessary wires to the CPU, printer, speakers, and scanner, we turned on the computer to see if it would work properly. That is when we discovered that something was not properly connected. The printer was not working at all and we knew the problem was not a software problem.

Comma Splices

Comma splices occur when you combine two independent clauses by splicing them together with a comma. Typically, you can correct a comma splice by creating two separate sentences, by adding a coordinating conjunction, or by separating the two independent clauses with a semicolon.

INCORRECT: We soon had to admit that we had failed to find the problem, whatever the problem was we were not going to discover it today.

CORRECT: We soon had to admit that we had failed to find the problem. Whatever the problem was, we were not going to discover it today.

Dangling or Misplaced Modifiers

Dangling modifiers occur when the sentence is worded in such a way that the modifying phrase or word does not modify the subject:

INCORRECT:	Opening the software package, the disk was not enclosed.
CORRECT:	Opening the software package, we realized that the disk was not enclosed.
INCORRECT:	Walking back to class, the notes blew away.
CORRECT:	Walking back to class, I dropped my notes and they blew away.
INCORRECT:	Having just finished taking the exam, the bell rang.
CORRECT:	As soon as I finished taking the exam, the bell rang.

Faulty Parallelism

Faulty parallelism occurs in sentences or lists whose component parts do not agree in form.

INCORRECT:	Connect the cable, install the printer driver, and the light will blink to show that the device is working.
CORRECT:	Connect the cable, install the printer driver, and check that the light is blinking to show that the device is working.

Subject–Verb Agreement

Subjects and verbs must work in pairs, agreeing in number. Singular subjects take singular verbs. Plural subjects take plural verbs. It is not always simple to determine whether a subject is singular or plural, however.

INCORRECT:	Either my CD-ROM drive or my scanner are causing the problem.
CORRECT:	Either my CD-ROM drive or my scanner is causing the problem.

A compound subject separated by *and* takes a plural verb. A compound subject separated by *or* takes a verb that agrees in number with the closer element of the subject.

Either the printer or the computers are always broken in our lab.

Either the computers or the printer is always broken in our lab.

Pronoun–Antecedent Agreement

Pronouns stand in for nouns or other pronouns. The nouns and pronouns that they stand for are their antecedents. A plural pronoun should stand for a plural antecedent.

INCORRECT:	Tell whoever wants to come that they can.
CORRECT:	Tell those who want to come that they can.

Pronoun Case

Pronouns have case just as nouns do, and the correct case to use depends on their function in the sentence. When pronouns are used as the subject of the sentence or clause, they are in the nominative case (*I, we, they*). When they function as an object of a verb or a preposition, they are in the objective case (*me, us, them*).

INCORRECT: The professor told Tom and I to leave the room.

CORRECT: The professor told Tom and me to leave the room.

Tense, Mood, Voice

Verbs have tense, mood, and voice.

Tense

Tense tells when an action occurred—in the past, present, or future. There are six tenses. Consider the verb *to go:* present tense (*I go*), past tense (*I went*), future tense (*I shall go*), present perfect tense (*I have gone*), past perfect tense (*I had gone*), and future perfect tense (*I shall have gone*). Use tenses consistently and in context:

- Present tense expresses action (or state of being) occurring now.
- Past tense expresses action (or state of being) that occurred in the past but did not continue into the present.
- Future tense expresses action (or state of being) at some time in the future (using *shall* or *will*).
- Present perfect tense expresses action (or state of being) occurring at no definite time in the past (formed with *have* or *has*).
- Past perfect tense expresses action (or state of being) completed in the past before some other past action or event (formed with *had*).
- Future perfect tense expresses action (or state of being) that will be completed in the future before some other future action or event (formed with *shall have* or *will have*).

Mood

Mood refers to whether the verb is stating something (indicative: *The printer is making a strange noise*), requesting something (imperative: *Then turn it off!*), or speculating about something contrary to fact or to be desired (subjunctive: *I wish it were working now*). Use the subjunctive mood in contrary-to-fact statements (after *if* or *as though*: If I *were* you, I'd buy this computer) and in statements expressing a wish (I wish it *were* true).

Voice

Voice refers to whether the subject of the verb is the agent of the action or the recipient of the action. A verb is in the active voice when it expresses an action performed by its subject (*The stylus tore the paper*). A verb is in the passive voice when it expresses an action performed upon its subject (*The paper was torn by the stylus*) or when the subject is the result of the action (*The paper was bought by my roommate*). Both active and passive voice may be used in many instances. However, the passive voice may produce awkwardness in writing, and, in general, a passive verb is weaker in its effect than an active verb. (See the "Active Voice" section in Chapter 7.)

Appendix C

Documentation Styles

Every discipline has a preferred documentation style. As with all of the other decisions you make about your document, you must choose a documentation style for the notes and bibliography that is suitable for the discourse community for which you are writing. Following are some of the major documentation style guides and examples of common citations.

HUMANITIES

MLA Style

The most widely used documentation style guides in the humanities are the *MLA Style Manual* and the *MLA Handbook for Writers of Research Papers.* These style guides offer an overview of writing and publication in the humanities, a guide to the mechanics of writing, tips on preparing the scholarly manuscript, rules for preparing the list of works cited, guidelines for documenting sources, a discussion of abbreviations, lists of reference words and proofreading symbols, and guidance on preparing theses and dissertations.

Chicago or Turabian Style

The Chicago or Turabian style, sometimes called documentary note or humanities style, places bibliographic citations at the bottom of a page or at the end of a paper. Although *The Chicago Manual of Style* and Kate L. Turabian's *A Manual for Writers of Term Papers, Theses, and Dissertations* offer guidelines for parenthetical documentation and reference lists as well, these styles are most commonly thought of as note systems.

SOCIAL SCIENCES

The *Publication Manual of the American Psychological Association* sets the documentation style not only for psychology, but also for the other behavioral and social sciences, as well as nursing, criminology, and personnel management.

If you are following the *Style Manual for Political Science* published by the American Political Science Association (APSA), use parenthetical citations within your text to indicate the source of borrowed ideas and quotations. At the end of your paper, provide a list of all of the references cited in the paper.

PHYSICAL SCIENCES

A number system of documentation is used in many scientific fields. Because details of number documentation differ according to discipline (and sometimes according to journals within the same discipline), ask your instructor or supervisor what specific style to use. For engineering publications, follow the requirements of individual journals. The Institute of Electrical and Electronics Engineers (IEEE) has a suggested citation style for its publications, but again there is some variation depending on the particular journal. Always follow the style required by the journal if it differs from what you see here. Documentation styles for chemistry, computer science, mathematics, physics, and medical sciences are summarized in James D. Lester's *Writing Research Papers,* 10th ed. (White Plains: Longman, 2001), an excellent source for a variety of documentation styles.

LIFE SCIENCES

The CBE (Council of Biology Editors, now the Council of Science Editors) manual, *Scientific Style and Format,* describes two systems of source documentation: the citation–sequence system and the name–year system. Both systems, often with variations, are used in scientific publications. For biomedical publications, the "Uniform Requirements for Manuscripts Submitted to Biomedical Journals" ("Vancouver" system) is typically followed. Since the CBE/CSE citation–sequence style is virtually the same as the Vancouver style, they are presented together in this appendix.

ELECTRONIC SOURCES

The organizations that provide guidelines for bibliographic formats in their fields are developing recommendations for citing electronic sources—newsgroup postings, mailing-list (listserver) messages, Web-page articles, e-mail messages, and the like. Because these types of sources are relatively new, many citation formats have been suggested, but most organizations have not yet codified them. For guidance on citing electronic sources, consult journals in your field to see how they are handling the question. Numerous individuals have suggested ways to treat online citations, and many of them have posted their suggestions on a variety of Web pages. Some of the Web pages have been written by graduate students or librarians at various universities, so when you look for these Web pages, they may have moved to another location. Try some of the following sites, and if you need more information, use a Web search engine for further references:

<http://bailiwick.lib.uiowa.edu/journalism/cite.html>.
   A Guide to Citation Style Guides.

<http://www.apastyle.org/elecref.html>.
   American Psychological Association.

WITHIN-THE-TEXT EXAMPLES: MLA, TURABIAN, APA

When you cite information in your work that you have derived from the works of others, you will have to inform your readers where the information can be found. You will do this on each occasion that you use the material you have either copied or paraphrased. Of course, you will also include a section called List of Works Cited, References, Bibliography, or a similar title at the end of your paper or report.

Page References in Paraphrased Material

MLA

To Spiekermann and Ginger, type families share many elements with musical ones (101).

Spiekermann and Ginger see letterforms as taking on lives of their own. "As soon as there are a bunch of letters gathered together, they fight for space, for the right to be recognized, to be read" (120).

Turabian

To Spiekermann and Ginger, type families share many elements with musical ones (1992, 101).

Spiekermann and Ginger see letterforms as taking on lives of their own. "As soon as there are a bunch of letters gathered together, they fight for space, for the right to be recognized, to be read" (1992, 120).

APA

To Spiekermann and Ginger(1992), type families share many elements with musical ones (p. 101).

Spiekermann and Ginger (1992) see letterforms as taking on lives of their own. "As soon as there are a bunch of letters gathered together, they fight for space, for the right to be recognized, to be read" (p. 120).

Author and Page References in Paraphrased and Quoted Material

MLA

Type families share many elements with musical ones (Spiekermann and Ginger 101).

Turabian

Type families share many elements with musical ones (Spiekermann and Ginger 1992, 101).

APA

Type families share many elements with musical ones (Spiekermann & Ginger, 1992, p. 101).

WORKS CITED EXAMPLES: MLA, TURABIAN, APA, IEEE, CBE, VANCOUVER

Books: One Author

MLA

Vaughan, Tay. *Multimedia: Making It Work*. 4th ed. Berkeley: Osborne-McGraw, 1998.

Turabian

Vaughan, Tay. *Multimedia: Making It Work,* 4th ed. Berkeley: Osborne-McGraw-Hill, 1998.

APA

Vaughan, T. (1998). *Multimedia: Making it work* (4th ed.). Berkeley, CA: Osborne-McGraw-Hill.

IEEE

Vaughan, T., *Multimedia: Making It Work,* 4th ed. Berkeley: Osborne-McGraw, 1998.

CBE (citation–sequence system) and Vancouver

Vaughan T. Multimedia: making it work. 4th ed. Berkeley (CA): Osborne-McGraw-Hill; 1998.

CBE (name–year system)

Vaughan T. 1998. Multimedia: making it work. 4th ed. Berkeley (CA): Osborne-McGraw-Hill.

Books: Two Authors

MLA

Strunk, William, Jr., and E.B. White. *The Elements of Style*. 4th ed. Needham Heights: Allyn and Bacon, 2000.

Turabian

Strunk, William, Jr., and E. B. White. *The Elements of Style,* 4th ed. Needham Heights: Allyn & Bacon, 2000.

APA

Strunk, W., & White, E. B. (2000). *The elements of style* (4th ed.). Needham Heights: Allyn & Bacon.

IEEE

Strunk, W., and White, E. B., *The Elements of Style,* 4th ed. Needham Heights: Allyn & Bacon, 2000.

CBE (citation–sequence system) and Vancouver

Strunk W, White EB. The elements of style. 4th ed. Needham Heights: Allyn & Bacon; 2000.

CBE (name–year system)

Strunk W, White E.B. 2000. The elements of style. 4th ed. Needham Heights: Allyn & Bacon.

Books: Many Authors

MLA

Absom, Gerald, Leonard Terry, Lucy Pushkin, Pedro Gonzales, Roberta Terrapin, and Jason Hazzard. *Telecommunications in the Twenty-First Century*. Dayton: Sagenton, 2001.

Turabian

Absom, Gerald, Leonard Terry, Lucy Pushkin, Pedro Gonzales, Roberta Terrapin, and Jason Hazzard. *Telecommunications in the Twenty-First Century*. Dayton: Sagenton, 2001.

APA

Absom, G., Terry, L., Pushkin, L., Gonzales, P., Terrapin, R., & Hazzard, J. (2001). *Telecommunications in the twenty-first century*. Dayton: Sagenton.

IEEE

Absom, G., Terry, L., Pushkin, L., Gonzales, P., Terrapin, R., and Hazzard, J., *Telecommunications in the Twenty-First Century*. Dayton: Sagenton, 2001.

CBE (citation–sequence system) and Vancouver

Absom G, Terry L, Pushkin L, Gonzales P, Terrapin R, Hazzard J. Telecommunications in the twenty-first century. Dayton (OH): Sagenton; 2001.

CBE (name–year system)

Absom G, Terry L, Pushkin L, Gonzales P, Terrapin R, Hazzard J. 2001. Telecommunications in the twenty-first century. Dayton (OH): Sagenton.

Corporate Author

MLA

New York Public Library. *Writer's Guide to Style and Usage.* New York:
HarperCollins, 1994.

Turabian

New York Public Library. *Writer's Guide to Style and Usage.* New York:
HarperCollins Publishers, 1994.

APA

New York Public Library. (1994). *Writer's guide to style and usage.* New York:
HarperCollins.

IEEE

New York Public Library, *Writer's Guide to Style and Usage.* New York:
HarperCollins, 1994.

CBE (citation–sequence system) and Vancouver

New York Public Library. Writer's guide to style and usage. New York:
HarperCollins; 1994.

CBE (name–year system)

New York Public Library. 1994. Writer's guide to style and usage. New York:
HarperCollins.

Reprint

MLA

Bernstein, Theodore M. *Miss Thistlebottom's Hobgoblins: The Careful Writer's
Guide to the Taboos, Bugbears and Outmoded Rules of English Usage.* 1971.
New York: Farrar, 1991.

Turabian

Bernstein, Theodore M. *Miss Thistlebottom's Hobgoblins: The Careful Writer's
Guide to the Taboos, Bugbears and Outmoded Rules of English Usage.*
New York: Farrar, Straus and Giroux, 1971; New York: Farrar, Straus and
Giroux, 1991.

APA

Bernstein, T. M. (1971/1991). *Miss Thistlebottom's hobgoblins: The careful
writer's guide to the taboos, bugbears and outmoded rules of English usage.*
New York: Farrar, Straus and Giroux.

IEEE

Bernstein, T. M., *Miss Thistlebottom's Hobgoblins: The Careful Writer's Guide to the Taboos, Bugbears and Outmoded Rules of English Usage.* New York: Farrar, Straus and Giroux, [1971] 1991.

CBE (citation–sequence system) and Vancouver

Bernstein TM. Miss Thistlebottom's hobgoblins: the careful writer's guide to the taboos, bugbears and outmoded rules of English usage. Reprint. New York: Farrar, Straus and Giroux; 1971/1991.

CBE (name–year system)

Bernstein TM. 1971/1991. Miss Thistlebottom's hobgoblins: the careful writer's guide to the taboos, bugbears and outmoded rules of English usage. Reprint. New York: Farrar, Straus and Giroux.

Chapter in a Book

MLA

Picard, Rosalind W. "Does HAL Cry Digital Tears? Emotions and Computers." *HAL's Legacy: 2001's Computer as Dream and Reality.* Ed. David G. Stork. Cambridge: MIT P, 1997. 279–303.

Turabian

Picard, Rosalind W. "Does HAL Cry Digital Tears? Emotions and Computers." In *HAL's Legacy: 2001's Computer as Dream and Reality,* ed. David G. Stork, 279–303. Cambridge: MIT Press, 1997.

APA

Picard, R. W. (1997). Does HAL cry digital tears? Emotions and computers. In D. G. Stork (Ed.), *HAL's legacy: 2001's computer as dream and reality* (pp. 279–303). Cambridge: MIT Press.

IEEE

Picard, R. W., "Does HAL cry digital tears? Emotions and computers," In *HAL's Legacy: 2001's Computer as Dream and Reality,* edited by D. G. Stork. Cambridge: MIT Press, 1997, pp. 279–303.

CBE (citation–sequence system) and Vancouver

Picard RW. Does HAL cry digital tears? Emotions and computers. In: Stork DG, editor. HAL's legacy: 2001's computer as dream and reality. Cambridge: MIT Press; 1997. p 279–303.

CBE (name–year system)

Picard RW. 1997. Does HAL cry digital tears? Emotions and computers. In: Stork DG, editor. HAL's legacy: 2001's computer as dream and reality. Cambridge: MIT Press. p 279–303.

Article in a Journal

MLA

Connatser, Bradford R. "A Phonological Reading Model for Technical Communicators." *Journal of Technical Writing and Communication* 27.1 (1997): 3–32.

Turabian

Connatser, Bradford R. "A Phonological Reading Model for Technical Communicators." *Journal of Technical Writing and Communication* 27, no. 1 (1997): 3–32.

APA

Connatser, B. R. (1997). A phonological reading model for technical communicators. *Journal of Technical Writing and Communication, 27,* 3–32.

IEEE

Connatser, B. R., "A phonological reading model for technical communicators," *Journal of Technical Writing and Communication,* vol. 27, pp. 3–32, 1997.

CBE (citation–sequence system) and Vancouver

Connatser BR. A phonological reading model for technical communicators. J Tech Writ Commun 1997;27:3–32.

CBE (name–year system)

Connatser BR. 1997. A phonological reading model for technical communicators. J Tech Writ Commun 27:3–32.

Article in a Journal: Two Authors

MLA

Grant, Stephen J., and James K. Cavers. "Further Analytical Results on the Joint Detection of Cochannel Signals Using Diversity Arrays." *IEEE Transactions on Communications* 48.11 (2000): 1788–1792.

Turabian

Grant, Stephen J., and James K. Cavers. "Further Analytical Results on the Joint Detection of Cochannel Signals Using Diversity Arrays." *IEEE Transactions on Communications* 48, no. 11 (Nov. 2000): 1788–92.

APA

Grant, S. J., & Cavers, J. K. (2000, November). Further analytical results on the joint detection of cochannel signals using diversity arrays. *IEEE Transactions on Communications, 48*(11), 1788–1792.

IEEE

Grant, S., and Cavers, J. K., "Further analytical results on the joint detection of cochannel signals using diversity arrays," *IEEE Transactions on Communications,* vol. 48, no. 11, pp. 1788–92, Nov. 2000.

CBE (citation–sequence system) and Vancouver

Grant S, Cavers JK. Further analytical results on the joint detection of cochannel signals using diversity arrays. IEEE Trans Commun 2000 Nov;48(11):1788–92.

CBE (name–year system)

Grant S, Cavers JK. 2000 Nov. Further analytical results on the joint detection of cochannel signals using diversity arrays. IEEE Trans Commun 48(11):1788–92.

Article in a Journal: Three or More Authors

MLA

Pascal, Andy, Erwin Peterman, and Claudiu Gradinaru. "Structure and Interactions of the Chlorophyll A Molecules in the Higher Plant Lhcb4 Antenna Protein." *Journal of Physical Chemistry B* 104.39 (5 Oct. 2000): 9317–9321.

Turabian

Pascal, Andy, Erwin Peterman, and Claudiu Gradinaru. "Structure and Interactions of the Chlorophyll A Molecules in the Higher Plant Lhcb4 Antenna Protein." *Journal of Physical Chemistry B* 104, no. 39 (5 Oct. 2000): 9317–9321.

APA

Pascal, A., Peterman, E., & Gradinaru, C. (2000, October 5). Structure and interactions of the chlorophyll a molecules in the higher plant Lhcb4 antenna protein. *Journal of Physical Chemistry B, 104*(39), 9317–9321.

IEEE

Pascal, A., Peterman, E., and Gradinaru, C., "Structure and interactions of the chlorophyll a molecules in the higher plant Lhcb4 antenna protein," *Journal of Physical Chemistry B,* vol. 104, no. 39, pp. 9317–21, 5 Oct. 2000.

CBE (citation–sequence system) and Vancouver

Pascal A, Peterman E, Gradinaru C. Structure and interactions of the chlorophyll a molecules in the higher plant Lhcb4 antenna protein. J Phys Chem B 2000 Oct 5;104(39):9317–21.

CBE (name–year system)

Pascal A, Peterman E, Gradinaru C. 2000 Oct 5. Structure and interactions of the chlorophyll a molecules in the higher plant Lhcb4 antenna protein. J Phys Chem B 104(39):9317–21.

Article in a Magazine or Newspaper

MLA

Kieran, Michael. "Image Management: Covering All the Bases." *Publish* Feb. 1997: 64–70.

Turabian

Kieran, Michael. "Image Management: Covering All the Bases." *Publish* Feb. 1997, 64–70.

APA

Kieran, M. (1997, February). Image management: Covering all the bases. *Publish, 12,* 64–70.

IEEE

Kieran, M., "Image management: covering all the bases," *Publish,* 64–70, Feb. 1997.

CBE (citation–sequence system) and Vancouver

Kieran M. Image management: covering all the bases. Publish 1997 Feb:64–70.

CBE (name–year system)

Kieran M. 1997 Feb. Image management: covering all the bases. Publish:64–70.

Appendix D

Other Documents

LITERATURE REVIEWS

Literature reviews discuss and assess some of the important published literature on a specific topic. (See Figure D.1.) They play a key role in most disciplines by summarizing, classifying, comparing, and evaluating the key existing works on a topic, area, or issue. Many literature reviews stand alone. Others may be part of a proposal, an article, a report, a scientific paper, or a chapter in a thesis or dissertation. In fact, a literature review is an essential part of a good grant or research proposal. You have to persuade your audience that you are making further contributions to a field of study, and to do this successfully,

---

In a perfect world, dedicated scientists would devise and perform experiments the results of which, expected or not, would be reported objectively and truthfully, so as to inform their peers of the progress of their work. In that perfect world, reports would accurately reflect the procedures followed and the active participation of all their authors. For various reasons that will be discussed here, that is not always the case. Over the last twenty years, celebrated cases of science fraud have shocked the scientific community and the lay public. The obvious questions are, how could this have happened so easily, and why weren't these lapses discovered sooner? The traditional assumption has been that science is a self-policing society with safeguards built into the system to filter out substandard results before they could enter the mainstream of collective knowledge. The inevitable conclusion has to be that the safeguards are insufficient in the presence of highly motivated individuals determined to publish no matter what. Society, both scientific and lay, must develop and institute effective procedures to protect itself from unscrupulous miscreants and not rely on peer review and replication to do the job.

Because science is performed by human beings, its playing field is as prone to human failures as other endeavors, despite the historical perception of science and its practitioners as being somehow "above all personal considerations." It is perhaps this widespread notion itself that is to blame for the extraordinary attention paid to the problem of science fraud, as a shocked public responds to report after report of improprieties in the "hallowed halls" of science. The sheer volume of material on this subject is overwhelming, and much of it quite recent. Some works are overviews, while others concentrate on one aspect of the problem or solution. In this review I will examine a sample of these sources and discuss their viewpoints. I will then synthesize the issues into a coherent whole and discuss responses to fraud and ideas for improving those responses.

Examining the Literature

William Broad and Nicholas Wade have written perhaps the most cited general book-length work on the subject of science fraud. *Betrayers of the Truth* was published in 1982, an early entry in literature of the field. Almost every source that deals broadly with the subject quotes this work. Its last chapter, "Fraud and the Structure of Science," appears in an anthology, *Ethical Issues in Scientific Research*, published in 1994, attesting to its relevance even twelve years later.

Broad and Wade provide an overview of the issues involved in science fraud. They see science as a process that is social, historical, and cultural. It is rational but also creative, imaginative, intuitive, and persistent. They take fraud to be the proof of those non-rational elements at work (75–76). They emphasize what other sources only point out or miss entirely, namely that fraud often arises out of conviction that the stated conclusions are true, even if the data do not support

---

FIGURE D.1

Literature Review

This excerpt from a literature review on fraud in science shows the introduction and a review of one source.

them *at this time*. History looks kindly upon scientists such as Newton, Mendel, and Millikan, because they turned out to be right; but some like Cyril Burt who "lied for truth [were] wrong" (69–70).

As science writing is the interface between scientists and their peers, Broad and Wade focus on rhetoric decisions made by science writers. They review the discrepancy between the conventions of scientific reporting and the realities of research (73–75). For them, "[i]t is only the literary conventions of scientific reporting that compel scientists to feign detachment. . . . Objectivity is an abstraction of the philosophers, a distraction for the researcher" (73).

The value of this work is apparent when one realizes that what Broad and Wade wrote nineteen years ago still stands as an authoritative text today. Their analysis of the problem and suggestions for its treatment are remarkable, considering that they wrote before so many of the more recent scandals in scientific publishing were known and before congressional committee investigations into science fraud were an annual event. Its continued appearance as citations in other works attests to its value today.

you must summarize the existing significant research on your topic. See Figure D.1 for an example of a literature review.

WRITING LITERATURE REVIEWS

- Define or identify the general topic, issue, or concern to provide some context for reviewing the literature.
- Discuss why you think it's necessary to review the literature on the topic.
- Explain how you will judge the literature you discuss and how you will organize the review.
- Comment on any specific trends identified by your research if you are simply informing your readers about the status of the research on a topic. Comment on any disagreements, controversies, or debates in the literature if your literature review is a specific argument in support of a point of view.
- Point to a specific dominant issue and discuss the merits of the issue if such an approach fits the information you have uncovered.
- Comment on why some literature on your topic has not been included in your review, if it's appropriate to do so.
- For the body of your literature review, decide on various strategies for grouping or classifying the literature you are discussing. Cover earlier literature first and then more recent literature; group according to the kinds of literature (reviews, journal articles, reports, case studies, Web documents); or group according to the conclusions of the authors or the purposes of each document.

- Summarize each work according to its importance and comment on the significance of each source you discuss. Some works contribute new thought to the topic; others add nothing new to the discussion. If the work is particularly important, devote more discussion to it in your literature review. Devote less discussion to less important works.
- Help your readers as much as possible in the literature review. Wherever possible, provide clear topic sentences at the beginnings of paragraphs. Provide brief summaries at various points in your discussion informing your readers of the importance of what you have covered so far.
- Reemphasize in the closing of the literature review the main points of the most important sources discussed in your review.
- Provide an overall evaluation of the state of knowledge concerning your topic. Comment on any gaps in the research, any inconsistencies, and any areas requiring further study.
- Wrap up by discussing how the topic of your literature review relates to the larger discipline or profession.

ANNOTATED BIBLIOGRAPHIES

Annotated bibliographies are organized lists of sources, with each source followed by a brief comment or annotation. Annotated bibliographies serve many valuable purposes in research, in that they describe the content and focus of sources; suggest the usefulness of the sources to your research or someone else's; evaluate the methods, conclusions, or reliability of sources; and record your reactions to sources.

Many annotated bibliographies are published as separate pamphlets or monographs. Some are published as journal articles, bibliographic essays, or literature reviews. Ideally, an annotated bibliography provides an up-to-date overview of the important literature on a well-focused topic.

You may be asked to write an annotated bibliography to show the quality of your own research, to provide additional information or background material to your reader, to explore a topic for further reading or research, or to give your research historical perspective or relevance. See Figure D.2 for an example of an annotated bibliography.

There are several major kinds of annotations:

- Summary annotations discuss the main argument of the book or article or other source.
- Descriptive annotations discuss what is included in the source.
- Evaluative annotations discuss what the writer thinks of the source.
- Combination annotations provide a blend of the above, offering, for example, a summary, a description, and an evaluation. The combination annotation is the most common type.

Annotated Bibliography

Spiekermann, Erik, and E. M. Ginger. *Stop Stealing Sheep and Find Out How Type Works.* Mountainview: Adobe, 1993

Type has personality in addition to size, weight, shape. Knowledge of historical and modern principles for using type enables document designers to create appropriate and elegant documents.

Stone, Sumner. *On Stone: The Art of Use of Typography on the Personal Computer.* San Francisco: Bedford Arts, 1991.

The designer of the Stone family of typefaces uses computer technology to develop and design type that benefits from his clear typographic knowledge and experience. Type designers today are empowered by computer technology and benefit greatly from the computer's powers to work more quickly and track changes automatically. The goal of information design is trouble-free navigation through the text. Many design decisions (headings, titles, justification, alignment, indentation) affect the readability of text. A history of type design, a case history in typographic design, and many specimens inform and educate the novice typographer.

———. "The Type Craftsman in the Computer Era." *Print* Mar./Apr. 1989: 84+.

Computer typography applies the old craft of making letterforms to the new context of computer science. The tools and materials may be new, but the letters are old. Today's typographer must become familiar with the original sources of the letterforms and make "faithful and lively versions" of them with the modern technology. The historical precedent of mixing alphabet styles is valid today in the mixing of different typefaces from the same family, for example the Stone typeface family.

Stopford, Charles. "Desk Top Type: Tradition and Technology." *Technical Communication* (1992): 74–79.

Despite technological changes over the centuries, reading has remained the same, so the requirements for readable text have not changed. Only typographic literacy will ensure that those presenting written material for others to read will provide aesthetically pleasing and usable documents.

Swann, Cal. *Language and Typography.* New York: Van Nostrand Reinhold, 1991.

Visible language consists of arbitrary symbols, including orthographic and paragraphological. The conventions of visible language are the visual expression of intonation. Letterforms have connotative qualities beyond their denotative ones, and their importance becomes clear when we examine posters, advertisements, and signs.

Wheildon, Colin. *Type & Layout: How Typography and Design Can Get Your Message Across—Or Get in the Way.* Berkeley: Strathmoor, 1995.

Research undertaken between 1982 and 1990 exposes those factors that make for effective, readable, legible text.

WRITING AN ANNOTATED BIBLIOGRAPHY

■ Once you have focused your research and finished finding all the sources you need, compile all of your sources. Photocopy the articles or print copies of the Web sources or borrow the books so that as many originals as possible are available to you when you begin the work on your annotations.

- Determine the documentation style you must use for the sources: MLA, Chicago/Turabian, APA, IEEE, CBE, or house style if your company has one. See Appendix C for information on choosing and using a documentation style.
- Determine whether you should write your annotations as phrases or complete sentences. Both are common. A phrase annotation simply offers the necessary few phrases to get the job done. A complete sentence annotation allows you to be a little more detailed.
- For a sentence annotation, vary the sentence length and avoid long and complex sentences. Sometimes you may be asked to provide a paragraph annotation. Each paragraph should be complete, unified, coherent, and ordered.
- Determine the kind of annotation you are required to do: a summary, a description, an evaluation, or a combination.
- To write a summary annotation, begin by stating the purpose or argument of the source. Develop the main argument with supporting points and examples and state the conclusion. Do not include phrases such as, "the author contends," "the article states," or "according to this book."
- To write a descriptive annotation, define the scope of the source, list the significant topics, and tell what the source is about. In this type of annotation, you shouldn't try to give actual supporting data or examples. Generally, you just include topics or chapter titles.
- To write an evaluative annotation, you need to determine the strengths and weaknesses of the source. Discuss why the source is interesting or helpful to you or why it is not interesting or helpful. Discuss the type, quantity, and usefulness of the information.
- To write a combined annotation, provide several sentences summarizing or describing the content and several sentences evaluating the source.
- Be brief. Highlight only the essential details or points.

RESOURCES

Booth, Wayne C., Gregory G. Colomb, and Joseph M. Williams. *The Craft of Research.* Chicago: U of Chicago P, 1995.

Council of Biology Editors. *Scientific Style and Format: The CBE Manual for Authors, Editors, and Publishers.* 6th ed. Cambridge: Cambridge UP, 1994.

Dolphin, Warren D. "Writing Lab Reports and Scientific Papers." Online. Available at <http://www.mhhe.com/biosci/genbio/maderinquiry/writing.html>. Accessed 20 August 2000.

Lester, James D. *Writing Research Papers: A Complete Guide.* 10th ed. White Plains: Longman, 2001.

Pyrczak, Fred. *Writing Empirical Research Reports: A Basic Guide for Students of the Social and Behavioral Sciences.* Los Angeles: Pyrczak, 1992.

Zimmerman, Donald E., and Dawn Rodrigues. *Research and Writing in the Disciplines.* Fort Worth: Harcourt, 1992.

Credits

Page abbreviations are as follows: (T)top, (B)bottom, (TL)top left, (TR)top right, (BL)bottom left, (BR)bottom right.

Text Credits

6 Copyright © 2001 The University of Central Florida. Used with permission. 21 "STC Ethical Principles for Technical Communicators" from *Technical Communication*, Vol. 47, No. 4, p. 587. November 2000. Copyright © 2000 STC. Used with permission from the Society for Technical Communication, Arlington, VA, www.stc.org. 26 From CROSSING THE GREAT DIVIDE: Can We Achieve Equity When Generation Y Goes to College?" Anthony P. Carnevale and Richard A. Fry, 2000. Reprinted by permission of Educational Testing Service, the copyright owner. 50 Adapted from "Stephen's Guide to Logical Fallacies" at http://www.datanation.com. Copyright © 2001. Used by permission of Stephen Downes. 57 Adapted from Table 1 in "The Technical Communicator's Role in Cross-functional Teams" by Marchwinski and Mandziuk, *Technical Communication*, p. 70, November 2000. Copyright © 2000 STC. Reprinted with permission from TECHNICAL COMMUNICATION, the journal of the Society for Technical Communication, Arlington, VA, www.stc.org. 99 © Microsoft Corporation, Inc. All rights reserved. 103 © 2001 by Experience In Software, Inc. Used with permission. 104 © 2001 Isbister International, Inc. Used with permission. 129 Copyright © 2001 The University of Central Florida Library. Used with permission. 131 Copyright © 2001 State University System of Florida. Used with permission. 132–135 From Applied Science & Technology Abstracts. © 2001 H. W. Wilson Company. 138–141 From Book Review Digest. © 2001 H. W. Wilson Company. 143 Copyright © 2001 State University System of Florida. Used with permission. 145–146 From www.onelook.com. Copyright © Study Technologies, 2001. Used with permission. 149, 150 Copyright © 2001 Altavista, Inc. All rights reserved. Used with permission. 152 Record retrieved from the RLG Union Catalog, reproduced by permission of the Research Libraries Group. 153(T) From VERONIS SUHLER COMMUNICATIONS INDUSTRY FORECAST, Fifteenth Edition, July 2001. Copyright © 2001. Used by permission. 153(B) Copyright © 2001 Dun & Bradstreet. All rights reserved. 154 "Macrodoctor, Come Meet the Nanodoctor," Kelly Morris, *The Lancet*, Vol. 357, Issue 9258, p. 778, 3/10/01. Copyright © 2001 The Lancet. Used by permission. 159 © Google, Inc. Used with permission. 163 Copyright © 2001 Yahoo, Inc. All rights reserved. 175 © 2001 ProCite Software. Used by permission from ISI ResearchSoft, Carlsbad, CA. 190 From THE TECHNICAL COMMUNICATOR'S HANDBOOK by Dan Jones. Copyright © 2000 by Allyn and Bacon. Reprinted with permission. 202, 217, 254 From THE NON-DESIGNER'S DESIGN BOOK, Robin Williams, p. 13, 100 © 1994 by Robin Williams. Reprinted by permission of Peachpit Press. 202 From SCIENCE AS WRITING, David Locke. Copyright © 1992 Yale University Press. Used with permission. 204 From TECHNOLOGY AND CREATIVITY, by Subrata Dasgupta. Copyright © 1996 by Oxford University Press, Inc. Used by permission of Oxford University Press, Inc. 205 Reprinted with the permission of Alpha Publishing, as represented by Pearson Computer Publishing, a Division of Pearson Education, from COMPLETE IDIOT'S GUIDE TO CREATING A WEB PAGE, 4/e by Paul McFedries. Copyright © 1999 by Alpha Publishing. 206 THE EVEN MORE INCREDIBLE MACHINE: Journal Entries June thru August, p. 1, p. 26. From Sierraonline.com. All rights reserved. 241 © 2000 InstallShield Software Corporation. All rights reserved. InstallShield is a registered trademark and service mark of InstallShield Software Corporation. Used with permission. 244 Reprinted with permission from AAAS. Copyright © 2001 American Association for the Advancement of Science. 244 © MIT Artificial Intelligence Laboratory. 265 Copyright © 2001 NuSphere. NuSphere is a trademark of NuSphere Corporation. Used with permission. 266 © 2001 Handspring, Inc. Used with permission. 267(TL) © DG Warehouse. Used with permission. 267(TR) Copyright © 2001 DBCORP Information Systems, Inc. Used with permission. 267(BL) Copyright © 2001 AGIdeas. Used with permission. 267(BR) United Airlines © 2001. All rights reserved. 280 Courtesy of Hoover's Online (www.hoovers.com). 281 Copyright © Thomas Register.

All rights reserved. **282** Reprinted with permission from Encyclopædia Britannica, Inc. © 2001 Britannica.com, Inc. (Fig. 8-29). **284** Copyright © HTML.com. All rights reserved. **285** Used with permission from University College London, School of Library, Archive and Information Studies at www.ecp.ucl.ac.uk. **298** Table "Top 10 List of Venture Capital Regions for the Year 2000" from *Infoworld*, 3/10/01. Copyright © 2001 Infoworld Media Group, Inc. Reprinted by permission via Copyright Clearance Center, Inc. **306** From "Fewer Newbies are coming Online" Jim Battey, *Infoworld*, 2/12/01. Copyright © 2001 Infoworld Media Group, Inc. Reprinted by permission via Copyright Clearance Center. **308** From *New York Times*, April 10, 2001. Copyright © 2001 New York Times Co., Inc. Used with permission. **331** Used with permission from *The Levels of Edit*, written by Robert Van Buren and Mary Fran Buehler, and published by the Society for Technical Communication, Arlington, Virginia. **556** "Guidelines for STC Special Opportunities Grants." Copyright © 1999 Society for Technical Communication. Reprinted with permission from the Society for Technical Communication, Arlington, VA. **634** Marc Pomplum et al., "Comparative Visual Search: A Difference That Makes a Difference," *Cognitive Science*, Vol. 25, No. 1, January–February 2001, pp. 3–36. Copyright © 2001 Cognitive Science Society. Reprinted by permission. **692** Excerpts from Dell Dimension XPSZ M166s and XPS M200s Systems Reference Guide. Copyright © 2000 Dell Computer Corporation. Reprinted by permission. **694** Excerpts from Dell Dimension XPSZ M166s and XPS M200s Systems Reference Guide. Copyright © 2000 Dell Computer Corporation. Reprinted by permission.

Photo Credits

10 Corbis Stock Market/Peter Beck, 1999. **14** Bettmann/CORBIS. **17** Photo courtesy of Apple Computer, Inc. **59(L)** Bettmann/CORBIS. **59(C)** Bettmann/CORBIS. **59(R)** Hulton Archive/ Getty Images. **137(L)** Bureau of Labor Statistics. **137(R)** Courtesy of NOAA and Best Publishing Company, Flagstaff, AZ. **286** Ron Fehling/Masterfile. **297** Index Stock Imagery/Erwin Nielsen. **318** Corbis Stock Market/John Zoiner. **319** Jeff Corwin/Getty Images/Stone. **324** NASA. **417** Bonnie Kamin/ PhotoEdit. **422** David Young-Wolff/PhotoEdit. **423** Corbis Stock Market/Jose L. Pelaez Inc., 1996. **442** Corbis Stock Market/Jim Erickson, 1999. **443** Corbis Stock Market/Jose L. Pelaez Inc., 1999. **448** Michael Newman/PhotoEdit. **449** Amy C. Etra/PhotoEdit. **450** Michael Newman/PhotoEdit. **451** Rob Brimson/Getty Images/FPG International LLC. **452** Jeff Greenberg/PhotoEdit. **453** Index Stock Imagery/Dave Mager. **455** Corbis Stock Market/Rob Lewine, 2000. **457** Corbis Stock Market/Chris Roger. **516** Center for Transportation Technologies and Systems, National Renewable Energy Laboratory. **627(T)** Brent Clingman/TimePix. **627(B)** Gary Braasch/CORBIS. **685(L)** Courtesy AIWA. **685(C)** © General Binding Corporation. **685(R)** Provided courtesy of Lexmark International, Inc. Used with Permission.

Index

Note: Page numbers followed by *f* refer to information in figures. Page numbers followed by *s* refer to information in sidebar quotations. Page numbers followed by *t* refer to information in tip lists.

abbreviations, 208–210, 732–733
  in e-mail, 506, 506*f*
  in formal reports, 650, 651*f*, 652
  in scannable résumés, 400*t*
abbrevomania, 210
abstractness
  on presentation slides, 456*t*
  in technical prose, 346–347
abstracts
  versus executive summaries, 645–646
  in formal reports, 642–644, 643*f*, 644*t*
  print and online, in research, 132–135*f*, 133
  in proposals, 552–553, 556, 556*f*
  in scientific papers, 634, 634*f*
academese, 212
accented letters (typography), 255
acceptance letters, 383–385, 384*f*
accessibility
  and bias, 225, 226*t*
  of Web sites, 283, 283*f*, 284*f*, 300
accuracy, 340–341, 355*f*
achievability of specifications, 528, 528*t*
achievements lists in résumés, 391
acknowledgment section (scientific papers), 635
acronyms, 209–210, 279*t*, 732–733
action verbs
  in résumés, 390
  in technical prose, 210, 738
active voice, 210–211, 743–744
activities lists (résumés), 391
address, forms of (correspondence), 469
addressee lines (memos), 495, 495*f*
addresses, 467, 469*f*, 736
ad hominem arguments, 49, 50f
adjectives, 738
adjustment letters, 487–490, 489*f*

adverbs, 738
age bias, 225, 226*t*
agendas, 71, 71*t*, 73*f*, 594*t*
agglomerese, 210
agreement
  pronoun–antecedent, 742
  subject–verb, 742
alerts and warnings (policies and procedures), 524*t*
alignment
  in design, 242–244, 242*f*, 244*f*
  in letters
    full-block, 476, 477*f*
    modified-block, 477–479, 478*f*
    personal, 480–481, 482*f*
    semiblock, 479–480, 479*f*
    simplified, 480, 481*f*
  in scannable résumés, 400*t*
  in text, 263–264, 264*f*
alternative order of steps (instructions), 692–694, 694*f*
ambiguity
  of modifiers, 214
  in prose, 347–348
  of references, 221
analogies in technical definitions, 513
analogy paragraphs, 218
analytical reports, 623–624, 624*f*. *See also* formal reports
anchoring illustrations to text, 301
and in specifications, 529
anecdotes in presentations, 437
anger and tone, 223
animation
  in GIF-format files, 300
  in online documents, 282–284
annotated bibliographies, 759–761, 760*f*
annual reports, 585*f*, 587–588, 590*f*
anti-aliasing (typography), 301
any in specifications, 529
APA citation style, 746, 748–755
apostrophes (punctuation), 728–729
appeal to force (logical fallacy), 50*f*
appearance predictability in print and online, 273*f*
appendixes
  in formal reports, 652–653

in policies and procedures, 524*t*
  in proposals, 562–563
applicability of specifications, 531–532
application letters, 376–379, 377*f*
appropriate language (presentations), 437
appropriateness
  of text, 341–342, 342*f*
  of visuals, 295–301
APSA citation style, 746, 748–755
archaic expressions, 207, 208*f*
archives in libraries, 137
argumentum ad hominem, 49, 50*f*
articles, journal
  design conventions for, 239*f*
  publishing in, 417–420, 418–419*f*
  writing, 417–420, 418–419*f*
artist's conceptions, 314–315
assembly-manual design, 238*f*
asymmetry in design, 242–244, 242*f*, 244*f*
attachments in e-mail, 501–503
attacking the person (logical fallacy), 49, 50*f*
attention line
  in letters, 468*f*, 469–470
  in memos, 495*f*, 496
attitude in prose, 222–225. *See also* jargon
audience
  appealing to (pathos), 45–46
  categorical approaches to, 35–40
  categories by knowledge level
    combined, 37, 40
    executives, 36–37
    experts, 37
    laypeople, 36
    multiple, 37, 40
    paraprofessionals, 37
    professionals, 37
    technicians, 37
  determining level of detail for, 220
  heuristic approaches to, 38–39
  and humor, 224*t*
  and persuasion, 34–51
  primary and secondary, 40
  and scope, 85
  for specific communications

audience *(cont.)*
    company policies, 523*t*
    formal reports, 636–638
    informal reports, 599
    instructions, 689
    presentations, 436
    proposals, 546, 548–549
    Web pages, 270
    and style, 198–199
    and tone, 47
audiovisual equipment for
    presentations, 440
author guidelines for journal articles,
    418–419*f*
awards and honors
    in portfolios, 401*t*
    in résumés, 391

background colors, 268, 269*f*, 318*t*
background reports, 624–625,
    659–681*f. See also* formal
    reports
background sections
    of proposals, 557–558
    of request for proposals, 549
back matter
    directives in style guides, 92
    elements of
        appendix, 524*t*, 562–563,
            652–653
        bibliography, 131*t*, 173, 175*f*,
            746–755, 759–761, 760*f*
        glossary, 513, 524*t*, 648–649, 688,
            697*t*
        index, 524*t*, 654, 654*t*
        list of symbols and abbreviations,
            650, 651*f*, 652
    in formal reports, 641
    in instructions, 697*t*
    in policies and procedures, 524*t*
balance in design, 242–244, 242*f*, 244*f*,
    247*t*
bandwidth and multimedia, 282–284,
    288–289
barbarisms, 207, 208*f*
bar graphs, 305–307, 306*f*, 307*t*
begging the question (logical fallacy),
    50*f*
bias, avoiding, 225, 226*t*
bibliographies. *See also* citation styles
    annotated, 759–761, 760*f*
    formats for, 131*t*, 746–755
    as research sources, 127*t*
    software for, 173, 175*f*

bibliography cards, 127*f*, 172–173
bitmaps, 323
blank space. *See* white space
block diagrams, 314–315
block format letters, 476, 477*f*
body language
    in interviews, 116*t*, 406–408
    in presentations, 442–443
body (paragraph) spacing in letters
    full-block, 476, 477*f*
    modified-block, 477–479, 478*f*
    personal, 480–481, 482*f*
    semiblock, 479–480, 479*f*
    simplified, 480, 481*f*
Boisjoly, Roger (*Challenger* engineer),
    14
bold styled text (boldface), 271, 271*f*,
    731
books
    conventions for design, 236, 236*f*
    as format for proposals, 548
    as research sources, 126, 135, 136*f*
Boolean searches, 142, 142*f*, 148*t*, 151*t*
Booth, Wayne (*The Craft of Research*),
    637
border graphics as design elements,
    250, 251*f*
bottom-up editing, 329–330, 330*f*
brackets (punctuation), 731
brainstorming, 85*e*, 86, 86*f*, 87*t*
brochures, designing, 237, 237*f*
browsers, 288, 301
budget-estimating programs, 105
budget section (proposals), 560–561,
    562–564*f*
bulleted lists, 250–253, 732
    in instructions, 686, 693, 693*f*
    in online design, 274
    in portfolios, 401*t*
    on presentation slides, 456*t*
    punctuation of, 253, 732
    and writing for the Web, 279*t*
bulletin-board online forums, 420–421
bureaucratese, 212
business correspondence. *See* e-mail;
    letters; memos
business stationery, 467, 469*f*
buttons (Web navigation), 250, 251*f*
buzzwords in scannable résumés, 400,
    400*t*

callouts
    in diagrams, 316*f*
    with figures, 297, 297*f*

in photographs, 318*t*
in pie graphs, 309*t*
readability of, 298
camcorders. *See* videos
capital letters
    in e-mail, 505
    on presentation slides, 456*t*
    usage, 723–724
captions
    in diagrams, 316*t*
    in figures, 297, 298*f*
    in photographs, 318*t*
    readability of, 298
    and writing for the Web, 279*t*
card catalogs, 131, 131*f*
career counseling assistance, 368–370,
    372
career development, 414–430
cartoon illustrations, 300, 314–315
cascading style sheets (CSS), 271–272,
    273*f*
case (pronoun), 743
catalogs
    library, 131, 131*f*
    online, 142–143, 162, 163–164*f*
categorical approaches to audience,
    35–38
cause-and-effect paragraphs, 218
cautions
    in instructions, 687–688, 688*f*
    in policies and procedures, 524*t*
CBE citation style, 747, 748–755
CD-ROM databases, 143–151
centered text, 263–264, 264*f*
certificate programs, 423
chalkboards (presentation tool), 446,
    447*f*, 449*f*
Challenger disaster, 14
chapter meetings, 425–426
chapter pages (books), 250
character. *See* credibility (ethos)
charts, 311–314. *See also* graphs
    flowcharts, 311, 311*t*, 312*f*
    Gantt charts, 313, 313*f*, 314*t*
    organizational charts, 312, 312*f*, 313*t*
    schedule charts, 313, 313*f*, 314*t*
checklist section of RFP, 550
Chicago citation style, 746, 748–755
chronological organization in technical
    descriptions, 515
chronological résumés, 388, 393–394,
    393*f*
chunking in online design, 289*t*
circle graphs. *See* pie graphs

circumlocutions, 344
citations
  examples, 748–755
  in research, 125*t*, 172–181
citation styles, 131*t*, 746–755
  APA, 746, 748–755
  APSA, 746, 748–755
  CBE, 747, 748–755
  Chicago, 746, 748–755
  IEEE, 747, 748–755
  MLA, 746, 748–755
  Turabian, 746, 748–755
  Vancouver, 747, 748–755
clarity, 214*t*, 347–348
classification paragraphs, 218
classified ads for employment, 371,
  371*f*
clichés
  avoiding, 214
  and cultural contexts, 227–228
clip art, 300, 319–320, 320*f*
clothing for interviews, 115*t*
clustering (mind mapping), 88, 88*t*, 89*f*
clutter
  and color, 268
  in design, 247
  in résumés, 392*t*
coherence
  in paragraphs, 220
  in presentations, 439
cohesion in paragraphs, 219
collaboration, 54–75
  advantages, 57–59
  disadvantages, 60–61
  evaluating, 62*f*
  face-to-face, 61–63, 61–63*t*
  listening skills, 67–68, 68*t*
  online, 63, 63*t*
  peer review, 64–67, 64*t*, 66*t*
  and professional development, 426
  pros and cons, 22
  resolving conflict, 68–69, 69*t*
  skills for, 67–70
  types, 54–57
    cross-functional, 56–57, 57*f*
    divided labor, 55–56
    horizontal, 55, 55*f*
    integrated, 56–57, 57*f*
    sequential, 55, 55*f*
    stratification, 55–56, 56*f*
    vertical, 55–56, 56*f*
colloquial diction, 205–206
Colomb, Gregory (*The Craft of
  Research*), 637

colon (punctuation), 726–727
color
  associations of, 268
  and clutter, 268, 269*f*
  cultural interpretations of, 266, 268
  for design consistency, 245
  as a design element, 265–266*f*,
    265–269, 267*f*, 269–270*t*, 269*f*
  messages conveyed by, 268
  in print documents *versus* online,
    273*f*
  in specific communications
    bar graphs, 307*t*
    drawings, 315*t*
    e-mail, 501
    graphs, 308*t*
    letters, 482*t*
    online illustrations, 300
    on-screen documents, 285, 287
    portfolios, 401*t*
    presentation slides, 456*t*
    schedule charts, 314*t*
color blindness, design considerations
  for, 268, 269*f*, 308*t*
color of type (density), 258, 260*f*
columns
  as design element, 249
  justification (typography), 264
  in scannable résumés, 400*t*
combination organization in technical
  descriptions, 515
combined audiences, 37, 40
comma splices, 741
commas (punctuation), 725–726
commercial databases in research, 146,
  147*f*
communication
  failures of, 12–15
  social contexts of, 11–17
  in the workplace, 8–11
companies, researching, 114, 376
company policies. *See* policies and
  procedures
comparison paragraphs, 218
comparisons in technical definitions,
  513
compiling copyrighted material,
  186–187
complaint letters, 486–487, 487*f*, 488*f*
complex prose, 207–208
complex style, 202–203
complimentary close in letters,
  473–474, 474*f*
  full-block, 476, 477*f*

modified-block, 477–479, 478*f*
personal, 480–481, 482*f*
semiblock, 479–480, 479*f*
simplified, 480, 481*f*
compressed letter spacing
  (typography), 262*f*
computerese, 212, 213
computer illustrations, 321–325
computer viruses and e-mail, 503
conciseness, 342–343, 343*t*
conclusion section
  in formal reports, 648
  in presentations, 439
  in progress reports, 587
  in proposals, 561
  in technical descriptions, 515
  in trip reports, 590
concreteness
  on presentation slides, 456*t*
  in technical prose, 346–347
conferences, professional, 374, 421–422
conflicts, resolving, 68–69, 69*t*
conjunctions, 739
connotations
  of colors, 268
  and denotations, 206–207*f*,
    341–342, 342*f*
consistency
  in design, 244–245, 245*f*, 250
  in instructions, 697*t*
  revising for, 347
contact information in résumés, 389
context
  in diagrams, 316*t*
  in letters, 472–473
continuing education, 422–424
contractions in reports, 606*t*
contrast in online illustrations, 301
contrast paragraphs, 218
controlled vocabularies in database
  searches, 151*t*
conventions
  for online documents, 279, 281, 282*f*
  for print documents, 235–239,
    236–237*f*
copyediting
  of documents, 333–334*t*, 333–336,
    334*f*, 335–336*f*
  symbols for, 334*f*
copyright, 185–191
  and clip art, 319–320, 320*f*
  and developmental editing, 332*t*
  fair-use doctrine, 187–188
  registration of, 191

corporate bias, 225, 226*t*
corporate culture and politics, 17–19
correctness, 340–341
correspondence, 238*f*, 375–388, 466–506. *See also* e-mail; letters; memos
correspondence courses, 423
cost-estimating software, 105
cost section (proposals), 560–561, 562–564*f*
courtesy copy notations
    in letters, 475, 476*f*
    in memos, 495*f*, 496
courtesy titles in business correspondence, 469, 470–471, 471*f*
cover letters
    for job applications, 376–379, 377*f*
    writing, 492, 494*f*
cover pages
    for formal reports, 642
    for policies and procedures, 524*t*
creative thinking (discovery and invention)
    brainstorming, 85*e*, 86, 86*f*, 87*t*
    freewriting, 89–90, 90–91*t*, 90*f*
    mind mapping, 88, 88*t*, 89*f*
creativity programs, 104–105
credibility (ethos)
    establishing, 46–47, 223, 348
    of online text, 278
    and presentations, 437
    strengthening in prose, 94
    and writing for the Web, 279*t*
cropping photographs, 318*t*
cross-functional collaborations, 56–57, 57*f*
Crotogino, Ron ("From the Workplace"), 604
cultural aspects of communication
    avoiding bias, 225, 226*t*
    understanding contexts, 227–228
    using color, 266, 268
    using humor, 224*t*
culture, corporate, 17–19
curriculum vitae (c.v.)
    preparing, 388–400
    in proposals, 560
cutaway views, 314–315
Cygnarowicz, Helen ("From the Workplace"), 406–407

danger notices in instructions, 687–688, 688*f*
dangling modifiers, 742

dashes (punctuation), 727–728
database-management programs, 105
databases
    commercial, for research, 126, 127*t*, 146, 147*f*
    of jobs, 375
    managing, 105
    and organizing research information, 173–175
    types, 151*t*
date lines
    in letters, 467, 469*f*
        full-block, 476, 477*f*
        modified-block, 477–479, 478*f*
        personal, 480–481, 482*f*
        semiblock, 479–480, 479*f*
        simplified, 480, 481*f*
    in memos, 495*f*, 496
dates, conventions for writing, 736
deadlines section of RFP, 550
decimal fractions, 735
decorative typefaces, 254*f*
decreased word spacing (typography), 262*f*
definition paragraphs, 218–219
definitions
    extended, 512*f*, 513, 514–515*f*
    formal, 512–513, 512*f*, 513*f*
    informal, 511–512, 512*f*
    technical, 511–513, 512*f*, 513*f*
degree programs, 423
denotation and connotation, 206–207*f*, 341–342, 342*f*
density of type, 258, 260*f*
dependencies in schedule charts, 314*t*
description paragraphs, 218
descriptions, technical, 513–516, 516*f*
descriptive abstracts in formal reports, 642–644, 643*f*
design, 235–289
    alignment in, 242–244, 244*f*
    balance in, 242–244, 244*f*
    color in, 265–266*f*, 265–269, 267*f*, 269–270*t*, 269*f*
    and credibility, 278
    determining in planning stage, 95
    and international audiences, 278
    and jargon, 278
    principles of, 240–246, 242*f*, 247*t*
        consistency, 244–245, 245*f*, 271
        readability, 245, 246*f*
        simplicity, 240–242, 243–244*f*
        symmetry, 242–244, 244*f*
        usability, 245–246
    for print *versus* online, 273*f*

repetition in, 244–245, 245*f*
reviewing for, 355*f*
in specific communications
    academic papers, 237, 239
    assembly manuals, 238*f*
    books, 236, 236*f*
    brochures, 237, 237*f*
    chapter pages, 250
    formal reports, 640
    hyperlinks, 278
    informal reports, 601
    instructions, 695–696*t*
    letters, 482*t*
    newsletters, 236–237, 237*f*, 238*f*
    online interfaces, 279–281, 280*f*
    on-screen documents, 270–289
    résumés, 392, 392*t*
    scannable résumés, 400*t*
    software manuals, 238*f*
    specifications, 527–528, 528*t*
    Web pages, 245, 270–289
and tone, 225
triage for, 289, 289*t*
detail, level of
    and conciseness, 343
    in paragraphs, 220
    in photographs, 318*t*
    in presentations, 439
    and tone, 223
developmental editing, 330–332, 332*t*
Dewey Decimal classifications, 136*f*
diagrams, 315–316, 316*f*, 316*t*
dictionaries, online, 145–146*f*, 151*t*
diction (word choice)
    appropriateness, 341–342, 342*f*
    levels of, 203–206
        colloquial, 205–206
        formal, 204
        informal, 205
        slang, 206
    and levels of technicality, 41–43
    in specific communications
        e-mail, 200*f*
        formal reports, 200*f*
        informal reports, 200*f*
        instructions, 200*f*
        letters, 199, 200*f*
        memos, 200*f*
        policies and procedures, 200*f*
        presentations, 437
        proposals, 200*f*
        scannable résumés, 399–400*t*
        specifications, 527, 529

style guides, 92
technical reports, 199–200
usage, 207, 208*f*
dingbats (typeface), 256, 256*f*
direct and indirect patterns, 483–485,
484*f*, 485*f*
for appealing to audiences, 46
for expressing purpose, 83–84
for international audiences, 228
in specific communications
adjustment letters, 487–490, 489*f*
complaint letters, 486–487, 487*f*,
488*f*
correspondence, 483–485, 484*f*,
485*f*
informal reports, 599
job decline letters, 385, 386*f*
refusal letters, 490, 491*f*
direct costs in budgets (proposals), 561
directives (company), 517*f*, 519–526
directories, online, 153*f*, 162, 163–164*f*
directories of periodicals, 128–129*f*
direct quotations, 183–185
discourse communities. *See* audience
discovery (initial ideas), 85–91
discussion groups, 420–421
discussion section (scientific papers),
635
displaying information visually,
295–325
distance education, 423
distance in prose. *See* formality; tone
diversity and technical communication,
23–27, 26*f*
divided-labor collaborations, 55–56
documentation styles, 746–755. *See
also* citations; citation styles
documenting sources, 172–181. *See
also* citations; citation styles
document plans, 98*t*, 101, 102*f*
documents. *See also specific document
types*
appropriate prose styles, 199–201,
200*f*
design conventions, 235–239,
236–237*f*
managing, 96–105, 98–99*t*
print *versus* online characteristics, 273*f*
double negatives, 348–349
doublespeak and doubletalk, 212
download speeds, 288–289
drafts
evaluating, 350–360
improving, 203–228, 329–350
in informal reports, 601, 603

in instructions, 696–697, 696*f*
drawing programs, 322–323
drawings, 300, 314–315, 314*s*, 315*f*,
315*t*
dressing for interviews, 115*t*
dry-erase boards (presentation tool),
446, 447*f*, 449*f*

each and *every* in specifications, 529
edit, levels of, 330, 331*f*
editing, 329–339
methods
bottom-up, 329–330, 330*f*
page-by-page, 329, 330*f*
top-down, 330, 330*f*
phases
copyediting, 333–334*t*, 333–336,
334*f*, 335–336*f*
developmental, 330–332, 332*t*
proofreading, 336–339, 337–338*f*,
338–339*t*
substantive, 332–333, 333*t*
of proposals, 547
education, continuing, 422–424
education section
in job application letters, 378
in résumés, 389–390
effective technical communication,
15–17
electronic collaboration, 22
electronic résumés, 395–400, 398*f*,
399–400*t*, 399*f*, 400*t*
electronic sources of information
citing, 747
indexes to, 128–129*f*
in libraries, 142–166
searching, 148*t*
elements of instructions, 684–689
ellipses (punctuation), 730–731
e-mail, 498–506, 499*t*
abbreviations in, 506, 506*f*
attachments to, 501–503
diction (word choice) in, 200*f*
formality in, 200*f*
as format for informal reports,
598–599*t*, 602–603*f*
netiquette in, 502
signature block for, 501–502, 502*f*,
505
e-mail discussion groups, 420–421
em dashes (punctuation), 727–728
emoticons (smileys), 506, 506*f*
emotions
appealing to, 45
in e-mail, 504

in letters, 486, 487*f*
in prose, 222–225
emphasis of sentences, 215–216
empirical research reports, 585*f*,
628–629, 629–632*f*, 632–633
employee handbooks, 520–522
employment, obtaining, 368–409
employment agencies, 371–373
enclosure notations
in letters, 475–476, 475*f*
full-block, 476, 477*f*
modified-block, 477–479, 478*f*
personal, 480–481, 482*f*
semiblock, 479–480, 479*f*
simplified, 480, 481*f*
in memos, 495*f*, 496
encyclopedia articles in research, 126*t*
en dashes (punctuation), 727–728
end notations in letters, 475–476, 475*f*
full-block, 476, 477*f*
modified-block, 477–479, 478*f*
personal, 480–481, 482*f*
semiblock, 479–480, 479*f*
simplified, 480, 481*f*
engineerese, 212
engineering drawings, 314–315
enumerative paragraphs, 218
environmental impact studies, 585*f*
equipment, audiovisual, 440
ethics
college and workplace standards,
20–22
defined, 19
and illustrations, 302
personal standards of, 73, 73*t*
and plagiarism, 181–183*t*
professional standards of, 21*f*
for quoting copyrighted material,
186–188
and reporting information, 182–191
Society for Technical
Communication code, 21*f*
ethos. *See* credibility (ethos)
etymology (word origins) in technical
definitions, 513
evaluating
drafts, 350–360
group work, 62*f*
interviews, 404
online sources, 163–164, 164–165*t*
print sources, 137–138, 138–141*f*,
139–141*t*
proposals, 549, 550, 565–567,
566–567*f*
every in specifications, 529

evidence and reasoning (logos), 47–49
example paragraphs, 217
examples in technical definitions, 513
exclamation points (punctuation), 725
executives (audience category), 36–37
executive summaries, 644–646, 645*t*
expanded letter spacing (typography), 262*f*
experience, listing
  in job application letters, 378
  in résumés, 391
experimentation, 122–124, 124*f*
experts (audience category), 37
expletive constructions (grammar), 345–346
exploded views in drawings, 314
extended character sets (typography), 255
extended definitions, 512*f*, 513, 514–515*f*
external proposals, 549, 549*f*

face-to-face collaborations, 61–63, 61–63*t*
facilitators
  in focus groups, 121
  in usability testing, 358
fair-use doctrine (copyright), 187–188, 298
fallacies, logical, 50*f*
false analogy (logical fallacy), 50*f*
false dilemma (logical fallacy), 50*f*
families of type, 255
FAQ. *See* Frequently Asked Questions (FAQ) lists
faulty parallelism, 350, 351–352*f*, 742
feasibility reports, 585*f*, 625–626
figures, 296–299, 297*f*, 299*f*
first drafts
  improving, 203–228, 329–350
  for instructions, 696–697, 696*f*
fixed order of steps (instructions), 692–694, 692*f*
flaming (abusive e-mail messages), 503
flat-file databases, 173–175, 174*f*
flip charts (presentation tool), 447*f*, 449–450, 451*f*
floating illustrations, 301
flourishes (typographic) in design, 250
flowchart programs, 105
flowcharts
  in documents, 311, 311*t*, 312*f*
  for planning, 179–180, 180*f*
  in Web design, 271*f*

flow in paragraphs, 219–220
focus
  achieving, 199, 199*f*
  determining, 80–85
  identifying key questions for, 637
  in specific communications
    formal reports, 636–638
    informal reports, 599
    instructions, 689
    surveys, 118
    Web pages, 270, 279*t*
focus groups, 121–122
foils (presentation tool), 405, 447*f*, 451*t*, 452*f*, 456*t*
foldout illustrations, 298
follow-ups
  for interviews, 408–409
  for job application letters, 379
fonts. *See* typefaces; typography
footers
  as navigation aids, 250
  in policies and procedures, 524*t*
footnotes in tables, 303*f*, 305*t*
formal definitions, 512–513, 512*f*, 513*f*
formal diction, 204
formality
  in documents, 200*f*
  in e-mail, 501, 504
  in presentation slides, 456*t*
  in prose, 222
formal outlines, 176–177, 177*f*
formal reports, 623–654
  diction (word choice) in, 200*f*
  elements of, 641–654
    abstract, 642–644, 643*f*, 644*t*
    appendix, 652–653
    conclusion, 648
    cover, 642
    executive summary, 644–646, 645*t*
    glossary, 648–649
    index, 654, 654*t*
    introduction, 646–647
    letter of transmittal, 641–642
    list of illustrations, 646
    recommendations, 648, 649*f*
    reference list, 654
    results, 647–648
    symbols and abbreviations, 650, 651*f*, 652
    table of contents, 646
    title page, 642
  and informal reports, 586
  strategies for preparing, 636–641
  style and format for, 200*f*

types
  analytical reports, 623–624, 624*f*
  background reports, 624–625, 659–681*f*
  empirical research reports, 628–629, 629–632*f*, 632–633
  feasibility reports, 625–626
  informational reports, 623–624, 624*f*
  recommendation reports, 610–621*f*, 623–624, 624*f*, 626–628
  scientific papers, 633–636
formal style in reports, 603
formal tables, 303–304, 303*f*, 304–305*t*, 304*f*
formats
  for memos, 494–497, 495*f*
  for policies and procedures, 523–524*t*
form reports, 596–597, 596–597*f*
fractions, 735
fragments of sentences, 741
freewriting, 89–90, 90*f*, 90*t*
Frequently Asked Questions (FAQ) lists, 687
"From the Workplace"
  Crotogino (research scientist and administrator), 604
  Cygnarowicz (mathematics courseware vice president), 406–407
  Hammack (consultant/trainer), 572–573
  Hansen (Web designer), 290–291
  Hartman (university information director), 458–459
  Hermansen-Eldard (course developer), 428–429
  Joshi (director of information technology and services), 356–357
  Lockwood (team leader), 188–189
  Mackler (engineering consultant), 534–535
  Maislin (information architect), 48–49
  Reed (engineering professor), 74–75
  Ricciardi (photographer and graphic artist), 322–323
  Rush (water-systems engineer), 24–25
  Shapiro (program manager), 504–505

Steinman (biomedical consultant), 652–653

Vogt (technical writer and Web developer), 106–107

Watts (fire-safety director), 226–227

Weber (science and technical writer and editor), 166–167

Williams (software development manager), 698–699

front matter

directives in style guides, 91

elements of

abstract, 551–553, 556, 556*f*, 634, 634*f*, 642–644, 643*f*, 644*t*

cover page, 524*t*, 642

executive summary, 644–646, 645*t*

list of figures, 299

list of illustrations, 646

list of tables, 299, 303

table of contents, 299, 524*t*, 646

title page, 633, 642

transmittal (cover) letter, 492, 494*f*, 641–642

in formal reports, 641

in instructions, 697*t*

in policies and procedures, 524*t*

full-block format letters, 476, 477*f*

full-justified text, 263–264, 264*f*

full-text databases, 151*t*, 154–155*f*

functional organization in technical descriptions, 515

functional résumés, 388, 394–395, 395–396*f*

function descriptions in technical definitions, 513

Gantt charts, 313, 313*f*, 314*t*, 354*f*

gathering information, 111–166

for formal reports, 638

for informal reports, 599

for instructions, 689–692, 690–691*f*

gender bias, 225, 226*t*

general reports, 624–625, 659–681*f*

general-to-specific paragraphs, 218

genre

as determining level of detail, 220

and developmental editing, 332*t*

and humor, 224*t*

and style, 199–201, 200*f*

genres (document types). *See specific document types*

GIF format for illustrations, 300, 323

global aspects of technical communication, 23–27

glossaries

about, 513

in formal reports, 648–649

in instructions, 688, 697*t*

in policies and procedures, 524*t*

goals and objectives in proposals, 558–559, 559–560*t*

gobbledygook, 213, 346

gopher (online searches), 156

governmentese, 212

government publications in research, 136–137, 137*f*

grammar, 738–739

graphics, 295–325

border, as design elements, 250, 251*f*

downloading, 288–289

online, 278

in portfolios, 401*t*

and simplicity, 241

in technical definitions, 513

and writing for the Web, 279*t*

graphics utilities, 324–325, 325*f*

graphs, 305–311

bar graphs, 305–307, 306*f*, 307*t*

line graphs, 307–308, 308*f*, 308*t*

pictographs, 310–311, 310*f*, 310*t*

pie graphs, 309–310*t*, 309*f*

grids, designing with, 249, 249*f*

group work. *See* collaboration; peer reviews

guidelines for authors (journals), 418–419*f*

halftones in photographs, 317

Hammack, Harlan ("From the Workplace"), 572–573

handbooks for employees, 520–522

handouts

of portfolio materials, 401*t*

in presentations, 445

Hansen, Lise ("From the Workplace"), 290–291

Hartman, Joel L. ("From the Workplace"), 458–459

headers

as navigation aids, 250

in policies and procedures, 524*t*

for second pages

of letters, 482*t*, 483*f*

of memos, 297*t*, 497*f*

headings

as design elements, 245

in online design, 274, 289*t*

in specific communications

chronological résumés, 394

letters, 467, 469*f*

memos, 495, 495*f*

policies and procedures, 524*t*

Web pages, 279*t*

hearing impairments, site accessibility and, 283, 284*f*

Hermansen-Eldard, Marjorie ("From the Workplace"), 428–429

heuristic approaches to audiences, 38–39, 38*f*

hierarchy in lists, 252

horizontal-model collaborations, 55, 55*f*

house style, reviewing for, 354, 355*f*

humor

and presentations, 437, 437*s*

in technical prose, 224*t*

and writing for the Web, 279*t*

hyperlinks, 278, 285

hyphens (punctuation), 728

hypothesis testing, 123, 124*f*

ideas, in creative thinking, 85–91

identification line

in letters, 475, 475*f*

full-block, 476, 477*f*

modified-block, 477–479, 478*f*

personal, 480–481, 482*f*

semiblock, 479–480, 479*f*

simplified, 480, 481*f*

in memos, 495*f*, 496

idiomatic expressions, 207, 208*f*

idioms as cultural issues, 227–228

IEEE citation style, 747, 748–755

illustrations, 295–325

accessibility online, 300

anchored to text, 301

appropriateness of, 295–301

color in, 300

computer creation of, 321–325

computer formats (GIF, JPEG), 300

contrast in, 301

and ethics, 302

fair-use doctrine (copyright) for, 298

floating, 301

in foldouts, 298

interlaced, 300

landscape format, 298

for online documents, 299–301

permissions for, 298

for print documents, 296–299

size, 301

in specific communications

illustrations *(cont.)*
    formal reports, 640
    informal reports, 601
    instructions, 695–696*t*
    types
        charts, 311–314
        clip art, 319–320
        diagrams, 315–316
        drawings, 314–315
        graphs, 305–311
        maps, 316–317
        photographs, 317–319
        tables, 302–305
    white space in, 297
imperative mood, 697*t*, 743
impersonality in prose, 222
impromptu presentations, 435
improprieties (word choice), 207, 208*f*
increased word spacing (typography),
    262*f*
indentions of paragraphs
    in full-block format letters, 476, 477*f*
    in modified-block format letters,
        477–479, 478*f*
    in personal format letters, 480–481,
        482*f*
    in semiblock format letters,
        479–480, 479*f*
    in simplified format letters, 480,
        481*f*
indexes
    in research
        online, 132–135*f*, 162, 163–164*f*
        for periodicals, 135
        print and electronic, 128–129*f*
    in specific communications
        formal reports, 654, 654*t*
        policies and procedures, 524*t*
indicative mood (verbs), 743
indirect and direct patterns, 483–485,
    484*f*, 485*f*
    for appealing to audiences, 46
    for expressing purpose, 83–84
    for international audiences, 228
    in specific communications
        adjustment letters, 487–490,
            489*f*
        complaint letters, 486–487, 487*f*,
            488*f*
        general correspondence, 483–485,
            484*f*, 485*f*
        informal reports, 599
        job decline letters, 385, 386*f*
        refusal letters, 490, 491*f*

indirect costs in budgets (proposals),
    561
indirect quotations, 184–185
ineffective technical communication,
    costs of, 15
inflated style (sentences), 216
informal definitions, 511–512, 512*f*
informal diction, 205
informality
    in e-mail, 504
    in prose, 222
informal outlines, 176, 176*f*
informal reports, 584–606
    audiences for, 40
    diction (word choice) in, 200*f*
    direct and indirect patterns in, 599
    and formal reports, 586
    formats for, 598–599*t*
    style and function for, 200*f*
    types
        form reports, 596–597, 596–597*f*
        lab reports, 591–594, 592–593*f*
        periodic activity reports, 587–588,
            590*f*
        progress reports, 586–587,
            588–589*f*
        trip reports, 588–590, 591*f*
informal style in reports, 603, 605*f*,
    606*t*
informal tables, 302, 302*t*, 304*f*
information
    determining needs of audience, 81
    displaying visually, 295–325
    electronic, 142–166, 143–151
    gathering, 111–166
    in instructions, 689–692, 690–691*f*
    interpreting, 44
    introducing new, 220–221
    managing, 172–191
    organizing, 172–191
    outlining, 175–177, 176*f*, 177–178*t*,
        177*f*
    qualitative *versus* quantitative, 118
informational interviews, 113–118
    obtaining, 402–403
    planning for, 114, 115*f*, 115*t*, 116*t*
    questions in, 115*f*, 116*t*
informational job interviews, 402–404,
    403*t*
informational reports, 623–624, 624*f*
informative abstracts (formal reports),
    642–644
informative presentations, 435–436
initial ideas, discovering, 85–91

initialisms, 209–210, 732–733
initials in identification lines (letters),
    475, 475*f*
inquiry letters, 490–492
inside addresses in letters, 468–469,
    470*f*
    full-block, 476, 477*f*
    modified-block, 477–479, 478*f*
    semiblock, 479–480, 479*f*
    simplified, 480, 481*f*
instructions, 683–699
    designing and illustrating, 695–696*t*
    diction (word choice) in, 200*f*
    elements of, 684–689
        Frequently Asked Questions
            (FAQ), 687
        introduction, 685
        materials, tools, and equipment,
            686
        steps, 686–687, 690–691*f*
        theory, 685–686
        troubleshooting, 687
    formality in, 200*f*
    ordering steps in, 692–694, 692*f*,
        693*f*, 694*f*
    versus procedures, 524
    versus processes, 517, 517*f*
    producing, 698
    strategies for preparing, 689–698
    style elements in, 697, 697*t*
    usability testing of, 698–699
    writing and revising, 696–697, 696*f*
integrated collaborations, 56–57, 57*f*
interactivity for online pages, 282
interests, lists of (résumés), 391
interfaces, designing for online,
    279–281, 280*f*
interjections, 739
interlaced illustrations, 300
interlibrary loans in research, 127*t*
internal proposals, 548–549, 549*t*
international audiences
    and color connotations, 266, 268
    communicating with, 227–228
    and design, 278
    and humor, 224*t*
    and jargon, 278
    persuading, 46*t*
    and technical communication,
        23–27
    and tone, 228
international correspondence and
    complimentary closes, 473–474
international date formats, 467

Internet mailing lists, 375
Internet research, 151–166
interpreting information
  in formal reports, 638
  in informal reports, 601
  in instructions, 689–692, 690–691*f*
  writer's role in, 44
interviews
  conducting, 116–117, 409, 409*t*
  evaluating, 404
  following up, 117
  informational, 113–118, 115*f*, 115*t*, 116*t*
  job informational, 402–404, 403*t*
  listening skills for, 116–117
  by mail, 117
  preparation for, 114, 115*f*, 115*t*, 116*t*
  questions for, 403–404
  as research tool, 113–118
  stages of, 406–408
  taking notes during, 117
  by telephone, 117–118*t*
introduction section
  in formal reports, 646–647
  in instructions, 685
  in proposals, 557
  in requests for proposals, 549
  in scientific papers, 634–635
invention. *See* creative thinking
  (discovery and invention)
italic styled text, 271, 271*f*, 731–732

"jaggies" (stair-step drawing effects),
  321
jargon, 212–213, 212*f*, 214*t*
  and attitude, 212
  and clarity, 214*t*
  cultural issues for, 227–228
  and international audiences, 278
  and online text, 278
  in scannable résumés, 400*t*
  and writing for the Web, 279*t*
job agencies, 371–373
job-application forms, 597
job-benefits forms, 597
job correspondence, 375–388
job counseling, 368–370
job databases, 375
job decline letters, 385, 386*f*
job fairs, 370
job interviews, 402–409, 403*t*
  conducting, 409, 409*t*
  preparing for, 404–405, 405*t*
job letters, 375–388

job-objective statements in résumés,
  389
job recruiters, 370
job searches, 368–409
Joshi, Yateendra
  "From the Workplace," 356–357
  Web publishing *versus* conventional
    publishing, 274
journal articles
  design conventions for, 239*f*
  publishing, 417–420, 418–419*f*
  as research sources, 126
  writing, 417–420, 418–419*f*
journals, trade, 370–371, 415
JPEG format for illustrations, 300, 323
justification of text, 263–264, 264*f*

key questions in narrowing focus, 637
keywords
  in abstracts, 643–644
  in online design, 274
  in scannable résumés, 399–400*t*
  searching, 148*t*
  in titles of scientific papers, 633
  and writing for the Web, 279*t*
knowledge, personal, 113
knowledge level and audience, 36–37

labels for figures, 296–297
laboratory reports, 239*f*, 585*f*,
  591–594, 592–593*f*
landscape format
  bindings for, 299
  in illustrations, 298
  for tables, 305*t*
layout
  of illustrations, 298
  online, 283*t*
laypeople (audience category), 36
leading (of type), 263, 263*f*
left-justified text, 263–264, 264*f*
legal issues
  and developmental editing, 332*t*
  in specifications, 527–528
legal reviews, 355*f*, 523*t*
legends
  in figures, 297
  in graphs, 308*t*
  in maps, 317*t*
  in pie graphs, 309*t*
  readability of, 298
legibility
  of presentation slides, 456*t*
  in typography, 253

length
  of instructions, 684
  of presentations, 445
  of proposals, 548
  of résumés, 394
  of sentences, 216
lettered lists, 250–253
letterhead stationery, 467, 469*f*
letters, 466–493
  conventions for design, 238*f*
  designing, 482*t*
  diction (word choice) in, 199, 200*f*
  formats, 476–482
    full-block, 476, 477*f*
    modified-block, 477–479, 478*f*
    personal, 480–481, 482*f*
    semiblock, 479–480, 479*f*
    simplified, 480, 481*f*
  parts, 467–476, 468*f*
    body, 472–473
    complimentary close, 473–474,
      474*f*
    courtesy copy (cc), 475–476,
      475*f*
    courtesy title, 469
    date line, 467, 469*f*
    enclosure indication, 475–476,
      475*f*
    end notations, 475–476, 475*f*
    headings, 467, 469*f*
    identification line, 475, 475f
    inside address, 468–469, 470*f*
    outside (return) address, 467, 469*f*
    salutation, 469, 470–471, 471*f*
    second page header, 482*t*, 483*f*
    signature block, 474, 474*f*
    subject line, 472, 472*f*
    typist's initials, 475, 475*f*
  as specific communications
    informal reports, 598–599*t*
    proposals, 548
  style and function of, 200*f*
  types, 485–493
    acceptance, 383–385, 384*f*
    adjustment, 487–490, 489*f*
    application, 376–379, 377*f*
    complaint, 486–487, 487*f*, 488*f*
    decline, 385, 386*f*
    employment, 375–388
    inquiry, 490–492
    job application, 376–379, 377*f*
    recommendation, 381, 382*f*
    refusal, 385, 386*f*, 490, 491*f*
    resignation, 385–388, 387*f*

letters, types *(cont.)*
    thank-you, 117, 379–381, 380*f*,
      408–409
    transmittal, 492, 494*f*, 641–642
    update, 381–383, 383*f*
letter spacing (typography)
  online, 287–288
  of text, 247, 260–262, 262*f*
levels of edit, 330, 331*f*
levels of technicality, 41–43
libraries, 124–155
Library of Congress
  classifications, 136*f*
  online catalog, 152
  subject headings, 126*t*, 127*t*, 151*t*
ligatures (typography), 255
lighting as design element, 273*f*
line drawings, 314–315
line graphs, 307–308, 308*f*, 308*t*
line length
  in scannable résumés, 400*t*
  typographic considerations for, 257,
    259, 259*f*
line spacing
  online, 287–288
  on presentation slides, 456*t*
  of text, 260–261, 263, 263*f*
linking on Web sites, 274, 285
listening skills
  in collaborations, 67–68, 68*t*
  in interviews, 116–117
lists, 250–253
  hierarchy in, 252
  in instructions, 686
listserver mailing lists, 420–421
lists of figures, 299
lists of illustrations, 646
lists of references in résumés, 391
lists of symbols and abbreviations,
  650, 651*f*, 652
lists of tables, 299, 303
literature reviews, 558, 757–758*f*,
  757–759
Lockwood, Paul ("From the
  Workplace"), 188–189
logical fallacies, 49, 50*f*
logic drawings, 314–315
logos (argument strategy), 47–49

Mackler, Scott ("From the Workplace"),
  534–535
magazines, trade, 370–371
mailing lists, 375, 420–421
mail interviews, 117

maintenance reports, 585*f*
Maislin, Seth ("From the Workplace"),
  48–49
management, project, 96–105, 98–99*t*,
  560
managing information, 172–191
  with databases, 173–175
  with flowcharts, 179–180, 180*f*
  with note cards, 172–173
  with outlines, 175–177, 177–178*t*
  with storyboards, 180–181, 181*f*
  with tree diagrams, 178–179, 178*f*,
    179*t*
manuals, procedure, 520–522
maps
  in libraries, 137
  in technical documents, 316–317,
    316–317*t*, 317*f*
margins and spacing
  as design elements, 245
  in online design, 289*t*
  in specific communications
    job application letters, 377
    letters, 482*t*
    policies and procedures, 524*t*
    résumés, 392*t*
  and tone, 225
materials, tools, and equipment
    sections (instructions), 686
materials and methods sections
    (scientific papers), 635
mathematical symbols (typography),
  255
measurements, 734–735
mechanics of good prose, 723–736
  determining, 95
  reviewing for, 355*f*
mechanization (diction), 213
meetings
  attending, 71–72, 71*t*
  chapters, 425–426
  minutes, 585*f*, 594, 594–595*t*, 595*f*
  professional organizations, 373–374,
    415, 421–422
  "Rules of Engagement" for, 72*e*
memo reports, 610–621*f*
memos, 493–497, 495*f*, 496–497*t*
  design conventions of, 238*f*
  diction (word choice) in, 200*f*
  formatting of, 494–497, 495*f*
  headings of, 495, 495*f*
  for specific communications
    informal reports, 598–599*t*
    proposals, 548

style and function of, 200*f*
mentoring, 426–429, 427*t*, 430*t*
metaphors as cultural issues, 227–228
meta search engines, 159–160
methods section
  in formal reports, 647, 647*f*
  in scientific papers, 635
mind mapping, 88, 88*t*, 89*f*
minutes of meetings, 585*f*, 594,
  594–595*t*, 595*f*
misplaced modifiers, 742
MLA style, 746, 748–755
models (presentation tool), 446, 447*f*,
  448*f*
moderators in focus groups, 121
modern typefaces, 254*f*
modified-block format letters,
  477–479, 478*f*
modifiers
  ambiguous, 214
  dangling or misplaced, 742
monitors (screens)
  designing for, 270–289
  illustrating for, 299–301
  resolutions of, 286*f*, 287, 300
monographs in research, 135, 136*f*
mood (verbs), 743
movies in online documents,
  282–284
multicultural aspects of technical
  communication, 23–27,
  227–228
multimedia, 282–284
multiple audiences, 37, 40

narration paragraphs, 218
navigation aids
  bars, 245
  buttons, 250, 251*f*
negation in technical definitions, 513
negative constructions, 348–349
negotiating skills, 69, 70*t*
netiquette, 502, 503–505
networking
  with business cards, 421*s*
  for employment, 373
  for professional development, 425
newsletters
  columns in, 264
  conventional design of, 236–237,
    237*f*, 238*f*
  for professional organizations, 415
newspapers and the job search, 371,
  371*f*

newspeak, 212
nominal group technique (focus groups), 121
nominalizations, 212
normal spacing (letters and words), 262*f*
normal typefaces, 257*t*
note cards, 172–173
note-taking
  in interviews, 117
  methods of, 172–173
  for research, 125*t*
noun phrases, 345
nouns
  as part of speech, 738
  in scannable résumés, 399*t*
noun strings, 211
novelty typefaces, 254*f*, 256, 256*f*
numbered lists, 250–253, 252*f*, 686, 692–693
numbering of figures, 296
numbers, mechanics of using, 733–736
numeric databases, 151*t*, 153*f*

objectives
  in proposals, 558–559, 559–560*t*
  of specifications, 532
objectivity
  establishing, 47
  in online text, 278
  in technical documents, 44
officialese, 212
oldstyle typefaces, 254*f*
online collaborations, 63, 63*t*
online documents
  characteristics of, 273*f*
  prose style of, 275–278, 279*t*
online forums, 420–421
online hyperlinks, 278
online research
  disadvantages, 162–163
  effective searches, 148*t*, 149–150*f*
  evaluating sources, 163–164, 164–165*t*
  library searches, 129–130*f*
  specific sources
    catalogs, 127–128*t*, 142–143, 152, 162, 163–164*f*
    CD-ROMs, 143–151
    databases, 127*t*, 143–151
    indexes, 128–129*f*, 132–135*f*, 133, 162, 163–164*f*
  using electronic sources, 142–166

online résumés, 396–397, 398*f*
oral presentations. *See* presentations
organization
  in complaint letters, 486–487, 487*f*, 488*f*
  in technical descriptions, 515
organizational charts, 312, 312*f*, 313*t*
organizations, professional, 373–374, 415–416
organizing. *See also* managing information
  for audience appeal, 45–46
  for specific communications
    formal reports, 639–640, 639*f*
    informal reports, 600–601
    instructions, 692–694
    portfolios, 401*t*
    presentations, 437
orientation as design element, 273*f*
or in specifications, 529
outlined presentations, 435
outlines
  creating, 104
  for formal reports, 639–640
  versus prewriting, 86
  of research results, 175–177, 176*f*, 177–178*t*, 177*f*
  versus tree diagrams, 179
outside addresses in letters, 467, 469*f*
overview section of RFP, 549

page-by-page editing, 329, 330*f*
paint programs, 323–324, 324*f*
paired bar graphs, 307*f*
paper
  for job application letters, 377
  for portfolios, 401*t*
  for résumés, 392
papers, academic, 237, 239
paragraph-level style, 216–221
paragraph spacing
  in letters
    full-block, 476, 477*f*
    modified-block, 477–479, 478*f*
    personal, 480–481, 482*f*
    semiblock, 479–480, 479*f*
    simplified, 480, 481*f*
  in policies and procedures, 524*t*
  and white space, 260–261
parallelism
  in chronological résumés, 394
  faulty, 742
  of sentences, 349–350, 351–352*f*
paraphrase cards, 126*f*

paraphrases, documenting, 125*t*
paraphrasing *versus* direct quotations, 183–185
paraprofessionals (audience category), 37
parentheses (punctuation), 731
parenthetical definitions, 511
passive voice, 211, 743–744
pathos (argument strategy), 45–46
patterns, direct and indirect, 483–485, 484*f*, 485*f*
peer reviews
  benefiting from, 67*t*
  collaborations for, 64–67
  as document usability testing, 354, 356–357
  for journal articles, 420
  sample questions for, 65*f*
pentagonese, 212
percentages, 736
performance requirements in specifications, 527, 528–529, 528*t*
periodic activity reports, 587–588, 590*f*
periodical indexes, 135
periodic reports, 585*f*
periods (punctuation), 724
permissions
  and copyright, 186–189
  and developmental editing, 332*t*
  for illustrations, 298, 320
  for recording interviews, 115*t*
personability in prose, 222
personal digital assistants (PDAs), 102–104, 104*f*
personal format letters, 480–481, 482*f*
personal information management software, 102–104, 104*f*
personal knowledge (research tool), 113
personification, 213
personnel evaluation forms, 597
perspective drawings, 314–315
persuasion
  and audience, 34–51
  and color, 266
  in presentations, 435–436
  strategies for, 44–49
philosophical bias, 225, 226*t*
photographs
  versus drawings, 314
  using, 317–319, 318*f*, 318*t*, 319*f*
phrase definitions, 511

phrases
  noun, 345
  prepositional, 344
  verb, 344–345
pictographs, 310–311, 310*f*, 310*t*
pie graphs, 309–310*t*, 309*f*
pixel programs, 323–324, 324*f*
plagiarism, avoiding, 181–183*t*
plain style, 201–202, 606*t*
planning, 80–105
  for interviews, 114, 115*t*
  for meetings, 72*t*
  for presentations, 436
  for quality in documents, 100
  for specific communications
    company policies, 523*t*
    proposals, 546
    Web pages, 270
  tools for, 101–105
plug-ins (browsers), 288
point sizes of type
  about, 257, 258*f*
  and margins, 259, 259*f*
  in memos, 497*t*
  in scannable résumés, 400*t*
policies and procedures, 519–526
  diction (word choice) in, 200*f*
  documents, 522*f*, 523–524*t*, 523*t*,
    539–544*f*
  versus processes and instructions,
    517*f*
political bias, 225, 226*t*
portfolios, 400–401, 401*t*
posters (presentation tool), 447*f*,
  448–449, 450*f*
precision, 340–341
predefined databases, 173–175, 174*f*
preparing for interviews, 404–405, 405*t*
prepositional phrases, 344
prepositions, 739
presentations, 434–460
  audiovisual tools
    setting up, 440
    using, 444, 446–460, 447*f*
  categories of, 435–436
  delivery of, 440–445
  diction (word choice) in, 437
  preparing for, 436–440
  tool types
    chalkboards and dry-erase boards,
      446, 447*f*, 449*f*
    computer displays, 105, 447*f*, 455,
      455*f*, 456*t*
    flip charts, 447*f*, 449–450, 451*f*

    models, 446, 447*f*, 448*f*
    posters, 447*f*, 448–449, 450*f*
    35-mm slides, 447*f*, 453–454,
      453*f*, 454*f*
    transparencies, 405, 447*f*, 451*t*,
      452*f*, 456*t*
    video, 447*f*, 456–457, 457*f*,
      459–460, 459*f*
pretentious words, 207–208, 209*f*, 212*f*
prewriting techniques. *See* creative
  thinking (discovery and
  invention)
primary audiences, 40
primer style (sentences), 216
print documents
  characteristics of, 273*f*
  illustrating for, 296–299
  planning for, 100
  quality of, 100
  versus Web publishing, 274
print sources in libraries, 125–129
  abstracts, 133
  evaluating, 137–138, 138–141*f*,
    139–141*t*
  indexes, 128–129*f*
privacy issues for e-mail, 500, 503
procedures, 524–526, 525*f*, 539–544*f*
procedures manuals, 520–522
processes, technical, 517–519, 517*f*,
  518*f*, 519*f*, 520*f*, 521*f*
producing
  instructions, 698
  policies and procedures, 523–524*t*
  print documents, 100
  proposals, 547
professional growth, 414–430
professionalism, 19–22
professional journals, 416–420,
  418–419*f*
professional meetings, 373–374, 415,
  425–426
professional memberships lists in
  résumés, 391
professional organizations, 415–416
professionals (audience category), 37
progress reports, 585*f*, 586–587,
  588–589*f*, 609*f*, 624
project (laboratory) reports, 239*f*, 585*f*,
  591–594, 592–593*f*
project management, 96–105, 98–99*t*,
  560
project reviews, 357–358
project-scheduling software, 102, 103*f*
pronoun–antecedent agreement, 742

pronouns
  case, 743
  as part of speech, 738
  in reports, 606*t*
proofreading
  about, 336–339, 337–338*f*,
    338–339*t*
  of job application letters, 379
  symbols for, 337
proposals, 546–574, 564–565*t*
  appearance, 573
  approval strategies, 566–567,
    573–574
  content and format specified in RFP,
    550
  design conventions, 238*f*
  diction (word choice) in, 200*f*
  as document plan, 101, 102*f*
  elements of, 551–563
    abstract, 552–553, 556, 556*f*
    appendix, 562–563
    background on problem or need,
      557–558
    budget, 560–561, 562–564*f*
    conclusion, 561
    description of what is proposed,
      558–559
    introduction, 557
    literature review, 558
    methods, 559–560*t*
    qualifications of participants, 560
    schedule, 560
    summary, 552–553, 556, 556*f*
  evaluating, 549, 565–567, 566–567*f*
  formats, 548
  internal and external, 548–549,
    549*f*
  solicited and unsolicited, 548–549,
    549*f*
  style and format, 200*f*
  types, 548–549
prose style. *See* style
proximity connectors (Boolean
  searches), 151*t*
public domain and clip art, 320
punctuation
  cultural issues of, 227–228
  of lists, 253, 732
  mechanics of, 724–732
  in print résumés, 392*t*
  in scannable résumés, 400*t*
purpose
  and controlling level of detail, 220
  and humor, 224*t*

in specific communications
    company policies, 523*t*
    formal reports, 636–638
    informal reports, 599
    letters, 473
    proposals, 546
    specifications, 527, 530–531
    surveys, 118
    Web pages, 279*t*
  stating, 82–84, 84*f*
  in Web design, 270

qualifications section of RFP, 550
qualitative information and surveys, 118
quality in print documents, 100
quantitative information and surveys, 118–119
question marks (punctuation), 725
questionnaires. *See* surveys and questionnaires
questions (informational interview), 115*f*, 116*t*, 403–404
question-to-answer paragraphs, 218–219
quotation marks (punctuation), 729–730
quotations
  direct
    documenting, 125*t*
    versus paraphrasing, 183–185
  indirect, 184–185

racial bias, 225, 226*t*
ragged-left and ragged-right text, 263–264, 264*f*
rare books in research, 136
Raskin, Jef (Macintosh Project), 16*s*
raster illustration programs, 323–324, 324*f*
readability
  of callouts, 298
  and design, 245, 246*f*
  of documents, 289*t*
  of e-mail messages, 501
  and justification, 264
  of résumés, 392, 392*t*
  in typography, 253
reader-friendly tone in instructions, 697*t*
read-only databases, 173–175, 174*f*
recommendation letters, 381, 382*f*
recommendation reports, 585*f*, 610–621*f*, 623–624, 624*f*, 626–628

recommendations section (formal reports), 648, 649*f*
recruiters, job, 370
Redish, Janice, 12–13, 13*f*
redundancies, 343–344
Reed, Gregory ("From the Workplace"), 74–75
reference letters, 381, 382*f*
references
  in formal reports, 654
  in résumés, 391
  in scientific papers, 636
reference sources
  citing, 125*t*, 131*t*, 172–181, 748–755
  electronic, 143–151
  in libraries, 132–133
refusal letters, 385, 386*f*, 490, 491*f*
rehearsing presentations, 439
relational databases, 173–175, 174*f*
reliability of surveys, 118
religious bias, 225, 226*t*
repetition in design, 244–245, 245*f*
reports
  designing, 238*f*
  diction (word choice) in, 199–200
  style and format of, 200*f*
  types, 584–586, 585*f*
    analytical, 623–624, 624*f*
    annual, 585*f*
    background, 624–625, 659–681*f*
    empirical research, 628–629, 629–632*f*, 632–633
    feasibility, 625–626
    formal, 623–654
    forms, 596–597, 596–597*f*
    general, 624–625, 659–681*f*
    government, 136–137, 137*f*
    informal, 584–606
    informational, 623–624, 624*f*
    laboratory, 591–594, 592–593*f*
    memo, 610–621*f*
    minutes of meetings, 585*f*, 594, 594–595*t*, 595*f*
    periodic activity, 587–588, 590*f*
    progress, 585*f*, 586–587, 588–589*f*, 609*f*, 624
    recommendation, 610–621*f*, 623–624, 624*f*, 626–628
    research, 628–629, 629–632*f*, 632–633
    scientific paper, 633–636
    trip, 585*f*, 588–590, 591*f*
request for proposal (RFP), 548, 549–551, 566–567*f*, 578–582*f*

research, 111–166
  beginning a search, 127*t*
  Boolean searches, 142, 142*f*
  citing sources, 172–181
  evaluating online sources, 163–164, 164–165*t*
  locating information
    books, 135, 136*f*
    electronic sources, 129–130*f*, 142–166, 148*t*, 149–150*f*
    library print sources, 125–129
    monographs, 135, 136*f*
    periodicals, 135
    rare books, 136
    special collections, 136
    on the Web, 151–166
  planning for, 125*t*
researching companies
  for interviews, 114
  for job search, 376
researching for specific communications
  formal reports, 638
  informal reports, 599–600
  informational job interviews, 402
  presentations, 437
  proposals, 547
resignation letters, 385–388, 387*f*
resolution
  design element, 273*f*
  for online illustrations, 300
  of screens, 286*f*, 287
results section
  in formal reports, 647–648
  in scientific papers, 635
résumés, 388–400
  designing, 239*f*, 392, 392*t*
  electronic, 395–400
    online, 396–397, 398*f*
    scannable, 397, 399–400, 399–400*t*, 399*f*
  organization
    chronological, 393–394, 393*f*
    functional, 394–395, 395–396*f*
  print, 393–395
  in proposals, 560
return addresses, 467, 469*f*, 480–481, 482*f*
review cycles, 350, 353–354, 354*f*
reviews
  for company policies, 523*t*
  of proposals, 550
  types of, 353–355, 355*f*

revising, 339–350, 340*t*
  of formal reports, 640–641
  of informal reports, 601, 603
  of instructions, 696–697, 696*f*
  of journal articles, 420
  of proposals, 547
  versus reviewing and evaluating, 340
RFP. *See* request for proposal (RFP)
Ricciardi, Peter ("From the
    Workplace"), 322–323
right-justified text, 263–264, 264*f*
rivers of white space, 261, 261*f*
Robert's Rules of Order, 594*t*
robots (Web programs), 162
roman typefaces, 257*t*
Rose, Caroline (Macintosh Project),
    16–17
rough drafts
  improving, 203–228, 329–350
  for instructions, 696–697, 696*f*
rules
  as design elements, 250
  in portfolios, 401*t*
  in tables, 303*f*
rules and regulations, 519–520
running heads. *See* headers
run-on sentences, 741
Rush, Stacey ("From the Workplace"),
    24–25

safety information
  in instructions, 687–688, 688*f*
  in policies and procedures, 524*t*
salutations
  in business correspondence, 469,
    470–471, 471*f*
  in full-block format letters, 476, 477*f*
  in modified-block format letters,
    477–479, 478*f*
  in personal format letters, 480–481,
    482*f*
  in semiblock format letters,
    479–480, 479*f*
  in simplified format letters, 480, 481*f*
sans serif typefaces, 254–255, 254*f*,
    255*f*, 256*f*, 287–288
sarcasm (tone), 224*t*, 504
scannable résumés
  designing, 400*t*
  diction (word choice) in, 397,
    399–400, 399–400*t*
  typefaces for, 392*t*
schedule charts, 313, 313*f*, 314*t*, 354*f*
schedule section (proposals), 560

scheduling
  for projects, 97–98, 98–99*t*
  for review cycles, 350, 353–354,
    354*f*
schematics, 314–315
scholarly journals in research, 127*t*
scientific method, 123, 124*f*
scientific papers, 633–636
  citation styles for, 636
  elements of
    abstract, 634, 634*f*
    acknowledgments, 635
    discussion, 635
    introduction, 634–635
    materials and methods, 635
    references, 636
    results, 635
    title page, 633
scientific theories, 123
scooters (Web programs), 162
scope
  and audience, 85
  determining for specific
    communications
    company policies, 523*t*
    formal reports, 636–638
    procedures, 524
    proposals, 546, 548, 549
  and level of detail, 220
  limiting, 84–85
screen-capture programs, 324–325,
    325*f*
screens (monitors)
  designing for, 270–289
  illustrating for, 299–301
  resolutions of, 286*f*, 287, 300
scripted presentations, 435
script typefaces, 254*f*
scrolling in online documents,
    284–285, 285*f*
search engines
  evaluating, 160–161, 161*t*
  using, 148*t*, 156–164, 157–158*f*,
    159–160*f*
search indexes and catalogs, 162,
    163–164*f*
searching
  in databases, 151*t*
  in libraries, 125–129
search trees, 162
secondary audiences, 40
second-page headers
  in letters, 482*t*, 483*f*
  in memos, 297*t*, 497*f*

semiblock format letters, 479–480,
    479*f*
semicolons (punctuation), 726
seminars, 423
sender lines (memos), 495*f*, 496
sentence definitions, 511
sentence emphasis, 215–216
sentence fragments, 741
sentence outlines, 177
sentences
  improving, 215–216
  length of, 216
  parallelism in, 349–350, 351–352*f*
  variety in, 606*t*
sequential-model collaborations, 55,
    55*f*
serif typefaces, 253–254, 254*f*, 255,
    255*f*
seven-steps rule (instructions), 686
sexism, 225, 226*t*
shall and *will* in specifications, 529
Shapiro, Bob ("From the Workplace"),
    504–505
shop talk, 213
signature block
  in e-mail, 501–502, 502*f*, 505
  in letters, 474, 474*f*
    full-block, 476, 477*f*
    modified-block, 477–479,
      478*f*
    personal, 480–481, 482*f*
    semiblock, 479–480, 479*f*
    simplified, 480, 481*f*
  in memos, 495*f*, 496
simple words, 207–208, 209*f*
simplicity (design principle), 240–242,
    242*f*, 243–244*f*
simplified format letters, 480, 481*f*
sincerity, 348
site accessibility, 283, 284*f*
size
  of documents and screens, 273*f*
  of figures, 297
  of online illustrations, 301
  of typefaces
    in documents, 257, 258*f*
    in e-mail, 501
    and margins, 259, 259*f*
    online, 287–288
    on presentation slides, 456*t*
    in résumés, 392*t*
size bias, 225, 226*t*
skills for collaborating, 67–70
slab serif typefaces, 254*f*

in specific communications
    e-mail, 501
    letters, 482*t*
    memos, 497*t*
    online documents, 287–288
    policies and procedures, 524*t*
    presentation slides, 456*t*
    résumés, 392*t*
    scannable résumés, 400*t*
  and tone, 225
typography. *See also* typefaces
  about, 253–264
  and color, 268, 269*f*

underlined styled text, 271, 271*f*,
    731–732
unnecessary words and phrases, 343
unsolicited letters of inquiry, 491–492,
    492*f*, 493*f*
unsolicited proposals, 548, 549*f*
update letters, 381–383, 383*f*
usability and design, 245–246
usability testing, 358–360, 359*f*
  compared with focus groups,
    121–122
  elements of, 359*f*
  of flowcharts, 311*t*
  for instructions, 698–699
  and peer reviews, 354, 356–357
  reviewing for, 355*f*
usage (word choice), 207, 208*f*

validity of surveys, 118
Vancouver citation style, 747, 748–755
variable order of steps (instructions),
    692–694, 693*f*
variety in sentences, 216
vector illustration programs, 321–323,
    321*f*
verb phrases, 344–345
verbs
  action, 210
  in instructions, 697*t*
  as part of speech, 738, 743–744

verifiability of specifications, 528,
    528*t*
vertical-division collaborations, 55–56,
    56*f*
videos
  in online documents, 282–284
  as presentation tools, 447*f*, 456–457,
    457*f*, 459–460, 459*f*
viewgraphs (presentation tool), 405,
    447*f*, 451*t*, 452*f*, 456*t*
visual impairments, site accessibility
  and, 283, 284*f*
visuals, 295–325, 440
vocabulary
  controlled, in database searches,
    151*t*
  specialized, 212
Vogt, Ann ("From the Workplace"),
    106–107
voice, active and passive (verbs),
    210–211, 743–744

warnings
  in instructions, 687–688, 688*f*
  in policies and procedures, 524*t*
Watts, John M. ("From the
    Workplace"), 226–227
Weber, Jean ("From the Workplace"),
    166–167
Web forms, 597
Web publishing *versus* conventional
    publishing, 274
Web research, 151–166
Web sites
  accessibility of, 283, 284*f*
  conventional elements of, 239*f*, 281,
    282*f*
  designing for, 180–181, 181*f*,
    270–289, 271*f*
  writing for, 279*t*
weight (density) of type, 258, 260*f*
white boards (presentation tool), 446,
    447*f*, 449*f*
white papers, 585*f*

white space
  about, 247–248, 248*f*
  as design element, 245
  in flowcharts, 311*t*
  in illustrations, 297
  in online design, 289*t*
  rivers of, 261, 261*f*
  and simplicity, 241
will and *shall* in specifications, 529
Williams, Joseph (*The Craft of
    Research*), 637
Williams, Rob ("From the Workplace"),
    698–699
wingdings (typeface), 256, 256*f*
word choice. *See* diction
  (word choice)
words
  and style, 203–214
  and unnecessary phrases, 343
word spacing
  online, 287–288
  of text, 247, 260–262, 262*f*
work experience
  in job application letters, 378
  in résumés, 390–391
workplace communications, 8–11
works cited. *See* bibliographies
writing
  planning for style of, 94
  for specific communications
    formal reports, 640–641
    informal reports, 601, 603
    instructions, 696–697, 696*f*
    proposals, 547
  techniques for improving drafts,
    203–228, 329–350

Yale catalog of libraries, 152
"yes/no" order in correspondence,
    483–485, 484*f*, 485*f*
"you attitude"
  in job application letters, 379
  in refusal letters, 490
  in reports, 606*t*

slang
  cultural contexts of use, 227–228
  as level of diction, 206
slashes (punctuation), 728
slippery slope (logical fallacy), 50*f*
SME (subject-matter experts), 113, 114
smileys (emoticons), 506, 506*f*
social customs and tone, 228
Society for Technical Communication
    (STC)
  code of ethics, 21*f*
  Special Opportunities Grant
    Guidelines (RFP), 578–582*f*
software, copyright of, 186
software-manual design, 238*f*
solicited letters of inquiry, 491–492,
    492*f*
solicited proposals, 548, 549*f*
SOPs (standard operating procedures),
    520–522
sound in online documents, 282–284
source citations
  documenting in note-taking, 125*t*
  in tables, 303*f*, 305*t*
spacing of paragraphs
  in letters
    full-block, 476, 477*f*
    modified-block, 477–479, 478*f*
    personal, 480–481, 482*f*
    semiblock, 479–480, 479*f*
    simplified, 480, 481*f*
  in policies and procedures, 524*t*
spacing of type
  between elements, 260–261
  online, 287–288
spatial organization in technical
    descriptions, 515
special collections, 136, 137
specialized experience (résumés), 391
specialized language, 212
specialty forms of type, 255
specifications, 526–534, 528*t*,
    530–532*f*, 533*f*
  achievability of, 528*t*
  applicability of, 531–532
  contents, 526–527
  defining purpose for, 530–531
  diction (word choice) in, 527, 529
  functional, 527
  objectives of, 532
  performance requirements in, 527,
    528–529, 528*t*
  standardization documents cited in,
    528*t*, 529

terminology in, 528*t*, 529
specifications section of RFPs, 549
specific plan statement (proposals),
    559–560*t*
specific-to-general paragraphs, 218
spelling, 723
spiders (Web programs), 162
stacked bar graphs, 306*f*
standardization documents cited in
    specifications, 528*t*, 529
standard operating procedures (SOPs),
    520–522
standards, setting and following, 91–96
stationery
  for job application letters, 377
  for letters, 482*t*
  for résumés, 392
statistical databases, 151*t*, 153*f*
statistics and presentations, 437
STC. *See* Society for Technical
    Communication (STC)
Steinman, Steve ("From the
    Workplace"), 652–653
steps in instructions, 686–687,
    690–691*f*
stereotypes
  and gender, 226*t*
  and humor, 224*t*
storyboards, 105, 180–181, 181*f*
strategies
  for Boolean searches, 151*t*
  for persuasion, 44–49
stratification-model collaborations,
    55–56, 56*f*
student memberships, 373–374
style, 198–228
  abstractness, 346–347
  accuracy, 340–341, 527–528
  appropriateness, 341–342, 342*f*
  and audience, 198–199
  circumlocutions, 344
  clarity, 347–348
  in complaint letters, 486–487, 487*f*,
    488*f*
  complex style, 202–203
  conciseness, 342–343, 343*t*
  concreteness, 346–347
  consistency, 347
  correctness, 340–341
  determination of, 94
  expletive constructions, 345–346
  and genre, 199–201, 200*f*
  gobbledygook, 346
  for informal reports, 603

for instructions, 697, 697*t*
in larger segments, 221–222
negative constructions, 348–349
noun phrases, 345
in online documents, 274–278,
    279*t*
at paragraph level, 216–221
plain style, 201–202
planning for, 94
precision, 340–341, 527–528
prepositional phrases, 344
redundancies, 343–344
revising for, 339–350, 340*t*
at sentence level, 215–216
sentence parallelism, 349–350,
    351–352*f*
sincerity, 348
telegraphic writing, 346
unnecessary words and phrases, 343
verb phrases, 344–345
at word level, 203–214
styled text, 271, 271*f*
style guides, 91–96, 92–93*t*, 93*f*, 131*t*
style reviews, 354
styles (bold, italic)
  in e-mail, 501
  in letters, 482*t*
  in memos, 497*t*
  in online page design, 271, 271*f*
  in résumés, 392*t*
  in scannable résumés, 400*t*
subheadings in online design, 274
subject
  in formal reports, 636–638
  narrowing, 81–82, 82*f*, 83*f*
  in proposals, 546
subject headings
  Library of Congress, 126*t*
  in research, 127*t*
subject lines
  in letters, 472, 472*f*
    full-block, 476, 477*f*
    modified-block, 477–479, 478*f*
    semiblock, 479–480, 479*f*
    simplified, 480, 481*f*
  in memos, 495*f*, 496
subject matter and humor, 224*t*
subject-matter experts (SME), 113, 114
subject search trees and online indexes,
    162
subject–verb agreement, 742
subjunctive mood (verbs), 743
submission information section of RFP,
    550

subscriptions to professional journals, 416
substantive editing, 332–333, 333t
substeps in instructions, 694
summarizing information, 183–184
summary (abstract) section of proposals, 552–553, 556, 556f
surveys and questionnaires, 118–121, 119f, 120–121t
symbols
for copyediting, 334f
in diagrams, 316t
in figures, 297
in maps, 317t
mathematical (typefaces), 255
for proofreading, 337
typefaces, 254f, 256, 256f
symbols and abbreviations (formal reports), 650, 651f, 652
symmetry in design, 242–244, 242f, 244f

table numbers, 302t, 303f
tables, 302–305
formal, 303–304, 303f, 304–305t, 304f
informal, 302, 302t, 304f
tables of contents
in formal reports, 646
for illustrations, 299
in policies and procedures, 524t
task analysis, 686–687, 690–692
teamwork. *See* collaboration
technical accuracy, reviewing for, 341, 355f
technical communication, defining, 4–5
technical definitions, 511–513, 512f, 513f
technical descriptions, 513–516, 516f
technicality, levels of, 41–43, 341
technical literature, indexes of, 128–129f
technical processes, 517–519, 517f, 518f, 519f, 520f, 521f
technical prose, audience and, 41–43
technical reports. *See* reports
technical specifications section of RFP, 549
technical terms, location in sentences, 215
technicians (audience category), 37

technobabble, 213
technology and technical communication, 26–27
technospeak, 212
telegraphic writing, 346, 697t
telephone interviews, 117–118t
templates
for documents, 95, 97f
for presentation slides, 455
tense (verbs), 743
terminology in specifications, 528t, 529
testing instructions, 698–699
text and color, 268, 269f
text links in online documents, 278
text lists, 250–253
thank-you letters (interviews), 379–381, 380f, 408–409
theories, scientific, 123
theory section (instructions), 685–686
thesauri in database searches, 151t
35-mm slides (presentation tool), 447f, 453–454, 453f, 454f
thumbnail sketches, 180–181, 181f, 301
time
conventions for writing about, 736
estimating schedules for projects, 97–98, 98–99t
timeline section of RFP, 550
time logs, 99f, 99t
title pages
of formal reports, 642
of scientific papers, 633
titles
of figures, 297, 298f
styling, 730, 732
of tables, 302t, 303f
tone, 222–225
in complaint letters, 486–487, 487f, 488f
controlling, for audience appeal, 47
in e-mail, 499, 500f
in online design, 274
and social customs, 228
and writing for the Web, 279t
tools
bibliography software, 173, 175f
cost-estimating software, 105
creativity programs, 104–105
database-management programs, 105
flowchart programs, 105
graphics utilities, 324–325, 325f

outlining programs, 104
paint programs, 323–324, 324f
personal digital assistants (PDAs), 102–104, 104f
personal information management, 102–104, 104f
pixel programs, 323–324, 324f
planning, 101–105
presentation programs, 105, 446–460, 447f, 455, 455f, 456t
project-scheduling software, 102, 103f
raster illustration programs, 323–324, 324f
screen-capture programs, 324–325, 325f
storyboard programs, 105
vector illustration programs, 321–323, 321f
top-down editing, 330, 330f
topics
of paragraphs, 217–218
for research, 86f
trade journals and magazines
publishing in, 417–420, 418–419f
reading, 370–371
trade shows, 374, 421–422
training courses, 423
transmittal (cover) letters, 492, 494f, 641–642
transparencies (presentation tool), 405, 447f, 451t, 452f, 456t
travel forms, 5
tree diagrams, 178–179, 178f, 179t
triage for document design, 289, 289t
trimming (sentence-emphasis technique), 215
trip reports, 585f, 588–590, 591f
trite phrases, 214
troubleshooting section (instructions), 687
trust, establishing, 47
Turabian citation style, 746, 748–755
typefaces. *See also* typography
about, 253–257, 254f, 255f, 256f, 257t
anti-aliasing of, 301
choosing, 257t
as design element, 245
families of, 255
for online use, 287–288
and readability, 245
sizes of, 257, 258f

Guidelines for Editing and Revision

Numbers indicate pages where topics are covered.

Abbreviations   732
Acronyms   732
Addresses   736
Bold   731
Bullets   732
Capitalization   723
Comma splices   741
Commonly confused words   739
Dangling modifiers   742
Dates   736
Decimals   735
Faulty parallelism   742
Fractions   735
Fragments   741
Initialisms   732
Italics   731
Measurements   734
Misplaced modifiers   742
Mood (verb)   743

Numbers   733
Parts of speech   738
  Adjective   738
  Adverb   738
  Conjunction   739
  Interjection   739
  Noun   738
  Preposition   739
  Pronoun   738
  Verb   738
Percentages   736
Pronoun case   743
Pronoun–antecedent
  agreement   742
Punctuation   724
  Apostrophe   728
  Brackets   731
  Colon   726
  Comma   725

Dash   727
Ellipsis   729
Exclamation point   725
Hyphen   728
Parenthesis   731
Period   724
Question mark   725
Quotation mark   729
Semicolon   726
Slash   728
Run-on sentences   741
Spelling   723
Subject–verb
  agreement   742
Tense (verb)   743
Time   736
Underline   731
Voice (verb)   743

Copyediting and Proofreading Symbols

See Figure 10.3 on page 334 for examples of how to use the symbols.

Marks	Explanation	Marks	Explanation	Marks	Explanation
℮	Delete	/	Make lowercase	⟨⟩	Add quotation marks
⌒	Close up	⊙	Make a period	—	Italicize
⌢	Delete and close up	⌃	Make a comma	∿	Make boldface
∧	Insert	=	Add a hyphen	· · ·	Stet (let it stand)
∿	Transpose	¶	Start a paragraph	⊗	Fix broken type
◯	Spell out	⌢	Run in	‖	Align type
≡	Capitalize	⌄	Add an apostrophe	ⓌⒻ	Fix wrong font